Lecture Notes in Computer Science 13873

The series Lecture Notes in Computer Science (LNCS), including its subseries Lecture Notes in Artificial Intelligence (LNAI) and Lecture Notes in Bioinformatics (LNBI), has established itself as a medium for the publication of new developments in computer science and information technology research, teaching, and education.

LNCS enjoys close cooperation with the computer science R & D community, the series counts many renowned academics among its volume editors and paper authors, and collaborates with prestigious societies. Its mission is to serve this international community by providing an invaluable service, mainly focused on the publication of conference and workshop proceedings and postproceedings. LNCS commenced publication in 1973.

Aurona Gerber · Richard Baskerville
Editors

Design Science Research for a New Society: Society 5.0

18th International Conference on Design Science Research
in Information Systems and Technology, DESRIST 2023
Pretoria, South Africa, May 31 – June 2, 2023
Proceedings

 Springer

Editors
Aurona Gerber (iD)
University of the Western Cape
Cape Town, South Africa

Richard Baskerville (iD)
Georgia State University
Atlanta, GA, USA

ISSN 0302-9743   ISSN 1611-3349 (electronic)
Lecture Notes in Computer Science
ISBN 978-3-031-32807-7   ISBN 978-3-031-32808-4 (eBook)
https://doi.org/10.1007/978-3-031-32808-4

This Springer imprint is published by the registered company Springer Nature Switzerland AG
The registered company address is: Gewerbestrasse 11, 6330 Cham, Switzerland

Preface

This volume of Springer LNCS (LNCS 13873) contains the revised accepted research papers of DESRIST 2023, the *18th International Conference on Design Science Research in Information Systems and Technology*. DESRIST 2023 was held from 31 May to 2 June 2023 at the Future Africa Conference Centre at the University of Pretoria (UP) Hatfield campus. The theme of the conference was *Design Science Research for a New Society: Society 5.0*.

Humanity experienced unprecedented technological developments during the past few decades. Few can deny that the lives we live and the societies we are part of are undergoing vast, often unexpected adjustments and transformation. More voices are requesting a rethink of the relationships we - as humans - have with technology in this new world. The term *Society 5.0* has emerged to describe the new society distinguished by the high degree of merging between physical space and cyberspace.

Due to its problem and solution orientation, which promises to drive innovation and address challenges on all levels of analysis (society, the business ecosystem, the enterprise, the workgroup and the individual), design science research (DSR) in information systems (IS) has received significant attention. In an immersed society, where there are numerous wicked problems on all levels of analysis, DSR is an ideal approach to understand complex challenges and support the design of useful solutions, making provision for rigour and relevance. Based on multi-stakeholder problem analysis and informed by existing descriptive and design knowledge, well-designed innovative methods, solution patterns, reference models and exemplary IS solutions promise to be effective means of addressing many of today's challenges and thus contribute to the further development of DSR's methodological foundations. The better we get at integrating humans, organisations and machines, the better we will be able to use all means possible to achieve sustainable development. The theme of DESRIST 2023 therefore challenged the DSR community to approach DSR from a more humanitarian perspective. Research papers, panels and workshops were encouraged to address the challenges faced by society, business ecosystems, organisations, workgroups and individuals, and the DESRIST 2023 conference tracks were selected to support the overarching conference theme and solicit submissions in areas that are key to DSR in Society 5.0.

With regards to DESRIST 2023 submissions, it is observable that the geography of society is transforming as a result of the progressive merger of physical and cyber spaces. The Covid-19 pandemic accelerated this transformation. Worries about the merger are everywhere: AI that seems out of control, technologies that seem inhuman and dangerous, and socio-technical spaces that seem impossible to govern. Is an Orwellian dystopia inevitable? In this book, we find how design science researchers are seeking out designs for technical artifacts that alleviate such worries by introducing principles for designing information systems that steer the social and the technical past such worries. The authors of papers in these proceedings build up themes such as explainable AI, keeping humans as co-creators in the design of technical artifacts (plus the consequent artifacts and the subsequent descendants of these artifacts) and setting aims for new artifacts that sustain and protect the well-being of humankind. Principles regarding design methods include co-creation, data as a product, national innovation, social markets, design accessibility, solution-driven design, cascading of co-design, and security that also delivers systems that are safe. Here, we focus not on an inevitable dystopia, but on a society that has technology to aid its social progress and sustainability. The track that received the most submissions was our theme track, which may attest to the fact that this new Society 5.0 we live in warrants such attention from DSR researchers. Other tracks that were popular include Innovation and Entrepreneurship, Emerging DSR Methods and Processes as well as Education and DSR. When considering the overall trends in submissions accepted for this book, a trend that is distinguishable is that DSR, with its associated focus on design knowledge, provides an appropriate paradigm for the study of the Society 5.0 phenomenon.

This DESRIST 2023 proceedings book contains 29 full research papers organized in their respective research tracks that were included for presentation in the program of DESRIST 2023. DESRIST 2023 aimed to strengthen the international DSR community and an additional 25 research-in-progress papers were accepted for presentation at the conference. With 101 papers submitted and 81 submissions sent out for review, the acceptance rate for full research papers was less than 37%. The review process was rigorous with every paper receiving at least three substantive double-blind reviews from an expert international program committee. A distinguished group of research track chairs managed the review process and supported the author teams to revise their papers to the quality results that are published in these proceedings. We send our deepest gratitude to these outstanding track chairs and program committee reviewers for their hard work and dedication on very aggressive time schedules. Thank you to the authors of all the submitted papers for sharing their exciting design science research projects. We hope the opportunity to participate in DESRIST 2023 will have a lasting impact on the quality and productivity of your future research.

We also acknowledge the enthusiasm and outstanding contributions of the local organizers of DESRIST 2023. The administration, faculty and staff of the University of Pretoria, as well as our conference organizer, Mongoose C&D, supported the planning, funding and execution of the conference with their generosity and energy. Thank you to everyone who contributed to the success of DESRIST 2023.

June 2023

Aurona Gerber
Richard Baskerville

Organisation

Conference Chairs

Alta van der Merwe   University of Pretoria, South Africa
Robert Winter   University of St. Gallen, Switzerland

Program Chairs

Aurona Gerber   University of the Western Cape and Centre for AI Research, South Africa
Richard Baskerville   Georgia State University, USA

Doctoral Consortium Chairs

Jeffrey Parsons   Memorial University, Canada
Tuure Tuunanen   University of Jyväskylä, Finland
Jan vom Brocke   University of Liechtenstein, Liechtenstein

Local Arrangement Coordinator

Reneé le Roux   Mongoose C&D, South Africa

Track Chairs

Design-Oriented Research for Society 5.0 (Theme Track)

Knut Hinkelmann   FHNW University of Applied Sciences and Arts Northwestern Switzerland, Switzerland and University of Pretoria, South Africa
Felix Härer   University of Fribourg, Switzerland

Design of Systems Using Emerging Technologies

Kaushik Dutta	University of South Florida, USA
Carson Woo	University of British Columbia, Canada

Human-Centered Artificial Intelligence (HCAI)

Pierre-Majorique Leger	HEC Montreal, Canada
Armel Quentin Tchanou	Université de Sherbrooke, Canada
Mahdi Mirhoseini	Concordia University, Canada

Healthcare Systems and Quality of Life

Reima Suomi	University of Turku, Finland
Monica Chiarini Tremblay	William and Mary University, USA
Debra VanderMeer	Florida International University, USA

Innovation and Entrepreneurship

Christoph Seckler	ESCP Berlin, Germany
Georges Romme	Eindhoven University of Technology, The Netherlands

Emerging DSR Methods and Processes

Hanlie Smuts	University of Pretoria, South Africa
John Venable	Perth University, Australia
Marie Hattingh	University of Pretoria, South Africa

Education and DSR

Asif Gill	Sydney University of Technology, Australia
Jean-Paul van Belle	University of Cape Town, South Africa

Human Safety and Cybersecurity

Mala Kaul	University of Nevada, USA
Paolo Spagnoletti	LUISS Guido Carli, Italy
H. Raghav Rao	University of Texas at San Antonio, USA

Co-design and Collective Creativity for Addressing Grand Challenges

Leona Chandra Kruse   University of Liechtenstein, Liechtenstein
Pascal Le Masson   Mines ParisTech, France

Sustainability and Responsible Design

Nigel Melville   University of Michigan, USA
Nicolas Prat   ESSEC Business School, France
Johann Kranz   LMU Munich, Germany

Programme Committee

Antragama Ewa Abbas   Delft University of Technology, The Netherlands
Shamel Addas   Queens University, Canada
Timothy Adeliyi   University of Pretoria, South Africa
Lubna Alam   Deakin Business School, Australia
Luis Alvarez Sabucedo   Universidade de Vigo, Spain
Yehia Alzoubi   American University of the Middle East, Kuwait
Memoona Anwar   University of Technology Sydney, Australia
Madhushi Bandara   University of Technology Sydney, Australia
Christian Bartelheimer   Paderborn University, Germany
Anol Battacherjee   University of South Florida, USA
Svein Bergum   Høgskolen i Lillehammer, Norway
Isabel Bienfuss   LMU Munich, Germany
Eva Bittner   Universität Hamburg, Germany
Saskia Bluhm   Karlsruhe Institute of Technology, Germany
Adele Botha   CSIR, South Africa
Robert Buchmann   Babeș-Bolyai University, Romania
Enrico Bunde   Ruhr-Universität Bochum, Germany
Marcel Cahenzli   University of St. Gallen, Switzerland
Gültekin Cakir   Maynooth University, Ireland
Arturo Castellanos Bueso   College of William & Mary, USA
Dilek Cetindamar   University of Technology Sydney, Australia
Samir Chatterji   Claremont University, USA
Tendani Chimboza   University of Cape Town, South Africa
Cecil Chua   Missouri University of Science and Technology,
                             USA
Jason Cohen   University of the Witwatersrand, South Africa
Colin Conrad   Dalhousie University, Canada
Stefan Cronholm   University of Borås, Sweden

Andre de la Harpe	Cape Peninsula University of Technology, South Africa
Retha de la Harpe	Cape Peninsula University of Technology, South Africa
Marne De Vries	University of Pretoria, South Africa
Ernestine Dickhaut	University of Kassel, Germany
Sifiso Dlamini	CSIR, South Africa
Brian Donnellan	Maynooth University, Ireland
Philippe Doyon-Poulin	Polytechnique Montréal, Canada
Andreas Drechsler	Victoria University of Wellington, New Zealand
Sven Eckhardt	University of Zurich, Switzerland
Joachim Ehrenthal	FHNW University of Applied Sciences and Arts Northwestern Switzerland, Switzerland
Sunet Eybers	University of South Africa (UNISA), South Africa
Mahdi Fahmideh	University of Southern Queensland, Australia
Leandro Feitosa Jorge	Université de Sherbrooke, Canada
Hans-Georg Fill	University of Fribourg, Switzerland
Thomas Fischer	University of Passau, Germany
Fabrizio Fornari	University of Camerino, Italy
Greg Foster	Rhodes University, South Africa
Sandro Franzoi	University of Liechtenstein, Liechtenstein
Michael Gau	University of Liechtenstein, Liechtenstein
Leonhard Gebhardt	ICN Business School, France
Rob Gleasure	Copenhagen Business School, Denmark
Shirley Gregor	Australian National University, Australia
Hannes Göbel	University of Borås, Sweden
Charles Gouin-Vallerand	Université de Sherbrooke, Canada
Shirley Gregor	Australian National University, Australia
Tobias Guggenberger	TU Dortmund, Germany
Amir Haj-Bolouri	University West, Sweden
Tom Hall	University of South Florida, USA
Moez Hamedani	University of South Florida, USA
Thomas Hanne	University of Applied Sciences Northwestern Switzerland, Switzerland
Magnus Rotvit Hansen	Roskilde University, Denmark
Savindu Herath	ETH Zurich, Switzerland
Marlien Herselman	CSIR and Nelson Mandela Metropolitan University, South Africa
Alexander Herwix	University of Cologne, Germany
Katharina Hölzle	University of Stuttgart, Germany
Juhani Iivari	University of Oulu, Finland
Pertti Jarvinen	Tampere University, Finland

Juergen Jung	Frankfurt University of Applied Sciences, Germany
Ilka Jussen	TU Dortmund, Germany
Dimitris Karagiannis	University of Vienna, Austria
Michael Kaufmann	Lucerne University of Applied Sciences and Arts, Switzerland
Arif Khan	University of Oulu, Finland
Bijan Khosrawi-Rad	Technische Universität Braunschweig, Germany
Henry Kim	York University, Canada
Gregor Kipping	Universität Liechtenstein, Liechtenstein
Paula Kotzé	University of Pretoria, South Africa
Aneesh Krishna	Curtin University, Australia
Jan Kroeze	University of South Africa, South Africa
Akshat Lakhiwal	Indiana University, USA
Emanuele Laurenzi	FHNW University of Applied Sciences and Arts Northwestern Switzerland, Switzerland
Christine Legner	University of Lausanne, Switzerland
David M. Lehmann	ESCP Business School, France
Florian Leiser	Karlsruhe Institute of Technology, Germany
Victoria Lemieux	University of British Columbia, Canada
Tobias Ley	University for Continuing Education Krems, Austria
Chenglong Li	Tampere University, Finland
Johanna Lorenz	Universität Hamburg, Germany
Hugo Lotriet	University of South Africa, South Africa
Roman Lukyanenko	University of Virginia, USA
Johannes Magenheim	Universität Paderborn, Germany
Negar Maleki	University of South Florida, USA
Munir Mandviwalla	Temple University, USA
Bartosz Marcinkowski	University of Gdansk, Poland
Andreas Martin	FHNW University of Applied Sciences and Arts Northwestern Switzerland, Switzerland
Carolin Marx	Hasso-Plattner-Institute, Germany
Jan Mendling	Humboldt-Universität zu Berlin, Germany
Tobias Mettler	University of Lausanne, Switzerland
Patrick Mikalef	Norwegian University of Science and Technology, Norway
Alok Mishra	Atılım University, Turkey
Stefan Morana	Saarland University, Germany
Solon Moreira	Fox School of Business, USA
Waseem Muhammad	University of Jyväskylä, Finland
Anik Mukherjee	IIM Calcutta, India

Matthew Mullarkey	University of South Florida, USA
Krishnakumar Nair	University of South Florida, USA
Peter Axel Nielsen	University of Aalborg, Denmark
Monelo Nxozi	Rhodes University, South Africa
Jacques Ophoff	Abertay University, Scotland
Edward Opoku-Mensah	HEC Montréal, Canada
Abhipsa Pal	Indian Institute of Management Calcutta, India
Mario Passalacqua	Polytechnique Montréal, Canada
Teijo Peltoniemi	University of Turku, Finland
Nargis Pervin	Indian Institute of Technology Madras, India
Erik Perjons	Stockholm University, Sweden
Fazlyn Petersen	University of the Western Cape, South Africa
Marco Piangerelli	University of Camerino, Italy
Andrea Polini	University of Camerino, Italy
Shweta Premanandan	Uppsala University, Sweden
Sandeep Purao	Bentley University, USA
Jaziar Radianti	University of Agder, Norway
Arindam Ray	University of South Florida, USA
Ulrich Reimer	Eastern Switzerland University of Applied Sciences, Switzerland
René Riedl	Johannes Kepler Universität Linz, Austria
Michael Rosemann	Queensland University of Technology, Australia
Matti Rossi	Aalto University, Finland
Daniel Rush	Boise State University, USA
Morteza Saberi	University of Technology Sydney, Australia
Viktor Salenius	University of Oxford, UK
Ian Sanders	University of the Witwatersrand, South Africa
Sandra Schlick	University of Applied Sciences and Arts Northwestern Switzerland, Switzerland
Ricarda Schlimbach	Technische Universität Braunschweig, Germany
Ulrich Schmitt	University of Stellenbosch, South Africa
Johannes Schneider	University of Liechtenstein, Liechtenstein
Isabella Seeber	Grenoble EM, France
Maung Sein	University of Southeastern Norway and Kristiania University College, Norway
Sylvain Senecal	HEC Montreal, Canada
Avijit Sengupta	University of Queensland, Australia
Janina Seutter	Paderborn University, Germany
Jun Shen	University of Wollongong, Australia
Dominik Siemon	LUT University, Finland
Vivek Singh	University of Missouri-St. Louis, USA
Stephen Smith	Macquarie University, Australia

Contents

Healthcare Systems and Quality of Life

Innovation and Entrepreneurship

Emerging DSR Methods and Processes

Education and DSR

Human Safety and Cybersecurity

Co-design and Collective Creativity for Addressing Grand Challenges

Sustainability and Responsible Design

Design-Oriented Research for Society 5.0 (Theme Track)

z-Commerce: Designing a Data-Minimizing One-Click Checkout Solution

Egor Ermolaev$^{(\boxtimes)}$, Iván Abellán Álvarez , Johannes Sedlmeir ,
and Gilbert Fridgen

Interdisciplinary Center for Security, Reliability and Trust,
University of Luxembourg, Luxembourg City, Luxembourg
{egor.ermolaev,ivan.abellan,johannes.sedlmeir,gilbert.fridgen}@uni.lu
https://wwwen.uni.lu/snt/research/finatrax

Abstract. E-commerce has grown rapidly over the past years, with prevailing e-commerce platforms aggregating large amounts of customer data. This practice has several undesirable side effects, such as facilitating profiling that may lead to price discrimination and data feedback loops that can hamper competition. Moreover, data hoarding carries security risks through data breaches and undermines customers' privacy expectations. On the other hand, convenience aspects and compliance regulation demand the processing and storage of user-related data. To address this tension field, we aim to conceptualize and iteratively refine a data-minimizinig e-commerce platform. Following a design science research approach, we identify design objectives and propose and implement a solution in which stakeholders receive only customer data that is indispensable for their part of the process. Our solution leverages digital identity wallets and general-purpose zero-knowledge proofs (zk-SNARKs). We aim to perform a criteria-based evaluation to assess our artifact's feasibility and fitness from an interdisciplinary perspective. With our results, we hope to illustrate that combining state-of-the-art cryptographic techniques and an emerging digital identity paradigm allows reaching the user experience of incumbent e-commerce platforms while mitigating the undesirable socio-economic side effects of avoidable data disclosure.

Keywords: Compliance · digital wallet · electronic commerce · platform · selective disclosure · privacy · zero-knowledge proof

1 Introduction

Electronic markets facilitate the discovery and coordination of stakeholders such as buyers and sellers, data trading, product matching, and payments through

This research was funded in part by the Luxembourg National Research Fund (FNR) through the PABLO project (grant reference 16326754) and by PayPal, grant reference "P17/IS/13342933/PayPal-FNR/Chair in DFS/Gilbert Fridgen" (PEARL). For the purpose of open access, the author has applied a Creative Commons Attribution 4.0 International (CC BY 4.0) license to any Author Accepted Manuscript version arising from this submission.

A. Gerber and R. Baskerville (Eds.): DESRIST 2023, LNCS 13873, pp. 3–17, 2023.
https://doi.org/10.1007/978-3-031-32808-4_1

digital means [56]. E-commerce is seen as a shift from traditional markets into the digital economy [40]. Corresponding digital platforms use digital technologies to fulfill business and market requirements, yet may also involve physical processes, for instance, for product delivery. E-commerce offers several benefits to merchants and consumers. First, the digital coordination of purchase-related processes, such as business-to-consumer interactions during payment and delivery, makes the corresponding markets ubiquitous [57] and more efficient, especially at large distances. Second, a single integrated platform, among other benefits, enables customers to efficiently discover products or services [65]. Third, e-commerce facilitates delivery based on customer preferences, such as shipment to door, to pick-up points, or just to the closest post office. It thus improves distant goods distribution [43] and benefits customers who would be limited to local sellers with a limited spectrum of available products. Fourth, e-commerce improves user experience by facilitating remote purchase agreements with integrated electronic payments [47]. Studies suggest that in 2022, e-commerce accounted for more than 5 trillion U.S. dollars in retail sales [35] and that e-commerce sales may further increase substantially over the next few years. Particularly large e-commerce platforms such as Amazon have grown enormously. This can be attributed to the presence of indirect network effects, as platforms with the greatest selection of merchants and their goods provide the highest utility to consumers and vice versa [4].

1.1 Benefits of Data Collection

Data processing is a key aspect of e-commerce due to multiple business requirements that include accounting, legal, recommender systems, and payment processing activities [47]. For instance, a legal requirement would be an age verification for purchasing alcohol, whereas a business requirement could be the disclosure of the residential address for product delivery. In this context, a user first obtains a user account on the e-commerce website by providing personal information. A registration process is not only used by merchants but also underlies payment, as banks or payment service providers (PSPs) need to conduct know-your-customer (KYC) processes based on verifiable personal data retrieved, for instance, from a national ID card [53]. As the registration process is time-consuming for the user and the verification of identity attributes may also be costly for the vendor, e-commerce providers store their customers' identity attributes to have them available for subsequent interactions. At the checkout process, platforms then ensure account ownership via authenticating their users [58]; typically using passwords and potentially additional factors. The inconvenience of registering with multiple service providers by filling out forms not only in e-commerce but also beyond has led to the appearance of identity providers (IdPs) who centrally collect users' identity information to offer single sign-on solutions [54]. To improve user experience, many e-commerce platforms and also independent merchants have integrated this federated identity model to allow users to authenticate with an existing account with their IdP and to transfer corresponding identity attributes without the need for repeated registration [31]. For instance, Amazon already acts as an IdP for many small vendors to provide their users with a one-click checkout without prior registration, and, thereby, extends its data collection even beyond consumers on its own e-commerce platform.

Data collection also benefits e-commerce platforms beyond improving user experience in the context of identity management. Targeted advertising to promote products is key in the e-commerce business model [3,7]. Recommender systems attract customers by advertising those offers that customers may be most interested in [65]. Personalized product recommendation is known to increase sales [66], which represents a major driver to improve the corresponding recommendation systems, for example, by training machine learning models on collected transaction data [66]. E-commerce platforms that aggregate multiple retail stores and small-sized merchants can, therefore, improve their service and provide more convenience to customers [40]. Data collection also improves the effectiveness of e-commerce platforms toward customer relationships [39]. Customer data gathering helps to tailor relationship management, for example, by making advertising campaigns more compelling, introducing effective customer retention techniques such as loyalty programs, or improving service quality to meet customers' expectations [39].

1.2   Problems in the Context of Data Collection

On the other hand, data collection through e-commerce platforms carries several economic, security, and privacy risks. Large-scale data collection allows for profiling customers, i.e., analyzing their transaction histories and modeling their behavior [34]. This profiling may lead to unfair treatment of customers, such as price discrimination [11]. Moreover, indirect network effects and the corresponding accumulation of market power to large e-commerce platforms are further increased: Direct access to customers' data may make dominant platforms feel tempted to practice anti-competitive measures, for instance, by placing lock-in practices through making data non-portable [15]. Additionally, platforms can also benefit from data feedback loops [29] and data network effects [25], so they could gain market share as advanced data analytics allows them to improve faster. Likewise, these marketplace aggregators, which offer convenience to both retailers and customers, can exploit other revenue streams, such as charging membership, service, or commission fees [40], allowing them to reduce fees and make them more attractive. All these practices significantly increase the market power of large, incumbent e-commerce platforms, ultimately hampering competition [29]. Additionally, collected data is generally stored in centralized silos [12], facing risk of being harvested without users' explicit consent [63]. As such, users have little control over whether their data is being sold to third parties [21]. Moreover, insufficient security measures or targeted attacks on "honey pots" can lead to data leaks or breaches. For instance, a hacker's raid on eBay led to a historic breach that leaked 145M user records in 2014 [48]. It is not only that data breaches pose a risk to privacy, as sensitive information may be exposed to third parties without consent. They also represent a substantial security threat, as users may be targeted for impersonation or social engineering attacks where publicly available information is exploited for malicious purposes [38]. Opaque data flows, advanced data analytics, and transaction monitoring also raise concerns among users who dislike disclosing personal information [39] or who fear the implementation of surveillance capitalism or an Orwellian state [67].

1.3   Searching for New Solutions

We conclude that the handling and processing of customer data need to navigate between convenience and business requirements on the one hand and security, privacy, and socio-economic risks on the other hand. Balancing users' privacy and business and compliance needs that require data collection is already a problem without an easy solution in electronic payments alone [41]. Arguably, balancing out this tension field in e-commerce may be even more challenging as it involves further business and compliance requirements, more complex processes, and additional stakeholders guided by their own interests. Some regulations and initiatives aim to address selected issues; for instance, the general data protection regulation (GDPR) aims to ensure the good and appropriate management of European citizens' personal data [62]. The Payment Services Directive (PSD2) enforces information security of payments conducted by financial institutions and PSPs [18]. Most recently, the Digital Services Act (DSA) introduced a set of measures to protect customer rights and ensure an accountable and fair competitive digital market, targeting "gatekeepers" that include e-commerce platforms such as Amazon [19]. Privacy-enhancing technologies have been proposed also in related areas, such as data markets for the Internet of Things (IoT) [22].

New trends in digital identity and privacy-enhancing technology, such as zero-knowledge proofs (ZKPs), may help pave the way toward convenient and yet privacy-oriented e-commerce solutions. In this paper, we investigate to which extent recent approaches to privacy-oriented digital interactions in the realm of identification [50,54] and payments [17,26,64] can be used for this purpose. Researchers have consistently encouraged the use of cryptography in this context [16,49], and corresponding solutions are increasingly discussed and explored [26,61]. Many approaches rely on ZKPs to facilitate the convenient, selective disclosure of information from users to relying parties, such as digital platforms, service providers, or blockchain-based applications, in a machine-verifiable way. For instance, requirements of an e-commerce transaction from a regulatory or business side should be verified effectively while reducing the processing of sensitive information to a minimum.

However, there has only been limited research on combining such tools in practical applications, particularly in the context of e-commerce. In contrast, most prior research has focused either on exchanging only identity-related data for specific business or administrative processes or on privacy-oriented payments but not on their combination. The work by Schanzenbach et al. [52] poses a notable exception that implements both decentralized identity management and a client-side payment system for e-commerce. However, it has a strong technical perspective, is subject to several limitations, and lacks consideration of how to coordinate the different stakeholders involved in an e-commerce purchase process. Related work has also not evaluated a data-minimal e-commerce (DMEC) solution with regard to stakeholders' expectations. We believe that the case of e-commerce may indeed illustrate the impact of novel data-minimizing technologies from an individual, economic, and societal perspective, combining both user and business perspectives. Integrating a corresponding wide variety of privacy features in a digital wallet may provide an alternative, "one-click registration and checkout" process that avoids unnecessary data processing and storage while maintaining a high level of user experience [28,32,51]. This direction could also shed light on new directions to preventing the privacy paradox [1].

Our work hence designs and evaluates a proof-of-concept that an alternative, data-minimizing approach to e-commerce is possible. Our system facilitates the selective disclosure of personal and payment information to stakeholders involved in a transaction on an e-commerce platform. We follow the design science research (DSR) methodology by Peffers et al. [45] to develop an artifact that addresses both users' and businesses' needs in the tension field between data use and data minimization. With our artifact, we aim to provide design knowledge on how to build data-minimizing e-commerce solutions. We plan to evaluate the artifact from an interdisciplinary perspective to demonstrate the feasibility and suitability of using digital wallets and ZKPs for achieving minimal information disclosure in e-commerce.

The remainder of this paper is structured as follows: In Sect. 2, we introduce background knowledge on ZKPs and where they are currently explored in practice in the form of privacy-oriented digital identity management and payments. We then review related work on privacy-oriented e-commerce solutions. Section 3 presents how we aim to conduct our design science research approach in detail and how we believe our research can contribute to the information systems domain.

2 Background and Related Work

2.1 Foundational Building Blocks

Zero-Knowledge Proofs: Goldwasser et al. [23] introduced the notion of zero-knowledge in interactive proof systems. It is a property of an interaction between two subjects, a "prover" and a "verifier". The prover probabilistically convinces the verifier of a statement while revealing no additional information about why the statement is true. For instance, the prover could convince the verifier that she knows a solution to a given Sudoku puzzle, without revealing any field of the solution to the verifier. The probability of a malicious prover convincing the verifier of a wrong statement decreases exponentially in the number of interactions between the prover and the verifier. zero-knowledge succinct non-interactive arguments of knowledge (zk-SNARK) are a family of ZKP that eliminates the need for interactions between the prover and the verifier by obtaining randomness using cryptography. zk-SNARKs also satisfy an additional property that makes them extremely efficient from the perspective of the verifier: They are succinct, i.e., the resulting proof is very short, and its verification is much quicker than verifying the statement directly through naive re-computation [27]. General-purpose zero-knowledge succinct non-interactive arguments of knowledge (zk-SNARKs) have rapidly evolved during the last few years because of their natural fit for solving technical challenges related to blockchain technology [9,55], with emerging domain-specific languages (DSLs) (e.g., Circom, ZoKrates), libraries (e.g. Circomlib) and tools (e.g. SnarkJS) that allow software engineers to implement ZKPs for a broad class of statements. This development has accelerated research and application of zero-knowledge technology also beyond blockchains, such as in digital identity [6], payment systems [26], and supply chains [42].

Digital Identity: Decentralized or self-sovereign identity (SSI) is a concept that involves representing and sharing attributes or authorizations of individuals or organizations, with the aim of providing a more convenient alternative to traditional IdPs while empowering individuals to control data disclosure using digital wallets. SSI's core principles were first described by Allen [2] and later extended with insights from practical experiences [54]. They include not only user-centric requirements such as convenience aspects, control, and data-minimization but also organizational requirements, such as verifiability and authenticity. For instance, a notable application of ZKP is "anonymous credentials" [14] in the realm of digital identity. A prover can ensure a verifier about adulthood without disclosing the date of birth registered in his digital identity by means of a digitally signed ID card issued, for instance, by a national institution [54]. In this context, ZKPs guarantee the verifiability of selectively disclosed attributes, although the underlying digitally signed attestation is never shared. Thereby, ZKPs can be used for selective disclosure – "the ability of an individual to granularly decide what information to share" [60] – and privacy-by-design solutions. A popular implementation is Hyperledger Aries, which presents one of the first efforts for technical specifications and implementation of SSI using blockchain technology [53]. It uses Hyperledger AnonCreds, a library, and specification of anonymous credentials conceptualized by Camenisch & Lysyanskaya [14] that facilitate advanced privacy features such as the selective disclosure of attributes and the avoidance of unique identifiers using special purpose ZKPs. Several public and private sector projects, such as the public-private consortium IDunion, use Hyperledger Aries to implement a SSI-based digital identity management solution that addresses businesses' needs and that is compliant with the EU GDPR [5]. Recently, ZKPs are discussed in the context of the revision of the electronic IDentification, Authentication and trust Services (eIDAS) regulation [13]. These and similar designs support limited functionalities due to the cryptographic primitives they use [6]. However, using these components in the context of e-commerce requires support for adoption at a large scale and more flexible and sophisticated predicates. Therefore, new research focuses on extending the data minimization capabilities of anonymous credentials using general-purpose ZKPs. For instance, several works including [50] and [6] adopt zk-SNARKs to prove complex composable statements about identity attributes without disclosing the signed attestation and to address some scalability shortcomings of the Anon-Creds implementation.

Payment systems represent an essential component of e-commerce. Cash is not sufficient for e-commerce due to limitations regarding convenience, such as remote purchasing, and security requirements for a safe transfer. Therefore, electronic payment systems seem more suitable. During the payment process, customers then need to reveal sensitive information to address compliance, technical, and processing requirements to their PSPs. Consequently, PSPs typically have access to transaction data and history. Also, the approach of sharing credit card information with the merchant, including legal name, credit card number, and security code, allows for transaction traceability and is far from data minimizing. To address privacy concerns in electronic payments. Chaum [16] introduced "e-cash" using blind signatures, which provides privacy to the payer. This solution is not flexible enough as the payee is fully transparent. ZeroCash [10] describes a completely anonymous digital currency leveraging ZKP. However, these approaches to anonymous payments do not comply with money laundering and terrorist financing regulation [26]. GNU Taler [17], another implementation of privacy-oriented payment systems based on Chaum's initial e-cash approach, addresses compliance issues by introducing the "auditor" role to which both users and payment processors are accountable. It provides a privacy-friendly payment system solution for the payer, who remains anonymous. Several recent works present alternative centralized or decentralized payment systems to address both privacy demands and compliance by enforcing turnover limits for anonymous transactions [26,64]. These architectures can be considered the next iteration of privacy-focused, ZKPs and blockchain-based cryptocurrencies such as Zcash [10] that in contrast have a solid chance of achieving regulatory compliance.

2.2 Related Work

Data Markets: DISSENS [52] provides decentralized identity management and a client-side payment system for e-commerce. It aims to be a regulatory-compliant solution built on a decentralized network, specifically a distributed hash table (DHT), that acts as an encrypted file storage for digital identity. Integrating the GNU Taler [17] payment system ensures client-side privacy features and provable regulatory compliance. However, several limitations prevail. Data, although encrypted, is shared on a public network, which may conflict with the GDPR's "right to be forgotten". Its functionality is limited to the disclosed attributes, so extensive functionality is not possible, such that proving general statements concerning one or multiple attributes. Agora [37] proposes a semi-private marketplace for data brokerage. Users generate encrypted data which upon payment brokers decrypt and batch. Brokers act as an unlinkability and aggregator service to interested data buyers, thus protecting users' data in front of end consumers. Due to the nature of the cryptographic algorithms used, their cryptographic protocols are limited in functionality. Agora only supports private data sharing of special mathematical function outputs, such as weighted averages and linear regressions. The paper highlights that functionality could be improved by leveraging ZKP. For instance, Garrido et al. [22] survey different privacy-enhancing technologies (PETs) in IoT data markets and illustrate their trade-offs. Data brokerage may use various PETs to enable aggregation and obfuscation of the initial private data that makes it irreversible and untraceable. Similarly, a centralized approach is proposed for data collection and service delivery [44]. Data generators use a particular cryptographic primitive to protect and preserve privacy by computing encrypted data. However, the system relies on a third party to create participants' identities, which may pose a risk to data privacy guarantees. If eventually, the registration center becomes corrupted, it could intercept and decrypt the data, thus correlating users to content. Additionally, a tamper-proof device is required, which usually poses an encumbrance to widespread adoption. Bella et al. [8] suggests an e-commerce architecture that balances privacy and trust by using differential privacy. Differential privacy introduces noise to make user data less sensitive, which brings fuzziness to the characteristics of each customer (e.g., adulthood). Hence, differential privacy approaches may not be adequate, particularly when clear boundaries are imposed by regulatory compliance considerations.

Besides some technical limitations of related work that we aim to address, we also note that related work, except for DISSENS [52], so far has not evaluated their solutions with stakeholders, for instance, to assess whether the approach can meet business needs and customers' user experience needs.

3 Method

In this paper, we outline how we aim to create general prescriptive knowledge on reducing the processing and storage of sensitive information in e-commerce following the DSR method [45]. Based on a demonstration of the feasibility of such a design, we want to identify how this approach can help avoid the aggregation of data by incumbent e-commerce platforms and the corresponding security and socio-economic challenges we discussed in Sect. 1. Our research hence provides an interdisciplinary perspective from an information systems lens by developing a solution based on novel cryptographic tools. Our research also addresses calls for more widespread applications of cryptography for "moral" reasons, for instance, to tackle increasing surveillance threats [49].

Our paper is structured according to the DSR best practices as described by Gregor & Hevner [24], yet considers the limitation of our paper's scope as it represents research in progress. We first comprehensively identify the problem and motivation. A valuable DSR artifact must satisfy a certain societal or business need [30] to determine the relevance and value of the contribution to the IS research field. According to Sect. 1, the accumulation of customer data and the corresponding economic implications (e.g., opportunities for price discrimination based on customer profiling and negative consequences for competition through data feedback loops), security threats, and moral issues pose such a need [49]. We aim to ensure both the relevance of our research and the fitness of our artifact by first more clearly identifying the research problem, identifying the roles, tasks, and requirements of the relevant stakeholders in a systematic literature review, and deriving comprehensive objectives of the solution in the future. As we argued in Sect. 1, the objectives will involve convenience expectations regarding end-user experience, regulatory compliance, and data minimization. We plan to validate and potentially extend these requirements based on expert interviews during the first evaluation cycle of our DSR. We plan to apply the convenience sampling method for interviews. We will form groups of interviewees with respect to their domain of expertise and involve also end-users to have a balanced sample. The selection criteria will correspond to the domains involved in our research, such as cryptographers or IT security researchers, and experts from the business side on e-commerce and adjacent service providers, such as logistics.

We follow the design science research methodology (DSRM) proposed by Peffers et al. [45]. Figure 1 features the corresponding iterative build-and-evaluation cycles. We aim to design and develop our artifact – a DMEC architecture and corresponding information flow that only shares and stores information that is indispensable for each stakeholder and, therefore, mitigates undesirable side effects such as price discrimination against consumers and accumulation of market power. The design will also define onboarding and end-to-end purchasing processes for customers. The build-and-evaluate process is at the core of DSR and helps IS researchers discover answers to problems that have not been resolved before [30]. The DSR method emerged to combine methods from engineering and social sciences for practically relevant, rigorous research [24]. Thus, one can apply the DSR approach to a broad spectrum of domains. The design of a DMEC platform addresses the tension field between convenience, compliance, and data minimization and, therefore, affects both technical and non-technical considerations that need to be incorporated in the development from an engineering and social sciences perspective. Yet, we believe that the implications of our DSR go far beyond e-commerce and may be applicable to adjacent realms such as e-government [20], healthcare [33], the industrial IoT [59], which also seem to involve tensions between data sharing needs and data protection considerations. Particularly blockchain-based applications require such data minimization by design owing to the inherent transparency of distributed ledgers [46,55].

During the process iterations of the DSRM process model, we also instantiate our artifact in the form of a prototype based on the architecture. We will use this instantiation both for the first set of more technical design iterations and for demonstration in the interview-based evaluation. For preparing the implementation, we will define the components of the high-level system architecture and their functionality. Then we will search for potential open-source solutions which can be used in the components. Particularly, we will analyze which open-source solutions could help us to implement the ZKP stack that provides selective disclosure. There will be multiple criteria for ZKP stack selection, such as the performance of proof generation (especially when considering a prototype for e-commerce on mobile devices). So far, we have closely analyzed several promising open-source solutions as candidates and assessed their potential extension for the needs of our architecture.

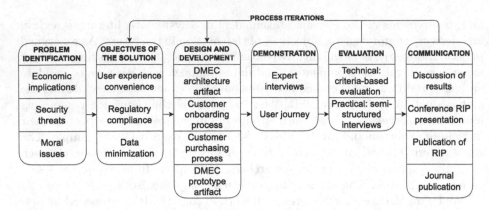

Fig. 1. Our applied DSR approach to design a DMEC architecture following Peffers et al. [45].

The Heimdall framework [6] promises a good fit for our technical requirements. As we highlighted in Sect. 2, related work on privacy-oriented e-commerce solutions still lacks essential features. The Heimdall framework provides several of these features as it implements anonymous credentials that facilitate seamlessly and verifiably sharing the minimum identity-related data required by the relying party in a scalable way [6]. In particular, Heimdall provides a modular set of tools to create, issue, verify, and manage verifiable credentials. Concretely, the framework supports "prover" and "verifier" functions. Users are able to manage and store issued verifiable credentials. They are also capable of generating data minimizing presentations upon verifiers' request in a private way (e.g., selectively disclosing personal information). They do so by means of ZKP, in particular zk-SNARK. Nonetheless, we envision the need to extend Heimdall's functionality to make it compatible with all the project's needs, which is feasible because zk-SNARKs are general-purpose and can be used to prove any statement. The envisioned artifact is in the form of an e-commerce architecture consisting of four main components, namely a checkout page, a digital identity wallet, a back-end architecture, and an agent. The checkout page implements potential checkout options of an e-commerce platform. The digital identity wallet, in which the customer manages identities, serves as a wallet application to share the minimal necessary information with the merchant. When customers indicate their intention to purchase through the website, this communicates with the e-commerce back-end so that the agent establishes a connection with the digital identity wallet. Customers are then able to generate proofs, which are based on the credentials stored in the wallet, in response to the agent's request. The agent verifies and confirms the user-generated proof and sends the appropriate user data to the checkout page.

During the iterations, we will synchronize the evolved design of the system architecture and development direction. The iterations will go in parallel for all the artifacts: the design, processes, and prototype. At the end of each iteration, the quality of the artifacts will be evaluated both technically (performance bench-marking, as mentioned before) and practically (interviews with relevant stake-holders). For demonstration and continuous improvement, we will conduct multi-ple interview cycles and evaluate user journeys with groups of people, which will contribute to the design and development as part of the process iterations by dis-seminating the intermediate progress with the stakeholders and receiving their feedback. Interviews will be essential for collecting feedback regarding the practi-cal side of the prototype to evaluate user experience. There are only a few studies on how users experience the use of digital wallets, particularly data minimiza-tion capabilities [36,51], and we believe that presenting users with a familiar flow, such as commerce, may help gain new insights. The collected feedback will also be implemented according to the DSRM process model.

The envisioned artifact is in the form of an e-commerce architecture con-sisting of four main components, namely a checkout page, a digital identity wallet, a back-end architecture (controller), and an agent. The checkout page implements a checkout option – "checkout with SSI". The digital identity wal-let allows customers to share the minimal identity information necessary with the merchant and other stakeholders, such as logistics service providers. We will use the design tools for layouts of both front-end components (checkout page and wallet). When a customer indicates their intention to purchase through the website, the checkout page communicates with the merchant back-end so that the agent establishes a connection with the digital identity wallet and sends a proof request to it. Upon the customer's confirmation, the wallet generates a corresponding cryptographic proof (SNARK) based on the credentials stored in the wallet that addresses the agent request and sends it back to the verifying component of the agent. The agent cryptographically verifies the proof and noti-fies the merchant's back-end, which transmits the verified identity attributes to the checkout page for a corresponding user.

At the evaluation stage, we will validate the objectives of the solution by means of criteria-based evaluation and semi-structured interviews with stake-holders from both interdisciplinary and specific domains (e.g., business, law, user experience, and software engineering). We also plan to conduct user expe-rience evaluations with our stakeholders. From the business-related interviews, we also aim to investigate the business opportunities of such a solution. At the communications stage, we will focus on the presentation and discussion of the research-in-progress paper at the conference. The second stage would be to pub-lish the full paper. In the end, we will open-source the code of our prototype on GitHub.

4   Conclusion

The increasing market growth of e-commerce has led to the aggregation of large amounts of customer data. With the proliferation of incidents related to sen-sitive data breaches and abuses, both users and regulators are taking steps to protect privacy rights. In this light, we follow the design science research methodology according to Peffers et al. [45] to identify the feasibility of an e-commerce solution that addresses the tension field between convenience aspects and compliance regulation demand the processing and storage of user-related data. Following DSRM, we aim to derive the system architecture of DMEC and build a corresponding prototype. Our proposed solution utilizes digital identities and zero-knowledge proof as core components for privacy-oriented e-commerce transactions. Using an interdisciplinary, criteria-based evaluation, we aim to demonstrate that our artifact can address the societal and business needs that we previously discussed and serve as a starting point for many relevant studies in information systems on usable privacy.

References

1. Alashoor, T., Keil, M., Smith, H.J., McConnell, A.R.: Too tired and in too good of a mood to worry about privacy: explaining the privacy paradox through the lens of effort level in information processing. Inf. Syst. Res. (2022)
2. Allen, C.: The path to self-sovereign identity (2016). http://www.lifewithalacrity.com/2016/04/the-path-to-self-soverereign-identity.html
3. Alt, R.: Electronic markets on business model development. Electron. Mark. 30(3), 405–411 (2020)
4. Alt, R.: Electronic markets on platform transformation. Electron. Mark. 32(2), 401–409 (2022)
5. Anke, J., Richter, D.: Digitale identitäten. HMD Praxis der Wirtschaftsinformatik (2023)
6. Babel, M., Sedlmeir, J.: Bringing data minimization to digital wallets at scale with general-purpose zero-knowledge proofs (2023). http://arxiv.org/abs/2301.00823
7. Baethge, C., Klier, J., Klier, M.: Social commerce - state-of-the-art and future research directions. Electron. Mark. 26(3), 269–290 (2016)
8. Bella, G., Giustolisi, R., Riccobene, S.: Enforcing privacy in e-commerce by balancing anonymity and trust. Comput. Secur. 30(8), 705–718 (2011)
9. Ben-Sasson, E., Bentov, I., Horesh, Y., Riabzev, M.: Scalable, transparent, and post-quantum secure computational integrity (2018). https://eprint.iacr.org/2018/046
10. Ben-Sasson, E., et al.: Zerocash: decentralized anonymous payments from Bitcoin. In: Proceedings of the IEEE Symposium on Security and Privacy, pp. 459–474 (2014)
11. Bergemann, D., Brooks, B., Morris, S.: The limits of price discrimination. Am. Econ. Rev. 105(3), 921–57 (2015)
12. Braud, A., Fromentoux, G., Radier, B., Le Grand, O.: The road to European digital sovereignty with Gaia-X and IDSA. IEEE Network 35(2), 4–5 (2021)
13. Busch, C.: eidas 2.0: digital identity service in platform economy (2022). https://cerre.eu/wp-content/uploads/2022/10/CERRE_Digital-Identity_Issue-Paper_FINAL-2.pdf
14. Camenisch, J., Lysyanskaya, A.: An efficient system for non-transferable anonymous credentials with optional anonymity revocation. In: Proceedings of International Conference on the Theory and Applications of Cryptographic Techniques, pp. 93–118 (2001)
15. Camp, L.J., Osorio, C.A.: Privacy-enhancing technologies for internet commerce (2002). https://papers.ssrn.com/abstract=329282

16. Chaum, D.: Security without identification: transaction systems to make Big Brother obsolete. Commun. ACM **28**(10), 1030–1044 (1985)
17. Dold, F.: The GNU Taler system: practical and provably secure electronic payments (2019). https://syntheses.univ-rennes1.fr/search-theses/notice.html?id=rennes1-ori-wf-1-12183&printable=true
18. European Central Bank: The revised payment services directive (PSD2) (2018). http://www.ecb.europa.eu/paym/intro/mip-online/2018/html/1803_revisedpsd.en.html
19. European Comission: The digital services act: Ensuring a safe and accountable online environment (2022). https://ec.europa.eu/info/strategy/priorities-2019-2024/europe-fit-digital-age/digital-services-act-ensuring-safe-and-accountable-online-environment_en
20. Fedorowicz, J., Gogan, J.L., Culnan, M.J.: Barriers to interorganizational information sharing in e-government: a stakeholder analysis. Inf. Soc. **26**(5), 315–329 (2010)
21. Fienberg, S.E.: Privacy and confidentiality in an e-commerce world: data mining, data warehousing, matching and disclosure limitation. Stat. Sci. **21**(2), 143–154 (2006)
22. Garrido, G.M., Sedlmeir, J., Uludağ, Ö., Alaoui, I.S., Luckow, A., Matthes, F.: Revealing the landscape of privacy-enhancing technologies in the context of data markets for the IoT: a systematic literature review. J. Netw. Comput. Appl. **207**, 103465 (2022)
23. Goldwasser, S., Micali, S., Rackoff, C.: The knowledge complexity of interactive proof systems. SIAM J. Comput. **18**(1), 186–208 (1989)
24. Gregor, S., Hevner, A.R.: Positioning and presenting design science research for maximum impact. MIS Q. **37**(2), 337–355 (2013)
25. Gregory, R.W., Henfridsson, O., Kaganer, E., Kyriakou, H.: The role of artificial intelligence and data network effects for creating user value. Acad. Manag. Rev. **46**(3), 534–551 (2021)
26. Gross, J., Sedlmeir, J., Babel, M., Bechtel, A., Schellinger, B.: Designing a central bank digital currency with support for cash-like privacy (2021). https://papers.ssrn.com/abstract=3891121
27. Groth, J.: On the size of pairing-based non-interactive arguments. In: Fischlin, M., Coron, J.-S. (eds.) EUROCRYPT 2016. LNCS, vol. 9666, pp. 305–326. Springer, Heidelberg (2016). https://doi.org/10.1007/978-3-662-49896-5_11
28. Guggenberger, T., Neubauer, L., Stramm, J., Völter, F., Zwede, T.: Accept me as I am or see me go: a qualitative analysis of user acceptance of self-sovereign identity applications. In: Proceedings of the 56th Hawaii International Conference on System Sciences (2023)
29. Hermes, S., Kaufmann-Ludwig, J., Schreieck, M.: A taxonomy of platform envelopment: revealing patterns and particularities. In: Proceedings of the 26th Americas Conference on Information Systems (2020)
30. Hevner, A., March, S.T., Park, J., Ram, S., et al.: Design science research in information systems. MIS Q. **28**(1), 75–105 (2004)
31. Jøsang, A., Fabre, J., Hay, B., Dalziel, J., Pope, S.: Trust requirements in identity management. In: Proceedings of the 44th Australasian Workshop on Grid Computing and e-Research, pp. 99–108 (2005)
32. Jørgensen, K.P., Beck, R.: Universal wallets. Bus. Inf. Syst. Eng. **64**(1), 115–125 (2022)
33. Kaye, J.: The tension between data sharing and the protection of privacy in genomics research. Annu. Rev. Genomics Hum. Genet. **13**(1), 415–431 (2012)

34. Kayes, I., Iamnitchi, A.: Privacy and security in online social networks: a survey. Online Soc. Netw. Media 3–4 (2017)
35. Keenan, M.: Global e-commerce: stats and trends to watch (2022). http://www.shopify.com/enterprise/global-ecommerce-statistics
36. Khayretdinova, A., Kubach, M., Sellung, R., Roßnagel, H.: Conducting a usability evaluation of decentralized identity management solutions. In: Friedewald, M., Kreutzer, M., Hansen, M. (eds.) Selbstbestimmung, Privatheit und Datenschutz. D, pp. 389–406. Springer, Wiesbaden (2022). https://doi.org/10.1007/978-3-658-33306-5_19
37. Koutsos, V., Papadopoulos, D., Chatzopoulos, D., Tarkoma, S., Hui, P.: Agora: a privacy-aware data marketplace. IEEE Trans. Dependable Secure Comput. 19(6), 3728–3740 (2022)
38. Krombholz, K., Hobel, H., Huber, M., Weippl, E.: Advanced social engineering attacks. J. Inf. Secur. Appl. 22, 113–122 (2015)
39. Kumar, V., Reinartz, W.: Customer privacy concerns and privacy protective responses. In: Customer Relationship Management. STBE, pp. 285–309. Springer, Heidelberg (2018). https://doi.org/10.1007/978-3-662-55381-7_14
40. Lee, C.: An analytical framework for evaluating e-commerce business models and strategies. Internet Res. 11(4), 349–359 (2001)
41. Maseeh, H.I., Jebarajakirthy, C., Pentecost, R., Arli, D., Weaven, S., Ashaduzzaman, M.: Privacy concerns in e-commerce: a multilevel meta-analysis. Psychol. Mark. 38(10), 1779–1798 (2021)
42. Mattke, J., Maier, C., Hund, A.: How an enterprise blockchain application in the U.S. pharmaceuticals supply chain is saving lives. MIS Q. Executive 18(4), 246–261 (2019)
43. Morganti, E., Seidel, S., Blanquart, C., Dablanc, L., Lenz, B.: The impact of e-commerce on final deliveries: alternative parcel delivery services in France and Germany. Transp. Res. Procedia 4, 178–190 (2014)
44. Niu, C., Zheng, Z., Wu, F., Gao, X., Chen, G.: Achieving data truthfulness and privacy preservation in data markets'. IEEE Trans. Knowl. Data Eng. 31(1), 105–119 (2019)
45. Peffers, K., Tuunanen, T., Rothenberger, M.A., Chatterjee, S.: A design science research methodology for information systems research. J. Manag. Inf. Syst. 24(3), 45–77 (2007)
46. Platt, M., Bandara, R.J., Drăgnoiu, A.-E., Krishnamoorthy, S.: Information privacy in decentralized applications. In: Rehman, M.H., Svetinovic, D., Salah, K., Damiani, E. (eds.) Trust Models for Next-Generation Blockchain Ecosystems. EICC, pp. 85–104. Springer, Cham (2021). https://doi.org/10.1007/978-3-030-75107-4_4
47. Qin, Z.: Introduction to E-commerce. Springer, Heidelberg (2009). https://doi.org/10.1007/978-3-540-49645-8
48. Reuters, CNBC: Hackers raid eBay in historic breach, access 145M records (2014). http://www.cnbc.com/2014/05/22/hackers-raid-ebay-in-historic-breach-access-145-mln-records.html
49. Rogaway, P.: The moral character of cryptographic work (2015). https://eprint.iacr.org/2015/1162
50. Rosenberg, M., White, J., Garman, C., Miers, I.: zk-creds: flexible anonymous credentials from zkSNARKs and existing identity infrastructure (2022). https://eprint.iacr.org/2022/878

51. Sartor, S., Sedlmeir, J., Rieger, A., Roth, T.: Love at first sight? A user experience study of self-sovereign identity wallets. In: Proceedings of 30th European Conference on Information Systems (2022)
52. Schanzenbach, M., Grothoff, C., Wenger, H., Kaul, M.: Decentralized identities for self-sovereign end-users (DISSENS). In: Proceedings of Open Identity Summit, pp. 47–58 (2021)
53. Schlatt, V., Sedlmeir, J., Feulner, S., Urbach, N.: Designing a framework for digital KYC processes built on blockchain-based self-sovereign identity. Inf. Manag. **59**(7), 103553 (2022)
54. Sedlmeir, J., Huber, J., Barbereau, T., Weigl, L., Roth, T.: Transition pathways towards design principles of self-sovereign identity. In: Proceedings of the 43rd International Conference on Information Systems (2022)
55. Sedlmeir, J., Lautenschlager, J., Fridgen, G., Urbach, N.: The transparency challenge of blockchain in organizations. Electron. Mark. **32**, 1779–1794 (2022)
56. Stahl, F., Schomm, F., Vossen, G., Vomfell, L.: A classification framework for data marketplaces. Vietnam J. Comput. Sci. **3**(3), 137–143 (2016)
57. Targett, D.: B2B or not B2B? Scenarios for the future of e-commerce. Eur. Bus. J. **13**(1) (2001)
58. Trautman, L.J.: E-commerce, cyber, and electronic payment system risks: lessons from PayPal (2016). https://papers.ssrn.com/abstract=2314119
59. Ukil, A., Bandyopadhyay, S., Pal, A.: IoT-privacy: to be private or not to be private. In: Proceedings of the Conference on Computer Communications Workshops, pp. 123–124 (2014)
60. W3C: Engineering privacy for verified credentials (2022). https://w3c-ccg.github.io/data-minimization/#selective-disclosure
61. Weigl, L., Barbereau, T.J., Rieger, A., Fridgen, G.: The social construction of self-sovereign identity: an extended model of interpretive flexibility. In: Proceedings of the 55th Hawaii International Conference on System Sciences, pp. 2543–2552 (2022)
62. Wolford, B.: What is GDPR, the EU's new data protection law? (2018). https://gdpr.eu/what-is-gdpr/
63. van der Wolk, A., Silva, K.: Insight: a slap on the wrist or show of force - GDPR fines reveal need for EU penalty guidelines (2019). https://news.bloomberglaw.com/privacy-and-data-security/insight-a-slap-on-the-wrist-or-show-of-force-gdpr-fines-reveal-need-for-eu-penalty-guidelines
64. Wüst, K., Kostiainen, K., Delius, N., Capkun, S.: Platypus: a central bank digital currency with unlinkable transactions and privacy-preserving regulation. In: Proceedings of the ACM SIGSAC Conference on Computer and Communications Security, pp. 2947–2960 (2022)
65. Zhuang, Y., Lederer, A.L.: An instrument for measuring the business benefits of e-commerce retailing. Int. J. Electron. Commer. **7**(3), 65–99 (2003)
66. Zhou, L.: Product advertising recommendation in e-commerce based on deep learning and distributed expression. Electron. Commer. Res. **20**(2), 321–342 (2020)
67. Zuboff, S.: Big other: surveillance capitalism and the prospects of an information civilization. J. Inf. Technol. **30**(1), 75–89 (2015)

Enabling the Evaluation of Production Scheduling Algorithms in Complex Production Environments Using Individually Deployable Scheduling Services

Michael Groth[✉], Alexander Dippel, and Matthias Schumann

University of Goettingen, Goettingen, Germany
{michael.groth,mschuma1}@uni-goettingen.de,
alexander.dippel@stud.uni-goettingen.de

Abstract. Changes in customer demands and technological advances increase the complexity of production scheduling. Hence, current production scheduling algorithms are not sufficiently good. Additionally, advances in the research of Machine Learning algorithms drive the development of new scheduling algorithms. Each algorithm's quality is problem-dependent, making it challenging to find the best algorithm for a given production scenario. Benchmark problems only provide guidance as they do not reflect real-world situations. To address this issue, in this article, we develop the software artifact *Simfia* that allows researchers and practitioners to evaluate production scheduling algorithms in highly customizable experiments. To create the solution, we follow a design science research approach. We identify 30 functional requirements, develop the solution prototypically and demonstrate it in an exemplary production scenario. The artifact is developed in a service-oriented architecture where scheduling algorithms are provided as individually deployable scheduling services that Simfia manages. This solution enables researchers and practitioners to experiment with production scheduling algorithms in highly configurable production scenarios.

Keywords: Production Scheduling Algorithms · Evaluation Environment · Simulation · Machine Learning

1 Introduction

Customers of manufacturing companies increasingly demand individualized products, summarized in the Mass Customization theory [1]. This demand change decreases batch sizes in production and thus creates the need for more frequent changeovers [2]. In addition, the demand for shorter delivery times is increasing, necessitating faster lead times in production [3]. Technological advances (e.g., cyber-physical systems) enable these demand changes [4]. Moreover, new schedules must be created quickly so that a delayed response to unforeseen situations (e.g., machine breakdowns and rush orders) does not reduce productivity [2]. This results in the need for fast production scheduling to

A. Gerber and R. Baskerville (Eds.): DESRIST 2023, LNCS 13873, pp. 18–32, 2023.
https://doi.org/10.1007/978-3-031-32808-4_2

handle the increased complexity, thus increasing efficiency of resource usage in industry [5].

Multiple approaches exist for creating schedules. Priority rules allow scheduling in a sufficiently fast time but only provide sub-optimal results, especially in complex situations [6, 7]. Additionally, Machine Learning algorithms, like Genetic Algorithms [e.g., 7] or Reinforcement Learning [e.g., 8], are researched to improve the quality of generated schedules. In Machine Learning, many algorithms exist, each offering specific advantages over other algorithms [8]. Since the quality of each algorithm is problem-dependent (e.g., setup times, machine buffers, scheduling of automated guided vehicles for transportation), finding the optimal algorithm for a production scenario is no trivial task. Benchmark problems, often used in the literature [9], can only provide guidance but not definite answers because they represent a specific problem. In addition, for more advanced problems, no benchmarks are available [10]. A tool is required to allow practitioners to find the most suitable algorithms for their production scenario and researchers to evaluate developed scheduling algorithms in a broad array of customizable scenarios against other independently developed algorithms.

Simulation tools are used to assess the quality of scheduling algorithms besides benchmarks [11]. These tools are tailored to specific production scenarios and do not allow extensive experiments with multiple scheduling algorithms independently deployed.

A solution is needed to allow practitioners and researchers to compare scheduling algorithms in highly customizable experiments adjusted to a company's individual needs or to cover a broad spectrum of scheduling problems. To provide such a solution and make the development reproducible, we answer the following research questions in this paper:

RQ1: *What are the requirements for a software artifact to evaluate production scheduling algorithms in complex production environments?*
RQ2: *How can a software artifact be designed to evaluate production scheduling algorithms in complex production environments?*

To answer these questions, the remainder is organized as follows: In the next section, the theoretical foundations and related research of production scheduling are presented to introduce the topic and provide a common understanding. After this, in Sect. 3, the research design is introduced, followed by the results of the conducted design science research process in Sect. 4, answering the research questions. Finally, we conclude our research and provide an outlook on future research in Sect. 5.

2 Theoretical Foundation and Related Research of Production Scheduling

Production Scheduling is part of production planning and control and is used in many manufacturing and services industries [12]. Production scheduling is the time-related allocation of production tasks to production resources for released production jobs [12].

The objectives of production schedules vary in companies. Often, the objective is minimizing lead times, tardiness, or costs [13]. Because scheduling is an np-hard problem, an optimal schedule cannot be found analytically, thus creating the need for heuristic methods to solve this problem [14]. To address this issue, heuristic methods are used to create "good" schedules. Priority rules (e.g., first-in-first-out [FIFO]) allow the fast creation of schedules that are easily understandable but lack quality [12, 15, 16]. To improve the quality of the solution, Machine Learning scheduling algorithms can also be used. Cyber-physical systems enable the use of Machine Learning methods for production scheduling by providing mass real-time data and thus enabling data-driven decisions [17].

Current research applies Genetic algorithms to generate production schedules by coding a sequence of operations or priority rules in the chromosomes [18, 19]. In addition, Genetic algorithms develop custom priority rules [20]. To incorporate real-world complexity into the algorithm, Nie et al. [21] use fuzzy processing times. Wei et al. [22] extend the scheduling problem by including the prioritization of jobs, while Yan et al. [23] consider transportation vehicles as additional production resources. Furthermore, other heuristic search algorithms are used. Zhang et al. [24] apply the Ant Colony Optimization algorithm, while Zhao et al. [25] use the Particle Swarm Optimization algorithm with Simulated Annealing. Also, Neural Networks can create production schedules [26]. Algorithms based on Reinforcement Learning show promising results while requiring a short time for calculating schedules [27, 28]. Instead of finding a global solution, articles suggest using an agent system where agents represent production resources and make their own decisions. Using agents reduces the complexity of the scheduling problem [29, 30].

The generated production schedules are generally evaluated using a Discrete Event Simulation. Discrete Event Simulation is a modeling technique [31] in which observed phenomena change value or state at discrete points in time, opposing to continuously with time [32]. Simulation also allows the incorporation of random events into the evaluation of production schedules [11]. Multiple commercial [33, 34] and open-source solutions [35–37] exist to simulate production schedules.

In these systems, practitioners design and test their factory layout and its influence on production. Therefore, it must be tailored to specific production scenarios. Besides scheduling, these systems are also used for strategic decision support, e.g., analyzing the layout and dimensioning of capacities. Therefore, the focus of these systems does not lie on the evaluation of production scheduling algorithms, and they do not allow extensive experiments with multiple different scheduling algorithms independently deployed.

3 Research Design

To answer the research question, we used the mixed-method Design Science Research approach adapted from Peffers et al. [38]. This problem-oriented approach includes the well-founded development of IT artifacts. In our research design, we followed the research process depicted in Fig. 1.

First, the design of the simulation environment is grounded in problem identification based on a structured literature review, according to vom Brocke [39] and Webster & Watson [40]. This literature review aimed to gain a holistic view of the research domain and define a solution's objectives (step 2). Therefore, we analyzed scientific literature databases with a search query combining search terms from the domains production scheduling (*(((industrial OR manufacturing) AND (scheduling OR sequencing)) OR "order dispatching" OR "flexible manufacturing"*), Machine Learning (*"machine learning" OR ML*), and application (*app OR application OR simulation*). While using the literature base for the problem identification, we found 16 publications relevant for defining an overarching objective and deriving the requirements of a solution, thus answering RQ1. According to the research design, we designed and developed (step 3) the software artifact based on the derived requirements. Finally, we demonstrated that the artifact works within a laboratory study in an exemplary production scenario.

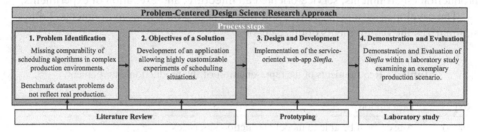

Fig. 1. Research design adapted from Peffers et al. [38]

4 Artifact to Evaluate Production Scheduling Algorithms

In the following sections, we will present the development and resulting artifact named *Simfia* for comparing production scheduling algorithms in highly customizable experiments. The structure follows the research design presented in Sect. 3.

4.1 Problem Identification

Good scheduling is required to deal with complex scheduling problems that arise from changing customer demands [2, 3]. In addition, the emerging technologies included in cyber-physical systems in production offer possibilities for data-driven decision-making that has to be taken into account by scheduling [4, 41].

Many algorithms are researched in production scheduling, making finding the best algorithm in a specific production environment challenging as algorithm performance is problem dependent [8]. The performance of algorithms may be measured in benchmark problems, but they only help guide the decision and cannot give a proficient answer because the real-world problem is different from benchmark problems. Additionally, benchmarks are not available for all problem classes [10].

Therefore, there is a need for a solution to compare scheduling algorithms in highly customizable experiments adjustable to individual needs. This is relevant for researchers to quickly evaluate developed algorithms in more complex scenarios and for practitioners to help find appropriate scheduling algorithms that work best in a company-specific situation.

4.2 Objective and Requirements

To solve these problems, the solution's objective is to provide an environment that allows practitioners and researchers to create and conduct highly customizable experiments to measure the performance of production scheduling algorithms in complex production scenarios. Following this objective, we derived 30 functional requirements based on the structured literature review described in Sect. 3 and following the approach of Sommerville [42]. We formulated the requirements by identifying and deriving them from literature on production scheduling algorithms [e.g., 27], decision support systems for production scheduling [e.g., 17], and research analyzing drivers and effects of production scheduling [e.g., 43]. We categorize the requirements into the representation of production environments, service-oriented architecture, and execution of experiments.

The developed system needs to be able to represent production environments. Table 1 summarizes the requirements of this category.

Table 1. Requirements of the representation of the production environment.

Req	Description
$R_{Prod}1$	A user must be able to model production scenarios
$R_{Prod}2$	A user must be able to use production scenarios in experiments
$R_{Prod}3$	A user must be able to define production resources
$R_{Prod}4$	A user must be able to define products
$R_{Prod}5$	A user must be able to define parts lists for products
$R_{Prod}6$	A user must be able to define a production process of products on production resources
$R_{Prod}7$	A user must be able to define the order of operations of a production process
$R_{Prod}8$	A user must be able to define the execution times of operations on production resources
$R_{Prod}9$	The system must visualize production processes and their operations
$R_{Prod}10$	A user must be able to define jobs that require a defined number of products and have a due date
$R_{Prod}11$	A user must be able to assign jobs to production scenarios
$R_{Prod}12$	The system must provide an aggregated view of jobs
$R_{Prod}13$	The system must display the properties of jobs, operations, and production resources

The system must allow users to model production environments in production scenarios [$R_{Prod}1$] and use them in experiments [$R_{Prod}2$]. Additionally, a user must be able to define production resources (e.g., machines) [$R_{Prod}3$], products [$R_{Prod}4$], and parts lists for products [$R_{Prod}5$]. Also, one must be able to define the production process on production resources consisting of operations [$R_{Prod}6$], the order of operations of a production process [$R_{Prod}7$], as well as the execution times of an operation on production resources [$R_{Prod}8$]. The production process should also be visualized for better understanding [$R_{Prod}9$]. In addition, users must be able to define jobs with a defined number of products and a due date [$R_{Prod}10$]. These jobs must be assignable to production scenarios [$R_{Prod}11$] and be visualized on an aggregated level to analyze all jobs of production scenarios [$R_{Prod}12$]. Finally, the system must display the properties of jobs, operations, and production resources [$R_{Prod}13$]. The scheduling problem is defined with these requirements, and scheduling services can create and simulate schedules using the information provided.

To support every possible scheduling algorithm, a service-oriented architecture is required, in which scheduling algorithms are implemented and provided in scheduling services. The developed system acts as a service consumer [44]. Table 2 presents the requirements regarding service-oriented architecture.

Table 2. Requirements of the service-oriented architecture

Req	Description
$R_{SOA}1$	A scheduling service must implement a scheduling algorithm
$R_{SOA}2$	A scheduling service must work independently
$R_{SOA}3$	A scheduling service must use a defined programming interface
$R_{SOA}4$	A scheduling service must provide a method to create production scenarios
$R_{SOA}5$	A scheduling service must save a production scenario and return an identifier
$R_{SOA}6$	A scheduling service must provide a method to delete a production scenario
$R_{SOA}7$	A scheduling service must provide a method to create production schedules
$R_{SOA}8$	The system must provide a directory of scheduling services
$R_{SOA}9$	The system must allow users to define connection data and other master data of a scheduling service
$R_{SOA}10$	The system must provide an automatic integration process for scheduling services
$R_{SOA}11$	The system must be able to deploy scheduling services

A scheduling service must implement a production scheduling algorithm [$R_{SOA}1$] and work independently of the developed system [$R_{SOA}2$]. For the system to work with the scheduling services, scheduling services must use a defined programming interface [$R_{SOA}3$]. The programming interface includes a method to transmit production scenarios and create them in the service [$R_{SOA}4$]. The service must persist the production scenarios and return an identifier of the persisted production scenario [$R_{SOA}5$]. In addition, the programming interface includes a method to delete production scenarios [$R_{SOA}6$]. It also includes a method to create a production schedule under the specification of a production scenario, including jobs and performance criteria returning a created production schedule [$R_{SOA}7$]. To work with scheduling services, the system must provide a directory of scheduling services [$R_{SOA}8$] and allow users to define properties, connection data, and other master data of a scheduling service [$R_{SOA}9$]. Hence the system should be easily usable, it must provide an automatic integration process of newly added scheduling services [$R_{SOA}10$] and offer the possibility to deploy scheduling services automatically [$R_{SOA}11$].

Finally, users must be able to conduct experiments. Table 3 lists the requirements for the execution of experiments.

First, the system must provide the possibility to define experiments referencing a production scenario and scheduling services on which the experiment should be conducted [$R_{Exp}1$]. Additionally, the user must be able to define the performance criteria of experiments. These criteria are used by the scheduling service to evaluate the resulting schedules in a simulation of the generated schedule and allow algorithms to optimize the creation of schedules regarding the performance criteria [$R_{Exp}2$]. After defining an experiment, the user must be able to start it [$R_{Exp}3$]. As a result, the system must display the resulting production schedules [$R_{Exp}4$] and provide a report with the aggregated results of the experiment [$R_{Exp}5$]. Finally, to allow for a more thorough analysis, the system must provide an export functionality of the raw data of experiments [$R_{Exp}6$].

Table 3. Requirements for the execution of experiments

Req	Description
$R_{Exp}1$	The user must be able to define an experiment using a production scenario and scheduling services
$R_{Exp}2$	The user must be able to define the performance criteria of experiments
$R_{Exp}3$	The user must be able to start experiments
$R_{Exp}4$	The system must display the resulting production schedules
$R_{Exp}5$	The system must report aggregated results of experiments
$R_{Exp}6$	The system must allow exports of raw data from experiments

4.3   Design and Development

To achieve the service-oriented architecture, we created a web-based application using the Python-based framework Django [45] as the backend server. The container virtualization platform Docker Engine [46] deploys and manages scheduling services. A container provides an application's runtime environment and encapsulates all software dependencies (e.g., program libraries, operating system packages). This separates software development from deployment and allows for automatic deployments [47]. Docker's REST API enables the developed system to manage containers programmatically [48]. This way, users only provide the container image or a link to the image of the scheduling service, which is used to create the container of the scheduling service. From this, scheduling services are not bound to one programming language, but the developers can use any desired programming language to develop the scheduling services. The required programming interface between scheduling services and *Simfia* is provided using the OpenAPI 3 specification [49], facilitating scheduling services developers to generate code fragments automatically. Therefore, developers can focus on the scheduling algorithm itself. We present our overall system architecture in Fig. 2 (left).

Based on the identified requirements, we derived the following key functionalities: Modeling of production environments, directory of scheduling services, and experiments.

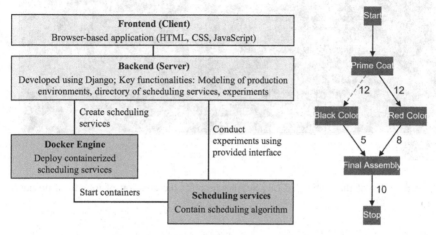

Fig. 2. Architecture of *Simfia* (left); Generated graph structure of a production process (right)

Modeling the production environment involves creating, editing, or deleting all data associated with the production environment. A production scenario represents a production environment. Production resources (e.g., machines) are defined in a production scenario. Each production resource has freely definable properties allowing any production environment to be mapped. These properties are key-value pairs. For example, they could be used to specify buffer sizes taken into account by the scheduling service. Additionally, products can be defined. These products can be final or intermediary products and contain a parts list. A production process consists of multiple process steps, each executing an operation, while a process step can have a following and an alternative process step. Figure 2 (right) shows an example of the resulting graph structure displayed in *Simfia*. The edges represent processing times, and the red edges show alternative branches. Operations are referred to in production process steps and are carried out using a production resource. Each operation can have freely definable properties. For example, they can be used to define the costs of an operation on a machine.

Finally, jobs can be defined for a production scenario. To enable a simple creation of complex job structures, jobs can be created using Lua Scripts [50]. A script interpreter can execute Lua Scripts. Different application domains have successfully used Lua Scripts in this embedded way [51, 52]. Figure 3 presents the embedded editor. The created jobs are presented in an aggregated view in the job overview of the production scenario showing the production parts distribution and the jobs per due date.

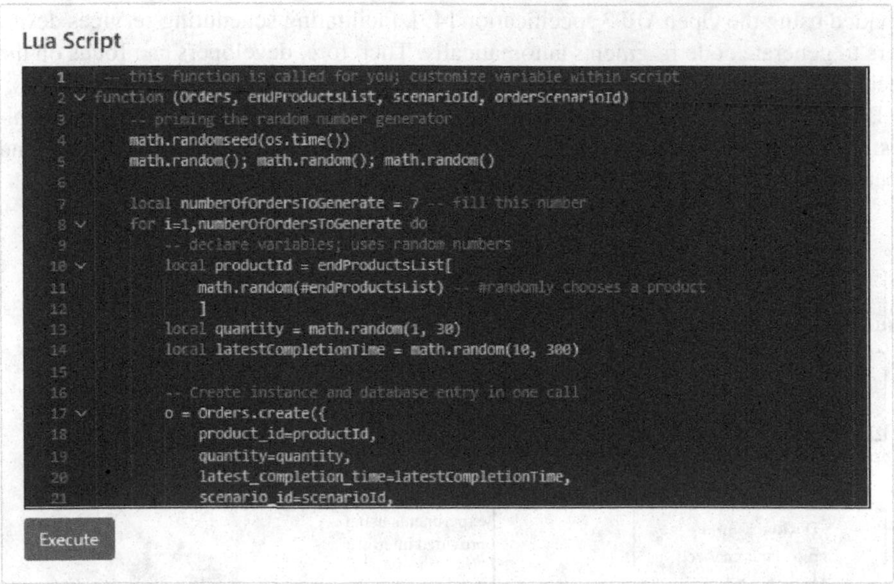

Lua Script

```
1     -- this function is called for you; customize variable within script
2  v  function (Orders, endProductsList, scenarioId, orderScenarioId)
3        -- priming the random number generator
4        math.randomseed(os.time())
5        math.random(); math.random(); math.random()
6
7        local numberOfOrdersToGenerate = 7  -- fill this number
8  v     for i=1,numberOfOrdersToGenerate do
9           -- declare variables; uses random numbers
10 v        local productId = endProductsList[
11             math.random(#endProductsList)  -- #randomly chooses a product
12          ]
13          local quantity = math.random(1, 30)
14          local latestCompletionTime = math.random(10, 300)
15
16          -- Create instance and database entry in one call
17 v        o = Orders.create({
18             product_id=productId,
19             quantity=quantity,
20             latest_completion_time=latestCompletionTime,
21             scenario_id=scenarioId,
```

Execute

Fig. 3. Screenshot of the embedded Lua Script editor for the creation of jobs for a production scenario

The second key feature is the directory of scheduling services. It is the connecting link between the simulation environment and scheduling services. For a scheduling service to be used, it must be integrated into the scheduling service directory. To integrate a scheduling service, the URL of the service has to be specified. Afterward, integration of the service can be conducted, resulting in an exchange of configuration options. A developer of a scheduling service can deploy it independently, or the developer can let *Simfia* deploy the service using the Docker Engine.

For a deployment by *Simfia*, a deployment template needs to be specified consisting of an image name and a container command for the startup. Optionally, credentials may be provided to allow the use of private container registries (e.g., GitLab's Container Registry [53]). This way, the deployment by *Simfia* can be integrated into a development process of a scheduling service. In a deployment template, additional configuration variables can be defined that will be passed to the created containers, making changes to the scheduling services possible without changes to the code base of these services. Based on the deployment template, containers can be created, which are integrated into the directory of scheduling services.

The goal of this key functionality is to enable the independent creation of production scheduling services which does not restrict developers from creating complex scheduling algorithms, potentially integrating Machine Learning methods into them. Furthermore, it offers an easy integration process of these services into *Simfia*.

The final key functionality is experiments, which combine the previously described functionalities. Herewith production scheduling algorithms can be evaluated. For an experiment, properties can be freely defined, e.g., the model ID of a neural network can be specified. In addition, performance criteria must be defined to evaluate the generated schedules. Finally, the used scheduling services are specified.

After creating an experiment, it can be conducted. The results are presented when all scheduling services calculated and simulated the production schedules and returned them. For each scheduling service, the resulting production schedule, as well as the results of the performance criteria, are presented. An export of the results of each scheduling service is available for more detailed analysis in different tools.

4.4 Demonstration

After implementing the artifact, we must demonstrate its feasibility and functionalities according to our research design. To accomplish this, we conducted a laboratory study of an exemplary production environment depicting a bicycle manufacturing process. We revise the functionalities and the implemented requirements in doing so.

The requirements of the representation of the production environment are implemented in the key functionality modeling of the production environment. The requirements $R_{Prod}1$, $R_{Prod}3$–8, $R_{Prod}10$–11, and $R_{Prod}13$ include defining data about the production environment. We used CRUD tables to have a similar user interface for all data management operations. CRUD tables offer the data operations "Create", "Read", "Update", and "Delete" in a table view [54]. Relationships between resources are also defined using the CRUD table. Figure 4 (top left) provides an exemplary screenshot showing a CRUD table for defining operations.

$R_{Prod}2$ is accomplished in the key functionality of experiments. $R_{Prod}9$ is implemented using the graph structure already presented in Fig. 2 (right). The aggregated view on jobs in a production scenario required by $R_{Prod}12$ is realized by diagrams showing the production parts distribution and the job distribution according to the due date. Figure 4 (top right, bottom) showcases these diagrams.

The requirements of the service-oriented architecture are implemented in the key functionality directory of scheduling services. The developer of the scheduling service must implement $R_{SOA}1$–7. To allow for a fast development process, the programming interface specification is provided using the OpenAPI 3 specification [49], enabling developers to generate methods to implement the programming interface automatically. The data of the requirements $R_{SOA}8$–9 are also defined using CRUD tables. The automatic integration process required by $R_{SOA}10$ is implemented by an integration function that tests the programming interface and exchanges configuration parameters. The automatic deployments required by $R_{SOA}11$ are enabled by providing the functionality to define container images within deployment templates. *Simfia* can then start these containers by calling the REST-API provided by the Docker Engine. *Simfia* manages the lifecycle of these containers.

The requirements of the execution of an experiment are implemented in the key functionality of experiments. Experiments [$R_{Exp}1$–2] are also defined in a CRUD table, referring to a production scenario and scheduling services and specifying the performance criteria. Afterward, a scheduling experiment can be started [$R_{Exp}3$]. *Simfia* then sends the required information to the scheduling services via the defined programming interface. Following the results returned by the scheduling services, they are presented according to $R_{Exp}4$–6. The individual results of each scheduling service are viewable, and

Fig. 4. Screenshot of the CRUD table for operations (top left); Screenshot of the aggregated view on jobs of a production scenario (top right, bottom)

the scheduling services are ranked according to the defined performance criteria making the best-performing scheduling algorithms in the experiment easily visible. Besides logs of the execution of a scheduling service, the raw data returned by the scheduling services can also be viewed and exported, which enables users to conduct a more in-depth analysis of the results in other tools.

5   Conclusion and Future Research

The presented research aimed to demonstrate how a software artifact could be designed to evaluate production scheduling algorithms in complex production environments. To achieve this goal, we followed a design science research approach. At first, based on a structured literature review, we identified the problem that changes in customer demands increase the complexity of production scheduling, and thus the demand to find the best algorithm in a specific production environment increases while, at the same time, the amount of available algorithms increases, enabled by advances in technology. To solve the problem of finding the best production scheduling algorithm, we derived the objective of the solution. The solution's goal is to provide an environment that allows practitioners and researchers to create and conduct highly customizable experiments to measure the performance of production scheduling algorithms in complex production scenarios. Based on the objective, we answered RQ1 and identified 30 requirements. The requirements were translated into the key functionalities representation of the production environment, service-oriented architecture, and execution of an experiment allowing the creation of complex real-world production scenarios by providing freely definable properties, answering RQ2. We demonstrated the functionalities based on a laboratory study. The developed solution uses the emerging technology of containerized, and thus independently deployable scheduling services and allows for the evaluation of Machine Learning scheduling algorithms.

However, we acknowledge that our research has some limitations. First, the structured literature review used for the problem identification and objective of a solution might not have found all literature of relevance and not all requirements. By following the structured approach, we tried to minimize subjective influences. Second, we conducted a laboratory study focused on our artifact's implemented requirements and functionalities. This way, we ensured the developed solution fulfills all requirements and meets the defined objective. Additionally, a qualitative study consisting of interviews with experts would be helpful to find potential additional requirements and to ensure practicability in practice and research. Finally, the developed artifact should be evaluated in practice using multiple production scheduling algorithms to find improvements to the developed solution. We plan to conduct a qualitative interview study and an application in practice with real-life data to evaluate and improve the developed solution in future research.

Nevertheless, the results show that *Simfia* can be used to evaluate production scheduling algorithms using highly customizable experiments. For practice, our research contributes a design concept and tool to find good production schedules efficiently. For research, our research contributes, in addition to the design concept and tool for scheduling researchers, a level 2 design science contribution presenting knowledge as operational principles in the form of requirements [55]. *Simfia* serves as an instantiation of the derived requirements. More iterations of the design science research process must be conducted to obtain a more general design theory (level 3).

References

1. Da Silveira, G., Borenstein, D., Fogliatto, F.S.: Mass customization: literature review and research directions. Int. J. Prod. Econ. **72**, 1–13 (2001). https://doi.org/10.1016/S0925-527 3(00)00079-7
2. Yang, W., Takakuwa, S.: Simulation-based dynamic shop floor scheduling for a flexible manufacturing system in the industry 4.0 environment. In: Chan, W.K.V. (ed) Winter Simulation Conference, pp. 3908–3916. IEEE (2017)
3. Schuh, G., Potente, T., Thomas, C., et al.: Web-based value stream oriented simulation of production control. In: Laroque, C. (ed) 2012 Winter Simulation Conference, pp. 1–10. IEEE (2012)
4. Lasi, H., Fettke, P., Kemper, H.-G., Feld, T., Hoffmann, M.: Industrie 4.0. Wirtschafts Informatik **56**(4), 261–264 (2014). https://doi.org/10.1007/s11576-014-0424-4
5. Baumol, W.J.: Economic theory and operations analysis. South. Econ. J. **28**, 305 (1962). https://doi.org/10.2307/1055453
6. Zhang, H., Jiang, Z., Guo, C.: Simulation-based optimization of dispatching rules for semiconductor wafer fabrication system scheduling by the response surface methodology. Int. J. Adv. Manuf. Technol. **41**, 110–121 (2009). https://doi.org/10.1007/s00170-008-1462-0

7. Wang, Z., Wu, Q., Qiao, F.: A lot dispatching strategy integrating WIP management and wafer start control. IEEE Trans. Automat. Sci. Eng. **4**, 579–583 (2007). https://doi.org/10.1109/TASE.2007.905991
8. Fazel Zarandi, M.H., Sadat Asl, A.A., Sotudian, S., Castillo, O.: A state of the art review of intelligent scheduling. Artif. Intell. Rev. **53**(1), 501–593 (2018). https://doi.org/10.1007/s10462-018-9667-6
9. Taillard, E.: Benchmarks for basic scheduling problems. Eur. J. Oper. Res. **64**, 278–285 (1993). https://doi.org/10.1016/0377-2217(93)90182-M
10. Li, W., Han, D., Gao, L., et al.: Integrated production and transportation scheduling method in hybrid flow shop. Chin. J. Mech. Eng. **35**, 1–20 (2022). https://doi.org/10.1186/s10033-022-00683-7
11. Banks, J.: Output analysis capabilities of simulation software. SIMULATION **66**, 23–30 (1996). https://doi.org/10.1177/003754979606600103
12. Pinedo, M.L.: Scheduling Theory, Algorithms, and Systems. Springer International Publishing, Cham (2016).https://doi.org/10.1007/978-3-319-26580-3
13. Toader, F.A.: Production scheduling in flexible manufacturing systems: a state of the art survey. J. Electr. Eng. Electron. Control Comput. Sci. **3**, 1–6 (2017)
14. Garey, M.R., Johnson, D.S.: Computers and Intractability, vol. 174. Freeman, San Francisco (1979)
15. Nguyen, S., Zhang, M., Johnston, M., et al.: Learning iterative dispatching rules for job shop scheduling with genetic programming. Int. J. Adv. Manuf. Technol. **67**, 85–100 (2013). https://doi.org/10.1007/s00170-013-4756-9
16. Blackstone, J.H., Phillips, D.T., Hogg, G.L.: A state-of-the-art survey of dispatching rules for manufacturing job shop operations. Int. J. Prod. Res. **20**, 27–45 (1982). https://doi.org/10.1080/00207548208947745
17. Freier, P., Schumann, M.: Design and implementation of a decision support system for production scheduling in the context of cyber-physical systems. In: Gronau, N., Heine, M., Poustcchi, K. et al. (eds) WI2020 Zentrale Tracks pp. 757–773. GITO Verlag, (2020)
18. Rolf, B., Reggelin, T., Nahhas, A., et al.: Assigning dispatching rules using a genetic algorithm to solve a hybrid flow shop scheduling problem. Procedia Manufact. **42**, 442–449 (2020). https://doi.org/10.1016/j.promfg.2020.02.051
19. Zhang, L., Wang, L., Tang, F.: Order-based genetic algorithm for flow shop scheduling. In: Proceedings of the International Conference on Machine Learning and Cybernetics, pp. 139–144. IEEE (2002)
20. Tamaki, H., Ochi, M., Araki, M.: Genetics-based machine learning approach to production scheduling-a case of in-tree type precedence relation. In: Proceedings of the IEEE International Symposium on Industrial Electronics ISIE 1998 (Cat. No.98TH8357), pp. 714–719. IEEE (1998)
21. Nie, L., Gao, L., Li, P., et al.: Application of gene expression programming on dynamic job shop scheduling problem. In: Proceedings of the 2011 15th International Conference on Computer Supported Cooperative Work in Design (CSCWD), pp. 291–295. IEEE (2011)
22. Wei, H., Li, S., Quan, H., et al.: Unified multi-objective genetic algorithm for energy efficient job shop scheduling. IEEE Access **9**, 54542–54557 (2021). https://doi.org/10.1109/ACCESS.2021.3070981
23. Yan, J., Liu, Z., Zhang, T., et al.: Autonomous decision-making method of transportation process for flexible job shop scheduling problem based on reinforcement learning. In: International Conference on Machine Learning and Intelligent Systems Engineering, pp. 234–238. IEEE (2021)
24. Zhang, R., Song, S., Wu, C.: Robust scheduling of hot rolling production by local search enhanced ant colony optimization algorithm. IEEE Trans. Ind. Inf. **16**, 2809–2819 (2020). https://doi.org/10.1109/TII.2019.2944247

25. Zhao, F., Zhang, Q., Yang, Y.: An improved particle swarm optimization (PSO) algorithm and fuzzy inference systems based approach to process planning and production scheduling integration in holonic manufacturing system (HMS). In: 2006 International Conference on Machine Learning and Cybernetics, pp. 396–401. IEEE (2006)
26. Liu, M., Dong, M.-Y., Wu, C.: An objective decomposing method based on IBMDC for solving complex production scheduling problem. In: Proceedings. International Conference on Machine Learning and Cybernetics, pp. 1676–1679. IEEE (2002)
27. Elsayed, A.K., Elsayed, E.K., Eldahshan, K.A.: Deep reinforcement learning based actor-critic framework for decision-making actions in production scheduling. In: 2021 Tenth International Conference on Intelligent Computing and Information Systems (ICICIS), pp. 32–40. IEEE (2021)
28. Qu, S., Wang, J., Shivani, G.: Learning adaptive dispatching rules for a manufacturing process system by using reinforcement learning approach. In: 2016 IEEE 21st International Conference on Emerging Technologies and Factory Automation (ETFA), pp. 1–8. IEEE (2016)
29. Waschneck, B., Reichstaller, A., Belzner, L., et al.: Deep reinforcement learning for semi-conductor production scheduling. In: 2018 29th Annual SEMI Advanced Semiconductor Manufacturing Conference (ASMC), pp. 301–306. IEEE (2018)
30. Park, I.-B., Huh, J., Kim, J., et al.: A reinforcement learning approach to robust scheduling of semiconductor manufacturing facilities. IEEE Trans. Automat. Sci. Eng. **17**, 1420–1431 (2019). https://doi.org/10.1109/TASE.2019.2956762
31. Jeffrey, P., Seaton, R.: The use of operational research tools: a survey of operational research practitioners in the UK. J. Oper. Res. Soc. **46**, 797–808 (1995). https://doi.org/10.1057/jors.1995.113
32. Fishman, G.S.: Discrete-Event Simulation. Springer New York, New York, NY (2001)
33. Plant Simulation: Plant Simulation (2023). https://plant-simulation.de/. Accessed 06 Jan 2023
34. anylogic: anylogic - Material Handling Library (2023). https://www.anylogic.de/features/libraries/material-handling-library/. Accessed 06 Jan 2023
35. SimPy: SimPy - Discrete event simulation for Python (2023). https://simpy.readthedocs.io/en/latest/. Accessed 06 Jan 2023
36. ManPy: ManPy - Discrete event simulation in python (2023). https://www.manpy-simulation.org/. Accessed 06 Jan 2023
37. Neal DeBuhr: SimRS (2022). https://simrs.com/. Accessed 06 Jan 2023
38. Peffers, K., Tuunanen, T., Rothenberger, M.A., et al.: A design science research methodology for information systems research. J. Manag. Inf. Syst. **24**, 45–77 (2007). https://doi.org/10.2753/MIS0742-1222240302
39. vom Brocke, J., Simons, A., Niehaves, B., et al.: Reconstructing the giant: On the importance of rigour in documenting the literature search process. In: Proceedings of the ECIS 2009 (2009)
40. Webster, J., Watson, R.T.: Analyzing the past to prepare for the future: writing a literature review. MIS Quarterly 26:xiii–xxiii (2002)
41. Lang, S., Reggelin, T., Jobran, M., et al.: Towards a modular, decentralized and digital industry 4.0 learning factory. In: 2018 Sixth International Conference on Enterprise Systems (ES), pp. 123–128. IEEE (2018)
42. Sommerville, I.: Integrated requirements engineering: a tutorial. IEEE Softw. **22**, 16–23 (2005). https://doi.org/10.1109/MS.2005.13
43. Kamaruddin, S., Khan, Z.A., Noor Siddiquee, A., et al.: The impact of variety of orders and different number of workers on production scheduling performance. J. Manuf. Technol. Manag. **24**, 1123–1142 (2013). https://doi.org/10.1108/JMTM-12-2010-0083
44. OASIS: Reference Model for Service Oriented Architecture (2006). https://www.oasis-open.org/committees/download.php/16587/wd-soa-rm-cd1ED.pdf

45. Django Software Foundation: Why Django? – Overview (2021). https://www.djangoproject.com/start/overview/. Accessed 21 Oct 2021
46. Docker Inc.: Docker Engine overview (2022). https://docs.docker.com/engine/. Accessed 13 Jun 2022
47. Boettiger, C.: An introduction to Docker for reproducible research. ACM SIGOPS Operating Syst. Rev. **49**, 71–79 (2015)
48. Docker Inc.: Docker Engine API (v1.41) (2021). https://docs.docker.com/engine/api/v1.41/. Accessed 10 Oct 2021
49. OpenAPI Initative: OpenAPI Specification - Version 3.1.0 (2021). https://spec.openapis.org/oas/v3.1.0. Accessed 15 Feb 2021
50. Ierusalimschy, R.: Programming in Lua, 3rd edn. Lua.org, Rio de Janeiro (2013)
51. Jordan, L., Greyling, P.: Embedding lua in android applications. In: Jordan, L., Greyling, P. (eds.) Practical Android Projects, pp. 155–192. Apress, Berkeley, CA (2011)
52. Tanimura, A., Iwasaki, H.: Integrating lua into C for embedding lua interpreters in a C application. In: Ossowski, S. (ed) Proceedings of the 31st Annual ACM Symposium on Applied Computing, pp. 1936–1943. ACM, New York, NY, USA (2016)
53. GitLab Inc.: GitLab Container Registry (2022). https://docs.gitlab.com/ee/user/packages/container_registry. Accessed 13 Jun 2022
54. Mashkoor, A., Fernandes, J.M.: Deriving software architectures for CRUD applications: the FPL tower interface case study. In: International Conference on Software Engineering Advances (ICSEA 2007), p. 25. IEEE (2007)
55. Gregor, S., Hevner, A.R.: Positioning and presenting design science research for maximum impact. MIS Q. **37**, 337–355 (2013)

Toward Cross-Company Value Generation from Data: Design Principles for Developing and Operating Data Sharing Communities

Hippolyte Lefebvre(✉) ⬡, Gabin Flourac ⬡, Pavel Krasikov ⬡,
and Christine Legner ⬡

Faculty of Business and Economics (HEC), University of Lausanne, 1015 Lausanne, Switzerland
{hippolyte.lefebvre,gabin.flourac,pavel.krasikov,
christine.legner}@unil.ch

Abstract. Unlike other assets, data's value increases when it is shared and reused. Whereas organizations have traditionally exchanged data vertically with other actors along the value chain, we observe that they increasingly share complementary data assets with others, even at times with their competitors, to address business and societal challenges. Research on these new forms of horizontal data sharing and the emerging data ecosystems is still scarce. Building on the theory of communities of practice, we study a pioneer data sharing community comprising more than 20 multinational companies that developed an innovative approach to pool data management efforts. We derive eight design principles for horizontal data sharing, which we cluster according to the following dimensions: domain of interest, shared practice, and community. By offering prescriptive design knowledge, our findings make an important contribution to the emerging literature on cross-company data sharing. Our research also provides practitioners with actionable insights on how to establish and operate data sharing communities effectively.

Keywords: Data Sharing Community · Design Principle · Data Ecosystem

1 Introduction

In the digital economy, companies consider data as assets that generate business value and enable innovation. Compared to other enterprise assets, however, data is characterized by unique properties and its value increases when shared and reused. Data sharing is therefore increasingly recognized as a key driver in the digital economy [1]. Recent estimates reveal that firms that "share data externally generate three times more measurable economic benefit than those who do not" [2]. The European data strategy [3] and the EU's underlying Data Act [4] underpin numerous data sharing benefits upfront, such as improved access to private and public data, the generation of new products and services, and the reduction of public services' costs, which will amount to 270 billion euros in additional GDP by 2028 [4]. Besides, data sharing contributes to the sustainable use and reuse of data, thus contributing, for instance, to energy and technological resources savings [3, 5].

A. Gerber and R. Baskerville (Eds.): DESRIST 2023, LNCS 13873, pp. 33–49, 2023.
https://doi.org/10.1007/978-3-031-32808-4_3

Whereas organizations have traditionally exchanged data vertically with other actors along the value chain (data sharing 1.0) [6], we observe that they are currently starting to share complementary data assets with others, even at times with their competitors, in order to address business and societal challenges. This new type of data sharing (data sharing 2.0) implies sharing common practices and seeking mutual benefits from doing so [7]. The emerging data sharing communities are closed ecosystems, similar to the gated communities and club goods concepts, which have strong boundaries, restricted access [8], and whose community outcome(s) should only benefit their members [9, 10].

The investigation of such communities is quite novel and of particular interest for researchers and practitioners, as it highlights a new paradigm for data sharing: from vertical to horizontal. Since cross-company data sharing is associated with challenges at all levels, more research is needed to support data sharing communities' successful establishment. We therefore pose the following research question: *How to develop and operate cross-company data sharing communities?*

Building on recent studies [11, 12], we conceptualize data sharing communities as communities of practice (CoPs) and aim to provide guidelines in the form of design principles as meta-artifacts [13]. Our research context is an action design research (ADR) project [14] during which we partnered with Business Partner Data Sharing Community, which is a pioneer data sharing community that a university spin-off operates. The community comprises more than 20 large multinational companies from different industries that share their business partner master data. Reflecting on this community's establishment and development, we extract design knowledge [15] and derive eight design principles (i.e., meta-artifacts) for developing and operating data sharing communities [16]. Our study enriches the emerging body of knowledge on cross-company data sharing. In addition, our research synthesizes prescriptive design knowledge as design principles of form and action [17], which address the following CoP characteristics [18], namely their domain of interest, their community, and shared practice. Thereby, we provide reusable and action-oriented guidelines as "how to do" knowledge [13] and offer firms and/or service providers concrete guidance on how to develop and operate data sharing communities.

The remainder of the paper is structured as follows: First, we provide a synthesis of the relevant literature on data sharing and CoPs. Second, we outline our research methodology and research process in greater detail. Third, we present our findings, i.e., the design principles. Finally, we discuss our findings, draw conclusions, and provide an outlook for future research.

2 Background

2.1 Data Sharing

Data sharing is defined as "the domain-independent process of giving third parties access to the data sets of others" [19]. It is enacted by providing and facilitating access for compliant use and the reuse of data [20, 21] between data providers and data consumers [19, 22]. During the last decade, data sharing's scope and its purpose in an enterprise context have evolved considerably [7]. For a long time, firms have exchanged mainly transactional data along their value chain, which is now referred to as *data sharing 1.0*

[7]. Further, firms mainly supported their existing business relationships with trusted partners, for example, a supplier would exchange data with retailers, distributors, and other sales intermediaries to derive data-driven decisions and insights [6]. However, firms have recently started to realize the economic potential of sharing complementary data assets with other organizations (*data sharing 2.0*) [7]. This has led to a new form of data sharing in which firms engage in "horizontal cooperation and collaboration" to achieve a common goal [6]. Figure 1 depicts the differences between vertical and horizontal cross-company data sharing. Contrary to vertical data exchange, which is primarily driven by enterprises' need to preserve an existing value proposition (e.g., to execute a transaction or comply with a regulation), horizontal data sharing is aimed at creating new value proposition by sharing relevant data assets outside the company's boundaries [7].

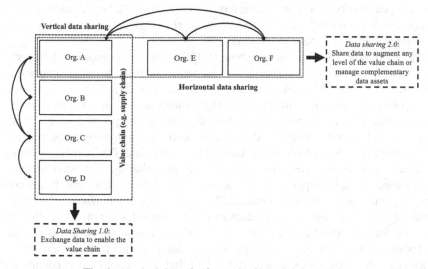

Fig. 1. Vertical data sharing vs horizontal data sharing

Overall, this paradigm shift enables companies to benefit from the sharing economy principles, such as minimizing the costs related to data's re-collection and re-utilization [23]. Concretely, actors share their data at the same level of the value chain, thereby augmenting the existing vertical data sharing. However, literature recently highlighted cases of purely horizontal data sharing with seemingly unrelated actors – i.e., from different industries and not part of the same value chain – concerned about the pooled management efforts for specific data or data types (e.g., master data) [12]. Such an evolution, combined with the involved actors' multifaceted nature, the varying degrees of responsibility that they hold, and their disparate levels of genuine willingness to participate, questions existing conceptualization of cross-company data sharing [24, 25]. Besides, in practice, cross-company data sharing, sometimes called B2B data sharing, still faces many challenges and barriers [26]. Many of the latter are related to the institutional setup, which allows secure and compliant data sharing. For instance, public and private actors are reluctant to share data outside their organizations, due to the incentives being misaligned, privacy concerns, and a lack of collaboration between the organization members [26–28]. Therefore, merely providing the technical infrastructure for data sharing is not sufficient, thus, specific standards and practices need to be developed [20].

2.2 Communities of Practice for Data Sharing

CoPs are conducive environment for cross-company data sharing [11, 12]. According to practice theory, CoPs are groups of people who share a concern, a set of problems, or a passion for a topic, and who deepen their knowledge of and expertise in this area by interacting on an ongoing basis [10, 18]. Data sharing communities (DSCs) are "composed of selected organizations (community members) sharing the same domain of interest who interact, collaborate, and commonly share/use any type of data to achieve a common goal and benefit from the created added value" [12]. DSCs can therefore be interpreted as "club goods," meaning that the value that the community creates from its data assets should only benefit its members [9].

Existing literature is often unclear about DSCs' scope and purpose, and, in vertical sharing contexts, mainly refer to them in various terms, such as data collaboratives, data donations, data partnerships, and even data exchanges [26, 29]. Although their actors (i.e., the roles) are clearly identified [22, 30], they emerge in the context of unidirectional data exchange, which does not align with CoP's participatory aspect, nor with data ecosystems' bidirectional nature, with the actors endorsing the roles of the producers and the consumers, also called data prosumers [31]. Horizontal DSCs, focusing on joint data use and innovation, emerge to extend vertical data sharing. For example, several airlines companies and components manufacturers join a DSC to share analytical insights to support planes' predictive maintenance [12]. However, purely horizontal data sharing is achieved if the DSC comprises members from different value chains who collectively endeavor to increase the data assets' value [12]. In the process, the members manage a shared pool of data assets (e.g., packaging supplier data), leading to the birth of a shared practice (e.g., developing new data quality rules) that will benefit independently each respective value chain.

Consequently, DSCs resonate with a data ecosystem's "network of multiple actors" of any kind (public-public, private-public, and private-private) that collaborates by sharing data to achieve a common goal benefiting the entire ecosystem [6, 22]. Inter-organizational collaboration requires "organizations [to] share resources and jointly create rules and structures that govern their organizational relationships in order to achieve a common goal through effective collaboration processes and high levels of information sharing that could not be accomplished by a single organization independently" [30]. Literature provides some hints about data sharing's underlying dimensions applicable to the DSC context, such as intermediaries, actors, and data types [12, 19]. However, Susha et al. [26] and the European Commission initiatives [32] point out academia and practice's lack of existing guidelines to develop and operate DSCs. This is critical, because the long-term operational aspect of CoP and especially their members' continuous commitment are typical challenges that communities face in order to continue and eventually create value from data [10, 33].

3 Research Context and Methodology

3.1 Research Context

We partnered a university spin-off, a data sharing pioneer with more than eight years of experience with developing and operating DSCs, when undertaking this research. The Business Partner Data Sharing Community (BP-DSC) is a horizontal data community comprising more than 20 multinational companies that collectively manage customer and supplier data (also called business partner data). The community emerged from a research consortium [34] composed of university researchers and practitioners from the mentioned European corporations, and aimed at jointly developing data management practices. At this time (2015), the firms shared a common concern about the high costs of managing data across business units or divisions (group data or corporate data). Each company performed very similar tasks to create and maintain their master data and had to invest significant skills and resources to ensure their data quality was high. This was especially true in the context of business partner data, which was business critical for each company, but which also overlapped significantly between the companies. Discussions of these pain points and shared practices allowed the group to develop the idea of applying the sharing economy's principles to corporate data and to pilot an approach through which the business partner data was shared and managed collaboratively. After a pilot phase, the first companies started sharing data productively in 2017. A university spin-off managing the data sharing platform and community supported the companies. Overall, the different data sharing stages reflected the gradual evolution of the community (see Table 1).

The first stage was to combine the company-specific perspectives and establish a common understanding of the business partner data. The BP-DSC first had to develop conceptual foundations and data sharing practices in order to share the business partner data across the company boundaries. This included data models, business rules, reference data, and processes, which had been jointly developed and were documented on the BP-DSC's wiki [35]. In the second stage, the external data sources (e.g., open government data from corporate registers, data acquired from specialized providers) that provide company information as a "trusted source" were identified. Building on these foundations, the third stage comprised the workflows' implementation to provide and validate datasets, as well as related updates on the data sharing platform. Important basic principles to keep in mind when sharing datasets are that the companies' anonymity needs to be maintained, while the four-eye principle (i.e., a second company's review) simultaneously ensures that the provided data is of a high quality and trustworthy.

As of today, the data sharing platform contains about 200 million records that are constantly maintained and expanded by using more than 2,100 data quality rules and that integrate more than 70 trustworthy reference data sources. By sharing business partner data, member companies realize economies of scale, while significantly improving their data's quality. The reduction in the data's lifecycle costs, i.e., the expenditure on the data creation and maintenance, as well as the reduction in the quality assurance's costs are also direct benefits. Improved data quality leads to more up-to-date, accurate, and complete data, which has positive, indirect effects on all the business processes involving business partners, i.e., primarily the purchasing, marketing, and sales processes. Further

Table 1. Data sharing stages at the beginning of the BP-DSC

Data sharing stages	Data Sharing Platform	Usage scenarios
Stage 1: Shared management of the data definitions and quality rules	Maintenance of a data model for business partners (including attributes such as the address, tax number, bank account, mapping to the operational systems). Maintenance of > 1,200 data quality rules comprising the completeness, correctness, and non-redundancy of the global coverage	Measurement of business partner data quality and detection of duplicates based on a comprehensive set of up-to-date rules
Stage 2: Shared management of external reference data	Maintenance of > 100 trusted external data sources, e.g., open data, commercial registers, and specialized databases with > 70 different identifiers for companies worldwide and > 3,000 legal forms	Validation of entries and enrichment with external reference data (e.g., addresses)
Stage 3: Shared management of datasets	Sharing of > 100 million datasets on business partners and their updates in the data sharing pool	Automated creation and updating of validated datasets

indirect benefits arise from the 360° view of the business partners, which enables better decisions and business insights, ensures compliance with regulatory requirements, and reduces risks. The university spin-off acts as an intermediary providing the technological infrastructure for sharing data, organizational support for the community (e.g., workshops five times a year), and ensures that the business develops.

In 2021, some of the BP-DSC's members proposed the idea of a new data sharing community in order to maintain the business partner data specific to the healthcare industry (HCO-DSC). This offered an opportunity to build, reflect, and learn from the BP-DSC's development and operation in order to support the following communities.

3.2 Research Process

The focus of our research collaboration was to design a reference process for developing and operating DSCs. In view of our research objectives, we adopted the action design research (ADR) approach, which is a "research method for generating prescriptive design knowledge through building and evaluating ensemble IT artifacts in an organizational setting" [14], i.e., the BP-DSC in our case. Overall, we followed the ADR framework's four stages (see Fig. 2).

From February 2021 to April 2022, one researcher was immersed in the BP-DSC activities, making observations, participating in workshops, and accessing the community documentation and platform. The strong cooperation not only allowed us to make direct observations, conduct semi-structured interviews, access physical artifacts, such as organization-specific documentation and tools, but also allowed our research results to influence the organizational setting. Moreover, the regular meetings and workshops created a common understanding and a controlled design process for artifacts.

As part of the *problem formulation*, we analyzed data sharing's specific challenges in the BP-DSC's development and operations context. We compared these challenges to a list of 38 challenges and barriers to data sharing collaboratives and partnerships from literature [26] that are currently not fully addressed due to academia and practice's lack of existing guidelines [32]. These challenges span the *regulatory, organizational, data-related,* and *societal* categories. In order to identify specific challenges for cross-company, horizontal data sharing, we subsequently subjected three senior data experts involved in the BP-DSC – two of whom were involved in its building – to a questionnaire asking them to rate the relevance of the each of the above-mentioned challenges. We developed an online evaluation form on which the participants had to rate the different challenges by using a Likert scale offering five options (Strongly disagree, disagree, neither agree nor disagree, agree, and strongly agree) and had to explain their rating. Data experts also had the possibility of suggesting other missing challenges based on their experience. Eventually, only challenges with two or more positive ratings (agree or strongly agree) were retained.

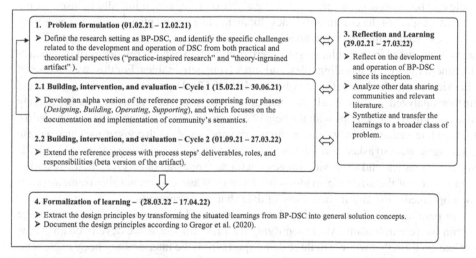

Fig. 2. ADR process followed for this research based on Sein et al. (2011)

The first *building, intervention, and evaluation* (BIE) cycle took place between February and May 2022 and was primarily aimed at designing an alpha version of the reference process in order to develop a data sharing community and implement a common semantic knowledge basis for it, such as a basic vocabulary. Following practice-inspired research and theory-ingrained artifact's principles [14], we built on the insights gained in the previous stage and initiated this first organization-dominant BIE cycle. We iteratively developed the alpha version of the reference process through analyzing existing data sharing processes, designing the artifact, and building and implementing a common ground of semantic knowledge for the community in a form of a data model hosted in a wiki. More specifically, this entailed the creation of a list of relevant terms for the community which were enriched with definitions, characteristics, and examples from several sources (e.g., member's own business glossaries, other existing communities, relevant online sources). This allowed the community to map the different terms (e.g., "health care organization") with industry-specific classification systems (SIC/NAICS). Another important step toward shared semantics was the definition of business rules to link terms and concepts (e.g., the minimum set of attributes/field required to consider pharmaceutical supplier data complete"). This phase resulted in our reference process's first version, which we, with key BP-DSC stakeholders, developed in five focus groups between February and April 2021: three representatives from the intermediary body, and six data experts from three member companies. Our artefact's initial form included the process's nominal phases (*designing, building, operating,* and *supporting*), as well as the underlying process steps in the corresponding phases. This version of the reference process was then presented for review in a new focus group with three representatives from the intermediary body, and nine data experts from three member companies. We used the collected feedback as input to initiate a new design cycle.

The second *BIE* cycle occurred from September 2021 to March 2022, focusing on refining the end-to-end reference process to develop and operate DSCs (see Fig. 2). This cycle can be viewed as an extension of the alpha version, which initially focused on the semantic aspect of the community's development. The design phases included gathering feedback from community members and extending the nominal process steps. These steps, formulated in the alpha version, were primarily expanded by means of exhaustive documentation, corresponding roles, and supporting deliverables. For this, we conducted interviews with the key actors involved in BP-DSC's development over the years and further analyzed its historical documentation. The reference process was intensively discussed in six workshops with the help of collaborative visualization tools (e.g., Miro) to stimulate exchanges between community members and reach consensus. During these exchanges, we also asked community members to challenge existing community's KPIs and other metrics, and to provide suggestion for new relevant ones. Overall, the resulting beta version of the artifact provides a more detailed and comprehensive framework for the implementation and management of data sharing communities.

In parallel with the two BIE cycles, we conducted a *reflection and learning* stage within the research team. After identifying the problem space, we developed an online evaluation form that we sent to three data experts from the intermediary body in November 2021, who also completed it. Two of them were involved in ramping up the BP-DSC, which was one of the first initiatives of its kind at the time. The participants had to rate the statements, namely the meta-requirements (MRs, see Sect. 4.1) by means of a Likert scale. The obtained results: MR1, MR2, MR3, and MR5 rated with 100% agreement, i.e., either agree or strongly agree with all statements; 83% agreement with MR4 (meaning that two-thirds strongly agreed and one-third neither agreed nor disagreed). This allowed us to reflect on the BP-DSC's development and operation, to analyze its differences and commonalities with other data sharing communities, and to transfer the learnings to a broader class of problem and goals. The *formalization of learning* stage consisted of extracting the design principles by transforming the situated learnings from the BP-DSC into general solution concepts, which subsequently allowed us to generate design principles of form and action.

3.3 Development of Design Principles

To ensure that the design principles for developing and operating the DSC were developed in a methodologically sound way, we followed the approach suggested by Möller et al. [16]. We therefore focused on extracting and making design knowledge available for cross-company data sharing's emerging paradigm (see Fig. 3).

Dimension	Characteristics				
Perspective	Supportive			Reflective	
Research design	DSR	A(D)R		Qualitative	Case study
MR Source	Literature	Theory	Interviews	Workshops / Focus groups	None
DP Design	Derived		Extracted	Responsive	
Iterations	Single			Multiple	
Evaluation	Expert / User feedback		Instantiation / Field testing	Argumentation	
Formulation	Free			Based on Template	

Fig. 3. Taxonomical approach followed for the design principle development based on [16]

With a strong focus on building prescriptive knowledge, our research design has a reflective research perspective, because design principles emerge after and during the reference process's design iterations [13]. The design principles were documented by following guidelines by Gregor, Kruse, and Seidel [17], who suggested a template to formulate the principles. They recommended that principles should be structured like common components, namely aim, context, and mechanism. These authors furthermore suggested that knowledge from the literature or empirical evidence should be used to justify principles. We utilized the CoP theoretical lens to extract design knowledge from the cases and then generalized the findings to form a set of empirically produced principles in order to generate the principles for designing cross-company data sharing communities.

4 Findings

4.1 Challenges and Meta Requirements

As part of the problem formulation, we analyzed horizontal data sharing's challenges (see Sect. 3.2) and identified the meta-requirements that would guide the processes for developing and operating these communities. Of the 18 general challenges retained, "measuring of impact and value," "lack of consistency of data and resources," "fear of losing control and lack of trust," and "differences in terminologies and frames of reference" were rated highly. For instance, one participant raised that its senior management does not support enough the community because it is not developed by them ("not invented here" syndrome). Examples of less-relevant challenges are "competitiveness between community members" and "public perception," because both contradict the idea of CoP and their members' willingness to collaborate. Overall, 16 challenges (one of *regulatory* type, 11 of *organizational* type, three of *data-related* type, and one of *societal* type) were raised and addressed in the meta-requirements.

First, to ensure that all the members share the same incentive, the DSC must offer a clear value proposition and ideally propose methods for measuring its impact or business value (**MR1**). This implies that the members should also acknowledge that they are not competitors in the community, but partners working toward shared benefits. This further entails that all the members must cooperate and collaborate fully, thereby endorsing the data prosumer role with corresponding responsibilities (**MR2**). Since their apparent loss of control over their data, or a general lack of trust could affect the members, procedures should specify the scope of the data sharing practices and of the community's institutional framework (**MR3**). In order to harmonize all the members' cultural and technical backgrounds, the reference process should clarify the semantics and other relevant data-related norms (**MR4**) of these various backgrounds by, for instance, establishing a common way of documenting business rules. Ultimately, the reference process should define the key data management practices performed in the data pool (**MR5**) in order to deliver in accordance with the community roadmap and to achieve the expected value proposition.

4.2 Design Principles for Developing and Operating Data Sharing Communities

Based on the learnings made throughout the development of the reference process, we identify eight design principles (DPs) to develop and operate data sharing communities. For each, we provide both justificatory knowledge and empirical examples (see Table 2). Building on our theoretical lens, we cluster these principles around a CoP's three characteristics: domain of interest, community, and shared practice.

Domain of Interest. A strong motivation and a "case for action" are required as a starting point when developing a data sharing community. This starting point can originate from industry (or from an existing community) where organizations (i.e., potential community members) raised common points regarding their data management practices. For example, firms from the healthcare industry faced challenges to comply with regulatory requirements that obliged them to classify the healthcare professionals with whom they interacted. After identifying a service provider (i.e., an intermediary), the community members were able to define a case for action that would clarify the community activities' purpose (**DP 1**). This step is critical to align the members' incentives [26]. Furthermore, since CoPs can fail rapidly when members' interests diverge [18], the intermediary body should therefore ensure that each member's expectation is thoroughly understood by, for example, having a one-to-one meetings with this member.

When individual and collective incentives are understood, a value proposition for shared data management should be formulated by the intermediary, which the community (**DP 2**) should approve. The community [18] and the intermediary should, in the form of "preliminary design," provide a description of the community, its scope, its domains of interest, its roles, the type of data shared, and the key expected benefits. By doing so, the members can acknowledge the community's competitive advantage and identify their data management practices' synergies.

Table 2. Overview of the design principles to develop and operate DSCs

CoP	Design principles based on Gregor et al. [17]	Rationale	Examples
Domain of Interest	**DP 1 – Case for action** **Aim:** To identify the data sharing community's scope and shared domains of interest **Mechanism**: Community members should pinpoint their shared data management challenges in a "case for action." **Context:** In the design phase	Aligned incentives are critical for a CoP's success [18, 26]. A data ecosystem aims to solve common challenges that actors face [36]	A list of pain points, needs, drivers, e.g., a survey; a synthesis of the shared challenges and potential actions
	DP 2 – Value proposition **Aim:** To communicate the data sharing community's value and impact **Mechanism**: The value proposition of shared data management should describe its expected direct and indirect benefits, as well as the methods for measuring its impact **Context:** In the design and the operating phases	A CoP's "preliminary design" should be built on a shared value proposition [18]. Shared data management is a typical value creation mechanism for data sharing communities [12]	Documentation of the benefits gained from shared data management, e.g., using quantitative and qualitative measures

(continued)

Table 2. (*continued*)

CoP	Design principles based on Gregor et al. [17]	Rationale	Examples
Community	**DP 3 – Community charter and guidelines** **Aim**: To clarify the institutional framework for the community **Mechanism:** Community guidelines and procedures should include a roadmap with deliverables, as well as the collaboration and participation mechanisms **Context:** In the design phase	Charters or procedures are necessary in the context of data-driven services [30]. A documentation of the activities and the responsibilities is key for CoP development [18]	A set of documents defining the community characteristics (e.g., the goals, planning, RACI matrix, and the collaborations)
	DP 4 – Community members as prosumers **Aim**: To ensure all the community members contribute actively to the shared practice **Mechanism:** Community members should endorse the roles of providers and consumers of the data assets in the data pool, thereby acting as data prosumers **Context:** In the building and the operating phases	Members of data ecosystems are often prosumers seeking mutual benefits [22]. A CoP entails all its members exchanging equivalent practices [18]	The members' commitment to contribute actively; data sharing policy; integrating data sharing at a member firm
	DP 5 – Community support **Aim**: To facilitate community operations in a trusted environment **Mechanism:** A neutral intermediary should provide organizational and technical support, and report the successes and KPIs regularly **Context:** In the building, operating, and supporting phases	The community moderator plays a central role in the community facilitation [27]. Measuring the success and value of a CoP is often challenging [10, 23]	Workshop planning and moderation; data sharing support; impact measurement and reporting

(*continued*)

Table 2. (*continued*)

CoP	Design principles based on Gregor et al. [17]	Rationale	Examples
Shared Practice	**DP 6 – Shared semantics** **Aim**: To standardize the community members' norms, practices, and terminologies **Mechanism:** A common business vocabulary and rulebook should be developed, accepted, and used by all the community members **Context:** In the building and the operating phases	Using the same language or semantic is critical to overcome knowledge obstacles in CoPs and to standardize the norms, practices, and terminologies [10]	Semantic wiki; tables and templates for data objects, or the documentation of the rules
	DP 7 – Shared data assets **Aim**: To expand the volume of share data assets **Mechanism:** The intermediary should provide periodic updates and communications about the community's data landscape, as well as communicate the external data sources that are relevant for enriching the pool **Context:** In the building and the operating phases	In a CoP, communication is essential for task completion [10]. External data sourcing emerges as key for value creation from the data [37]	List of relevant external sources that examine the existing data pool. An overview of the data pool's composition
	DP 8 – Data management practices **Aim**: To grow the community and its benefits **Mechanism:** Community members should continuously refine the required data management practices that need to be implemented on the data sharing platform **Context:** In the building and the operating phases	The refinement and development of shared practice are central to a CoP and its members' collective empowerment and learning [18]. Knowledge exchanges in CoPs generate a shared understanding of the problems and solutions [38]	Obtain community agreement to update the solution; decisions on whether to integrate a new dataset or to formulate new data quality rules

Community. The community operations should be explained in a detailed planning that the members build collaboratively, and which includes the phases, tasks, milestones, roadmap, and related deliverables. Accordingly, the resources, roles, and responsibilities (e.g., RACI matrix) should be mapped out. The community members define the basic community rules, and all the stakeholders should follow these. All these requirements and specificities should be grouped to create community guidelines that the entire community acknowledges (**DP3**). This could be considered a "commonly agreed collaboration charter" [30], defining the community's basic principles, the community members' acceptable behavior, and generally aimed at strengthening the community members' cohesion with the community [10]. Overall, as one member reflected: "*Looking back at the community development process, it would have been valuable to set up a general community guideline (i.e., non-technical) at the beginning and then set up more technical guidelines (e.g., about the storage). It is also valuable to reuse existing guidelines, such as a GS1*".

A CoP's success relies on all of its participants being active and sharing their experiences proactively [10]. For DSCs, this also entails that all the members endorse the role of providers and consumers of data assets in the shared data pool, thereby acting as data prosumers (**DP 4**) [31]. Consequently, the members should ensure their data's availability, as agreed in the community guidelines, in order to ensure the value proposition. The members should therefore trust the community data sharing policies and contracted service agreements.

Furthermore, the members benefit from a wide range of services, such as the organizational (e.g., agenda, workshops, facilities) and technical support (e.g., use of the solution and the technical integration) that the intermediary provides, who also ensures progress and the tracking of success (**DP 5**). In fact, the community moderator plays a central role in the community's life, because his/her main role is to plan and facilitate community events [18]. Measuring data sharing communities' success and value against the initial expectations is often perceived as a challenge [26]. Reporting success-related KPIs is therefore a suitable way of convincing the members of a DSC's benefits (e.g., the data pool's growth or the number of shared data assets managed).

Shared practice. Using the same language or semantics is crucial to overcome a CoP's knowledge obstacles and to standardize the norms, practices, and terminologies [10]. All data sharing community's members should develop and agree on a common business vocabulary in order to clarifying the shared elements' meanings and how they are represented in the community data model (**DP 6**). Owing to the large and evolving volume of data in the pool, the intermediary must document, for example, tables or ideally in a machine-readable semantic wiki. The community should also settle on a definition and the synonyms, parent types, subtypes, and key characteristics of each data object. Similarly, the intermediary should document other data that is relevant for the shared practice, such as the business rules (e.g., the business partner's name is missing) and update this when necessary. Besides maintaining the data model, the intermediary must ensure the regular update of the community's data landscape, including the externally sourced data required to enrich the data pool (**DP7**). First, the intermediary should screen the data that community members contribute and assess their quality before sharing them. Moreover, such verification helps to identify data concepts and rules that could impact the pool. However, to achieve the community's objectives and support the shared practice, the intermediary (the customer success managers in this case) should search for external sources that might enrich the pool. For instance, external data used in the BP-DSC includes reference data (e.g., country codes), an official institution's datasets (e.g., The European Medicines Agency's dataset containing all the healthcare organizations and their related addresses), and business registers. However, they can only be integrated after a proper sourcing process [37], an assessment of their quality, and approval by their members. Focus groups, workshops and regular meetings support these data management practice exchanges. Consequently, new practices requiring the intermediary to maintain the data sharing platform and integrate the changes (**DP8**) might emerge. Examples of such practices include, for instance, new data quality and business rules.

5 Summary and Conclusion

Data sharing, and especially cross-company data sharing, have gained momentum in IS research. In this study, we focus on a special type of data ecosystem that stimulates cross-company data sharing in order to manage complementary data assets. Using action design research, we provide guidelines in the form of design principles as reusable meta-artifact with which to develop and operate data sharing communities. By applying a rigorous methodology to generate design principles and by using a leading data sharing community comprising more than 20 multinational companies as a knowledge base, we identify eight DPs. Furthermore, by building on communities of practice theory, we cluster the DPs according to the three following characteristics: domain of interest (2 DPs), community (3 DPs), and shared practice (3 DPs). In addition, our results highlight horizontal data sharing's specific nature as a new paradigm for data sharing 2.0, which requires new design knowledge. This study's limitation lies in the partner community only including multinational companies with a certain maturity, resources, and experience with data, thereby hindering smaller firms from applying the DPs.

Anchored into the growing body of data sharing knowledge and grounded to the emerging discourse on business and data ecosystems, we believe our study offers opportunities for further research on data prosumers' routines and joint business value creation from firms that seem to be unrelated and that do not necessarily share the same value chain.

Overall, we provide empirically and theoretically grounded guidelines that could help practitioners develop and operate data sharing communities. While such communities could vary considerably in terms of shared practices, we believe our results provide practitioners with relevant guidelines, while they can still customize these guidelines to accommodate different situations.

References

1. Jarke, M., Otto, B., Ram, S.: Data sovereignty and data space ecosystems. Bus. Inf. Syst. Eng. **61**(5), 549–550 (2019).

2. Gartner: Data Sharing Is a Business Necessity to Accelerate Digital Business. https://www.gartner.com/smarterwithgartner/data-sharing-is-a-business-necessity-to-accelerate-digital-business. last accessed 2022/01/05
3. European Commission: A European Strategy for data. https://digital-strategy.ec.europa.eu/en/policies/strategy-data. last accessed 2022/10/01
4. European Commission: Data Act: Measures for a Fair and Innovative Data Economy,. https://ec.europa.eu/commission/presscorner/detail/en/ip_22_1113. last accessed 2022/10/01
5. Jarvenpaa, S.L., Essén, A.: Data sustainability: data governance in data infrastructures across technological and human generations. Inf. Organ. **33**, 100449 (2023)
6. Otto, B., et al.: Data Ecosystems. Conceptual Foundations, Constituents and Recommendations for Action. Fraunhofer Institute for Software and Systems Engineering (2019)
7. Wixom, B.H., Sebastian, I.M., Gregory, R.W.: Data Sharing 2.0: New Data Sharing, New Value Creation. MIT CISR (2020)
8. Blakely, E.J.: Fortress America Separate and Not Equal. In: Platt, R.H. (ed.) The Human Metropolis: People and Nature in the 21st-Century City. University of Massachusetts Press in association with the Lincoln Institute of Land Policy (2006)
9. Buchanan, J.M.: An Economic Theory of Clubs. Economica **32**, 1–14 (1965)
10. Nicolini, D., Pyrko, I., Omidvar, O., Spanellis, A.: Understanding communities of practice: taking stock and moving forward. Acad. Manag. Ann. **16**, 680–718 (2022)
11. Jarvenpaa, S.L., Markus, M.L.: Data sourcing and data partnerships: opportunities for IS sourcing research. In: Hirschheim, R., Heinzl, A., Dibbern, J. (eds.) Information Systems Outsourcing. PI, pp. 61–79. Springer, Cham (2020).
12. Lefebvre, H., Krasikov, P., Flourac, G., Legner, C.: Toward cross-company value generation from data: investigating the role of data sharing communities. In: Proceedings of the Pre-ICIS Workshop of the AIM, Copenhagen, Denmark (2022)
13. Gregor, S.: The nature of theory in information systems. MIS Q. **30**, 611 (2006)
14. Sein, M.K., Henfridsson, O., Purao, S., Rossi, M., Lindgren, R.: Action design research. MIS Q. **35**, 37–56 (2011)
15. Chandra, L., Seidel, S., Gregor, S.: Prescriptive knowledge in IS research: conceptualizing design principles in terms of materiality, action, and boundary conditions. In: Proceedings of the 48th Hawaii International Conference on System Sciences (HICSS). Kauai, Hawaii, USA (2015)
16. Möller, F., Guggenberger, T.M., Otto, B.: Towards a method for design principle development in information systems. In: Hofmann, S., Müller, O., Rossi, M. (eds.) Designing for Digital Transformation. Co-Creating Services with Citizens and Industry 2020. LNCS, vol. 12388, pp. 208–220. Springer, Cham (2020).
17. Gregor, S., Kruse, L., Seidel, S.: Research perspectives: the anatomy of a design principle. JAIS **21**, 1622–1652 (2020)
18. Wenger, E., McDermott, R.A., Snyder, W.: Cultivating Communities of Practice: A Guide to Managing Knowledge. Harvard Business School Press, Boston, Mass (2002)
19. Jussen, I., Schweihoff, J., Dahms, V., Möller, F., Otto, B.: Data sharing fundamentals: characteristics and definition. In: Proceedings of the 56th Hawaii International Conference on System Sciences (HICSS). Maui, Hawaii, USA (2023)
20. Tenopir, C., et al.: Data sharing by scientists: practices and perceptions. PLoS ONE **6**, e21101 (2011)
21. Lefebvre, H., Legner, C., Fadler, M.: Data democratization: toward a deeper understanding. In: Proceedings of the 42nd International Conference on Information Systems (ICIS). Austin, Texas (2021)
22. Azkan, C., Mã, F.: Hunting the Treasure: Modeling Data Ecosystem Value Co-Creation In: Proceedings of the 43rd International Conference on Information Systems. Copenhagen, Denmark (2022)

23. Legner, C.: Data sharing in business ecosystems. In: TREO Talks in conjunction with the Fortieth International Conference on Information Systems (ICIS). Munich, Germany (2019)
24. Weyzen, R., van Hesteren, D., Huyer, H.: Advanced Technologies for Industry – AT WATCH: Technology Focus on Data Sharing. European Commission (2021)
25. Graef, I., Prüfer, J.: Governance of data sharing: A law & economics proposal. Res. Policy **50**, 104330 (2021)
26. Susha, I., Grönlund, Å., Van Tulder, R.: Data Driven social partnerships: exploring an emergent trend in search of research challenges and questions. Gov. Inf. Q. **36**, 112–128 (2019)
27. Skatova, A., Ng, E., Goulding, J.: Data Donation: Sharing Personal Data for Public Good. Presented at the Digital Economy All Hands Meeting, London, England: N-Lab (2014)
28. Susha, I., Janssen, M., Verhulst, S.: Data collaboratives as a new frontier of cross-sector partnerships in the age of open data: taxonomy development. In: Proceedings of the 50th Hawaii International Conference on System Sciences. Manoa, Hawaii, USA (2017)
29. Hale, S.S., et al.: Managing troubled data: coastal data partnerships smooth data integration. In: Coastal Monitoring Through Partnerships, pp. 133–148. Springer (2003).
30. Schlosser, S.R.: Design principles for collaborative data services (2016)
31. Otto, B., Aier, S.: Business models in the data economy: a case study from the business partner data domain. In: Proceedings of the 11th International Conference on Wirtschaftsinformatik (2013)
32. European Commission: Study on data sharing between companies in Europe: executive summary. Publications Office, LU (2018)
33. Lefebvre, H., Legner, C.: How communities of practice enable data democratization inside the enterprise. In: Proceedings of the 30th European Conference on Information Systems (ECIS). p. 16. Timisoara, Romania (2022)
34. Österle, H., Otto, B.: Consortium research: a method for researcher-practitioner collaboration in design-oriented IS research. Bus. Inf. Syst. Eng. **2**, 283–293 (2010)
35. CDQ AG: Data Sharing Community Wiki. https://meta.cdq.com/Data_Sharing_Community. last accessed 2023/01/25
36. Gelhaar, J., Bergmann, N., Müller, P., Dogan, R.: Motives and incentives for data sharing in industrial data ecosystems: an explorative single case study. In: Proceedings of the 56th Hawaii International Conference on System Sciences (HICSS). Maui, Hawaii, USA (2023)
37. Krasikov, P., Eurich, M., Legner, C.: Unleashing the potential of external data: a DSR-based approach to data sourcing. In: Proceedings of the 30th European Conference on Information Systems. Timișoara, Romania (2022)
38. Pyrko, I., Dörfler, V., Eden, C.: Communities of practice in landscapes of practice. Manag. Learn. **50**, 482–499 (2019)

Neuro-Adaptive Interface System to Evaluate Product Recommendations in the Context of E-Commerce

Bella Tadson[1]([✉]) [ID], Jared Boasen[1,2] [ID], François Courtemanche[1] [ID],
Noémie Beauchemin[1] [ID], Alexander-John Karran[1] [ID], Pierre-Majorique Léger[1] [ID],
and Sylvain Sénécal[1] [ID]

[1] Tech3Lab, HEC Montréal, Montréal, Canada
{bella.tadson,sylvain.senecal}@hec.ca
[2] Faculty of Health Sciences, Hokkaido University, Sapporo, Japan

Abstract. Personalized product recommendations are widely used by online retailers to combat choice overload, a phenomenon where excessive product information adversely increases the cognitive workload of the consumer, thereby degrading their decision quality and shopping experience. However, scientific evidence on the benefits of personalized recommendations remains inconsistent, giving rise to the idea that their effects may be muted unless the consumer is actually experiencing choice overload. The ability to test this idea is thus an important goal for marketing researchers, but challenging to achieve using conventional approaches. To overcome this challenge, the present study followed a design science approach while leveraging cognitive neuroscience to develop a real-time neuro-adaptive interface for e-commerce tasks. The function of the neuro-adaptive interface was to induce choice overload and permit comparisons of cognitive load and decision quality associated with personalized recommendations, which were presented according to the following three conditions: (a) not presented (control), (b) perpetually presented, or (c) presented only when a real-time neurophysiological index indicated that cognitive workload was high. Formative testing cycles produced a neuro-adaptive system in which the personalization of recommendations and neuro-adaptivity function as intended. The artifact is now ready for use in summative testing regarding the effects of personalized recommendations on cognitive workload and decision quality.

Keywords: Neuro-adaptive interface · digital technologies · e-commerce · choice overload · cognitive load · decision-making · design science

1 Introduction

Personalized product recommendation systems are being increasingly used in e-commerce. A 2019 Forrester report approximated that 67% of large-scale online retailers employed recommendation systems [1] to aid users in decision-making and combat choice overload, a phenomenon where consumers are unable to analyze and compare

A. Gerber and R. Baskerville (Eds.): DESRIST 2023, LNCS 13873, pp. 50–68, 2023.
https://doi.org/10.1007/978-3-031-32808-4_4

excessive quantities of products and product information [2–4]. Choice overload has been recognized to adversely increase cognitive workload [5–8], and thereby degrade purchase decision quality [9–12], or lead consumers to delay [13] or abandon their purchase [2, 4, 14]. However, e-commerce interfaces that offer personalized recommendations generally do so without considering whether a consumer is experiencing choice overload. Coincidentally, empirical research based on such interfaces has yielded inconsistent results regarding the benefits of personalized recommendations against choice overload [15–19]. This has given rise to the idea that the effects of personalized recommendations may be muted or counterproductive unless the consumer is in fact experiencing choice overload. Correspondingly, there has a been a call from e-commerce researchers for the development of a more robust system to evaluate the effects of personalized product recommendations [15, 18].

Answering this call to research requires the development of a system that detects the occurrence of choice overload in real-time and provides personalized product recommendations accordingly. However, to our knowledge, no such system exists, and commonly-used retrospective self-reported measures [15–17, 20–22] are not appropriate. To develop the needed system, we applied the design science research (DSR) approach, as it has demonstrated effectiveness for e-commerce interface design for both industrial and academic purposes [23–26]. We classified our development as a Type 4 research problem, which is characterized by an absence of relevant data available for manipulation, combined with yet unknown operations and methods to address the research problem [27, 28]. One viable approach to measure choice overload in real-time is to target cognitive workload using neurophysiology such as Electroencephalography (EEG). With its high temporal resolution, EEG provides the capability to measure brain activity continuously, and is also an established tool to measure cognitive workload [29–33]. Moreover, recent advances in cognitive neuroscience technology have now made it possible to analyze EEG-derived brain activity in real-time, thereby permitting the development of interfaces that adapt according to changes in a brain activity index (i.e. neuro-adaptive interface) [34–38].

Thus, we asked the following research question: *How can we address the aforementioned call to research by following a DSR approach while leveraging cognitive neuroscience to develop a real-time neuro-adaptive interface for e-commerce evaluation?* Specifically, we sought to design a system with a neuro-adaptive interface that could induce choice overload and permit neuropsychophysiological comparisons of cognitive load to assess the effects associated with personalized recommendations on choice overload and decision quality. The system presented recommendations according to the following three conditions: (a) not presented (control), (b) perpetually presented, or (c) presented only when a real-time neurophysiological index indicated that cognitive workload was high. This study demonstrates the applicability of DSR to neuro-adaptive system design and contributes a novel artifact to the field of e-commerce which answers the call to design a more rigorous means of evaluating the effects of personalized product recommendations against choice overload.

2 Foundations and Related Work

2.1 Choice Overload and Decision-Making

Choice overload is a form of information overload that occurs when a user is confronted with excessive quantities of information used to support decision-making [5–8]. Consequently, choice overload degrades decision quality, defined as the extent to which a purchase decision is objectively or subjectively optimal in relation to other product options [39]. The relationship between choice overload and decision quality is non-linear. As illustrated in Fig. 1, decision quality (accuracy) is thought to improve with information quantity up to a certain point, but then deteriorates thereafter with the onset of choice overload (information overload) [11]. As decision quality decreases, negative emotions and impulsive behaviour increase [7, 40, 41]. Consequently, users express less satisfaction with their shopping experience [42], and less confidence in their selections compared with those who did not experience choice overload [12, 17, 42]. Thus, assessing the decision-making process through the lens of decision quality, decision-making behaviour, and psychological measures of satisfaction and confidence are crucial to understanding choice overload and the effectiveness of strategies against it.

Many researchers attempted to predict the exact quantity of information required to induce choice overload [41, 43, 44]. Recently, a few studies have demonstrated that presenting as few as 24 products [2, 45] and 9 attributes [45] at a time is sufficient for inducing choice overload. However, it is also recognized that the threshold for choice overload differs between individuals as a function of level of expertise and cognitive workload capacity [7, 10, 42–44]. In other words, there is no universal threshold of information quantity which will induce choice overload. Therein likely lies a predominant reason why strategies against choice overload such as personalized product recommendations have yielded inconsistent results regarding their effects [15–19], as it is not clear when precisely a given user might be overloaded and thus needs the recommendations. For this reason, studies on choice overload might benefit from targeting measures of cognitive workload.

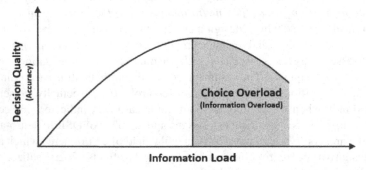

Fig. 1. Relationship between choice overload and decision quality. Based on [11].

2.2 EEG and Neuro-Adaptive Systems

EEG is a well-established neurophysiological modality which has been used to index cognitive workload [29–33]. A notable recent study used an EEG and event-related potentials to identify cognitive overload and link it with poor decision quality [46]. However, if using personalized product recommendations to counteract choice overload, it is important to not merely know whether choice overload occurred, but also to identify when it is happening in real-time to present recommendations to users at the appropriate time, both achievable using an EEG-based solution.

Recent advances in data processing technology have now made it possible to process neurophysiological data such as EEG in real-time [47–49]. This has given rise to a new technology known as neuro-adaptive systems [34–36]. A neuro-adaptive system is one that continuously evaluates the neurophysiological activity of its user, processing an index of cognitive or affective state in real time. Then, when changes in the cognitive or affective state index are detected, the system adapts, often via visual changes on the interface [34–36]. Due to its high temporal fidelity, portability, and customizability, EEG remains a predominant modality for neuro-adaptive applications [50].

Having originated in the field of biomedical engineering, neuro-adaptive systems have recently broadened their application into other fields. For example, some research teams attempted to establish remote communication and control systems between a user and a device [51–53]. Other instances vary from applying neuro-adaptive systems to support learning [37] and reading [34] in education, to maintaining vigilance and attention for air traffic control [38]. While some neuro-adaptive systems have relied upon cognitive indices of user attention and engagement [46, 54], others have targeted cognitive load [34, 37]. However, the application of such systems in the field of e-commerce, albeit relevant and of high potential, remains scant. Consequently, we sought to leverage this neuro-adaptive technology to capture consumers' state of choice overload in real-time via a neurophysiological index of high cognitive workload, which when detected, would cause an e-commerce interface to adapt and display personalized product recommendations.

2.3 Personalized Product Recommendations

The personalization of product recommendations is a strategy widely employed across the e-commerce industry. Most global e-commerce sites, including market leaders like Amazon [55], use an algorithm called collaborative filtering [56–58]. Though many variations of it exist, the most common ones are user-based, where individual product preferences are compared to those of other similar users to predict potential purchases, or product-based, where recommended items are similar to those previously liked or visited by a user [57, 59]. Another emerging trend has recently been to add a social component to the computation, such as social tags prediction, based on blogs and online communities [60] or social network graph algorithms, centered on recommendations from friends and other peers [61].

While sophisticated and effective, the algorithmic computational approaches employed by the industry to create personalized product recommendations are not practical for e-commerce research. This is because the historical product viewing or purchasing behaviour required to use industrial algorithms is nearly impossible to acquire for exper- imental participants within a typical data collection timescale. Instead, a simpler, more expedient method is required which nevertheless yields effective personalization. One commonly employed method is the Multi-Attribute Decision-Making (MADM) method [62], particularly the Simple Additive Weighting (SAW) approach. MADM-SAW per- mits comparison between large groups of products, taking into consideration the impor- tance an individual places on each product attribute simultaneously [63]. MADM-SAW has been shown to facilitate optimal decision-making in the contexts of education [64, 65] and internships [66], media consumption [67], and e-commerce [68].

2.4 Application to Design Science Research

The multi-component and multidisciplinary complexity of a neuro-adaptive system arti- fact calls for a structured definition of requirements, as well as flexible iteration cycles of subcomponents of the solution, making the DSR framework the optimal approach. More specifically, given that current neuro-adaptive systems based on users' cognitive load exist in other fields, our research to extend and refine its application into the realm of e-commerce thereby constituted an exaptation solution, according to the knowledge con- tribution framework [28]. The envisioned contribution was thus twofold. First, creating an artifact to support the problem in e-commerce research regarding the lack of a rigor- ous means of evaluating the effect of product recommendations on consumers' choice overload. Secondly, contributing to the body of knowledge in IS through our proof-of- concept, which can serve as a prescriptive theory [69, 70] to successfully implement such an artifact.

3 Methodology and Research Design

To provide a logical framework for constructing the neuro-adaptive e-commerce system, we followed the DSR framework by Peffers et al. [71]. Following this approach was deemed appropriate given its widely-acknowledged application among DSR models [26, 28], and its cyclic nature that provides for various entry points into the process [26, 71]. Figure 2 illustrates said DSR approach, adapted to our study.

In Step 1, a literature review was performed regarding the problem at hand: the lack of a robust system to evaluate the effect of personalized product recommendations on choice overload and identify the state of currently deployed solutions. In Step 2, we derived and refined objectives of a system to solve the problem using a Rigor Cycle [72] grounded in the current body of knowledge and methods regarding e-commerce interfaces and recommendation systems. We also performed a Relevance Cycle [72], building upon neuro-adaptive interface artifacts from different fields and drawing upon exploratory testing formerly conducted at our lab. Step 3 comprised internal Design Cycles [72] over 8-months, cycling between design-related decisions, their implemen- tation, evaluation, and refinement, until the objectives of the solution were fulfilled [73]. This and the following steps of the study were integrated in a research certificate ID 5071 approved by the institution's ethics review board (Comité d'éthique de la recherche de HÉC Montréal - CÉR). In Step 4 we demonstrated that the artifact adapts according to cognitive load classifications via real-time testing with a sample of 42 voluntary participants recruited through convenience sampling. All participants were adults aged 18 years old or older, fluent in English, right-handed, neurotypical and not taking any medication for neurological or behavioural disorders. Their consent and confidentiality were ensured through CÉR's protocols. Then in Step 5, the artifact was evaluated based on validity and quality criteria [28]. The "proof-of-concept" demonstrated through simulations revealed that all design requirements (discussed in the following section) were fulfilled, and interface adaptations occurred as intended. The artifact is now ready for the second evaluation phase, in which we intend to execute summative experimental testing [28]. Approximately 50 new participants are expected to be recruited through random sampling and the same inclusion criteria for this phase. In Step 6, the communication of our designed system will be achieved through two phases: 1) publication of the present manuscript, and 2) via implementation of the system throughout usability testing by practicing professionals, potentially with various customizations of on-screen adaptation elements and conditions.

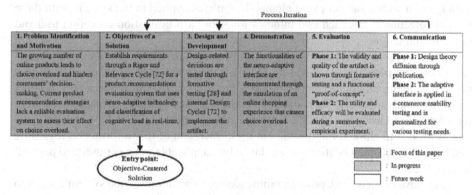

Fig. 2. DS Research methodology by Peffers et al. [71], adapted for this study.

4 Objectives of a Solution

Our overarching objective was to rigorously evaluate the effect of product recommendations on choice overload using neuro-adaptive technology. This technology permitted recommendations to be presented according to real-time EEG measurements of cognitive load. The components of this system were dissected based on Rigor and Relevance Cycles [72], translated into design requirements, and then prioritized according to resource availability and cost-benefit analyses.

First, the system had to comprise an assortment of selectable products and remain complex enough to potentially elicit choice overload (Table 1, DR 1). We used laptop computers as products due to their numerous attributes which complexify decision-making [9, 74]. Based on e-commerce research and formative testing, products and their attributes were displayed in a series of product comparison matrices, each with

24 products [2, 45], and 8 attributes per product [45], thereby permitting a trial-based approach for subsequent summative testing.

Next, product recommendations needed to be easily identifiable, yet not obstruct non-recommended products (DR 2). Iterative Relevance Cycles [72, 75] achieved this by highlighting a product row as an indicator of recommendation. The system was furthermore designed to be capable of highlighting (recommending) three product rows out of the 24 on each product matrix trial, with 3 products considered a small enough assortment size [9].

With an interest in comparing the effectiveness of our system to historical all-or-nothing approaches to investigating responses to product recommendations, we addressed the research problem (DR 3) by designing the system to present recommendations according to three conditions: (a) control (i.e. an interface which provides only the list of products and their attributes without any decisional aid in the form of recommendations), (b) static, perpetually presented from the onset of each product selection trial, and (c) neuro-adaptive, presented only when a real-time neurophysiological index has indicated that cognitive workload is high. To maximize the number of trials per participant, a within-subject experimental design was applied to the system, with three product selection trials, each two minutes long, in each evaluation condition to avoid experimental fatigue.

The next requirement was to personalize the recommendations to ensure their trustworthiness and pertinence (DR 4) [20, 21]. This was planned to be achieved by implementing a questionnaire to identify a user's preferences regarding the laptop product device attributes (DR 4.1). Then, the three highest-ranked products to recommend were to be determined using the MADM-SAW calculation method (DR 4.2) [62]. Lastly, the system needed to allow for a manual, but rapid insertion of this information regarding which product recommendations to display, when applicable, on a per user and per trial basis (DR 5).

To achieve the neuro-adaptive recommendations condition (c), the system needed to be capable of recording raw EEG signals (DR 6), which could also serve post-experiment analyses. Then, the system needed to calculate a cognitive load index in real-time based on raw EEG signals (DR 7), and transmit a classifier based on the index to the product recommendation interface (DR 8). Classifier transmission required both a send and receive component which ensured the classifier transmission was properly synchronized. Additionally, the interface required a set of rules on when to present recommendations, i.e. when to trigger the recommendations (DR 9). Given that display conditions required potential adjustment through formative testing, the system design needed to enable a modifiable field to input adaptation triggering rules. Finally, the system needed to support collection of self-reported measures and extraction of behavioural quantitative data for use in post-hoc analyses (DR 10). Self-reported questionnaires were to target choice overload, choice confidence and satisfaction (DR 10.1). Behavioural data would include decision time and product selections and recommendations (when applicable) for each trial (DR 10.2).

Table 1. Overview of design requirements (DR)

Design requirement	Description
User interface	
DR 1: Interactive user interface that displays a matrix of products and attributes to choose from, capable of inducing choice overload	A difficult-to-process product comparison matrix with 24 laptops [2, 45] (rows) and 8 attributes for each [45] (columns). Images and brand names are removed to avoid bias. To select a product, users may click on the chosen product and click the "Submit" button to confirm their selection
DR 2: A small number of product recommendations appear clearly, yet without interfering with the decision-making process	Recommendations appear in form of a highlight of three rows of products. Users are still free to select any product, i.e. to follow the recommendation or not. Three products of 24 are recommended to simplify decision making and reduce choice overload [9]
Experimental design	
DR 3: System permits isolation of recommendation effects for rigorous summative testing	The artifact presents recommendations according to three conditions: (a) no recommendations (control), product matrix only, (b) static, with recommendations always displayed, and (c) neuro-adaptive, with recommendations being triggered by a real-time EEG index of high cognitive load (signaling choice overload) The system uses a within-subject experimental design, with three product selection trials in each experimental condition
Personalized recommendations	
DR 4: Personalize product recommendations for each user	**DR 4.1** – Gather personal user preferences: determine the relative importance each user allocates to different product attributes through a self-reported questionnaire **DR 4.2** – Determine the three highest-ranked products to recommend per trial, when applicable, according to the MADM-SAW method [62]
DR 5: Inform the system of what personalized recommendations to display	Create a manual input field to inform the system of which products to recommend (obtained in DR 4), when applicable, for each trial and for each user

(continued)

Table 1. (*continued*)

Design requirement	Description
Real-time classification of neurophysiological data	
DR 6: Measure raw neurophysiological data throughout the experiment	Measure and record EEG data for cognitive load classification (DR 7) and post-experimental analyses
DR 7: Classify raw neurophysiological data as low or high cognitive load	Calculate an EEG cognitive load index and classify it in real-time in a format readable by the interface
Neuro-adaptation of the interface	
DR 8: Continuously transmit cognitive load classifiers to the user interface	Ensure synchronized and continuous transmission and receipt of cognitive load classifiers by the system throughout all trials
DR 9: Conditions to initiate the presentation of product recommendations	Enable a modifiable input field for recommendation display rules, based on the continuously received cognitive load classifiers
Self-reported evaluations/Trial performance data	
DR 10: Enable capture and extraction of trial performance data and self-reported measures for post-hoc analyses	**DR 10.1** – Behavioural quantitative data: ensure capture and extractability of trial data regarding the classifiers received, products and (when applicable) recommendations displayed, product selected, and decision time **DR 10.2** – Perceptual quantitative data: enable a pause after each trial to present post-trial questionnaires on choice overload, choice confidence and satisfaction

5   Design and Development

5.1   Classification and Transmission of Cognitive Load to the Interface

Real-time processing of neurophysiological activity (DR 6 from Table 1 above) and classification of cognitive load (DR 7) were designed using Simulink in MATLAB (version R2021b, IBM). The Simulink model was built to sample neurophysiological activity at 250 Hz from a g.tec Research: a 32-channel wireless, gel-based active electrode electroencephalographic (EEG) hardware, installed according to the 32-channel standard montage by g.tec. Real-time processing blocks for channel selection and band-power extraction were incorporated, in addition to Butterworth low-pass and high-pass filtering and a notch filter. A block was added to classify cognitive load as low (0), medium (1), or high (2), based on mean alpha-band power output over six-second intervals. Low and high cognitive workload band power thresholds were calibrated for each individual participant using EEG signals sampled during a 0-Back and a 2-Back task, respectively. The N-Back working memory paradigm is a well-established task for differentiating cognitive workload [76–78]. The raw and processed EEG data, and derived classifications, were set up to be recorded in parallel to permit post-hoc analysis and investigation of our phase 2 evaluation step (Fig. 2). Cognitive load classifications (0, 1, 2) were continuously transmitted to the interface (DR 8), as they were derived (every six seconds) over the local network via Lab Streaming Layer (LSL). The classification was then communicated to the web interface through a Python-based LSL receiver and a WebSocket client on a web server at the same rate of one classifier every six seconds.

5.2 Neuro-Adaptation Logic

Neuro-adaptation was designed such that the interface presented recommendations to users according to primary and secondary cognitive load classification logic. The primary logic consisted of the aforementioned classification of cognitive load sent from Simulink via LSL (transmitted values being 0, 1, or 2). The secondary logic, applied downstream from this using a Python script, converted the output value into a "3" if it satisfied a best out of three condition. In other words, if at least two 2's were received within the last three classifiers, the script would transform the next value that it would relay to the interface into a "3". The interface adaptation rules and conditions were implemented through a web application (see Sect. 5.4 below).

5.3 Product Recommendations

To enable users to attribute personal importance to each of the 8 laptop product criteria (DR 4.1), a 5-point Likert scale (with 1 being "Not important at all" and 5 being "Very important") was utilized in an online Qualtrics questionnaire. These attribute ratings were then input into an Excel file, which was designed to determine the three highest-ranked products per trial for each user (DR 4.2), according to the MADM-SAW method [62]. The calculation takes into account the total database of 360 fictitious, but plausible laptop products and their attributes which we included in the system, objectively assessing them in accordance with the subjective importance of the attributes reported by each user.

5.4 User Testing Interfaces

The front-end (DR 1, DR 2, and DR 3) of the system was developed in HTML and enhanced with CSS formatting, executed on a web browser with a computer operating on Windows 11. A front-end web application was developed in Google's AngularJS MVC framework, internally called Metamorph, to launch a separate interface for each recommendation presentation condition (control, static and neuro-adaptive) through a link generated on a per participant basis.

For the static and neuro-adaptive condition interfaces, the Metamorph application included a field to integrate the product ID's of the top-three laptops for each user and each trial – identified in the previous step – to inform the interface of which products to recommend, when applicable (DR 5).

For the neuro-adaptive condition interface, the application also comprised a rule engine library, that is, a functionality that permitted upload of a set of conditions into the database in form of a JSON file, meant to dictate the rules to display product recommendations (DR 9). These rules use Javascript objects to control the presentation of product recommendations. They were designed such that no recommendations would display the first and last 12 s of each trial, to give users the chance to read the entire matrix and react to recommendations if they were presented. Outside of these two time windows, the display of recommendations was triggered when the value received through the WebSocket client was "3" (see Sect. 5.2).

Meanwhile, the interface was designed such that users could select only one product with a left mouse click, and then submit their selection by pressing a "Submit" button on the bottom of the screen. After a selection was submitted, the interface presented a transition screen thanking the user and then paused. This pause permitted to present the post-trial questionnaires on choice overload, choice confidence and satisfaction via Qualtrics (DR 10.1). After the questionnaires were completed, the transition screen of the interface was redisplayed and the user was instructed to press a "Continue" button, which initiated the subsequent trial. The transition screen on the last trial displayed a message requesting users to await further instructions and had no "Continue" button.

Lastly, in provision of the second phase of our evaluation (Fig. 2) (DR 10), a feature was integrated in the application to enable capture and extraction of per-trial post-study behavioural quantitative data. The generatable output is in form of a JSON file, which compiles: a) the different values of classifiers received every six seconds throughout the trial, b) the time users took to complete their product selection, c) the products included in the trial, d) the three products that were recommended (for the static and the neuro-adaptive conditions, when applicable), and e) the product that the user selected.

6   Demonstration and Preliminary Evaluations

Daily to weekly iterations were executed over a period of 8 months and included 42 formative testing participants. These formative testing cycles were concluded with proof-of-concept simulations to establish the validity and quality [28] of the system we built, thereby completing the first phase of our evaluation defined in Fig. 2. A simplified mock-up of the resulting product comparison matrix of the user interface is shown in Fig. 3, with an example of what a product recommendation looked like. From a technical standpoint, the system now operates consistently and dependably to satisfy sought goals and design requirements defined in previous steps. This development and implementation serve as the main result of our paper. The proof-of-concept demonstration of the artifact working as intended is illustrated in Fig. 4.

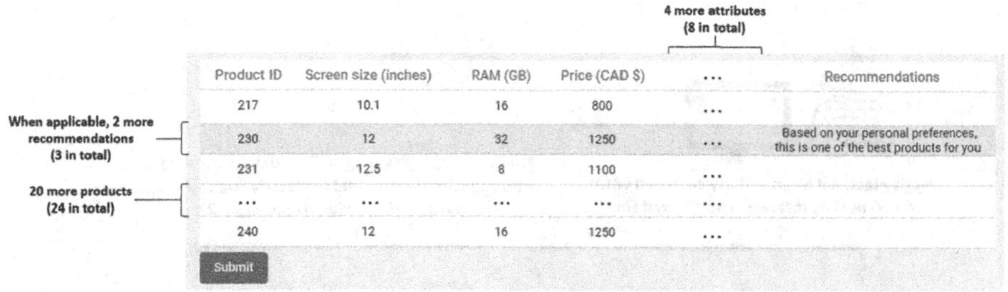

	Product ID	Screen size (inches)	RAM (GB)	Price (CAD $)	4 more attributes (8 in total) ...	Recommendations
	217	10.1	16	800	...	
When applicable, 2 more recommendations (3 in total)	230	12	32	1250	...	Based on your personal preferences, this is one of the best products for you
	231	12.5	8	1100	...	
20 more products (24 in total)	...	...	...	...	...	
	240	12	16	1250	...	
Submit						

Fig. 3. Simplified illustration of the product comparison matrix of the user interface. When applicable, recommendations take the form of a green highlight across the entire product row.

The results of our research carried out during the Rigor Cycle [72] (step 3 in Fig. 2) suggest a high level of potential utility of the constructed artifact. Given the limited availability of evaluation tools to assess the effectiveness of product recommendations, the value our system can bring outside of the development environment [28, 71] is highly promising. However, the system's utility and efficacy are yet to be evaluated in a second evaluation phase (Fig. 2) to assess its practical application in summative and empirical research.

7 Discussion

7.1 Implications for Design Science

The present study followed a DSR methodology to build a neuro-adaptive system which would permit more rigorous assessment for e-commerce research regarding the effects of personalized product recommendations on choice overload. Formative testing through live simulations revealed that the design requirements of the system [28] functioned as intended. This effectively demonstrated the success of our approach to answer our research question and the call for solutions from e-commerce researchers. The novel application of neuro-adaptive technology in the development of an e-commerce evaluation artifact can now be formalized into a dependable prescriptive (Type V) design theory [69, 70] to guide the choice of functionalities and construction of similar tools. Table 2 outlines our acquired design knowledge using the Jones and Gregor framework [79].

62 B. Tadson et al.

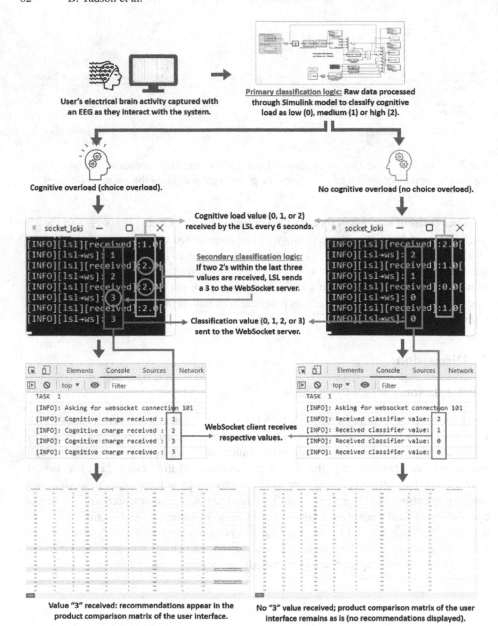

Fig. 4. Demonstration of neuro-adaptivity through simulation.

Table 2. Components of a design theory for the evaluation of personalized recommendations in the context of e-commerce, adapted from Jones and Gregor [79].

Type	Component
Purpose and scope	Development of a more robust and reliable evaluation system to assess the effects of personalized product recommendations in an e-commerce context. To efficiently isolate the effect of recommendations, the system includes three recommendations conditions: (a) no recommendations (control), (b) recommendations displayed perpetually, or (c) recommendations triggered by a real-time neurophysiological classification of cognitive workload as high, captured through an EEG
Constructs	Choice overload, cognitive load, decision quality, decision confidence, satisfaction
Principles of form and function	A difficult-to-process product comparison matrix with 24 products (rows) and 8 attributes for each (columns). Recommendations appear in form of a highlight of the rows with recommended products
Artifact mutability	The system is an exaptation of a neuro-adaptive artifact based on cognitive load to apply it to the field of e-commerce evaluation, which constitutes a novel solution that has not yet been explored
Testable propositions	1. The interface presents a number of products and product attributes that are sufficiently high to induce choice overload 2. Provided recommendations are personalized 3. When applicable, personalized recommendations are provided according to a neurophysiological cognitive load index measured in real-time through an EEG
Justificatory knowledge	The artifact builds on current knowledge from e-commerce user experience, choice overload theory, decision-making theory, cognitive workload theory, real-time neurophysiological processing theory (current neuro-adaptive technology), product recommendations strategies
Principles of implementation	The tool is intended for use by researchers, as well as industry practitioners in marketing, IS, user experience, etc. to better assess e-commerce strategies to cope with choice overload, in controlled experimental settings, where the users (participants) must be healthy and autonomous adults

7.2 Implications for Stakeholders

There are three main advantages of the system. One, whereas past approaches predominantly have relied upon retrospective self-reports of choice overload, the present system permits continuous, real-time assessment of choice overload via an EEG cognitive workload index. Two, the continuous assessment of choice overload via EEG-based cognitive workload permits delivery of personalized recommendations only when choice overload is being experienced by the user, rather than an all or nothing approach. And three, the use of three recommendation conditions and recording of raw EEG along with behavioural and self-reported data permits rigorous evaluation of the hypothesis that personalized product recommendations are most effective against choice overload when it is indeed being experienced at the time of recommendation delivery.

The implications of the present system for stakeholders, particularly marketing and user experience researchers, are manifold. The flexibility of the system permits manipulation of adaptivity elements, conditions, and overall interface design. Not only can the content of the matrices in the e-commerce interface be modified to match different e-commerce contexts, but the HTML-based graphics could be redesigned to model real-world websites while still retaining the neuro-adaptive functionality. Moreover, the brain activity index used for classification can easily be changed, thereby permitting researchers to study responses based on cognitive factors other than cognitive load, such as fatigue or attention. Thus, the present system could potentially be used to investigate behavioural responses to recommendations driven by a multitude of cognitive factors, which could then be leveraged in the industrial domain. Correspondingly, studies using the present system could potentially derive insights about context-dependent information display preferences. The present system could potentially even be used to accurately identify behavioural indices of choice overload, which could then be employed industrially. Ultimately, the present system could drive a change in personalized recommendation strategies, improving their effectiveness along with the experience for consumers.

7.3 Limitations and Directions for Future Research

Though overarching objectives have been achieved, there are some limitations to the current iteration of the designed system. First, recommendation conditions were not centralized within the rules agent of the Metamorph application, necessitating the more cumbersome approach of two-step adaptation logic discussed in the Design and Development section (see Sect. 5.2). Additionally, the identification and input of personalized recommendation criteria for each user (DR 4 and DR 5 from Table 1) must currently be performed manually using an online Qualtrics questionnaire, Excel spreadsheet, and an input field in the Metamorph application. However, these limitations do not fundamentally impede system function and can thus be addressed in future development cycles. Indeed, the present system functioned smoothly and appropriately, as was demonstrated through formative testing and proof-of-concept simulations.

8 Conclusion

This study demonstrates the applicability of DSR to neuro-adaptive interface design to solve Type 4 research problems, and contributes a novel, functional artifact to the field of e-commerce which answers the call to design a more rigorous means of evaluating the effects of personalized product recommendations against choice overload. The system is now ready for summative testing, which should further cement its contribution to the fields of e-commerce and DSR. The present publication marks an important milestone in dissemination of the DSR knowledge gained. Going forward, the system's inherent flexibility should permit improvement of operational efficiency, and context-independent evolution of visual design and adaption based on other cognitive constructs.

References

1. Kodali, S.: The State of Retailing Online 2019. In: Editor (Ed.)^(Eds.): Book The State of Retail-ing Online 2019 (Forrester, 2019, edn.), p. 25 (2019)
2. Iyengar, S.S., Lepper, M.R.: When choice is demotivating: can one desire too much of a good thing? J. Pers. Soc. Psychol. **79**(6), 995–1006 (2000)
3. Scheibehenne, B., Greifeneder, R., Todd, P.: Can there ever be too many options? a meta-analytic review of choice overload. J. Consum. Res. **37**, 409–425 (2010)
4. Özkan, E., Tolon, M.: The effects of information overload on consumer confusion: an examination on user generated content. Bogazici J. **29**, 27–51 (2015)
5. Bawden, D., Robinson, L.: Information Overload: An Overview: Oxford Encyclopedia of Political Decision Making. Oxford University Press, Oxford (2020)
6. Fehrenbacher, D.D., Djamasbi, S.: Information systems and task demand: an exploratory pupillometry study of computerized decision making. Decis. Support Syst. **97**, 1–11 (2017)
7. Deck, C., Jahedi, S.: The effect of cognitive load on economic decision making: a survey and new experiments. Eur. Econ. Rev. **78**, 97–119 (2015)
8. Peng, M., Xu, Z., Huang, H.: How does information overload affect consumers' online decision process? An event-related potentials study. Front. Neurosci. **15**, 695852 (2021)
9. Chernev, A., Böckenholt, U., Goodman, J.: Choice overload: a conceptual review and meta-analysis. J. Consum. Psychol. **25**(2), 333–358 (2015)
10. Chen, Y.-C., Shang, R.-A., Kao, C.-Y.: The effects of information overload on consumers' subjective state towards buying decision in the internet shopping environment. Electron. Commer. Res. Appl. **8**(11), 48–58 (2009)
11. Eppler, M.J., Mengis, J.: The concept of information overload: a review of literature from organization science, accounting, marketing, mis, and related disciplines. Inf. Soc. **20**(5), 325–344 (2004)
12. Calvo, L., Christel, I., Terrado, M., Cucchietti, F., Pérez-Montoro, M.: Users' cognitive load: a key aspect to successfully communicate visual climate information. Bull. Am. Meteor. Soc. **103**(1), E1–E16 (2022)
13. Kurien, R., Paila, A.R., Nagendra, A.: Application of paralysis analysis syndrome in customer decision making. Procedia Econ. Finance **11**, 323–334 (2014)
14. Deng, L., Poole, M.S.: Affect in web interfaces: a study of the impacts of web page visual complexity and order. MIS Q. **34**(4), 711–730 (2010)
15. Aljukhadar, M., Senecal, S., Daoust, C.-E.: Using recommendation agents to cope with information overload. Int. J. Electron. Commer. **17**(2), 41–70 (2012)
16. Liang, T.-P., Lai, H.-J., Ku, Y.-C.: Personalized content recommendation and user satisfaction: theoretical synthesis and empirical findings. J. Manag. Inf. Syst. **23**(3), 45–70 (2006)
17. Zhang, H., Zhao, L., Gupta, S.: The role of online product recommendations on customer decision making and loyalty in social shopping communities. Int. J. Inf. Manage. **38**, 150–166 (2018)
18. Konstan, J.A., Riedl, J.: Recommender systems: from algorithms to user experience. User Model. User-Adap. Inter. **22**(1), 101–123 (2012)
19. Wertenbroch, K., et al.: Autonomy in consumer choice. Mark. Lett. **31**(4), 429–439 (2020). https://doi.org/10.1007/s11002-020-09521-z

20. Chen, C.C., Shih, S.-Y., Lee, M.: Who should you follow? Combining learning to rank with social influence for informative friend recommendation. Decis. Support Syst. **90**, 33–45 (2016)
21. Wang, W., Benbasat, I.: Recommendation agents for electronic commerce: effects of explanation facilities on trusting beliefs. J. Manage. Inf. Syst. **23**, 217–246 (2007)
22. Rose, J.M., Roberts, F.D., Rose, A.M.: Affective responses to financial data and multimedia: the effects of information load and cognitive load. Int. J. Account. Inf. Syst. **5**(1), 5–24 (2004)
23. Sia, C., Shi, Y., Yan, J., Chen, H.: Web personalization to build trust in E-commerce: a design science approach. World Acad. Sci. Eng. Technol. **64**, 325–329 (2010)
24. Ball, N.L.: Design science II: the impact of design science on e-commerce research and practice. Communications of the Association for Information Systems **7**, 2 (2001)
25. Karmokar, S., Singh, H.: Improving the website design process for SMEs: a design science perspective (2012)
26. van der Merwe, A., Gerber, A., Smuts, H.: Guidelines for conducting design science research in information systems. In: ICT Education, pp. 163–178 (2020). https://doi.org/10.1007/978-3-030-35629-3_11
27. McKenny, J.L., Keen, P.G.W.: How managers' minds work. In: Editor (Ed.)^(Eds.): Book How Managers' Minds Work (1974, edn.), pp. 79–90 (1974)
28. Gregor, S., Hevner, A.R.: Positioning and presenting design science research for maximum impact. MIS Q. **37**(2), 337–355 (2013)
29. Fernandez Rojas, R., et al.: Electroencephalographic workload indicators during teleoperation of an unmanned aerial vehicle shepherding a swarm of unmanned ground vehicles in contested environments. Front. Neurosci. **14**, 40 (2020)
30. Antonenko, P.P., Paas, F., Grabner, R., Gog, T.: Using electroencephalography to measure cognitive load. Educ. Psychol. Rev. **22**, 425–438 (2010)
31. Gredin, N.V., Broadbent, D.P., Findon, J.L., Williams, A.M., Bishop, D.T.: The impact of task load on the integration of explicit contextual priors and visual information during anticipation. Psychophysiology **57**(6), 1–13 (2020)
32. Guan, K., Zhang, Z., Chai, X., Tian, Z., Liu, T., Niu, H.: EEG based dynamic functional connectivity analysis in mental workload tasks with different types of information. IEEE Trans. Neural Syst. Rehabil. Eng. **30**, 632–642 (2022)
33. Al-Samarraie, H., Eldenfria, A., Zaqout, F., Price, M.L.: How reading in single- and multiple-column types influence our cognitive load: an EEG study. Electron. Libr. **37**(4), 593–606 (2019)
34. Andreessen, L.M., Gerjets, P., Meurers, D., Zander, T.O.: Toward neuroadaptive support technologies for improving digital reading: a passive BCI-based assessment of mental workload imposed by text difficulty and presentation speed during reading. User Model. User-Adap. Inter. **31**(1), 75–104 (2020). https://doi.org/10.1007/s11257-020-09273-5
35. Krol, L.R., Zander, T.O.: Passive BCI-based neu-roadaptive systems. In: Editor (Ed.)^(Eds.): Book Passive BCI-Based Neuroadaptive Systems (2017, edn.), pp. (2017)
36. Wolpaw, J.R., Millán, J.d.R., Ramsey, N.F.: Chapter 2 - brain-computer interfaces: definitions and principles. In: Ramsey, N.F., Millán, J.d.R. (eds.): Handbook of Clinical Neurology, pp. 15–23. Elsevier (2020)
37. Eldenfria, A., Al-Samarraie, H.: Towards an online continuous adaptation mechanism (OCAM) for enhanced engagement: an EEG study. Int. J. Hum.-Comput. Interact. **35**(20), 1960–1974 (2019)
38. Di Flumeri, G., et al.: Brain-computer interface-based adaptive automation to prevent out-of-the-loop phenomenon in air traffic controllers dealing with highly automated systems. Front. Hum. Neurosci. **13**, 296 (2019)
39. Xiao, B., Benbasat, I.: E-commerce product recommendation agents: use, characteristics, and impact. MIS Q. **31**(1), 137–209 (2007)

40. Wheeler, P., Arunachalam, V.: The effects of multimedia on cognitive aspects of decision-making. Int. J. Account. Inf. Syst. **10**(2), 97–116 (2009)
41. Appiah Kusi, G., Azmira Rumki, Z., Hammond Quarcoo, F., Otchere, E., Fu, G.: The role of information overload on consumers online shopping behavior. J. Bus. Manage. Stud. **4**(4), 162–178 (2022)
42. Lee, B.-K., Lee, W.-N.: The effect of information overload on consumer choice quality in an on-line environment. Psychol. Mark. **21**(3), 159–183 (2004)
43. Ho, E.H., Hagmann, D., Loewenstein, G.: Measuring information preferences. Manage. Sci. **67**(1), 126–145 (2021)
44. Lurie, N.H.: Decision making in information-rich environments: the role of information structure. J. Consum. Res. **30**(4), 473–486 (2004)
45. Greifeneder, R., Scheibehenne, B., Kleber, N.: Less may be more when choosing is difficult: choice complexity and too much choice. Acta Physiol. (Oxf) **133**, 45–50 (2009)
46. Chen, Z., Jin, J., Daly, I., Zuo, C., Wang, X., Cichocki, A.: Effects of visual attention on tactile P300 BCI. Computat. Intell. Neurosci., 1–11 (2020)
47. Khorshidtalab, A., Salami, M.J.E.: EEG signal classification for real-time brain-computer inter-face applications: a review. In: Editor (Ed.)^(Eds.): Book EEG signal classification for real-time brain-computer interface applications: A review (2011, edn.), pp. 1–7 (2011)
48. Guarnieri, R., Zhao, M., Taberna, G.A., Ganzetti, M., Swinnen, S.P., Mantini, D.: RT-NET: real-time reconstruction of neural activity using high-density electroencephalography. Neuroinformatics **19**(2), 251–266 (2020). https://doi.org/10.1007/s12021-020-09479-3
49. Zanetti, R., Arza, A., Aminifar, A., Atienza, D.: Real-time EEG-based cognitive workload monitoring on wearable devices. IEEE Trans. Biomed. Eng. **69**(1), 265–277 (2022)
50. Aricò, P., Borghini, G., Di Flumeri, G., Sciaraffa, N., and Babiloni, F.: Passive BCI beyond the lab: current trends and future directions. Physiol. Meas. **39**(8), 08tr02 (2018)
51. Yangyang Miao, M.C., et al.: BCI-based rehabilitation on the stroke in sequela stage. Neural Plasticity, 2020 (2020)
52. Ron-Angevin, R., Garcia, L., Fernández-Rodríguez, Á., Saracco, J., André, J.M., Lespinet-Najib, V.: Impact of speller size on a visual P300 brain-computer interface (BCI) system under two conditions of constraint for eye movement. Computational Intelligence & Neuroscience, 1–16 (2019)
53. Velasco-Álvarez, F., Fernández-Rodríguez, Á., Vizcaíno-Martín, F.-J., Díaz-Estrella, A., Ron-Angevin, R.: Brain–computer interface (BCI) control of a virtual assistant in a smartphone to manage messaging applications. Sensors (14248220) **21**(11), 3716 (2021)
54. Perry, N.C., Wiggins, M.W., Childs, M., Fogarty, G.: Can reduced processing decision support interfaces improve the decision-making of less-experienced incident commanders? Decis. Support Syst. **52**(2), 497–504 (2012)
55. Linden, G., Smith, B., York, J.: Amazon.com recommendations. In: Editor (Ed.)^(Eds.): Book Amazon.com Recommendations (IEEE Computer Society, 2003, edn.), pp. 76–80 (2003)
56. Sharma, J., Sharma, K., Garg, K., Sharma, A.K.: Product recommendation system a comprehensive review. IOP Conf. Ser. Mater. Sci. Eng. **1022**(1), 12–21 (2021)
57. Huang, Z., Zeng, D., Chen, H.: A comparison of collaborative-filtering recommendation algorithms for e-commerce. IEEE Intell. Syst. **22**(5), 68–78 (2007)
58. Sarwar, B., Karypis, G., Konstan, J., Riedl, J.: Analysis of recommendation algorithms for e-commerce. In: Editor (Ed.)^(Eds.): Book Analysis of Recommendation Algorithms for E-Commerce (University of Minnesota, 2000, edn.), pp. 158–167 (2000)
59. Pandey, S., Kumar, T.S.: Customization of recommendation system using collaborative filtering algorithm on cloud using mahout. IJRET: Int. J. Res. Eng. Technol. **3**(7), 39–43 (2014)

60. Yuan, Z.-m, Huang, C., Sun, X.-y, Li, X.-x, Xu, D.-r: A microblog recommendation algorithm based on social tagging and a temporal interest evolution model. Front. Inf. Technol. Electron. Eng. **16**(7), 532–540 (2015). https://doi.org/10.1631/FITEE.1400368

61. Adabi, A., de Alfaro, L.: Toward a social graph recommendation algorithm: do we trust our friends in movie recommendations? In: Herrero, P., Panetto, H., Meersman, R., Dillon, T. (eds.) OTM 2012. LNCS, vol. 7567, pp. 637–647. Springer, Heidelberg (2012). https://doi.org/10.1007/978-3-642-33618-8_83

62. Adriyendi, M.: Multi-attribute decision making using simple additive weighting and weighted product in food choice. Int. J. Inf. Eng. Electron. Bus. **7**(6), 8–14 (2015)

63. Sun, P., Yang, J., Zhi, Y.: Multi-attribute decision-making method based on Taylor expansion. Int. J. Distrib. Sens. Netw. **15**(3), 1550147719836078 (2019)

64. Pratiwi, D., Putri, J., Agushinta, D.: Decision support system to majoring high school student using simple additive weighting method. Int. J. Comput. Trends Technol. **10**, 153–159 (2014)

65. Aminudin, N., et al.: Higher education selection using simple additive weighting. Int. J. Eng. Technol. (UAE) **7**(2.27), 211–217 (2018)

66. Santoso, P.A., Wibawa, A.P., Pujianto, U.: Internship recommendation system using simple additive weighting. Bull. Soc. Inform. Theory Appl. **2**(1), 15–21 (2018)

67. Hdioud, F., Frikh, B., Ouhbi, B.: Multi-criteria recommender systems based on multi-attribute decision making. In: Proceedings of the International Conference on Information Integration and Web-based Applications & Services (2013)

68. Engel, M.M., Utomo, W.H., Purnomo, H.D.: Fuzzy multi attribute decision making simple additive weighting (MADM SAW) for information retrieval (IR) in E commerce recommendation. Int. J. Comput. Sci. Softw. Eng. **6**(6), 136–145 (2017)

69. Gregor, S.: The nature of theory in information systems. MIS Q. **30**(3), 611–642 (2006)

70. Kuechler, W., Vaishnavi, V.: On theory development in design science research: anatomy of a research project. EJIS **17**, 489–504 (2008)

71. Peffers, K., Tuunanen, T., Rothenberger, M.A., Chatterjee, S.: A design science research methodology for information systems research. J. Manag. Inf. Syst. **24**, 45 (2008)

72. Hevner, A.: A three cycle view of design science research. Scandinavian J. Inf. Syst. **19**, 4 (2007)

73. Simon, H.A.: The Sciences of the Artificial. The MIT Press (1996)

74. Okfalisa, O., et al.: Decision support system for smartphone recommendation: the comparison of fuzzy Ahp and fuzzy Anp in multi-attribute decision making. Sinergi **25**(1), 101–110 (2020)

75. Hevner, A., Park, J., March, S.T.: Design science in information systems research. MIS Q. **28**(1), 75–105 (2004)

76. Wang, S., Gwizdka, J., Chaovalitwongse, W.A.: Using wireless EEG signals to assess memory workload in the N-Back task. IEEE Trans. Hum.-Mach. Syst. **46**(3), 424–435 (2016)

77. Kirchner, W.K.: Age differences in short-term retention of rapidly changing information. J. Exp. Psychol. **55**(4), 352–358 (1958)

78. Karran, A.J., et al.: Toward a hybrid passive BCI for the modulation of sustained attention using EEG and fNIRS. Front. Hum. Neurosci. **13**, 393 (2019)

79. Jones, D., Gregor, S.: The anatomy of a design theory. J. Assoc. Inf. Syst. **8**(5), 312–335 (2007)

Measuring the Actual Office Workspace Utilization in a Desk Sharing Environment Based on IoT Sensors

Arnold F. Arz von Straussenburg$^{(\boxtimes)}$ ⓘ, Mevludin Blazevic ⓘ,
and Dennis M. Riehle ⓘ

University of Koblenz, Universitätsstraße 1, 56070 Koblenz, Germany
arz@uni-koblenz.de

Abstract. Businesses that follow the trend of flexible work arrangements with home offices and hybrid work models are increasingly utilizing desk sharing to allocate available desks in the office efficiently. In this work, we investigate the utilization of flexible work arrangements, specifically the implementation of desk sharing in hybrid work models. To optimize the occupancy rate of shared desks and simultaneously meet demand and save costs, it is crucial to have real-time knowledge of their availability which can be obtained by recording occupancy over time. We utilize the Design Science Research (DSR) methodology to develop a prototype solution for real-time monitoring of shared desks occupancy in hybrid work models. The proposed prototype is a low-cost solution utilizing Internet of Things (IoT) technology consisting of a motion sensor and accelerometer that collect occupancy data and transmit it via Long Range Wide Area Network (LoRaWAN). Signal processing utilizing cloud computing is employed to enhance the quality and accuracy of the data, which is subsequently made available through a web dashboard. The prototype's effectiveness is evaluated through a small-scale pilot deployment in a real-world environment over a two-week period, with reference values obtained during periods of non-use serving as a benchmark for the evaluation.

Keywords: Internet of Things · Flexible Office · Desk Sharing · Workplace Utilization

1 Introduction

The Internet of Things (IoT) has been driving technological change since its first appearance, transforming the way we live and work in the future. It has become one of the significant subjects of research and industry in the area of Information and Communications Technology (ICT) [9–11]. One of the focus points of research in the area of IoT aims to investigate social, organizational, economic, individual, and technological impact [6,11,31].

In recent years, there has been a drastic increase in the number of employees working from home [19], due in part to the Covid-19 pandemic. This has

© The Author(s), under exclusive license to Springer Nature Switzerland AG 2023
A. Gerber and R. Baskerville (Eds.): DESRIST 2023, LNCS 13873, pp. 69–83, 2023.
https://doi.org/10.1007/978-3-031-32808-4_5

prompted companies to reevaluate their current working methods and consider long-term alternatives to the traditional model of mandatory office presence. As a result, more companies are establishing various modern working models, including hybrid work models [18]. These models represent a mixture of office and home-based work and offer several advantages such as health protection during a pandemic, a reduction of travel costs, and a better work-life balance.

However, hybrid work models can also introduce difficulties, such as the need to optimize the utilization of available workspaces in order to save costs. One way to achieve this is to provide shared desks that employees book in advance, but this requires accurate recording of the times employees are present and absent from the office, representing additional effort and duty of care for the employees. Another option is to capture real-time workplace utilization using a combination of IoT sensors.

This paper aims to develop a prototypical development of an application based on IoT sensors to record the presence at workstations as accurately as possible. The following two research questions are derived from this goal: How can IoT sensors be used to measure the occupation of shared desks in a flexible office ($RQ1$) and how can a prototype for measuring desk occupation be deployed in an organization ($RQ2$)?

The theoretical foundations for approaching the research questions are presented in the following (Sect. 2), as well as the research method used (Sect. 3). The focus of this paper is on developing the prototype (RQ1) with the associated application explained in Sect. 4. The prototype is exposed to a test scenario (Sect. 5) which serves as the basis for the subsequent evaluation, fulfilling RQ2. Finally, the insights gained are discussed and summarized in the conclusion (Sect. 6).

2   Background and Related Work

IoT is an extension of the Internet and a subset of Cyber Physical Systems (CPS), where intelligent objects are connected to each other [1,8]. The core concept of IoT is that "everyday objects can be equipped with identifying, sensing, networking, and processing capabilities that will allow them to communicate with one another and with other devices and services over the Internet to achieve some useful objective" [7, p. 261].

Another definition pertains to the properties of objects or things. IoT can be viewed as "a system of interconnections between digital technologies and physical objects that enable such (traditionally mundane) objects to exhibit computing properties and interact with one another with or without human intervention" [6, p. 557].

Desk sharing or hot-desking or Flexi-desks "refers to workstations that are shared by more than one individual and typically claimed/booked on a daily/temporary basis" [23]. Thereby, desk sharing may reduce cost by increasing the average number of employees per workstation [23].

Many application areas of IoT exist today. The so-called IoT domains are very diverse and permeate all areas of life, such as smart homes, smart cities, healthcare, industry, and agriculture, among others [2–4,15]. This paper focuses on the application of IoT in workplace management and hybrid work models, especially in supporting desk sharing.

Existing literature explores using IoT to detect occupancy at desks, achieving 87.5% accuracy compared to manual observations [20]. This study aims to enhance accuracy with inexpensive sensors. This work focuses on developing, demonstrating, and evaluating a solution to improve accuracy using lower-cost sensors. Other related work focuses on different network protocols, such as WiFi and Bluetooth, as well as utilizing various types of sensors including carbon dioxide sensors [26–29]. However, while some of the research touches on the sensors used, it fails to provide detailed information about whether entry-level or industrial sensors were utilized and little attention is given to the description of how the data quality of the sensors was achieved.

3   Research Method

The research questions proposed in Sect. 1 require a technical solution to the problems raised. In consequence, the Design Science Research (DSR) methodology according to [5, 24] is employed in this work, who suggest different steps to follow (cf. Fig. 1).

The first step consists of identifying and motivating a research problem. While we have already contributed to the motivation in the introduction, in the section, we will provide a more precise identification of IoT sensors for measuring workplace utilization, and define the objectives of our solution by selecting a suitable communication technology and IoT sensor stack.

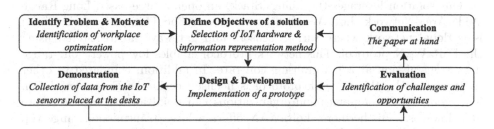

Fig. 1. Design Science Research Cycle (adapted from [5,24]).

The section holds the development and demonstration of a prototypical application and contributes to steps three and four of [5] DSR cycle. In Sect. 5, our prototype is analyzed and evaluated by testing it in a real-life deployment at a small Information Technology (IT) organization. The analysis and evaluation correspond to the evaluation phase of the DSR process [5]. Lastly, this paper itself contributes to the communication of our research results. The DSR approach by [5] features multiple feedback loops enabling multiple iterations of the DSR process. However, this paper presents only the latest iteration for clarity and comprehensibility.

4   Development of a Sensor-Based Prototype

4.1   Hardware Components

The underlying hardware for the sensor system consists of developer boards (microcontrollers) and the sensors themselves. Specifically, the prototype employs the *Arduino MKR WAN 1310* board and two types of sensors.

The *Arduino MKR WAN 1310* was chosen as the development board due to its diverse analog and digital inputs and outputs, which enable the software to perform necessary tasks. Moreover, it facilitates the attachment of sensors and control of electronic components. Compared to the classic *Arduino Uno* board, the *Arduino MKR WAN 1310* boasts a faster microprocessor and a radio module with an antenna connector for Long Range (LoRa) connectivity [17]. Additionally, it is smaller and more energy-efficient, and it includes a connector and charge controller for an external battery.

To detect motion, the prototype utilizes an *HC-SR501* Passive InfraRed (PIR) motion detector. This type of detector is capable of sensing the infrared radiation emitted by humans and animals due to body heat. To avoid false triggers due to air temperature changes, the motion detector is set up to activate only when there is a significant difference between the triggers of the detector's two PIR-sensors [14,22].

In addition to the motion detector, we also use an *InvenSense GY-521* sensor, which integrates an acceleration sensor and a gyroscope on a single chip. This type of sensor is commonly used in smartphones to determine their orientation and position in three-dimensional space. Figure 2 depicts a schematic representation of the sensors.

Our solution leverages the Things Stack, an open source-based Long Range Wide Area Network (LoRaWAN) network server. The Things Network (TTN) is a global network where various sensors and gateways are registered using the LoRaWAN protocol. This network protocol enables low-power, long-range data transmission at a low transmission rate. In addition, compared to other radio standards, this network protocol is license-free in the European Union. Therefore, small companies and organizations can build an IoT infrastructure at a low cost. Furthermore, LoRaWAN offers a large transmission range (up to 15km out of town). [16]. The chosen development board is fully supported by *TTN* and includes a factory-configured End-device Identifier (DevEUI) to identify the board in the LoRaWAN.

Several other sensors and developer boards of different price ranges exist on the market. The use of cameras would also be conceivable for recording workstation occupancy, but this option is problematic because of European data protection guidelines. Our goal is to ensure the high quality and accuracy of the captured data by combining different sensors in the low price range so that even small companies can implement a workplace occupancy system with little financial effort.

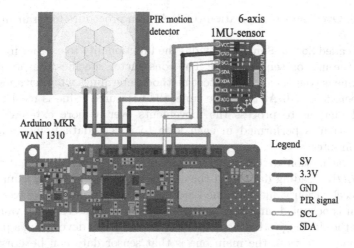

Fig. 2. Schematic depiction of the sensors.

4.2   Programming of IoT Devices

Although the devices used offer various sensors, only a portion is operated to evaluate the data. Notably, only the acceleration sensor of the *GY-521* is used. The accelerometer detects vibrations on the table, such as when an object is placed or bumped, or even minor disturbances like typing on a keyboard. This could indicate that the table is currently being used or cleaned, making it unavailable.

In the prototype, the motion detector was mounted under the tabletop to only detect the area under the workstation. Similarly, [20] mounted and tested various PIR sensors under work tables. This way of attaching the sensors leads it only to detect movements of the lower body parts of a person sitting or standing at the table, and the likelihood that nearby persons will trigger the sensor is reduced (c.f. [20]). In order to obtain the most fine-grained data possible, the triggering duration was set to the minimum value possible. Thus, the sensor sends a *HIGH* signal for only a few seconds when motion is detected. A USB power supply was used for constructing the prototype, which was connected via the micro USB socket with 5 V.

After connecting the LoRa antenna to the Arduino module, the next step is installing the Arduino software *Sketch*, which interprets the sensors' raw data. As usual with such development boards, it consists of the setup method, executed once the Arduino is started, and a method called loop, which is then repeated continuously as long as the device remains switched on. Subsequently, the sensors and LoRaWAN interface are initialized and calibrated in the setup method. The main loop caches the acquired sensor data and triggers various calculations to send the results in predefined intervals via LoRaWAN.

A `LoRaInterface` serves as an interface for critical functions of the `LoRaModem` class, located in another library. The `LoRaInterface` is initialized with an Application Identifier (AppEUI) and AppKey, which provides the access data for the Over the Air Activation (OTAA) join procedure for transmission to TTN.

A class called `MotionSensor` provides the functionality to extract meaningful data from the motion sensor signal. The constructor specifies the pin to which the signal line is connected. The detect method determines whether a movement has just been detected. At the same time, the measured value is used to enable further calculations to process the movements over a more extended period. This calculation is performed in each loop to collect data points within the transmission intervals.

Unlike the motion detector, which has a simple signal line that is either *HIGH* or *LOW*, reading data from the acceleration sensor is more complicated. The raw acceleration values obtained are not enough to determine whether the workstation is occupied, and thus must be compared to a reference value.

Among the challenges that need to be addressed when developing a prototype for occupancy detection, the main one is that sensor data can be noisy, which can make it difficult to detect when someone is actually using the workstation. Additionally, the data needs to be aggregated and compared on a web dashboard in a meaningful way to ensure it is reliable.

The sensor data are read out in the detection method of the respective sensor and, in the case of the acceleration sensor, initially abstracted as a Boolean. *True* corresponds to a detected movement or detected vibrations, and *False* the absence of these.

The result is sent in predefined intervals and is initially buffered. The individual sensor values of each loop do not need to be stored. Instead, the average value of the respective sensors within the current transmission interval is of interest, which is implemented as an average of the possible values *True (1)* and *False (0)*. This calculation takes place in an `Utility` class. In this class, a continuous average calculation is implemented. The current values of the average and the counter are passed on as pointers are incremented. The result is the proportion of the values corresponding to the case of detection as a double between [0; 1]. The Double value is converted to a Byte Array and transmitted via LoRaWAN. The Byte Array has two fields: a Byte Array of type `asBytes` and a Double of type `asDouble`.

No Booleans are read from the accelerometer, but Integer values are. The Integers are to be interpreted according to the defined measuring range. For the prototype, the Integer values are mapped to Boolean values, which define whether an acceleration (e.g. due to vibrations) has occurred.

In the detection method of the accelerometer, their deviations from the reference are determined. After the values have been read out, the current acceleration values of each axis are written to a variable of the type Ring Buffer. A *Ring Buffer* is a data structure to be overwritten repeatedly after reaching capacity. Usually, separate pointers are used for writing and reading operations.

The buffer is iterated through in each loop without using an explicit read pointer. The write index is kept within the array's limits using a modulo calculation of the incremented index and the array's length. As the data for all axes are collected in sequence and the three ring buffers are stored in a 2D array, only one write index is needed for all buffers. In the next step, the difference between the current values and the corresponding average is calculated based on the average values. If the difference of at least one axis exceeds the limit, the result is mapped to *True*.

The data is transmitted to the TTN via LoRaWAN using a LoRa gateway. This data is stored and processed centrally in the Microsoft Azure Cloud, using Azure Functions, where, e.g., conversion from byte array to double takes place. For storage, an Azure Table is used (see [30] for an overview of IoT database storage solutions). Raw data is stored separately via Cold Path to enable data analysis afterwards. Reference data is determined through an Azure Function to detect false positive measurements of the sensors. Detecting these should improve the data quality in general and increase accuracy.

In the prototype, the storage of reference data also has the advantage of detecting erroneous data early and recognizing it later in productive operation. Nevertheless, the reference values are calculated in Azure Functions for periods when it is highly likely that no one is occupying the desks.

4.3   Development of the Web Dashboard

As specified in RQ1, the dashboard has two pages showing current and historical occupancy data. A simple backend was created to access the data stored in Azure tables, aggregate and present it to the frontend. The backend was implemented in JavaScript with *Node.js* and the *Express Framework* and consists of a small Application Programming Interface (API) that accepts HTTP requests. Two distinct methods are defined in the backend that both request data from Azure Tables to be displayed in the dashboard. Simple filters restrict timestamps to a specific period, which can be defined according to the *Open Data Protocol (OData)* standard.

The frontend is built on *Vue.js* version 3, a framework designed for single-page web applications, while the *Chart.js* library (version 3.7.0) is employed for diagram display. A custom dashboard implementation was preferred over available solutions such as *Grafana* or *Node-RED*, ensuring maximum flexibility in user-friendly design and seamless integration with an existing tech stack.

In Fig. 3, the content of the index page is depicted. There, shared desk areas with tables and occupancy information are displayed. The information is randomly generated to simulate realistic values in an application with many sensor modules.

The dashboard's historical data page presents occupancy information over time through simple charts, covering the current week from Monday to Friday or until the latest data point. It begins with a bar chart for general occupancy rates during various time slots, followed by line charts offering additional details, such as the difference between recorded sensor data and daily-changing reference values, which are displayed for each sensor to contextualize raw data.

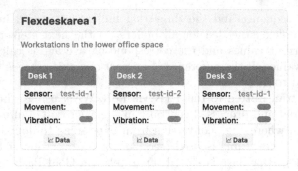

Fig. 3. Home page content with live data.

5 Demonstration and Evaluation

The IoT devices were tested in an experimental setting under real-world conditions in a small company in order to answer RQ2. It will be demonstrated that the prototype maintains reliable operation for several weeks and sends the occupancy data at the defined interval. Additionally, the demonstration period is used to simultaneously collect all occupancy data, which can evaluate how accurately the prototype operates. Different scenarios are conducted based on the collected data to determine how the data can be interpreted in the best possible way. Based on this, it can be decided when the raw data should be classified as occupied or unoccupied.

The demonstration period started on March 28, 2022 at noon and ran until Aprirl 8, 2022 at 11:59am. During this period, occupancy data is collected from two work desks, each with two sensor modules. The redundancy of the sensor modules is intended to provide additional information in the event of potential discrepancies in sensor data. Both workstations have the same users who have agreed to perform this test throughout the demonstration period. The work desks are used both by standing and sitting employees. The possibility of other employees approaching the tables is also encouraged, demonstrating that the sensors cover only the area under the table. However, these two circumstances are not enforced, representing ordinary office and workstation use.

The users record the time at their desks accurately for testing purposes. These time recordings serve in the evaluation as ground truth. In order to establish comparability and to better classify the results, the accuracy of the prototype is calculated. Accuracy as a metric is also recorded in studies in the Heating, Ventilation and Air-conditioning (HVAC) field, as comparable sensors are often used in this field (c.f. [13]). Measuring the accuracy allows the results to be compared with those of [20], who performed similar experiments. The authors provide the following equation to calculate the accuracy:

$$accuracy = \frac{TP + TN}{TP + TN + FP + FN} \qquad (1)$$

In this case, True Positives (TPs) and True Negatives (TNs) represent the amounts of correct assignments corresponding to the ground truth of the occupancy status of a measured value. On the other hand, False Positives (FPs) reflect the number of false detections of an assignment and False Negatives (FNs) the number of unrecognized assignments. Other important characteristics are the False Positive Rate (FPR) and the False Negative Rate (FNR) or their specificity and sensitivity inversion. Thus, sensitivity describes the proportion of detected occupancies in the application case out of all cases where occupancy is observed. Opposite to the sensitivity is the FNR, which describes the inverse probability that occupancy is not detected.

The proportion of negative occupancy statuses among the cases in which the workplace was not occupied is called specificity. In order to summarize all these characteristics in one feature, the Youden index is suitable. This index can assume a value in the range $[-1; 1]$ and ideally has the value 1. The Youden index is calculated as follows (c.f. [12,21]):

$$J = \frac{TP}{TP + FN} + \frac{TN}{FP + TN} - 1 \tag{2}$$

The research of [20] is very similar to this work, but the authors achieved an accuracy of only 87.7% (see Table 1, showing the FPR, FNR, and the Youden index.).

Table 1. Accuracy achieved by [20].

Accuracy	FPR	FNR	Youden-Index
87.70%	15.21%	7.75%	0.7705

While demonstrating at the company, a sensor failure was detected and rectified quickly. After the end of the demonstration, the sensor data was exported in Comma-separated Values (CVS) format for further evaluation afterwards. The prototype's FPR and FNR were considered under different conditions and reference values. Three main scenarios are to be considered.

The first scenario corresponds to the accuracy evaluation without data processing by Azure Functions. In the second scenario, the accuracy is determined with one reference value per day. In a third scenario, it is checked whether the accuracy can be further increased by calculating the reference based on a more extensive reference period.

Table 2. Accuracy, FPR and FNR from Scenario 1 (sensor data only), 2 (daily reference) and 3 (daily reference).

Char.	Scenario	Movement	Vibration	Mov. AND Vib.	Mov. OR Vib.
Accuracy	1	41.65%	77.72%	38.89%	78.48%
	2	94.19%	90.02%	93.42%	90.80%
	3	95.00%	90.85%	95.86%	90.00%
FPR	1	79.69%	27.82%	83.82%	23.69%
	2	4.70%	2.32%	6.58%	0.44%
	3	2.95%	1.63%	4.17%	0.41%
FNR	1	1.34%	14.83%	0.45%	15.71%
	2	8.88%	31.14%	6.59%	33.43%
	3	6.91%	29.95%	4.06%	32.80%

In the first scenario, only the accuracy of the sensors is evaluated (see Table 2). If vibrations or movements are detected, the Boolean value *True* is determined; otherwise, *False*. A high accuracy assumes an error-free measurement of the sensors at the point, which was not the case in practice. The motion detector, in particular, has an exceptionally high FPR and a low accuracy. If only the data of the motion detector is evaluated, it is not sufficient for determining the work occupancy. Table 2 lists the main features of the measurement. The motion detector has a higher accuracy when measuring vibrations.

The occupancy data is evaluated in the second scenario considering daily references to increase the accuracy, corresponding to the implemented state. First, it should be ensured that the reference values calculated by the Azure Function are correct. For this purpose, the reference values for the reference periods are calculated manually. In the current state of development, a desk is considered occupied if the values of at least one sensor are above the reference with k-factor 2.5. Thus, the motion or acceleration sensor must have a value above its reference to detect occupancy.

Nevertheless, all theoretical options are considered in this scenario, i.e., the individual sensors and an *AND* combination of the sensors. The corresponding results are summarized in Table 2. Comparing and calculating the sensor data with reference data can achieve a higher accuracy of Movement and Vibration. The accuracy is over 90% in all cases and thus already higher than in the first scenario. Thus, using the reference values, the prototype is already more accurate than the PIR sensors used in the comparison study from [20]. The accuracy of the implemented case (Mov. || Vib. column) is 93.42%.

FPRs and FNRs are about the same, indicating that the detection provides an outstanding balance between FPs and FNs in determining the occupancy status. Moreover, the FPR is reduced in this approach, but the FNR is increased simultaneously by using this calculation. However, requiring both sensors to strike out is not recommended here due to the high FNR of 33.43%. Expanding on the results from the second scenario, there is opportunity for enhancement as the previously chosen k-factor of 2.5 was arbitrarily selected. To ensure a more sensible value is chosen, alternative values were tested for daily reference. The accuracy and previously introduced Youden index were employed to evaluate the results.

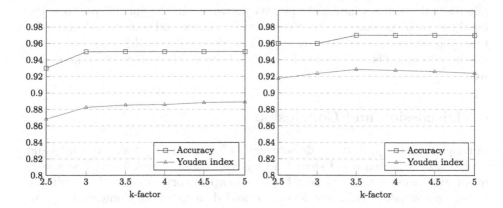

(a) Accuracy and Youden index of daily reference as a function of the k-factor in scenario 1

(b) Accuracy and Youden index of the total reference as a function of the k-factor in scenario 3.

Fig. 4. Accuracy and Youden index of different scenarios.

The accuracies up to the value five increase more and more with increasing k-factor. The Youden index reaches its maximum at about five, as shown in Fig. 4. In this case, the accuracy is 95.32%, and the Youden index is 0.8889. This accuracy improvement is mainly due to the additional data processing. After completing the evaluation, the k-factor in the implementation was set to the optimal value of 5.

In the last scenario, the data basis is broader in time. This scenario is intended to show further potential for improvement of the current implementation, but it still needs to be implemented. Instead of being calculated daily, the reference is calculated over the demonstration period. Only the period between midnight and 4 AM is still considered a reference, but this time from all days. The reference values change randomly, and there is no clear trend over time in which direction the values develop. Table 2 shows the results of the third scenario. The broader reference calculation again leads to a significant improvement in accuracy.

In particular, when the sensors are OR-linked (Mov. || Vib.), the accuracy increases, and FPR and FNR decrease. The other characteristics show minimally better values than in scenario 2. Overall, a comprehensive reference calculation with both sensors being OR-linked achieves better accuracies.

Furthermore, in this scenario, the k-factor can be optimized. The accuracies keep increasing up to a limit with increasing k-factor. The Youden index reaches its maximum at a factor of approx. 3.5. Then the accuracy is 97.11%, and the Youden index is 0.9286. Concerning the comparison study, this is an improvement in accuracy of +9.41% and for the Youden index of +0.1581. Thus, the optimal reference for this scenario is 3.5 times the standard deviation from the mean.

Afterward, we investigate whether data was sent at the set interval of one minute to determine whether the prototypes work reliably. For this purpose, the database with the sensor data was sorted by sensor and date to calculate the time differences between any two rows. The mean value of the time intervals is one minute and 234 ms. All in all, sending in time intervals works remarkably well.

6   Discussion and Conclusion

In conclusion, the prototype's demonstration for measuring desk occupancy and deployment in a real-world shared desk environment, coupled with the subsequent evaluation detailed in Sect. 5, proved satisfactory. As a result, a solution to research question RQ2 was developed and demonstrated. Compared to similar studies, our approach exhibits significantly higher accuracy and reliability, achieved through data processing and interpretation using statistical methods. Consequently, this presents a lower-cost, higher-accuracy solution for measuring actual office workspace utilization in a desk-sharing environment.

The first research question, RQ1, requires that the prototype determines the occupancy status, is transmitted via LoRaWAN, and is further processed visually via a dashboard. If no reference data is collected, the transmitted detection of motion and shaking from the accelerometer and motion detector can be used or combined with an *AND* relationship to achieve an accuracy of 78.48% (see Table 2). In this respect, part of RQ1 is already achieved under these circumstances, albeit only with moderate accuracy and moderate Youden index.

A new, more accurate detection method was developed due to the inefficiency of the previous motion detector. Data processing is performed in the Microsoft Azure cloud and has a 95.32% accuracy rate with a Youden index of 0.8889, achieved through daily reference. This performance could be further increased with minor changes if the reference values are formed over an extended period, which also helps to reduce the impact of exceptions on performance.

However, the reference for past and future periods should be similar because there was no clear trend in the reference determination. Calculating reference data for each prototype individually or together did not yield a significant difference for evaluation. Calculating the reference for the first week of demonstration and applying it to the second week yields an accuracy of 97.06% and a Youden index of 0.9189, corresponding to an overall reference calculation over the last week. So, based on the barely measurable deviations, everything indicates that the sensors can use the same reference values regardless of the time and the specific specifications. Theoretically, the reference values can also be defined as constants in the source code so that reference values may be unnecessary. Since the data sent via LoRaWAN must be stored centrally, the currently implemented version with data processing in the cloud proved to be an appropriate approach.

Moreover, well-founded reference values can be formed in the long term since the data is determined daily without disrupting ongoing operations. Higher-quality sensors could achieve better accuracies so that the formation of reference values would not be necessary, but for cost reasons, products below 20€ had to be procured. Nevertheless, good accuracy could also be achieved with these models with reference values. The low cost constitutes another benefit of our solution over others presented in the literature.

Further prototype development can use raw data from the sensor itself. The same applies to the accelerometer data. Instead of calibrating this initially and abstracting it to truth values, it could be investigated whether the pure absolute values of the acceleration data are suitable for data processing in the cloud. Another improvement could reduce the impact of delays between the sensor and data storage.

In order to attach the sensors better and more compactly, housing would be advantageous in the long term, which has not been done so far to preserve the flexibility of possible sensor changes. Since the prototype is based on a commercially available developer board with a reasonable amount of connection pins, it can easily be expanded modularly.

For example, if additional sensors are desired, an ultrasonic sensor could be mounted under the tabletop to measure the set table height. Additionally, sound and other environmental sensors can be integrated to ensure a productive working atmosphere. To accomplish this, all that is required is to configure them on the Arduinos, map them into the Azure Tables, and display them in a meaningful way on the dashboard.

An answer to research question RQ1 was achieved through the development of a suitable dashboard, which displays both current occupancy data and past weeks' data. Employed during the demonstration, the dashboard effectively displayed plausible data and functioned without issues. While it currently includes only essential features for data display, the dashboard can be readily expanded with additional Vue components or desired charts.

This approach, which employs low-cost, high-accuracy sensors and cloud-based data processing, can be utilized in various IoT domains for future research, including occupancy management in areas such as conference room availability and retail store customer tracking. While the design proposed here tackles hot-desking, it can also serve as a foundation for creating smart working spaces more broadly when combined with other IoT solutions.

In future research, we plan to further evaluate our artifacts using the Fitness-Utility Model (FUM) as part of the DSR approach, with a focus on long-term design impact. However, due to the extensive time horizon required, we couldn't draw conclusions about fitness and utility in our short evaluation period. The FUM outlines design fitness characteristics like "Interesting", "Elegant", and "Malleable", which can be assessed through qualitative and quantitative methods [25].

References

1. Atzori, L., Iera, A., Morabito, G.: The internet of things: a survey. Comput. Netw. **54**, 2787–2805 (2010)
2. Perwej, Y., Haq, K., Parwej, F., Mumdouh, M.: The internet of things (IoT) and its application domains. Int. J. Comput. Appl. **182**, 36–49 (2019). https://www.ijcaonline.org/archives/volume182/number49/perwej-2019-ijca-918763.pdf
3. Ibarra-Esquer, J., González-Navarro, F., Flores-Rios, B., Burtseva, L., Astorga-Vargas, M.: Tracking the evolution of the internet of things concept across different application domains. Sensors **17**, 1379 (2017). https://www.mdpi.com/1424-8220/17/6/1379
4. Gardašević, G., et al.: The IoT architectural framework, design issues and application domains. Wirel. Pers. Commun. **92**, 127–148 (2017). https://doi.org/10.1007/s11277-016-3842-3
5. Peffers, K., Tuunanen, T., Rothenberger, M., Chatterjee, S.: A design science research methodology for information systems research. J. Manag. Inf. Syst. **24**, 45–77 (2007). https://www.tandfonline.com/doi/full/10.2753/MIS0742-1222240302
6. Baiyere, A., et al.: Internet of things (IoT) - a research agenda for information systems. Commun. Assoc. Inf. Syst. **47**, 21 (2020)
7. Whitmore, A., Agarwal, A., Da Xu, L.: The internet of things-a survey of topics and trends. Inf. Syst. Front. **17**, 261–274 (2015). https://doi.org/10.1007/s10796-014-9489-2
8. C Henshaw, M.: Systems of systems, cyber-physical systems, the internet-of-things...whatever next? Insight **19**, 4 (2016)
9. Ramirez, A., González-Carrasco, I., Jasper, G., Lopez, A., Lopez-Cuadrado, J., García-Crespo, A.: Towards human smart cities: internet of things for sensory impaired individuals. Computing **99**, 107–126 (2017). https://doi.org/10.1007/s00607-016-0529-2
10. Georgakopoulos, D., Jayaraman, P.: Internet of things: from internet scale sensing to smart services. Computing **98**, 1041–1058 (2016). https://doi.org/10.1007/s00607-016-0510-0
11. Atzori, L., Iera, A., Morabito, G.: Understanding the Internet of Things: definition, potentials, and societal role of a fast evolving paradigm. Ad Hoc Netw. **56**, 122–140 (2017)
12. Hedderich, J., Sachs, L.: Angewandte Statistik. Springer, Heidelberg (2016)
13. Jung, W., Jazizadeh, F.: Human-in-the-loop HVAC operations: a quantitative review on occupancy, comfort, and energy-efficiency dimensions. Appl. Energy **239**, 1471–1508 (2019). https://linkinghub.elsevier.com/retrieve/pii/S030626191930073X
14. Lee, M., Guo, R., Bhalla, A.: Pyroelectric sensors. J. Electroceram. **2**, 229–242 (1998)
15. Lohiya, R., Thakkar, A.: Application domains, evaluation data sets, and research challenges of IoT: a systematic review. IEEE Internet Things J. **8**, 8774–8798 (2021). https://ieeexplore.ieee.org/document/9311636/
16. Blenn, N., Kuipers, F.: LoRaWAN in the Wild: Measurements from The Things Network. arXiv (2017)
17. Sub-G Module Data Sheet (2018). https://static6.arrow.com/aropdfconversion-/8b033f4fa36fb9e2c8464263592495ee5b-833573-/type_abz.pdf
18. Pacchi, C.: Sharing economy: makerspaces, co-working spaces, hybrid workplaces, and new social practices. In: Milan, pp. 73–83 (2017)

19. Poulten, G.: Why trust and autonomy are essential factors when working from home (2020). https://www.rolandberger.com/en/Insights/Publications/The-home-office-becomes-the-new-normal.html
20. Sheikh Khan, D., Kolarik, J., Anker Hviid, C., Weitzmann, P.: Method for long-term mapping of occupancy patterns in open-plan and single office spaces by using passive-infrared (PIR) sensors mounted below desks. Energy Build. **230**, 110534 (2021). https://linkinghub.elsevier.com/retrieve/pii/S0378778820318958
21. Youden, W.: Index for rating diagnostic tests. Cancer **3**, 32–35 (1950)
22. Yun, J., Song, M.: Detecting direction of movement using pyroelectric infrared sensors. IEEE Sens. J. **14**, 1482–1489 (2014). https://ieeexplore.ieee.org/document/6697828/
23. Kim, J., Candido, C., Thomas, L., De Dear, R.: Desk ownership in the workplace: the effect of non-territorial working on employee workplace satisfaction, perceived productivity and health. Build. Environ. **103**, 203–214 (2016). https://www.sciencedirect.com/science/article/pii/S036013231630138X
24. Mullarkey, M., Hevner, A.: An elaborated action design research process model. Eur. J. Inf. Syst. **28**, 6–20 (2019). https://www.tandfonline.com/doi/full/10.1080/0960085X.2018.1451811
25. Gill, T., Hevner, A.: A fitness-utility model for design science research. ACM Trans. Manag. Inf. Syst. **4**, 1–24 (2013). https://dl.acm.org/doi/10.1145/2499962.2499963
26. Wagner, D., Mathur, A., Boor, B.: Spatial seated occupancy detection in offices with a chair-based temperature sensor array. Build. Environ. **187**, 107360 (2021). https://linkinghub.elsevier.com/retrieve/pii/S0360132320307290
27. Elkhoukhi, H., Bakhouya, M., El Ouadghiri, D., Hanifi, M.: Using stream data processing for real-time occupancy detection in smart buildings. Sensors **22**, 2371 (2022). https://www.mdpi.com/1424-8220/22/6/2371
28. Pan, J., Cho, T., Bardhan, R.: Occupancy level prediction based on a sensor-detected dataset in a co-working space. In: Proceedings of the 9th ACM International Conference on Systems for Energy-Efficient Buildings, Cities, and Transportation, pp. 340–347 (2022). https://dl.acm.org/doi/10.1145/3563357.3566133
29. Sood, T., Janssen, P., Miller, C.: Spacematch: using environmental preferences to match occupants to suitable activity-based workspaces. Front. Built Environ. **6**, 113 (2020). https://www.frontiersin.org/article/10.3389/fbuil.2020.00113/full
30. Blazevic, M., Riehle, D.: University of things: opportunities and challenges for a smart campus environment based on IoT sensors and business processes. In: Proceedings of the 8th International Conference on Internet of Things, Big Data and Security, pp. 105–114 (2023). https://doi.org/10.5220/0011761900003482. ISBN 978-989-758-643-9, ISSN 2184-4976
31. Wolters, A., Blazevic, M., Riehle, D.: On-premise Internet of Things (IoT) data storage: comparison of database management systems. In: Proceedings of the 8th International Conference on Internet of Things, Big Data and Security, pp. 140–149 (2023). https://doi.org/10.5220/0011851200003482. ISBN 978-989-758-643-9, ISSN 2184-4976

Design of Systems Using Emerging Technologies

Introduction to the Design of Systems Using Emerging Technologies Track

Kaushik Dutta and Carson Woo

1 Introduction

In today's rapidly changing, interconnected global economy, concepts such as Fin-Tech and blockchain have become commonplace from the newsroom to the boardroom. Recently, disruptions from the global pandemic have worked to accelerate change and increase demand for new knowledge, leadership, innovation, and solutions to emerging complex challenges in the public and private sectors. As a result, rapidly evolving, technology-driven research domains and industry sectors such as those involving FinTech and blockchain systems are having broad based transformational impacts on a range of diverse market spaces including (although not limited to) banking, finance, financial services, healthcare, insurance, manufacturing, supply chain, transport, government, legal, energy, cyber security, and utilities, among others.

In this track, we received 3 full papers and 3 research-in-progress (RIP) papers. After review we accepted one full paper for this proceedings and 2 RIP in this track. The papers accepted in this track follows the theme of the track. The accepted full paper describes the design of a tool in augmented reality along with the evaluation of the tool on several dimensions including effectiveness, efficiency, quality, cognitive load, mental effort and ease of use. The two RIP papers also describe the work-in-progress in development of two different systems using emerging technology such as blockchain - traceability system for supply chain and distributed version control system. All the systems described in these three papers are very timely, have practical application and are using emerging technology platform. We want to thank the authors to submit such high-quality paper in this track at DESRIST 2023.

We want to acknowledge the expert opinion of our reviewers in reviewing the papers in this track. The dedication of the review team in timely submission of review is essentials for the success of a track.

Designing an Augmented Reality Authoring Tool to Support Complex Tasks. A Design Science Study Using Cognitive Load Theory

Kay Hönemann(✉) [iD], Björn Konopka[iD], and Manuel Wiesche[iD]

TU Dortmund University, Dortmund, Germany
{kay.hoenemann,bjoern.konopka,manuel.wiesche}@tu-dortmund.de

Abstract. Despite the potential of augmented reality (AR) to support and guide complex industrial tasks, the technology is still not broadly applied. One possible reason for this is that the creation of AR content is highly complex and requires programming skills and deep spatial knowledge. AR authoring tools can help address this complexity by enabling non-developers to create self-sufficient AR content. Therefore, this paper proposes a theory-driven design for AR authoring tools that allows non-developers to create self-sufficient AR-based instructions to support complex tasks. Based on ten interviews with experts working with AR authoring tools and a following focus group with eight participants, we propose three design principles for future AR authoring tools in the engineering context. These design principles are instantiated in two prototypes of different richness and evaluated in an experiment with 23 students. Our study shows that the cognitive load is slightly increased when using the extensive AR authoring tool, but it also shows that significantly better results can be achieved with the extensive AR authoring tool. We contribute by providing design principles for AR authoring tools for creating AR-based instructions, which extend the existing AR authoring research in the industrial context.

Keywords: Augmented Reality · AR Authoring · Design Science Research · Cognitive Load Theory

1 Introduction

We often find ourselves in situations where we encounter problems in our daily work. When we are not able to handle the issues on our own, we either seek help from people with more experience and expertise [1], or we are supported by specific technologies that help us to handle the problem and at the same time ensure that we complete our work in a compliant manner [2]. Especially in complex work environments and in the execution of knowledge-intensive tasks, these technologies are needed. The tasks include activities that, on the one hand, have a strong contextual reference, influenced by several environmental factors. On the other hand, the task requires an enormous amount of knowledge. An example is the complexity of designing and developing new information systems [3]. Another example would be the use of AR in the safety-critical service process of soil

© The Author(s), under exclusive license to Springer Nature Switzerland AG 2023
A. Gerber and R. Baskerville (Eds.): DESRIST 2023, LNCS 13873, pp. 87–101, 2023.
https://doi.org/10.1007/978-3-031-32808-4_6

sounding [4] or the maintenance and repair of technical assets [5]. For instance, in software engineering, users are supported by a specific technology during the development phase to improve process compliance [6]. In recent years, digitally enriched guidance has increased significantly through augmented reality (AR) technology for these tasks. Very early on, researchers and practitioners recognized the enormous potential of these digitally enriched guidance systems [7]. Yet, the technology has mainly been applied in the engineering context only in prototype form. One reason could be that creating AR content is very complex and requires strong programming skills and deep spatial knowledge [8]. Consequently, 64% of all AR applications in the engineering sector are individual developments [9]. Individual developments are often not very practical for SMEs, as even small changes, which are part of the daily work for such volatile things as instructions, mean significant development costs.

AR authoring tools can help address this challenge. Authoring tools are software programs that allow users to create and publish AR experiences on different platforms on different types of hardware [8, 10]. However, a closer look at the existing tools reveals that they are still used by experienced software developers, as some of the more complex functions require extensive programming knowledge and 3D modeling skills [8]. Therefore, the creation of AR content by non-developers remains a challenge.

Many AR studies consider how the ideal work instruction looks like in augmented reality. For example, one study examines what information is needed to depict an instruction in AR [11]. Even the effectiveness of AR guidance compared to the usual paper guidance has been researched in recent years [12]. Other studies, in turn, have explored which type of AR representations are most suitable for AR guidance [13]. In contrast, the creation of AR content, so-called AR authoring, is still an unknown area of research. These findings refer exclusively to the use of AR content and do not provide any information about which AR content has which kind of impact on users during the creation process. For example, in the literature, it was determined that complex visualization elements are better suited for using AR instructions [13]. However, it might be possible that the users find it more difficult to create these complex visualization elements, which could then influence the quality of the AR instructions. To the best of our knowledge, there is no study on how the complexity of AR visualizations affects the mental and cognitive abilities of the creator during the creation process. Therefore, we aim to answer the following research question: *"How does the richness of AR visualizations affect task performance, ease of use, and mental and cognitive load during the creation process?"*.

To answer the research question, we follow a comprehensive Design Science Research (DSR) methodology [14] focusing on designing innovative artifacts. The research is structured as follows. The conceptual background and related work are considered in the next chapter. The third chapter gives an overview of the DSR approach, which was applied in the study. The fourth chapter describes the design principles, the software artifact, and the evaluation. Finally, in the last chapter, the practical and theoretical contribution paper is discussed, as well as the limitations and future research.

2 Conceptual Background and Related Work

2.1 AR Authoring

Despite the broad application of AR in recent years in many fields, there are still several challenges in creating AR content. Ashtari et al. identified eight key barriers defining the complexity of AR content creation [15]. These range from the initial difficulties in choosing suitable tools to the lack of clear design guidelines to the challenges in testing and evaluating AR applications. With AR authoring tools, these barriers should be overcome in the future. Nebeling & Speicher analyzed existing AR/VR authoring tools in their research. As a result, they could divide the existing tools into five groups [8]. In the first group are tools like InVision or Sketch, non-developers can use them, but they do not offer an AR/VR interface yet. Tools such as Unity or Unreal are assigned to the fifth group, where individual customizations with these tools require strong programming skills and deep spatial knowledge. In the second group, tools are assigned which can be used exactly like in the first group by non-developers. Tools in this class are no-code/low-code tools for developing AR content. They differ from conventional no-code/low-code tools from software development because they provide an AR interface allowing 3D content to be anchored in the real environment. This aspect makes the AR authoring tools unique.

One of the first examples is the AR authoring tool DART from 2005 [16]. This tool allows users to create complex relationships between the real and virtual worlds. This first approach led to new tools for different application areas to create AR content to support context-intensive tasks [17, 18]. Another important research area is AR authoring tools, which are applied to Head Mounted Displays (HMD). For example, non-developers can use tools such as HoloWFM [19] to create workflows that increase the efficiency of task execution.

2.2 AR Tools Supporting Complex Tasks

Due to the continuous implementation of smart connected products, more and more data is available to users. This rising flood of data leads to a fundamental disconnection from the real environment [20]. Thus, some researchers argue that while the real environment is three-dimensional, the data we use daily to make new decisions are trapped in two-dimensional spaces like displays [20]. The gap between the real and virtual environment hinders the ability to make the best possible decisions [20]. Researchers and practitioners are already well aware of this gap, which is why one of the biggest use cases for AR is to provide process guidance based on data directly in situ [21]. Kortekamp et al. identified that this use case is the most frequently applied in the manufacturing environment [22]. In this use case, information is displayed to the users in situ, which is required to work in a compliant manner. For example, service technicians need to know the sequence of maintenance steps and how to perform them.

AR is often used for complex tasks in the field of aerospace technology to complete the work in a process-compliant manner. For example, authors Chen et al. initiated and evaluated an AR application that guides service technicians through the assembly process of cables in large spacecraft components [23]. In another AR application, service technicians are guided through installing an aircraft's wiring harness. Using AR reduced the time required to identify the parts to be installed. As a result, maintenance time was reduced by 90% [7]. These are just two examples of how AR can be used to support complex tasks. Many more AR applications in this context exist in the literature [5, 12]. In addition to the AR applications, researchers have identified six information types (i.e., identity, location, way-to, notification, order, and orientation) with which a maintenance manual can be fully represented in AR [11].

2.3 Cognitive Load Theory

For this research, we draw on a kernel theory concerned with conceptualizing and representing design knowledge. This research draws on Cognitive Load Theory (CLT), which originates in educational psychology [24]. The basic assumption of CLT is that individuals are limited in their ability to absorb and process information during the learning process. Furthermore, the CLT framework provides guidance on how to structure information to achieve better learning outcomes [25]. We argue that using new technologies (i.e., AR authoring tool) to achieve a specific goal (i.e., creating an AR instruction) is a learning process. As the design principles must have a long-term learning impact on the users, we use the CLT as the kernel theory.

The cognitive impact of AR instructions during use is frequently studied in the literature. For example, early research has shown that AR assembly instructions in the user's field of view require fewer cognitive resources than traditional assembly instructions on display [12]. This is just one example. Recent studies have also highlighted the potential of AR instructions to reduce cognitive load [26]. However, creating AR instructions using AR authoring tools has not yet been considered from a cognitive load perspective.

3 Methodology

Our study is part of a large ongoing DSR project that provides an innovative solution to a real-world problem [27]. More specifically, we address the lack of design knowledge about how non-developers can create AR content. In this way, we want to improve SMEs' access to AR technology. We adapted Küchler & Vaishnavi's [14] approach. Therefore, we separated the overall DSR project into three successive design cycles. The study focuses on the second design cycle based on the first design cycle. It forms the basis for the final design cycle. The following section briefly describes the entire DSR project to provide additional information and highlight the overall research goal. We started the first design cycle by investigating the challenges related to task execution in the engineering context, for which we conducted a first literature review. The findings highlight that in the literature, AR applications have been predominantly instantiated and evaluated in various contexts. Many of these studies point to an enormous savings potential of AR [5, 12]. The literature also showed that despite the existing AR authoring tools, there are still enormous difficulties in creating AR content [8]. There is a significant need for research to understand better the needs of the different types of users trying to get into AR development [15]. Therefore, we conducted an evaluation study with an industrial plant supplier with a subsequent focus group. For instance, we found out that the use of HMDs is prototypically excellent for these types of tasks, but in practice, these devices are not yet suitable for daily operation due to various boundary conditions (i.e., the already dark operating environments become much darker with an HMD) [28]. The literature review and evaluation study findings form our initial meta-requirements. Based on these, we developed our first software prototype and evaluated it in a field study. In the second design cycle, we adapted the design principles based on the findings of the first design cycle and were thus able to instantiate a first software prototype and subsequently evaluate it in a laboratory experiment. In the third design cycle, we intend to replicate the results of the second design cycle in a real application context. In doing so, we want to respond to the request of Peffers et al. to evaluate DSR artifacts in more real environments [29].

4 Design Science Research Project

4.1 Problem Awareness

To further deepen our understanding of the problem, we conducted ten semi-structured interviews with experts who work with AR authoring tools in their daily work. We also conducted a focus group with eight participants to triangulate and validate the findings from the interviews. Three AR authoring experts and five users from the identified target group (i.e., service technicians) participated in the focus group. The focus group is used to gain a better understanding of the results and to facilitate and further enrich the results. The experience of the individuals with AR authoring tools differed, so 30% could be classified as beginners, 40% as intermediates, and 30% as specialists.

In line with the literature, existing AR authoring tools are empowering for AR authoring experts, but in practice, these are not used by non-developers [8]. Their justification for this is straightforward. The fault lies with the user. For example, one participant said: *'[I]... is some kind of painting tool that is so simple that customers can use it to create AR experiences without any additional help. [I] I find the solution very fast and find it correspondingly interesting that people still don't jump on it. [I] The fact that the authoring is not done by the customers themselves is due to the customers and their lack of capacity, not due to the tool'*. Another important aspect some participants mentioned was that the existing tools are designed for a specific application domain. In their opinion, this makes sense since the requirements for a marketing application differ from those for an engineering application. *'[IV]... is specialized in maintenance/service instructions. For marketing applications, it is not suitable because special requirements like font size, font, special image size are not feasible.'*. Some participants also mentioned requirements in AR authoring from which design suggestions emerged. For example, almost all participants agreed that the most time-consuming and biggest challenge for an AR authoring tool user is to obtain the correct data (i.e., CAD models) and then compress them [30].

Another challenging aspect of AR authoring is choosing the appropriate tracking method and its implementation. Tracking is unique for AR applications in this form so far. Thus, it can be assumed that non-developers have no experience in this area, but it forms the basis of nearly every AR application. Without tracking, virtual objects cannot be anchored in the user's real environment [28]. Making decisions about AR hardware also causes challenges for users. Although the interviews revealed several advantages of AR authoring tools, they also highlighted the complexity of the approach. Especially topics like tracking or handling 3D data are complex and require some prior experience. Therefore, future AR authoring tools must guide non-developers through these processes.

4.2 Suggestion

We obtained substantial evidence about the design of AR authoring tools from the industrial context from the interviews. The first meta-requirement (**MR1**) refers to the effective use of a system, which results from the co-dependence between the system and the task. To counteract this representative complexity, the system should be designed so that the user is supported in the execution of the task and at the same time that only a few semantic understandings are necessary for the execution of the task [31]. The authors vom Brocke et al. propose ten principles of how good process management can be implemented in practice. First, the system should be designed to fit into the organizational context on the one hand, and on the other, the system should make opportune use of AR technology [32]. The creation of AR-based instructions differs significantly from the creation of conventional instructions, as digital content is anchored in the user's real environment [33]. Users must therefore be able to create both two-dimensional and three-dimensional processes. Our first design principle (DP), which we propose, is based on this meta-requirement: **DP1**: *Provide the system with various process steps in order to clearly separate the creation of pure 2D and 3D content for non-developer.*

The second meta-requirement (**MR2**) refers to a library of 2D and 3D elements to completely represent an instruction in AR. The authors Gattullo et al. identified six types of information that can be used to represent work instructions in AR. For this reason, the users must be able to access different 2D and 3D elements [11]. Both distinguishing intrinsic and extraneous cognitive load are related to the difference between novices and experts in their learning process [25]. These effects imply that novices need more detailed information about a system to be able to use it to overcome the knowledge gap. On the other hand, experts with a greater knowledge level in using AR draw on their prior knowledge. Since users use an AR authoring tool with different levels of prior knowledge, the system must provide a set of AR elements requiring different information levels to create AR instructions of different complexities [34]. The third meta-requirement (**MR3**) relates to the ability of users to create their media. The decision between using complex and abstract AR representations is a matter of disagreement among researchers. Some studies indicate that using complex AR representations distracts users, negatively affecting the error rate [35]. On the other hand, some studies demonstrate that much better results can be achieved with complex AR representations. However, these also show that similarly good results can be achieved with abstract AR representations in combination with media like photos or videos [13]. The two meta requirements described above form the foundation for the second design principle we propose: **DP2**: *Provide the system with a library of display and information elements which requires different information levels so that non-developers can entirely visualize instruction in Augmented reality of different complexities.*

The fourth meta-requirement (**MR4**) refers to the general design approach regarding the target group, the non-developers. On the one hand, just-in-time access to information during task performance reduces cognitive load, and on the other hand, it enables learning [36]. With augmented reality instructions, only the required information is displayed in the right place in the real environment at the right time. The non-developers are empowered to create self-sufficient AR content to increase their learning outcomes sustainably [25]. In order for users to adopt new interactive technologies, they must be able to adapt the technologies to their practice [37]. This perspective leads to discourse in research about the end-user development approach. This is defined as various methods, techniques, and tools that allow non-developers to create, adapt and extend the software for themselves [38]. According to Nebeling and Speicher, these tools belong to the second group of AR authoring tools [8]. The fifth meta-requirement (**MR5**) relates to the environment of the industrial context. Asset maintenance often occurs at the customer's site in inaccessible locations. Many studies use HMDs for this application context and show the great potential associated with them [7, 39]. Nevertheless, the hardware is not yet mature enough for daily use since most HMDs are heavy and have short battery life and a limited field of view [40]. For this reason, the AR authoring tool must be used on application-grade hardware. The two meta requirements thus form our final design principle that we propose: **DP3**: *Provide the system with an end-user development and just-in-time access to information approach empowering non-developers with different levels of experience to create self-sufficient Augmented Reality content for a specific application domain.* By initiating the prototypes based on all these approaches, we intend to evaluate these approaches and then adapt the design principles accordingly.

4.3 Development

To instantiate our design principles, we developed an AR authoring tool prototype. The first design principle specifically maps onto the possibility of creating a process flow for the instructions. The instructions' structure and sequence are determined in the so-called Node-Editor. Here three different node types are available to users. The first node type is the Info-Node, where only 2D elements (i.e., text) can be added. An Instruction-Node reflects one step in an instruction manual, and an Exploration-Node, where only location-dependent content can be displayed. The second design principle specifically maps onto the display and information elements used to represent the instructions in AR. For this purpose, a library of seven annotations is available to the users, which can be anchored in the users' real environment. These range from simple arrows, which refer to a position in the real environment, to complex tethers, which act as navigation through the real environment. In addition to the 3D elements, 2D elements such as media or text can be added to an instruction step. The third design principle maps onto the foundational design of a standalone AR authoring tool that operates on a tablet without installing additional software or plugins or deploying additional hardware. The tool can be used to create AR instructions as well as to support the execution of complex tasks. Through the use of an end-user development approach, the Graphical User Interface does not allow users to implement their code. Instead, users can create instructions by drag and drop and enrich them with 2D and 3D elements. Figure 1 shows the node editor on the left and the authoring environment of the AR authoring tool on the right.

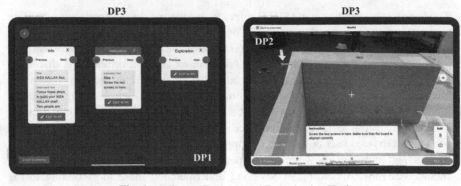

Fig. 1. Software Prototype: AR Authoring Tool

Since participants' preferences varied widely and there is disagreement in the existing literature about the complexity of AR visualizations, we developed a second prototype with different AR visualizations (DP2). Based on the evaluation results, we want to identify the most important display and information elements and adapt our design principles accordingly. As described above, the first prototype provides users with a total of seven different annotations. In the second prototype, only two annotations are available to users (i.e., arrow and point of interest). Furthermore, users do not have the option to add media to an instruction step. Figure 2 shows the AR authoring environment of both prototypes. The right side shows the prototype with extensive visualization elements (i.e., various abstract AR elements, including media), and the left side shows the prototype with reduced visualization elements (i.e., a few abstract AR elements without media).

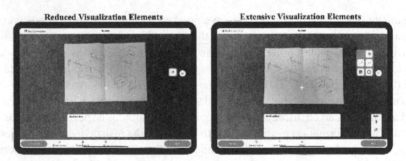

Fig. 2. AR Authoring environment of both prototypes

4.4 Evaluation

To examine task performance, we examined the effectiveness, efficiency, and quality of the created AR instruction as key performance indicators. We also analyzed the mental effort, cognitive load, and ease of use to assess important performance indicators related to the CLT. The following hypotheses regarding task performance and the CLT when using the AR authoring tool were investigated in this experiment.

- **H1a:** Increased richness of the tool positively affects effectiveness.
- **H1b:** Increased richness of the tool positively affects efficiency.
- **H1c:** Increased richness of the tool positively affects the AR instruction quality.
- **H2:** Increased richness of the tool negatively affects mental effort.
- **H3:** Increased richness of the tool negatively affects the cognitive load.
- **H4:** Increased richness of the tool negatively affects the ease of use.

We conducted a between-subjects laboratory experiment to test our hypotheses, in which different participants tested one of the two AR authoring prototypes. For example, one participant group used an AR authoring prototype with a reduced feature set. The other participant group used a more extensive AR authoring prototype with an extended feature set. We choose a between-subject design to minimize possible learning effects when the same participants use both types of AR authoring tools sequentially to create instructions, as repetition could introduce bias to the collected data.

As part of our experiment, we collected qualitative and quantitative data using our AR authoring tool prototypes. The effectiveness, efficiency, and quality of the authored AR instructions were evaluated as dependent variables. Furthermore, the participants evaluated cognitive load, mental effort, and ease of use through self-reports as part of the post-experiment survey. As an independent variable, the richness of the AR authoring tool was examined using two AR authoring tool prototypes with different levels of richness.

At the beginning of each experiment session, we briefed our participants about our research objective - evaluating our AR authoring tool - as well as the experiment procedure. In addition, a pre-experiment written survey was used to collect demographic data and insights into participants' previous experiences with AR.

Before starting the experiment, we demonstrated the tool to the participants and explained its functions and how to operate it. After introducing the tool, a simple demonstration task was presented to the participants. Then, participants had to solve it autonomously to verify whether they understood how to use the tool. Following this introduction to the tool and successful completion of the demonstration task, no further information on how to use the tool was provided to the participants.

As the main task of the experiment, we requested participants to assemble a 2x2 IKEA KALLAX shelf following IKEA's paper-based instruction manual, which features eight assembly steps. We asked participants to use the AR authoring tool to create an AR assembly instruction, which means replicating the eight steps of the paper-based instruction and improving this instruction through AR visualizations. Participants were given 20 min to create their AR instruction. The experiment task is concluded when it is completed or time runs out. During the experiment, quantitative data was collected. While participants were working on the experiment task, a screen recording of their activities was captured on the tablet computer used to run the AR authoring prototype. In addition, a camera placed in the corner of the lab room was used to record video of the participant's actions. The variable effectiveness was measured based on how many of the eight steps of the IKEA paper instructions were implemented by the participants in AR using the tool. For the variable efficiency, the time required in seconds to reproduce the second step of the IKEA instructions in AR was measured. The quality variable is based on the average of two AR authoring experts' ratings for the AR instructions created by the experiment participants.

To conclude the experiment, we asked participants to complete a post-experiment survey. Among other questions, we used NASA-TLX [41] and RSME [42] questionnaires to measure perceived task load and perceived mental effort, respectively. For collecting data on participants' perceptions of the ease of use of our tool, we used the scale ease of use by Wixom and Todd [43].

We recruited 23 student participants for our laboratory experiment, ten male and thirteen female. Of these student participants, 18 are enrolled in business administration and five in industrial engineering. Although participation in the experiment was voluntary as a reward, participants received three bonus points for a written exam.

Regarding the experience with AR, 18 participants stated that they have experience with using AR to varying degrees, mainly AR games, social media filters, and shopping applications. Five participants indicated that they had never used any AR application before. Two participants stated that they'd developed AR applications before. None of the participants used an AR authoring tool before this study.

5 Results

We conducted a statistical analysis of the dependent variables collected through our laboratory experiment to test our hypotheses. Given that t-test postulates normally distributed and homogeneous variables tested our variables for normal distribution with the Shapiro-Wilk-Test [44] and for homogeneity of variance using Levene's test [45]. As shown in Table 1, the two tests show that a normal distribution and homogeneity can be assumed for all examined dependent variables, as all values are significant at the $\alpha <$ 0.05 level.

G*Power [46] was used to calculate the achieved power for an independent group's t-test for two groups of 11 and 12 participants, respectively. We chose an alpha level of $\alpha = 0.05$, and the effect size was estimated to be d = 0.5 based on Cohen's [47] guidelines, as there is no comparable study yet from which the effect size could be adapted. Using these values, the study achieved a power level of 0,21, which shows that the study is underpowered. Therefore, any statistical results obtained must be considered with caution.

Hypothesis H1a states that increasing tool richness has a positive effect on effectiveness, which cannot be confirmed through our t-test due to a lack of statistical significance $(t(21) = 0,393, p < 0,699)$. However, descriptive statistics imply the opposite of our hypothesis. Higher richness slightly decreases the effectiveness. The mean effectiveness of all participants is 0.367 (SD = 0.238). The mean effectiveness of the group using the reduced tool is 0,387 (SD = 0,265), and the mean value for the more extensive tool is lower at 0,348 (SD = 0,22).

Hypothesis H1b states that increasing tool richness positively affects efficiency. This cannot be confirmed through our t-test due to a lack of statistical significance $(t(21) = -1,142, p < 0,266)$. Our descriptive results indicate that increased richness could positively affect efficiency. The mean efficiency of all participants is 204,391 (SD = 132,608). The mean efficiency of the group using the reduced tool is 171,636 (SD = 117,150), and the mean value for the more extensive tool is higher at 234,417 (SD = 143,655).

Table 1. Calculated results for normal distribution and homogeneity.

	Shapiro Wilk Test		Levene Test	
Dependent Variable	Sig. (p)	Result	Sig. (p)	Result
Effectiveness	0,104	ok	0,466	ok
Efficiency	0,516	ok	0,707	ok
Quality	0,103	ok	0,993	ok
Cognitive Load	0,376	ok	0,191	ok
Mental Effort	0,013	ok	0,828	ok
Ease of Use	0,132	ok	0,626	ok

Hypothesis H1c states that increasing tool richness positively affects the quality of the AR instruction. Our t-test results show that there is a statistically significant difference between the group using the reduced prototype and the group using the extensive prototype (t(21) = -2,301, p < 0,032). Descriptive statistics also show a difference in the quality of the two groups. The mean quality score of all participants is 2,935 (SD = 1,048). The mean quality of the group using the reduced tool is 2,455 (SD = 1,011), and the mean for the extensive tool is higher at 3,375 (SD = 0,908).

Hypothesis H2 states that increasing tool richness negatively affects cognitive load, which is increased when richness is increased. This cannot be confirmed through a t-est due to a lack of statistical significance (t(21) = -0,517, p < 0,61). However, the descriptive statistics indicate a higher cognitive load when using the extensive tool. The mean cognitive load of all participants is 4,522 (SD = 1,380). The mean cognitive load of the group using the reduced tool is 4,364 (SD = 1,132), and the mean for the extensive tool is higher at 4,667 (SD = 1,611).

Hypothesis H3 states that increasing tool richness negatively affects mental effort, which is increased when richness is increased. This cannot be confirmed through our t-test due to a lack of statistical significance (t(21) = -0,683, p < 0,502). The descriptive statistics also show a higher mental load when using the extensive tool. The mean mental effort of all participants is 41,478 (SD = 30,336). The mean mental effort of the group using the reduced tool is 36,909 (SD = 30,989), and the mean value for the extensive tool is higher at 45,667 (SD = 30,455).

Hypothesis H4 states that increasing tool richness negatively affects the ease of use, which is decreased when richness is increased. This cannot be confirmed through our t-test due to a lack of statistical significance (t(21) = 0,466, p < 0,646). However, the descriptive statistics show higher ease of use of the reduced tool. The mean ease of use reported by all participants is 4,246 (SD = 1,429). The mean ease of use reported by the group using the reduced tool is 4,394(SD = 1,497), and the mean value for the extensive tool is lower at 4,111 (SD = 1,417).

6 Discussion

This paper presents an AR authoring tool that enables non-developers to create AR instructions to support complex tasks. The proposed design principles contribute theoretically to design knowledge by guiding the development of an AR authoring tool for the industrial context. The laboratory experiment results show that the design principles and their instantiation in a software prototype enable non-developers to create AR instructions self-sufficiently. Along with the existing AR literature, we found that creating AR content with complex visualization elements (i.e., various abstract AR elements, including media) can achieve better results [13, 35]. Thus, the laboratory experiment demonstrated the significantly better quality of the AR instructions without significantly increasing the participants' cognitive load and mental effort. Furthermore, there was no significant difference in the ease of use of the tools. When instating the design principles in a software prototype, we implemented passive tracking that is not perceived by the participants, intending to reduce the tool's richness [28] and thus improve the learning outcome [25]. Consequently, the AR content could not be placed precisely enough, which some participants perceived as a hindering factor. The next design cycle should investigate how active tracking affects the cognitive load and the participants' task performance. To sum up, our three theoretically grounded design principles provide prescriptive knowledge about the design of AR authoring tools for creating AR instructions. Following the DSR contribution framework of Gregor and Hevner, we consider our contribution as an improvement since we propose, on the one hand, a software prototype for a real-world problem and, on the other hand, knowledge in the form of operational design principles [27].

Although we conducted the DSR project and evaluation described in this research according to established guidelines, there are limitations that require further research. First of all, the evaluation was conducted only with participants who do not correspond to the target group (i.e., service technicians). In order for the results to be richer and more generalizable, the evaluation must be conducted with participants from the target group. Second, this study evaluates only a first step toward examining cognitive load during AR creation. Further evaluations are needed to make a validated statement about the progression of cognitive impact on users. Considering social cognitive theory and associated application self-efficacy may also raise new insights regarding cognitive effects during the AR creation process. Third, although two AR authoring experts evaluated the quality of AR instructions created by participants, a representative target group may perceive the quality of AR-based instructions differently. In a two-stage evaluation, the AR-based instructions created by the non-experts could be assessed by other non-experts, which could lead to new and representative results. Finally, due to the small sample size and limited statistical significance of the results of the t-test analysis, some caution must be exercised in regard to the generality of our findings. Nevertheless, our current statistical data, including those from the descriptive analysis, seems to confirm our formulated hypotheses. The hypotheses of this study will be tested again in an upcoming study with a larger sample size.

Acknowledgments. This research was sponsored by the German Federal Ministry for Education and Research in the project WizARd under the reference 02K18D180. Further information can be found at: https://wizard.tu-dortmund.de/

References

1. Zolnowski, A., Schmitt, A.K., Böhmann, T.: Understanding the impact of remote service technology on service business models in manufacturing: from improving after-sales services to building service ecosystems. In: 19th European Conference on Information Systems (2011)
2. Morana, S., Schacht, S., Scherp, A., Maedche, A.: A review of the nature and effects of guidance design features. Decis. Support Syst. **97**, 31–42 (2017)
3. Kaul, M., Storey, V.C., Woo, C.: A framework for managing complexity in information systems. J. Datab. Manag. **28**, 31–42 (2017)
4. Bräker, J., Osterbrink, A., Semmann, M., Wiesche, M.: User-centered requirements for augmented reality as a cognitive assistant for safety-critical services. Bus. Inf. Syst. Eng. (2022)
5. Choi, T.-M., Kumar, S., Yue, X., Chan, H.-L.: Disruptive technologies and operations management in the Industry 4.0 era and beyond. Prod. Oper. Manag. **31**, 9–31 (2022)
6. Becker-Kornstaedt, U., et al.: Support for the process engineer: the spearmint approach to software process definition and process guidance. In: 11th International Conference on Advanced Information Systems Engineering, CAiSE 1999 (2011)
7. Serván, J., Mas, F., Menéndez, J.L., Ríos, J.: Using augmented reality in AIRBUS A400M shop floor assembly work instructions. In: The 4th Manufacturing Engineering Society International Conference, vol. 1431, pp. 633–640 (2011)
8. Nebeling, M., Speicher, M.: The trouble with augmented reality/virtual reality authoring tools. In: 17th IEEE International Symposium on Mixed and Augmented Reality, pp. 333–337 (2018)
9. Palmarini, R., Erkoyuncu, J.A., Roy, R., Torabmostaedi, H.: A systematic review of augmented reality applications in maintenance. Robot. Comput.-Integr. Manufact. **49**, 215–228 (2018)
10. Konopka, B., Hönemann, K., Brandt, P., Wiesche, M.: WizARd: a no-code tool for business process guidance through the use of augmented reality. In: Demonstration & Resources Track, Best BPM Dissertation Award, and Doctoral Consortium at BPM 2022 Co-located with the 20th International Conference on Business Process Management (2022)
11. Gattullo, M., Laviola, E., Uva, A.E.: From therbligs to visual assets: a technique to convey work instructions in augmented reality technical documentation. In: International Joint Conference on Mechanics, Design Engineering and Advanced Manufacturing, pp. 1327–1339 (2022)
12. Tang, A., Owen, C., Biocca, F., Mou, W.: Comparative effectiveness of augmented reality in object assembly. In: Proceedings of the SIGCHI Conference on Human Factors in Computing Systems, pp. 73–80 (2003)
13. Jasche, F., Hoffmann, S., Ludwig, T., Wulf, V.: Comparison of different types of augmented reality visualizations for instructions. In: CHI Conference on Human Factors in Computing Systems (2021)
14. Kuechler, B., Vaishnavi, V.: On theory development in design science research: anatomy of a research project. Eur. J. Inf. Syst. **17**, 489–504 (2008)
15. Ashtari, N., Bunt, A., McGrenere, J., Nebeling, M., Chilana, P.K.: Creating augmented and virtual reality applications: current practices, challenges, and opportunities. In: CHI Conference on Human Factors in Computing Systems (2020)

16. MacIntyre, B., Gandy, M., Dow, S., Bolter, J.D.: DART: a toolkit for rapid design exploration of augmented reality experiences. In: 17th Annual ACM Symposium on User Interface Software and Technology, pp. 197–206 (2004)
17. Zhu, J., Ong, S.K., Nee, A.: A context-aware augmented reality assisted maintenance system. Int. J. Comput. Integr. Manuf. **28**, 213–225 (2015)
18. Krings, K., Weber, P., Jasche, F., Ludwig, T.: FADER: an authoring tool for creating augmented reality-based avatars from an end-user perspective. In: Mensch und Computer 2022, pp. 52–65 (2022)
19. Damarowsky, J., Kühnel, S.: Conceptualization and design of a workflow management system front end for augmented reality headsets. In: 30th European Conference on Information Systems (2022)
20. Porter, M.E., Heppelmann, J.E.: Why every organization needs an augmented reality strategy. Harv. Bus. Rev. 1–13 (2017)
21. Klinker, K., et al.: Structure for innovations: a use case taxonomy for smart glasses in service processes. In: Multikonferenz Wirtschaftsinformatik, pp. 1599–1610 (2018)
22. Kortekamp, S.S., Werning, S., Ickerott, I., Thomas, O.: The future of digital work - use cases for augmented reality glasses. In: 27th European Conference on Information Systems - Information Systems for a Sharing Society (2019)
23. Chen, H., Chen, C., Sun, G., Wan, B.: Augmented reality tracking registration and process visualization method for large spacecraft cable assembly. In: Augmented reality tracking registration and process visualization method for large spacecraft cable assembly, vol. 612 (2019)
24. Miller, G.A.: The magical number seven, plus or minus two: some limits on our capacity for processing information. Psychol. Rev. **63**, 81–97 (1956)
25. Sweller, J.: Cognitive load during problem solving: effects on learning. Cognit. Sci. **12**, 257–285 (1988)
26. Hou, L., Wang, X., Bernold, L., Love, P.E.D.: Using animated augmented reality to cognitively guide assembly. J. Comput. Civ. Eng. **27**, 439–451 (2013)
27. Gregor, S., Hevner, A.R.: Positioning and presenting design science research for maximum impact. MIS Q. **37**, 337–355 (2013)
28. Azuma, R.T.: The most important challenge facing augmented reality. Pres.: Teleoper. Virt. Environ. **25**, 234–238 (2016)
29. Peffers, K., Rothenberger, M., Tuunanen, T., Vaezi, R.: Design science research evaluation. In: Peffers, K., Rothenberger, M., Kuechler, B. (eds.) DESRIST 2012. LNCS, vol. 7286, pp. 398–410. Springer, Heidelberg (2012). https://doi.org/10.1007/978-3-642-29863-9_29
30. Hönemann, K., Osterbrink, A., Wiesche, M.: Enabling non-professionals users to bring physical processes into the industrial metaverse. In: 21st Annual Pre-ICIS Workshop on HCI Research in MIS (2022)
31. Lauterbach, J., Mueller, B., Kahrau, F., Maedche, A.: Achieving effective use when digitalizing work: the role of representational complexity. MIS Q. **44**, 1023–1048 (2020)
32. vom Brocke, J., Schmiedel, T., Recker, J., Trkman, P., Mertens, W., Viaene, S.: Ten principles of good business process management. Bus. Process. Manag. J. **20**, 530–548 (2014)
33. Azuma, R.T.: A survey of augmented reality. Pres.: Teleoper. Virt. Environ. **6**, 355–385 (1997)
34. Gassen, J.B., Mendling, J., Thom, L.H., de Oliveira, J.P.M.: Towards guiding process modelers depending upon their expertise levels. In: Advanced Information Systems Engineering Workshop (2015)
35. Lavric, T., Bricard, E., Preda, M., Zaharia, T.: A low-cost AR training system for manual assembly operations. Comput. Sci. Inf. Syst. **19**, 1047–1073 (2022)
36. Subramani, M., Wagle, M., Ray, G., Gupta, A.: Capability development through just-in-time access to knowledge in document repositories: a longitudinal examination of technical problem solving. MIS Q. **45**, 1287–1308 (2021)

37. Dourish, P.: The appropriation of interactive technologies: some lessons from placeless documents. Comput. Support. Coop. Work **12**, 465–490 (2003)
38. Lieberman, H., Paternò, F., Klann, M., Wulf, V.: End-user development: an emerging paradigm end user development. Hum.-Comput. Interact. Ser. **9**, 1–8 (2006)
39. Klinker, K., Wiesche, M., Krcmar, H.: Digital transformation in health care: augmented reality for hands-free service innovation. Inf. Syst. Front. **22**, 1419–1431 (2020)
40. Park, S.-M., Kim, Y.-G.: A Metaverse: taxonomy, components, applications, and open challenges. IEEE Access **10**, 4209–4251 (2022)
41. Hart, S.G., Staveland, L.E.: Development of NASA-TLX (Task Load Index): results of empirical and theoretical research human mental workload. Adv. Psychol. **52**, 139–183 (1988)
42. Zijlstra, F.R.H., van Doorn, L.: The construction of a scale to measure perceived effort (1985)
43. Wixom, B.H., Todd, P.A.: A theoretical integration of user satisfaction and technology acceptance. Inf. Syst. Res. **16**, 85–102 (2005)
44. Shapiro, S.S., Wilk, M.B.: An analysis of variance test for normality (complete samples). Biometrika **52**, 591 (1965)
45. Levene, H.: Robust tests for equality of variances. In: Olkin, I., Ed., Contributions to Probability and Statistics, pp. 278–292 (1960)
46. Faul, F., Erdfelder, E., Lang, A.-G., Buchner, A.: G*Power 3: a flexible statistical power analysis program for the social, behavioral, and biomedical sciences. Behav. Res. Methods **39**, 175–191 (2007)
47. Cohen, J.: A power primer. Psychol. Bull. **112**, 155–159 (1992)

Human-Centered Artificial Intelligence (HCAI)

Introduction to the Human-Centered Artificial Intelligence (HCAI) Track

Pierre-Majorique Léger[1], Armel Quentin Tchanou[2], and Mahdi Mirhoseini[3]

[1] HEC Montreal
pierre-majorique.leger@hec.ca
[2] Université de Sherbrooke
armel.quentin.tchanou@usherbrooke.ca
[3] Concordia University
mahdi.mirhoseini@concordia.ca

The fast-paced world of artificial intelligence (AI) never seems to take a break, as each day brings captivating new advances and breakthroughs that are likely to impact our society significantly. The current arms race on generative artificial intelligence (AI) between major technology players around the globe has accelerated the pace of innovation to an unprecedented level[1]. ChatGPT, an AI chatbot developed by OpenAI, has become the first technology in history to reach 100 million users in less than two months[2].

Our 2023 research track on Human-Centered Artificial Intelligence (HCAI) could not be more relevant and timely. Despite the widespread use of AI, its successful and satisfactory adoption by humans remains a challenge [1]. As citizens, employees, or consumers, issues such as bias, distrust, and low user satisfaction can impede our willingness to embrace AI in different domains [2]. Therefore, a comprehensive and integrated approach to AI is necessary to promote its adoption and overcome these challenges.

The interdisciplinary research area of HCAI is concerned with designing, evaluating, and implementing AI systems for human use [3]. With DESRIST 2023 track, we aim to continue the discussion on HCAI with two main contributions. First, Reinhard and colleagues propose a conceptual model incorporating a value-co-creation perspective to address the problem of data quality in supervised or semi-supervised intelligent systems. Designers try to involve users in the learning mechanisms by methods such as human-in-the-loop to ensure data quality. However, this process requires employees to have enough motivation and incentive to annotate and label data. Reinhard and colleagues contribute by showing how value co-creation can be central to self-learning systems. Second, Bunde and colleagues propose principles for improving the design of explainable AI-based medical decision support systems. User acceptance of predictions and categorizations provided by AI-based systems remains a challenge despite tremendous effort in the explainable AI field to alleviate limitations in the explainability of several AI techniques. Well-designed explainable AI is part of the

---

[1] https://time.com/6255952/ai-impact-chatgpt-microsoft-google/.

[2] https://www.reuters.com/technology/chatgpt-sets-record-fastest-growing-user-base-analyst-note-2023-02-01/.

solutions to improve the acceptability of AI-based decision support systems. Bunde and colleagues contribute by proposing design principles for AI-based medical applications through rigorously grounded applied methods.

References

1. Jiang, J., Karran, A.J., Coursaris, C.K., Léger, P.M., Beringer, J.: A situation awareness perspective on human-AI interaction: Tensions and opportunities. Int. J. Hum. Comput. Interact. 1–18 (2022)
2. Korosec-Serfaty, M., et al.: Understanding the nature and constituent elements of artificial intelligence-based applications: a scoping review research in progress. In: Chen, J.Y.C., Fragomeni, G., Degen, H., Ntoa, S. (eds.) HCII 2022. LNCS, vol. 13518, pp. 319–328 (2022). Springer, Cham. https://doi.org/10.1007/978-3-031-21707-4_23
3. Léger, P.M., Maedche, A., Weber, B.: Intelligent systems and human interaction. In: Drechsler, A., Gerber, A.J., Hevner, A.R. (eds.) DESRIST 2022, St Petersburg, FL, USA, 1–3 June 2022 Proceedings, vol. 13229, pp. 112–114 (2022). Springer. https://doi.org/10.1007/978-3-031-06516-3

Giving DIAnA More TIME – Guidance for the Design of XAI-Based Medical Decision Support Systems

Enrico Bunde[1]([✉]), Daniel Eisenhardt[1], Daniel Sonntag[2], Hans-Jürgen Profitlich[2], and Christian Meske[1]

[1] Ruhr-University Bochum, Bochum, Germany
{enrico.bunde,daniel.eisenhardt,christian.meske}@rub.de
[2] German Research Center for Artificial Intelligence (DFKI), Oldenburg University, Oldenburg, Germany
{sonntag,profitlich}@dfki.de

Abstract. Future healthcare ecosystems integrating human-centered artificial intelligence (AI) will be indispensable. AI-based healthcare technologies can support diagnosis processes and make healthcare more accessible globally. In this context, we conducted a design science research project intending to introduce design principles for user interfaces (UIs) of explainable AI-based (XAI) medical decision support systems (XAI-based MDSS). We used an archaeological approach to analyze the UI of an existing web-based system in the context of skin lesion classification called DIAnA (Dermatological Images – Analysis and Archiving). One of DIAnA's unique characteristics is that it should be usable for the stakeholder groups of physicians and patients. We conducted the in-situ analysis with these stakeholders using the think-aloud method and semi-structured interviews. We anchored our interview guide in concepts of the Theory of Interactive Media Effects (TIME), which formulates UI features as causes and user psychology as effects. Based on the results, we derived 20 design requirements and developed nine design principles grounded in TIME for this class of XAI-based MDSS, either associated with the needs of physicians, patients, or both. Regarding evaluation, we first conducted semi-structured interviews with software developers to assess the reusability of our design principles. Afterward, we conducted a survey with user experience/interface designers. The evaluation uncovered that 77% of the participants would adopt the design principles, and 82% would recommend them to colleagues for a suitable project. The findings prove the reusability of the design principles and highlight a positive perception by potential implementers.

Keywords: Design Science Research · Design Principles · Explainable Artificial Intelligence · Medical Decision Support Systems · Healthcare

1 Introduction

For future developments in the healthcare sector, human-centered ecosystems that integrate artificial intelligence (AI) are becoming indispensable [1]. Novel healthcare technologies like AI-based medical decision support systems (MDSS) can promote good

A. Gerber and R. Baskerville (Eds.): DESRIST 2023, LNCS 13873, pp. 107–122, 2023.
https://doi.org/10.1007/978-3-031-32808-4_7

health, well-being, and support access to healthcare globally [2]. In addition, such AI-based technologies can help make medical analysis more efficient [3] and outperform human experts in tasks like classifying pigmented skin lesions [4]. However, AI also introduces unique challenges. For example, Tschandl et al. [5] concluded that faulty AI could mislead a spectrum of clinicians, including experts. Additionally, many modern AI approaches are black boxes and thus not interpretable, which leads to questions regarding accountability, liability, fairness, and explainability [6].

Scholars from the field of explainable AI (XAI) work on such challenges and aim to introduce transparent AI models or techniques that explain black box models [7]. XAI-based MDSS have already entered clinical practice, and researchers have investigated them in contexts like in-hospital mortality, intensive care unit admissions, or incidences of leukemia and cancer [8]. When designing such systems, involving relevant stakeholder groups like physicians or patients to consider human factors is highly important [9]. Well-designed XAI-based MDSS can facilitate the acceptance of AI predictions, support detecting errors, or aid in establishing appropriate levels of trust toward the system [7, 10, 11]. However, there is only little prescriptive design knowledge that guides practitioners when developing XAI-based MDSS and their user interfaces (UIs) as the first entry point of the Human-XAI interaction [9, 10]. We address this research gap by establishing the following research question:

RQ: Which design principles for UIs can be derived from an in-situ analysis of an XAI-based MDSS for skin-related diagnoses that consider multiple stakeholders?

We have conducted a design science research (DSR) project to answer the research question. Following an archaeological approach [12], we have analyzed an existing XAI-based MDSS in-situ called *Dermatological Images – Analysis and Archiving* (DIAnA). The unique characteristic of DIAnA is that it aims to be accessible and usable by multiple stakeholders, including physicians and patients [13]. Therefore, we involved two physicians, four physicians in training, and six patients during the analysis to consider their individual information needs [10, 14]. For the analysis, we used think-aloud protocols and semi-structured interviews [15]. Since the Theory of Interactive Media Effects (TIME) formulates UI features as causes and user psychology as effects [16], it provided a valuable knowledge base for deriving our applied interview guide. Based on the insights, we derived 20 design requirements (DRs) associated with the needs of physicians, patients, or hybrid nature if they address the needs of both stakeholder groups. We addressed these DRs with nine design Principles (DPs), which were formalized according to the scheme of Gregor et al. [17]. We anchored the DPs in concepts of TIME, which explains the effect of technologies on humans in terms of affordances and thus provides valuable insights on perceived system properties that could drive users to operate the system in nuanced ways [16, 18]. We evaluated the DPs qualitatively with four software developers and quantitatively with 66 user interface and user experience designers regarding their reusability [19]. The evaluation ensured that the DPs introduced are applicable in practice and revealed a positive perception.

We present the DSR project in the following structure. First, in Sect. 2, we provide the background. Then, we describe our research design and the methodologies used in Sect. 3. Afterward, we derive and present the prescriptive design knowledge in Sect. 4, followed by a presentation of the evaluation and the results in Sect. 5, which we discuss in Sect. 6. We conclude the article with Sect. 7.

2 Background

2.1 Explainable Artificial Intelligence in Medical Decision Support Systems

The pervasiveness of AI has significantly increased across domains, which also applies to the healthcare industry [7, 10]. AI can outperform human experts in medical contexts like the classification of pigmented skin lesions and can reduce the time required in processes of medical analysis [3, 5]. The influence of AI in a medical context is so powerful that surgeons or physicians may even change their decisions [20]. However, the lack of transparency and explainability is still a major obstacle to the usage of AI in a high-risk context like health [10]. Therefore, the relevance of XAI for AI-based MDSS becomes steadily more relevant [8]. Nevertheless, the sheer presence of explanations may not improve human-computer interaction or interpretation of AI-based results [7, 9]. Although XAI has entered health-related research streams, there is still much need for research on XAI-based MDSS to generate user benefits [8, 10]. Especially the design of XAI-based MDSS and their UIs is under-researched [9, 10].

2.2 The Multi-stakeholder Perspective

When designing MDSS that are efficient and supportive, it is highly relevant to involve individual stakeholder groups and take a human-centered perspective [8, 9]. Different stakeholder groups can use MDSS, like physicians or patients [10]. Prior research uncovered clinicians prefer systems to quickly gain an overview and identify critical information immediately [21, 22]. Because MDSSs for patients are no longer viewed as a repository [23], new requirements for this specific stakeholder group need to be derived. For example, from the user experience perspective, patients prefer essential information on conditions and treatments to better evaluate their health status and physician decisions [24]. Due to patients' high possibility of misinterpretation of information, it is necessary to understand how information can be optimally communicated to them [25]. Design-oriented studies can therefore improve the accessibility of novel healthcare technologies and may reduce the barriers for patients to participate in their treatment [2].

2.3 Theory of Interactive Media Effects (TIME)

TIME considers two individual routes of affordances, the action route and the cue route [16]. The action route considers the psychological impacts on users' knowledge, attitudes, and behaviors. In contrast, the cue route focuses on the presence of individual cues in the UI and their effect on users' perception. Overall, TIME includes four models to explain its propositions regarding the predictors, mediating variables, and outcomes. The models are *Interactivity Effects Model, Agency Model, Motivation Technology Model*, and the *Modality-Agency-Interactivity-Navigability (MAIN) Model*. The first three models explain the action route of TIME, and the MAIN model the effects of the cue route. Since TIME consists of four underlying models focusing on different psychological facets [16], we adopted suitable elements for designing UIs of XAI-based MDSS, including interactivity, navigability, perceptual bandwidth, or interface and content perception.

TIME further posits that UIs provide interactive features which influence user engagement in nuanced ways. They involve various technological affordances and psychological variables [16]. To consider these factors, we grounded our DPs in TIME, which predicts affordances that affect user psychology [16]. Transferred to an AI context, afforded user actions can influence user engagement and experience through the provided interactions with the system [18]. Similarly, the features of UIs influence content perception [26]. Moreover, a well-designed interaction between users and AI systems can increase trust in the system [27]. TIME looks at different aspects of the interaction between users and the medium and explores how these influences can affect the behavior of users toward the UI [18].

3   Method: The Design Science Research Process

For our DSR project, we adapted the framework of Kuechler and Vaishnavi [28]. Figure 1 provides a concise overview of the process steps, methods used, activities conducted, and outputs. The first step, *awareness of problem*, was initiated by a literature review and the in-situ artifact analysis. In the second step, *suggestion*, we investigated existing literature to identify a suitable theoretical basis for the DPs. During the third step, *development*, we conceptualized the DPs and integrated insights from TIME. The *evaluation* is the fourth step. Finally, we evaluated the reusability of the proposed qualitatively and quantitatively. By reflecting and interpreting the proposed DPs in combination with the evaluation results, we complete the last step of the *conclusion*.

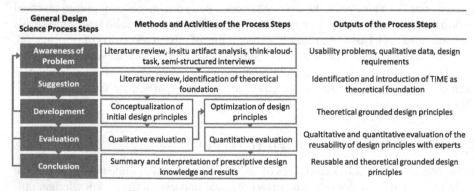

Fig. 1. Overview of the adapted DSR process.

We applied an archaeological perspective with an in-situ analysis inspired by Chandra Kruse et al. [12]. We approached the in-situ analysis by combining methods from human-computer interaction and usability research. In the in-situ analysis, we chose an archaeological perspective to take a human-centered approach and involve the relevant stakeholder groups (i.e., physicians and patients) [8, 9]. While we took the archaeological perspective, we analyzed dimensions like the aesthetic and symbolic one. Moreover, we considered intended and unintended effects, which XAI-based MDSS can trigger, like misleading decision support [5, 20]. The analyzed XAI-based MDSS, DIAnA [13], provides features like classifying skin lesions, generating XAI-based explanations, and managing patient-related data. DIAnA is currently available online via https://iml.dfki.de/demos/diana/index.html (2023/01/23). The following Fig. 2 depicts two exemplary screens of DIAnA.

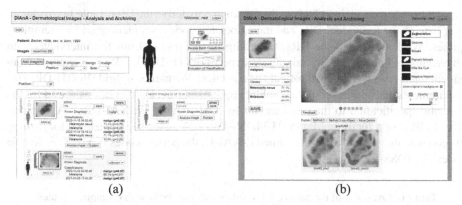

(a)   (b)

Fig. 2. Screenshots of DIAnA: (a) overview for a patient and (b) XAI-based diagnosis.

We started with think-aloud protocols since they allow users to communicate usability problems freely since we, as scholars, exert no influence on participants. Overall, we involved 12 participants in the in-situ analysis: two physicians, four physicians in training, and six patients. After the 12 interviews, we did not identify new insights, reached theoretical saturation, and did not conduct further interviews. The analysis started with a think-aloud part based on the cognitive task analysis [15]. The participants had to work through simple tasks to get familiar with the XAI-based MDSS while verbalizing their thoughts and actions during the interaction. After the think-aloud part, we conducted the semi-structured interviews guided by our TIME-inspired interview guide. Finally, we conducted follow-up semi-structured interviews to discuss concepts from TIME, focusing on UI features and their psychological effects on users [16; 18]. We followed an interview guide developed based on the before-mentioned aspects and dimensions of TIME, supplemented by questions focusing on the XAI features. The resulting data were analyzed using the thematic analysis of Braun and Clarke [29]. The codes were inductively derived using a descriptive coding method [30].

To formalize the DPs according to the status quo in DSR, we applied the scheme for specifying DPs for information technology-based artifacts in sociotechnical systems by Gregor et al. [17]. During the evaluation, we used the reusability dimensions and the associated template provided by Ivari et al. [19]. In the first and qualitative evaluation, we derived an interview guide based on the template. Four experienced software developers participated in the qualitative evaluation. For the second quantitative evaluation, we measured the reusability dimensions using a Likert scale ranging from 1 (strongly disagree) to 7 (strongly agree). Within the quantitative evaluation, we recruited 66 experienced user interface and user experience designers through Prolific and applied statistical analysis using *R*.

4   The Development of Prescriptive Design Knowledge

4.1   The Derivation of Design Requirements Based on Empirical Insights

The qualitative data analysis laid out the foundation to derive the DRs. Table 1 provides an overview of the individual DRs and the associated codes, supplemented by exemplary quotes. We have named the DRs, according to the results from the interviews with physicians and physicians in training, as expert DRs (E-DRs). DRs that resulted from patient interviews were named patient DRs (P-DRs). We named hybrid DRs (H-DRs) for requirements that address both stakeholder groups. For traceability reasons, we added the thematic specification to the requirements as XAI-focused (H-XAI-DRs), AI-focused (H-AI-DRs), or a focus on MDSS (H-MDSS-DRs). We used the same logic for naming the codes so that expert codes are named E-XAI-C, the patient codes P-AI-C, and hybrid codes H-MDSS-C.

Table 1. Overview of the defined DRs and associated codes with exemplary quotes.

Requirements	Codes and Exemplary Quotes
E-AI-DR1: If a MDSS is based on artificial intelligence, the system should provide the medical staff with information about the performance of the artificial intelligence in order to enable an evaluation of the system's recommendation	**E-AI-C1 System Information:** *"I might need more data on that, like what is the success rate of the AI, or how often has the AI been wrong."* (Interviewee 5)
E-MDSS-DR2: If the development of the patient-related object of analysis (e.g., melanoma) over time is critical to the diagnosis, the system should provide the possibility to compare historical patient data	**E-MDSS-C2 Diagnostic Timeline:** *"Then of course that would be great if you can compare old photos, see the analysis, let's say 2020 the system says 20% malignant, 2023 it says 60% malignant and 2026 it's going to scare the hell out of me, and we have to cut that out now."* (Interviewee 4)
E-MDSS-DR3: If multiple patients are managed by one MDSS, it should provide the medical staff with the ability to uniquely identify each patient	**E-MDSS-C3 Patient Identification:** *"The patient identification is done by the date of birth and the name, [...]. Often there are several Becker Hilde which are born perhaps in 1990, therefore it would be important to display all information [...]."* (Interviewee 5)

(continued)

Table 1. (*continued*)

Requirements	Codes and Exemplary Quotes
E-MDSS-DR4: If the medical staff feels the need to adjust the appearance and accessibility of task-related functionalities, the system should provide the individual with the ability to customize the interface to optimize the workflow	**E-MDSS-C4 Customization:** *"But that would be cool, of course, if you could really drag your most popular function right where you want it. Or you could set a favorite. That's a good way to save time."* (Interviewee 5)
H-MDSS-DR5: If diagnosis-relevant patient data is displayed (e.g., images or tabular data), the system should provide the user with the ability to customize the presentation of corresponding data (e.g., zooming in/out of an image) in order to enhance the cognitive processing of information	**H-MDSS-C5 Visual Adjustment:** *"So some photos are very big, and some photos are very small probably it's the original file size I don't know. In some cases, I cannot see everything equally well."* (Interviewee 4)
H-MDSS-DR6: If the MDSS is used by individuals with different linguistic backgrounds (e.g., German, English), the system should be able to display user interfaces in different languages in order to increase its comprehensibility	**H-MDSS-C6 Language Barrier:** *"If my mother had to use the system, she doesn't know much about English. I think she would be overwhelmed. Maybe it would be cool to offer it in different languages."* (Interviewee 6)
H-MDSS-DR7: If the MDSS provides information within separate, modal windows and stakeholders are able to adjust these windows with regards to their size (e.g., to full screen), the user interface should be designed in a responsive way so that the presentation of data is automatically adjusted (e.g., enlargement of images)	**H-MDSS-C7 Automatic Scalability:** *"It's kind of difficult because you don't know which button to press here and what the buttons belong to, whether it's unknown benign or malignant."* (Interviewee 4)
E-MDSS-DR8: If the medical staff feels the need to get a second opinion, the system should provide the medical staff with the ability to communicate with other experts in order to enable a professional exchange	**E-MDSS-C8 Communication Between Experts:** *"[…] it is nice when you could contact a colleague for a second opinion […]"* (Interviewee 7)
H-MDSS-DR9: If the MDSS is used by multiple stakeholders (e.g., patients/layperson and professionals/experts), the system should provide the stakeholders with the ability to communicate with each other in order to enable a corresponding discourse	**H-MDSS-C9 Expert-Patient Communication:** *"I didn't think of that at first, but that would certainly be an interesting function as well. It would certainly be a good function for patients."* (Interviewee 9)

(*continued*)

Table 1. *(continued)*

Requirements	Codes and Exemplary Quotes
H-MDSS-DR10: If the MDSS offers options to communicate between multiple stakeholders (e.g., patients/laymen and professionals/experts), the system should enable the stakeholders to reference specific (patient) data for a precise and unambiguous communication	**H-MDSS-C10 Communication clarification:** *"If there are multiple lesions. Yes, that would be the most important to me that you can refer very specifically to one. Maybe like on WhatsApp, you can click specifically on a message and then answer the quote, so to speak."* (Interview 2)
P-MDSS-DR11: If the MDSS processes patient-related data (e.g., images or tabular data), the system should provide the patient with information on where the data is stored, how the data is processed and by whom or what the data is analyzed in order to increase the transparency of the data handling	**P-MDSS-C11 Information on data processing:** *"I think I might also need contextual information about whom I'm actually sending this to and what kind of person it is from which institute, so contextual information about who is processing it."* (Interviewee 2)
H-MDSS-DR12: If the MDSS presents information and functionalities on different subpages, the system should provide the user with an efficient and consistent navigation in order to increase the user's orientation when interacting with the system	**H-MDSS-C12 Navigational consistency:** *"I've pressed the wrong button several times now when trying to close the window because I'm always looking for an X somewhere, but you have to press it [the window] again."* (Interviewee 4)
H-MDSS-DR13: If a MDSS uses separate, modal windows to present information, the system should provide the windows with a standardized graphical design (e.g., same buttons or icons and their locations as on the main page) in order to have a consistent presentation of information and interface functions	**H-MDSS-C13 Continuity of System Display:** *"It is questionable to me in several places how things are arranged."* (Interviewee 10)
H-MDSS-DR14: If the MDSS provides different kind of data (e.g., tabular and/or image data), its presentation should have a clear structure with easy to interpret labels so that users can quickly gain an overview of the content	**H-MDSS-C14 Over Information:** *"Partly, you are overwhelmed with information in the different subpages and functions which are perhaps not so important."* (Interviewee 9)
H-MDSS-DR15: If the MDSS is used by multiple stakeholders with varying levels of experience with such systems, the MDSS should provide an on-demand walkthrough on how to operate it in order to increase the stakeholders' independency and effectivity of their system usage	**H-MDSS-C15 Introduction to the System:** *"My feeling is […] somewhat overwhelming, so at first glance when you see so much data, what it could mean and why so many data is given, and everything is just on top of each other. […] Maybe I would be happy, and the feeling would be better if you were eased into it a little friendlier."* (Interviewee 2)

(continued)

Table 1. (*continued*)

Requirements	Codes and Exemplary Quotes
H-MDSS-DR16: If the MDSS is used by multiple stakeholders with varying levels of experience with such systems, it should provide the stakeholders with possibilities to inform themselves (e.g., help functions) about the provided functionalities so that the stakeholders can get familiar with the system	**H-MDSS-C16 Information on Demand:** *"A wiki, a FAQ section or something like that, [...]"* (Interviewee 2)
H-MDSS-DR17: If the MDSS uses imaging techniques to support the diagnostic process, the system should enable the stakeholders to compare images from other cases so that they can expand their knowledge base by identifying relevant similarities or differences across the analyses of image data	**H-MDSS-C17 Comparison Options:** *"In addition to filtering options, it would, of course, be interesting to be able to compare cases with each other and different classifications, I have not seen this function so far."* (Interviewee 9)
P-AI-DR18: When the MDSS communicates the results of its analysis, the system should provide recommendations for action (e.g., to export the data and contact a specialist) so that the patients are assisted in planning the next steps	**P-AI-C18 Recommendation for Action:** *"Because the website doesn't currently tell me what I have to do now, i.e., a recommendation for action or something similar."* (Interviewee 6)
H-AI-DR19: If the MDSS provides automated, diagnostic recommendations to support the analytical process, it should integrate techniques to generate explanations for the given recommendations so that stakeholders can comprehend and evaluate the output, and to develop an appropriate level of trust into the system	**H-AI-C19 Explanation Necessity:** *"Of course, it is always difficult to rely on a program. But if you can now see why, it has decided this way, that's good. It is also possible that something was misinterpreted or that something strange was marked, which could be an error in the system. That's why I think it's important and makes sense."* (Interviewee 7)
H-XAI-DR20: If the MDSS provides explanation functionalities for the automated recommendations, the system should provide guidance on how to interpret the specific explanation so that stakeholders can develop an accurate mental model of the system's output	**H-XAI-C20 XAI Interpretation:** *"It confused me now because it was called Heatmap, and I thought it had something to do with the blood flow and temperature. But after an additional explanation, it was clear with what it correlates, and then I also found the XAI-tool clear."* (Interviewee 1)

4.2 The Development of Theoretically Grounded Design Principles

The developed DRs build the foundation for the initial set of DPs, which we derive and describe in the following. Figure 3 provides an overview of the relationship between the derived DRs and DPs.

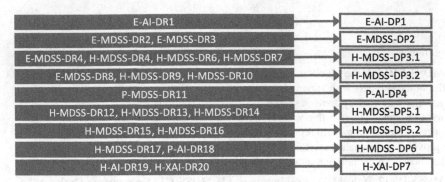

Fig. 3. Overview and summary of the relationship between DRs and DPs.

Transparency and explainability are important aspects of AI-based MDSS, which can influence users' acceptance [10]. AI performance metrics are essential information that can further increase transparency [9]. Providing competencies as information in a UI can lead to a positive perception of the underlying system and positively influence trust [18]. Consequently, we establish **E-AI-DP1**: *To provide an AI-MDSS, which clearly communicates its performance in the context of health-related diagnoses, the system should provide AI-related performance metrics as well as the probability of its classification in an easy-to-understand way, so that medical professionals without knowledge in computer science can appropriately interpret the system's recommendation.*

TIME proposes completeness and level of detail as essential quality criteria of information systems [16]. Since participants of the interviews communicated that a specific amount of information is necessary to identify patients and work effectively with the system, it should provide selected information for the user. Presenting relevant information will also influence the ease of use and the identification of critical information immediately [21, 22]. Furthermore, during the interviews, it was mentioned that time-related information like timespans is vital for a holistic overview. Consequently, we establish **E-MDSS-DP2**: *To provide an MDSS, which supports unique identification of patients and provides a trackable overview of their health status for medical professionals in the context of health-related diagnoses, the system should provide unique patient-related information as well as timestamps of previous diagnoses, so that the experts can quickly gain an overview of a specific patient's medical history.*

Prior research has proven that customizing systems to individual needs can strengthen information intake [31]. Customization can also enhance users' ability to manage tasks [16]. Moreover, customization can be valuable as it enhances self-efficacy beliefs and increases learning performance [32]. Consequently, we establish **H-MDSS-DP3.1**: *To provide an MDSS, which allows the customization of the user interface regarding the appearance, the interaction with information, and system level settings in the context of health-related diagnoses, the system should provide intuitive customization features, so that the system can be adjusted on a graphical and functional level, provide filter options, and options to interactively explore the information, so that all stakeholders can customize the system according to their cognitive needs and individual workflows.*

A valuable feature with beneficial aspects is the interactivity of exchange between users that use the same system [33]. Interactivity with other users positively affects users' perception of the content quality and the value of the information [16]. Participants of the interviews also communicated the desire to exchange with other users. For example, physicians may want a second opinion and a feature to reference specific information to avoid miscommunication. Consequently, we establish **H-MDSS-DP3.2**: *To provide an MDSS, which allows an unambiguous communication between medical experts or between medical experts with patients in the context of health-related diagnoses, the system should provide the possibility for professional exchange, which enables the stakeholders to reference specific data points of analyses, so that an effective discussion can take place.*

According to TIME, trustworthiness is an important aspect when users evaluate the credibility of systems [16]. Therefore, influencing and appropriately calibrating trust is another integral objective pursued by XAI [6]. During the interviews, we uncovered specific aspects that users would desire and could influence their credibility assessment and trust towards the AI-based MDSS, for example, regarding information for data storage or information processing methods used in the underlying system. Consequently, we establish **P-AI-DP4**: *To provide an AI-MDSS, which includes transparent information of the collected and analyzed data for patients in the context of health-related diagnoses, the system should provide a separate feature for patients to retrieve information regarding the storage, processing, and analysis of their personal data, so that they understand how their data is handled.*

To ensure the usability and efficiency of AI-MDSS, the UI of the system must be consistently designed [18; 33]. Designing functionalities and consistently navigating through a UI leads to usability enhancements, for example, by guiding users through the system [16]. We discussed these aspects also with both stakeholder groups during the interviews. Consequently, we establish **H-MDSS-DP5.1**: *To provide an MDSS, which includes an efficient navigational flow, concise labels, and descriptions in the context of health-related diagnoses, the system should maintain a consistent structure as well as the appearance of the graphical user interface elements, so that multiple stakeholders can navigate intuitively as well as effectively through the system resulting in a satisfying user experience.*

An easy way to navigate through systems and additional information that support the user in getting familiar with the system can influence the user's judgment regarding its credibility [16]. In TIME it is a helper heuristic. Both stakeholder groups also addressed these aspects during the interviews. Moreover, guiding users through actions can trigger the scaffolding heuristic, which can positively impact users' perception of systems [16]. We include both heuristics. Consequently, we establish **H-MDSS-DP5.2**: *To provide an MDSS, which includes assistance regarding the operation of the system's functionalities and information presented in the context of health-related diagnoses, a series of walkthroughs in combination with a help function to get detailed information about the system should be integrated, so that multiple stakeholders can independently and effectively work with the system.*

Clinicians prefer to learn case-based and the integration of practical cases. It involves comparing or recognizing essential characteristics, which is more beneficial for them than just being confronted with problems that need to be solved [10]. This aspect is also represented in TIME as self as source which describes that engaging users enable them to critically reflect on decisions and draw conclusions by themselves [16]. This authority heuristic is vital for patients since it requires recommendations and guidance for initiating appropriate actions. Especially if they lack the expertise to understand and analyze medical cases alone. Consequently, we establish **H-MDSS-DP6**: *To provide an MDSS, which extends the stakeholders' knowledge base regarding the specific diagnostic context, and enables an informed decision-making in the context of health-related diagnoses, the system should provide a functionality to compare and connect information across diagnostic cases as well as to recommend appropriate actions within the corresponding medical scope that a patient can initiate, so that the stakeholders can operate the system in a self-effective manner and initiate informed follow-up actions.*

Following TIME, trustworthiness and understandability are essential to perceiving a system's credibility [16]. Similarly, XAI can help to improve the credibility assessment, trustworthiness, and understandability of AI-based systems [6; 34; 35]. Furthermore, the role of explanations is also crucial for the acceptance of AI-based systems in clinical practice [10]. Moreover, we discussed these aspects during the interviews, and both stakeholder groups communicated the need for additional information to interpret the explanations correctly. Consequently, we establish **H-XAI-DP7**: *To provide an AI-MDSS, which includes explanations for its diagnostic recommendations and that enables an accurate interpretation of these explanations in the context of health-related diagnoses, the system should provide supplementary information on how to interpret the explanations, so that the stakeholders can develop an understanding as well as an appropriate level of trust towards the system.*

5   Evaluation and Results

As described, we have conducted two evaluation cycles with potential implementers focusing on the reusability of the proposed DPs. The four software developers in the first qualitative evaluation had experience in versatile domains, including web development, mobile app development, and machine learning. We started with a practitioner-oriented introduction to the concept of DPs and the type of system they are intended for (i.e., XAI-based MDSS). Subsequently, we worked through the different dimensions of the reusability evaluation. All participants perceived the proposed DPs as valuable and perceived them positively. We uncovered only little potential for optimization, which focused on the wording rather than the content. Two exemplary quotes from the qualitative evaluation to highlight the positive perception: *"Overall, the design principles are very comprehensible and also understandable."* (Interview 1); *"I can imagine that such design principles can have a positive impact on my productivity."* (Interview 2).

Afterward, we used the questionnaire template for a quantitative evaluation, which we implemented in a survey via Prolific. We measured each reusability dimension with a Likert scale ranging from 1 (strongly disagree) to 7 (strongly agree). We recruited 75 participants with experience in either user interface design or user experience design. From these 75 participants, we excluded nine participants for speeding. We included the responses of the remaining 66 participants in the analysis. Overall, the positive perception of the qualitative evaluation episode was confirmed in the quantitative evaluation. The analysis yielded the following results: accessibility ($\alpha = 0.83$; $M = 4.9$; $SD = 1.2$); importance ($\alpha = 0.88$; $M = 4.5$; $SD = 1.4$); novelty and insightfulness ($\alpha = 0.64$; $M = 5.1$; $SD = 1.1$); actability and appropriate guidance ($\alpha = 0.82$; $M = 5.2$; $SD = 0.84$); effectiveness ($\alpha = 0.82$; $M = 5.2$; $SD = 0.97$). 77% of the 66 participants indicated they would adopt the DPs, and 82% would recommend them to a colleague for a suitable project.

6   Discussion

6.1   Summary of Findings

Through our DSR project, we provide in-depth insights into the perception and design of XAI-based MDSS and their UIs for skin-related diagnosis. Research characterizes this research area still as under-researched [9, 10]. Therefore, we aimed to take a human-centered approach to analyze DIAnA by involving relevant stakeholder groups using an archaeological approach from a user perspective [12]. In doing so, we considered the individual information needs of versatile stakeholder groups vital to achieving a high acceptance of XAI-based systems and AI predictions [7; 10; 14]. The in-situ analysis led us to 20 empirically grounded DRs for XAI-based MDSS for skin-related diagnosis. By applying concepts of TIME and using the scheme of Gregor et al. [17], we introduced nine DPs for guiding the design of XAI-based MDSS. Through our qualitative and quantitative reusability evaluation with experienced practitioners, we ensured that the proposed DPs are transferrable into practice, a desirable characteristic of DPs [19]. Therefore, practitioners and scholars can adopt suitable DPs for their use cases and particular application context. Following Gregor and Hevner's [36] DSR contribution framework, we consider our contribution an improvement. We used a human-centered archaeological approach to derive prescriptive design knowledge (i.e., design principles) to improve the human-centered design of solution artifacts (i.e., XAI-based MDSS) [36]. Our findings can therefore support the development of XAI-based MDSS and align with related research that highlighted the high relevance of human-centeredness when designing XAI-based systems [7; 9; 10; 35].

6.2   Limitations and Opportunities for Future Research

Like any other research project, ours is not without its limitations. At the same time, this also creates a range of opportunities for future research. For example, the derivation of design features, their instantiation in an MDSS, and their evaluation were not part of this project. Therefore, our future research aims to instantiate the theoretically grounded DPs and evaluate the resulting MDSS in a controlled laboratory or real-world setting. Other areas that were not part of our research are subjects like data protection or regulation of such classes of MDSS. Therefore, scholars from these disciplines could investigate how to protect the privacy of patient-related data or the regulation of such MDSS in the real world. We have also not focused on how to integrate the investigated MDSS in human-centered health ecosystems [1], which could be a flourishing area of research in the future. Consequently, many research opportunities arise around MDSS, especially with a multi-stakeholder perspective and human-centeredness.

7 Conclusion

In our DSR project, we investigated the design of XAI-based MDSS. These systems can be an influential driving force for future human-centered health ecosystems. During different stages of the DSR project, we involved multiple stakeholders, including physicians, physicians in training, patients, software developers, user interface, and user experience designers. We summarize the results of our project as empirically grounded DRs, which we address with a set of reusable DPs that potential implementers positively perceive. Consequently, we propose a set of reusable DPs, grounded in empirical insights and theoretical concepts of TIME.

Acknowledgements. This research is partly funded by the pAItient project (BMG, 2520DAT0P2).

References

1. Bulc, V., Hart, B., Hannah, M., Hrovatin, B.: Society 5.0 and a human centred health care. In: Simini, F., Bertemes-Filho, P. (eds.) Medicine-Based Informatics and Engineering. LNB, pp. 147–177. Springer, Cham (2022). https://doi.org/10.1007/978-3-030-87845-0_9
2. Rojas, C.N., Penafiel, G.A.A., Buitrago, D.F.L., Romero, C.A.T.: Society 5.0: a Japanese Concept for a super intelligent society. Sustainability **13**, 1–16 (2021)
3. Sahoo, P.R., Chatterjee, S.M.: Threats and challenges of artificial intelligence in healthcare industry. In: Zhang, Y.D., Senjyu, T., So-In, C., Joshi, A. (eds.) Smart Trends in Computing and Communications, LNNS, vol. 396, pp. 761–770. Springer, Singapore (2023)
4. Tschandl, P., et al.: Comparison for the accuracy of human readers versus machine-learning algorithms for pigmented skin lesion classification: an open, web-based, international, diagnostic study. Lancet oncology **20**(7), 938–947 (2019)
5. Tschandl, P., et al.: Human-coputer collaboration for skin cancer recognition **26**, 1229–1234 (2020)
6. Arrieta, A.B., et al.: Explainable Artificial Intelligence (XAI): concepts, taxonomies, opportunities and challenges toward responsible AI. Inf. Fusion **58**, 82–115 (2020)
7. Adadi, A., Berrada, M.: Peeking inside the black-box: a survey on explainable artificial intelligence (XAI). IEEE Access **6**, 52138–52160 (2018)
8. Payrovnaziri, S.N., et al.: Explainable artificial intelligence models using real-world electronic health record data: a systematic scoping review. J. Am. Med. Inform. Assoc. **27**(7), 1173–1185 (2020)
9. Schoonderwoerd, T.A.J., Jorritsma, W., Neerincx, M.A., van den Bosch, K.: Human-centered XAI: developing design patterns for explanations of clinical decision support systems. Int. J. Hum. Comput. Stud. **154**, 1–25 (2021)
10. Barda, A.J., Horvat, C.M., Hochheiser, H.: A qualitative research framework for the design of user-centered displays of explanations for machine learning model predictions in healthcare. BMC Med. Inform. Decis. Mak. **20**, 1–16 (2020)
11. Meske, C., Bunde, E.: Transparency and trust in human-AI-interaction: the role of model-agnostic explanations in computer vision-based decision support. In: Degen, H., Reinerman-Jones, L. (eds.) HCII 2020. LNCS, vol. 12217, pp. 54–69. Springer, Cham (2020). https://doi.org/10.1007/978-3-030-50334-5_4

12. Chandra Kruse, L., Seidel, S., vom Brocke, J.: Design archaeology: generating design knowledge from real-world artifact design. In: Tulu, B., Djamasbi, S., Leroy, G. (eds.) DESRIST 2019. LNCS, vol. 11491, pp. 32–45. Springer, Cham (2019). https://doi.org/10.1007/978-3-030-19504-5_3

13. Sonntag, D., Nunnari, F., Profitlich, H.-J.: The Skincare project, an interactive deep learning system for differential diagnosis of malignant skin lesions. DFKI Tech. Rep. **H2020**, 1–20 (2020)

14. Meske, C., Bunde, E., Schneider, J., Gersch, M.: Explainable artificial intelligence: objectives, stakeholders, and future research opportunities. Inf. Syst. Manag. **39**(1), 53–63 (2022)

15. Fernandez, A., Insfran, E., Abrahao, S.: Usability evaluation methods for the web: a systematic mapping study. Inf. Softw. Technol. **53**, 789–817 (2011)

16. Sundar, S.S., Jia, H., Waddell, T.F., Huang, Y.: The Handbook of Psychology of Communication Technology, 1st edn. Wiley, Hoboken (2015)

17. Gregor, S., Chandra Kruse, L., Seidel, S.: Research perspectives: the anatomy of a design principle. J. Assoc. Inf. Syst. **21**(6), 1622–1652 (2020)

18. Sundar, S.S.: Rise of machine agency: a framework for studying the psychology of Human-AI Interaction (HAII). J. Comput.-Mediat. Commun. **25**, 74–88 (2020)

19. Ivari, J., Hansen, M.R.P., Haj-Bolouri, A.: A proposal for minimum reusability evaluation of design principles. Eur. J. Inf. Syst. **30**(3), 286–303 (2021)

20. Dwivedi, A., Dwivedi, S.S., Tariq, M.R., Qiu, X., Hong, S., Xin, Y.: Scope of artificial intelligence in medicine. J. Res. Med. Dent. Sci. **8**(3), 137–140 (2020)

21. Westerbeek, L., et al.: Barriers and facilitators influencing medication-related CDSS acceptance according to clinicians: a systematic review. Int. J. Med. Inform. **152**, 1–14 (2021)

22. Westerbeek, L., de Bruijn, G.-J., van Weert, H.C., Abu-Hanna, A., Medlock, S., van Weert, J.C.M.: General practitioners' needs and wishes for clinical decision support systems: a focus group study. Int. J. Med. Inform. **168**, 1–7 (2022)

23. Fuji, K.T., Abbot, A.A., Galt, K.A., Drincic, A., Kraft, M., Kasha, T.: Standalone personal health records in the United States: meeting patient desires. Health Technol. **2**, 197–205 (2012)

24. Attfield, S.J., Adams, A., Blandford, A.: Patient information needs: pre- and post-consultation. Health Inform. J. **12**(2), 165–177 (2006)

25. Jefford, M., Tattersall, M.H.: Informing and involving cancer patients in their own care. Lancet Oncol. **3**(10), 629–637 (2002)

26. Hwang, A.H.-C., Oh, J.: Interacting with background music engages E-Customers more: the impact of interactive music on consumer perception and behavioral intention. J. Retail. Consum. Serv. **54**, 1–15 (2020)

27. Sun, Y., Sundar, S.S.: Exploring the effects of interactive dialogue in improving user control for explainable online symptom checkers. In: Extended Abstracts of the 2022 CHI Conference on Human Factors in Computing Systems, pp. 1–7. Association for Computing Machinery, New Orleans, LA, USA (2022)

28. Kuechler, W., Vaishnavi, V.: A framework for theory development in design science research: multiple perspectives. J. Assoc. Inf. Syst. **13**(6), 395–423 (2012)

29. Braun, V., Clarke, V.: Using thematic analysis in psychology. Qual. Res. Psychol. **3**(2), 77–101 (2006)

30. Xu, W., Zammit, K.: Applying thematic analysis to education: a hybrid approach to interpreting data in practitioner research. Int. J. Qual. Methods **19**, 1–9 (2020)

31. Kreuter, M.W., Strecher, V.J., Glassman, B.: One size does not fit all: the case for tailoring print materials. Ann. Behav. Med. **21**, 276–283 (1999)

32. Ku, O., Hou, C.-C., Chen, S.Y.: Incorporating customization and personalization into game-based learning: a cognitive style perspective. Comput. Hum. Behav. **5**, 359–368 (2016)

33. Sundar, S. S., Oh, J., Bellur, S., Jia, H., Kim, H.-S.: Interactivity as self-expression: a field experiment with customization and blogging. In: Proceedings of the SIGCHI Conference on Human Factors in Computing Systems, pp. 395–404. Association for Computing Machinery, Austin, Texas, USA (2012)
34. Bunde, E., Kühl, N., Meske, C.: Fake or credible? towards designing services to support users' credibility assessment of news content. In: Proceedings of the 55th Hawaii International Conference on System Sciences, pp. 1883–1892 (2021)
35. Meske, C., Bunde, E.: Design principles for user interfaces in AI-based decision support systems: the case of explainable hate speech detection. Inf. Syst. Front. 1–31 (2022)
36. Gregor, S., Hevner, A.R.: Positioning and presenting design science research for maximum impact. MIS Q. 37(2), 337–355 (2013)

A Conceptual Model for Labeling in Reinforcement Learning Systems: A Value Co-creation Perspective

Philipp Reinhard[1]([✉]) [iD], Mahei Manhai Li[1] [iD], Ernestine Dickhaut[1] [iD],
Cornelius Reh[1], Christoph Peters[1,2] [iD], and Jan Marco Leimeister[1,2] [iD]

[1] University of Kassel, Kassel, Germany
{philipp.reinhard,mahei.li,ernestine.dickhaut,christoph.peters,
leimeister}@uni-kassel.de
[2] University of St.Gallen, St.Gallen, Switzerland
{christoph.peters,janmarco.leimeister}@unisg.ch

Abstract. Artificial intelligence (AI) possesses the potential to augment customer service employees e.g. via decision support or solution recommendations. Still, its underlying data for training and testing the AI systems is provided by human annotators through human-in-the-loop configurations. However, due to the high effort for annotators and lack of incentives, AI systems face low underlying data quality. That in turn results in low prediction performance and limited acceptance by the targeted user group. Faced with the enormous volume and increasing complexity of service requests, IT service management (ITSM) especially, relies on high data quality for AI systems and incorporating domain-specific knowledge. By analyzing the existing labeling process in that specific case, we design a revised to-be process and develop a conceptual model from a value co-creation perspective. Finally, a functional prototype as an instantiation in the ITSM domain is implemented and evaluated through accuracy metrics and user evaluation. The results show that the new process increases the perceived value of both labeling quality and the perceived prediction quality. Thus, we contribute a conceptual model that supports the systematic design of efficient and interactive labeling processes in diverse applications of reinforcement learning systems.

Keywords: Human-in-the-loop · Interactive labeling · Artificial intelligence · Value co-creation

1 Introduction

Artificial Intelligence (AI) based information systems are becoming a key factor in today's workplaces [1]. Especially knowledge-intensive organizations, such as customer service support [2], aim to augment employees by employing machine learning and deep learning [3]. In the realm of ITSM, augmentation is required to cope with the ever-increasing number of customer problems and the challenge of having high turnover rates [4]. Even before the pandemic, the average annual turnover rate of help desks reached 40%, with ITSM domain showing the highest overall turnover rate [5]. Overall, the technological capabilities of AI possess a large potential improving workplaces by relieving service employees from monotone and repetitive tasks [6] and supporting problem-solving capabilities through AI-enabled recommender systems [7]. However, implementing intelligent systems and the subsequent adoption of AI-based systems at the workplace comes with two major challenges, which is this paper's DSR focal challenge: The first challenge refers to the lack of data quality caused by limited incentives to label and maintain data [8]. AI and in particular supervised or semi-supervised hybrid intelligence systems typically rely on high-quality data to train their models [9]. Yet, employees are typically not eager to annotate data given the processing effort [10] and the lack of incentives and lack of immediate returns, resulting in subpar data quality [8]. The second challenge refers to a lack of trust and confidence in AI-based systems. For example, experienced support agents are especially skeptical of AI systems, also known as algorithm aversion [11]. A lack of trust may induce resistance to the suggestions of AI [12]. Therefore, designers of human-AI collaboration tools and especially decision support and recommendation systems aim at increasing trust in these AI-based systems by ensuring a high prediction performance and emphasizing the capabilities of the systems [13]. Other approaches address the role of explainability (XAI) and transparency concerning trust [14]. Explanations of performance, functionality, and limitations of AI systems can increase trust in their prediction results [12].

Interactive machine learning approaches [15] try to integrate the human user into the learning mechanism as a so-called human-in-the-loop (HITL) [16] - for example by interactive labeling processes [17]. Prior research on interactive labeling aimed at improving the upfront labeling activities by increasing user engagement [18] or gamifying the annotation tasks [19]. Still, prior approaches have yet not considered the underlying cause of the mentioned challenges. Users are either only incentivized extrinsically or are rewarded with a delay. However, HITL-based labeling processes constitute a value co-creation phenomenon as different actors – here AI-based systems and human users – create value through a value-driven interaction. Thus, by incorporating a value co-creation perspective and a service-dominant logic as our input knowledge [20, 21], we aim to overcome the challenges of data quality and trust and facilitate the co-creation of value in human-ai interaction via labeling activities. Co-creation of value in human-ai systems is going to motivate users to label data during use and show more trust as the realized value-in-use is higher. Therefore, we state the following research question: *How can we design a conceptual model for interactive labeling for reinforcement learning by incorporating a value co-creation perspective?*

By following the DSR process, we propose a conceptual model as a solution for designing value co-creation-based labeling processes in interactive machine learning. With the configured labeling process and the derived design principles, we aim at emphasizing and strengthening the role of humans in the development and application of AI [22]. We focus primarily on the interaction between the AI-based system and the end user. The role of the operator is out of scope. Finally, an instantiation and an evaluation of the derived design conclude the design process.

2 Related Work

2.1 Interactive Machine Learning and Labeling

Machine learning (ML) in complex environments, such as ITSM, is in demand of high amounts of high-quality domain-specific user input [23]. Meza Martínez, Nadj, Maedche [24] differentiate between two possible strategies to overcome the lack of domain-specific knowledge in ML. The first approach suggests ML practitioners learn from domain experts when designing and developing ML models [23]. As users are not involved in the development at all, there is a lack of user engagement and a lack of trust because the systems are being considered a "black box" [25, 26]. Another approach, which represents the underlying theoretical foundation for this research project, is interactive ML. Interactive ML [15, 26], sometimes referred to as hybrid intelligence [9], induces a hybrid of human and machine intelligence by joining both – humans and machines – in a learning mechanism. Thereby, complementary strengths can be leveraged, especially for scaling services where human interaction is key [27]. A common practice among developers involves employing HITL mechanisms to ensure that users are directly involved and that the models learn continuously and iteratively as users provide domain-specific input [25]. Meza Martínez, Nadj, Maedche [24] distinguish between supervised learning, active learning, and reinforcement learning as HITL learning mechanisms. This paper focuses only on a ticket recommender system that relies on reinforcement learning as its underlying learning mechanism [28]. Reinforcement learning is characterized by a self-learning mechanism based on rewards and punishments during use [29].

Interactive labeling is an important part of building high-performance interactive ML systems [17]. Interactive labeling constitutes a field of practice and research, in which the role of the human is especially prevalent for providing domain-specific knowledge for training the models. Whereas other approaches see the role of domain experts in the development of the functionalities, for example in low-code development projects [30]. One of the goals of this approach aims at removing noisy annotated data [31]. Another goal is to inspect the most uncertain label instances [31]. Most of the prior work on interactive labeling concern the number of high-quality labels as the main objective. Therefore, optimizing labeling processes and motivating human users to contribute labeled data is of certain interest in practice as well as in literature [8, 10, 17, 26]. Facilitating labeling processes by providing interactive modes and incentives can contribute to not only increasing the available data quality but also for example incorporating more valuable domain knowledge into other systems and artifacts. Within this research, we emphasized facilitating value co-creation through interactive labeling.

2.2 Value Co-creation

When applying the service-dominant logic (SDL) as a theoretical lens on interactive ML, the interaction between humans and the AI can be seen as a value co-creation where both actors provide and integrate resources [21]. Human users or annotators contribute domain-specific knowledge and offer feedback while the prediction model learns certain patterns, provides useful recommendations, and thereby augments the human workplace. A key aspect of SDL is the co-creation of value, which emphasizes the collaborative and interactive creation of value between actors and entities through the mutually beneficial integration of resources [32–34]. Following the theories on value co-creation, customers – here support agents – are not only consuming a service, but they are also active participants in the value creation process through interaction [21]. The creation of value is defined as a process by which the user is made better off in some way [35] – for instance by reducing the time for finding a solution or by receiving high-quality recommendations. The unique nature of SDL is that there is more meaning to the value-in-use than there is to the value-in-exchange [36]. Value-in-use refers to the individually perceived value when using the AI-based system instead of only for example consuming a recommended solution [21, 37]. In contrast to value-in-exchange, value-in-use accumulates over time [20]. Grönroos, Voima [20] differentiate between three spheres in which value is created: The provider sphere (here: AI-based system) acts as a facilitator and enables a potential value. On the other side, within the customer sphere, the support agents create value independently by translating and adjusting recommended solutions to fit the special problem and by communicating with the end user. Between these two spheres exists the joint sphere, in which both – the value facilitator and the value recipient - create real value through direct interaction [20]. Thus, following a value co-creation and value-in-use perspective, we derive design knowledge for a value-driven interactive labeling process for reinforcement learning-based AI systems.

3   Methodology

Following the DSR approach our overall goal is to design a solution for the case of problem-solving tasks in ITSM and infer design knowledge for a generally improved value-driven interactive labeling process in HITL configurations, presented as a conceptual model (Fig. 1).

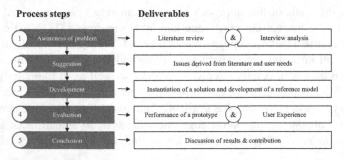

Fig. 1. DSR procedure according to Kuechler & Vaishnavi (2008)

According to Kuechler, Vaishnavi [38], in *Phase 1* (Awareness of problem) we conducted a review of the literature on HTL and interactive labeling. We additionally enriched our fundamental awareness and base of theories by incorporating literature on human-centered AI including trust, control, explainability, and transparency. The retrieved knowledge and theories ensure the rigor of our research [39]. In addition, value co-creation serves as a theoretical base. To consider practical relevance, we performed semi-structured interviews with eight support agents. The focus was placed on problem-solving capabilities and the interaction with AI-based systems within the service workplace. The interview analysis ensures practical relevance and allows for identifying pressing issues. In *Phase 2* (Suggestion) we aggregated common issues along the existing labeling process, which was derived from the case of ticket recommender systems in the realm of ITSM. Business Process Model and Notation (BPMN) is applied to visualize the current situation and outline the as-is process of currently developed AI systems in a larger DSR project that has been running for 3 years within a consortium. Afterward, in *Phase 3* (Development), we derive design principles from the identified issues and the proposed to-be process. The design principles are then translated into a to-be process model for value-driven interactive labeling [40, 41]. Furthermore, we instantiate the to-be process by developing a multi-armed contextual bandit system for IT support ticket recommendation and conceptualize a conceptual model of value co-creating labeling processes. The to-be process and the corresponding design principles in form of the instantiated AI-based system are evaluated in *Phase 4* (Evaluation) utilizing labeling performance as well as perceived value, sense of control, usability, and overall usefulness. We follow the Framework for Evaluation in Design Science Research (FEDS) [42] to evaluate prototypical instantiation, a technical experiment, and a user evaluation including 11 interviews [41] to provide the necessary validation of the efficiency of the proposed process. Finally, we reflect on the design process and the developed conceptual model and conclude with a discussion.

4 Design and Development

4.1 As-is Labeling Process

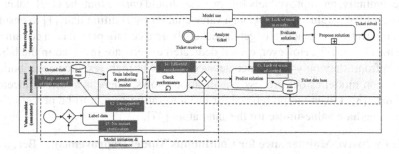

Fig. 2. As-is labeling and model training process for TRS.

To a large extent, literature on developing and operating supervised- or semi-supervised AI models refers to two different roles in terms of model initialization and model use. The group of "annotators" label data and provide the ground truth for training and testing the model during the initialization phase. However, annotators typically do not use the system afterward and are incentivized intrinsically [43]. For the case of supporting service employees in ITSM organizations, we differentiate between the roles of annotators and users – here support agents using a ticket recommender system. The ticket recommender system augments the problem-solving activities of support agents by recommending already solved problems as possible solutions. We analyzed and visualized the as-is labeling and model use process. As Fig. 2 shows, the ground truth is utilized to train a model, that predicts a recommended solution ticket given an incoming request. The human in the loop then evaluates the prediction and decides how to adapt or reject the solution. Along the as-is process, we identified six major issues justified by practical relevance and literature:

Issue 1: A Large Amount of Data is Required Upfront. Currently, annotators are meant to label a large amount of data upfront to categorize a ticket (Expert (E) 2) and to train and test the model [23]. This approach is time-intensive and costly (E2, E3, E4, E7) [10, 44]. An improved labeling process should therefore reduce the required volume of ground truth data during the initial incorporation of domain-specific knowledge and generate labeled data during operation.

Issue 2: Unsupported Labeling. The upfront labeling efforts are not being supported by the traditional labeling processes and act as an oracle. Typically, samples for labeling are selected by the development team and then forwarded to the annotators uncured. This hampers labeling efficiency, discourages annotators in the long term, and reduces data quality. In practice, a knowledge manager is responsible for providing domain knowledge (E4, E7) and agents are under large pressure (E6). An improved process should therefore aim at augmenting and semi-automate at least a part of the labeling tasks [45].

Issue 3: No Intrinsic Gratification. Usually, annotators do not benefit from labeling the data [43]. As such the relationship between the task giver and the annotator can be described by the principle-agent theory, where both actors strive for different goals [46]. Accordingly, an improved labeling process should ensure that the HTIL takes over both – the role of a value recipient and a value enabler by auditing data [1] to ensure an intrinsic motivation – "practically get the tickets from a certain period on a certain topic as an extract" (E1, E7). However, even if dedicated experts are involved in the labeling process upfront, they only experience delayed effects of their resource contribution to the prediction model as our process visualization shows. There is a lack of incentives to label data [8]. Given the preference for instant gratification, a to-be process should provide immediate value-in-use for the annotators [47].

Issue 4: Extensive Maintenance for Continuous Model Improvement. Because of the increasing number of incoming tickets for IT support, new data is generated during the use rapidly. Therefore "it [the knowledge base] is very high-maintenance, outdated and you can't find anything" (E4). To improve the model continuously and adapt to data drift [48], model operators have to monitor the performance and initiate new labeling phases. In sum, the effort for observing data drift and performing model maintenance is high [49]. For that reason, an interactive labeling process and self-learning system should autonomously improve its performance and its underlying data quality continuously and simultaneously (E4, E8).

Issue 5: Lack of Sense of Control. The theory of IS identity concerns the impact of AI in workplaces in terms of a lack of control [50]. Employees are being more and more replaced in knowledge-sharing and extraction activities [51]. In the context of human-ai interaction, it is important to give humans control over the results and the adaption of AI recommendations. We propose that service employees should experience more interaction with AI, where they act as supervisors [52] and verify machine outcomes [9, 53]. In addition, Dietvorst, Simmons, Massey [54] showed that giving users some degree of control can reduce algorithm aversion. In conclusion, a labeling process for HITL configurations should enable humans to control in terms of adjusting, evaluating, and accepting or rejecting results.

Issue 6: Lack of Trust in the Results. Prior research has examined the phenomenon of algorithm aversion [54] and emphasized the importance of trust in AI systems [12, 14]. Generally, AI systems possess a lack of trust of humans. Especially in complex problem-solving tasks like IT support, trust is limited by the restricted performance and reliance on recommender systems and the difficulty to recommend optimal solutions [55]. Support agents state that they typically need a lot of time to find a certain ticket in the database and thus rely on colleagues instead of using an AI-based system (E1, E5). As AI is perceived as being a "black box", researchers and practitioners aim at increasing transparency and explainability to increase trust [14, 55]. However, simply increasing trust in AI predictions is not ideal, as it could lead to over-reliance. An improved labeling mechanism therefore should increase trust by enhancing the perceived accuracy while at the same time giving users an indication and transparency of when to trust the systems' predictions.

4.2 To-Be Process: Value-Driven Labeling Process

By addressing the issues, we developed a revised process for value-driven labeling (Fig. 3). Starting with the role of the user as the annotator, we removed the bottom lane to illustrate the removal of the dichotomy between value enablers and value recipients. Still, the process requires an initial set of ground truth data for pre-training the system. However, we ensured that the initial required data remains manageable. As in the as-is process, the ground truth data is applied for training a labeling and prediction model. Given an incoming ticket, the system proposes a labeling of the content by highlighting relevant entities. The subsequent prediction model processes the pre-labeled ticket and directly presents solutions to the user. Now, the user can check whether the proposed recommendations are of use and whether the pre-labels are correct. If not, it is possible to adjust the labels and start a new prediction. Finally, the user evaluates the suggested solutions and gives feedback back to the reinforcement learning system.

4.3 Conceptual Model for Value-Driven Labeling

From the identified issues of the as-is process and components of the developed to-be process, we derived a conceptual model (Fig. 4) that incorporates a value co-creation perspective [20, 21] on interactive labeling and interactive ML. By including the principles

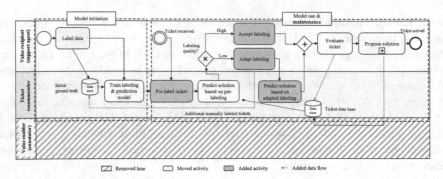

Fig. 3. To-be value-driven and interactive labeling process.

of service-dominant logic [21] and value co-creation [20], finally, four generalized design principles for value-driven interactive labeling systems constitute the value co-creation model for labeling:

DP1: Augment the Labeling Process.   The labeling process is augmented by a pre-trained model, that provides automatically generated labels initially. Based on a small size of ground truth data, that requires less effort to generate, a labeling model is being initiated. This initialization phase is required to augment the labeling process more automatically and effectively. Therefore, a traditional annotation phase is placed upfront involving domain experts who at the same time are the users. The automatically retrieved labels themselves should provide a benefit for the users by providing the user additional information or support for the problem-solving or decision task. According to the theory of value co-creation customers are meant to act as value creators [20]. Thus, the design principle proposes that the role of external annotators as value enablers should be dismissed. Instead, the actual user must label voluntarily during the phase of model use. The user thereby decides which labels need to be improved to improve model prediction [31]. This overall results in a removal of the dichotomy between value enabler and value recipient. By minimizing the initial need for data and domain-specific knowledge, the design downsizes the so-called provider sphere [20].

DP2: Enable Control Over Value Creation Through Labeling.   From a service perspective, the second design principle ensures accumulating value throughout the user's value-creation process [21]. The role of the user as a value creator is emphasized by the gained control and the enablement of co-producing value [20]. After receiving a pre-labeled ticket, the user decides whether to adjust the labels and share knowledge with the system [47]. In addition, the designed process enables users to evaluate the recommendation results and return feedback (e.g., selection of a ticket, 5-star rating, thumbs up/thumbs down). Our research suggests maintaining "human-in-control" as a key paradigm of ML-based recommender systems [16].

DP3: Provide Immediate Value-in-Use for Labeling Activities.   Due to the high effort [10] and the low immediate incentives of labeling [8], data quality for ML models remains extremely precarious in the complex and context-specific environment. For

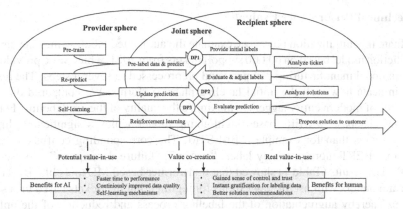

Fig. 4. Conceptual model for co-creation-based labeling based on [20]

such complex domains, interactive systems provide particular value [17]. An interactive labeling process should therefore reward labeling activities immediately to motivate and incentivize labeling and thereby increase the perceived relevance for annotators [17]. Such rewards can be better decision support or more personalized recommendations and must be provided immediately after contributing high-quality domain knowledge as part of the value-in-use [21]. The long-term benefit – delayed benefits – of providing the system with labels can only be hardly presented. The conceptual model places the focus on value-in-use and not primarily on potential or prospective use.

The following conceptual model summarizes the key activities of value co-creation in interactive ML systems and the abstracted design principles within that ML value chain. Additionally, the visualization shows how the complementary strengths generate added value above mere solution recommendations for both humans and machines. According to Grönroos, Voima [20], we differentiate between a (1) provider sphere, (2) recipient sphere, and (3) joint sphere. The ML system represents the provider sphere as it supports the human user through recommendations. The ML system itself only generates a potential value-in-use, that is being activated within the joint sphere and realized by the user within the recipient respectively customer sphere.

5 Evaluation

We evaluate our design and its instantiation by applying FEDS [56] to answer our research question within an artificial and a naturalistic summative evaluation. At first, a technical performance evaluation is conducted [42]. We apply common accuracy measures (accuracy, precision, recall, F1-Score) to validate the usefulness of the pre-highlighting model[57]. Afterward, our prototypical instantiation is presented in a naturalistic summative evaluation where 11 users work with the system and provide feedback in a subsequent interview.

5.1 Technical Performance Evaluation

To evaluate the initialization phase, we evaluate the automated labeling mechanism and the prediction model based on 60,000 support tickets from 2021, which were provided by an international manufacturing company and preprocessed in several steps. The results should indicate how well the initial labeling phase performs. We compared different approaches of modern entity taggers to maximize the quality of the pre-labeling. For our underlying database, a BERT-based highlighting model achieves significantly higher accuracy scores than for example a Bi-LSTM. The corresponding confusion matrix reveals that BERT more precisely labels "system", "failure description" and "service request". The results (Table 1) showed that transformer-based ML tools like BERT can provide annotators with useful suggestions for highlighting the tickets based on a small database. Thereby augmentation of the labeling process and reduction of the upfront labeling effort takes place (DP1). However, overall, the pre-labeling model possesses a comparatively low performance. This is reasoned by the unstructured and informal character of most of the problem descriptions.

Table 1. Performance metrics of the pre-trained labeling system[1]

	Accuracy	Precision	Recall	F1-Score
BERT-based	0.806	0.769	0.806	0.773
Bi-LSTM	0.249	0.392	0.249	0.299

5.2 User Evaluation

Within a naturalistic user evaluation, we instantiated the process and enabled a walk of the designed interactive labeling process. The goal of this evaluation was to account for the perceived immediate value of manual labeling (DP3) and the perceived sense of control (DP2). For the sake of simplicity, the ticket recommender system only presented 3 solution tickets in each case. The involved participants were instructed to first-rate the recommended solution based on pre-labeled tickets, then manually adjust the labels if necessary and rate the new predictions on a scale of 1 to 5. Solving the tickets took an average of 20 min. The interview partners were on average 26 years old and all possess a technical background and experience with IT. Afterward, the 11 interviewees (I) were asked to answer questions regarding their experience during interviews. Finally, we conducted a short survey. In total, the user evaluation lasted about 60 min.

We interviewed the participants regarding the overall experience of the value-driven labeling process. Regarding the augmentation of the labeling process (DP1), the interviewed participants stated that the tool intuitively supported the labeling, and annotating the data was perceived as being straightforward. In addition, interviewees mentioned that the labeling supported their cognitive processing of the presented problem cases

---
[1] Weighted precsion, recall and F1-score.

and understanding of the recommended solutions. The interviewees expected that the recommended labels were correct, and showed signs of reliance and blind trust. The automated labeling could be extended to the presented solutions as well, to enable an easier matching of problem-solution pairs: *"I think next time I would label first and then read the tickets, to be able to match the problem with the recommended tickets easier"* (I3). Overall, the participants did not perceive highlighting the data as being effortful, unnecessary, or meaningless. Nevertheless, to make the process more convenient, the system could give agents information and examples on the different categories and make the highlighting clickable (I7).

Providing the system with domain-specific knowledge in the form of labeling the text phrases, stimulated a sense of control (DP2) (I2, I4, I6). Interestingly, the willingness to contribute to higher data quality through interactive labeling was broadly confirmed and reasoned by the benefit of receiving better recommendations (DP3): *"Because then I noticed that with correct labeling I also get immediately meaningful solution possibilities"* (I4). The users understood that labeling the data supported the AI to *"narrow down the problem request"* (I1) or *"filter based on important phrases"* (I2). An interviewee compared the labeling to providing prompts to ChatGPT: *"you have to specify the input to the AI so that it can answer your question exactly – that's similar to this ChatGPT"* (I1). In conclusion, the system motivates users to input their knowledge and justifies the effort of highlighting the text. The immediate adjustment of the recommendation was thus perceived as valuable. Subsequently, trust in the system was raised (DP3). Asking the participants whether bad recommendations were caused by insufficient labeling or the underlying system, they showed more confidence in their labeling activities and blame the machine to be inaccurate (I1). This was confirmed by others that stated that the system presented single recommendations that were extremely unsuitable (I1, I4, I5). During operations, the system must ensure the extraction of such distrust-generating results as trust is strongly influenced by the quality of recommendations. Furthermore, trust was generated by matching the labeled keywords with the solution recommendations: *"So if you see the same keywords again at the bottom. So the same topic then you always think well the results fit"* (I7). The effects should be examined within larger quantitative research as a few interviewees did not deduce a connection between labeling and recommendations. However, this could be caused by single inferior recommendations. Following the interviews, we measure the usability of our system using the system usability scale (SUS) [58]. Given the 11 responses, we achieved a 73.5 SUS score which in the interpretation speaks for "good usability" confirming the qualitative feedback.

6   Implications, Limitations, and Conclusion

We developed a conceptual model for value-driven interactive labeling by incorporating a value co-creation perspective. Along with the research project, we analyzed the as-is process and identified six key issues that restrict the potential of AI systems. After developing a to-be labeling process, we derived a generalized conceptual model which integrates a service perspective [20, 21]. As one of the first papers in the literature stream on interactive ML [15], hybrid intelligence [9], and HITL configurations [1], we show how value co-creation can be the core of self-learning systems and how an integrated interactive labeling process removes the dichotomy between value recipients and value facilitators. With enabling value-in-use in terms of immediate perceived value and providing a sense of control, we contribute novel mechanisms to the knowledge of designing interactive labeling systems [17]. From a practical perspective, the model can be used to improve ML development and operations in terms of efficient initialization, continuous usage, and model maintenance. The approach outlines a way to incentivize users to contribute domain-specific knowledge. The optimized interaction between humans and AI will lead to a higher prediction and subsequent service performance.

Our research comes with limitations and provides room for future research. Given the scope of this research, the role of operators and how they are integrated into the conceptual model remains neglected. One limitation refers to the selected interactive ML type. Considering aspects of other types such as active learning can provide additional insights into value co-creation-based labeling. For example, a system could only request new labels or feedback when the data is needed to improve the model or the results. Thereby researchers and practitioners could further reduce the demand on users to label data [17]. In addition, our evaluation does not consider labeling quality and performance as key metrics. Calculating the differences between automated labels and manual labels through similarity scores, our evaluation results could have been enhanced by revealing the user's contribution and engagement. Another limitation points to the challenge of bad labels but good recommendations which require additional feedback mechanisms. It is not revealed whether users will first check the labels or check the recommendations as our test setup asked the user to first-rate the pre-predictions. That way we ensured that a comparison of recommendations based on pre-labeled and manually labeled could be drawn. Overall, further research has to be conducted to ensure an accumulation of value and value co-creation in the long term by evaluating the performance of the automated labeling model after adding manual labels. A future large-scale experiment should aim for quantitative analysis that could underline the effects mentioned by the interviewees.

We expect that our resulting conceptual model for value-co-creation-based labeling can be applied to different labeling tasks and different learning mechanisms as well. In conclusion, our evaluation suggests that the perceived immediate value can stimulate the willingness to co-create value in HITL configurations and thus improve data quality and subsequent recommender performance. Thus, we provide novel insights into solving the challenge of data quality in AI.

References

1. Grønsund, T., Aanestad, M.: Augmenting the algorithm: emerging human-in-the-loop work configurations. J. Strateg. Inf. Syst. **29**, 101614 (2020). https://doi.org/10.1016/j.jsis.2020.101614
2. Li, M.M., Peters, C., Leimeister, J.M.: Designing a peer-based support system to support shakedown. In: International Conference on Information Systems (ICIS), Seoul, South Korea (2017)
3. Al-Hawari, F., Barham, H.: A machine learning based help desk system for IT service management. J. King Saud Univ. – Comput. Inf. Sci. **33**, 702–718 (2021). https://doi.org/10.1016/j.jksuci.2019.04.001
4. Dostál, M.: Service desk onboarding training environment. Acta Informatica Pragensia **11**, 265–284 (2022)

5. Rumburg, J.: Metric of the Month: Annual Agent Turnover (2018)
6. Schmidt, S., Li, M., Peters, C.: Requirements for an IT support system based on hybrid intelligence. In: HICSS (2022)
7. Li, M., Löfflad, D., Reh, C., et al.: Towards the design of hybrid intelligence frontline service technologies – a novel human-in-the-loop configuration for human-machine interactions. In: HICSS (2023)
8. Kubiak, P., Rass, S.: An overview of data-driven techniques for IT-service-management. IEEE Access 6, 63664–63688 (2018). https://doi.org/10.1109/ACCESS.2018.2875975
9. Dellermann, D., Ebel, P., Söllner, M., et al.: Hybrid intelligence. Bus. Inf. Syst. Eng. 61, 637–643 (2019)
10. Choi, M., Park, C., Yang, S., et al.: AILA: attentive interactive labeling assistant for document classification through attention-based deep neural networks. In: Proceedings of the 2019 CHI Conference on Human Factors in Computing Systems. ACM, New York (2019)
11. Luo, X., Qin, M.S., Fang, Z., et al.: Artificial intelligence coaches for sales agents: caveats and solutions. J. Mark. 85, 14–32 (2021). https://doi.org/10.1177/0022242920956676
12. Kim, T., Song, H.: Communicating the limitations of AI: the effect of message framing and ownership on trust in artificial intelligence. Int. J. Hum.–Comput. Interact. 1–11 (2022). https://doi.org/10.1080/10447318.2022.2049134
13. Jacovi, A., Marasović, A., Miller, T., et al.: Formalizing trust in artificial intelligence. In: Proceedings of the 2021 ACM Conference on Fairness, Accountability, and Transparency. ACM, New York (2021)
14. Schmitt, A., Wambsganss, T., Janson, A.: Designing for conversational system trustworthiness: the impact of model transparency on trust and task performance. In: ECIS, vol. 172 (2022)
15. Holzinger, A.: Interactive machine learning for health informatics: when do we need the human-in-the-loop? Brain Inform. 3(2), 119–131 (2016). https://doi.org/10.1007/s40708-016-0042-6
16. Wiethof, C., Bittner, E.: Hybrid intelligence - combining the human in the loop with the computer in the loop: a systematic literature review (2021)
17. Nadj, M., Knaeble, M., Li, M.X., Maedche, A.: Power to the Oracle? Design principles for interactive labeling systems in machine learning. KI - Künstliche Intelligenz 34(2), 131–142 (2020). https://doi.org/10.1007/s13218-020-00634-1
18. Viana, L., Oliveira, E., Conte, T.: An interface design catalog for interactive labeling systems. In: Proceedings of the 23rd International Conference on Enterprise Information Systems. SCITEPRESS - Science and Technology Publications (2021)
19. Warsinsky, S., Schmidt-Kraepelin, M., Thiebes, S., et al.: Gamified expert annotation systems: meta-requirements and tentative design. In: Drechsler, A., Gerber, A., Hevner, A. (eds.) The Transdisciplinary Reach of Design Science Research. DESRIST 2022. Lecture Notes in Computer Science, vol. 13229, pp 154–166. Springer, Cham. https://doi.org/10.1007/978-3-031-06516-3_12
20. Grönroos, C., Voima, P.: Critical service logic: making sense of value creation and co-creation. J. Acad. Mark. Sci. 41, 133–150 (2013)
21. Vargo, S.L., Lusch, R.F.: The four service marketing myths: remnants of a goods-based, manufacturing model. J. Serv. Res. 6, 324–335 (2004)
22. Zanzotto, F.M.: Viewpoint: human-in-the-loop artificial intelligence. JAIR 64, 243–252 (2019)
23. Porter, R.B., Theiler, J.P., Hush, D.R.: Interactive machine learning in data exploitation. Office of Scientific and Technical Information (OSTI) (2013)
24. Meza Martínez, M.A., Nadj, M., Maedche, A.: Towards an integrative theoretical framework of interactive machine learning systems. In: ECIS (2019)

25. Amershi, S., Cakmak, M., Knox, W.B., et al.: Power to the people: the role of humans in interactive machine learning. AIMag **35**, 105–120 (2015). https://doi.org/10.1609/aimag.v35i4.2513
26. Jiang, L., Liu, S., Chen, C.: Recent research advances on interactive machine learning. J. Vis. **22**(2), 401–417 (2018). https://doi.org/10.1007/s12650-018-0531-1
27. Kleinschmidt, S., Peters, C., Leimeister, J.M.: How to scale up contact-intensive services: ICT-enabled service innovation. JOSM **31**, 793–814 (2020). https://doi.org/10.1108/JOSM-12-2017-0349
28. Afsar, M.M., Crump, T., Far, B.: Reinforcement learning based recommender systems: a survey. CoRR (2021)
29. Kaelbling, L.P., Littman, M.L., Moore, A.W.: Reinforcement learning: a survey. JAIR **4**, 237–285 (1996). https://doi.org/10.1613/jair.301
30. Elshan, E., Ebel, P.A., Söllner, M. et al.: Leveraging low code development of smart personal assistants: an integrated design approach with the SPADE method. J. Manag. Inf. Syst. (JMIS) (2022)
31. Bernard, J., Hutter, M., Zeppelzauer, M., et al.: Comparing visual-interactive labeling with active learning: an experimental study. IEEE Trans. Vis. Comput. Graph. **24**, 298–308 (2018). https://doi.org/10.1109/tvcg.2017.2744818
32. Schüritz, R., Farrell, K., Wixom, B., et al.: Value co-creation in data-driven services: towards a deeper understanding of the joint sphere (2019)
33. Blaschke, M., Riss, U., Haki, K., Aier, S.: Design principles for digital value co-creation networks: a service-dominant logic perspective. Electron. Mark. **29**(3), 443–472 (2019). https://doi.org/10.1007/s12525-019-00356-9
34. Peters, C.: Designing work and service systems. Doctoral Dissertation (2020)
35. Grönroos, C.: Service logic revisited: who creates value? And who co-creates? Eur. Bus. Rev. **20**, 298–314 (2008). https://doi.org/10.1108/09555340810886585
36. Vargo, S.L., Lusch, R.F.: Service-dominant logic: continuing the evolution. J. Acad. Mark. Sci. **36**, 1 (2008). https://doi.org/10.1007/s11747-007-0069-6
37. Grönroos, C.: Value co-creation in service logic: a critical analysis. Mark. Theory **11**, 279–301 (2011). https://doi.org/10.1177/1470593111408177
38. Kuechler, B., Vaishnavi, V.: On theory development in design science research: anatomy of a research project. Eur. J. Inf. Syst. **17**, 489–504 (2008)
39. Hevner, A.R., March, S.T., Park, J., et al.: Design science in information systems research. MIS Q. **28**, 75 (2004). https://doi.org/10.2307/25148625
40. Winter, R.: Design science research in Europe. Eur. J. Inf. Syst. **17**, 470–475 (2008). https://doi.org/10.1057/ejis.2008.44
41. Peffers, K., Rothenberger, M., Tuunanen, T., et al.: Design science research evaluation. In: Peffers, K., Rothenberger, M., Kuechler, B. (eds) Design Science Research in Information Systems. Advances in Theory and Practice. DESRIST 2012. Lecture Notes in Computer Science, vol. 7286, , pp. 398–410. Springer, Heidelberg (2012). https://doi.org/10.1007/978-3-642-29863-9_29
42. Venable, J., Pries-Heje, J., Baskerville, R.: FEDS: a framework for evaluation in design science research. Eur. J. Inf. Syst. **25**, 77–89 (2016). https://doi.org/10.1057/ejis.2014.36
43. Cao, H.-A., Wijaya, T.K., Aberer, K., et al.: A collaborative framework for annotating energy datasets. In: 2015 IEEE International Conference on Big Data (Big Data). IEEE (2015)
44. Yan, Yang, J., Hauptmann: Automatically labeling video data using multi-class active learning. In: Proceedings Ninth IEEE International Conference on Computer Vision. IEEE (2003)
45. Desmond, M., Duesterwald, E., Brimijoin, K., et al.: Semi-automated data labeling. In: NeurIPS 2020 Competition and Demonstration Track, pp. 156–169 (2021)

46. Eisenhardt, K.M.: Agency theory: an assessment and review. AMR **14**, 57–74 (1989). https://doi.org/10.5465/amr.1989.4279003
47. Ranjan, K.R., Read, S.: Value co-creation: concept and measurement. J. Acad. Mark. Sci. **44**(3), 290–315 (2014). https://doi.org/10.1007/s11747-014-0397-2
48. Mallick, A., Hsieh, K., Arzani, B., et al.: Matchmaker: data drift mitigation in machine learning for large-scale systems. Proc. Mach. Learn. Syst. **4**, 77–94 (2022)
49. Pianykh, O.S., Langs, G., Dewey, M., et al.: Continuous learning AI in radiology: implementation principles and early applications. Radiology **297**, 6–14 (2020). https://doi.org/10.1148/radiol.2020200038
50. Mirbabaie, M., Brünker, F., Möllmann, F., Nicholas, R.J., et al.: The rise of artificial intelligence – understanding the AI identity threat at the workplace. Electron. Mark. **32**, 73–99 (2022). https://doi.org/10.1007/s12525-021-00496-x
51. Vorobeva, D., El Fassi, Y., Costa Pinto, D., et al.: Thinking skills don't protect service workers from replacement by artificial intelligence. J. Serv. Res. **25**, 601–613 (2022). https://doi.org/10.1177/10946705221104312
52. Braun, M., Greve, M., Riquel, J., et al.: Meet your new colle (AI) GUE–exploring the impact of human-AI interaction designs on user performance. In: ECIS (2022)
53. Hemmer, P., Schemmer, M., Riefle, L., et al.: Factors that influence the adoption of human-AI collaboration in clinical decision-making. In: ECIS (2022)
54. Dietvorst, B.J., Simmons, J.P., Massey, C.: Overcoming algorithm aversion: people will use imperfect algorithms if they can (even slightly) modify them. Manag. Sci. **64**, 1155–1170 (2018)
55. Lockey, S., Gillespie, N., Holm, D., et al.: A review of trust in artificial intelligence: challenges, vulnerabilities and future directions. In: HICSS (2021)
56. Venable, J., Pries-Heje, J., Baskerville, R.: A comprehensive framework for evaluation in design science research. In: Peffers, K., Rothenberger, M., Kuechler, B. (eds.) Design Science Research in Information Systems. Advances in Theory and Practice. DESRIST 2012. Lecture Notes in Computer Science, vol. 7286, pp. 423–438. Springer, Heidelberg (2012). https://doi.org/10.1007/978-3-642-29863-9_31
57. Shani, G., Gunawardana, A.: Evaluating recommendation systems. In: Ricci, F., Rokach, L., Shapira, B., Kantor, P.B. (eds.) Recommender Systems Handbook, pp. 257–297. Springer, Boston, MA (2011). https://doi.org/10.1007/978-0-387-85820-3_8
58. Brooke, J.: SUS: A 'quick and dirty' usability scale. In: Usability Evaluation in Industry. CRC Press, pp. 207–212 (1996)

Healthcare Systems and Quality of Life

Introduction to the Healthcare Systems and Quality of Life Research Track

Reima Suomi[1] 🆔, Monica Chiarini Tremblay[2] 🆔,
and Debra VanderMeer[3] 🆔

[1] University of Turku, Finland
reima.suomi@utu.fi
[2] William and Mary University, USA
monica.tremblay@mason.wm.edu
[3] Florida International University, USA
vanderd@fiu.edu

The healthcare industry is grappling with a variety of complex issues, as evidenced by the recent Covid-19 pandemic. Addressing these challenges requires collaboration across multiple disciplines, with healthcare professionals, regulators, and technology suppliers all playing important roles. Ultimately, the patient/citizen is the most crucial stakeholder and actor in the healthcare ecosystem. In healthcare organizational settings, there are often complicated relationships between clinical, IT, and administrative personnel. These all are further divided into powerful subgroups.

Clinical work, including clinical research, is characterized by its stringent rules, process specifications, and structures. Design Science Research easily finds an accepting home in clinical settings due to shared values with this field, including a problem-solving orientation, a structured approach to the activity, and a commitment to quality.

Improving general well-being and quality of life is a less structured area of clinical research than in other fields. Developing effective solutions in this area requires careful research and support from Design Science Research. While there are countless ideas and activities that people engage in to improve their quality of life, only some things can be achieved through careful planning and problem-solving.

In health and well-being settings, solutions in one environment may not necessarily work in others. Moreover, organizational boundaries often need to be respected, and integrative solutions are needed to address complex issues that cut across multiple domains. Therefore, wide-reaching solutions that integrate different perspectives and stakeholders are required to enhance people's well-being and quality of life effectively.

The Healthcare Systems and Quality of Life Research Track makes two important contributions. Firstly, it provides a conceptual IT governance framework focusing on interoperable health information systems. This work addresses the core problems facing modern healthcare, where individual organizations may have sophisticated systems, but integration between different organizations remains a significant challenge. This lack of integration often leads to low service quality, suboptimal results, and high costs.

The second contribution of the research track focuses on blood donation. Blood donation is a voluntary activity critical to delivering life-saving blood to needy people. However, streamlined arrangements and processes can make blood donation more efficient and satisfactory. The article highlights the potential of inexpensive and simple solutions, such as mobile apps, to improve the blood donation process.

Our two submissions describe two elegant solutions, but we challenge that there are many opportunities for Design Science Research to enhance well-being in various domains. The potential of Design Science Research lies in its ability to create innovative and effective solutions to complex problems that can improve people's lives. We provide two examples.

The first is in mental health, a crucial aspect of well-being. Design Science Researchers can contribute with research that guides practice in developing effective solutions to support individuals in managing their mental health. This can include mobile apps, chatbots, or other digital tools that help people cope with stress, anxiety, and depression. Care must be taken, that the solutions increase, not decrease, individual and society well-being.

Second, as the world's population ages and people live longer, there is an increasing need for technologies and systems that promote healthy aging and support independent living. Design Science Research can contribute to this area by developing solutions that improve accessibility for all, including those with disabilities or mobility challenges. Examples of solutions that can be developed through Design Science Research in this area include smart home technologies, wearable devices, and assistive technologies that help individuals with daily living activities. These solutions can enhance the quality of life for older adults and individuals with disabilities, enabling them to remain independent and engaged in their communities for longer.

Guiding the Development of Interoperable Health Information Systems: A Conceptual IT Governance Framework

Lebogang Matshaba[1]([⊠]) [iD], Monelo Nxozi[1] [iD], and Marlien Herselman[2] [iD]

[1] Department of Information Systems, Rhodes University, Makhanda 6139, South Africa
Lebomatshabba@gmail.com

[2] NGEI Cluster, CSIR, Pretoria and Department of Industrial Engineering, University of Stellenbosch, Stellenbosch, South Africa

Abstract. In the midst of dynamic healthcare needs, health information systems' lack of interoperability continues to hinder the health sector's ability to provide healthcare services. For instance, the recent COVID-19 epidemic has sparked discussion about the health department's ability to meet healthcare needs and the readiness of the National Health Insurance initiative in South Africa. Moreover, operating in resource-constrained circumstances presents a further obstacle and raises questions as to whether quality healthcare services can be delivered to patients. Following the Design Science Research Methodology (DSRM) process, this paper developed an IT governance conceptual framework, termed the HISIG-CF, to inform the interoperability of health information systems. The HISIG-CF was developed using literature and insights garnered from qualitative data using expert reviews from practitioners in the healthcare industry. The results indicated a need for more guidance to inform interoperability interventions and strengthen current health information systems through the use of well-defined IT Governance frameworks and mechanisms. Furthermore, the HISIG-CF was deemed adequate to improve health information systems interoperability within the healthcare sector in the North West, with prospects for usage across South Africa.

Keywords: IT governance · Health information systems · Interoperability · National Health Insurance · Design Science Research

1 Introduction

South Africa continues to experience poor health outcomes rooted in historic inequalities that continue to burden the current healthcare systems [1]. The World Health Organisation (WHO) notes that "at the center of this humanitarian crisis is a failure of health systems" [2]. Maintaining the current trajectory will create health systems lacking adaptability and continue to lessen the quality of healthcare and social value [3].

Health systems are a collection of organisations and people who contribute to providing and promoting healthcare to a large population [4]. Across different health systems, health information is stored with the purpose of [5]:

© The Author(s), under exclusive license to Springer Nature Switzerland AG 2023
A. Gerber and R. Baskerville (Eds.): DESRIST 2023, LNCS 13873, pp. 143–156, 2023.
https://doi.org/10.1007/978-3-031-32808-4_9

- Collecting health data stored across health systems.
- Analysing health data to make more meaningful sense of its use.
- Reporting on analysis results to enhance the efficiency of health services.

Across South Africa, Health Information Systems (HIS) are largely "driven by donor-funded vertical programmes" that often operate as pilot projects that are not in alignment with the overall national health strategies set [1]. Furthermore, electronic health (eHealth) systems implementations are crippled by the lack of coordination at the highest level of government [6]. Where there is evidence of health systems, a considerable fraction are unable to share crucial information needed to effectively deliver health services [7]. The different systems are spread across different healthcare facilities, operating as silos. Subsequently resulting in the fragmentation of health information, which continues to hamper the potential realisation of health systems benefits [7, 8].

Central to the delivery of health services, is the exchange of health information stored as Electronic Health Records (EHR) [9]. EHRs provide the history of a patient's health records in a digital format, allowing access as required. This enables stakeholders to gain access to health data needed to effectively deliver much-needed healthcare.

Interoperability relates to how systems (or components thereof) communicate towards mutual goals through exchanging and sharing information [10]. Through interoperability, healthcare providers could form knowledge-sharing networks that contribute to the reduction of health information duplication [11]. Additionally, the value of interoperable health systems allows key decision-making stakeholders to gain access to information needed to strengthen the provision of quality healthcare services [11]. In South Africa, interoperability in healthcare forms part of a broader digital health ecosystem [9]. Considerable progress has been made in defining interoperability constructs and its implementation, however, interoperability is not yet at a stage of being fully enacted [11–13]. Where interoperability is present, only about 30% are able to exchange information [7]. Furthermore, a large fraction of the health systems do not adhere to standards set, at both a national and international level [7]. Without a standardized guide that can be implemented across the different systems, the lack of quality healthcare provision will remain a recurring challenge. Considering this, there is a need to explore approaches that can improve the current health systems across South Africa and how interoperability can be well-governed.

The National Department of Health (NDoH) has identified leadership, governance, and multi-sector engagement as one of the key enablers of a progressive health environment [14]. Furthermore, the "use of mechanisms, expertise, coordination and partnerships to implement the eHealth strategy and develop or adopt eHealth components (e.g. standards)" as a priority in implementing the eHealth strategy [7]. The health ministry has prioritised governance in the delivery of quality healthcare facilitated through well-functioning health systems, which calls for an improvement in governance efforts. Although governance has been acknowledged to be of great significance, its value within the health environment is yet to be realised [15]. IT Governance (ITG) still lags behind in making provisions for interoperability.

The lack of clear implementation measures to improve health systems further impedes South Africa's progress towards attaining Universal Health Coverage (UHC) through the National Health Insurance (NHI) program [14]. The NHI envisions an ideal

state of health provision to enable accessible, high-quality healthcare services, regardless of individuals' economic status [14]. However, if the focus is not on providing quality healthcare by strengthening local systems, UHC will produce unrealistic outcomes
through the NHI.

In this paper, constructs of an ITG conceptual framework are proposed to aid in
improving the governance of interoperable HISs. This is achieved by building on ITG
mechanisms developed by van Grembergen, De Haes and Guldentops [16]. The development of the conceptual framework (HISIG-CF) follows the Design Science Research
Methodology (DSRM). Furthermore, the paper provides the theoretical grounding,
results and analysis, conclusion, and recommendation for similar further studies.

2 Conceptual Framework (viz. HISIG-CF)

In defining the constructs of the HISIG-CF, the design was created in accordance with
three overarching themes, namely; ITG, HIS, and Interoperability. Within the ITG theme,
the design focused on the ITG mechanisms and the sectoral nuances in effect. The HIS
theme delves into the eHealth maturity levels and eHealth building blocks capable of
enhancing health systems. Lastly, the Interoperability theme concentrates on the various layers of interoperability and adoptable standards. This section concludes with a
synthesised design of the HISIG-CF artefact.

2.1 IT Governance Mechanisms

Health systems require significant IT investments to operate effectively. However, such
investments will be in vain without well-defined ITG. ITG can be defined as "Enterprise
governance of IT is an integral part of corporate governance, exercised by the Board,
overseeing the definition and implementation of processes, structures and relational
mechanism in the organisation" [17]. The application of ITG aims to assist organisations
align their operations with their information technology.

It is essential to note that meaningful value can be achieved by establishing pragmatic
approaches to implementation. According to Van Grembergen, Haes and Guldentops
[16], the deployment of ITG is facilitated by a mix of structures, processes, and relational
mechanisms. Selig [18] adds to this by stating that ITG mechanisms are introduced as
the critical enablers in the implementation of ITG.

The central theme of the structure mechanism is on leadership with the intent of
ensuring that clear channels of responsibility are defined from the onset. Further creating
an enabling environment with a definition of who the key stakeholders are and their
respective responsibilities [19]. This study draws from the COBIT 2019, RACI matrix
which is a tool that can be used to define who is Responsible, Accountable, Consulted,
and Informed (RACI) for executing ITG activities [20].

Creating an environment conducive to the implementation of ITG far extends defining the roles and responsibilities. It also entails setting the practices that may be followed
to reach the desired end goal. In ITG, processes are viewed as arrangements of formali-
ties involved in decision-making [21]. Additionally, the process mechanism guides the

design of the forms of monitoring that are essential during the rollout of an ITG programme. As part of the process mechanism, this study focused on employing adaptive frameworks, standards and monitoring tools include the: Information Technology Infrastructure Library (ITIL) which can be used for planning and the support of IT services; VAL IT, which is useful for identifying and defining connections between functions of an organisation and IT; as well as COBIT etc., [21]. An organisation's IT goals primarily drives the selection of appropriate frameworks, standards, or tools. For instance, an ITIL framework may be adopted if an organisation's IT goal is to standardise IT delivery because it offers the relevant tools. In addition to ITG standards, this study defines the implementation process using the Continual Improvement Life Cycle Approach as determined in COBIT 2019 [20]. The approach identifies three interconnected areas of development necessary to make ITG a reality namely, program management, change enablement and the continual improvement lifecycle.

Lastly, relational mechanisms can be identified as a significant cohesive tool that enables structures and processes to operate efficiently [21]. Through relational mechanisms, the emphasis moves from strictly technical aspects of ITG and towards the integration of socio-technical factors. According to Wu, et al., [19], a range of crucial factors is necessary to implement ITG. These include (but not limited to) the active involvement of senior or critical stakeholders in an organisation, the use of well-coordinated communication processes to promote ITG, and the establishment of a relational culture to foster collaboration.

2.2 Sectoral Differences

Organisations operate under different sectoral regulations that guide their activities. Misuraca and Viscusi [22] argue that the domain in which organisations exist places a requirement for specific governance implementation strategies. Therefore, to implement the correct ITG mechanisms, it is vital to understand the pre-existing norms in a given sector. The two main sectors in which organisations exist as addressed in this study include the private and public sectors [23, 24].

Private sector organisations are characterised by their ability to generate positive profit margins with the intent of delivering shareholder value. ITG is considered to the extent of its influence on profit projections [21, 23]. On the other hand, public sector organisations orientate their functions towards providing value for public and societal benefits [22]. At the forefront of public organisations are the social and political goals on which their decisions making occurs.

In South Africa, healthcare services are accessible through two broader and parallel systems namely, the private and public healthcare sectors [25]. The former accounts for a large proportion of resources used to deliver health services. Over 80% of the population is reliant on public healthcare, further straining an already frail health system [26]. Additionally, 60% of resources are directed towards the private sector, which is only accessible to approximately 20% of the population [13]. These disparities not only continue the cycle of unequal access to quality healthcare but also infringe on a fundamental human right that "everyone has the right to have access to healthcare services" [27].

2.3 eHealth Maturity Levels

What eHealth aims to achieve is to address healthcare challenges through ICT [28]. It is concerned with supporting health information delivery, using electronic methods, and improving how information flows across different systems [1, 13].

It is also crucial in the implementation of ITG to consider the eHealth systems' maturity levels. Embarking on a journey to change any health system requires a clear understanding of the state of functionality characterising each system. According to NDoH and CSIR [7], eHealth systems maturity levels assist in the decision-making processes to determine the best course of action:

- **Level 1: Local paper-based systems:** Define the lowest level of recording health information (e.g., patient information). In these types of health systems, medical records are manually stored, and information is only accessible in a local health facility.
- **Level 2: Local paper-based health systems with limited IT support:** At this level of maturity, health systems are predominately paper based however, IT features are used to store patient's demographical information used to uniquely match each medical records to each patient. Information mainly remains at a single health care facility.
- **Level 3: Centralised electronic health systems with both paper-based and electronic features:** In this instance, the use of a paper-based system would occur when a healthcare worker records a patient's health information and medical record in a patient's file. To maintain consistency, standardised forms are used to record patient's information. Furthermore, paper-based functions would also be used to record samples e.g., blood tests, sent to pathologies however, the results obtained would then be electronically recorded.
- **Level 4: Fully integrated national shared health system:** This level of eHealth maturity represents the desired, end goal for a fully electronic-based Electronic Health Records (EHR) system that enables health information exchange to occur. At this level of eHealth maturity, patient's health records are stored at the localised healthcare facility's EMR. The relevant aspects of a patient's health record are then stored onto a shared EHRs system, accessible across different networks.

2.4 eHealth Building Blocks

The strength of HIS is not only reliant on its technical attributes but draws from a range of contributing building blocks as depicted in Table 1 below. The building blocks can also be used as a measure of progress made to improve health systems currently in place [2, 9].

It is imperative to state that the leadership and governance layer is at the core of each of the identified building blocks for health systems. This is aimed at ensuring accountability across the various blocks. In the South African context, the National Department of Health (NDoH) has outlined leadership, governance and multi-sector engagement as one of the key components in creating an enabling environment for eHealth. The components further describe the "use of mechanisms, expertise, coordination and partnerships to implement the eHealth strategy and develop or adopt eHealth components

Table 1. Building blocks of health systems [2, 9]

Building block	Description
Health service delivery	Quality health services delivery is a vital component for health systems. Health systems need to deliver efficient and quality health services while doing so in a secure manner
Health workforce	A sound health system relies on human capital, skills and the knowledge set it possesses to deliver quality health services while efficiently utilizing the resources available
Health information systems	Reliable and timely information is the foundation required for decision making related to health systems. Useful HISs need to achieve the following: collect relevant health data, analyse information to ensure and maintain quality and reliability, then convert the data to information that can be used to make decisions
Access to essential medicines	Health systems must provide access to essential medication of quality, that is safe and cost-effective
Health financing	At the core of health financing is ensuring that health services can be received by any individual that requires health care. Additionally, health systems need to accumulate funds that can be used for the supply of health services
Leadership and governance	Strategic policy frameworks coupled with effective oversight, the building of partnerships, regulation, and accountability are essential for efficient health systems

(e.g. standards)" as a priority in implementing the eHealth strategy [7]. Although the significance of governance has been acknowledged, its value in the health environment is yet to be realised [29]. Therefore, improving governance in the healthcare environment is fundamental as it serves as the foundation for all the other building blocks.

2.5 Interoperability Layers

Adding to the complexity of interoperability, Amin et al., [30] notes that its facilitation is a multifaceted approach that focuses on organisational, technical, semantic or syntactical interoperability. Hardware requirements are examined at a technical and organisational level whereas software requirements are documented at a semantic and syntactical level [31]. Depending on the needs of the different healthcare facility and the maturity level at which the health system used is in, a decision can be made on the type of interoperability considered. Furthermore, different actors (doctors, healthcare providers, pharmacies) all participate in healthcare delivery and may require different sets of data relevant to their specific needs [32].

2.6   Standards of Interoperability

To guide the process of interoperability, standards play a critical role. Understanding what standards exist and how best to use them to identify effective approaches is critical to facilitating interoperability in the healthcare context. Standards define specifications that have been mutually agreed upon to achieve and maintain consistently [33]. In this study, constructs of the National Health Normative Standards Framework for Interoperability in eHealth in South Africa (HNSF), were utilised to provide a foundation for how to implements interoperability using a standards-based approach [7].

Furthermore, the specifications of a standard defined as Fast Healthcare Interoperability Resources (FHIR) is gaining prominence in healthcare [4]. FHIR has been developed to provide standards for exchanging healthcare information electronically. The standard offers an opportunity that may significantly contribute to industry and health research in the future. Figure 1 below provides a synthesized view of the constructs of the HISIG-CF.

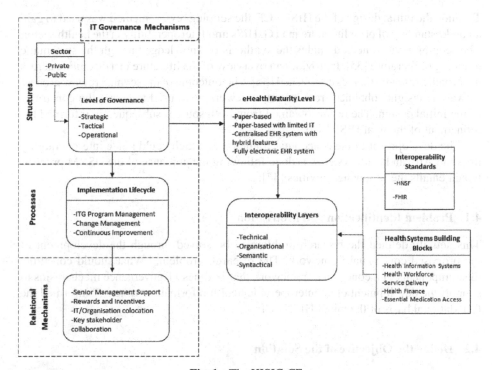

Fig. 1. The HISIG-CF

3   Theoretical Grounding

This study drew from the Institutional Theory and the DSRM process, grounded in DSR and related design theory. The Institutional Theory aided in defining the setting and contextual influences present in the healthcare environment [34]. Through this, it was possible to establish the complexities associated with integrating an IS/IT-based solution (through the HISIG-CF) in context to the health environment.

The proposed HISIG-CF, as shown in Fig. 1, considers the goals set out by the National Department of Health to define the extent of interoperability interventions [14, 20].

In addition, this study followed the guidance of the DSRM (detailed in the next section) which aided the evaluation of the utility and efficacy of the conceptual framework. The use of the DSRM aimed to align the final artefact (HISIG-CF) with the main research question: What should constitute the components of a conceptual framework that outlines IT governance mechanisms to support the development of an interoperable health information system?

4   Research Methods

To guide the initial design of the HISIG-CF, the scoping review method was used to gain an understanding of prior literature in ITG, HISs and Interoperability in the health sector. The scoping review method guides the synthesis of knowledge through the systematic mapping of literature [35]. It provides an overview of the literature in a discipline across the broader research themes established [36]. The outcome of the scoping review process as well as insights obtained from expert reviewers were used to assess the constructs of the initial design. The results obtained from both sources subsequently informed the refinement of the final HISIG-CF.

The development of the conceptual framework, which could guide interoperability in South African health systems, is done following the guidance of the DSRM process, which entails the following activities [37]:

4.1   Problem Identification and Motivation

This activity defined the research problem to be solved through the development of the proposed conceptual framework. The research problem, "What should constitute the components of a conceptual framework that outlines IT governance mechanisms to support the development of an interoperable health information system?" informed the foundational basis of the initial HISIG-CF.

4.2   Define the Objective of the Solution

Considering the motivation of the research, as presented by the research problem, the main objective of this study was driven by the need to provide a solution through an IT governance conceptual framework that would enhance the knowledge of health information systems interoperability. The HISIG-CF serves as a blueprint to understand the areas of inquiry [38] and this study followed this notion to provide a solution that would be relevant for the healthcare environment.

4.3 Design and Development

The aim of this activity was to create the actual conceptual framework, as motivated by the research problem and overall objective. The process entailed the use of knowledge drawn from literature to form the constructs of the solution, to position this study in the broader research field of IT governance in the health environment.

4.4 Demonstration

This activity involved demonstrating the use of the solution that has been designed to establish the feasibility of practical implementation [39]. The demonstration process was guided by the qualitative methodological approach undertaken for this study through conducting a thorough literature review to define the constructs of the HISIG-CF design. The literature was analysed using Thematic Analysis to search for patterns across the data sets [40].

4.5 Evaluation

Saunders, Lewis and Thornhill [41] note that evaluations enable a researcher to judge the methods used based on accuracy and consistency. Importantly, it is also a valuable measure of determining the comprehensiveness of a solution designed. Through evaluations, the researcher was able to determine the extent to which the initial conceptual framework met its intended outcome in producing a novel solution to the management of healthcare information [42]. The outcome of the evaluation contributed to the process of refining the initial proposed HISIG-CF. Evaluating the rigour of the HISIG-CF required the contribution of expert reviewers.

4.6 Communication

The final stage of this process involves communicating the knowledge a study contributes and the overall importance of the solution as informed by disciplinary knowledge. Using assumptions associated with IS research development and the different phases that this research underwent, the HISIG-CF as presented in Fig. 1 was developed.

5 Results and Analysis

To evaluate the constructs of the HISIG-CF, expert reviews were used to gain insights. The experts consisted of five individuals in management positions that have either practical or academic experience with health systems. The selection of five expert reviewers was guided by Nielsen [43], who explains that the point of saturation can be met when evaluating an artefact or research beyond five individuals. For this reason, the expert reviewers selected for this study included five experts with senior management experience in the health environment and expertise in health systems.

In order to draw meaning from the results obtained, the hermeneutics was employed. Hermeneutics is rooted in the interpretive paradigm with the intent of understanding various parts that contribute to the functions of a whole [1]. For purposes of this study, hermeneutics functioned as a valuable analysis approach that enabled the researcher to gain an in-depth understanding of the various actors and systems involved in the healthcare environment [44].

To assess the foundations upon which the HISIG-CF was defined, it was necessary to ascertain the holistic significance of the constructs used. This was done to demonstrate how the experts perceived the design of the conceptual framework. As a result, the experts were requested to respond by indicating (using a Likert scale of 1–5) which HISIG-CF construct they would consider significant for developing interoperable HISs. According to the feedback obtained, none of the experts disputed, disagreed, or was indifferent about any stated constructs.

To comprehend data was distributed among the participants, variance and mean were calculated for the sample population. Based on the results presented in Table 2 below, the variance is relatively low (i.e. 0.2). Variance is used to determine the average difference between the values in a data set [41]. Furthermore, the mean was calculated to determine the average results obtained from the data collected from the various experts. Considering the sample size used, the average mean was relatively high in terms of the agreeability between the respondents (i.e. 4.8). Both variance and mean results depict a positive outcome across the data set, which further validates the constructs that have been identified as being relevant for HIS interoperability intervention using ITG.

Table 2. Expert Review Results

	Sample size	Variance	Mean
Overall results per HISIG-CF construct	5	0.2	4.8

The results were analysed following the guidance of the Framework for Evaluating Design Science (FEDS) as a strategy for evaluation [42]. Furthermore, this study followed the criteria established by [4] to evaluate the utility of the HISIG-CF, which is founded on the belief that the usefulness of a DSR artefact should demonstrate: validity, utility, quality and efficacy.

On the grounds of utility, the results revealed that the HISIG-CF was necessary for the healthcare environment. Expressed by one of the experts, it was noted that the HISIG-CF "acknowledges the other challenges experienced, namely the varying levels of eHealth maturity, which is a major challenge when considering that also the key decision-makers in healthcare are exposed to and familiar with different levels of eHealth maturity." As such, the framework's utility goes as far as considering the contextual influences of the health environment, which could be an essential contributor towards further development.

To further evaluate the efficacy of the designed framework, the experts needed to determine whether the HISIG-CF would produce results for the healthcare environment. Another reviewer indicated that they could already identify aspects of the framework that could be used to provide direction and structure from the provincial departments of health to the management of hospitals in the district. Thus, revealing the value of the implementing the framework within the healthcare environment.

The experts were requested to provide their views on the rigour of the conceptual framework and how it has been developed. All expert that took part expressed that the framework was rigorously done. One of the experts revealed that the linkage of the SRQs to the constructs and how these have been applied to the actual HISIG-CF demonstrates a logical outline of its use and further enabled the constructs to be critically synthesised.

The last aspect of evaluation related to the efficiency of the HISIG-CF. The experts were requested to provide their view of the efficiency of the conceptual framework and determine whether the constructs used were simplistic enough to understand in their current form. The consensus was that the HISIG-CF was simple to follow through and to make sense of. One of the experts expressed their opinion regarding the efficiency by stating that the order of the structures and the differentiation between structures, processes, and relational mechanisms provide a logic of sequence and causality. Thus, showing that the HISIG-CF presents potential value for the healthcare environment.

6 Conclusion

Society's changing health needs call for an improvement in HISs that can adapt to ensure that efficient health services are adequately provided. HISs operating across different health facilities with no ability to share the most crucial health information require solutions to improve operation. However, in seeking ways to improve and strengthen current operational health systems, a multi-faceted approach to development is required. In light of the National Health Insurance (NHI), which is currently being piloted across South Africa, and the need for overall improved healthcare through interoperable health systems, this study sought to develop an ITG conceptual framework that would assist in this regard.

Although well-defined policies are in place to guide health interventions, implementation is still lagging in South Africa. The novelty of this research was illustrated by drawing from IT governance, health information systems, and interoperability literature to develop the HISIG-CF. Experts evaluated the conceptual framework in the health environment and academia to assess and validate its constructs and the foundation on which the framework design occurred. The designed HISIG-CF is suitable for the health environment (health systems) to guide management on using ITG to drive HIS interoperability.

7 Recommendations and Future Research

The primary focus of interoperability should not be solely on defining implementation based on technical aspects, but rather on formalised provisions and understanding the contextual needs being solved. This could include integrating social factors into technical solutions. As a consequence, interventions in HIS interoperability will reduce the perception of strictly technical solutions being out of reach or too complex. This, when combined with health literacy, has the potential to lead to more effective solutions that people can maximise.

Although the findings in this study were primarily drawn from a South African context, the foundation and literature used to provide a comprehensive study drew from global studies. Furthermore, the HISIG-CF employed constructs that are applicable in a variety of healthcare settings. The HISIG-CF is yet to be empirically tested, but its design has been approved as fit for purpose by health professionals and health researchers.

References

1. Herselman, M., Botha, A., Toivanen, H., Myllyoja, J., Fogwill, T., Alberts, R.: A digital health innovation ecosystem for South Africa. In: 2016 IST-Africa Week Conference, pp. 1–11 IEEE (2016)
2. World Health Organization: Monitoring the Building Blocks of Health Systems: a Handbook of Indicators and their measurement instruments. World Health Organization (2010)
3. Kruk, M.E., et al.: High-quality health systems in the Sustainable Development Goals era: time for a revolution. The Lancet global health, 6. 11, pp. e1196–e1252 (2018)
4. Fogwill, T., et al.: MomConnect: an exemplar implementation of the Health Normative Standards Framework in South Africa. South African Health Rev. 1, 125–135 (2016)
5. Hammond, W.E.: Standards for Global health information systems. In: Global Health Informatics, pp. 94–108. Academic Press (2017)
6. Adebesin, F., Kotzé, P.: A process for developing an e-health standards selection method artefact using design science research. J. Des. Res. 15, 258–287 (2017)
7. NDoH, CSIR: South African National Health Normative Standards Framework for Interoperability in eHealth: Complete Version, pp. 1–57 (2014)
8. Jouko, M., et al.: Conceptualising of a South African Digital Health Innovation Ecosystem. CSIR Meraka Institute, Pretoria (2016)
9. Iyawa, G.E., Herselman, M., Botha, A.: Digital health innovation ecosystems. Int. J. Reliable Qual. E-Healthcare 8(2), 1–14 (2019)
10. Wimmer, M.A., Boneva, R., Di Giacomo, D.: Interoperability governance: a definition and insights from case studies in Europe. In: ACM International Conference Proceeding Series (2018)
11. Desai, S.: Health information exchange, interoperability, and network effects. University of Pennsylvania Scholarly Commons, vol. 102 (2015)
12. Clarke, J.M., Warren, L.R., Arora, S., Barahona, M., Darzi, A.W.: Guiding interoperable electronic health records through patient-sharing networks. Npj Dig. Med. 1(1), 1–6 (2018)
13. Katuu, S.: Transforming South Africa's health sector: The eHealth Strategy, the implementation of electronic document and records management systems (EDRMS) and the utility of maturity models. J. Sci. Technol. Policy Manage. 7(3), 330–345 (2016)
14. National Department of Health: National Digital Health Strategy for South Africa 2019–2024. In National Department of Health (2019)
15. Benedict, M., Schlieter, H.: Governance guidelines for digital healthcare ecosystems. Stud. Health Technol. Inform. 212, 233–240 (2015)
16. Van Grembergen, W., De Haes, S., Guldentops, E.: Structures, processes and relational mechanisms for IT governance. In: Strategies for Information Technology Governance, pp. 1–36. IGI Global (2004)
17. Haes, S., Grembergen, W.: Enterprise governance of IT. In: Enterprise Governance of Information Technology. MP, pp. 11–43. Springer, Cham (2015). https://doi.org/10.1007/978-3-319-14547-1_2
18. Selig, G.J.: IT governance—an integrated framework and roadmap: How to plan, deploy and sustain for competitive advantage. In: 2018 Portland International Conference on Management of Engineering and Technology (PICMET), pp. 1–15. IEEE (2018)

19. Wu, S.P.J., Straub, D.W., Liang, T.P.: How information technology governance mechanisms and strategic alignment influence organizational performance. MIS Q. **39**(2), 497–518 (2015)
20. ISACA.: Designing an Information and Technology Governance Solution. COBIT 2019 (2018)
21. Levstek, A., Hovelja, T., Pucihar, A.: IT governance mechanisms and contingency factors: towards an adaptive IT governance model. Organizacija **51**(4), 286–310 (2018)
22. Misuraca, G., Viscusi, G.: Shaping public sector innovation theory: an interpretative framework for ICT-enabled governance innovation. Electron. Commer. Res. **15**(3), 303–322 (2015). https://doi.org/10.1007/s10660-015-9184-5
23. Campbell, J., McDonald, C., Sethibe, T.: Public and private sector IT governance: identifying contextual differences. Austral. J. Inform. Syst. **16**, 2 (2010)
24. Winkler, T.J.: IT governance mechanisms and administration/IT alignment in the public sector: a conceptual model and case validation (2013)
25. Nicol, E., Hanmer, L.A., Mukumbang, F.C., Basera, W., Zitho, A., Bradshaw, D.: Is the routine health information system ready to support the planned national health insurance scheme in South Africa? Health Policy Plan. **36**(5), 639–650 (2021)
26. Brauns, M.: Public healthcare in a post-apartheid South Africa: a critical analysis in governance practices. PhD diss (2016)
27. South African National Department of Health: Strategic Plan 2020/21–2024/25 (2020). https://www.health.gov.za/wp-content/uploads/2020/11/depthealthstrategicplanfinal2020-21to2024-25-1.pdf
28. Adebesin, F., Kotzé, P., Van Greunen, D., Foster, R.: Barriers & challenges to the adoption of E-Health standards in Africa (2013)
29. Benedict, M., Schlieter, H.: Governance guidelines for digital healthcare ecosystems. In: eHealth. pp. 233–240 (2015)
30. Amin, M.M., Sutrisman, A., Stiawan, D., Ermatita, E., Alzahrani, M.Y., Budiarto, R.: Interoperability framework for integrated e-health services. Bull. Electric. Eng. Inform. **9**(1), 354–361 (2020)
31. European Commission: European Interoperability Framework - Implementation Strategy, p. 9 (2017)
32. Iroju, O., Soriyan, A., Gambo, I., Olaleke, J.: Interoperability in healthcare: benefits, challenges and resolutions. Int. J. Innov. Appl. Stud. **3**(1), 262–270 (2013)
33. Han, L., Liu, J., Evans, R., Song, Y., Ma, J.: Factors influencing the adoption of health information standards in health care organizations: a systematic review based on best fit framework synthesis. JMIR Med. Inform. **8**. 5, e17334 (2020)
34. Raynard, M., Johnson, G., Greenwood, R.: Institutional theory and strategic management. Advanced Strategic Management: A Multi-Perspective Approach, pp. 9–34 (2015)
35. Levac, D., Colquhoun, H., O'Brien, K.: Scoping studies: advancing the methodology. Implement. Sci. **5**(69), 1–9 (2010)
36. Booth, A., Sutton, A., Papaioannou, D.: Systematic approaches to a successful literature review (2016)
37. Peffers, K., Tuunanen, T., Rothenberger, M.A., Chatterjee, S.: A design science research methodology for information systems research. J. Manag. Inf. Syst. **24**(3), 45–77 (2007)
38. Bharti, K., Agrawal, R., Sharma, V.: Literature review and proposed conceptual framework. Int. J. Mark. Res. **57**(4), 571–604 (2015)
39. Vaishnavi, V., Kuechler, W.: Design Science Research in Information Systems
40. Bell, E., Bryman, A., Harley, B.: Business Research Methods. 5th edn. Oxford University Press, Oxford (2013)
41. Saunders, M., Lewis, P., Thornhill, A.: Research Methods for Business Students, 7th edn. Pearson, Harlow (2016)

156   L. Matshaba et al.

42. Venable, J., Pries-Heje, J., Baskerville, R.: FEDS: a framework for evaluation in design science research. Eur. J. Inf. Syst. **25**(1), 77–89 (2016)
43. Nielsen, J.: Why you only need to test with 5 users. Nielsen Norman Group (2000). https://www.nngroup.com/articles/why-you-only-need-to-test-with-5-users. ISSN, 0737-8939
44. Kroeze, J.H., Van Zyl, I.: The theme of hermeneutics in is - the need for a structured literature review. In: Twenty-first Americas Conference on Information Systems, AMCIS 2015 (2015)

Persuasive Blood Donation App Design for Individualist and Collectivist Cultures

Helena M. Müller [ID] and Melanie Reuter-Oppermann[✉][ID]

Technical University of Darmstadt, Hochschulstr. 1, 64289 Darmstadt, Germany
{mueller,oppermann}@is.tu-darmstadt.de

Abstract. The two African countries South Africa and Ghana both suffer from low recruitment and retention of blood donors and daily face the challenge of matching supply and demand of blood products. When addressing this challenge, it is important to note that the blood donation cultures of both countries differ, with South Africa representing an individualist and Ghana a collectivist blood donation culture. In order to support donor management in both countries, we argue that blood donation apps can play an important role. By applying the design science methodology, we evaluate and analyse a set of previously defined design features with regard to their importance for a blood donation app in those two countries. By means of an online survey, we establish the overall usefulness of a blood donation app. We additionally conclude that for both countries personal and social features are important for the design, but that for South Africa personal features like reminders or rewards are even more important, while for Ghana social features dominate.

Keywords: Blood donation cultures · App design · Design science

1 Introduction

In many countries worldwide, donor management is one of the most important and challenging tasks within the blood supply chain nowadays. Not least due to the COVID-19 pandemic, donation numbers decreased, increasing the shortage of blood products [25]. This is especially challenging in countries like South Africa or Ghana, which already had a comparably low percentage of blood donors pre-COVID - less than 1% of the population donated blood [24]. As blood products also only have a short shelf-life, fulfilling the demand for blood products on average days is already a major challenge in South Africa and Ghana [28]. As Dei-Adomakoh et al. stated, "the low recruitment and retention of blood donors in sub-Saharan Africa is a grave concern for blood transfusion services in the region" [4, p. 770]. Based on previous research which has shown the potential and importance of a blood donation app for donor management [17], we argue that such an app can also be beneficial for blood donor management in African countries. For our work, we have chosen South Africa and Ghana as an individualist and a collectivist blood donation culture. We applied the design science research (DSR) methodology in order to design such an app and predominantly evaluate design features for blood donation apps in both countries with respect to their different donation cultures. Consequently, we address the following research question in this work: *How to design culture-tailored persuasive blood donation apps?*

The remainder of the paper is structured as follows. In Sect. 2, we summarise relevant literature, especially with regard to persuasive system design. Our design science research project is described in Sect. 3. The following Sect. 4 presents the design of a persuasive blood donation app for South Africa and Ghana. In Sect. 5, we discuss the results of our evaluation with respect to cultural influences that differ between the two countries. We conclude our work with a summary and an outlook on future research in Sect. 6.

2 Persuasive System Design for Blood Donation Cultures

According to Fogg [7], socio-technical systems whose design is deliberately aimed at influencing behaviour are classified as persuasive technologies. Persuasion itself means communicating in a way that behavioural change is the outcome of the interaction [27]. It is obvious that persuasion as a means of intentional communication looks different depending on the culture. In the context of blood donation, cultural influences should not be neglected as predictors of blood donor behaviour such as the mechanisms of altruism vary across cultures [6]. For communicating effectively in the sense of persuasion, knowing the specific predictors is crucial in order to induce behavioural changes. For instance, in Black, Asian and Ethnic Minority (BAME) communities, donating blood is primarily motivated by reciprocity (knowing exactly whose life is being saved), whereas in Western communities (non-BAME) donors do not know for whom they have donated blood (saving the life of strangers) [14]. Because of the culturally driven variation in blood donation practices grounded on the different conceptualisations of altruism, we introduced the term "blood donation culture". In line with Hofstede's [10] "Individualism vs. Collectivism" dimension, we distinguish between an individualist (non-BAME communities) and a collectivist (BAME communities) blood donation culture. Originally emerged from a country-level analysis, this is one out of six dimensions Hofstede introduced to facilitate the comparison between national cultures by providing six scores for each country [11]. According to him, culture means "the collective programming of the mind which distinguishes the members of one human group from another" [10, p. 260]. The difference between individualist and collectivist cultures is that the behaviour of the former is mainly guided by individual needs following a self-driven approach, whereas, in feeling responsible for the belonging group in exchange for loyalty, the latter are primarily influenced by group needs [10]. These interdependences have been demonstrated by several cross-cultural studies of the theory of planned behaviour, showing that the behaviour of individualists is primarily determined by attitudes while norms are the main determinant for collectivists (e.g., [1]).

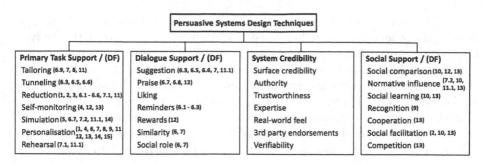

Persuasive Systems Design Techniques			
Primary Task Support / (DF)	**Dialogue Support / (DF)**	**System Credibility**	**Social Support / (DF)**
Tailoring (6.9, 7, 8, 11)	Suggestion (6.3, 6.5, 6.6, 7, 11.1)	Surface credibility	Social comparison (10, 12, 13)
Tunneling (6.3, 6.5, 6.6)	Praise (6.7, 6.8, 12)	Authority	Normative influence (7.2, 10, 11.1, 13)
Reduction (1, 2, 3, 6.1 - 6.6, 7.1, 11)	Liking	Trustworthiness	Social learning (10, 13)
Self-monitoring (4, 12, 13)	Reminders (6.1 - 6.3)	Expertise	Recognition (9)
Simulation (5, 6.7, 7.2, 11.1, 14)	Rewards (12)	Real-world feel	Cooperation (13)
Personalisation (1, 4, 6, 7, 8, 9, 11, 12, 13, 14, 15)	Similarity (6, 7)	3rd party endorsements	Social facilitation (2, 10, 13)
Rehearsal (7.1, 11.1)	Social role (6, 7)	Verifiability	Competition (13)

Fig. 1. Mapping of blood donation app DFs to DPs of the PSD model (based on [20]).

Many DSR and Information Systems researchers made use of the link of Hofstede's dimensions to certain design aspects to investigate the differences in the users' design preferences between cultures assuming that they are similar within one culture (e.g., [23]). However, these aspects are rather abstract with regard to, for example, the handling of content, colours and images mainly applicable to websites (cf., [15]). To the best of our knowledge, Oyibo [21] (qualitative approach) as well as Oyibo and Vassileva [22] (quantitative approach) have been the first to link Hofstede's "Individualism vs. Collectivism" dimension to specific fitness app design features by mapping them to the Persuasive System Design (PSD) model proposed by Oinas-Kukkonen and Harjumaa [19] to design and evaluate persuasive systems. The applicability of the PSD model as a comparative framework seems obvious when looking at its four categories: Primary Task Support (i.e., support in focusing the target behaviour), Dialogue Support (i.e., support through system-user interaction by providing feedback), System Credibility (i.e., support in assessing a system's credibility) and Social Support (i.e., support through social influences). It is reasonable to assume that the former is more important to the individualist compared to the collectivist culture, whereas for the latter category it is the other way round. In the quantitative study of Oyibo and Vassileva [22], this assumption is confirmed, whereas in the qualitative study of Oyibo [21] not social support but dialogue support was more important to the collectivist compared to the individualist group. This finding was obtained by the aforementioned researchers' comparison of the users' perceived persuasiveness of the applied persuasive systems design techniques of each category (except System Credibility). In total, the PSD model comprises 28 techniques, seven out of each category, that describe how a system can be designed to be persuasive (Fig. 1). In this paper, we take a similar approach by first mapping of our blood donation app design features (DFs) to the design principles of the PSD model to evaluate if the proposed design of our app (described in our prior study [17]) generally is persuasive and secondly by investigating the differences in the DFs' perceived persuasiveness between the two blood donation cultures. In line with Oyibo [21] as well as Oyibo and Vassileva [22], the System Credibility category is not considered, because its PSD techniques are rather abstract compared to them of the other categories regarding the target behaviour and therefore they are not represented by our blood donation app design features (see Fig. 1: no assignment of DFs - an explanation of the assignment to the other categories follows in Sect. 4). However, in contrast to the study of Oyibo [21], our participants are not biased towards their perceived persuasiveness by showing them a mock-up with a preconceived selection of DFs and parallelly asking them to reveal the feature most requested, as our DFs had already been exploratively derived in our prior design science study [17] and thus all of our DFs were shown to the participants asking them to assess the persuasiveness of each of the DFs separately. In the context of blood donation, to the best of our knowledge, our study is the first to examine culture-tailored persuasive system design.

3   Design Science Research Project

With regard to blood donation, there are several calls on the need to design theory-based recruitment and retention interventions and to tailor them to different cultures, as there is a lack of effective practical solutions (e.g., [2,6]). We argue that the DSR approach [9] is particularly suited for addressing this challenge and answering our research question, since we target the blood donor management as a real-world problem by the iterative design and evaluation of a persuasive blood donation app in the specific context of potential blood donors in South Africa and Ghana. To increase the relevance of our research, we purposefully selected the two countries as our use cases because, with the majority of blood donors being white [18], South Africa represents the non-BAME communities, i.e., the individualist blood donation culture, whereas Ghana represents the BAME communities, i.e., the collectivist blood donation culture. This is consistent with Hofstede's classification based on the country scores on the "Individualism vs. Collectivism" dimension with South Africa scoring 65 (above 50) and Ghana 15 (below 50) on the dimension scale ranging from zero to 100 [12]. Increasing the rigor of our research, besides behavioural change models our design is grounded on, we include the PSD model for evaluating our design in terms of its persuasiveness. As shown in Fig. 2, our DSR project with three subsequent design cycles is based on the framework proposed by Kuechler and Vaishnavi [13]. As this study focuses on our last design cycle, in the following, we only summarise design cycle three. A detailed description of our first two design cycles including our research results is presented in [17].

We started our third design cycle with further reading on culture and persuasive system design theory in order to be able to evaluate if our proposed blood donation app design generally is persuasive and to better understand how different blood donation cultures might differ in their perceived persuasiveness. For the evaluation of our proposed design, we first mapped the design features of our blood donation app to the design principles of the PSD model. Subsequently, before evaluating the perceived persuasiveness of the different blood donation cultures with the help of our conceptual model developed in our second design cycle, we used the online survey of our first design cycle to determine if our blood donation app is also perceived as useful by potential end users from Africa and if it is also the tool of choice for them when competing with a website or chatbot

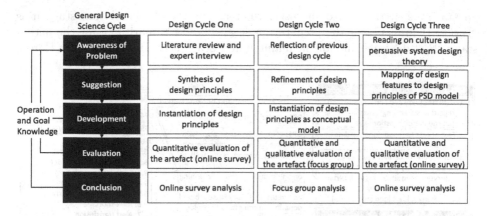

Operation and Goal Knowledge	General Design Science Cycle	Design Cycle One	Design Cycle Two	Design Cycle Three
	Awareness of Problem	Literature review and expert interview	Reflection of previous design cycle	Reading on culture and persuasive system design theory
	Suggestion	Synthesis of design principles	Refinement of design principles	Mapping of design features to design principles of PSD model
	Development	Instantiation of design principles	Instantiation of design principles as conceptual model	
	Evaluation	Quantitative evaluation of the artefact (online survey)	Quantitative and qualitative evaluation of the artefact (focus group)	Quantitative and qualitative evaluation of the artefact (online survey)
	Conclusion	Online survey analysis	Focus group analysis	Online survey analysis

Fig. 2. Design cycles with respective research activities (based on [17]).

as our app was originally designed for and evaluated with potential end users from Germany. Two snapshots of our conceptual user interfaces representing all of our blood donation app design features were added to the survey in order to evaluate the DFs' perceived persuasiveness of individualist (South Africa) compared to collectivist (Ghana) blood donation cultures, quantitatively by asking the potential African end users for their rating of each DF in order to prioritise them (similar to the evaluation in our second design cycle with the German focus group) and qualitatively by the comparison of the participants' statements on the usage potential of the app.

4   Persuasive Blood Donation App Design

In this section, we explain the mapping of our blood donation app design features to the design principles of the PSD model (see Fig. 1). Figure 3 shows all proposed design features (DF1 - DF15). As shown in Fig. 1, most of our DFs can be assigned to the Primary Task Support category promoting to keep focus on donating blood. In order not to lose this focus, our blood donation app **tailors the information to its particular user** through the integrated chatbot that, according to the user's determined stage of change, reacts appropriately with regard to its initiated exchange of expectations and experiences (DF6.9) as well as motivational (DF7.1) and awareness-raising approaches (DF7.2) engendered during its conversation with the user. In line with the proposal of Sardi et al. [26], the user's initial stage of change (one out of five according to the transtheoretical model) is determined by answering four questions when first registering and logging into the app. Based on the staging algorithm developed by Burditt et al. [2], users are asked 1) to assess their eligibility to donate blood, 2) to specify their past donations within last year as well as 3) to assess their willingness to donate blood within the next six months and 4) next month. Similarly to Sardi et al. [26], if the result depending on the respective answers is "precontemplation", no status is attributed to the user, whereas for the contemplation stage it is "Blood Beginner", for the preparation stage "Good Samaritan", for the action stage "Blood Ninja" and for the maintenance stage it is "Blood Donation Hero".

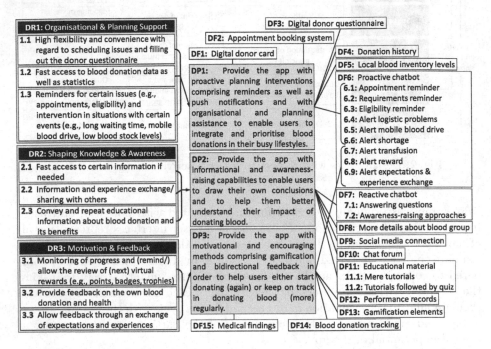

Fig. 3. Derivation of design principles and their mapping to design features [17].

During the use of the blood donation app the users can always look up their current status on the start page's progress bar and, by clicking on the corresponding icon, they receive a description of what the stage of change they are currently in means and why making further progress is worth it. Additionally, depending on the users' determined stage of change, the app provides appropriate educational material in the form of tutorials (DF11.1) and subsequent quizzes (DF11.2). Moreover, regardless of the stage of change, the users can look up information about their own blood group (DF8) at any time by clicking on their profile (e.g., compatibility of blood groups).

Furthermore, the app also **triggers the users along the way** by sending them push notifications with subsequent appointment setting options through reminding them when they are eligible to donate blood again (DF6.3), letting them know when there will be a mobile blood drive taking place in their immediate vicinity (DF6.5) and when their blood donation with their specific blood group is urgently needed due to low blood stock levels (DF6.6).

For focusing on donating blood, the app **makes it easier for users to handle everything related to blood donation**. With the donor card being integrated digitally (DF1), the card cannot be left behind as users usually have their smartphone with them at all times. Containing all the necessary data, after the scan of the donor card when entering the blood donation centre, the user is able to complete the blood donation process more quickly as all data has already been transferred with one click. It works similarly with the donor questionnaire to be filled in digitally (DF3) through the generation of a QR code that enables the blood service to read out the result immediately. The blood donation appointments can be arranged quickly and straightforwardly with the help of an integrated appointment booking system (DF2). Even when seeking for information about donating blood, the users do not need to call the blood service or search the internet as the chatbot answers all of their questions promptly (DF7.1) and fitting tutorials (DF11.1) further illustrate the content enabling the user to control their knowledge gain by taking part in subsequent quizzes (DF11.2). Additionally, the chatbot reminds users of their upcoming blood donation appointment (DF6.1), the requirements to be met (DF6.2), when they are eligible to donate blood again (DF6.3) and notifies where and when the donation centre can be visited and how long the stay will probably last (DF6.4), so that they do not need to think about all that by himself/herself. The chatbot's push notification about nearby mobile blood drives (DF6.5) enables the users to spontaneously donate blood in their vicinity and being notified about low blood stock levels (DF6.6) lets the users know that their blood donation is urgently needed and they can make a difference.

The app **enables the users to track their blood donations or blood donation status** by showing them where and when they have donated blood by now (DF4), which score, badges, trophies and rankings related to the amount of blood donations they have achieved so far (DF12) and, with the help of the progress bar, what kind of status (stage of change) they are currently in (DF13).

Moreover, the app **enables the users to observe the interplay of cause and effect in terms of donating blood** by displaying the local blood stock levels, which are high when people come and donate and low when they do not (DF5), by showing videos with stories of patients in need of blood who survived due to blood donations of other people (DF11.1) and by the chatbot casually telling the user during their conversation, for example, that they can save up to three lives with their blood donation (DF7.2). Additionally, the chatbot immediately notifies the user as soon as his/her donation has been transfused to a patient (DF6.7). The latter can also be observed by the user him-/herself through the tracking of the path of the own donation from the blood collection, processing, testing and storage to the blood transfusion (DF14).

The app **offers the user personalised content and services** through the blood donation app design features mentioned before (i.e., DF1, DF4, DF6, DF7, DF8, DF11, DF12, DF13, DF14) as well as through the app's connection to the users' social media channels (DF9) allowing users to post their blood donation appointment, performance records and/or blood journey (i.e., the path of the own blood donation) in order to, for example, make others aware of donating blood and through the insight into the users' vital parameters measured directly before tehir blood donation was made as well as into the users' results of the blood tested afterwards (DF15).

Additionally, in a simulating way, the blood donation app **enables the user to go through all the steps involved in the blood donation process** by the chatbot offering a virtual 3D tour explaining how the whole process works if the users ask for (DF7.1) as well as by clicking on the relevant tutorials illustrating every single step of the process (DF11.1).

The app also provides dialogue support by interacting with the users and giving them feedback with regard to their blood donation behaviour. For this purpose, with the help of the chatbot, the app **suggests the users to set up an appointment for donating blood** after being reminded when they are eligible to give blood again (DF6.3) as well as after being notified that there will be a mobile blood drive in the immediate vicinity (DF6.5) and that the users' blood donation is urgently needed (DF6.6). Additionally, at random during the conversation with the users, the chatbot suggests appointment booking when it makes the users aware of their impact of donating blood (DF7.2). With the help of the chatbot (DF7.1) and the tutorials (DF11.1), the app **suggests the user to fulfil all relevant pre- and post-donation criteria** such as general requirements in terms of weight and age as well as specifics like the recommendation to eat iron-rich food and not to do any strenuous physical exercises.

The app also **praises the users whenever they donates blood** via push notifications of the chatbot as soon as their blood donation has been transfused (DF6.7) and in line with that as soon as they have achieved a new score, badge, trophy or ranking (DF6.8) as part of their performance records (DF12). Via push notifications of the chatbot, the app **reminds the users of donating blood**. This includes the users' reminder of their upcoming appointment (DF6.1), of the requirements to be met in preparation for their appointment (DF6.2) as well as of tehir eligibility to donate blood again (DF6.3). As another form of feedback, the app **rewards users for donating blood** by virtually providing points, badges, trophies and rankings (DF12). Moreover, the app **imitates the users** with the help of the chatbot being human-like (DF6, DF7) and due to that **embodies a social role for the user** in the form of a companion that provides stage-matched guidance and feedback to the users supporting them to either start donating (again) or keep on track in donating blood (more) regularly. The PSD technique "Liking" meaning that the app should have a look and feel appealing to the user is not represented by our blood donation app design features, because similar to the techniques of the System Credibility category, this technique is rather abstract with regard to blood donor behaviour change.

Besides primary task support and dialogue support, our blood donation app also provides social support through social influences with regard to donating blood. This means that the app **enables the users to compare their own blood donor behaviour** to that of other users by looking at the profiles of the users in the chat forum showing their total amount of blood donations to date as well as the blood donation status they are currently in (DF10). In the chat forum, the users can also share and compare information related to their blood donor behaviour via instant messaging. Here as well as in other connected social media channels, the users can post their achieved points, badges, trophies and rankings (DF12) for comparison with other donors. Additionally, the leader boards showing the ranking of the users in terms of the app's integrated challenge of earning the most points for donating blood (DF13) enable the users to compare their own blood donor behaviour to that of other users.

The app **makes the users feel norms** by having the leader boards not only at individual but also at team level (DF13), which leverages the users' feeling of peer pressure. The latter can also happen in the chat forum (DF10), where people with the same goal of donating blood for saving lives come together and share their thoughts. Feeling norms can also be evoked during a user's conversation with the chatbot casually telling the users, e.g., how many lives they can save with their blood donation (DF7.2) and when watching tutorials showing, e.g., mass casualty incidents with people in need of blood (DF11.1). In addition, the blood donation app **enables the users to observe other users donating blood and see their outcomes** by looking at the users' profiles in the chat forum showing respective blood donor statistics (DF10) as well as at the leader boards displaying the different rankings of the users (DF13). As another form of social support, the app **enables users to be recognised publicly for donating blood** through the connection to the users' social media channels (DF9), where they can share their appointment, performance records and/or blood journey (i.e., the path of the own blood donation). Furthermore, the app **enables the user to cooperate with other users** by taking part in the app's integrated challenge of earning the most points for donating blood at team level (DF13). Besides that, the blood donation app **enables users to discern other users donating blood along with them** by looking at the users being active in the chat forum (DF10), at the leader boards showing the rankings of other users (DF13) as well as at the map integrated in the appointment booking system that, apart from the users' own blood donation footprint, also shows that of a blood donor friend to the user (DF2). Additionally, the app **enables the user to compete with other users** by taking part in the app's integrated challenge of earning the most points for donating blood at individual as well as team level (DF13).

5   Cultural Influences on Perceived Blood Donation App Persuasiveness

As described in Sect. 3, our online survey to evaluate the perceived blood donation app persuasiveness of individualist (South Africa) compared to collectivist (Ghana) blood donation cultures was based on the online survey of our first design cycle for the determination of the app's perceived usefulness as well as selection as tool of choice competing with a website or chatbot from the perspective of potential African end users due to the app's original design for and evaluation with potential German end users. With this, we first wanted to find out whether our blood donation app design is generally transferable to other countries, as what seems to be useful for Germans may not necessarily apply to Africans. We asked the African participants to evaluate the importance of each DF on a rating scale ranging from 1 (not important) to 5 (very important). We took a similar approach to the evaluation in our second design cycle with the German focus group, with the difference that in the survey format it was not possible to show our clickable app prototype developed with the platform Marvel [16] to our participants, why we included two snapshots instead. After our eight closed-ended questions about the respondent's demographics and characteristics, the online survey consisted of two main parts: 1) ten fictional blood donation scenarios representing our identified requirements (e.g., booking a blood donation appointment), for which our respondents had to choose one out of three alternatives, i.e., website, chatbot or app, that meets the presented requirement best and 2) questions divided into five categories referring to the two snapshots of our conceptual user interfaces representing all of our blood donation app design features, for which we asked our participants to assess the persuasiveness of each of them separately and to make statements about the usage potential of the app in general. In line with Fig. 3, the categories have been: 1) push notifications of the chatbot (DF6), 2) organisational and planning support (DP1), 3) shaping knowledge and awareness (DP2), 4) motivation and feedback (DP3) and 5) usage potential of the app.

Our survey was designed as a structured, self-administered questionnaire with the tool Unipark and was available online for participation within one week (South Africa) and three weeks (Ghana) respectively, after we had conducted pretests with our research project partners from the Western Cape Blood Service (WCBS) in South Africa, the South African National Blood Service (SANBS) and the National Blood Service Ghana (NBSG) to test the framing and timing for data collection. Even though in South Africa donating blood is allowed from the age of 16 and in Ghana from 17, for comparability with our study conducted with potential blood donors from Germany, we recruited participants who were at least 18 years old. From 4 January 2023 to 11 January 2023, with the help of the platform Clickworker [3], we randomly recruited participants from South Africa, which resulted in 434 complete responses. In total, we received 228 complete responses from our Ghanaian participants, of which 174 were randomly recruited between 4 January 2023 and 25 January 2023 by Clickworker and 54 between 11 January 2023 and 25 January 2023 by NBSG via their different social media channels and blood donation sessions. Table 1 displays the statistics of our respondents from South Africa and Ghana.

The online survey revealed that for our participants from South Africa in eight out of ten and from Ghana in seven out of ten scenarios the app was chosen as the most preferred tool, in line with our previous research for Germany [17]. Among the Ghanaians, for one scenario the chatbot was the most preferred tool - probably because they rather want to use follow-up questions to ask for the address of the blood donation centre, its opening ours as well as parking facilities. The website was clearly not perceived as useful to them as it was for the German participants. The differences in perceived usefulness between the German and African participants are probably due to the fact that Africa has skipped the desktop era and predominantly came in touch with the internet via mobile devices such as smartphones, through which apps and chatbots are quickly and easily accessible [8]. In the future, more than half of the participants

Table 1. Characteristics of the respondents from South Africa and Ghana (in italics).

Variable	N = 434 *N = 228*	%	Variable	N = 434 *N = 228*	%	Variable	N = 434 *N = 228*	%
Gender			**Age (y)**			**Chatbot Used**		
female	289	66.59	18 to 25	100	23.04	yes	332	76.50
	52	*22.81*		*65*	*28.51*		*130*	*57.02*
male	143	32.95	26 to 29	94	21.61	no	102	23.50
	175	*76.75*		*48*	*21.05*		*98*	*42.98*
diverse	2	0.46	30 to 39	174	40.10	**Donor Group**		
	1	*0.44*		*83*	*36.40*	non-donors	137	31.57
Pref. Tool			40 to 49	47	10.83		*69*	*30.26*
website	79	18.20		*28*	*12.28*	first-time donors	85	19.59
	46	*20.18*	50 to 60	15	3.46		*77*	*33.77*
chatbot	109	25.12		*3*	*1.32*	lapsed donors	115	26.50
	67	*29.39*	≥ 61	4	0.92		*54*	*23.68*
app	246	56.68		*1*	*0.44*	regular donors	97	22.35
	115	*50.44*					*28*	*12.28*

from South Africa and Ghana would rather use an app (56.68% and 50.44%) than a website (18.20% and 20.18%).

The difference between South Africa as an individualist and Ghana as a collectivist blood donation culture is also reflected in Table 1, when looking at the different proportions of the four individual donor groups: non- (nd), first-time (fd), occasional and lapsed (ld) as well as regular donors (rd) [5,18]. Looking at the Ghanaian participants, it is not surprising that the proportion of the first-time donors is the highest, because as a collectivist blood donation culture, the Ghanaians donate blood out of reciprocity knowing exactly who they are donating their blood for, which is why they often donate blood only once in their lives. The distinction between the different types of donors is also crucial when figuring out how both blood donation cultures differ in their perceived persuasiveness of the blood donation app design features (see Table 2). Table 2 and Table 3 summarise the results for the five categories mentioned before. It can be seen that reminders (DF6.1 - DF6.3), especially eligibility reminders (DF6.3), are generally more important to the individualist than the collectivist blood donation culture. Note that with only 28 participants the regular donors from Ghana represent a smaller sample size compared to the other donor groups (see Table 1). The fact that reminders are perceived as more persuasive by the individualist compared to the collectivist blood donation culture is also reflected in the survey participants' statements on the app's usage potential (see Table 3). In our fifth category of the survey, we asked our participants why or why not they could imagine the app supporting potential blood donors to increase their willingness to donate blood or to positively change their blood donation behaviour in the long term. Whenever the statement was specific by addressing individual design features, we assigned it to one or more appropriate PSD techniques. As shown in Table 3, while almost 50% of all South African respondents' statements belonging to the Dialogue Support category can be attributed to the fact that for the respective participants reminders are perceived as most persuasive, this was only the case for ca. 30% of all Ghanaian respondents' statements. Within this category, the social role embodied by the chatbot is almost as important to the Ghanaian participants as the reminders, whereas for the South African respondents it is hardly perceived as persuasive. Another social feature within this category that is more important to the participants from Ghana than from South Africa is the suggestion provided by the chatbot or the tutorials. Conversely, the rewards as a further personal feature in addition to the reminders are perceived as more persuasive by the South African compared to the Ghanaian respondents. The participants from South Africa, in contrast to those from Ghana, rated watching tutorials followed by quizzes to increase their score within their performance records (DF11.2) slightly better than watching mere tutorials (DF11.1). Additionally, the rating as part of DP1 shows that the appointment booking system (DF2) as well as the digital donor questionnaire (DF3) are perceived as more persuasive by the South African than the Ghanaian respondents - presumably because it is more important to them to reduce the waiting time on site in order to use the time saved for other important tasks to be accomplished. This is in line with Table 3, when comparing the proportion of the South African respondents' statements belonging to the Primary Task Support category that are assigned to the PSD technique "Reduction" to that from the Ghanaian participants' statements. While the blood donation trigger along the way ("Tunneling") is another personal feature within this category that is perceived as more persuasive by the South African compared to the Ghanaian respondents, it is the other way round for the tracking of the own blood donations or blood donation status ("Self-monitoring"). The latter can also be seen as a social feature in this context, because when looking more closely at the individual statements of the participants from Ghana, the statements reveal that they do not track their donations or status for themselves, but they track their loyalty to their community by looking up the numbers to see how many lives they have saved. Within the Primary Task Support category, for both, South African and Ghanaian participants, most statements were assigned to the PSD techniques "Tailoring" and "Simulation", which are perceived as equally persuasive in both blood donation cultures. For the Social Support category, "Normative Influence" was the technique most statements from the respondents of both countries were assigned to, with the difference that for the Ghanaian respondents, with a proportion of about 20% more assigned statements, this social feature is perceived as more persuasive than for the participants from South Africa. This is consistent with the rating as part of DP2 in Table 2, as the respondents from Ghana with more experience in donating blood (ld and rd) rated the chat forum (DF10) for the exchange of thoughts, opinions and experiences as more important than those with experience from South Africa. In addition, the rating as part of DP3 shows that gamification elements (DF13) such as blood donation quizzes to compete with other users are perceived as more persuasive by South African compared to Ghanaian respondents. Overall, the results of Table 2 and Table 3 revealed that for both, South Africa as an individualist as well as Ghana as a collectivist blood donation culture, personal as well as social features are important, whereby for the former personal features (Reminders, Rewards, Tunneling, Reduction, Competition) and for the latter social features (Suggestion, Social role, Self-monitoring (in the sense of group loyalty), Normative influence) predominate in their perceived persuasiveness.

Table 2. Rating of the blood donation app design features.

DF	South Africa (SA)					Ghana (GH)				
	Mean	nd	fd	ld	rd	Mean	nd	fd	ld	rd
6.1	4,36	4,26	4,36	4,31	4,46	4,20	4,01	4,19	4,17	4,40
6.2	4,31	4,36	4,42	4,17	4,23	4,34	4,28	4,25	4,41	4,30
6.3	4,18	4,03	4,18	4,28	4,29	4,07	3,85	4,05	4,00	4,40
6.4	4,36	4,31	4,39	4,38	4,35	4,31	4,20	4,26	4,10	4,55
6.5	4,13	3,93	4,29	4,24	4,21	4,22	3,97	4,20	4,14	4,40
6.6	4,10	3,93	4,18	4,03	4,24	4,01	3,82	3,96	4,00	4,55
1	4,15	4,15	4,08	4,11	4,23	4,10	3,97	3,99	4,17	4,40
2	4,44	4,36	4,42	4,38	4,51	4,24	4,16	4,13	4,24	4,70
3	4,36	4,34	4,25	4,44	4,46	4,19	4,13	4,10	4,31	4,35
4	4,14	4,15	4,17	3,95	4,26	4,20	4,06	4,13	4,25	4,63
5	3,84	3,77	3,98	3,61	3,91	3,86	3,64	3,88	3,93	3,95
6	4,17	4,09	4,21	4,06	4,30	4,22	4,01	4,14	4,32	4,45
7.1	4,31	4,30	4,33	4,17	4,39	4,22	4,17	4,05	4,28	4,60
7.2	3,79	3,71	3,98	3,64	3,84	3,93	3,91	3,92	3,48	4,25
8	4,33	4,36	4,42	4,27	4,30	4,42	4,36	4,34	4,45	4,45
9	3,18	3,12	3,39	2,94	3,18	3,26	2,94	3,54	3,10	3,50
10	3,43	3,38	3,74	3,02	3,45	3,56	3,27	3,57	3,69	4,00
11.1	3,9	3,89	3,96	3,61	3,88	4,09	3,91	4,09	4,14	4,40
11.2	3,91	3,82	3,98	3,72	4,01	3,96	3,79	4,05	3,97	4,30
6.7	4,29	4,25	4,27	4,20	4,37	4,29	4,25	4,23	4,07	4,50
6.8	3,96	3,82	4,01	3,91	4,05	4,06	3,94	4,03	3,83	4,35
6.9	4,12	4,10	4,19	3,80	4,22	3,95	3,88	3,82	4,00	4,25
12	4,08	3,85	4,24	4,14	4,24	4,11	4,03	4,01	3,93	4,40
13	3,93	3,85	4,00	3,79	3,96	3,87	3,79	3,83	3,55	4,15
14	4,17	4,06	4,32	4,03	4,29	4,20	4,15	4,13	4,07	4,20
15	4,40	4,34	4,44	4,38	4,49	4,40	4,39	4,27	4,52	4,45

Table 3. Assignment of the survey participants' statements.

Dialoque Support	N = 80 (SA)	%	N = 36 (GH)	%
Suggestion	7	8.75	5	13.89
Praise	7	8.75	4	11.11
Liking	1	1.25	0	0.00
Reminders	37	46.25	12	33.33
Rewards	21	26.25	4	11.11
Similarity	1	1.25	0	0.00
Social role	6	7.50	11	30.56
Primary Task Support	N = 186 (SA)	%	N = 71 (GH)	%
Tailoring	74	39.78	29	40.85
Tunneling	21	11.29	4	5.63
Reduction	25	13.44	7	9.86
Self-monitoring	7	3.76	8	11.27
Simulation	37	19.89	13	18.31
Personalisation	19	10.22	8	11.27
Rehearsal	3	1.61	2	2.82
Social Support	N = 72 (SA)	%	N = 42 (GH)	%
Social comp	2	2.78	0	0.00
Norm. influence	49	68.06	38	90.48
Social learning	5	6.94	3	7.14
Recognition	5	1.39	0	0.00
Cooperation	1	2.78	0	0.00
Social facil	4	5.56	0	0.00
Competition	6	8.33	1	2.38

6   Conclusion and Outlook

In this work, we have performed a design science study on blood donation apps with the focus on the two African countries South Africa and Ghana. As the main results with relation to Tables 2 and 3 we concluded that for both countries personal and social features are important for the design. With South Africa having a more individualist blood donation culture, personal features like reminders or rewards are even more important, while for Ghana with a collectivist blood donation culture social features, e.g., suggestion or social role, dominate.

From our findings we can conclude that having knowledge of the cultural differences will help researchers, designers and developers create better and more effective blood donation apps tailored to the two types of blood donation culture. We recommend that, while personal and social persuasive features can be implemented to motivate blood donor behaviour change in individualist and collectivist blood donation cultures, personal persuasive features should be given priority in individualist cultures and social persuasive features should be given priority in collectivist cultures.

We also want to report a few limitations of our work. It was difficult to get equal/balanced sample sizes for the two cultures as we were working with two different countries. The individualist group (n = 434) had a significantly larger sample size than the collectivist group (n = 228). Within the survey, we could not implement a clickable demonstrator, but could only display snapshots. We therefore aim to perform another evaluation with a prototype in the following design cycle. Lastly, our culture-specific findings were based on participants whose countries of origin and residence are South Africa and Ghana. As such, our findings might not generalise to other individualist and collectivist cultures. Hence, there is a need to conduct similar studies in other individualist and collectivist cultures as well in the future to test the generalisability of our findings.

As future work, we work towards the implementation of a prototype and aim for an evaluation of the final design, also including aspects like user experience in a real-life setting. Based on our findings, the prototype for Ghana will be developed as a "Digital Companion" to account for the importance of "Social Role". Like a companion, the included chatbot can provide stage-matched guidance and feedback to the user to promote the developmental process of the user's blood donor career. We aim to extent the existing chatbot as part of the app to allow for actively contacting donors, reminding them about appointments and informing them about current demand, for example. To further support the overall challenge of donor management, we will develop and integrate appointment planning services into the app, potentially making the use of operations research methods for appointment planning as well.

References

1. Bontempo, R., Rivero, J.: Cultural variation in cognition: the role of self-concept and the attitude-behavior link. In: Meeting of the American Academy of Management, Las Vegas, Nevada (1990)
2. Burditt, C., Robbins, M., Paiva, A., Velicer, W., Koblin, B., Kessler, D.: Motivation for blood donation among African Americans: developing measures for stage of change, decisional balance, and self-efficacy constructs. J. Behav. Med. 32(5), 429–442 (2009)
3. Clickworker Homepage. https://www.clickworker.de/umfragen/. Accessed 10 Jan 2023

4. Dei-Adomakoh, Y., Asamoah-Akuoko, L., Appiah, B., Yawson, A., Olayemi, E.: Safe blood supply in sub-Saharan Africa: challenges and opportunities. Lancet Haematol. **8**(10), 770–776 (2021)
5. Ferguson, E., Bibby, P.: Predicting future blood donor returns: past behavior, intentions, and observer effects. Health Psychol. **21**(5), 513–518 (2002)
6. Ferguson, E., et al.: Blood donor behaviour, motivations and the need for a systematic cross-cultural perspective: the example of moral outrage and health- and non-health-based philanthropy across seven countries. ISBT Sci. Ser. **13**(4), 375–383 (2018)
7. Fogg, B.: Persuasive computers: perspectives and research directions. In: Proceedings of the SIGCHI Conference on Human Factors in Computing Systems, Los Angeles, USA, pp. 225–232 (1998)
8. Gilbert, P.: SA smartphone numbers jump, but fixed broadband subs drop. Connecting Africa (ed.). https://www.connectingafrica.com/author.asp?section_id=761&doc_id=761473. Accessed 10 Jan 2023
9. Hevner, A., March, S., Park, J., Ram, S.: Design science in information systems research. MIS Q. **28**(1), 75–105 (2004)
10. Hofstede, G.: Culture's Consequences: International Differences in Work-Related Values. Sage, Beverly Hills (1980)
11. Hofstede, G.: Dimensionalizing cultures: the Hofstede model in context. Online Read. Psychol. Cult. **2**(1), 1–26 (2011)
12. Hofstede Insights Homepage. https://www.hofstede-insights.com/country-comparison/ghana,south-africa/. Accessed 10 Jan 2023
13. Kuechler, W., Vaishnavi, V.: On theory development in design science research: anatomy of a research project. Eur. J. Inf. Syst. **17**(5), 489–504 (2008)
14. Ma, L., Tunney, R., Ferguson, E.: Does gratitude enhance prosociality?: a meta-analytic review. Psychol. Bull. **143**(6), 601–635 (2017)
15. Marcus, A., Gould, E.: Crosscurrents: cultural dimensions and global web user-interface design. ACM Interact. **7**(4), 32–46 (2000)
16. Marvel Homepage. https://marvelapp.com/. Accessed 10 Jan 2023
17. Mueller, H., Reuter-Oppermann, M.: A design science approach to blood donation apps. In: Drechsler, A., Gerber, A., Hevner, A. (eds.) DESRIST 2022. LNCS, vol. 13229, pp. 221–232. Springer, Cham (2022). https://doi.org/10.1007/978-3-031-06516-3_17
18. Muthivhi, T., et al.: Motivators and deterrents to blood donation among Black South Africans: a qualitative analysis of focus group data. Transfus. Med. **25**(4), 249–258 (2015)
19. Oinas-Kukkonen, H., Harjumaa, M.: Persuasive systems design: key issues, process model, and system features. Commun. Assoc. Inf. Syst. **24**(28), 485–500 (2009)
20. Oinas-Kukkonen, H.: Behavior change support systems: the next frontier for web science. In: Web Science Conference, Raleigh, USA (2010)
21. Oyibo, K.: Investigating the key persuasive features for fitness app design and extending the persuasive system design model: a qualitative approach. In: Proceedings of the International Symposium on Human Factors and Ergonomics in Health Care, pp. 47–53 (2021)
22. Oyibo, K., Vassileva, J.: Investigation of the moderating effect of culture on users' susceptibility to persuasive features in fitness applications. Information **10**(11), 1–21 (2019)
23. Reinecke, K., Bernstein, A.: Knowing what a user likes: a design science approach to interfaces that adapt to culture. MIS Q. **37**(2), 427–453 (2013)

24. SANBS Homepage. https://sanbs.org.za/. Accessed 10 Jan 2023
25. SANBS Statement (2020). https://sanbs.org.za/wp-content/uploads/2016/09/PARTNER-WITH-THE-SANBS-TO-GIVE-HEALTH-AND-HOPE-TO-SOUTH-AFRICA_FINAL.pdf
26. Sardi, L., Kharbouch, M., Rachad, T., Idri, A., de Gea, J.M.C., Fernández-Alemán, J.L.: Blood4Life: a mobile solution to recruit and retain blood donors through gamification and trans-theoretical model. In: Rocha, Á., Adeli, H., Reis, L.P., Costanzo, S. (eds.) WorldCIST'19 2019. AISC, vol. 932, pp. 3–12. Springer, Cham (2019). https://doi.org/10.1007/978-3-030-16187-3_1
27. Simons, H., Morreale, J., Gronbeck, B.: Persuasion in Society. Sage Publications, Thousand Oaks, London, New Delhi (2001)
28. Vermeulen, M., et al.: Assessment of HIV transfusion transmission risk in South Africa: a 10-year analysis following implementation of individual donation nucleic acid amplification technology testing and donor demographics eligibility changes. Transfusion 59(1), 267–276 (2019)

Innovation and Entrepreneurship

Introduction to the Innovation and Entrepreneurship Track

Christoph Seckler[1] and Georges Romme[2]

[1] ESCP Business School, Berlin, Germany
cseckler@escp.eu
[2] Eindhoven University of Technology, The Netherlands
a.g.l.romme@tue.nl

Abstract. Design science has gained significant traction in the fields of innovation and entrepreneurship. The Innovation and Entrepreneurship track offers an excellent platform for scholars to exchange ideas, discuss future research directions, provide mutual support, generate innovative research ideas, and cultivate professional relationships with peers across various career stages. The accepted papers in this track address diverse challenges related to Society 5.0 in a rigorous manner. These papers add significant value to the existing body of design knowledge, demonstrating highly interesting applications of design science across various levels of analysis and offering various practical insights.

Keywords: Design science · Innovation · Entrepreneurship

1 Introduction

Design science (DS) is gaining momentum in the domains of innovation management and entrepreneurship. A growing number of scholars publish their DS work in top-tier journals (e.g., Berglund et al. 2020; Dimov 2022; Romme and Holmström 2023; Seckler et al. 2021). The *Journal of Business Venturing* initiated a pioneering platform solely dedicated to design and design science, which is known as the *Journal of Business Venturing Design* (Berglund 2021). A recent editorial in *Entrepreneurship Theory and Practice* paves the way for more design science work (Dimov et al. 2022). And *Technovation* appointed a dedicated area editor for DS submissions (Romme and Holmström 2023).

Against this backdrop, the Innovation and Entrepreneurship Track at DESRIST 2023 offers a unique opportunity for scholars in this field to exchange ideas on design science, discuss future research directions, develop novel research ideas, and build relationships with peers at all career stages. The track received a large number of submissions, with four full papers accepted for publication in the proceedings.

The four accepted papers represent excellent examples of outlining clear and strong contributions to the body of design knowledge, being positioned within relevant literature, drawing on the best available background knowledge, and using appropriate methods (Seckler et al. 2021). They tackle various challenges related to Society 5.0 with scientific rigor; they focus on data product design (Hasan and Legner 2023), business models for sustainability (Gebhardt and Hölzle 2023), funding of deeptech food startups (Nacke and Seckler 2023), and design principles for national innovation agencies in social market economies (Lehmann and Salenius 2023).

Taken together, the DESRIST 2023 Innovation and Entrepreneurship Track includes high-quality design science projects on prevailing challenges in the innovation management and entrepreneurship domains. The included submissions make a strong contribution to the body of design knowledge, showcase how to publish design science work on different levels of analysis, and provide significant practical value.

References

Berglund, H.: Entrepreneurship as design and design science. J. Bus. Ventur. Des. **1**(1), 100012 (2021)

Berglund, H., Bousfiha, M., Mansoori, Y.: Opportunities as artifacts and entrepreneurship as design. Acad. Manag. Rev. **45**(4), 825–846 (2020)

Dimov, D., Maula, M., Romme, A.G.L.: Crafting and assessing design science research for entrepreneurship. Entrepreneurship Theory Pract. (2022, forthcoming) https://doi.org/10.1177/10422587221128271

Gebhardt, L., Hölzle, K.: Scaling Sustainable Entrepreneurship for Impact: Design Knowledge for the Use of Digital Technologies. LNCS (2023)

Hasan, M.R., Legner, C.: Data Product Canvas - A Visual Inquiry Tool Supporting Data Product Design. LNCS (2023)

Lehmann, D.M., Salenius, V.M.: Design Principles for National Innovation Agencies in Social Market Economies. LNCS (2023)

Nacke, R., Seckler, C.: How to Invest in the Future of Food: An Exploration Design Science Project. LNCS (2023)

Romme, A.G.L., Holmström, J.: From theories to tools: calling for research on technological innovation informed by design science. Technovation **121**, 102692 (2023)

Seckler, C., Mauer, R., vom Brocke, J.: Design science in entrepreneurship: conceptual foundations and guiding principles. J. Bus. Ventur. Des. **1**(1), 1–12 (2021)

Scaling Sustainable Entrepreneurship for Impact: Design Knowledge for the Use of Digital Technologies

Leonhard Gebhardt[1,2](✉) and Katharina Hölzle[3,4]

[1] ICN Business School, CEREFIGE, University of Lorraine, Rue Baron Louis 3-25, 54000 Nancy, France
leonhard.gebhardt@icn-artem.com
[2] University of Potsdam, August-Bebel-Straße 89, 14482 Potsdam, Germany
[3] Institute for Human Factors and Technology Management, University of Stuttgart, Allmandring 35, 70569 Stuttgart, Germany
[4] Fraunhofer Institute for Industrial Engineering, Nobelstraße 12, 70569 Stuttgart, Germany
katharina.hoelzle@iao.fraunhofer.de

Abstract. Digital transformation helps organisations become more efficient while increasing their outreach and targeting new markets. However, it also makes the organisational design more malleable and can blur or even disrupt a firm's boundaries. For sustainable entrepreneurs who develop business models for sustainability (BMfS), this is a Faustian bargain, as they trade independence for more potential. In this in-depth case based on action and design science research, we accompanied and evaluated the design of a BMfS with digital technologies. To evaluate for rising tensions, we looked at the relevant dynamics within the entrepreneurial firm and the digital business ecosystem. Besides a proposed solution model and its evaluation, we present design principles of contingency, re-configuration, and alliancing. This nascent design knowledge explains dynamics that occur when developing business models with digital technologies.

Keywords: Sustainable Entrepreneurship · Business Models for Sustainability · Digital Business Ecosystems

1 Introduction

Digital technologies promise to be key to unleashing business models' potential [1, 2]. However, implementing digital technologies and digitally transforming an organisation to become part of Society 5.0, in which physical and cyber-physical space are increasingly merged [3], risks firms' individual sovereignty. The introduced digitalisation becomes a constant, as the organisation is increasingly embedded in a digital business ecosystem [4]. Given that digital transformation makes organisational designs more malleable and blurs or even disrupts a firm's boundaries [5, 6], it is not yet fully understood how best to balance an increasing external influence while preserving an individual firm's sovereignty.

A. Gerber and R. Baskerville (Eds.): DESRIST 2023, LNCS 13873, pp. 177–190, 2023.
https://doi.org/10.1007/978-3-031-32808-4_11

Trading sovereignty to unleash business model potential might come as a Faustian bargain, particularly for sustainable entrepreneurs. These entrepreneurs develop Business Models for Sustainability (BMfS), adapting sustainability innovations to create value for a diverse set of stakeholders in order to transform markets and society [7, 8] in the direction of sustainable development [9]. Deploying digital technologies enables niche business models to gain a broader audience and challenge existing market structures and incumbents [10]. However, this can also raise tensions between digital and sustainability logics [11], especially in BMfS. In addition, the sustainability commitments of other stakeholders can create a lock-in effect for sustainable entrepreneurs [10], making it even harder for them to scale for impact.

While a plethora of research exists on embedding digital technologies in organizations, it has often failed to critically reflect on the negative consequences [12]. Literature on the development of BMfS using digital technologies is scarce. To get a comprehensive picture, not only the first-order features of digital technologies are relevant, but also the second-order consequences: the embeddedness of organisational design within the digital business ecosystem that comes with utilising digital technologies. In this study, we investigate how sustainable entrepreneurs employ digital technologies in their business model with a design science research. We aim to present design knowledge useful for embedding digital technology in BMfS. Our research question is the following: *How can sustainable entrepreneurs (successfully) embed digital technologies in BMfS without compromising their sustainability value logics?*

To outline the related problem space, we define the application context as the development of BMfS, and the goodness criteria as the stipulation that sustainable value logics remain intact while increasing the output of BMfS [13]. First, building on the theory as well as practical needs, we identify promising digital technologies to overcome the lock-in situation and propose a possible solution model. For evaluation purposes, we document tensions that arise from their use as well as the dynamics at work in a digital business ecosystem. We further seek to highlight the acquired design knowledge that may prove useful when embedding digital technologies in BMfS. To that end, we provide design principles that can support sustainable entrepreneurs in reconciling the various dynamics involved.

We chose an approach that combines action research with design science research, enabling us to connect a relational paradigm—pursuing "worthwhile purposes, for the flourishing of persons, communities, and the ecology of which we are all a part" [14]—with forward-orientated, prescriptive features of design science research for entrepreneurship [15, 16]. To do so, we accompanied the development of a BMfS for a year and evaluated its outcomes within the overall digital business ecosystem. In the process, we gathered a diverse set of data from the firm and its involved stakeholders, including field notes, transcribed interviews, workshop proceedings, and supplementary information. We link our process study with the kernel theory of sustainable entrepreneurs developing BMfS [7] and outline the practical implications.

The tensions can be understood as relating to the transference of responsibilities within the firm and the increasing dependence on digital technology providers with distinct value-creation logics. As a solution, we encourage entrepreneurs to engage their evolving digital business ecosystem proactively.

2 Theoretical Background

2.1 Niche-BMfS Have Only Limited Impact

Concerned with societies' challenges, sustainable entrepreneurs pursue economic as well as environmental and social objectives in their businesses to positively influence their systemic environment and resolve existing sustainability issues with their products and services [17]. Business Models for Sustainability (BMfS) conceptualise business sustainability as "sustainable value creation with and for a broad range of stakeholders" [7], seeking a "creation of fit between strategy, organisation, innovations, and a firm's business environment" (p. 670).

Agents of fit, so to speak, are sustainable entrepreneurs who commercialise their innovations with their business models [7], effectively creating business cases by contextualising sustainability innovation. These are either anchored in market niches or diffused into the mass market, which translates to their respective impact on sustainable development [18]. However, niches can be adhesive. Such lock-in effects may be caused by *market barriers related to resistant users* [19] or *existing policies* [20]. Furthermore, some sustainable entrepreneurs hesitate to compromise their own and stakeholders' idealistic *sustainability commitments* or are simply afraid of being outspent in *R&D expenses* by incumbents [10].

2.2 Unleashing BMfS with Digital Technology Affects Value Logics

Indeed, digital technologies may be able to help remedy the niche lock-in effects. Building on a study of sustainable entrepreneurs using digital technologies [11], we identify the following potential: digital technologies can *enable an effective and efficient connection with customers* that could remedy the market barrier of resistant users by either identifying a broader audience or integrating complementary offerings into platforms. Furthermore, the increased *scalability can overcome existing policy restrictions,* e.g. by increasing geographical independence. Last but not least, the co-creative function of digital technologies *enables customers' participation in developing products and services* and could compensate for the lack of R&D funds.

However, aiming for scalability with digital technologies can still compromise the *sustainability commitments* of sustainable entrepreneurs or their existing stakeholders: digital technologies have properties that must be considered when embedding these technologies in business models. Digital technologies can be categorised as digital artefacts, digital platforms, and digital infrastructure, as "distinct but related elements" [1]. Their use renders organisational designs more malleable, with the consequence that organisational change becomes permanent [4]. It is their embedding in digital business ecosystems that pilots the continuous adaption of these organisational designs. These digital business ecosystems are defined as "sociotechnical network[s] of individuals, organisations and technologies" affecting a firm's value creation [21].

Consequently, embedding digital technologies to develop sustainable business models needs to be investigated on multiple levels, grounded on the observation that a technology's value creation and capture builds on a system of firm-level and ecosystem-level activities [22]. Technology's value creation and capture relate to both technology-applying firms and technology providers. Digital technologies, in particular, augment the implications of embedding, as "a large part of the technological set-up may lie outside the control of a particular firm" [4]. Thus, embedding digital technologies in BMfS is a question of organisational change concerning the firm, its boundaries, and environmental contingencies, i.e. stakeholder relationships [7].

2.3 A Design Science View of BMfS Development with Digital Technologies

Introducing market alternatives for institutional change, as sustainable entrepreneurs do, results in a paradoxical tension between expansion and the 'purity' of organisational logics that needs to be dynamically balanced [23]. Consequently, we aim to identify design knowledge that guides sustainable entrepreneurs in their attempt to increase impact when selecting and embedding digital technologies into their business models.

The use of design science in entrepreneurship combines usefulness with rigour [24]. We aim at identifying design object knowledge revealing ways to digitalise business models in sustainable entrepreneurship (usefulness), as their introduction bears certain risks as outlined above (design problem). We consider the entrepreneur and the organisation as a triad consisting of *individuals*—entrepreneurs—creating *artefacts* that are intended to unfold selected properties under certain *conditions* [15], i.e. keeping the sustainability value logics intact. Entrepreneurship as design is defined "as the purposive, gradual, and uncertainty-facing process of establishing a new venture [...] given environmental circumstances, which are themselves sometimes transformed as part of the process" [25]. Design science is suitable for investigating the issues and underlying reasons related to tensions (problem space) that occur when embedding digital technologies in BMfS by entrepreneurs—a real-world challenge [26]—as well as for delivering prescriptive knowledge on how to mitigate them (solution space) [27, 28].

Starting from the kernel theory of sustainable entrepreneurship and business model development, we investigate the entrepreneurial process of embedding digital technologies in BMfS to develop a design theory, i.e. design knowledge.

3   Research Method

Our process study applies a design science research (DSR) approach [13]. We chose this approach because its level of analysis is the triad of transforming business models by an entrepreneur in changing environments. Design science research "aims to generate prescriptive knowledge about the design of Information Systems (IS) artefacts, such as software, methods, models, or concepts" [29], to generate design knowledge in the form of artefacts, design principles, or design theories [13]. In our case, we generate design knowledge about the development of BMfS with digital technologies, i.e. a designed artefact as a solution model or, in other words, a conceptual model of representative value [30]. We also suggest design principles for scaling BMfS without losing the sovereignty to retain the firm's original sustainability value logic. Design principles have been described as "prescriptive statements that indicate how to do something to achieve a goal" [31].

With the design science research approach, our endeavour adds to the action design research genre in DSR [32, 33]. Through a publicly funded digital transformation project, we actively participated in an innovation process and accompanied in real-time the identification of suitable technologies for BMfS development over the course of one year. The entrepreneur contacted the research project staff for help selecting the digital technologies. Independent of the research project, we continuously accompanied the implementation of digital technologies by the sustainable entrepreneur for his BMfS, following and adapting the *framework for developing a business model development tool* [34]. Our approach allowed us to understand the process as "shaped by the temporal, spatial and historical context" and how "the lived experiences of entrepreneurs and [...] their interactions play out in context and place" [35]. As we do research with people, not on people [36], we treat entrepreneurs as co-investigators. Their actions and interactions generate the data we interpret further in our investigation. To remain at a distance for analytical purposes, the second author of the paper was not involved in the in-person fieldwork in order to allow critical reflection.

We collected our data using different techniques, including workshops, field visits, observations, and interviews. In the beginning, we applied the Business-Model-Canvas approach [37] to record the business model, select suitable technologies, and reflect on potential changes. Furthermore, in-person interactions from the workshops, interviews, and observations provided the data points from which to generate inferences (see Table 1, data types and data description). Building on our data points, a refined catalogue of measures pertaining to the implementation of digital technologies and the entrepreneurial ecosystem's activation was discussed, formulated, and iterated. With the further support of the involved digital business ecosystem stakeholders, we prototyped solutions and documented them with respect to existing tensions. The process and its outcomes were documented and analysed in MAXQDA 2020, a qualitative data analysis software featuring text as well as audio-visual coding and evaluations. We documented paper and electronic representations as indicators of the changing organisation and its BMfS, including images and contextual material [38].

To understand the problem space (needs) and delineate a solution model and, later, the design principles, our data analysis builds on the triangulation of experiences with theory [39]. We distinguished between qualitative results according to contextual, organisational, and entrepreneurial needs (problem space). We then coded our heterogeneous data set from scratch before we matched it with dimensions of sustainability value logic [40] to generate the relevant design knowledge (solution space). Similar to the process of axial coding, similarities within our categories that transcend given theoretical explanations enabled us to further elaborate on the theory of sustainability value logic concerning the digital transformation of BMfS. The subsequent evaluation indicated whether the prototyping with digital technologies created a "misfit" with the sustainability value logics that stem from the use of digital technologies.

Table 1. Description of Data.

Data Types	Amount and Location	Use in Analysis
Primary data		
Calls & Emails	Uncounted	Understanding situational needs
Observations	Half-day observations, incl. Routine sales at the store (3), field notes	Understanding situational and organisational needs
Workshops	Two workshops (via Zoom) about organisational needs and digital technologies	Developing a catalogue of digital technologies to be prototyped ("digital agenda"), reflecting on tensions and adding a capability perspective
Interviews	Two informal interviews (field notes) at the store and manufacturing plant	Contextual information
	Two interviews with verbatim transcription from audio recordings at the store and workshop (22 pages, 171 paragraphs)	
Web conferences with stakeholders	Three sets of field notes, incl. From the consultant and providers	Contextual information, e.g. about digital business ecosystem
Secondary data		
Online appearance	Webpage (virtual)	Follow-up on the potential of digital technologies

4 Results

4.1 Case Description and the Need for Solutions

Klein Lieblingsschuh GmbH is a case of a Business Model for Sustainability (BMfS). It "[a]dopt[s] a stewardship role" and "[e]ncourage[s] sufficiency" [41]. Its *stewardship* role is grounded in consumer care, ethical trade, and resource stewardship. The firm further educates its prospective consumers about the links between kids' shoe features and posture. All the shoes' materials are carefully selected for their sustainable origin and wearable comfort. In terms of sufficiency, the design and manufacturing respect the in-house orthopaedic knowledge gained from experience, education, and industrial design expertise to create lasting products.

Furthermore, a considerable role is played by the store, including production facilities that offer transparency about the production process. Shoes are also sold online. The value proposition that sets the firm apart is: offering kids' footwear that does not compromise growing up with a healthy posture. While professional education enables the sustainable entrepreneurs to adhere to the outlined sustainable value proposition, religious belief motivates them. Christian beliefs guide the entrepreneurial decision-making and actions.

While the belief system of the sustainable entrepreneurs initiated the sustainability value logic [40], emphasising a proposition that adopts a stewardship role by engaging with stakeholders and customers on the matter of health and well-being [41], the high degree of in-person involvement has inhibited the organisation's growth and impact. For example, we observed the entrepreneur to be highly involved in educating parents about why and how to use their shoes. Besides the theoretical aspects explained above, we identified the need to make the value creation process more independent of the entrepreneur, while at the same time not compromising on the sustainability value logics.

4.2 Solution Model to Identify Digital Technologies for BMfS

In Fig. 1, we summarise the identified needs based on theory and our practical findings. Furthermore, we added the potential for digital technology use (co-create, connect, scale-away). We assigned them to business model value dimensions.

First, in a workshop in October 2020 and meetings in February and March 2021, we pondered the option of developing a business model platform for used shoes, as kids grow out of shoes relatively fast. Enabling customers to sell shoes second-hand might strengthen the notion of a *value proposition* encouraging sufficiency. Besides a proposal from the design science researcher, the platform idea was also suggested by a customer, as noted in one of the observations in November 2020.

Second, we identified the increased use of social media as a potential avenue for the digital transformation of BMfS. Social media platforms have the potential to educate customers about the importance of choosing the right shoes for children's health, as well as to encourage sufficiency. Separating value creation from the entrepreneurs' involvement would give them more freedom for the design, production, and quality control of the manufactured shoes.

Third, we saw potential in integrating the existing software subsystems to reduce individual workload and help with scaling. An external sales platform with Enterprise Resource Planning (ERP) functionalities could help with integrating existing subsystems. Taking the company's size into account, we found the use of an independent ERP system not feasible. Instead, the adaption of an online sales platform (*value exchange*) with an adequate merchandise management system (*value capture*) was examined further.

4.3 Evaluation of the Solution Model: Observed Tensions

To evaluate our suggested solution model, we examined the embedding of digital technologies in BMfS. The interventions were evaluated with regard to the digital business ecosystem's involvement, situational turn-out, and organisational change, and scrutinised for potential value logic tensions. We identify tensions when implementing digital technologies contradicts sustainability logic principles and values [40]. Tensions arise when ventures attend to divergent goals, values, norms, and identities [42]. We evaluated the projection of a platform for used shoes, as it could develop the value proposition. In terms of value creation, the adoption of existing social media platforms was of interest to

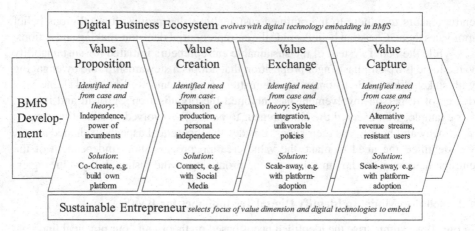

Fig. 1. Solution model for needs and potentials of digital technology use in BMfS.

increase the storytelling potential. We considered the adaption of e-commerce platforms, e.g. Shopify, for the purpose of value capture and exchange.

Adopting social media platforms to amplify value creation may backfire when in-person communication is eliminated. Hence, the tension affects the dimension of value exchange, and the sustainable entrepreneur stated accordingly: "we now have the advantage that people already know us. People are sympathetic, empathetically connected with us." The tension arises from a virtualization of value creation, in which not the content but the context is decisive. Instead of adopting a stewardship role and encouraging sufficiency person-to-person in the workshop's operating environment, a platform's adoption indeed offers only a virtual statement on the value creation. It might reduce the overall experience, although the potential to reach more people quantitatively, even to sell more in combination when drawing on paid services, is high. Besides the potential for growth, the subsequent need to involve investors with divergent logics to finance the project and account for their aspirations was perceived as alienating for the entrepreneur. Consequently, adopting social media platforms may serve as an extension of the company's value creation (education and stewardship), but it cannot serve as a substitution. Adding to the above-described tension of non-organic growth, the entrepreneur found paying platform providers for their ad services controversial, as it would inhibit him from using the money to renovate the workplace and develop the ecological aspects of his products.

Adopting an e-commerce platform for value exchange would entail switching from the current online-shop solution that cannot fully incorporate online sales logistics to a solution that would include payment services and stock management. To investigate the contextual effects of this promising option, the entrepreneur involved an e-commerce consultant that offered pro-bono advice. We ascertained that including digital technologies in the value exchange as envisioned might indeed compromise both the value capture and value exchange. The tensions we identified as inhibiting a wholesome integration are threefold: first, integrating a new solution would translate into sharing profits with the platform provider. Secondly, a wholesome integration could create a vendor lock-in effect associated with services based on cloud computing. While the first tension is self-explanatory, the second is non-trivial: the lock-in effect may carry substantial costs, legal constraints, or technical incompatibilities associated with a change of platforms [43]. A third downside of expanding digitalisation to the detriment of the firms' sovereignty is that relying on a new shop platform would immensely limit SEO activities and forego successful positioning in search engines.

Developing a new platform for used shoes would enable value to be co-created with the customers. It would indeed represent a value co-creation and not only a "co-exchange", as opening up a platform for high-quality shoes would allow platform participants to co-ideate, co-evaluate, co-design, co-test, and co-launch products [44]. Developing the firms' value capture this way would bring with it serious tensions involving the value proposition logics expressed early on by the entrepreneur. In addition, value co-creation with customers can inhibit the entrepreneur from controlling the quality of products offered or their fit with the value proposition, which emphasised high quality: it could endanger this deliberately chosen and proudly held proposition. While it might offer the potential to increase value capture, it would put the claim of guaranteeing the highest-possible product quality at risk. Thus, the aspect of supporting the sufficiency of the value proposition, which might be strengthened in building a platform for used shoes, would not play a role. As a second-degree consequence, creating such a platform could risk 'cannibalising' the incoming sales streams from the manufacturing business. In the following, we highlight the design principles for developing BMfS with digital technologies.

4.4 Design Principles for Artefact Development

To resolve the identified tensions, we infer design knowledge, i.e. design principles, that sustainable entrepreneurs need in order to mediate the tensions that can arise from applying certain technologies, as outlined in Table 2. In that vein, we offer useful, prescriptive advice on the selective use of digital technologies. With the first design principle of contingency, we address the match between the entrepreneur and the artefact to be designed. Secondly, the design principle of re-configuration aims at overcoming path dependency in artefact development. Third, the design principle of alliancing aims at closing or avoiding blind spots that cannot be remedied with the first two principles.

> Embed digital technologies in BMfS contingent on sustainable entrepreneurs' traits in order to amplify the entrepreneurs' thoughts and actions so that existing sustainability value logics are complemented but not jeopardised.

The successful implementation of digital technologies builds on their internal and external contingency. The re-contextualisation of a value proposition may be of complementary value but not sufficient for the substitution of in-person involvement. However, it raises the question regarding the extent to which the entrepreneur limits development of the BMfS. Protecting sustainability value logics while embedding digital technologies in a BMfS does not, however, mean that the value creation, exchange, and capture will remain unaltered, leading to the second design principle:

> Given the willingness to uncouple the sustainability value logics of the firm and the entrepreneur, assess the organisational and ecosystem-related consequences of digital technology use in BMfS in order to balance trade-offs and sustainable impact in the re-configuration of value logics.

Value logics that are not integral for keeping the sustainability value logics intact may be adapted. Mainly operational duties but also core activities can be delegated, e.g. educating consumers. We observed and reflected with the entrepreneur on the need to balance operational duties with organizational development. The third design principle addresses supporting entrepreneurs in delegation and development decisions:

> Increase transparency within the digital business ecosystem so that sustainable entrepreneurs can proactively curate their business model ecosystem by involving like-minded stakeholders in order to remain sovereign when embedding digital technologies into their business models.

Especially the partial outsourcing of value creation, enabled by digital technologies, requires a technological understanding and the capacity to identify a partner who can help implement the required digital solution. For a Society 5.0 characterised by increasing complexity, we identify the third design principle of alliancing as an important condition allowing entrepreneurs to make informed choices and anticipate effects on their business models' operational sovereignty.

Table 2. Integration of Problem and Solution Spaces.

Digital technology potential	Possible tensions	Design principles to resolve tensions
Connect: Virtualization of sustainable value proposition to increase personal independence and create persistence in stakeholder connections, e.g., with *Social media*	- Less personal exchanges, less customized advice (value creation-related tensions) - Resource use (value proposition and capture related tensions)	*Embed digital technologies in BMfS contingent on sustainable entrepreneurs' traits*
Scale-away: Removing barriers to the diffusion of sustainable innovation by finding new and effective forms of value exchange, e.g., by *adopting a platform*	- Margin-share (value capture-related tension) - System lock-in (value capture and creation-related tensions) - SEO-fallout	*Re-negotiate value logics in line with sustainability logics*
Co-create: Involve digital business ecosystem stakeholders in value creation processes, e.g., *building a platform*	- Lack of quality - insurance (value proposition-related tension) - Possible cannibalisation (value capture-related tension)	*Pro-actively curate a digital business ecosystem*

5 Discussion and Conclusion

Sustainable entrepreneurs can embed digital technologies in BMfS successfully without compromising sustainability value logics when they proactively reflect on their role, re-negotiate the status quo, and curate their digital business ecosystem. Like Wagner in Goethe's Faust, the ecosystem stakeholders' role can be to introduce debates or warnings as tensions arise from digital technologies when previously unconnected business model elements are linked [45], but also to provide encouragement [46]. Their involvement inhibits digital technologies from presenting a Faustian bargain, even if the entrepreneur lacks technological domain knowledge.

Regarding our first design principle, we confirm the findings of "imprinting" research that emphasise the role of founders' different self-concepts when making critical decisions in ventures [47]. In this case study, our founder's "missionary identity" is indispensable for selecting suitable digital technologies. As the entrepreneur stated, his personal beliefs are key in motivating his engagement in a firm that serves as a "platform" from which to pursue "particular causes, generally of a social or environmental nature" (p. 944). This "imprinting" effect entails the selective use of digital technologies and shapes external stakeholder engagement.

Regarding the second design principle, we found evidence for the impeding role of path dependencies and the threatening role of anticipated lock-in effects. This adds to BMfS research—which has found innovation with digital technologies to improve the given design elements [48]—the notion that design elements may be changed, i.e. reduced or even discarded, to keep sustainability value logics intact.

For the third and last design principle, we argue that sustainable entrepreneurs should proactively curate their ecosystems by engaging stakeholders in the process of selecting digital technologies. In so doing, they may cultivate alliances that can help them bridge knowledge gaps, implement technologies, and identify threats. We confirm the importance of engaging a wide array of stakeholders in the business ecosystem to increase a firm's likelihood of innovating its business [49]. Just as the initial partners have an impact on the evolving networks of ventures [50], the careful arrangement of the digital business ecosystem creates the path for digital transformation.

We infer from our solution model that the development of BMfS with digital technologies is dependent on internal and external contingencies and driven by the mechanisms of imprinting and digital business ecosystem involvement. Internally, the entrepreneur expresses his missionary identity in the organisation. Externally, the interaction with the digital business ecosystem ensures the embedding of the organisation. Hence, the firm's change is contingent on the entrepreneur's imprinting identity and the technology-related business ecosystem.

We see it as a strength of our study that we accompanied the digitalisation process in real time and were heavily involved in identifying the organisation's needs and suitable solutions. By applying a design science research approach, we aimed not only to generate general insights, but also to add value to our research partner in the analytical and implementation phases. Although we cannot generalise from our case, we have outlined design knowledge on how to mediate tensions with potentials. Further research could assess our principles in other contexts and across organisations, such as with more quantitative research designs. This would increase the confidence in the design knowledge

[13]. In this respect, prudence is crucial when implementing technologies with BMfS that might put their value logics at stake.

We encourage researchers to conceptually develop an imprinting perspective of the selective decision-making regarding digital technologies. We expect different digitalisation trajectories for BMfS development. Our study helps entrepreneurs to select digital technologies. It also should incentivise policy designers to foster collaborations in digitalisation-related activities in order to support sustainable entrepreneurs' ability to make use of digital technologies.

Acknowledgement. Our work received funding from the Senate Department for Economics, Energy and Public Enterprises Berlin (DIGITAL+, Masterplan Industriestadt Berlin 2018–2021) and the Commission for Research and Young Scientists (FNK), HTW Berlin. We thank Holger Lütters and Katharina Erdle for insightful collaboration in the workshops conducted to identify the business models' needs and potential digital solutions, as well as Tim Leipelt for his help with the data-analysing process.

References

1. Nambisan, S.: Digital entrepreneurship: toward a digital technology perspective of entrepreneurship. Entrep. Theory Pract. **41**, 1029–1055 (2017). https://doi.org/10.1111/etap.12254
2. von Briel, F., Davidsson, P., Recker, J.: Digital technologies as external enablers of new venture creation in the IT hardware sector. Entrep. Theory Pract. **42**, 47–69 (2018). https://doi.org/10.1177/1042258717732779
3. Deguchi, A., et al.: What is society 5.0? In: Society 5.0, pp. 1–23. Springer, Singapore (2020). https://doi.org/10.1007/978-981-15-2989-4_1
4. Hanelt, A., Bohnsack, R., Marz, D., Antunes Marante, C.: A systematic review of the literature on digital transformation: insights and implications for strategy and organizational change. J. Manage. Stud. **59** (2020). https://doi.org/10.1111/joms.12639
5. Burgelman, R.A., Grove, A.S.: Cross-boundary disruptors: powerful interindustry entrepreneurial change agents. Strateg. Entrep. J. **1**, 315–327 (2007). https://doi.org/10.1002/sej.27
6. El Sawy, O.A., Malhotra, A., Park, Y., Pavlou, P.A.: Research commentary—seeking the configurations of digital ecodynamics: it takes three to tango. Inf. Syst. Res. **21**, 835–848 (2010). https://doi.org/10.1287/isre.1100.0326
7. Lüdeke-Freund, F.: Sustainable entrepreneurship, innovation, and business models: integrative framework and propositions for future research. Bus Strat Env **29**, 665–681 (2020). https://doi.org/10.1002/bse.2396
8. Schaltegger, S., Lüdeke-Freund, F., Hansen, E.G.: Business models for sustainability. Organ. Environ. **29**, 264–289 (2016). https://doi.org/10.1177/1086026616633272
9. Patzelt, H., Shepherd, D.A.: Recognising opportunities for sustainable development. Entrep. Theory Pract. **35**, 631–652 (2011). https://doi.org/10.1111/j.1540-6520.2010.00386.x
10. Hockerts, K., Wüstenhagen, R.: Greening goliaths versus emerging davids—theorising about the role of incumbents and new entrants in sustainable entrepreneurship. J. Bus. Ventur. **25**, 481–492 (2010). https://doi.org/10.1016/j.jbusvent.2009.07.005
11. Gregori, P., Holzmann, P.: Digital sustainable entrepreneurship: a business model perspective on embedding digital technologies for social and environmental value creation. J. Clean. Prod. **272**, 122817 (2020). https://doi.org/10.1016/j.jclepro.2020.122817

12. Trittin-Ulbrich, H., Scherer, A.G., Munro, I., Whelan, G.: Exploring the dark and unexpected sides of digitalisation: toward a critical Agenda. Organization **28**, 8–25 (2021). https://doi.org/10.1177/1350508420968184

13. vom Brocke, J., Winter, R., Hevner, A., Maedche, A.: Special issue editorial – accumulation and evolution of design knowledge in design science research: a journey through time and space. JAIS **21**, 520–544 (2020). https://doi.org/10.17705/1jais.00611

14. Reason, P.: Choice and quality in action research practice. J. Manag. Inq. **15**, 187–203 (2006). https://doi.org/10.1177/1056492606288074

15. Berglund, H.: Entrepreneurship as design and design science. J. Bus. Venturing Des. **1**, 100012 (2021). https://doi.org/10.1016/j.jbvd.2022.100012

16. Gregor, S.: The nature of theory in information systems. MIS Q. **30**, 611–642 (2006)

17. Dyllick, T., Muff, K.: Clarifying the meaning of sustainable business. Organ. Environ. **29**, 156–174 (2016). https://doi.org/10.1177/1086026615575176

18. Fichter, K., Clausen, J.: Diffusion of environmental innovations: sector differences and explanation range of factors. Environ. Innov. Soc. Trans. **38**, 34–51 (2021). https://doi.org/10.1016/j.eist.2020.10.005

19. Long, T.B., Blok, V., Coninx, I.: The diffusion of climate-smart agricultural innovations: systems level factors that inhibit sustainable entrepreneurial action. J. Clean. Prod. **232**, 993–1004 (2019). https://doi.org/10.1016/j.jclepro.2019.05.212

20. Pinkse, J., Groot, K.: Sustainable entrepreneurship and corporate political activity: overcoming market barriers in the clean energy sector. Entrep. Theory Pract. **39**, 633–654 (2015). https://doi.org/10.1111/etap.12055

21. Senyo, P.K., Liu, K., Effah, J.: Digital business ecosystem: literature review and a framework for future research. Int. J. Inf. Manage. **47**, 52–64 (2019). https://doi.org/10.1016/j.ijinfomgt.2019.01.002

22. Kapoor, R., Teece, D.J.: Three faces of technology's value creation: emerging, enabling, embedding. Strat. Sci. **6**, 1–4 (2021). https://doi.org/10.1287/stsc.2021.0124

23. Kim, S., Schifeling, T.: Good corp, bad corp, and the rise of b corps: how market incumbents' diverse responses reinvigorate challengers. Adm. Sci. Q. **67**, 674–720 (2022). https://doi.org/10.1177/00018392221091734

24. Seckler, C., Mauer, R., vom Brocke, J.: Design science in entrepreneurship: conceptual foundations and guiding principles. J. Bus. Ventur. Des. **1**, 100004 (2021). https://doi.org/10.1016/j.jbvd.2022.100004

25. Berglund, H., Bousfiha, M., Mansoori, Y.: Opportunities as artifacts and entrepreneurship as design. AMR **45**, 825–846 (2020). https://doi.org/10.5465/amr.2018.0285

26. Becker, J., vom Brocke, J., Heddier, M., Seidel, S.: In search of information systems (grand) challenges. Bus. Inf. Syst. Eng. **57**(6), 377–390 (2015). https://doi.org/10.1007/s12599-015-0394-0

27. vom Brocke, J., Hevner, A., Maedche, A.: Design Science Research. Cases. Springer International Publishing, Cham (2020). https://doi.org/10.1007/978-3-030-46781-4

28. van Aken, J.E.: Management research as a design science: articulating the research products of mode 2 knowledge production in management. Br. J. Manage. **16**, 19–36 (2005). https://doi.org/10.1111/j.1467-8551.2005.00437.x

29. vom Brocke, J., Maedche, A.: The DSR grid: six core dimensions for effectively planning and communicating design science research projects. Electron. Mark. **29**(3), 379–385 (2019). https://doi.org/10.1007/s12525-019-00358-7

30. Winter, R., Aier, S.: Design science research in business innovation. In: Hoffmann, C.P., Lennerts, S., Schmitz, C., Stölzle, W., Uebernickel, F. (eds.) Business Innovation: Das St. Galler Modell. BIUSG, pp. 475–498. Springer, Wiesbaden (2016). https://doi.org/10.1007/978-3-658-07167-7_25

31. Gregor, S., Kruse, L., Seidel, S.: Research perspectives: the anatomy of a design principle. JAIS **21**, 1622–1652 (2020). https://doi.org/10.17705/1jais.00649
32. Sein, M.K., Henfridsson, O., Purao, S., Rossi, M., Lindgren, R.: Action design research. MIS Q. **35**, 37–56 (2011). https://doi.org/10.2307/23043488
33. Peffers, K., Tuunanen, T., Niehaves, B.: Design science research genres: introduction to the special issue on exemplars and criteria for applicable design science research. Eur. J. Inform. Syst. **27**, 129–139 (2018). https://doi.org/10.1080/0960085X.2018.1458066
34. Ebel, P., Bretschneider, U., Leimeister, J.M.: Leveraging virtual business model innovation: a framework for designing business model development tools. Info. Syst. J. **26**, 519–550 (2016). https://doi.org/10.1111/isj.12103
35. van Burg, E., Cornelissen, J., Stam, W., Jack, S.: Advancing qualitative entrepreneurship research: leveraging methodological plurality for achieving scholarly impact. Entrep. Theory Pract. **46**, 104225872094305 (2020). https://doi.org/10.1177/1042258720943051
36. Heron, J., Reason, P.: The practice of co-operative inquiry: research 'with'rather than 'on' people. Handbook Action Res. **2**, 144–154 (2006)
37. Osterwalder, A., Pigneur, Y.: Business Model Generation: A Handbook for Visionaries, Game Changers, and Challengers. Wiley (2010)
38. Corley, K.G., Gioia, D.A.: Identity ambiguity and change in the wake of a corporate spin-off. Adm. Sci. Q. **49**, 173–208 (2004). https://doi.org/10.2307/4131471
39. Futonge Nzembayie, K., Buckley, A.P.: entrepreneurial process studies using insider action research: opportunities & challenges for entrepreneurship scholarship. Eur. Manage. Rev. **17** (2020). https://doi.org/10.1111/emre.12422
40. Laasch, O.: Beyond the purely commercial business model: organisational value logics and the hetero-geneity of sustainability business models. Long Range Plan. **51**, 158–183 (2018). https://doi.org/10.1016/j.lrp.2017.09.002
41. Bocken, N.M.P., Short, S.W., Rana, P., Evans, S.: A literature and practice review to develop sustainable business model archetypes. J. Clean. Prod. **65**, 42–56 (2014). https://doi.org/10.1016/j.jclepro.2013.11.039
42. Smith, W.K., Gonin, M., Besharov, M.L.: Managing social-business tensions: a review and research agenda for social enterprise. Bus. Ethics Q. **23**, 407–442 (2013). https://doi.org/10.5840/beq201323327
43. Opara-Martins, J., Sahandi, R., Tian, F.: Critical analysis of vendor lock-in and its impact on cloud computing migration: a business perspective. J. Cloud Comput. **5**(1), 1–18 (2016). https://doi.org/10.1186/s13677-016-0054-z
44. Russo-Spena, T., Mele, C.: "Five Co-S" in innovating: a practice-based view. JOSM **23**, 527–553 (2012). https://doi.org/10.1108/09564231211260404
45. Boons, F., Lüdeke-Freund, F.: Business models for sustainable innovation: state-of-the-art and steps towards a research Agenda. J. Clean. Prod. **45**, 9–19 (2013). https://doi.org/10.1016/j.jclepro.2012.07.007
46. von Goethe, J.W.: Faust, A Tragedy. Part one. Yale University Press, New Haven, CT (1992)
47. Fauchart, E., Gruber, M.: Darwinians, communitarians, and missionaries: the role of founder identity in entrepreneurship. Acad. Manag. J. **54**, 935–957 (2011). https://doi.org/10.5465/amj.2009.0211
48. Hahn, R., Spieth, P., Ince, I.: Business model design in sustainable entrepreneurship: illuminating the commercial logic of hybrid businesses. J. Clean. Prod. **176**, 439–451 (2018). https://doi.org/10.1016/j.jclepro.2017.12.167
49. Acebo, E., Miguel-Dávila, J.-Á., Nieto, M.: External stakeholder engagement: complementary and substitutive effects on firms' eco-innovation. Bus. Strat. Env. **30** (2021). https://doi.org/10.1002/bse.2770
50. Milanov, H., Fernhaber, S.A.: The impact of early imprinting on the evolution of new venture networks. J. Bus. Ventur. **24**, 46–61 (2009). https://doi.org/10.1016/j.jbusvent.2007.11.001

Data Product Canvas: A Visual Inquiry Tool Supporting Data Product Design

M. Redwan Hasan(✉) ⓘ and Christine Legner ⓘ

Faculty of Business and Economics (HEC), University of Lausanne, 1015 Lausanne, Switzerland
{mredwan.hasan,christine.legner}@unil.ch

Abstract. Data products (DP) are considered a key enabler of data-driven innovation. However, suitable methodologies and tools supporting DP design are still
scarce. The emerging body of practitioner literature mostly focuses on analytics-
based products and their technical design and architecture but lacks a more comprehensive product perspective on data. To address this gap, we propose the Data
Product Canvas (DPC) as a visual inquiry tool that supports cross-functional teams
in understanding, designing, and analyzing DPs. The DPC was developed in an
iterative design science process involving focus groups with 15 global companies
and was demonstrated for selected DPs. Building on the core ideas of the Business
Model Canvas, the DPC outlines the critical elements for designing DPs focusing
on three key themes: desirability from the customer perspective, feasibility from
the technical perspective, and viability from an economic perspective. The DPC
instantiates the design principles for visual inquiry tools and comprises a conceptual model, shared visualization, and directions for use. The DPC is the first step
toward a systematic approach and shared language in designing DPs in ways that
technical experts and business users understand.

Keywords: Visual Inquiry Tools · Data Product Canvas · Data Product Design

1 Introduction

Recent forecasts envisage that the amount of data is likely to exceed the 175 zettabyte
mark by 2025 [1]. By acquiring the data, analyzing and using it in various assignments,
enterprises are able to create business value and foster data-driven innovations [2]. Since
data comes in different forms, combining, packaging, and delivering selected units as
a data product (DP), end users' information needs can be fulfilled, which creates value
[3]. DPs come in various forms and features, such as datasets, lists, metrics, ML models,
or data-driven physical products [3]. However, high volumes of data lead to increasing
the burden on analytics, as well as to lower data reuse and to unclear ownership [4] –
implying the need to design DPs in a way that facilitates effective consumption and
governance. As stated in one of the earlier papers, *"data products aren't about the data;
they're about enabling their users to do whatever they want, which most often has little
to do with data"* [3].

DPs have recently been popularized by the data mesh concept which encourages
domain teams to build DPs as a way of scaling analytics, delegating responsibilities, and

A. Gerber and R. Baskerville (Eds.): DESRIST 2023, LNCS 13873, pp. 191–205, 2023.
https://doi.org/10.1007/978-3-031-32808-4_12

ensuring ownership [4]. Here, DPs are associated with the so-called DATSIS principles, which means they should be discoverable, addressable, trustworthy, self-describing, interoperable, and secure. Building on these ideas, the emerging body of literature on DPs [5, 6] mostly focuses on the technical design and architecture of analytics-based DPs.

Hence, harmonizing the technical and business perspectives to build appropriate DPs remains a challenge [7]. [8] emphasize that creating a DP should commence with a broad conceptualization phase involving the collaboration of relevant subject-matter experts prior to any data collection activities. To date, we lack suitable methodologies and tools that could help the different stakeholders – business, data, and IT experts – to collaborate in DP design. Therefore, we propose the following research question: *How to support organizations in designing data products?*

To answer this question, we propose the Data Product Canvas (DPC), as visual inquiry tool that facilitates DP design by merging the technical and business perspectives. The DPC was developed following a design science research (DSR) approach [9], involving 15+ global companies, through two design iterations, three focus groups, three demonstrations, and two expert evaluations. Building on the core ideas of the Business Model Canvas (BMC) [10], the DPC outlines the critical elements for designing DPs around three key themes: desirability from the customer perspective, feasibility from the technical perspective, and viability from an economic perspective. The DPC also instantiates the design principles for visual inquiry tools, which comprises the conceptual model, shared visualization, and directions for use.

The remainder of the paper is structured as follows: Sect. 2 provides a background on DPs and visual inquiry tools, Sect. 3 outlines the methodology, Sect. 4 describes all the building blocks of the DPC, and Sect. 5 provides a demonstration of the DPC.

2   Background

2.1   Evolution of Data Products

Although DPs have recently become very popular [8], we should note that the product perspective on information was already introduced more than three decades ago in seminal papers on data quality management. Referring analogously to a manufacturing supply chain, an MIT researcher, Richard Wang, and his co-authors [11] argued that data moves through an information supply chain where it undergoes several transformation processes to reach end consumers in the form of an information product (IP). These scholars suggested four principles for treating information as a product: (1) understanding consumers' information needs, (2) managing well-defined production processes, (3) managing the lifecycle of information products, and (4) appointing an IP manager to handle the processes and the product [11]. IPs have been studied in multiple contexts [12–14], such as within data supply chains. In the early understanding of IPs, they were mostly associated with information in a tangible form that fulfills simple end-user needs, such as bank statements, with a finite scope and containing only a limited amount of information.

In the 2010s, the notion of data-driven enterprises gained traction and the term DP gained prominence [3]. One of the first papers [3] asserting this term highlighted that a DP should be designed in such a way that consumers can use it without understanding its intricacies. Depending on the need, broadly two types of DPs exist: *overt* DPs where data itself is the output (such as spreadsheets, lists) and *covert* DPs where data is invisible and works in the background (such as recommendation engines) [3, 15]. To enable good design practice around DPs, [7] suggested using the drivetrain approach – a systematic design method to couple business needs and analytical methods – to produce actionable output for data consumers. However, this method centers very specifically on data science.

As the need for sophisticated approaches to create more value from data emerged, more analytics-based DPs appeared. For instance, [8] argued that the Google Analytics Dashboard is a DP offering descriptive insights, whereas Predictive Maintenance is a software-based DP that provides predictive insights. They further argue that certain DPs can be delivered as mobile applications with some level of analytics in the background. In contrast, more advanced DPs are driven by analytical techniques (e.g., regression, classification, or clustering) [15] to instill self-learning capabilities, thereby facilitating prescriptive knowledge creation. In addition to the technical aspects, successful DP creation involves skills related to data management, DP design, as well as data visualization, to transmit hidden patterns to end-users through creative data storytelling [16]. Therefore, such analytics-based DPs facilitate decision making across the wider enterprise, and hence, prior to initiating any ETL activities, its design should include a proper conceptualization stage involving all stakeholders [8]. To achieve this, [17] proposed intersecting the value proposition design framework [18] with analytical techniques as a starting point in DP design.

Table 1. Data product examples in the literature

Source	Data product example	Data product form
[19] [12] [20] [13] [21] [14]	Client account data, certificates, bills, transcripts, bank statements, invoices, business reports, prescriptions, birth certificate, mailing labels, sales orders, news products	Paper-based
[3, 5, 22, 23]	Spreadsheets, monetizable datasets, raw data, domain sales data, online profit data, personal data, financial data, pharmaceutical data	Dataset
[5, 8, 17]	KPIs, metrices, reports, insights	Dashboard
[3, 5, 8, 15]	Recommendation engines, ML models, predictive maintenance, property price prediction, APIs, 'Quantified self'	Algorithm-based
[3, 6]	Self-driving cars, nest thermostat, autonomous devices	Data-driven physical products

More recently, the data mesh concept has pushed the design of DPs toward the domains responsible for creating and managing their respective data [4]. The underlying principles that drive the DP design thinking in a data mesh environment are the DATSIS principles. [4] argues that such characteristics ensure the creation of high-quality DPs that are well governed and have a greater possibility of meeting stakeholder needs, both internally and externally. Hence, recent practitioner publications have adopted a technical-focused view of DPs [24, 25]. Academically, DPs have been investigated using other lenses, such as service science [17] or the data marketplace [26]. In summary, we observe that DPs come in various shapes and sizes to address the diversity of use-cases data consumers have (Table 1). Nonetheless, we lack common guidelines that underpin the design of these DPs. More specifically, to ensure a proper DP design, we need to combine the technical perspective with the user-centric product view on data, and to integrate economic perspectives.

2.2 Visual Inquiry Tools as Part of Joint Inquiry Techniques

Given the challenges of designing DPs, visual inquiry tools appear to be suitable supportive instruments. By leveraging joint inquiry techniques, they have emerged as a popular choice in design thinking. Joint inquiry techniques allows for an iterative process through which many individuals are able to collaboratively define, explore, and evaluate potential solutions to a particular problem [27]. Such techniques motivate cross-functional teams to cooperate and align their work on a certain topic creatively [27], thereby offering a problem-solving mechanism through which firms can foster innovation and value creation [28]. Visual inquiry tools help organizations navigate wicked and difficult strategic management problems by providing a shared and framed design space where practitioners can brainstorm together [27]. Some well-known examples are the BMC [10], Value Proposition Canvas [18], and Team Alignment Map [29]. More specifically, these tools allow an alternative way of handling complex management issues, i.e., they support building prototypes that can be iteratively improved to capture all design requirements [27]. Consequently, they help transform abstract and uncertain challenges into a tangible form that allows practitioners to find solutions to situations for which there are no straightforward answers [30]. The BMC, for instance, highlights the economic, operational, and managerial elements of a business model and provides utility by *"describing the business logic of an idea, product and service in a simple and visual representation"* [31].

Regarding DP design, we observe an increasing number of canvases, mostly from practitioners [24, 25]. However, they focus mainly on analytics and emphasize the DPs' technical design. They also lack a thorough theoretical foundation. In the academic literature, only one recent study [5] developed a canvas related to DPs. First, the canvas is analytics-oriented in focusing on the types of technique to be used for the DP. Second, the business and economic aspects – elements critical to any product development process – are missing [32]. Third, the canvas development is not grounded on established design principles for visual inquiry tools, which reduces its academic rigor. Hence, we see an opportunity to create visual inquiry tools for DP design, which integrate the different DP design perspectives and follow the design principles for visual inquiry tools outlined in [27] – *conceptual model* to structure and describe the building blocks of the problem, *shared visualization* using a visual problem space to facilitate communication between users, and *directions for use* to define and specify techniques that allow for joint inquiry.

3 Methodology

3.1 Research Methodology and Process

To develop the DPC as a visual inquiry tool, we engaged in a DSR project over a period of eight months between May 2022 and December 2022. The DSR setting allows researchers to collaborate with practitioners on research problems, finding common ground regarding rigor and relevance, to create practically meaningful and academically sound solutions [33]. Our approach is also consistent with the work of [34] where the proposed cycles of diagnosis, design, and implementation coincide with DSR phases, allowing for various entry points. In our case, the research team (a PhD student and a senior researcher) collaborated with more than 30 experts from 15 global companies, all with significant professional experience in the field of data management and with a strong overview of the data initiatives in their organizations. The firms are members of a research consortium which, alongside the research team, engages in industry-research collaboration and are part of the DP research program.

Following the DSR process outlined by [9], we started with the *problem identification*. During our initial focus group meeting with 18 data experts from 12 companies in May 2022, we observed a growing concern about the large volumes of data being created within the organizations or captured from external sources. Specifically, data consumers find it difficult to discover, repurpose, and reuse such data in analytical workflows to drive novel use-cases and take the right decisions. Thus, to ensure a better product-market fit for DPs, the companies require a way of disclosing their consumers' needs. Additionally, challenges related to data ownership, access provision, and compliance persist. These issues become inflated due to the size of the enterprises and because they are globally dispersed, which inhibits a harmonized approach in managing these data resources. Scholars identified building DPs as one way of dealing with these challenges and of enhancing the reuse of data. Practitioners confirmed that DPs enable streamlined data governance with a clear allocation of roles, responsibilities, and tasks [35], which ensures high data quality and good value generated in steering novel use-cases [4]. However, we still lack clear guidelines on how to design such DPs that will be available for consumption by a wide variety of users. Therefore, the *objective of the solution* would be to facilitate conceptualization of DPs using a simple visual brainstorming space, which blends the technical, business, and user perspectives on DP. Concretely, the participants agreed to create a canvas that will foster fruitful interaction between various key stakeholders in their contribution to the design of a DP. We named this canvas the DPC. Since it aims to support DP design in organizations, our artifact falls into the theory type V (theory for design and action) of Gregor's taxonomy of IS research [36].

The *first design phase* took place between June 2022 and September 2022, resulting in a first version of the DPC. To inform our design, we scanned both the academic and practitioner literature on DPs and visual inquiry tools. Although a few studies highlighted the definition of a DP and gave examples from a specific perspective, such as data science [6] or the data marketplace [26], there was no research discussing DP design.

Interestingly, we came across a few canvases in non-academic publications [24, 25] that claimed to support the process of DP design. Upon inquiry, we discovered that such canvases are analytics-driven, heavily focusing on the technical aspects of the DP. Being mainly practitioner-oriented, they are not academically rigorous in their formulation. We now adopt the product-perspective on data since we intend to go beyond the technical design elements to explicitly cover the consumer and economic perspectives of the DP. They capture consumers' perceived value regarding the DP and explain the cost-benefit analysis – both of which play a critical role in deciding whether to invest in a DP. The high-level DPC design was inspired by the BMC [37] and by design thinking tools and methods [31] that outline three spaces, i.e., desirability (the user perspective), feasibility (the technical perspective), and viability (the economic perspective), which should be addressed in innovation. These perspectives and the BMC building blocks are widely discussed in the product design and development literature [32, 38] and are also relevant for DPs. Therefore, we revisited the BMC building blocks and adapted them to the DP context. For each block, we proposed guiding questions and examples to facilitate the conceptualization of the DP and to avoid missing any important details. With the first version of our DPC, we conducted two focus group discussions for evaluation. One group consisted of 28 data experts from 14 companies and the second group consisted of 8 consultants working with a data service provider. The overall feedback was satisfactory in that the building blocks and their adaptation to DPs made good sense. However, some major modifications were proposed for the next steps, such as "… *the title in each section needs to be reframed for better clarity*" (manufacturing company), "… *these questions are very generic so you need to make sure they are concrete enough for non-specialists to answer accurately*" (packaging company), and "…*where do I see the version of the data product being designed? It is key in agile approaches*" (data service provider).

The *second design phase* took place between October 2022 and December 2022. We responded to the feedback by formulating the block titles between two to four words, reformulating the questions by breaking them up into multiple smaller, more precise questions, and by adding a header block to capture the name, category, and version of the DP being designed. Additionally, we colored the different blocks aiming thereby to offer the participants an intuitive sequence to fill the canvas. We used red for the blocks inquiring about the consumer perspective, yellow for the block om data requirements, and green for the blocks that highlight economic viability. Subsequently, we conducted the first demonstration round of the DPC. Based on the discussions with participants, we selected *Sustainability Report* as an example because most were familiar with this DP. Relying on a third focus group which consisted of 15 data experts from 8 companies, we filled in the empty spaces, using sticky notes to capture aspects of the report relevant for each block. Following up on the demonstration, we received positive feedback regarding the ease-of-use and colorfulness of the canvas. A few reflections on this version of the DPC mentioned "…*I think we have to mention how this data product would be discovered by the user*" (pharmaceutical company) and "…*the canvas should capture both monetary and non-monetary benefits*" (telecommunication company). We incorporated such feedback by adding another guiding question on discoverability and modifying an example to mention non-monetary benefits in one of the blocks.

The final *demonstration and evaluation* phase took place in December 2022. It consisted of two in-depth, one-hour long expert evaluations, of which one represented a global packaging firm and the other a global medical device producer. With minimal support from the research team, the experts filled up and evaluated the canvas by using real-life candidate DPs that their organizations are planning to create. Specifically, the packaging company evaluated the DPC using the 'Account and Hierarchy Data Product', while the medical device producer evaluated it using the 'Product 360 Cube'. The feedback we received was strongly positive as the experts were satisfied with the final outcome, finding that DPC to be simple, take up less time and preparatory work, and that it would interactively challenge the various perspectives that cross-functional teams bring. Additionally, on reflection, they mentioned "*... this facilitates a standard approach to clearly mapping the data to ensure good quality of the data products*" (packaging company), "*... the canvas really helps us to be precise in the early stages of the data product development*" (medical device producer), "*... we can make good portfolio decisions on whether to promote a data product, or not*" (medical device producer), and "*... this activity can help us decide concretely on what the next steps should be; however, how to go about the next steps is really the question*" (packaging company).

4 A Visual Inquiry Tool Facilitating Data Product Design

4.1 Purpose and Overview

The DPC's purpose is to support cross-functional teams – composed of business users, data and analytics experts, product owners, and sponsors – in designing DPs. This goes beyond the strictly technical view on data in encouraging users to perceive it as a product, which implies a focus on end users' information needs. Further, attention turns to coordinating critical business resources and activities that play a key role in generating value through this product. Conceptualizing a suitable business model enables companies to meets consumer demand by offering the most appropriate product, while also considering the required resources and economic viability [10]. Similarly, articulating the relevant business elements would help companies create a DP that has a strong product-market fit and satisfies consumers' information needs. Hence, to design the high-level structure of the DPC, we have adopted the perspectives the BMC used [10], as well as innovation and design thinking tools [39]: *desirability* (customer relationships, channels, and customer segments), a vital step in product design approaches to gauge consumers' DP requirements [32]; *feasibility* (key partners, key activities, and key resources) that fulfills the consumer requirements in underscoring various technical capabilities and tasks as discussed in numerous DP publications [3, 16, 17, 21–23], and *viability* (cost structures and revenue streams) that helps us understand the economic suitability of investing in the DP, akin to similar assessments made during product development [32]. The three perspectives serve as high-level structure in which to organize the nine building blocks for our DPC (Fig. 1).

4.2 Value Proposition

The *value proposition* is located at the center of the DPC canvas for two reasons: First, it outlines the unique aspects of a DP and gives reasons why a consumer would use the DP rather than alternative offerings. Second, the *value proposition* connects the *desirability, feasibility,* and *viability* themes and thereby provides a common ground to explicate its relationship with a product's consumer, technical, and economic aspects [40]. This block is instantiated by two questions. Since seminal literature [11] indicates the need to first articulate users' desire before starting to create a DP, the first question inquires what information needs the DP is expected to satisfy or which existing problems the DP is meant to solve. Deliberating on this question supports users in formally noting the information challenges they face and facilitates discussion on whether a solution already exists. If not, they can consider the potential of investing in a new DP. The second question asks about the concrete value that would be realized if this information need were to be met. The goal here is to encourage users' reflection on whether the added value the DP can bring is significant enough to merit developing it.

4.3 Desirability Perspective

The desirability perspective establishes a combined view on the target consumers and how the DP addresses their needs. Such an outlook enables logically arranging the DP consumers' different priorities and outlines the relevant delivery mechanisms and relationships.

The *consumers* block encourages describing the target consumers, the relevant segments or groups, and their types (internal/external). Before DP development, a key objective is to understand the consumers' tasks and how the DP could support them [11]. This allows users to gauge the usage scope and highlight relevant stakeholders. Further, the distinction between internal and external users has substantial governance implications in terms of access, compliance, and the DP's security, as recent literature [35] has also highlighted. The next question inquires more deeply about relevant use-cases for the identified consumers, which allows users to deduce the concrete tasks and the level of detail required in the DPs. For example, a logistics specialist may need minute-by-minute oversight on outbound drug temperatures, while a senior manager would need only annual KPIs.

The *delivery mechanism* block considers the ways in which consumers would like to have the DP packaged and consumed [17]. The first question attempts to grasp the most suitable format in which the DP should be presented. This delivery aspect must reflect the consumers' aptitude and ensure that DPs are available in a form and layout they would find most convenient. For example, a business analyst might prefer working with datasets, whereas a group president could require a single-page dashboard. The subsequent question encourages users to determine the most appropriate interface through which the DP will be accessed. The key idea here is to reflect on the appropriate access points through which consumers can attain the required insights in the shortest possible time. Also important is how secure these access points are, as the literature [4] also point out.

The *consumer relationship* block is meant to reflect on how to maintain relationships with the identified consumers, starting with discovering the DP and collecting feedback and suggestions for further DP releases/versions. This building block comprises the method through which companies can inform the intended audience about the DP, such as data catalogs [41] or data marketplaces [26]. Quite evidently, the need to discover and address DPs has steadily gained traction in the literature [23]. Similarly, product management literature [32] has put out calls to provide high-quality customer support. Hence, the next question draws information on the nature of support, technical or non-technical, that consumers expect regarding the DP. This should allow users to determine the type and frequency of assistance that must be guaranteed. For instance, service level agreements are required between the DP producer and consumers regarding expected performance, new releases, and retirement procedures.

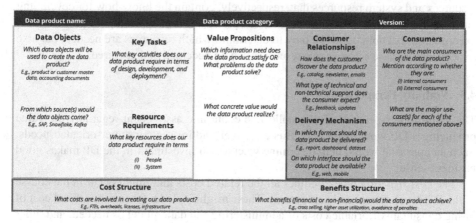

Fig. 1. The Data Product Canvas

4.4 Feasibility Perspective

The feasibility perspective captures how the DP is created. It outlines the steps and resources required to convert the identified data needs of the DP into a minimum viable product. Such transformation, in particular, outlines the provisions required in terms of data, human resources, and technology.

The *data objects* block considers which raw materials need to be assembled in building the DP, similar to processes building any physical product. More precisely, the first question's purpose is to challenge users to identify the exact data required to empower the DP. It builds on previous reflections on identified problems, the types of consumers, and their use-cases. In most situations, data from different functional areas has to be combined to address complex needs [16], hence, this activity pushes users to intuitively ponder the existence and quality of the data. Utilizing as much relevant data as possible allows companies to extract the most value from their data assets [42]. The next question motivates users to consider the various source systems or enterprise platforms present in the organization and to reflect on whether they hold the required data. Additionally, key external sources could be identified to acquire data for the organizations [43].

The *key tasks* block explores the concrete actions required to build and deploy the DP. The palette of tasks is not only data-centric but can also include developing and testing the product itself [44]. Only a few methods for creating DPs, such as the drivetrain approach [7], have been discussed in the literature so far. In the DPC, users can deliberate on tasks such as requirement collection, prototyping, testing, performance monitoring, and versioning of the DP. Such an exercise will ensure the required set of tasks has been sequentially brainstormed to avoid any misalignment in the DP development process.

The *resource requirements* block builds on the task deliberation in the previous step. To accomplish the set of jobs identified, users have the opportunity to set out all the necessary resources presumed to be important. These resources could be both intellectual resources and system resources that, respectively, contain the know-how for developing and managing the DPs [45], and the tools and platforms for supporting the process. This exercise could enable users not only to determine which resources are needed, but also to decide how these often-scarce resources can be accessed and acquired.

4.5 Viability Perspective

The viability perspective offers a collective economic assessment regarding the value producing a DP would generate. This effectively addresses consumer-oriented needs. Such an appraisal would help determine whether an investment in the DP makes good business sense.

The *cost structure* block outlines all the related costs that might occur in the course of the DP development and deployment. These might include, for instance, fixed cost of hiring consultants, variable costs of administering the data model as needed, and other overhead costs that would be similar to any product development costs [32]. Further, maintenance costs such as licensing fees or infrastructure cost for hosting the DP are considered here. Conversely, the *benefits structure* block encourages users to articulate all the tangible and non-tangible positives of creating the DP. Possible benefits are not only limited to tangible financial figures, hours saved, or cost reduction, but could also accrue in terms of brand perception and goodwill [46].

4.6 Evaluation and Demonstration

To ensure that our artifact is theoretically grounded, we exhibit how the DPC addresses the three design principles outlined by [27] that are pertinent in visual inquiry tools, i.e., a conceptual model, shared visualization, and directions for use. Table 2 provides the summary of this evaluation.

We conducted demonstrations with practitioners; yet, due to lack of space, here we give only a short summary and the main highlights. The 'Account and Hierarchy Data Product' from the packaging company is meant to provide complete, high-quality information about customer accounts and their parent-child relationship. This DP supports that payments go to the correct cost centers, thereby reducing operational costs of reinvoicing and the risk of fiscal penalties, while improving customer relationships owing to less payment errors.

In contrast, the 'Product 360 Cube' DP from the medical device producer helps employees optimize portfolio management to improve online presence. This DP saves product data search time by offering consumers a single source of truth which they attain by harmonizing fragmented data from multiple sources and which also ensures data quality. We observe that the first DP has a broader scope with direct implications for external stakeholders, whereas the second DP is narrowly focused on certain internal functions as consumers. Such findings indicate varying scope and complexity levels in DPs aligned with the larger requirements of the organization [11]. Further, the first DP

Table 2. Mapping the DPC to the design principles for visual inquiry tools

Principles	Implementation in the DPC
DP1 Conceptual model	
DP1.1 Frame	The DPC blocks represent the components on which teams should inquire to design DPs. They are mutually exclusive and collectively exhaustive in capturing three central perspectives related to a DP: desirability (focused on user), feasibility (focused on technical), and viability (focus on business)
DP1.2 Rigor and relevance	The DPC is designed following the DSR process outlined by [9]. To ensure practical relevance, over a period of more than eight months, we involved more than 30 practitioners from 15 + global firms in design, demonstration, and evaluation. Further, the DPC is academically grounded and it satisfies the design principles for visual inquiry tools [27]
DP1.3 Parsimony	The DPC has nine building blocks that are structured into three higher-order perspective components. We avoid offering a prohibitive level of detail, thus we explicate, maximally, the two most-relevant questions per building block
DP2 Shared visualization	
DP2.1 Functionality	The DPC exhibits the building blocks as empty problem spaces that allow cross-functional teams to freely represent any facts, ideas, hypotheses, or reflections regarding DP design
DP2.2 Arrangement	The value proposition block is positioned in the middle as it relates to all three perspectives. The desirability aspect is captured on the right to understand consumer needs, and feasibility is on the left to gauge the technical capabilities to meet those needs; viability is at the bottom to foster economic sensemaking
DP2.3 Facilitation	The DPC perspectives are aesthetically presented using three colors to intuitively guide the sequence in which they should be filled. Most DPC blocks also contain examples intended to reduce ambiguity for the average participant
DP3 Directions for use	
DP3.1 Ideation	The DPC is a domain-independent tool that allows cross-functional teams to tap into their knowledge and expertise in exchanging creative ideas. Such ideas and reflections can easily be aggregated, rearranged, or removed by using sticky notes which facilitate a flexible collaborative process

(continued)

Table 2. (*continued*)

Principles	Implementation in the DPC
DP3.2 Prototyping	The DPC was demonstrated in workshop settings to exhibit how it functions. Further, the canvas captures the type and version of the DP being worked on, which helps users to revisit and rework certain blocks depending on the progress of the DP design project
DP3.3 Presentation	The DPC can be displayed and interacted with in a versatile manner through online (e.g., Miro board) or offline settings (e.g., printed as poster) for workshop and seminars. Sticky notes can be used to visibly present all the creative ideas and individuals outside of the teams can easily view and critique them

falls under the master data management domain, whereas the latter goes beyond basic master data to integrate transactional data that provides a comprehensive view.

This underscores both groups' needs to provide reusable DPs for broader use instead of being use-case specific. This also explains both firms' aim, as stated during the demonstration, to deliver their respective DPs in a basic dataset format, to thereby offer the flexibility of repurposing and reusing the data based on the data consumers' highly diverse and specific analytical needs [47] on introducing it into the wider organization at a later stage. Interestingly, we further observe that the findable, accessible, interoperable, and reusable (FAIR) principles [41] also become manifest while the companies fill up the canvas. The relationships block captures the findable aspect in asking how the DP will be discovered, while the delivery mechanism block captures the accessible aspect by developing an understanding of where and in which format the DP will be made available. Finally, the feasibility blocks together capture the interoperable and reusable aspect by clearly outlining which data must be integrated from which sources and clearly defining their metadata for future DP creation. Further, during the demonstration and evaluation rounds, we learnt that the DPs might be developed in several iterations and could require cross-functional teams to revisit the DPC. Additionally, the teams might have to conceptualize a new version of the DP altogether. Such approaches are quite frequently taken in companies using agile methodologies [48]. Evidently, our canvas is also able to track these changes over time by capturing the name, category, and version of the DP being worked on in the canvas header.

5 Conclusion

Leveraging a DSR approach, we propose a DPC as visual inquiry tool that supports cross-functional teams – composed of business users, data and analytics experts, product owners, and sponsors – in designing DPs. To the best of our knowledge, this is one of the first tools supporting DP design that goes beyond the purely technical aspects of a DP and embraces relevant business and consumer perspectives. We also apply the established design principles for visual inquiry tools to ensure further academic rigor. To evaluate, we relied on three focus groups, three demonstrations, and two expert evaluations.

The DPC contributes to research as well as practice. For academics, our research conceptualizes DP design by harnessing the desirability, feasibility, and viability aspects of the DP as a mechanism to facilitate data-driven innovation. For practitioners, the canvas provides an interactive, yet systematic, approach to brainstorm all the vital elements that play an important role in creating DPs.

Although we followed a rigorous DSR approach, we need to acknowledge certain limitations. For instance, our work is limited by the specific research context and the type of companies we collaborated with. While the BMC offers the economic, operational, and managerial perspectives that match the DPC goals, the BMC and DPC can differ in terms of potential end-users since the former is more strategic in nature, whereas the DPC can help design both strategic and operational DPs. In most cases, the experts taking part in our study were also the potential consumers of the DP. Further, we aimed to create a general DP canvas that accommodates the design of any DP type, implying that the suggested DPC goes beyond other canvases developed for specific analytics products. Hence, future work could center on adapting the DPC for internal or external users. We also see opportunities to study how different canvases and other visual inquiry tools are applied in DP design to help diffuse DP thinking in firms.

References

1. Reinsel, D., Rydning, J., Gantz, J.F.: Worldwide Global DataSphere Forecast, 2020–2024: The COVID-19 Data Bump and the Future of Data Growth (2020). https://www.idc.com/get doc.jsp?containerId=US44797920. Accessed 3 Nov 2020
2. Grover, V., Chiang, R.H.L., Liang, T.-P., Zhang, D.: Creating strategic business value from big data analytics: a research framework. J. Manag. Inf. Syst. **35**, 388–423 (2018). https://doi.org/10.1080/07421222.2018.1451951
3. Loukides, M.: The Evolution of Data Products. O'Reilly Media, United States of America (2011)
4. Dehghani, Z.: Data Mesh - Delivering Data-Driven Value at Scale. O'Reilly, United Stated of America (2021)
5. Fruhwirth, M., Breitfuss, G., Pammer-Schindler, V.: The data product canvas: a visual collaborative tool for designing data-driven business models. In: Proceedings of the 33RD Bled eConference Enabling Technology For A Sustainable Society, pp. 1–14. TU Graz (2020)
6. Bengfort, B., Kim, J.: Data Analytics with Hadoop. O'Reilly Media, United States of America (2016)
7. Howard, J., Zwemer, M., Loukides, M.: Designing great data products. O'Reilly Media, United States of America (2012)
8. Davenport, T.H., Kudyba, S.: Designing and developing analytics-based data products. MIT Sloan Manag. Rev. **58**, 83–89 (2016)
9. Peffers, K., Tuunanen, T., Rothenberger, M.A., Chatterjee, S.: A design science research methodology for information systems research. J. Manag. Inf. Syst. **24**, 45–77 (2007). https://doi.org/10.2753/MIS0742-1222240302
10. Osterwalder, A., Pigneur, Y.: Business Model Generation: A Handbook for Visionaries, Game Changers, and Challengers. Wiley (2010)
11. Wang, R.Y., Lee, Y.W., Pipino, L.L., Strong, D.M.: Manage your information as a product. Sloan Manage. Rev. (1998)
12. Shankaranarayanan, G., Wang, R.Y., Ziad, M.: IP-MAP: Representing the manufacture of an information product. In: Proceedings of the 2000 Conference on Information Quality, pp. 1–16 (2000)

13. Davidson, B., Lee, Y.W., Wang, R.: Developing data production maps: meeting patient discharge data submission requirements. IJHTM **6**, 223 (2004). https://doi.org/10.1504/IJHTM. 2004.004978
14. Nam, J., Lamb, R.: The news: examining perceptions of Information Product Quality (IPQ). In: Proceedings of Americas Conference on Information Systems (AMCIS 2006), pp. 425–429. AIS Electronic Library (AISeL) (2006)
15. Meierhofer, J., Meier, K.: From data science to value creation. In: Za, S., Drăgoicea, M., Cavallari, M. (eds.) IESS 2017. LNBIP, vol. 279, pp. 173–181. Springer, Cham (2017). https:// doi.org/10.1007/978-3-319-56925-3_14
16. Stadelmann, T., Klamt, T., Merkt, P.H.: Data centrism and the core of Data Science as a scientific discipline. Arch. Data Sci. Ser. A **8**, 1–16 (2022). https://doi.org/10.5445/IR/100 0143637
17. Meierhofer, J., Stadelmann, T., Cieliebak, M.: Data products. In: Braschler, M., Stadelmann, T., Stockinger, K. (eds.) Applied Data Science: Lessons Learned for the Data-Driven Business, pp. 47–61. Springer International Publishing, Cham (2019). https://doi.org/10.1007/978-3-030-11821-1_4
18. Osterwalder, A., Pigneur, Y., Bernarda, G., Smith, A.: Value Proposition Design: How to Create Products and Services Customers Want. Wiley (2015)
19. Wang, R.Y.: A product perspective on total data quality management. Commun. ACM **41**, 58–65 (1998). https://doi.org/10.1145/269012.269022
20. Cai, Y., Ziad, M.: Evaluating completeness of an information product. In: Proceedings of Americas Conference on Information Systems (AMCIS 2003), pp. 1–9 (2003)
21. Wang, Y.-Y.R., Pierce, E.M., Wang, R.Y., Madnik, S.E., Fisher, C.W.: Information Quality. M.E. Sharpe (2005)
22. Chen, P., Yang, J., Beheshti, A., Su, J.: Towards data economy: are products and marketplaces ready? In: Proceedings of the 48th International Conference on Very Large Data Bases (VLDB), pp. 1–4. Sydney, Australia (2022)
23. Machado, I., Costa, C., Santos, M.Y.: Data-driven information systems: the data mesh paradigm shift. In: Proceedings of the 29th International Conference On Information Systems Development (ISD2021), pp. 1–6. AIS, Valencia (2021)
24. InnoQ: Data Mesh Architecture: Designing Data Products. https://datamesh-architecture. com. Accessed 19 Jan 2023
25. Carvalho, L.: Data Product Canvas—a practical framework for building high-performance data products (2022). https://medium.com/@leandroscarvalho/data-product-canvas-a-practi cal-framework-for-building-high-performance-data-products-7a1717f79f0. Accessed 19 Jan 2023
26. Eichler, R., Gröger, C., Hoos, E., Schwarz, H.: From data asset to data product – the role of the data provider in the enterprise data marketplace. In: Proceedings of the 16th Symposium and Summer School On Service-Oriented Computing (SummerSoc 2022), pp. 1–21. University of Stuttgart (2022)
27. Avdiji, H., Elikan, D., Missonier, S., Pigneur, Y.: A design theory for visual inquiry tools. J. Assoc. Inform. Syst. **21** (2020). https://doi.org/10.17705/1jais.00617
28. Gruber, M., de Leon, N., George, G., Thompson, P.: Managing by Design. AMJ. **58**, 1–7 (2015). https://doi.org/10.5465/amj.2015.4001
29. Avdiji, H., Missonier, S.: A design approach to team coordination. Revue Tranel. **68**, 97–106 (2018)
30. Dalsgaard, P.: Understanding the nature and role of tools in design. Int. J. Des. **11**, 13 (2017)
31. Chasanidou, D., Gasparini, A.A., Lee, E.: Design thinking methods and tools for innovation. In: Marcus, A. (ed.) DUXU 2015. LNCS, vol. 9186, pp. 12–23. Springer, Cham (2015). https://doi.org/10.1007/978-3-319-20886-2_2

32. Ulrich, K., Eppinger, S.: EBOOK: Product Design and Development. McGraw Hill (2011)
33. Hevner, A.R., March, S.T., Park, J., Ram, S.: Design science in information systems research. MIS Q. **28**, 75–105 (2004)
34. Mullarkey, M.T., Hevner, A.R.: An elaborated action design research process model. Eur. J. Inf. Syst. **28**, 6–20 (2019). https://doi.org/10.1080/0960085X.2018.1451811
35. Fadler, M., Legner, C.: Data ownership revisited: clarifying data accountabilities in times of big data and analytics. J. Bus. Anal. **5**, 123–139 (2021)
36. Gregor, S.: The nature of theory in information systems. MIS Q. **30**, 611–642 (2006). https://doi.org/10.2307/25148742
37. Osterwalder, A., Pigneur, Y., Tucci, C.L.: Clarifying business models: origins, present, and future of the concept. Commun. Assoc. Inf. Syst. **16**, 1–25 (2005)
38. Morris, R.: The Fundamentals of Product Design. Bloomsbury Publishing (2016)
39. Brown, T.: Change by Design - How Design Thinking Transforms Organizations and Inspires Innovation. HarperBusiness, New York (2009)
40. Fritscher, B., Pigneur, Y.: Supporting business model modelling: a compromise between creativity and constraints. In: England, D., Palanque, P., Vanderdonckt, J., Wild, P.J. (eds.) TAMODIA 2009. LNCS, vol. 5963, pp. 28–43. Springer, Heidelberg (2010). https://doi.org/10.1007/978-3-642-11797-8_3
41. Labadie, C., Eurich, M., Legner, C.: Data democratization in practice: fostering data usage with data catalogs. In: Communications of the 20th Symposium of the Association Information and Management (AIM), p. 1541. Marrakesh, Morocco (2020)
42. Hannila, H., Silvola, R., Harkonen, J., Haapasalo, H.: Data-driven begins with DATA; potential of data assets. J. Comput. Inform. Syst. **62**, 29–38 (2022). https://doi.org/10.1080/08874417.2019.1683782
43. Krasikov, P., Legner, C., Eurich, M.: Sourcing the right open data: a design science research approach for the enterprise context. In: Chandra Kruse, L., Seidel, S., Hausvik, G.I. (eds.) DESRIST 2021. LNCS, vol. 12807, pp. 313–327. Springer, Cham (2021). https://doi.org/10.1007/978-3-030-82405-1_31
44. Porter, M.: The value chain and competitive advantage. In: Understanding Business Processes, pp. 50–66. Routledge (2001)
45. Fadler, M., Legner, C.: Toward big data and analytics governance: redefining structural governance mechanisms. In: Proceedings of the 54th Hawaii International Conference on System Sciences. Hawaii, USA (2021)
46. Franzak, F., Makarem, S., Jae, H.: Design benefits, emotional responses, and brand engagement. J. Prod. Brand Manage. **23**, 16–23 (2014). https://doi.org/10.1108/JPBM-07-2013-0350
47. Woodall, P.: The data repurposing challenge: new pressures from data analytics. J. Data and Information Quality. **8**, 11:1–11:4 (2017). https://doi.org/10.1145/3022698
48. Nerur, S., Balijepally, V.: Theoretical reflections on agile development methodologies. Commun. ACM. **50**, 79–83 (2007). https://doi.org/10.1145/1226736.1226739

Design Principles for National Innovation Agencies in Social Market Economies

David M. Lehmann[1]([✉]) [iD] and Viktor M. Salenius[2] [iD]

[1] ESCP Business School, 14059 Berlin, Germany
dlehmann@escp.eu
[2] University of Oxford, Oxford OX1 1HP, UK

Abstract. This paper reports on a design science research project that develops a design framework for national innovation agencies in line with the principles and values of the social market economy. The study conceptually examines the tension between the state's interventions in the economic process to foster technology-based innovation and the social market economy's pursuit of a privilege-free and competitive economic order. The chosen design science approach encompasses five steps: problem definition, diagnosis, solution design, evaluation, and learning. Based on the design requirements and case studies of four existing national innovation agencies, the study suggests twelve design principles for national innovation agencies. Drawing on feedback from leading German economists, the paper proposes general lessons for implementing innovation policies in social market economies, using the CIMO logic. This study contributes to the knowledge base on how to support technology-based innovation through national innovation agencies and provides practical implications for policymakers and innovation agency executives.

Keywords: National Innovation Agency · Social market economy · Design knowledge · Design Principles

1 Introduction

Social market economies build on the division of labour between the private sector and the state: While private businesses deliver products and services, the state is responsible for maintaining the rule of law and providing a stable as well as reliable legal market framework for the private sector to operate in. These roles are often described through the analogy of a football match: The referee is represented by the state and the private sector is represented by the teams of players who compete in a fair game against each other. While this football analogy might be static or incomplete, it illustrates the potential problems that can occur when the state supports individual private sector players who should be in fair competition with each other. The allocation of responsibilities between the private sector and the state is based on the principles of Ordoliberalism, an economic philosophy that underscores the necessity of a robust state and intergovernmental organisations to establish a competitive and privilege-free market economy. This philosophy highlights

A. Gerber and R. Baskerville (Eds.): DESRIST 2023, LNCS 13873, pp. 206–220, 2023.
https://doi.org/10.1007/978-3-031-32808-4_13

the significance of private property and competition in promoting innovation and posits that the state's role in the economy should primarily focus on ensuring that markets function efficiently, with the objective of promoting prosperity for all [1, 2]. While this economic philosophy was developed in the 20th century, it is still highly relevant for contemporary political discourse, particularly in Europe and German-speaking countries [3]. In fact, the multifaceted challenges facing industry stakeholders and decision-makers today call for even more rigorous discussion about the strategy and practice of innovation policy in different contexts.

Over the last century, we have witnessed an extraordinary amount of technology-based innovation. One example for this technological progress is the exponential development of the density of transistors on microprocessors [4]. In many cases, the state has played an essential role in giving rise to new products and services, beyond financing basic research at universities. For example, the jet engine, internet, or GPS could arguably not have come into existence without early government financing, demand-building, or legislative support. For this reason, many states have set up dedicated national innovation agencies (NIA), which are serving as an interface between the state, research institutions, and the private sector and are designed to play an enabling role for technology-based innovation through entrepreneurial activity in the private sector.

The cases of NIA-supported innovation in the last century pose both a challenge and an opportunity to the concept of the social market economy: A challenge because the state leaves the role of being solely a referee and becomes an economic actor in the innovation process instead of exclusively relying on competition between private actors as the main discovery process for novel products and services. From a social market economy viewpoint, these interventions could lead to inefficiencies in resource allocation. However, NIA-supported technological innovation can also be seen as an opportunity: If we review the structure and policies of NIAs through a social market economy lens, we can delineate design knowledge on how to maximise the overall welfare (economic growth and societal development through innovation) while minimising potential adverse outcomes (reduced competition, power agglomeration, cronyism), which might lead to a decrease in innovation.

To address this complexity in the rationale of NIAs, we conducted a design science research project. Design science is an approach for the development of prescriptive knowledge using scientific methods [5]. The approach can be "conceptualized as a research strategy, aimed at knowledge that can be used in an instrumental way to design and implement actions, processes or systems to achieve desired outcomes in practice" [6]. We follow van Aken's & Berends' [6] design science methodology which encompasses the following five research steps: (1) problem definition, (2) diagnosis, (3) solution design, (4) evaluation, and (5) learning. The outcome is a design framework for policy makers and agency executives, as well as design principles for its application in practice. With this paper, we contribute to the emerging literature on the application of design science research in public policy and administration [7]. Furthermore, the paper advances design knowledge around technology-based innovation through NIAs [8–10]. It presents a design framework aligned with the values and principles of the social market economy, offers expert insights on the implementation of policies to support technology-based innovation in such economies, and contributes to the discussion on purpose and design of NIAs in Germany and beyond.

2 Problem Definition and Analysis

2.1 Research Question

Entrepreneurship and innovation research provides two key arguments for the emergence of innovation policies that aim to support private sector innovation in general and NIAs in particular: Firstly, corporate R&D projects are often connected to substantial investment in time and resources but the knowledge and expertise these investments create tend to transcend organisational boundaries. There are many ways in which that happens, e.g., through business partnerships, changes in staff or other social networks. This means that companies cannot reap the full potential of the investments that they make, and their investment strengthens others around them. Secondly, technology-based innovation projects involve a substantial amount of risk and uncertainty. Of a larger set of projects, only a few will generate knowledge or expertise that will improve the company's business prospects. Furthermore, it is uncertain how projects will develop over time and which of them will ultimately be successful from the firm's perspective. Oftentimes companies thus prefer to invest in incremental improvements of their current business than to engage in long-term, high-risk discontinuous innovation projects [11]. NIAs aim to address this lack of incentives for investment into technology-based innovation that requires high-risk or long-term discontinuous innovation projects.

This study addresses the practical problem of public policy and government actors in social market economies seeking to develop design knowledge on NIAs. The problem can be described as follows: While NIAs have internationally become common government institutions to support high-risk, uncertain, long-term innovation projects, related design knowledge taking into account the specific principles and values of social market economies is scarce. Social market economies are a particular context for NIAs as they aim to avoid direct interference with economic processes and aim to minimise the influence of policy on the private sector (and vice versa). We thus aim to initiate a conversation on NIA design in the context of social market economies and provide a first step in addressing the following research question: *How to design national innovation agencies in alignment with the principles and values of social market economies?*

2.2 What Stakeholders Need: Principles and Values of the Social Market Economy

The concept of the social market economy developed after the Second World War was shaped by the ideas of the German Freiburg School, a group of researchers who focused on market-oriented economic policy. Members of the Freiburg School, such as Eucken, Böhm and Miksch, directly influenced economic policy through their involvement in the German Ministry of Economics and their contributions to legislation such as the 1948 law abolishing price controls ("Gesetz über die Leitsätze für die Bewirtschaftung und Preispolitik nach der Geldreform") and the 1958 competition law ("Gesetz gegen Wettbewerbsbeschränkungen"). Their greatest influence, however, came from their inspiration of two politicians, Ludwig Erhard and Alfred Müller-Armack, who were responsible for shaping post-war German economic policy in government [1, 2].

The social market economy is based on the principles of the free market economy. It emphasises the role of privilege-free competition among private actors as an efficient search routine for the creation and diffusion of innovative products and services. The state focuses on creating a supportive environment for innovation by enforcing antitrust laws, protecting property rights, and providing funding for basic research. Economic policy in social market economies focuses on creating and maintaining this competitive order, rather than intervening directly in economic processes. Ideally, therefore, government agencies would not engage in direct economic (process) intervention or industrial policy to support innovation, as this type of action could lead to inefficiencies and distortions of competition. For example, government subsidies to projects, industries or technologies could lead to a less efficient allocation of resources, which could hamper overall economic growth and innovation. At the same time, the social market economy is concerned with the common good and human dignity. Thus, social welfare such as insurance against unemployment and universal healthcare aim to correct potential hardships of free market outcomes. These policies are merely corrective, so they are not replacing the competitive order but rather complementing or adjusting it for national social welfare. The table below presents a digest of relevant aspects of social market economy political philosophy in the form of design principles (Table 1).

Table 1. Social Market Economy Design Principles

No	Design Principle
1	*Avoid interventions in the economic processes*
2	*Ensure fair competition, without special interest group influence*
3	*Do not replace private sector activity*
4	*Be technology and industry agnostic*
5	*Ensure transparency and accountability*

2.3 What Can Be Built: National Innovation Agency Models

During World War II, the United States and other state actors developed a range of state-led innovation projects that worked on breakthrough technologies for their war efforts. These projects involved connected activities of government, university, and industry actors, resulting in technologies such as sonar and radar, the jet engine, atomic weapons, and large-scale computer technology. However, after the war ended, these military innovation activities were largely dismantled due to shrinking budgets and a greater focus on civilian goods and services [12].

In the 1950s, with the Soviet Union successfully launching its Sputnik satellite into space, the US went back to a more connected approach to defence research with the creation of the Defense Advanced Research Agency (DARPA) and the National

Aeronautics and Space Administration (NASA). However, in the 1980s, the US was increasingly economically outcompeted by Japan and Germany through their strong continuous innovation activities. To address this gap, the US government created a variety of initiatives such as the Bayh-Dole Act, Small Business Innovation Research (SIBR) and the Small Business Technology Transfer (STTR) to address different issues along the innovation funnel and to fill the gap between scientific invention and commercialisation as innovative products and services, which was labelled as the "valley of death" [12].

To understand what can be built, we review the international landscape of NIAs. They aim to foster innovation with a systematic national approach, but often have an international cooperation component as well. However, they are quite idiosyncratic in their general set-up, funding, scope, beneficiaries, and partnerships. In addition, they are usually part of a larger innovation ecosystem of several types of innovation support organisations, such as basic research funding councils and university technology transfer offices. To explore the potential NIA solutions, we gathered data through interviews with NIA staff and independent think tanks and complemented this data through archival research on existing international agencies specifically outside the German social market economy context.

For our comparative interviews and desk-based research, we purposefully selected four illustrative agency models to explore in greater depth, and to delineate potential design characteristics from them. The selected agencies have all been established for several years, meaning they have institutionalised governance structures and a track record of engaging with their respective national economies and innovation systems. The selected NIAs are all located in advanced knowledge economies that have a tradition of research-based industry development and score highly on international innovation scoreboards. Moreover, for our selection we focused on NIAs that are placed in a variety of different national industry contexts that have varying characteristics in age, staff size, funding, and types of available support instruments. In addition, none of the selected cases are too similar to the German context, where the logic of the social market economy originates and is most actively applied, thereby further enhancing the strength of comparative analysis. As a result of these characteristics weighing into the selection of cases, we arrived at the following four NIAs.

Innosuisse is a Swiss federal institution under public law that promotes innovation through funding and support. It was founded in 2018 and developed out of the former Commission for Technology and Innovation. Innosuisse's funding comes directly from the federal state budget and its approach is designed to be bottom-up, meaning it only supports projects that are interesting for research institutes and industry. Until recently, Innosuisse did not directly fund the development of companies of any size, but a change in legislation now allows for more direct support of start-ups before market entry. Beneficiaries are selected through application-based and rolling competitions, with the goal of supporting the best and most promising ideas that would not otherwise be able to evolve and enter competitive markets.

DARPA (Defense Advanced Research Projects Agency) is the NIA for discontinuous innovation in defence technology of the United States of America. Its goal is to ensure the technological situational awareness and superiority of the United States armed forces. It was founded in 1958 with a lean structure and a mission to make pivotal investments in breakthrough technologies for national security. DARPA receives its funding from the US Department of Defense and its budget is 25% of DoD's total science and technology funding and 2% of all federal research and development funding. DARPA has a clear military focus and aims at revolutionary breakthroughs that could be transformative for their armed forces, but their technologies can also enter the civilian market later. Its portfolio is overseen by six technical offices and two more support offices.

Innovate UK is an NIA established in 2007 that supports business-led innovation across the United Kingdom. It is part of UK Research and Innovation and is governed by an Innovate UK Council. The agency is publicly funded by the government and in late 2022, a rise was announced to the yearly budget allocation to Innovate UK. Innovate UK's funding decisions are based on an assessment of whether a grant proposal is likely to provide added value from the perspective of UK taxpayers. The agency is active across all industry sectors in the country and has a role in advising and influencing government innovation policy. About 80% of the grant funding is targeted at applicants that fall into specific thematic areas identified by the agency and the remaining 20% is awarded to the development of tools-based innovations. The innovation grants are mostly awarded following a 50/50 (pari passu) principle where the volume of private funding is expected to match the granted public innovation support. Around 90% of the beneficiaries of Innovate UK are Small and Medium Enterprises (SMEs).

The Israel Innovation Authority is the primary NIA in Israel. It was formed in 1965 as the Office of the Chief Scientist and changed its name in 2016. The agency is politically independent and has a strong mandate in innovation policy that gives it a strong position in Israel's wider innovation ecosystem. The agency has played a strong role in promoting university-industry collaboration, the growth of venture capital funding, and R&D investment in high-technological sectors. It is publicly funded by the Israeli government and the two largest shares of the available funding are channelled to grants towards growth-focused R&D and start-up support. The agency also gets revenue from royalties accrued on successful innovations that have earlier received grant funding. The agency has a wide range of support structures and programs that are tailored to specific industry niches and ventures with specific bottlenecks or development stages in their innovation activities. The agency's goal is to support and strengthen market-driven innovation, not to actively reshape it. The agency's funding stake in its support schemes are flexible, they often represent less than half of the total budget for an innovation project, but can also sometimes be over 50% if there is deemed to be a particular benefit to the development of the innovation ecosystem.

Our view of what can be built is further informed by the existing body of literature on NIA design, that does not consider the specificities of social market economies. In particular, we build on Breznitz et al. [8], who developed insights into different types of NIA as well as their means and ends, Glennie et al. [9], who (based on the work of Bresnitz) developed a practice guide on NIA at the UK-based innovation agency NESTA, as well as Atta et al. [10], who focus on the particular design features of DARPA.

3 Solution Design

Based on the preceding problem definition and analysis and anchored in the empirical work conducted as part of the research project, this paper now moves to apply the variety of observed design features and principles into a conceptual NIA design.

3.1 Design Requirements

Design requirements are qualities that the solution design must have while also taking into account the user groups' expectations. There are four groups of design requirements: Functional requirements describe the fundamental functions that are responsible for the performance of the solution; User requirements are the requirements provided by the solution's intended users; Boundary conditions describe the conditions that must be satisfied without exception; and Design restrictions are the solution space that the target user group prefers [6].

The functional requirement in the case of designing NIAs is to deliver a solution design that adheres to the principles and values of the social market economy and covers the constitutional elements of NIAs, including following: Scope, people, instruments, and governance. The user requirement is to design the solution in an easy-to-understand fashion to ensure that it is understandable by all stakeholders involved in the public discourse on innovation policy, from policy-makers to journalists. As a boundary condition, the solution design should focus on industrialised countries with established institutions, as prior research has shown that non-industrialised context require substantially different approaches to building innovation infrastructure [13]. The only design restriction is to ensure that the solution design is in line with the values and principles of the social market economy.

3.2 Solution Design

Based on the outlined requirements, a set of twelve design principles for NIAs in social market economies was developed. To this end, we used a combination of induction from our cases studies and deduction from the social market economy principles. Figure 1 provides an overview of the key aspects that are discussed as design principles in greater detail below.

Scope. *Design principle 1–Clear agency mission.* The NIA design should be specifically tailored to address the "valley of death" and/or the diffusion of innovation. Both missions require different approaches: while bridging the "valley of death" primarily aims to encourage and finance projects between research institutions and the private sector, the diffusion involves not only knowledge dissemination and support in experimenting with technologies, but also work on the development of market institutions and regulatory environments.

Design principle 2–Supporting competition for innovation. The agency should not engage in activities that could create barriers to entry for new market participants or undermine the ability of private companies to innovate and compete. Thus, the agency's

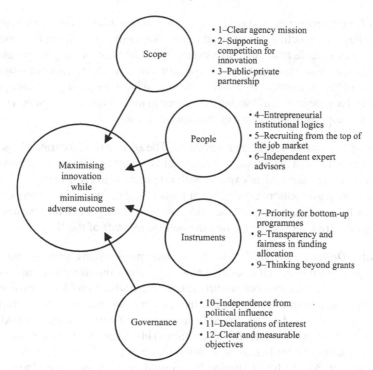

Fig. 1. Design Principles Overview

role should ideally be limited to indirectly supporting private firms, rather than paying direct subsidies to them. Direct funding can be directed towards research partners (such as universities or research institutions), who are not market participants. All support functions should be designed to be open to all applicants, independent of their size, although tailored approaches to different kind of stakeholders can be a useful way to ensure diverse and accessible participation in the innovation ecosystem.

Design principle 3–Public-private partnership. The agency should not replace private sector activity but rather complement where the market fails to deliver. To this end, the agency should partner with the private sector (e.g., venture capital firms, corporate R&D units) but also universities (e.g., transfer offices, entrepreneurship centres) and government institutions (e.g., military procurement) to leverage their expertise and resources in achieving the agency's goals.

People. *Design principle 4–Entrepreneurial institutional logics.* The agency should be as independent as possible from other government bodies. Flexibility and autonomy on organisational and programme level should support the development of entrepreneurial instead of government/administrative institutional logics. Bureaucracy needs to be kept to a minimum.

Design principle 5–Recruiting from the top of the job market. The agency leadership and the programme managers should be recruited from the top of the job market. This means they have relevant research experience at top universities or comparable industry experience. Pay and benefit schemes need to be competitive, so joining the innovation agency becomes a viable alternative to a career in academia or joining corporate R&D units. However, to ensure constant renewal and influx of new talent, tenure of programme managers should be limited to three to five years, making it necessary to move projects along quickly. Experienced staff leaving the agency to join private firms can be a valuable component of supporting innovation in the private sector.

Design principle 6–Independent expert advisors. The agency should curate a large group of international experts in the relevant research fields. Funding recommendations should be made by multiple independent experts, with no personal interest in the project. Furthermore, a wide participation from different parts of the economy in the work to draw up strategies for the functioning of the NIA can be a strong asset that harnesses the opportunity of shared knowledge beyond the permanent staff of the NIA itself.

Instruments. *Design principle 7–Priority for bottom-up programmes.* As the capacity of the agency to possess all relevant knowledge about on-going innovation is limited, the NIA should prioritise bottom-up programmes, where problems drive solution development, where both formal and informal pre-existing networks for learning and innovation are boosted and not overruled from above, and where exceptional skills and learning capabilities drive successful innovation. This means that market participants and research institutions are free to apply with whatever they think can be a promising innovation project. After a first screening by programme managers, the innovativeness will be judged by the external experts. Thematic top-down competitions around a particular problem (e.g., energy storage) can complement this focus on bottom-up projects, but innovation challenges should be outcome-centred and sufficiently open to different technological approaches.

Design principle 8–Transparency and fairness in funding allocation. The agency should have a transparent and fair process for allocating funding, to ensure that all applicants have an equal opportunity to compete for funding. Funding decisions should be based on evaluations made by external experts in the subject matter, without interest in the particular project.

Design Principle 9–Thinking beyond grants. The agency should aim to fill the functions in the innovation ecosystem that the market is not providing. Depending on the situation in the given ecosystem, the NIA could engage in a portfolio of activities beyond financially supporting promising innovation projects. For example, this could be collaboration with universities to provide entrepreneurship education, particularly to research staff, or providing technical assistance to small businesses and entrepreneurs to help them navigate the process of adoption and implementation of new technologies and ideas. Furthermore, assistance to participate in public procurement could help create initial demand for innovative products and services.

Governance. *Design principle 10–Independence from political influence.* The agency should be independent from political influence, to ensure that funding decisions are made based on merit rather than political considerations. This is important to ensure that the agency does not engage in activities that could result in privileges for particular groups or create barriers to entry for new market participants.

Design Principle 11–Declarations of interest. Everyone involved in decision making should declare their interests in written form for every project, with substantial penalties for breach of contract. This is to ensure fair competition for the limited resources of the NIA and to reduce the likelihood of any type of cronyism or narrowing of the applicant pool to only "usual suspects" who knew about funding opportunities from before.

Design principle 12–Clear and measurable objectives. The agency should have clearly defined and measurable objectives, to ensure that funding is directed towards projects that are most likely to achieve the agency's goals. The agency should be accountable to both the government and the public and should be subject to regular audits and evaluations to ensure that it is achieving its goals and using its resources effectively. The agency should engage with the public through all possible media and provide transparency through regular open events.

Overall, these twelve design principles aim to align the NIA with the principles and values of the social market economy. Their goal is to optimise national welfare through entrepreneurship and innovation by filling gaps in the innovation ecosystem without compromising privilege-free private sector competition.

4 Evaluation

To evaluate our solution design, we gathered written expert feedback from six leading German economists that are intellectually associated with the social market economy. Below we present brief summaries of their statements.

Economist 1 emphasises that innovations and their external effects justify market interventions, but a competitive structure is crucial for research and development. Innovation agencies can play a vital role in promoting riskier projects and transferring successful projects to the market. However, innovation policy must align with the market economy to be effective. It should encourage collaboration between universities, research institutes, companies, and private venture capital. It is essential to prevent market participants from crowding out self-sustaining activities and engaging in excessive rent-seeking. Poorly designed innovation policies can end up working against themselves. Innovation agencies can promote riskier projects and transfer successful ones to the market by focusing on future markets and venture capitalists at an early stage.

Economist 2 underlines that innovations, driven by private companies' research and development, drive economic growth and development. However, private companies only consider their own benefit when making investment decisions, resulting in too little investment in new knowledge from a macroeconomic perspective. This justifies government intervention in the form of education and basic research funding, as well as setting framework conditions and incentives for private-sector innovation. However, calls for government intervention to promote discontinuous innovations have been met with scepticism. These innovation projects can be costly and risky, and some argue that government agencies are not as efficient or effective as private venture capital firms in identifying and promoting them. In market-based economies, competition serves as a discovery process for innovation, and state intervention may be expensive and counterproductive in the long run.

Economist 3 states that only through its innovativeness is it possible for an otherwise resource-poor economy such as Germany to achieve a high national welfare, provide a high level of public goods and play a key role in international value chains. To intervene in the innovation process at the right place and at the right time, different types of NIAs have been established. These agencies, in contrast to the usual state administration, must have an agile structure that quickly adapts to the dynamic innovation process and ensures a high degree of competition in the allocation of funding. This requirement profile can only be fulfilled if considerable competencies are available in the agencies, which can hardly be built up in the administrative apparatus itself.

Economist 4 reminds us of how innovation economics argues that firms' investment in innovation may be insufficient in a laissez-faire market due to externalities and limited access to funding. However, the effectiveness of NIAs in addressing these market failures varies and depends on the agency's structure and the particular innovation ecosystem. The historical success of NIAs is not always as clear as it seems as we cannot know what would have happened without their intervention. While NIAs might nevertheless play a positive role, it is still worthwhile to consider policy instruments that rely less on the ability of only a few experts to make correct judgments. Tax incentives for investments into R&D and also for funding early-stage, innovative firms are one type of example. The German success story of establishing a network of institutes of applied science ("Fraunhofer-Gesellschaften") with the purpose of intensive industry co-creation is another example.

Economist 5 underlines that the private sector, especially early-stage start-ups, has the potential to innovate and commercialise new technologies. However, major breakthroughs in "grand challenges" like addressing climate change often require long development cycles and specialised expertise based on basic research. These breakthroughs often require "high risk-high reward" research, which can be difficult for start-ups to provide due to the pressure to generate short-term returns. NIAs can bridge this gap by providing funding and mentorship to start-ups and small firms. These agencies focus on specific sectors or technologies and provide not only financial grants but also direct mentoring and technological exchange with hired scientists. This approach has been successful in fostering innovation, bridging the gap between basic and applied research, and commercialising breakthrough technology.

Economist 6, finally suggests practicing humility. Modernity is fuelled by the innovative dynamism of individuals who continually contribute their knowledge to market processes. This includes countless small entrepreneurs who enhance their products and processes every day. Focusing solely on prominent founders fails to recognise the contributions of these micro-innovators. The state's role in innovation policy should be to foster a culture of innovation by providing an institutional climate for micro-innovation through education, taxation, and legal structures. Additionally, the state should facilitate the flow of innovations from basic research institutions to the private sector. While the state's support is vital in this process, innovation policy should exercise humility: the state can establish goals but should avoid claiming to know the best means to achieve them.

In summary, the economists highlight a wide range of issues for designing NIA in context of social market economies. In particular, economist 1 emphasises the importance of designing such agencies in line with market principles–otherwise, the agency could potentially become its own adversary. This suggests that the agency should operate in a way that leverages market dynamics through supporting competition, rather than trying to supplant them. Economist 2 emphasises the need to focus on competition as a way of discovery. This suggests that innovation policy should encourage competition among firms to promote innovation, rather than simply funding individual projects. Economist 3 underlines the need for agencies to have sufficient agility and competence to fulfil their mission. This suggests that the agency should be designed to be adaptable and responsive to changing circumstances and that the programme managers of the agency should be highly competent and well-trained. Economist 4 reminds us that policy should also consider other instruments, such as tax incentives, to foster innovation. This suggests that the agency's design should take into account other policy instruments that can be used in conjunction with the agency to achieve its goals. Economist 5 suggests that high-risk, high-reward projects could benefit from support through national innovation agencies. This suggests that the agency's design should incorporate mechanisms for identifying and supporting particularly such projects. Lastly, economist 6 calls for humility, noting that while government agencies may set goals, they should not assume to have all the knowledge needed to achieve them. This suggests that the agency's design should remain solution-agnostic and incorporate mechanisms for seeking input and feedback from a broad range of stakeholders, including industry experts, academics, and the public. In other words, the reading emerging from both existing literatures, the undertaken review of four independent NIAs, and the feedback and discussion by leading experts, all suggest that NIAs are not necessarily the proper forum for political involvement and debate surrounding innovation policy and its direction.

5 Learning

The learnings from the study are transformed into design propositions on innovation policy by applying the CIMO logic [14]. The CIMO logic offers a structured approach for deriving propositions by integrating the context with particular interventions, which correspond to particular mechanisms and produce defined results. The details of the design propositions are summarised in the illustration below (Fig. 2).

Following the CIMO logic, the findings and design principles of our study can be summarised as follows: This paper develops a type of NIA tailored to the needs of the social market economy (C) with a curated set of principles the agency scope, people, instruments and governance. These consider the risks of interventions in the economic process (I) by promoting a market-based and complementary way of fostering long-term, high-risk, uncertain projects (M) to support technology-based innovation in the private sector and maximise national welfare (O).

The existing literature such as Breznitz et al. [8], Glennie et al. [9], or Atta et al. [10] provide design suggestions for different aspects of NIA setups. In contrast, this paper complements the existing literature by proposing design principles for NIAs in line

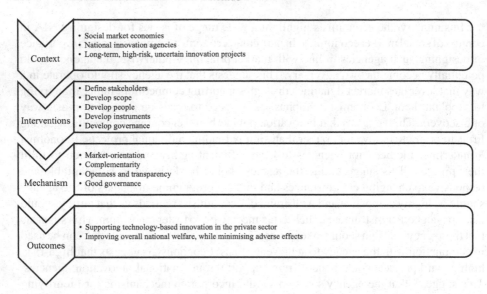

Fig. 2. Design Proposition with CIMO logic

with the principles and values of the social market economy. The solution design suggested takes into account the delicate balance between the potential benefits of market-interventions and the risks of adverse outcomes such as reduced competition, through particular design features.

Furthermore, based on the preceding analysis, we provide three general propositions on innovation policy: Firstly, our review of the principles and values of the social market economy in the context of NIA suggests that the overall aim of innovation policy should be on correcting the economic order for the shortcomings of laissez-faire market outcomes in terms of innovation, to maximise overall national welfare. Secondly, NIAs are not the only option that policy makers and industry have to support innovation. It remains unclear if innovations would not have been brought to the market without intervention by the state. Thus, other options, such as tax incentives, industry initiatives, or other more general economic policy measures should be taken into consideration as well. Thirdly, while some proponents of the social market economy see justification for interventions in the economic process through NIAs, some experts argue that a free market should be able to serve as a sufficient method of discovery for the creation and diffusion of technology-based innovative products and services. Therefore, in order to maximise the benefits from NIAs, the question remains to identify where exactly the market fails to deliver the desired outcomes in an innovation ecosystem, and to assess whether interventions in the economic process are justified by these potential failures.

6   Conclusion

The proposed solution design is a conceptual approach to the tension between the interventions of NIAs in the economic process and the social market economy's pursuit of a privilege-free and competitive economic order. With our twelve design principles in four domains, we provide the user group with a lightweight and approachable guidance framework in decision making on the setup and funding of NIAs. By aligning the two concepts, we suggest a variant of the NIA that could support the creation and diffusion of technology-based innovation and national welfare while not leading to adverse effects like cronyism and reduced competition.

The limitation of this study is that the conceptual solution covers only higher-level principles of NIA design rather than operational details. Furthermore, it has not yet been implemented and tested on its practicability. This evaluation could involve contributions of policy makers, investors, entrepreneurs, company executives, and technology researchers to increase the diversity of perspectives. To better understand the impact of NIAs in social market economies, future studies could evaluate the impact of individual design features of NIAs on innovation outcomes in different social market economies. Here, basic research based on quantitative and qualitative and qualitative data on outcomes of NIA interventions could be helpful to inform further design science research projects. However, as pointed out by economist 4, testability might be limited as technology-based innovations could have alternative pathways to be realised without state intervention. Here the lack of a control group for the treatment might be an issue in evaluating the success of NIAs.

This paper contributes to the body of design knowledge on supporting technology-based innovation through an NIA and has practical implications for policy makers and innovation agency executives. Firstly, we contribute to the body of design knowledge by developing a design framework for NIAs in line with the values and principles of the social market economy. Secondly, based on expert reflections on this project, we provide more general insights for the implementation of policies for technology-based innovation in social market economies. Thirdly, we contribute to the emerging literature on design science in public policy and administration [7]. Lastly, with our project, we contribute directly to the ongoing policy conversations on the purpose and design of NIAs in Germany and beyond.

References

1. Feld, L.P., Köhler, E.A., Nientiedt, D.: Ordoliberalism and the Social Market Economy. Freiburg Discussion Papers on Constitutional Economics (2019)
2. Kolev, S.: Neoliberale Staatsverständnisse im Vergleich. Walter de Gruyter, Berlin/Boston (2017). https://doi.org/10.1515/9783110489910
3. Dold, M., Krieger, T.: The ideological use and abuse of Freiburg's ordoliberalism. Public Choice. (2021). https://doi.org/10.1007/s11127-021-00875-0.
4. Moore, G.E.: Cramming more components onto integrated circuits. Electronics **38**, 114–117 (1965)
5. Seckler, C., Mauer, R., vom Brocke, J.: Design science in entrepreneurship: conceptual foundations and guiding principles. J. Bus. Ventur. Des. **1**, 100004 (2021). https://doi.org/10.1016/j.jbvd.2022.100004
6. van Aken, J.E., Berends, H., Bij, H.V., Der,: Problem Solving in Organizations: A Methodological Handbook for Business and Management Students. Cambridge University Press, Cambridge, UK (2012)

7. Romme, A.G.L., Meijer, A.: Applying design science in public policy and administration research. Policy Polit. **48**, 149–165 (2020). https://doi.org/10.1332/030557319X15613699981234

8. Breznitz, D., Ornston, D., Samford, S.: Mission critical: the ends, means, and design of innovation agencies. Ind. Corp. Chang. **27**, 883–896 (2018). https://doi.org/10.1093/icc/dty027

9. Glennie, A., Bound, K.: How innovation agencies work: International lessons to inspire and inform national strategies. London (2016)

10. Atta, R. Van, Windham, P., Bonvillian, W.B.: Lessons from DARPA's Experience. Open Book Publishers, Cambridge, UK (2019). https://doi.org/10.11647/OBP.0184

11. Christensen, C.M.: The Innovator's Dilemma. Harvard Business Review Press, Boston (1997)

12. Bonvillian, W.B.: The new model innovation agencies: an overview. Sci. Public Policy **41**, 425–437 (2014). https://doi.org/10.1093/scipol/sct059

13. Intarakumnerd, P., Chaminade, C.: National innovation system policies in less successful developing countries: the case of Thailand. Res. Policy **31**, 1445–1457 (2007)

14. Denyer, D., Tranfield, D., Van Aken, J.E.: Developing design propositions through research synthesis. Organ. Stud. **29**(3), 393–413 (2008)

How to Invest in the Future of Food: An Exploration Design Science Project

Richard Henry Nacke and Christoph Seckler[✉] [iD]

ESCP Business School, Berlin, Germany
richard_henry.nacke@edu.escp.eu, cseckler@escp.eu

Abstract. The food production sector is one of the largest industries globally, yet it is confronted with significant challenges. While food tech startups are viewed as a promising means of addressing some of these obstacles, they frequently encounter the issue of being highly research-intensive and risky investments. In this project, we pose the following question: How can we effectively design investment vehicles and strategies to support food tech startups? To address this question, we undertook an exploration design science research project. In collaboration with a corporate venture fund, we initially explored opportunities and subsequently developed a solution design for one of the most promising prospects. This study contributes to the body of design knowledge in three primary ways. Firstly, it contributes by providing a situated artifact that outlines the design of a closed-ended deep science food tech fund engaged in production and input supply. Secondly, it contributes by establishing design principles for investment vehicles and strategies in ventures that are highly research-intensive and risky. Lastly, this study makes a methodological contribution by showcasing how a methodology for addressing exploration design science projects could look like.

Keywords: Food tech · Investment vehicle · Investment strategy · Design science · Exploration project

1 Introduction

The global food and agricultural sector is one of the largest industries worldwide, estimated to be worth $8.7 trillion [28], and it contributes to almost 10% of the global gross domestic product [28]. Despite its size and economic significance, this industry faces significant challenges that are expected to exacerbate in the future. The current food system is unlikely to be capable of feeding the global population [30]. Natural disasters such as the locust blight in East Asia or pandemics such as swine fever and Covid-19 pose a threat to the food value chain. Additionally, the current global food supply chain is extremely unsustainable [29] and results in health and healthcare issues like obesity, diseases, deaths, and high healthcare costs [45].

Food tech startups are addressing critical issues related to the global food supply chain by utilizing novel technologies such as plant-based protein, gene-editing, drones, indoor farming, satellite imaging, precision farming, and computational biology. These

A. Gerber and R. Baskerville (Eds.): DESRIST 2023, LNCS 13873, pp. 221–231, 2023.
https://doi.org/10.1007/978-3-031-32808-4_14

startups are likely to bring significant changes to the food and agriculture system through technology.

However, financing these often highly research-intensive and risky ventures poses a challenge. Little is known about how to effectively finance food tech startups. Previous literature has mainly focused on outlining the opportunities of food tech topics such as edible insect production [20], vertical farming [10], and cellular agriculture on the meat industry [40]. On the other hand, literature on developing venture funding has focused mainly on the different types of investment vehicles and provides some generic ideas on how to develop venture funds [34]. Yet, both literatures provide little guidance on how to design investment vehicles and strategies that account for the specific characteristics of food tech startups. Thus, this research project seeks to answer the question, "How can we design an effective investment vehicle and strategy for food tech startups?".

To answer the research question of how to design an effective investment vehicle and strategy for food tech startups, we undertake a design science research project [35, 37, 42]. Specifically, we conduct an exploration project in collaboration with a venture fund, we refer to as "The Firm." The project illustrates a methodology to address exploration design science projects [37, 38], which consists of two main phases. In the first phase, we explore the problem space (i.e., the needs of food tech startup stakeholders) and the solution space (i.e., potential investment vehicles and strategies) [44]. Based on this exploration, we identify and create multiple promising opportunities and select the most viable one. In the second phase, we develop and evaluate a design object [43] for an investment vehicle and strategy for food tech startups.

This design science project contributes to the body of design knowledge in three main ways. First, this article contributes by developing a situated artefact outlining the design of a closed-ended deep science food tech fund active in production and input supply [20, 34]. Second, we develop more generalizable design principles on investment vehicles and strategies to financially support research intensive and risky deep tech ventures such as food tech startups [20, 34]. Third, this study makes a methodological contribution to the design science discourse [11, 22, 44] by showcasing how a methodology to address exploration design science projects [37, 38] could look like.

The paper is structured according to the two main phases of the exploration design science project methodology that was utilized [37, 38]. Firstly, we present the phase of opportunity exploration, which entails analyzing both the problem and solution space, and serves as the foundation for identifying and selecting the most promising opportunity. Secondly, we outline the phase of opportunity exploitation, which involves developing and evaluating a situated artifact for the investment vehicle and strategy of the chosen opportunity. Finally, we conclude with a discussion of the key contributions to the literature, limitations of the study, and future research opportunities.

2 Opportunity Exploration

2.1 Methodical Approach

Opportunity exploration can be described as a search process of identifying promising novel opportunities, that is, means-end relationships or problem-solution combinations

[37, 38, 44]. To discover and create novel opportunities, we engage in two main activities. First, we explore the problem and solution space [44], and subsequently generate novel opportunities, and evaluate them [37, 38]. We followed the guiding principles for design science in entrepreneurship to draw on the best available knowledge and to use fitting methods to develop complementing knowledge. This means we reviewed relevant literatures to explore the solution space (what can be built), and the problem space (what is needed) and complemented these insights with 10 semi-structured interviews with relevant stakeholders (i.e., fund managers, investors, and startups). In the following, we outline our findings in exploring the solution space and the problem space (Sect. 2.2), as well as the opportunities that we have generated and chosen (Sect. 2.3).

2.2 Analyzing the Solution Space and the Problem Space

2.2.1 Analyzing the Solution Space – What Can Be Built?

A review of the literature on designing investment vehicles and strategies, we identified several key design parameters to consider with regard to both the investment vehicle, as well as the investment strategy. There are various investment vehicles that can be built. An investment vehicle is an asset aiming to generate returns for investors [21]. For The Firm, the relevant types of investment vehicles are venture capital (VC) funds. VC is the 'professionalized financial activity consisting of investing in companies which are in the start-up or expanding stages' [3]. VC funds can be differentiated into two distinct models depending on the time frame in which capital can be raised and returned: They can either be a closed-ended VC investment fund or an open-ended VC investment fund. Closed-ended funds are limited partnerships with a fixed term that are only liquidated on termination day. Open-ended funds are limited liability companies without a fixed term that can continuously invest, raise, repay, and transfer capital. Closed-ended and ever-green funds offer similar returns for investors from a total value perspective but differ in value creation, distribution of returns and taxation.

The fund portfolio size and structure depends on the target sector and portfolio construction. Empirical analyses suggest that medium-sized funds ($84–365 million) with vintage years from 1995–2005 outperformed both smaller and larger funds in internal rate of return (IRR) [25]. Furthermore, specialized funds perform better than general funds [17]. Regarding the target sector, funds investing in companies based on deep science technology tend to require larger fund sizes than funds investing in companies based on software technology [24, 34]. To construct a portfolio, the VC fund needs to define the portfolio size, average total investment, and average holding period at the time of exit [34]. The portfolio size depends on the type of companies that a VC fund invests in. VC funds focused on software companies tend to have a larger portfolio and lower total average investments. Reversely, funds focused on deep science companies usually have smaller portfolios and higher total average investments [7, 34]. Funds can either invest in companies with a similar risk profile or distribute investments across risk profiles. Generally, the portfolio construction should resemble the level of risk agreed on by both fund managers and fund investors [18].

The investment strategy is the "raison d'être" of a VC fund and outlines how the targeted market approached [34]. Most VC funds use an emergent strategy which can be adapted over time [34]. According to Arnold [2], there are three approaches to create a competitive edge with an investment strategy: (1) Sourcing better investments, (2) making better deals, and (3) supporting investments better. First, deal sourcing can be done from inbound and outbound sources and determines the quality of the subsequent investment funnel. Sourcing is particularly important because it determines the quality of leads that get into the funnel and consequently the portfolio [2]. Second, making better deals is related to the investment thesis. An investment thesis summarizes the beliefs of the VC fund about a sector on a high level and sets the parameters to evaluate and decide on potential investments [41]. Third, VC funds can support portfolio companies through operational support, network, and expert industry knowledge. The level of operational involvement of VC funds varies and can have a great impact on a portfolio company's performance [13].

The targeted food market can be differentiated into three segments: food tech deep science, food tech software, or food brands companies. Food tech deep science companies innovate through novel technical competencies in the natural or physical sciences. These sciences include biology, chemistry, physics, or computer sciences. Food tech software companies harness existing digital technologies enabled by internet software and focus primarily on business model innovation. Food brands companies do not feature novel, proprietary technology, business models, or production facilities. They rather innovate through branding and follow more routine innovations.

The three types of food companies differ in their required capital, timeline, overall revenue potential, and VC growth trajectory. Food tech deep science companies have very high capital and timeline requirement [24]. Consequently, food tech deep science companies pose high risks to investors but also the biggest rewards. In contrast, food tech software companies require less capital and time because the product is based on software and can be developed in a shorter time frame. These attributes accelerate the time to market as the product can be quickly released to the market via the internet and demand can be tested effectively. Consequently, they have the best growth trajectory and pose the lowest risk to investors. Lastly, food brands companies possess high capital and time requirements due to the physical products involved and reliance on traditional channels. While food tech companies have the potential to dominate an entire market, it is highly unlikely for food brands as they are missing a technological edge over other products. This missing potential and their comparably low level of innovation increases the risk for investors, limits the overall revenue potential, and flattens the growth trajectory compared to food tech companies.

2.2.2 Exploring the Problem Space - What Stakeholders Actually Want

We explored the needs of three main stakeholder groups: investment professionals, fund investors, and founders of food tech startups. First, our interviews suggest unsurprisingly that one need for investment professionals is that the investment vehicle produces positive financial returns. Besides the annual management fee, carried interest is often the opportunity for investment professionals to earn money with the investment vehicle. Furthermore, multiple interviewed investment professionals highlighted their altruistic perspective on investments and focused on positive social and environmental impacts.

Finally, investments professionals described their desire to pass on their expertise to support the founders of their portfolio companies.

Second, we explored what fund investors are looking for in a food tech investment vehicle. We find that to meet fund investors' needs we should design an investment vehicle and strategy that produces a competitive financial return (>20%). Furthermore, our interviews indicated that the investment vehicle should offer them the opportunity to explore business models and industries, access digital technologies and collaborate with startups. Exploring business models and industries through VC funds is an important tool particularly for corporate investors to spot trends and develop their company. Lastly, fund investors were interested in satisfying the ESG criteria.

Third, founders of food tech companies indicated the following needs. First, they highlighted investment ticket size and valuation as the most important criteria for selecting an investor. Also, founders suggested that they actively look for investors that have enough capital reserved for follow-up rounds and that there is a mission alignment. Interviewed founders also highlighted how valuable and important the operational support of an investor is for them in both primary and support activities. Finally, we find that founders actively look for investors that have a good network within the food industry.

2.3 Opportunity Generation and Evaluation

Based on the analysis of the problem and the solution space, we generated and evaluated multiple promising opportunity candidates, that is problem-solution candidates [38]. We used a morphological box approach to first determining a promising fit between targeted market (e.g., food tech deep science, food tech software, or food brands companies) and investment vehicle (i.e., different fund models). Based on the matrix of all possible combinations, we chose four opportunity candidates with the best fit: (1) closed-ended fund focused on food tech software companies, (2) closed-ended fund focused on food tech deep science companies, (3) evergreen fund focused on food tech deep science companies, and (4) evergreen fund focused on food brands companies and companies from the food tech innovative food investment category.

After comparing the parameters set for the four opportunities to the needs of involved stakeholders, we decide to select the second opportunity to be the most promising one, that is a "closed-ended deep science food tech fund". Although evergreen funds exceed closed-ended funds in satisfying non-financial customer needs and offer unique advantages, closed-ended funds outperform evergreen fund models from a financial perspective in the geographical region that "The Firm" is located in. Furthermore, we decided for the opportunity to invest in food tech deep science companies. Our analyses indicated that deep science companies possess more power to solve the outlined problems associated with the current food system. The input supply and production steps of the value chain account for more than 80% of GHG emissions for most foods [31], withdraw 70% of global freshwater, and use 50% of global habitable land [32].

3 Opportunity Exploitation

3.1 Methodical Approach

After choosing a promising opportunity, we designed an outline design for an investment vehicle and strategy [38]. An outline design is created by determining all design parameters, assigning values to them, and detailing them out [43]. An outline design transforms a generic opportunity into a situated artefact that provides detailed guidance on how to seize the opportunity [43]. In the following, we outline the design of the investment vehicle and strategy and evaluate them.

3.2 Investment Vehicle

As we have chosen a closed-ended fund, the fund is set-up as a limited partnership. The fund model includes the fund investors as limited partners (LPs), the partners of the VC fund as general partners (GPs), and an investment management company. We set the timeline of the fund at 10 years including two one-year extension options. The investment period lasts three years and the harvesting period for seven to nine years. We conducted a separate analysis to showcase that the set timeline is feasible to invest in food tech deep science companies within the targeted market.

Due to the high-risk profile of deep science companies, we pursue a homerun investment logic for the fund. Consequently, we are counting on a few companies in the portfolio to generate the targeted return of the entire fund. The fund targets an ROI of 20–30% to be competitive with other investment vehicles. As previously introduced, the most successful funds had a higher share of money-losing investments than mediocre funds over the course of 1975 to 2014 [12] and 20% of deals produced around 90% of returns for funds with an ROI > 5x [19]. Hence, the logic is to invest in high risk-high return startups which pursue disruptive ideas that can change the rules and capture their entire market.

We have decided to set the fund size at $120 mn. Medium-sized funds ($84–365 million) with vintage years from 1995–2005 outperformed both smaller and larger funds in IRR [25] and deep science funds tend to require larger funds [24]. The $120 mn fund size seems realistic since other European food tech funds have raised similar fund sizes [6]. The fund conducts its first investment in a company either in the seed or series A round. 65% of the funds are dedicated to seed investments and the remaining 35% to series A investments. We do not conduct series B investments because we want to focus on younger companies and the fund size is not sufficient for later stage investments.

The envisioned portfolio size is 36 companies in total. This portfolio size is big enough to increase the chance of a homerun. Out of the 36 investments, 24 are seed investments and 12 series A investments. After deducting the management fee from the fund size, it translates into $2.5 mn available per company starting at seed investment and $3.2 starting at series A investments. For seed investments, 50% of the available capital is invested in the seed round and 50% across the following rounds. For series A investments, 80% is invested in the seed round and 20% across the following rounds. However, since companies are written-off in the process, there is significantly more capital available per company in later stages than the average to double-down on winners. Thus, we plan to follow-up approximately 50% of our seed investments. The assumptions for the portfolio development are based on a study of CBInsights [4].

Finally, the fund aims to make syndicate investments with other investors since deep science companies are too capital-intense for a single fund of the envisioned fund size [24]. The fund targets 6% ownership for first-round seed and 4% for first-round series A investments. The fund participates in all subsequent rounds until an exit and try to increase ownership percentage. Combining all these assumptions, the fund achieves a multiple of 2.68 of the invested capital. This represents an ROI of 26.8% for the regular fund timeline and 22.4% if both extension options are activated. Hence, it is favorable to avoid the extension options if not necessary.

3.3 Investment Strategy

The investment strategy is designed as follows. The sourcing strategy focuses on outbound sources. Besides the network of the team with other VCs, founders, and angel investors, we focus our efforts on targeting the right incubators, accelerators, and universities to spot opportunities early on. Optimally, a brand as a leading investor is developed and increases inbound sourcing.

The fund should aim to have approximately 20% of the portfolio companies in the vertical farming area. We deem hydroponic systems, aeroponic systems, and lightning equipment particularly promising. Also, we target to have around 5% of the portfolio in the insect production area. Another 20% of the portfolio companies are aimed to be active in cellular production. To us, cellular production is promising because the end product is not distinguishable from conventional meat. We believe that companies working on the whole production process of cultured meat are still attractive investment targets in the short- to long-term. In addition, companies specializing in the value chain, or building enabling platforms may be attractive investment targets, too. Most importantly, we aim to appoint the largest share of portfolio companies to acellular production at 45% because our analysis indicated great potential for the future of food. We deem all opportunities in both the B2B and B2C segment promising. Lastly, we dedicate 10% of the portfolio to companies in adjacent areas with a focus on growth mediums.

The geographical focus of the designed fund is on Europe and North America. The fund operates from Europe and the target is to conduct 70% of all investments in Europe to participate in the recent surge in European food tech funding [1]. The remaining 30% is invested in North America, the most active and largest food tech country [1]. Moreover, the fund should aim at leading each initial investment round that is entered. Also, the fund focuses on first-round seed to series A investments. Accordingly, the fund is likely to show more volatility in IRR [5] but also to produce better fund performance than later-stage focused funds [25].

The VC fund should support portfolio companies through its network, expert industry knowledge, and operational support while taking a medium level and frequency of involvedness. Hence, the partners join the management board and founders can always approach the fund for advice and operational support. In the early-stage development phase, the focus of operational support is on enabling the development of the technology and prototype through personal advice, support in hiring, access to laboratories, attracting more funding, and connections to other scientists. In the scale and manufacturing phase, the focus of support is to help attract sufficient investors to finance the actual production facilities and support operations and the value chain development. Lastly, the support in the revenue growth phase is around branding, pricing, retailer selection, marketing, sales, and distribution.

The best possible exit strategy is to achieve an IPO. However, more likely is a strategic acquisition by an existing corporate. According to Decker et al. [8], 23% of all agriculture executives indicated Mergers & Acquisitions (M&A) as their preferred way of investing while only 8% are currently pursuing M&A deals. The strategic acquisitions market for the targeted investment categories is especially attractive because the targeted companies disrupt not only the producers of food but ultimately also the large CPG brands that have to change their offering and procurement strategy. Also, the food industry M&A market has drastically grown during the past 15 years totaling 591 deals in 2017 [36]. Correspondingly, the number of global food unicorns increased from 35 in 2018 to 45 in 2019 with an increasing number of food tech deep science companies. Together, they were valued at €214 bn [16].

3.4 Evaluation of the Outline Design

We engaged in a first evaluation of the solution design by performing a descriptive evaluation [22, 37, 38]. A descriptive evaluation is an informed argument for the artifact's utility [22]. We compare the solution design to the identified actual needs of the stakeholder groups to judge how well the solution design satisfies them.

First, the solution design satisfies the identified needs by founders and investment professionals. The solution design meets the demand for competitive returns of investment professionals and fund investors by yielding a ROI of 20–30%. Similarly, the fund fulfils the need to generate a positive impact through targeting investment areas that foster sustainable practices and having ESG accordance as one of the investment criteria. On the other hand, the solution design only offers the opportunity to mentor, advise, and support founders operationally to a medium degree due to the larger portfolio size and closed-ended fund model. Moreover, it offers no educational program to founders because it does not feature pre-seed investments and incubation. It also only offers a timeline of medium length compared to evergreen funds. Finally, the solution design only has a medium capability to enable fund investors to explore business models and industries since they are not as operationally involved as in evergreen funds. Besides these compromises, we believe the solution design achieves the highest degree of need satisfaction in comparison to alternative designs.

4 Discussion

This design science research project was motivated by the question of how an investment vehicle and strategy might look like to support food tech startups. Using a design science approach, we first explored the opportunity space of promising alter-natives. Based on the choice for the most promising opportunity candidate, we developed a detailed solution design. This design science projects contributes to both the body of design knowledge on creating investment vehicles and strategies for food tech startups and showcases how a methodology for exploration projects [37, 38] could look like.

First, the project makes a significant contribution by providing a detailed blueprint of an investment vehicle and strategy to invest in food tech startups. While previous literature on food tech has mainly focused on specific topics, such as edible insect production [20], vertical farming [10] and cellular agriculture [40], and literature on venture funding has provided generic ideas on developing venture funds [34], our study presents a situated artefact with direct practical implications for venture capital firms interested in investing in food startups. This blueprint can also be applied to other domains with high research intensity and investment risks through a case-to-case transfer logic [15, 44]. This contribution has the potential to bring significant changes to the food and agricultural system by supporting the development of innovative food technologies.

A second contribution is that we inferred more generalizable design principles based on this project [42]. The design principles follow a CIMO logic [9]. Two key design principles can be summarized as follows: First, to successfully invest in the future of food (C), investors should invest in companies active in controlled environment agriculture and food-as-software (I), which will through their competitive advantage over industrial agriculture (M) ensure the long-term viability of the investor's investment strategy (O). A second design principles is the following: To design an investment vehicle and strategy that optimally meets corporate fund investors' non-financial needs (C), fund operators for corporates or the corporate itself can use an evergreen fund model (I), which will through the more flexible timeline, better operational support, and corporate's higher involvement in the fund (M) attract more companies to the vehicle and yield increased non-financial benefits for the corporate (O).

A third contribution of this study is that it illustrates a methodology for exploration design science projects. Existing design science methodologies from the field of information systems [27, 39], management [43] and operations management [23] mostly provide guidance for so called improvement projects [11, 37]. Yet, there is little guidance for a particularly interesting type of design science project for the entrepreneurship field, namely exploration projects [11, 37]. Exploration projects aim at exploring novel means-ends relationships [11, 37]. Exploration projects need methodological guidance for exploring and seizing novel opportunities. This project illustrates initial ideas on how such methodology could look like.

5 Limitations and Future Research

In light of the limitations of this study, there exist numerous prospects for future research. Firstly, the initial designs of the investment vehicle and strategy that we proposed ought to be subjected to further evaluation and development in subsequent research endeavors. Secondly, the design principles that we inferred warrant further refinement and testing. Thirdly, the methodology we illustrated can be considered a preliminary step towards the development of a complete design science methodology for exploration projects, one that should align with the guiding principles for design science elucidated in the literature [22, 37].

References

1. AgFunder AgFunder Agri-Food Tech Investing Report '19. Year in Review. AgFunder (2020)
2. Arnold, P.: There Are Only Three Venture Capital Strategies. Switch Ventures; Valley Voices. Forbes (2019)
3. Balboa, M., Martí, J.: An Integrative Approach to the Determinants of Private Equity Fundraising. SSRN(2003). https://doi.org/10.2139/ssrn.493344
4. Insights, C.B: Venture Capital Funnel Shows Odds of Becoming A Unicorn Are About 1%. The venture capital funnel highlights the natural selection inherent in the venture capital process (2018)
5. John, C.H.: The risk and return of venture capital. J. Financ. Econ. **75**(1), 3–52 (2005)
6. Cosgrove, E.: French Agrifood Tech VC Capagro Doubles Fund to €124m. AgFunder (2017)
7. Cumming, D.J.: The determinants of venture capital Portfolio size: empirical evidence. J. Bus. **79**(3), 1083–1126 (2006). https://doi.org/10.1086/500670
8. Walker, D., Kurth, T., Van Wyck, J., Tilney, M: Lessons from the Frontlines of the AgTech Revolution. BCG; AgFunder (2016)
9. Denyer, D., Tranfield, D., Van Aken, J.E.: Developing design propositions through research synthesis. Organ. Stud. **29**(3), 393–413 (2008)
10. Despommier, D.D.: The vertical farm. Feeding the world in the 21st century. With assistance of Majora Carter. New York (N.Y.): Picador (2011)
11. Dimov, D., Maula, M., Romme, A.G.L.: Crafting and assessing design science research for entrepreneurship. Entrepreneurship Theory Pract. 10422587221128271 (2022)
12. Dixon, C.: Performance Data and the 'Babe Ruth' Effect in Venture Capital. Edited by Andreesen Horowitz (2015)
13. Edelman, L.F.: German venture-capital firms and portfolio-company performance: what types of management support make a difference? Acad. Manag. Perspect. **16**(1), 156–157 (2002). https://doi.org/10.5465/ame.2002.6640238
14. EVCA: Annual Survey of Pan-European Private Equity and Venture Capital Activity (2012)
15. Firestone, W.A.: Alternative arguments for generalizing from data as applied to qualitative research. Educ. Res. **22**(4), 16–23 (1993)
16. Five Seasons Ventures; Dealroom.co The State of European Food Tech 2019 (2019)
17. Gao, L.S.: Portfolio industry strategy in venture capital investments. J. Private Equity **14**(2), 59–71 (2011). https://doi.org/10.3905/jpe.2011.14.2.059
18. Kendrick, G.K.: Diversification in Venture Portfolio Construction. Hone Capital. Medium (2018)
19. Graham, A.: Three Core Principles of Venture Capital Portfolio Strategy. Toptal (2017)
20. Halloran, A., Flore, R., Vantomme, P., Roos, N.: Edible in-sects in sustainable food systems. New York NY: Springer Science+Business Media (2018)
21. Harris, L.: Investment Vehicles. CFA Institute (2014)
22. Bichler, M.: Design science in information systems research. Wirtschaftsinformatik **48**(2), 133–135 (2006). https://doi.org/10.1007/s11576-006-0028-8
23. Holmström, J., Ketokivi, M., Hameri, A.P.: Bridging practice and theory: a design science approach. Decis. Sci. **40**(1), 65–87 (2009)
24. Jamison, D.W., Waite, S.R., Anderson, M.: Venture Investing in Science. Columbia Business School Publishing, New York (2017)
25. Lerner, J., Pierrakis, Y., Collins, L., Bravo Biosca, A.: Atlantic Drift. Venture capital performance in the UK and the US. Nesta (2011)
26. Mullarkey, M.T., Hevner, A.R.: An elaborated action design research process model. Eur. J. Inf. Syst. **28**(1), 6–20 (2019)

27. Peffers, K., Tuunanen, T., Rothenberger, M.A., Chatterjee, S.: A design science research methodology for information systems research. J. Manag. Inf. Syst. **24**(3), 45–77 (2007)
28. Plunkett Research Plunkett's Food Industry Market Research. Global Food Industry Statistics and Market Size Overview. Plunkett Research (2018)
29. Poore, J., Nemecek, T.: Reducing food's environmental impacts through producers and consumers. Science **360**(6392), 987–992 (2018). https://doi.org/10.1126/science.aaq0216
30. Ray, D.K., Mueller, N.D., West, P.C., Foley, J.A.: Yield Trends are insufficient to double global crop production by 2050. PLoS ONE **8**(6), e66428 (2013). https://doi.org/10.1371/journal.pone.0066428
31. Ritchie, H.: You want to reduce the carbon footprint of your food? focus on what you eat, not whether your food is local. Our World Data (2020)
32. Ritchie, H., Roser, M.: Environmental impacts of food production. Our World Data (2020)
33. WHO: Obesity and overweight. World Health Organization (2020)
34. Ramsinghani, M.: The Business of Venture Capital. Insights from Leading Practitioners on the Art of Raising a Fund, Deal Structuring, Value Creation, and Exit Strategies, 2nd edn. John Wiley & Sons, Hoboken, New Jersey (2014)
35. Romme, A.G.L.: Making a difference: organization as design. Organ. Sci. **14**(5), 558–573 (2003)
36. Rowan, J.: Food Industry M&A: Buying Innovation. The Food Institute (2018)
37. Seckler, C., Mauer, R., vom Brocke, J.: Design science in entrepreneurship: conceptual foundations and guiding principles. J. Bus. Ventur. Des. 1(1), 1–12 (2021)
38. Seckler, C., Mauer, R., vom Brocke, J.: A design science methodology for entrepreneurship research. In: Paper accepted for presentation at the 83rd Annual Meeting of the Academy of Management, Boston, MA, USA (2023)
39. Sein, M.K., Henfridsson, O., Purao, S., Rossi, M., Lindgren, R.: Action design research. MIS Q. **35**(1), 37–56 (2011)
40. Shapiro, P.: Clean Meat. Gallery Books, New York (2018)
41. Szyzdek, P.: All you should know about the Investment Thesis. Data Driven Investor. Medium (2019)
42. van Aken, J.E.: Management research based on the paradigm of the design sciences: the quest for field-tested and grounded technological rules. J. Manage. Stud. **41**(2), 219–246 (2004)
43. van Aken, J.E., Berends, H.: Problem Solving in Organizations. Cambridge University Press, Cambridge, UK (2018)
44. vom Brocke, J., Winter, R., Hevner, A., Maedche, A.: Accumulation and evolution of design knowledge in design science research: a journey through time and space. J. Assoc. Inf. Syst. **21**(3), 520–544 (2020)
45. WHO: Obesity and overweight. World Health Organization (2020). https://www.who.int/news-room/fact-sheets/detail/obesity-and-overweight. Accessed 23 May 2020

Emerging DSR Methods and Processes

Introduction to the Emerging DSR Methods and Processes Track

John R Venable[1], Hanlie Smuts[2], and Marié Hattingh[2]

[1] Curtin University
j.venable@curtin.edu.au
[2] University of Pretoria
{hanlie.smuts,marie.hattingh}@up.ac.za

Abstract. This introduction describes the track theme, types of contributions sought, number of submissions, review process, acceptances, and accepted submissions to the Emerging DSR Methods and Processes track.

Keywords: Design science research · Research method · Research process · Research technique · Research tool · Design theory · Artificial intelligence

1 Introduction

Design Science Research (DSR) methods, tools, techniques, and processes guide DSR researchers in planning and conducting DSR. The Emerging DSR Methods and Processes track sought both conceptual and empirical contributions, especially submissions addressing the conference theme - Design Science Research for a New Society: Society 5.0. Conceptual studies could address foundations of DSR, e.g. paradigms, ontologies, epistemologies, ethics, the nature of artefacts and human purposes. Empirical studies could contribute evidence concerning the strengths, weaknesses, requirements, efficacy, effectiveness, efficiency, and/or ethicality of existing and emerging DSR methods and processes and facilitate improvement of DSR methods and processes. We particularly welcomed submissions addressing the theme of the conference.

We received 11 submissions. Submissions were reviewed by a minimum of 2 highly-qualified reviewers, with all but one submission receiving three or more reviews. Four submissions (36%) were selected for publication in the proceedings and two were selected as research-in-progress (RIP) papers for conference presentation only.

Of the papers accepted for publication in the proceedings, one (Akoka et al.) developed an overview of how the field of DSR has progressed, one (Gau et al.) addressed the important issue of the accessibility of design knowledge, and two (Reinhartd et al. and Daase and Turowski) addressed the increasingly important area (to Society 5.0 and beyond) of DSR for Artificial Intelligence. Both RIP papers (Trierweiler and Krumay, and Knapp) developed promising ideas for reconceptualising key aspects of DSR methods. Taken together, these six papers address current issues as well as raise new directions for Design Science Research.

Design Science Research: Progression, Schools of Thought and Research Themes

Jacky Akoka[1] , Isabelle Comyn-Wattiau[2] , and Veda C. Storey[3(✉)]

[1] CEDRIC-CNAM, Paris, France
jacky.akoka@lecnam.net
[2] ESSEC Business School, Cergy-Pontoise, France
wattiau@essec.edu
[3] Computer Information Systems, J. Mack Robinson College of Business, Georgia State
University, Atlanta, Georgia
vstorey@gsu.edu

Abstract. Design science research, a well-established research approach to solving complex real-world problems, has evolved over time. This research characterizes design science research in information systems. By performing a bibliometric analysis, we show that design science research has progressed in the information systems field through three main phases, which we call *periods of inquiry*. A co-citation analysis shows that the progression has been largely influenced by a few main pioneering studies, leading to three schools of thought. Bibliographic coupling analysis suggests that research in design science can be classified into several distinct intellectual areas corresponding to different research themes. This bibliometric analysis proposes a broad viewpoint of design science and design research, serving as a basis for shaping further research.

Keywords: Design science research · periods of inquiry · design knowledge · bibliometric analysis · co-citation analysis · bibliographic coupling analysis

1 Introduction

Design science research (DSR) addresses complex problems in the real world to which there is no easy, or obvious, solution. Design science research has matured in the production of knowledge and its evaluation and develops theories, methods, and knowledge bases of design. Just like other fields that mature, its evolution can be informative in understanding its potential for future progression. Design science research has both design and science components and is pluralistic and dynamic. Scientific research in all fields evolves and progresses through various stages. As a field matures, it is useful to understand its importance, relevance, and impact on society. Society also evolves with its increasing emphasis on digitalization and the adjustments and transformations that continue to occur. Baskerville et al. [5] argue that, unlike traditional approaches to information systems (IS) development that focuses on how to represent the real world, the inverse must now be considered. The digital world may happen first and influence reality. Society 5.0 refers to our new society with emergence between the digital and physical spaces, and an unprecedented relationship with technology that can be both new and transformative [10]. Since design science research focuses on complex problems of the real world, one can assume that design science research will continue to significantly shape the role of information systems in this evolving digital society.

Design science research has emerged into a paradigm, with its foundations in Herbert Simon's *Sciences of the Artificial* [31]. Over the past 60 years, design science has evolved based on many efforts to define it, understand the types of problems it can address, and identify what we can learn from trying to solve such problems. Methods and theories have been developed and contributions to design knowledge identified. Generally, design science research focuses primarily on the design and creation of artifacts that are useful to society and the methods and assessment measures to do so. However, although there are many notions specific to design science research, there is less known about how these have progressed over time, even though design science is regarded as a dynamic field. Although some papers published in design science research have been regarded as seminal, the reasons for this designation are not described; nor is the maturing of the field that lead to them being identified or articulated.

Design Science Research is one of the five research streams of the information systems discipline [3] and increasingly expanding. Therefore, the research question is: *How can we characterize the progression of design science research?* This research question can be decomposed into three sub-questions. *How do the DSR publications evolve over time (RQ1)? What are the different schools of thought characterizing DSR's sintellectual base (RQ2)? What are the main research themes covered by DSR scholars (RQ3)?* Our goal is to characterize this research stream by undertaking a retrospective view of the research contributions that constitute the foundational knowledge of DSR. In doing so, we aim to identify what design science is, and how it differs from other areas of research in information systems, as well as to develop a strong sense of its identity and importance in Society 5.0. Our contribution may be useful for doctoral students and researchers wishing to participate in this field.

We review the intellectual base of DSR, and the intellectual communities of DSR that have formed over the period 1969–2022; that is, from Simon's *Sciences of the Artificial* [31] until present. By applying bibliometrics analysis, we show that DSR has progressed through three main phases, which we call *periods of inquiry*. The co-citation analysis (CCA) shows that DSR has been developed under the influence of two pioneering studies. Finally, a bibliographic coupling analysis (BCA) suggests that DSR can be classified into several distinct intellectual areas.

2   Related Research

There have been many different approaches to categorizing and classifying the characteristics of design science research, motivated by the need to understand the status of current research in order to progress the field. Of the efforts to understand how to properly conduct design science research, highly abstracted processes have been identified, including Walls et al. [37], March and Smith's focus on the artifact [19], Hevner et al.'s [15] guidelines, Peffers et al.'s [26] generic methodology and Sein et al.'s [30] proposal for action design research, and Venable et al.'s [36] and Prat et al.'s [28] work on evaluation. Tremblay et al. [33] conducted a scientometric study. Larsen et al. [17] address validity. Others address design theory [18] and ethics [14].

Recognizing the dynamic and pluralistic nature of DSR [4], this research considers knowledge development as it has progressed over time. Other studies attempted to capture the essence of design science research, but with a limited corpus or analysis (e.g., Aviji and Winter [2], Thuan et al. [32], Deng and Ji [9], Nagle et al. [21], Dwivedi et al. [11], Peffers et al. [25], and van der Merwe et al. [35]).

Piirainen et al. [27] performed a co-citation analysis to examine the patterns in design research to uncover the structures in Design Science. One finding is that the most cited and citing papers are from IS, management, engineering, design research, and computer science. Their findings are used as a basis for our co-citation and bibliographic coupling analysis.

Akoka et al. [1] identified several clusters representing an overview of the structure of the DSR body of knowledge. By analyzing 233 DESRIST proceedings papers (2009–2015) they identified the most cited DSR publications and authors and describe the structure of DSR knowledge for that period. Most of the clusters found in their analysis deal with theories or methodologies of DSR as opposed to applications to specific domains. Our study aims to confirm some of these findings and discover additional ones.

Herwix and Rozenkranz [13] present a systematic literature review of design science to propose a framework for the classification of knowledge contributions within the context of general scientific inquiry. Their study provides a systematic overview of the diversity of knowledge scope and goal design oriented IS research.

Pascal and Renaud [24] performed a co-citation analysis of 192 ISDSR (Information Systems Design Science Research) articles published in the AIS basket of eight journals (1992–2018). They identified five schools of thought: qualitative methodological foundations, reflections on the IS discipline, IS design theory, action research in ISDSR, and general guidelines for ISDSR. There are several limitations to their study, notably the small size of the sample, and the fact that only articles published in the basket of eight IS journals were considered. There is no investigation of DSR research themes. Our study will go beyond in terms of sample size, data sources, and analysis by including bibliographic coupling.

There are two complementary themes. The first one is bibliometric methods, which has been used in a wide variety of disciplines. Boyack and Klavans [6] compare the accuracies of cluster solutions of a large corpus of articles from the biomedical literature using four similarity approaches: co-citation analysis, bibliographic coupling, direct citation, and a bibliographic coupling-based citation-text hybrid approach. They found that bibliographic coupling slightly outperforms co-citation analysis. Direct citation has been found to be the least accurate mapping approach by far, whereas a hybrid approach improves upon the bibliographic coupling results. We combine co-citation analysis and bibliographic coupling since they are complementary. The second is related to the periods of academic inquiry. Like other areas of academic inquiry, as a field matures, it passes through various stages in its maturity. For example, within our society, humans are organized by the "generation" to which they belong which is determined primarily by the year in which they were born. For people, these generations are now based mostly on a 15-year cycle. In prior generations they were delineated by shared experiences. This labelling of generations has often been used to attribute a set of common characteristics to a set of people (and workforce) who were born around the same time. Similarly, in psychology, there are important approaches or schools of thought (structuralism, functionalism, psychodynamic, behaviourism, cognitive, and social-cultural [7]).

Hirschheim and Klein [16] examine a 40-year history of research in the entire IS field and divide it into four eras, albeit with some overlap. For each era, they identify important "events", which are somewhat analogous to the "turning points" we identify in this research. They also identify research themes for each of the eras. Their reasons for the review were: to help researchers identify and understand what information systems are; to identify how the information systems field is different from other disciplines; and to help create a sense of identity for the information systems field. Our work is analogous in that we can use our results to: understand what design science is; identify how it differs from other areas of research in information systems; and develop a stronger sense of identity of design science research and its importance in today's society. Niederman [22] simply uses three distinct time categories, which he labels as *past*, *now* and *future*. More formally, the *periodization of history* reflects how temporal continuity relates to inside periods and the discontinuity between periods, as turning points. These can become phrases or periods of inquiry within a field.

3 Methodology

This paper is intended to be a first attempt to characterize the DSR domain using a methodology that combines co-citation analysis and bibliographic coupling analysis. Our methodology is comprised of five main steps (Fig. 1):

1. *Data extraction*: We first identify the relevant data sources and define a querying strategy for extracting a suitable dataset. Seeking to obtain the most comprehensive database, we used Scopus since it contains abundant citation data of research publications.
2. *Publications periodization*: Periodization consists of dividing time into distinct periods for the purpose of analysis. It allows us to elicit research periods based on the dynamics of publications over time.
3. *Schools of thoughts identification*: Our objective is to discover patterns and trends in DSR publications that would lead to the identification of different schools of thoughts. We seek to identify the key themes representing DSR studies using co-citation analysis.
4. *Research themes identification*: This requires determining the key themes or research traditions in DSR. Bibliographic coupling allows us to classify DSR research into a set of intellectual communities where the papers in each group are strongly linked together.
5. *DSR field characterization:* The analyses performed during the previous steps allow us to provide an understanding of the field on three dimensions: temporal, intellectual base, and current themes.

Overall, we combine two types of analyses. Co-citation analysis is used for investigating the intellectual base of DSR studies. Bibliographic coupling analysis is introduced to explore the intellectual communities in DSR.

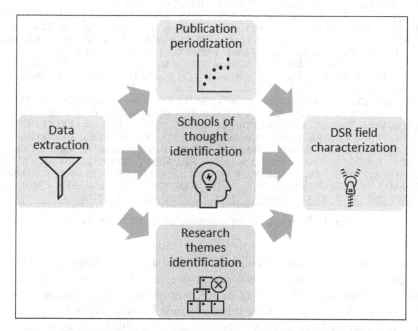

Fig. 1. Methodology: Systematic Overview of DSR Literature

Phase 1. Data Extraction. We collected the data (DSR research papers) from the Scopus database. Our choice of Scopus was motivated by the fact that it has one of the largest amounts of indexed data. Then, we searched the Scopus database to retrieve all articles that cite "design science" or "design research". These two keywords are general enough to include most papers that present a design-based approach. We checked that using only the keyword "design science research" was too restrictive. "Design science" keyword subsumes "Design science research". The choice of these keywords alone allows us to detect possible communities related to design, but which do not necessarily have the same approaches to this concept and do not claim to be information systems, even if they are very related. We also tested the same query by adding the keyword "information systems", which considerably reduced the sample. The search was performed on the titles, abstracts, or keywords. We retrieved only papers published in journals and conference proceedings related to the domains of management, computer science and decision sciences. The time span was from 1969 to 2022 to account for the influence of Simon's *Sciences of the Artificial* [31] to present day. The data cleaning operations was performed using the ARTIREV [38] software, with the final set (after cleaning) of 3473 articles. The articles published in journals represent **32%** while those published in conference proceedings represent **68%**. Note that the journals and the conferences are

the most recognized in the information systems (IS) and DSR communities. The query
used to generate the final set of papers is given in Fig. 2.

```
( TITLE-ABS-KEY ( "design science" ) OR TITLE-ABS-KEY ( "design re-
search" ) ) AND ( DOCTYPE ( ar ) OR DOCTYPE ( re ) OR DOCTYPE ( cp ) ) AND LANGUA
GE ( english ) AND PUBYEAR BEF 2023 AND PUBYEAR AFT 1968 AND ( SRCTYPE ( j )
OR SRCTYPE ( p ) ) AND ( SUBJAREA ( comp ) OR SUBJAREA ( deci ) OR SUBJAREA ( busi
) ) AND ( EXCLUDE ( LANGUAGE , "French" ) OR EXCLUDE ( LANGUAGE , "Portu-
guese" ) OR EXCLUDE ( LANGUAGE , "German" ) OR EXCLUDE ( LANGUAGE , "Ital-
ian" ) ) AND ( EXCLUDE ( LANGUAGE , "Korean" ) OR EXCLUDE ( LANGUAGE , "Span-
ish" ) OR EXCLUDE ( LANGUAGE , "cata-
lan" ) ) AND ( EXCLUDE ( PUBSTAGE , "aip" ) ) AND ( EXCLUDE ( SUBJAREA , "MATH" )
OR EXCLUDE ( SUBJAREA , "ARTS" ) OR EXCLUDE ( SUBJAREA , "ECON" ) OR EXCLU
DE ( SUBJAREA , "PSYC" ) OR EXCLUDE ( SUBJAREA , "MATE" ) ) AND ( EXCLUDE ( SU
BJAREA , "ENGI" ) OR EXCLUDE ( SUBJAREA , "SOCI" ) OR EXCLUDE ( SUBJAREA , "E
NVI" ) OR EXCLUDE ( SUBJAREA , "ENER" ) OR EXCLUDE ( SUBJAREA , "MEDI" ) OR E
XCLUDE ( SUBJAREA , "PHYS" ) OR EXCLUDE ( SUBJAREA , "BIOC" ) ) AND ( EXCLUDE
( SUBJAREA , "AGRI" ) OR EXCLUDE ( SUBJAREA , "CENG" ) OR EXCLUDE ( SUBJAREA
, "CHEM" ) OR EXCLUDE ( SUBJAREA , "EART" ) OR EXCLUDE ( SUBJAREA , "MULT" )
OR EXCLUDE ( SUBJAREA , "NEUR" ) OR EXCLUDE ( SUBJAREA , "PHAR" ) )
```

Fig. 2. Scopus query for generation of dataset of papers

The query allows us to search for relevant DSR literature using Scopus and to identify
articles published in journals and conference proceedings. The inclusion criteria points
to a period spanning from 1969 to 2022, as well as areas such as management, computer
and decision sciences. The exclusion criteria include language and sub-areas such as
mathematics, engineering, etc. They were progressively refined in order to reduce the
size of the data set without missing relevant literature. The strings "design science" and
"design research" were searched in the titles, abstracts, and keywords.

Phase 2. Publication Periodization. The periodization of publications allows us to
elicit research periods based on the dynamics of publications over time. In general,
periodization consists of dividing time into distinct periods for the purpose of analysis.
It can be performed using different methods including chronological periodization, and
theme-based periodization, which consists in dividing time into periods based on a specific DSR research theme. Event-based periodization divides time into periods based on
specific events or *turning points*; for example, events corresponding to the publication
of seminal papers. For our purposes, we choose a chronological periodization, which
consists of representing the number of published papers per year. Figure 3 depicts the
distribution of DSR publications over the entire period spanning from 1969 to 2022.
Before 1982, figures are very low, and have been omitted.

As shown in Fig. 3, during the "emergence" period, the number of the yearly publications was relatively small (67 papers, less than two papers per year on average),
indicating that the DSR topics were starting to capture an attention from scholars. During this period, the foundational knowledge needed to develop DSR was laid. The DSR
research stream entered a new phase in 2004 with the publication of some seminal papers.
During this "take-off" period, or initiation phase, the number of DSR publications follows an ascending trend (2823 papers, about 176 per year on average). This indicates

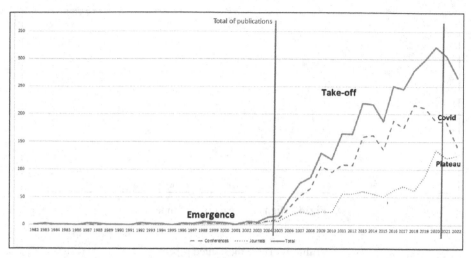

Fig. 3. Distribution of DSR papers (1969–2022) for conferences, journals, and globally

that this stream of IS research has attracted the interest of many more researchers. Note that the year 2020 realized the largest number of publications (i.e., 322 in total). Clearly a new period starts after 2020. In terms of journal papers, the curve describes a plateau whereas the number of conference papers is decreasing, perhaps due to the impact of the COVID-19 pandemic. However, the length of this third period is too short to deduce any meaningful tendency. If there is a decrease in interest in this area, based on the sample used in this research, such a decreasing phenomenon would need to be confirmed in future years. It is possible, of course, that researchers were distracted by the need to conduct research into COVID-19-related issues. Or it is also feasible that productivity decreased over this timeframe as promotion and tenure decisions were delayed due to the pandemic, as were some of the deadlines for reviews and decisions at many journals.

The transition from period 1 to period 2 is also marked by the impact of several seminal articles, the most cited in the sample (Fig. 4). The curve represents the number of citations for the 100 most cited papers in the sample. The analysis of this curve shows two remarkable events in 2004 and 2007 related to the three most cited papers of the entire period (Table 1). In other words, this event-based periodization confirms the chronological periodization represented in Fig. 3. In some sense, these three periods cover the past, present, and future of DSR.

Phase 3. Schools of Thoughts Identification. Our aim is to identify the key themes that DSR covers, leading to the identification of the schools of thought being represented. Co-citation analysis is a method used to identify the relationship between two or more documents based on the number of times they are cited together. In our case, it enables the identification of patterns and trends in DSR. We use it to identify important published papers in DSR, assuming that research papers that are frequently cited together are likely to be related, such as being part of the same research tradition. It allows us to identify significant schools of thoughts in DSR. We, thus, started by considering the dataset of articles obtained in phase 1. We compiled all of the papers cited in the 3473 papers

J. Akoka et al.

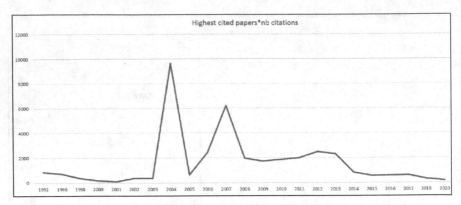

Fig. 4. High cited papers over time

Table 1. Three most cited papers

Authors	Title	Year	Source title	Cited by
Hevner A.R., March S.T., Park J., Ram S.	Design science in information systems research	2004	MIS Quarterly: Management Information Systems	8473
Peffers K., Tuunanen T., Rothenberger M.A., Chatterjee S.	A design science research methodology for information systems research	2007	Journal of Management Information Systems	3808
Gregor S.	The nature of theory in Information Systems	2006	MIS Quarterly: Management Information Systems	2078

provided by Scopus. Then we created a co-citation matrix, which is a table that shows how often each pair of publications has been cited together in the corpus of 3473 papers. We used a clustering algorithm (Leiden) implemented in the ARTIREV software. The latter groups the publications based on their co-citation patterns, leading to a set of clusters of publications that have similar co-citation patterns. However, ARTIREV requires the user to select a threshold value, representing the minimum number of citations that a document must have to be considered. We tried several threshold values and compared the results before making a final decision, considering the size of the sample and the desired level of cluster granularity. Figure 5 shows the results of the co-citation analysis for a threshold value of 92. Twenty papers are cited more than 92 times and constitute the three clusters.

To explore the intellectual base of DSR we have to detect the key publications that are highly cited by the articles of the dataset obtained in phase 1. Analyzing the results presented in Fig. 5, we found that Hevner et al. [15] is the key paper with the most cited publications over almost the last twenty years. This work influences DSR with the idea that "the design-science paradigm seeks to extend the boundaries of human and organizational capabilities by creating new and innovative artifacts." The second most important articles in the intellectual base are: Peffers et al. [26], March and Smith [20] and Simon [31]. Peffers et al. [26] proposed a methodology for conducting design science research in information systems. March and Smith [19] stated that "real problems must be properly conceptualized and represented." Simon [31] introduced the concept of the science of artificial. Figure 5 shows that Schön [29] and Nunamaker et al. [23] are the earliest publications among these most cited ones. Schön advocated a greater interaction between researchers and practitioners, and was the first researcher after Simon to introduce a new approach to cognitive design theory. Nunamaker et al. [23] are the first to propose using IS development methodologies as research methodologies.

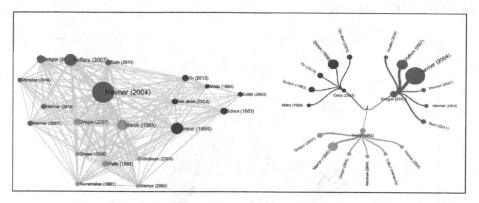

Fig. 5. Co-citation graph and associated dendrogram

As can be seen in Fig. 5, we obtained three clusters. To interpret the clusters, we analyzed the content of the publications in each group and identified the key themes they represent. The first cluster, in red, corresponds to the development of DSR **methodologies and frameworks**. The two main groups of authors of this cluster (Hevner et al. [15]; Peffers et al. [26]) contributed to the foundations of DSR by proposing DSR methodologies and guidelines. They capitalized on previous work in computer science and decision support systems. Venable et al. [36] proposed a framework for evaluation. Sein et al. [30] proposed action design research. The second cluster, in green, is composed of seven core papers dedicated to **design research and design theory**. The seminal work of March and Smith [19] proposed that design science should be considered as a new methodological approach in IS research. They presented a two-dimensional framework based on types of design and natural science research activities and on types of outputs produced by design research. Walls et al. [37] provided a template for the structure of design theories. The third cluster, in blue, is comprised of six papers that focus mainly on **experimentation and field testing**. The contributions of Simon [31] and Schön [29] are mainly qualitative. Van Aken [34] proposes a qualitative approach to building design rules with kernel theories. Yin [39] discusses the role of validity and generalization in case study evaluations. Thus, the co-citation analysis reveals three interrelated clusters corresponding to three schools of thoughts. Each cluster contributes to the development of DSR by providing methodologies and frameworks, design theories, and field experimentations.

Phase 4. Research Themes Identification. Bibliographic coupling is a method used to identify the relationships between different publications in DSR. It is based on the idea that publications that share a significant number of references are likely to be related in some way, such as being part of the same research tradition. We, therefore, examine the references that two DSR publications share together. The choice of a threshold value can greatly affect the results of bibliographic coupling analysis. Using the dataset obtained in phase 1, we compiled all the citations used in each of the publications in the dataset. Then, we created a bibliographic coupling matrix, which is a table that shows how often each pair of publications shares references. We tested different threshold values based on the size of the data sample.

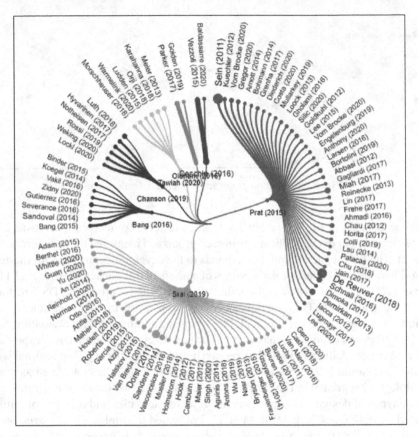

Fig. 6. Bibliographic coupling graph (references available)

Bibliographic coupling analysis requires defining a relevant time window. ARTIREV recommends a six-year time window. Because our sample spans more than fifty years, a good perception of the themes covered requires a larger time window. Therefore, we conducted several experiments and opted for a time window of ten years. Using ARTIREV's clustering algorithm (Leiden), with a threshold value of 44, we grouped the publications over the past ten years, based on their bibliographic coupling patterns. The result, depicted in Fig. 6, shows a set of seven clusters that have similar bibliographic coupling patterns. Each cluster corresponds to a current research theme. Given the differences between the sizes of the clusters, we will concentrate on the first two, having 42 and 40 documents, respectively.

The first cluster, in red, contains 42 papers which concentrate on **Methods in DSR and applications**. Ten years after the publication of the seminal papers mentioned above, the latter constitute a common body of knowledge referred to in nearly all the papers of this cluster. The 42 papers either implement DSR or complete its guidelines and frameworks. An important subset of this cluster is devoted to big data. Sein et al. [30] is an example of a paper in the DSR methodological toolkit, focusing mainly on action design research. De Reuver [8] develops a research agenda for digital platforms research in IS. Goldkuhl [12] proposes an integration of action research and design research in a project.

The second cluster, in green, contains 40 papers devoted to different aspects of design, including design thinking and product design. Most use a design science approach to solve problems in different domains, such as healthcare, environment, etc. This cluster illustrates essentially research that solves problems by adopting a design approach, including design science. Therefore, the main research theme of this cluster can be defined as **Design at large**. The other five clusters are much smaller and more homogeneous. As a result, they are easier to characterize. Cluster 3 (9 papers) is devoted to education and learning. Cluster 4 (7 papers) concerns blockchain research. Cluster 5 (7 papers) focuses mainly on gamification. Cluster 6 (3 papers) tackles the issues of work and job design. Finally, sustainability is the main subject of cluster 7 (3 papers).

Phase 5. DSR Field Characterization. Our chronological analysis of publications mentioning "design science" and "design research" reveals a three-period dynamic. We note the convergence between the chronological analysis and the co-citation analysis: several seminal articles published between 2004 and 2007 will boost the publication dynamics and justify the passage from the emergence of the field to its takeoff, which was identified in the chronological analysis. To date, there is no other more recent article that is the subject of so many citations. However, there are two explanations for this: as the publication is more prolific, citations are more evenly distributed across all articles in the field (64 articles published between 2008 and 2015 have more than 100 citations each). Explaining the transition from the take-off period to the next is very difficult. At this stage, even the experts are not able to ascertain whether this period will be a plateau or a decline in research in this field.

To our knowledge, there is no cross analysis of CCA and BCA techniques. However, combining CCA and BCA really enriches the lenses of the analysis. It is not meaningful to map the three schools of thoughts revealed by the CCA and the seven clusters emerging from the BCA. The latter elicited two main clusters. Cluster 1 puts together papers that cite Hevner et al. [15], Peffers et al. [26], and others. Cluster 2 is essentially another community that does not implement the DSR frameworks: they are design-based or design-oriented but not DSR. Our BCA reveals the emergence of small communities around new topics such as blockchain or sustainability. Other clusters are very homogenous, but not all can be considered as DSR.

4 Discussion

Design science research has a long history, leading to a significant body of work. From our bibliometric analysis, we conclude that this field has progressed from being considered a more applied field to one based on well-established concepts, constructs, and methodologies. We performed our analysis over a long period of time (over 50 years). The analysis of the distribution of DSR publications over the entire period revealed three different periods. There are challenges, of course, including how to identify appropriate turning points and label the periods. Other limitations of periodization that are generally known, include reductionism, duration, consistency, and a false sense of progress.

The BCA revealed three clusters related to new topics (gamification, blockchain and sustainability). Big data and Machine Learning are part of the main DSR cluster. It is obvious that the digital world in which we live will continue to evolve; therefore, design science research needs to continue to address important, societal challenges that emerge from digitalization (e.g., how to build and deploy models to address the need to distribute digital technologies on a global scale). Technologies continue to emerge and the methods being developed around these new technologies will be important to use in design science research (machine learning, general AI (artificial intelligence), multiple languages). Using our advances in design science research to identify and address the grand problems of today will require transdisciplinary research.

There are several limitations. We used Scopus to identify a good dataset encompassing all DSR papers. However, it might have provided more papers, due to the difficulty of identifying exact keywords. It is not easy to access the metrics that the ARTIREV software provides in order to assess the quality and the strength of the clusters obtained. Both the choice of thresholds and the time window of BCA might have introduced biases. Moreover, given the size of the samples analyzed, it would have been impossible to obtain any meaningful results manually. We relied on software that may also introduce a bias due to the algorithms implemented and to design choices inherent to them. Finally, as a bibliometric study, we focus on past research categorization to help understand the structure and dynamics of a field and its possible evolutions.

A future bibliometric analysis of the type presented in this paper could be useful to researchers to identify potential publication targets by considering topics dealing with digital trends. The impacts of emerging digital technologies may influence how we carry out future research with bibliometric techniques as knowledge transfer is sought [21]. This research is intended to be an initial start in that direction and possibly contribute to the literature in periodization as a concrete application to an evolving field.

5   Conclusion

This research has proposed that design science research has matured to a stage where it is possible to identify its periods of inquiry and their major publications that have contributed to transforming research in this field. After considering previous approaches to categorizing DSR publications, we conducted a bibliometric analysis composed of five steps: data extraction, publication periodization, schools of thought identification, research themes identification, and field characterization. These analyses both complement and reinforce each other. Three periods were distinguished by analyzing the dynamics of publications. The first two are *emergence* and *take-off* periods. Interpreting trends for the third period (beginning in 2021) is more complex due to the lack of hindsight and its short duration.

This study considers a span of over fifty years (1969 to 2022) to include many papers encompassing design science and design research domains, from journals and conference proceedings, and covering computer science, management, and decision sciences. With the resulting data set being very large, only automated techniques could be used to analyze it. Hence, the research themes elicited constitute a very broad meaning of design science research. The results indicate that the research has progressed since Simon's 1969 vision of the *Sciences of the Artificial* to a set of stable constructs and methodologies today. By choosing a large sample, an important contribution is to identify, in a single cluster, the scope of other studies mentioned in the state of the art and to highlight additional clusters that belong to related communities not imbued with the design principles, guidelines and frameworks of the DSR field. The design community (which includes design thinking and product design) is an example. It produces and evaluates artifacts without claiming the fundamental frameworks that have been defined for two decades in the DSR community, typified by DESRIST conferences. The other clusters reveal smaller, more recent communities foreshadowing emerging topics such as blockchain, sustainability, and characteristics of Society 5.0. Future research should focus on the resulting clusters, including the three schools of thought and the seven BCA clusters, each a subfield of interest in itself. An example is the analysis of the evolution of schools of thought over time. Another is how DSR can contribute to the study of problems related to Society 5.0 and the link between reality and artificiality.

Acknowledgements. The authors thank sincerely the reviewers for their enlightening suggestions and Nicolas Prat for his helpful comments.

References

1. Akoka, J., Comyn-Wattiau, I., Prat, N.: The structure of DSR knowledge as reflected by DESRIST – a citation analysis (2009–2015). In: Parsons, J., Tuunanen, T., Venable, J., Donnellan, B., Helfert, M., Kenneally, J. (eds.) DESRIST 2016. LNCS, vol. 9661, pp. 177–185. Springer, Cham (2016). https://doi.org/10.1007/978-3-319-39294-3_12
2. Avdiji, H., Winter, R.: Knowledge gaps in design science research. In: 40th International Conference on Information Systems. Munich, Germany (2019)
3. Banker, R.D., Kauffman, R.J.: The evolution of research on information systems: a fiftieth year survery of the literature in management science. Mgt. Sc. **50**(3), 281–298 (2004)
4. Baskerville, R.L., Kaul, M., Storey, V.C.: Genres of inquiry in design-science research: justification and evaluation of knowledge production. MIS Q. **39**(3), 541–564 (2015)
5. Baskerville, R.L., Myers, M.D., Yoo, Y.: Digital first: the ontological reversal and new challenges for information systems research. MIS Q. **44**(2) (2020)
6. Boyack, K.W., Klavans, R.: Co-citation analysis, bibliographic coupling, and direct citation: which citation approach represents the research front most accurately? J. Am. Soc. Inform. Sci. Technol. **61**(12), 2389–2404 (2010)
7. Campus, B.: Psychology evolution (2023). https://opentextbc.ca/introductiontopsychology/
8. De Reuver, M., Sørensen, C., Basole, R.C.: The digital platform: a research agenda. J. Inf. Technol. **33**(2), 124–135 (2018)
9. Deng, Q., Ji, S.: A review of design science research in information systems: concept, process, outcome, and evaluation. Pac. Asia J. Assoc. Inf. Syst. **10**(1), 2 (2018)
10. DESRIST 2023 Call for Papers

11. Dwivedi, N., Purao, S., Straub, D.W.: Knowledge contributions in design science research: a meta-analysis. In: Tremblay, M.C., VanderMeer, D., Rothenberger, M., Gupta, A., Yoon, V. (eds.) DESRIST 2014. LNCS, vol. 8463, pp. 115–131. Springer, Cham (2014). https://doi.org/10.1007/978-3-319-06701-8_8

12. Goldkuhl, G.: Pragmatism vs interpretivism in qualitative information systems research. Eur. J. Inf. Syst. **21**, 135–146 (2012)

13. Herwix, A., Rosenkranz, C.: Making sense of design science in information systems research: insights from a systematic literature review. In: Designing for a Digital and Globalized World: 13th International Conference, DESRIST 2018, Chennai, India, June 3–6, 2018, Proceedings 13, pp. 51–66. Springer International Publishing (2018)

14. Herwix, A., Haj-Bolouri, A., Rossi, M., Tremblay, M.C., Purao, S., Gregor, S.: Ethics in information systems and design science research: five perspectives. Commun. Assoc. Inf. Syst. **50**(1), 589–616 (2022)

15. Hevner, A., March, S., Park, J., Ram, S.: Design science in information systems research. MIS Q. **28**(1), 75–105 (2004)

16. Hirschheim, R., Klein, H.K.: A glorious and not-so-short history of the information systems field. J. Assoc. Inf. Syst. **13**(4), 5 (2012)

17. Larsen, K.R., Lukyanenko, R., Mueller, R.M., Storey, V.C., VanderMeer, D., Parsons, J., Hovorka, D.S.: Validity in design science research. In: Hofmann, S., Müller, O., Rossi, M. (eds.) DESRIST 2020. LNCS, vol. 12388, pp. 272–282. Springer, Cham (2020). https://doi.org/10.1007/978-3-030-64823-7_25

18. Lukyanenko, R., Parsons, J.: Research perspectives: design theory indeterminacy: what is it, how can it be reduced, and why did the polar bear drown? J. Assoc. Inf. Syst. **21**(5), 1 (2020)

19. March, S., Smith, G.: Design and natural science research on information technology. Decis. Support Syst. **15**(4), 251–266 (1995)

20. March, S., Storey, V.C.: Design science in the information systems discipline: an introduction to the special issue on design science research. MIS Q. 725–730 (2008)

21. Nagle, T., et al.: The research method we need or deserve? A literature review of the design science research landscape. Commun. Assoc. Inf. Syst. **50**, 358–395 (2022)

22. Niederman, F.: Why future studies provides a critical opportunity for the IS discipline. In: Proceedings of the 56th Hawaii International Conference on System Sciences (2023)

23. Nunamaker, J.F., Chen, M., Purdin, T.D.: Systems development in information systems research. J. Manag. Inf. Syst. **7**(3), 89–106 (1990)

24. Pascal, A., Renaud, A.: 15 years of information system design science research: A bibliographic analysis. In: Proceedings of the 53rd Hawaii International Conference on System Sciences (2020)

25. Peffers, K., Tuunanen, T., Niehaves, B.: Design science research genres: Introduction to the special issue on exemplars and criteria for applicable design science research. Euro. J. Inf. Syst. **27**(2) 129–139 (2018)

26. Peffers, K., et al.: A design science research methodology for information systems research. J. Manag. Inf. Syst. **24**(3), 45–77 (2007)

27. Piirainen, K., Gonzalez, R.A., Kolfschoten, G.: Quo vadis, design science?–A survey of literature. In: Winter, R., Zhao, J.L., Aier, S. (eds.): DESRIST 2010. LNCS, vol. 6105, pp. 93–108. Springer, Heidelberg (2010). https://doi.org/10.1007/978-3-642-13335-0

28. Prat, N., Comyn-Wattiau, I., Akoka, J.: A taxonomy of evaluation methods for information systems artifacts. J. Manag. Inf. Syst. **32**(3), 229–267 (2015)

29. Schön, D.A.: The Reflective Practitioner: How Professionals Think in Action. Basic Books. New York (1983)

30. Sein, M.K., et al.: Action design research. MIS Q. **35**(1), 37–56 (2011)

31. Simon, H.A.: The Sciences of the Artificial, pp. xiv-xiv. MIT Press, Cambridge, Mass (1996)

32. Thuan, N.H., Drechsler, A., Antunes, P.: Construction of design science research questions. Commun. Assoc. Inf. Syst. **44**(1), 20 (2019)

33. Tremblay, M., VanderMeer, D., Beck, R.: The effects of the quantification of faculty productivity: perspectives from the design science research community. Commun. Assoc. Inf. Syst. **43**, 625–661 (2018)

34. van Aken, J.: Management research based on the paradigm of the design sciences: the quest for field-tested and grounded technological rules. J. Manage. Stud. **41**(2), 219–246 (2004)

35. van der Merwe, A., Gerber, A., Smuts, H.: Guidelines for conducting design science research in information systems. In: Tait, B., Kroeze, J., Gruner, S. (eds.) SACLA 2019. CCIS, vol. 1136, pp. 163–178. Springer, Cham (2020). https://doi.org/10.1007/978-3-030-35629-3_11

36. Venable, J., Pries-Heje, J., Baskerville, R.: FEDS: a framework for evaluation in design science research. Eur. J. Inf. Syst. **25**(1), 77–89 (2016)

37. Walls, J.G., Widmeyer, G.R., El Sawy, O.A.: Building an information system design theory for vigilant EIS. Inf. Syst. Res. **3**(1), 36–59 (1992)

38. Walsh, I., Renaud, A., Medina, M.J., Baudet, C. Mourmant, G., ARTIREV: an integrated bibliometric tool to efficiently conduct quality literature reviews. Systèmes d'information et management, **27**(4), 5-50 (2022)

39. Yin, R.K.: Validity and generalization in future case study evaluations. Evaluation **19**(3), 321–332 (2013)

Conducting Design Science Research in Society 5.0 – Proposal of an Explainable Artificial Intelligence Research Methodology

Christian Daase[✉] [iD] and Klaus Turowski

Otto-Von-Guericke University, Magdeburg, Germany
{christian.daase,klaus.turowski}@ovgu.de

Abstract. Every technological or scientific advance is accompanied by a change in social structures, moral concepts, laws and education. As more and more people gain access to the digital world and the technical possibilities increase at the same rate, the excitement to carry out computer-based engineering projects increases. This in turn leads to an elevated demand for appropriate design-oriented methodologies, especially from the field of design science research (DSR), which in a sense democratize digital engineering. The idea of Society 5.0 is one of the major shifts in perspective on the role of technology, humans and their interaction in a shared living world. As a core component, artificial intelligence (AI), together with the Internet of things and big data analytics, is expected to have the most significant impact on the transformation toward smart societies. In this study, a systematic literature review of a total of 137 published articles addressing AI projects using DSR methodologies is conducted with the purpose of establishing a unified methodology for explainable AI-focused DSR projects. The proposed methodology further takes into account the particularities of AI at the varying advanced levels of artificial narrow intelligence (ANI) to the presumed necessities for approaching artificial general intelligence (AGI), which has not yet been fully realized. By allowing AI researchers to rely on a generalized methodological approach, the gap between behavioral science and design science is bridged, with the former laying the foundation for understanding living reality and the latter developing the means to mimic that reality as part of artificiality.

Keywords: Design Science Research · Artificial Intelligence · Behavior Analysis · Society 5.0 Research Methodology · Systematic Literature Review

1 Introduction

Every technological or scientific progress is accompanied by shifts in social structures, moral codes, laws, and education [1]. As more and more people are getting access to the digital world and the technical capabilities are increasing equally accelerated, the excitement of conducting computer-based engineering projects is expanding [2]. This leads to an enlarged need for design-oriented methodologies, especially from the field of *design science research* (DSR), whose popularity today draws sufficient attention to

© The Author(s), under exclusive license to Springer Nature Switzerland AG 2023
A. Gerber and R. Baskerville (Eds.): DESRIST 2023, LNCS 13873, pp. 250–265, 2023.
https://doi.org/10.1007/978-3-031-32808-4_16

devote special journal issues, conference tracks, and even dedicated conferences to this branch of research [3, 4]. Since DSR is highly context-dependent, lots of contributions have been made in the past years and a wide range of methodologies for different DSR project's peculiarities are already existing [5, 6]. While these can be differentiated mainly in terms of participants, objectives, and philosophy [6], the specific technologies used are usually not the distinguishing factor for choosing a DSR methodology. However, since Hevner et al. [7] published their manifesto on DSR in information systems in 2004, there has been a technological evolution in several directions. These technologies, including big data analytics, the Internet of things (IoT), cloud computing, artificial intelligence (AI), and robotics, mean that research efforts using highly adaptable DSR methodologies must tailor each research activity and justify research design decisions. In light of strict space constraints in publications, it can be argued that a preconfigured methodology specifically for AI projects would mitigate the need to devote space to methodological customization, as it could be more precise from the outset.

The idea of *Society 5.0*, first proposed by the Japanese government as an initiative addressing societal shifts through digitization [8–11], is one of the major perspective changes nowadays internationally recognized on the role of technology, humans, and their interaction in a common living environment. Not only is Society 5.0 a set of emerging technologies, but it is also a principle for innovation, stimulating the simultaneous shift towards human-centric, sustainable, and resilient economies as an advancement of *Industry 4.0* to *Industry 5.0* [8, 10]. Although it is disputed whether humans are psychologically prepared for machine-intervention on a human-like level [12], AI is viewed as a core element of a leap towards the *smart society* along with supporting technologies for data gathering and interconnectivity [9, 10]. Jiang et al. [1] call this close integration of the virtual and the physical world a shift from *"connected things"* to *"connected intelligence"*. While there is a contrast between the core of DSR, which is to develop and instantiate innovative artifacts to improve their environment, and behavioral science, which focuses on understanding and explaining phenomena [4, 13], the two will become more closely linked as part of the larger scheme of information systems research. The American computer scientist John McCarthy, who is attributed to have coined the term AI in 1956, defined it as making a machine behave in a way that could be considered as *intelligent* for human standards [1, 14–16]. In contrast to tools that must be designed to solve a particular problem, AI-based systems are ideally based on an existing, yet partially difficult to formalize, design: human-like rational behavior. Since the main object of study in DSR is the artifact being designed [4] and AI reflects a real-world model, behavioral science is not only complementary to DSR in AI projects, but an integral part of a suitably adapted research methodology.

This paper addresses how a proposal for a methodology developed specifically for DSR projects in the field of AI could be assembled. The next Sect. 1 discusses the role of AI in Society 5.0 and explains the different stages of AI. The Sect. 3 describes the process of conducting a systematic literature review (SLR) of work by other researchers who have applied DSR methodologies for building AI-enabled artifacts. In Sect. 4, the articles reviewed are placed within the larger scheme of DSR. Sect. 5 compiles a unified methodology that takes into account the specifics of AI integration as well as the social and behavioral science background. Sect. 6 concludes with an overview of the scientific contribution of the proposed methodology.

2   AI in Society 5.0

After the initial draft of the concept by John McCarthy, scholars tried to explain what AI means with varyingly abstract definitions based on literature or legislations (e.g., [14, 16]). In terms of the present article, the key points of the explanation attempts can be sorted into three pillars. First, AI may describe systems that have the ability to perceive information multimodal in ways that are usually associated with human senses, such as visual analytics, speech recognition, translation, or tactile sensing. Second, the processing of incoming data is similar to human abilities, such as adaptability to unforeseen scenarios and building a wealth of experience. Third, defining AI may focus on the purpose of a development endeavor, such as finding an optimal solution to a particular problem or making the most advantageous decision possible, as a rational human would strive to do. The difficulty of drawing a clear line between what can and cannot be considered AI becomes tangible when looking at the technical side. Properly programmed software usually mimics behavior that the respective developer considers rationally correct and advantageous, even if the code consists only of *if-then* operations. So-called *expert systems*, which are rule-based software with an underlying knowledge base intended to help with decision making in complex scenarios, are either considered as AI [17] or not [16], depending on the source. Other explanation attempts broaden the space of AI capabilities to more advanced human traits, such as emotional knowledge, consciousness, and creativity [15].

While the exact definitions vary, there is great unanimity over the fact that AI is influencing large portions of society, such as education, business, government, and healthcare [16]. The human-centric nature of Society 5.0 is underpinned by AI adaptation in retail and marketing for personalized offers and purchase decision-support [9, 18], in financial services for credit scoring and risk assessment [19], for social service digitization [8], and even in the media industry in which AI is applied to artificially generate news articles [12]. As a key aspiration of Society 5.0 is to ensure a better life for the people in it, healthcare is certainly one of the most important areas where AI can bring benefits, for example, using facial recognition to aid in diagnosis, medication, and surgery support [11, 20]. However, AI is no exception when it comes to human fears of transformation. One of the most dominant reasons for reluctance is the fear of job loss due to AI [19], although it may bring new professions in turn [14]. Moreover, there is a fear that AI could commit criminal acts on its own since it knows no moral principles to refrain from such behavior due to emotional conflicts, while on the other hand effective punishments cannot be enforced without a conscience [20, 21]. Another significant setback for AI acceptance was the global financial crisis between 2007 and 2009, in whose course several AI systems ceased working properly [19].

To classify these considerations correctly, the broad understanding of AI has to be broken down to its widely recognized three stages: *artificial narrow intelligence* (ANI), *artificial general intelligence* (AGI), and *artificial super intelligence* (ASI). In general, ANI, termed as "weak" AI, describes a form of intelligence capable of performing a singular task well that may involve different kinds of perception and decision making, such as playing chess, driving a vehicle autonomously, or answering customer questions [1, 14, 16]. Most of today's AI systems comply with these requirements to perform a very limited scope of clearly defined tasks [15]. ANI has no independent judgement and acts only within the boundaries of previously by human developers established procedures

[21]. In contrast, AGI, as the next big step in AI, is intended to extend the scope to solving problems for which it has not been trained, through independent planning and reasoning [16]. Although it is disputed whether this advanced stage of AI can ever be reached at all [22], the human-like cognitive abilities necessary would certainly require massively extended computing capacities, for example realized with quantum computing [15]. On the ethical side, AGI is mainly connected to concerns regarding autonomous criminal acts of machines since it is not limited to a developer's intentions [21]. The last and currently purely hypothesized stage of AI, ASI, is conceptualized as a form of intelligence capable of designing AGI itself better than a human could do and altering its own firmware, leading to unpredictable characteristics [1]. Since humans are largely bound by biological constraints that can hardly be changed, a machine capable of changing its functioning and perhaps its building materials would potentially outperform humans in every way, making them redundant [16]. However, the occurrence of a "strong" AI, how ASI and partially AGI are called, is not expected earlier than 2045 according to most experts, assuming that this kind of artificially created cognitive potential is possible to be realized at all [15].

Strengthening the role of AI for Society 5.0 and regaining public trust should be the central aspiration of any AI related project. Hence, a subtopic of research called *explainable AI* (XAI) has emerged to better understand the decision making processes of such systems in order to reduce fears of unforeseen malicious behavior [1]. The methodology proposed in this paper takes into account that the foundation for constructing AI systems should be made clear for the developer as well as for the intended user group. Figure 1 summarizes the explained pillars and stages of AI evolution.

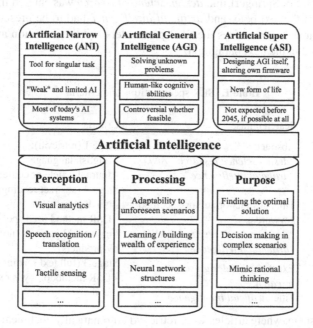

Fig. 1. Pillars and stages of artificial intelligence

3   Systematic Literature Review

The literature foundation that can be regarded as relevant in terms of the objective to streamline existent approaches addressing DSR projects in the AI domain is based on an SLR, following the guidelines proposed by Kitchenham and Charters [23]. Therefore, conducting the SLR as clearly, comprehensibly, and reproducibly as possible is a necessity. The review protocol includes information on the databases used, the search queries, imposed constraints, inclusion and exclusion criteria, and the review phases in which they were applied. In addition, test searches were conducted to identify appropriate configurations to limit the literature found to a manageable selection without excluding potentially relevant articles based on overly stringent criteria. As a primary source of literature, the abstract and citation database *Scopus*, which links to several full text databases, and *SpringerLink* are used, since the former claims to be the largest database of its kind while the latter extents the literature body with a selection of own high-quality journals and conference articles [23]. The secondary sources added to supplement the literature, especially in consideration of the emerging nature of the field under investigation, are the full text databases *IEEE Xplore*, *ScienceDirect*, and *Web of Science*. Although it was expected that most of the articles retrieved from these databases are duplicates of the results from Scopus, some highly topical articles were not yet indexed. The search phrase chosen consisted simply of a conjunction of the terms *design science research* and *artificial intelligence*, each placed within quotations marks to only search for exact matches. The phrase was searched for in abstracts for the databases Scopus, IEEE Xplore, and Web of Science, and in the joint field for abstracts, titles, and keywords in ScienceDirect. For SpringerLink, *design science research* was entered in the field for exact matches in the text body and *artificial intelligence* had to be present in the title of an article. Table 1 summarizes the SLR parameters and the inclusion and exclusion criteria described in the next paragraph.

Table 1. SLR specifications and criteria

Database	Search phrase	Criteria
Scopus	Abstract:	Stage 1 (retrieval):
IEEE Xplore	*"design science research"* AND *"artificial intelligence"*	- English language - Journal article or conference paper
Web of Science		Stage 2 (abstract reading):
ScienceDirect	Title, abstract or author-specified keywords: *"design science research"* AND *"artificial intelligence"*	- No duplicate - DSR method used specifically for finalized AI projects (not only for by-products)
SpringerLink	Exact phrase: *design science research* Title: *artificial intelligence*	Stage 3 (full text reading): - DSR methodology is explained in detail

In the first stage, where articles were retrieved automatically, technical criteria were applied that could be enforced directly through the mechanisms of the databases. These included restriction to journal articles and conference papers in English. In the second phase of reading the abstracts, duplicates were excluded and it was checked whether a DSR methodology was actually applied to carry out an AI-related development project. In the final phase of reading the full texts with special attention to the methodological sections, only articles explaining a sufficiently detailed research methodology and suitable for synthesizing a unified methodological approach were considered.

The aforementioned databases yielded a total of 137 results, which served as the basis for the SLR. 45 articles were identified as duplicates across the various databases. They were therefore excluded from further investigation. Five additional articles could not be evaluated due to technical inaccessibility. Of the remaining 87 articles, 34 were found not to be specific to AI projects using DSR methodologies. Thirteen articles were excluded because they were either pure reviews, introductions to proceedings or journal issues, or ongoing research that did not cover the entire development cycle of a DSR project. Of the remaining 40 publications, 17 were excluded in the full-text reading phase because they did not contain detailed explanations of the DSR approach used. Figure 2 illustrates the completed workflow of the SLR.

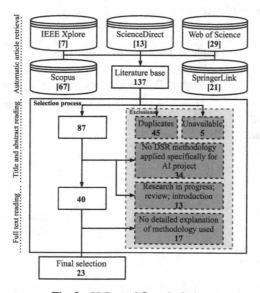

Fig. 2. SLR workflow depiction

4 AI Use Cases

The literature provides applied examples which can superficially be sorted into the four originally proposed types of artifacts: constructs, models, methods, and instantiations [7]. However, drawing a clear line between different outcomes of the same research endeavor is not always feasible. In Table 2, the retrieved scientific contributions and the primary DSR guidelines applied therein are listed with the presumed most fitting outcome designations. Considering the stages of AI evolution, it can be observed that most applications remain on the level of ANI, addressing specific tasks such as classification and prediction [24–31], supporting decision making [32–37], or providing conversational agents [38–40] (i.e., chatbots). Some practical integrations of AI furthermore utilized different technologies that are expected to play an important role in Society 5.0, such as augmented reality in retailing [41] or the Internet of Things [42].

Noteworthy, the phenomenon of XAI is mentioned frequently in the design justifications [28, 30, 33, 35–37, 41, 43]. In [36], the authors refer to Jobin et al. [44] and the five principles of *responsible AI* as a term that goes one step further by not only aspiring to make AI tangible for the larger audience but also proposing ethical guidelines in doing so. The principles are *transparency* (explaining the source codes and origins of used data in non-technical terms), *justice* (using diverse datasets to avoid discrimination due to trained bias), *non-maleficence* (preventing harmful behavior by monitoring and assessing solutions after deployment), *accountability* (aligning solution behavior with human values and identifying legal responsibilities), and *privacy* (ensuring secure data storage while masking private information). The proposal of a tailored methodology for DSR projects in the AI domain in the subsequent section incorporates these principles of responsible / explainable AI.

Table 2. Literature basis overview

Publication	Primary DSR guidelines	Outcome
Smart Space Design–A Framework and an IoT Prototype Implementation [42]	Hevner and Chatterjee [45]	IoT framework/instantiation
An ontological artifact for classifying social media: Text mining analysis for financial data [29]	Geerts [46]	Classifier/instantiation
AI and public contests: a model to improve the evaluation and selection of public contest candidates in the Police Force [28]	Self-developed	Theoretical framework/model
DELEN – A Process Model for the Systematic Development of Legitimate Digital Nudges [47]	Peffers et al. [48]	Model
An investigation on trust in AI-enabled collaboration: Application of AI-Driven chatbot in accommodation-based sharing economy [39]	Hevner et al. [7]	Chatbot/instantiation

(*continued*)

Table 2. *(continued)*

Publication	Primary DSR guidelines	Outcome
Towards Design Principles for User-Centric Explainable AI in Fraud Detection [43]	Ostrowski et al. [49]	Design principles/construct
Finding the unicorn: Predicting early stage startup success through a hybrid intelligence method [31]	Hevner et al. [7], Gregor and Hevner [50]	Prediction/method
Enhancing Collaborative Rationality between Humans and Machines through Data-Driven Decision Evaluation [33]	Peffers et al. [48], Sonnenberg and vom Brocke [51]	Model
Developing Purposeful AI Use Cases – A Structured Method and Its Application in Project Management [37]	Hevner et al. [7]	Method
A Nudge-Inspired AI-Driven Health Platform for Self-Management of Diabetes [24]	Drechsler and Hevner [52]	Web application/instantiation
Digital transformation to mitigate emergency situations: increasing opioid overdose survival rates through explainable artificial intelligence [35]	Hevner et al. [7]	Model/instantiation
Responsible Artificial Intelligence in Healthcare: Predicting and Preventing Insurance Claim Denials for Economic and Social Wellbeing [36]	Peffers et al. [48]	Prediction/instantiation
Supporting customer-oriented marketing with artificial intelligence: automatically quantifying customer needs from social media [27]	Kuechler and Vaishnavi (B) [53]	Social media analytics/instantiation
Designing an AI-based advisory platform for design techniques [54]	Peffers et al. [48]	Platform/instantiation

(continued)

Table 2. (*continued*)

Publication	Primary DSR guidelines	Outcome
Artificial intelligence-based method for forecasting flowtime in job shops [34]	Peffers et al. [48]	Method
Testing acoustic scene classifiers using Metamorphic Relations [26]	Wieringa [55]	Classifier/instantiation
COVID-Bot, an Intelligent System for COVID-19 Vaccination Screening: Design and Development [38]	Peffers et al. [48]	Chatbot/instantiation
Design and Evaluation of a Conversational Agent for Facilitating Idea Generation in Organizational Innovation Processes [40]	Peffers et al. [48]	Chatbot/model/instantiation
Utilizing Evidence in Asset Management in the Era of Industry 4.0 and Artificial Intelligence [56]	Peffers et al. [48]	Asset management/instantiation
Designing Transparency for Effective Human-AI Collaboration [32]	Hevner et al. [7], Sonnenberg and vom Brocke [51]	Design principles/construct
Designing a feature selection method based on explainable artificial intelligence [30]	Kuechler and Vaishnavi (A) [57]	Design framework/instantiation
The Design of Reciprocal Learning Between Human and Artificial Intelligence [25]	Gregor and Hevner [50], Sein et al. [58]	Conceptual framework/instantiation
Enhancing brick-and-mortar store shopping experience with an augmented reality shopping assistant application using personalized recommendations and explainable artificial intelligence [41]	Gregor and Hevner [50]	Augmented reality assistant/instantiation

5   Explainable AI Artifact Design Methodology (XAIADM)

In response to current developments in Society 5.0 and due to the increasing complexity of AI systems, there is pressure to streamline research efforts and to make the results understandable to the target audience by considering them not only as users but also as co-creators [8]. Therefore, we propose the *Explainable AI Artifact Design Methodology*

(XAIADM) to both enable researchers and practitioners to formalize their research to keep pace with the expected growing complexity of future AI systems [1], and to encourage researchers to conduct design science studies in such a way that the target audience (e.g., non-technical users) can understand the underlying AI behavior, thereby adhering to XAI standards and increasing user confidence in the research results.

The XAIADM consists of five research steps and a concurrent explanatory feedback loop (EFL). First, the problem to be solved and the perspective on it must be defined. Second, a human-centric subject analysis of the available domain knowledge is performed to assess expected human behavior in the stated problem situation and to evaluate environmental and technical conditions. This is done by aggregating the human knowledge base, collecting data from the environment in which the solution is to be applied, and observations of existing technological solution approaches. In addition, soft requirements definitions that take into account human behavior and biases can be derived from this step. The third step focuses on defining the AI scope of the project on a scale from simple ANI to feasible AGI. Simultaneously in the EFL, the requirements for a solution are consolidated and retrospectively compared with the soft requirements definitions. In the fourth step, a behavioral model is designed in which the formalized behavioral requirements are matched with the technical capabilities. In the fifth step, the solution is evaluated through prototyping, simulation, and qualitative and quantitative feedback, depending on the type of artifact being developed. The corresponding activity in the EFL is to inform the target group by making the implementation tangible and involving the audience in the evaluation. In the feedback loop, the observed realized AI behavior can be compared with the intended AI behavior.

5.1 Problem (Perspective) Definition

AI use cases can be considered from two perspectives: either to solve existing problems or to explore organizational opportunities for beneficial AI integration [37]. In this step, researchers are asked to specify the perspective to enable an assessment of whether the targeted approach can be considered experimental, with the risk of not solving a particular problem or not improving the current state. The potential outcomes should also be defined. To increase scientific rigor and precision, clearly defined research questions (RQs) can be formulated at this step. The lack of sufficiently delineated questions is considered a major shortcoming, with a notable proportion of DSR projects tending to omit RQs [4]. In addition, considerations of the generalizability of an identified problem can be made in this step.

5.2 Human-Centric Subject Analysis

The research step of a necessary human-centric subject analysis concerns three aspects. Since AI generally describes the imitation of human cognition and behavior [14, 20], a knowledge base for understanding human behavior must be aggregated for artificial imitation. In addition to the universally applicable method of (systematic) literature review, human-oriented methods such as surveys, (expert) interviews, and brainstorming sessions are often used [29, 31, 33, 42, 43]. The second aspect of analysis concerns the collection of environmental data. Related to the identified problem, the intended application context is clarified, for example, based on social media or organizational data. While the former also provide information on human bias and articulation, the latter can be used to match subjective public statements with objective data. The third aspect of this step is an assessment of existing technological solution approaches to select the means for the present research project. While algorithms are studied from a technical perspective, legal regulations must be carefully considered as well. Since one promise of XAI is to provide transparency to the users [28, 30, 36, 43], any threats of a solution must be highlighted, including failures that could occur if a human were to perform the tasks for which the AI is designed. Technological limitations should be pointed out, both from the perspective of limitations in solving the given problem and from the perspective of what harmful behavior would not be possible due to technical inability.

The outcome of this step serves two purposes. First, it lays the knowledge base for the subsequent AI scope declaration. Second, it establishes the first element of the parallel EFL, the soft requirement definitions, meaning the subjectively expected situational human behavior that can be formalized as a set of reactions that draw a line from the identified problem to the assumed appropriate human behavior (i.e., the reaction that the AI artifact should suggest or execute, depending on the type of artifact).

5.3 AI Scope Declaration

As illustrated in Fig. 1, AI can be divided in the three stages ANI, AGI, and ASI [1, 14, 16]. However, there are shades between the stages rather than a clear demarcation. On a scale from largely realized ANI to rudimentary approximations of AGI, a number of attributes can be defined that determine the degree of progress. In the methodology proposed here, AI systems range from purely defining rules (i.e., expert systems [16, 17]), to enabling learning, to extending adaptability to unknown scenarios, to an integration of human-like cognitive variance, to the ability to self-adapt reasoning. The scope declaration can be derived from any advanced level. In the EFL, the AI scope declaration is accompanied by the consolidation of requirements. Here, the identified problem is linked to the intended scope of the AI solution and the AI behavior is described in detail, formalizing the technological perspective of the DSR project. The consolidated requirements are then used to compare the conceptualized intended AI behavior with previously observed human behavior.

5.4 Behavioral Model Design

The behavioral model design as the core of a DSR project is introduced as the fourth research step. Based on the requirements and technical specifications, the problem to be solved is first matched with the intended AI behavior. In a loop, the preliminary model is then compared with ethical and legal specifications and adapted if necessary. To make the artifact comprehensible, the model can then be simplified or illustrated to make the design intuitively understandable. In particular, the input and expected output parameters in decision making scenarios should be made transparent and can later be a basis for evaluation in collaboration with domain experts as well as regular users.

5.5 Solution Assessment

The fifth research step covers the artifact's journey from development to commissioning to evaluation. Depending on the type of artifact, prototyping may proceed to a stage of self-development through training if the AI solution has integrated learning capabilities through machine learning or similar. Then, the artifact can be put into operation through simulations supervised by domain experts or in the context of a user study [30, 40, 42, 56]. Knowledge about the artifact is extracted through two types of evaluation: qualitative (i.e., subjective characteristics such as ease of use, generalizability, and proximity to human behavior) and quantitative (i.e., measurable characteristics such as efficiency, accuracy, and precision) [34]. The practically designed artifact and the underlying blueprint form the basis for the last corresponding activity in EFL, informing the target audience. From the knowledge about the behavior of the AI artifact, the perceived impact of certain features, especially for learning enabled applications, is extracted and communicated either with experts to ask their opinion, or with users via a survey, or both. Given the need for XAI to be transparent about the entire process, it is concluded that the results of the study should be published. In order to improve the design in a next design iteration of the same or similar artifact, the result of this activity in the EFL is again to be used to compare the realized AI behavior with the intended AI behavior, like in the previous activity in the EFL. The proposed XAIADM is illustrated in Fig. 3.

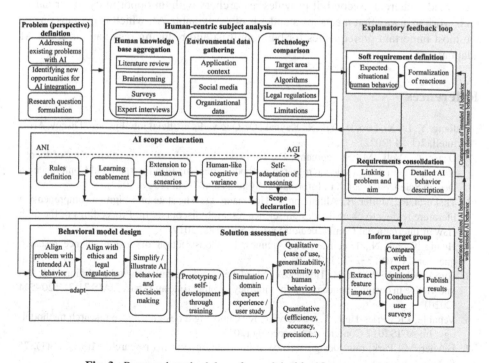

Fig. 3. Proposed methodology for explainable AI systems design

6 Methodological Contribution and Future Research

In times of economic and social transformation such as Industry 4.0 and Society 5.0, design researchers in the field of artificial intelligence are embracing the challenge of developing concepts and applications that benefit individuals and society at large while setting new standards for digital responsibility [9, 10, 19]. In this article, the pillars of AI and the resulting stages of ANI, AGI, and ASI are explained and placed in context with the Society 5.0 paradigm. A proposal for an *Explainable AI Artifact Design Methodology* (XAIADM) is presented and the five research steps accompanied by a parallel explanatory feedback loop are described in detail. However, future research needs to focus on the empirical evaluation of the proposed research steps. This article provides the DSR community access to a tailored methodology for AI-focused projects. Thus, practical formative and summative evaluation can take place in the adoption by scholars. Furthermore, perspective further steps may include an extensive literature review of projects that are, in contrast to publications reviewed here, not explicitly based on design science principles but can might be mapped to the approach presented here in order to underpin the profoundness of the XAIADM by literature validation. Two major contributions to design science are made in this article: First, by providing a DSR methodology specifically for the technological field of AI, corresponding research articles are relieved from the burden of fine-grained adaptation of more generic methodologies, as AI peculiarities are already inherent. Second, it provides researchers with an opportunity to formalize their work in a way that meets the standards of explainable AI, which is perhaps one of the most important prerequisites for building trust and reducing reservations about AI adaptations.

References

1. Jiang, Y., Li, X., Luo, H., Yin, S., Kaynak, O.: Quo vadis artificial intelligence? Discov. Artif. Intell. **2**(1), 4 (2022)
2. Daase, C., Volk, M., Staegemann, D., Turowski, K.: Addressing the dichotomy of theory and practice in design science research methodologies. In: 17th International Conference on Design Science Research in Information Systems and Technology (2022)
3. Thakurta, R., Müller, B., Ahlemann, F., Hoffmann, D.: The state of design - a comprehensive literature review to chart the design science research discourse. In: Proceedings of the 50th Hawaii International Conference on System Sciences (2017)
4. Hoang Thuan, N., Drechsler, A., Antunes, P.: Construction of design science research questions. CAIS, 332–363 (2019)
5. vom Brocke, J., Winter, R., Hevner, A., Maedche, A.: Accumulation and evolution of design knowledge in design science research: a journey through time and space. JAIS **21**(3), 520–544 (2020)
6. Venable, J.R., Pries-Heje, J., Baskerville, R.: Choosing a design science research methodology. In: ACIS2017 Conference Proceeding (2017)
7. Hevner, M.: Park, ram: design science in information systems research. MIS Q. **28**(1), 75 (2004)
8. Carayannis, E.G., Morawska-Jancelewicz, J.: The futures of Europe: society 5.0 and industry 5.0 as driving forces of future universities. J. Knowl. Econ. **13**(4), 3445–3471 (2022)

9. Muslikhin, M., Horng, J.-R., Yang, S.-Y., Wang, M.-S., Awaluddin, B.-A.: An artificial intelligence of things-based picking algorithm for online shop in the society 5.0's con-text. Sensors (Basel, Switzerland) **21**(8), 2813 (2021)
10. Nair, M.M., Tyagi, A.K., Sreenath, N.: The future with industry 4.0 at the core of society 5.0: open issues, future opportunities and challenges. In: 2021 International Conference on Computer Communication and Informatics (ICCCI), pp. 1–7 (2021)
11. Al Mamun, S., Kaiser, M.S., Mahmud, M.: An artificial intelligence based approach towards inclusive healthcare provisioning in society 5.0: a perspective on brain disorder. In: Mahmud, M., Kaiser, M.S., Vassanelli, S., Dai, Q., Zhong, N. (eds.) BI 2021. LNCS (LNAI), vol. 12960, pp. 157–169. Springer, Cham (2021). https://doi.org/10.1007/978-3-030-86993-9_15
12. Owsley, C.S., Greenwood, K.: Awareness and perception of artificial intelligence operationalized integration in news media industry and society. AI Soc. (2022)
13. vom Brocke, J., Hevner, A., Maedche, A.: Introduction to design science research. In: vom Brocke, J., Hevner, A., and Maedche, A. (eds.) Progress in IS, Design Science Research. Cases, pp. 1–13. Springer International Publishing, Cham (2020). https://doi.org/10.1007/978-3-030-46781-4_1
14. Girasa, R.: AI as a disruptive technology. In: Artificial Intelligence as a Disruptive Technology, pp. 3–21. Springer, Cham (2020). https://doi.org/10.1007/978-3-030-35975-1_1
15. Cisek, G.: How much and what kind of artificial intelligence can humans bear? In: The Triumph of Artificial Intelligence, pp. 1–6. Springer, Wiesbaden (2021). https://doi.org/10.1007/978-3-658-34896-0_1
16. Kaplan, A., Haenlein, M.: Siri, Siri, in my hand: Who's the fairest in the land? on the interpretations, illustrations, and implications of artificial intelligence. Bus. Horiz. **62**(1), 15–25 (2019)
17. Russell, S.J., Norvig, P.: Artificial Intelligence: A Modern Approach, 3rd edn. Prentice-Hall, Upper Saddle River, NJ (2010)
18. Jarek, K., Mazurek, G.: Marketing and artificial intelligence. CEBR **8**(2), 46–55 (2019)
19. Elliott, K., et al.: Towards an equitable digital society: artificial intelligence (AI) and corporate digital responsibility (CDR). Society **58**(3), 179–188 (2021)
20. Shastry, K.A., Sanjay, H.A.: Cancer diagnosis using artificial intelligence: a review. Artif. Intell. Rev. **55**(4), 2641–2673 (2021). https://doi.org/10.1007/s10462-021-10074-4
21. Huang, H.: Analysis on the criminal subject of artificial intelligence. In: Huang, C., Chan, Y.-W., Yen, N. (eds.) Advances in Intelligent Systems and Computing, Data Processing Techniques and Applications for Cyber-Physical Systems (DPTA 2019), pp. 317–321. Springer Singapore, Singapore (2020). https://doi.org/10.1007/978-981-15-1468-5_40
22. Fjelland, R.: Why general artificial intelligence will not be realized. Hum. Soc. Sci. Commun. **7**(1), 1–9 (2020)
23. Kitchenham, B., Charters, S.: Guidelines for performing Systematic Literature Reviews in Software Engineering: Technical report, Version 2.3 EBSE Technical Report (2007)
24. Joachim, S., Forkan, A.R.M., Jayaraman, P.P., Morshed, A., Wickramasinghe, N.: A nudge-inspired AI-driven health platform for self-management of diabetes. Sensors (Basel, Switzerland) **22**(12), 4620 (2022)
25. Zagalsky, A., et al.: The design of reciprocal learning between human and artificial intelligence. Proc. ACM Hum.-Comput. Interact. **5**(CSCW2), 1–36 (2021)
26. Moreira, D., Furtado, A.P., Nogueira, S.: Testing acoustic scene classifiers using metamorphic relations. In: 2020 IEEE International Conference on Artificial Intelligence Testing (AITest), pp. 47–54 (2020)
27. Kühl, N., Mühlthaler, M., Goutier, M.: Supporting customer-oriented marketing with artificial intelligence: automatically quantifying customer needs from social media. Electron Mark. **30**(2), 351–367 (2020)

28. Bailao Goncalves, M., Anastasiadou, M., Santos, V.: AI and public contests: a model to improve the evaluation and selection of public contest candidates in the Police force. TG **16**(4), 627–648 (2022)
29. Alzamil, Z., Appelbaum, D., Nehmer, R.: An ontological artifact for classifying social media: text mining analysis for financial data. Int. J. Acc. Inf. Syst. **38**, 100469 (2020)
30. Zacharias, J., Zahn, M. von, Chen, J., Hinz, O.: Designing a feature selection method based on explainable artificial intelligence. Electron Mark. 1–26 (2022)
31. Dellermann, D., Lipusch, N., Ebel, P., Popp, K.M., Leimeister, J.M.: Finding the unicorn: predicting early stage startup success through a hybrid intelligence method (2021)
32. Vössing, M., Kühl, N., Lind, M., Satzger, G.: Designing transparency for effective human-AI collaboration. Inf. Syst. Front. **24**(3), 877–895 (2022)
33. Elgendy, N.: Enhancing collaborative rationality between humans and machines through data-driven decision evaluation. In: Proceedings of the 21st International Conference on Perspectives in Business Informatics Research (BIR), Rostock, Germany, pp. 20–23 (2022)
34. Modesti, P., Ribeiro, J.K., Borsato, M.: Artificial intelligence-based method for forecasting flowtime in job shops. VJIKMS (2022)
35. Johnson, M., Albizri, A., Harfouche, A., Tutun, S.: Digital transformation to mitigate emergency situations: increasing opioid overdose survival rates through explainable artificial intelligence. IMDS, **123**(1), 324–344 (2021)
36. Johnson, M., Albizri, A., Harfouche, A.: Responsible artificial intelligence in healthcare: predicting and preventing insurance claim denials for economic and social wellbeing. Inf. Syst. Front. 1–17 (2021).https://doi.org/10.1007/s10796-021-10137-5
37. Hofmann, P., Jöhnk, J., Protschky, D., Urbach, N.: Developing purposeful AI use cases – a structured method and its application in project management, In: Gronau, N., Heine, M., Poustcchi, K., Krasnova, H. (eds.), WI2020 Zentrale Tracks, pp. 33–49. GITO Verlag (2020)
38. Okonkwo, C.W., Amusa, L.B., Twinomurinzi, H.: COVID-Bot, an intelligent system for COVID-19 vaccination screening: design and development. JMIR Formative Res. **6**(10), e39157 (2022)
39. Cheng, X., Zhang, X., Yang, B., Fu, Y.: An investigation on trust in AI-enabled collaboration: Application of AI-Driven chatbot in accommodation-based sharing economy. Electr. Comm. Res. Appl. **54**, 101164 (2022)
40. Poser, M., Küstermann, G.C., Tavanapour, N., Bittner, E.A.C.: Design and evaluation of a conversational agent for facilitating idea generation in organizational innovation processes. Inf. Syst. Front. **24**(3), 771–796 (2022)
41. Zimmermann, R., et al.: Enhancing brick-and-mortar store shopping experience with an augmented reality shopping assistant application using personalized recommendations and explainable artificial intelligence. JRIM (2022)
42. Alsamani, B., Chatterjee, S., Anjomshoae, A., Ractham, P.: Smart space design–a frame-work and an IoT prototype implementation. Sustainability **15**(1), 111 (2023)
43. Cirqueira, D., Helfert, M., Bezbradica, M.: Towards design principles for user-centric explainable AI in fraud detection. In: Degen, H., Ntoa, S. (eds.) HCII 2021. LNCS (LNAI), vol. 12797, pp. 21–40. Springer, Cham (2021). https://doi.org/10.1007/978-3-030-77772-2_2
44. Jobin, A., Ienca, M., Vayena, E.: The global landscape of AI ethics guidelines. Nat. Mach. Intell. **1**(9), 389–399 (2019)
45. Hevner, A., Chatterjee, S.: Design science research in information systems. In: Hevner, A., Chatterjee, S. (eds.) Integrated Series in Information Systems, Design Research in Information Systems, pp. 9–22. Springer US, Boston, MA (2010). https://doi.org/10.1007/978-1-4419-565 3-8_2
46. Geerts, G.L.: A design science research methodology and its application to accounting information systems research. Int. J. Account. Inf. Syst. **12**(2), 142–151 (2011)

47. Barev, T.J., Schöbel, S., Janson, A., Leimeister, J.M.: DELEN – a process model for the systematic development of legitimate digital nudges. In: Chandra Kruse, L., Seidel, S., Hausvik, G.I. (eds.) DESRIST 2021. LNCS, vol. 12807, pp. 299–312. Springer, Cham (2021). https://doi.org/10.1007/978-3-030-82405-1_30
48. Peffers, K., Tuunanen, T., Rothenberger, M.A., Chatterjee, S.: A design science research methodology for information systems research. J. Manag. Inf. Syst. **24**(3), 45–77 (2007)
49. Ostrowski, Ł, Helfert, M., Hossain, F.: A conceptual framework for design science research. In: Grabis, J., Kirikova, M. (eds.) BIR 2011. LNBIP, vol. 90, pp. 345–354. Springer, Heidelberg (2011). https://doi.org/10.1007/978-3-642-24511-4_27
50. Gregor, S., Hevner, A.R.: Positioning and presenting design science research for maximum impact. MIS Q. **37**(2), 337–355 (2013)
51. Sonnenberg, C., vom Brocke, J.: Evaluations in the science of the artificial – reconsidering the build-evaluate pattern in design science research, In: Hutchison, D. et al. (eds.) Lecture Notes in Computer Science, Design Science Research in Information Systems. Advances in Theory and Practice, 381–397. Springer Berlin Heidelberg, Berlin, Heidelberg (2012)
52. Drechsler, A., Hevner, A.: A four-cycle model of is design science research: capturing the dynamic nature of is artifact design. In: Proceedings of the 11th International Conference on Design Science Research in Information Systems and Technology (DESRIST), pp. 1–8 (2016)
53. Kuechler, W., Vaishnavi, V.: A framework for theory development in design science research: multiple perspectives. JAIS **13**(6), 395–423 (2012)
54. Liu, X., He, S., Maedche, A.: Designing an AI-based advisory platform for design techniques. In: 27th European Conference on Information Systems - Information Systems for a Sharing Society, ECIS 2019 (2020)
55. Wieringa, R.J.: Design Science Methodology for Information Systems and Software Engineering. Berlin, Heidelberg: Springer Berlin Heidelberg (2014)
56. Tervo, J., Kortelainen, H., Purhonen, A.: Utilizing evidence in asset management in the era of industry 4.0 and artificial intelligence. In: Borzemski, L., Selvaraj, H., Świątek, J. (eds.) ICSEng 2021. LNNS, vol. 364, pp. 271–280. Springer, Cham (2022). https://doi.org/10.1007/978-3-030-92604-5_24
57. Kuechler, B., Vaishnavi, V.: On theory development in design science research: anatomy of a research project. Eur. J. Inf. Syst. **17**(5), 489–504 (2008)
58. Sein, M.K., Henfridsson, O., Purao, S., Rossi, M., Lindgren, R.: Action design research. MIS Q. **35**(1), 37 (2011)

Accessing the Design Science Knowledge Base - A Search Engine for the Accumulation of Knowledge Across Decentrally Organized Publications

Michael Gau[1,2]([✉]) [ID], Alexander Maedche[1] [ID], and Jan vom Brocke[2] [ID]

[1] Karlsruhe Institute of Technology (KIT), Karlsruhe, Germany
michael.gau@uni.li, {michael.gau,alexander.maedche}@kit.edu
[2] University of Liechtenstein, Vaduz, Liechtenstein
jan.vom.brocke@uni.li

Abstract. Design science research (DSR) intends to contribute design knowledge to the scientific discourse in the field of Information Systems. However, such design knowledge is typically produced in isolated DSR projects and does not follow a systematic knowledge accumulation strategy in terms of refining or extending previous design knowledge. Towards a first step in fostering design knowledge reuse and supporting knowledge accumulation in DSR, we propose a design knowledge search engine facilitating access to existing design knowledge. In this paper, we present a knowledge extraction template, a mechanism to automatically extract design knowledge of existing DSR publications based on this template as well as a search interface. Applying DSR ourselves we report on the preliminary results and findings of the first design cycle and deliver (1) design requirements derived from the literature, (2) propose an initial set of design principles, (3) a prototypical implementation called DEKNOWSE, and (4) an evaluation of the first design cycle in a focus group with DSR researchers. We contribute design knowledge for the class of design knowledge extraction and search systems.

Keywords: Design Science Research · Knowledge Accumulation · Design Knowledge Search

1 Introduction

Scientific research—including the Information System (IS) field—is based on the concept of systematic knowledge accumulation [16]. Knowledge accumulation leads to a body of knowledge that is relevant to both theory and practice [26]. In the context of IS different forms of knowledge are produced, such as descriptive or prescriptive knowledge [17]. Design Science Research (DSR) aims to produce prescriptive knowledge in the form of designed artifacts, design principles, or design theories [15, 17, 19]. These findings are described using different representations [9] and are shared with researchers through the process of publishing. Such publications can be either presented at conferences, manuscripts in journals, or books.

A. Gerber and R. Baskerville (Eds.): DESRIST 2023, LNCS 13873, pp. 266–278, 2023.
https://doi.org/10.1007/978-3-031-32808-4_17

However, researchers observed that DSR does not follow a systematic knowledge accumulation strategy in terms of refining or extending previous design knowledge [30, 33]. A recent JAIS Special Issue Editorial on accumulation and evolution of design knowledge in DSR states that typical DSR contributions are rather isolated and the provided design knowledge has a monolithic structure [6]. Additionally, DSR is a multidisciplinary field and a recent MISQ editorial alludes to the diversity of methods and concepts applied by design science researchers [29]. DSR has been intensively discussed in the IS research community, however, it is increasingly applied in other disciplines, too, such as in entrepreneurship and management [3, 34]. Consequently, design knowledge contributions are widely spread across different fields and types of publication outlets and often remain fragmented. The potential for knowledge accumulation is insufficiently exploited.

In order to enhance knowledge accumulation, the design knowledge has to be made accessible so that single contributions can build on one another. Currently, however, existing design knowledge is usually embedded in unstructured documents like manuscripts of conference proceedings, journal publications, or books. Although these documents may be structurally kept in electronic libraries, the findings and the knowledge they contain are not [10]. Moreover, the academic knowledge base is growing and the number of publications is increasing rapidly over time [5]. Hence, to foster knowledge accumulation in the field of DSR, we argue that existing design knowledge has to be made more accessible. In order to keep up with the pace, we argue in favor of a decentralized organization of design knowledge, and we ask the following research question (RQ):

RQ: How to design a search engine to facilitate design knowledge access from decentrally organized publications?

In this paper, we develop a bottom-up approach by crawling DSR publications to automatically extract the contained design knowledge based on a defined extraction template. Moreover, we aim to provide simple access via a search engine interface to make the design knowledge accessible to design researchers. Applying the design science research methodology described by [19] we follow the process proposed by [23], we report on the preliminary results and findings of the first design cycles and deliver (1) design requirements derived from the literature, (2) propose an initial set of design principles, (3) a prototypical implementation called DEKNOWSE (DEsign KNOWledge Search Engine), and (4) an evaluation of the first cycle in a focus group including design science researchers. With our prototype, we contribute to the class of novel IS systems supporting design knowledge extraction and search.

2 Related Work

DSR aims to solve real-world problems by designing innovative artifacts [19]. There exist many frameworks, guidelines, and process models supporting design science researchers in conducting DSR projects [19, 23, 28, 36]. During the design process, one objective is to produce design knowledge on how to build solutions for important problems effectively [6]. Such design knowledge is about means-end relationships between problem and solution spaces [39]. In DSR design knowledge is primarily divided into two different types of knowledge. Descriptive knowledge—describes the natural phenomena—and prescriptive knowledge—describes human-built artifacts [17]. More broadly, design knowledge provides knowledge about the problem space including knowledge about contexts and goodness criteria and the solution space including knowledge about artifacts and the design processes [6]. Furthermore, design knowledge can have different forms of representation, such as instantiations, models, methods, constructs, or design theories [17]. To express design knowledge several alternative forms can be found, including design patterns [4, 12], technology rules [1], and design principles. The latter, design principles are often used by design researchers to conceptualize and express design knowledge in natural language [8, 15]. Furthermore, there exist templates supporting researchers to express design principles in a comprehensive and precise way [15].

In DSR knowledge accumulation relies on the communication of existing design knowledge to foster reuse and accumulation of knowledge over time. In the literature there exist several suggestions to establish knowledge accumulation in DSR. For instance, Barquet et al. provide a framework supporting researchers in systematically communicating knowledge contributions [2]. Reining et al. developed an evolutionary process model illustrating the importance of scientific progress based on a synthesis of different streams in the philosophy of science [30]. Additionally, they provide actions and quality criadera for DSR contributions regarding each step in the process model. Rothe et al. propose a process model illustrating knowledge creation including different mechanisms and their impact on design knowledge accumulation [32]. Others suggest an ontology-based approach as a knowledge-sharing mechanism in DSR projects to increase knowledge accumulation [25]. A base for the systematic and usable formulation of design theories is presented by Gregor and Jones [18]. In their study, they provide a template to describe design knowledge based on predefined components to describe the anatomy of design theories in a structured way.

In other disciplines tool support to extract knowledge for reuse and knowledge accumulation already exists. For instance, in behavioral research, a tool called TheoryOn processes existing knowledge and provides a search engine to access it [24]. The main objective of TheoryOn allows researchers to directly search for constructs, construct relationships, antecedents and consequents, and easily integrate related theories into other research projects. A similar approach is DSIKNET, a tool for building a consistent body of knowledge for structural equation model (SEM) based studies within the IS discipline by systematic knowledge accumulation [10]. Furthermore, Wagner et al. outline how the use of artificial intelligence in literature reviews can transform traditional research practices and how researchers benefit from such tool support [40].

However, in the field of DSR, tool support facilitating access to existing design knowledge is missing. Therefore, we investigate how to design knowledge extraction and search engines enabling access to existing design knowledge in order to foster knowledge reuse and knowledge accumulation in DSR.

3   Method

Applying DSR ourselves we followed the approach described by Kuechler and Vaishnavi [23] and present the results of the first design cycle. We first derived a set of design requirements originating from the literature and introduced in the related work section. Second, based on the derived requirements we proposed a set of design principles. We rely on existing design knowledge on how to design knowledge accumulation systems presented by Dan et al. [10] and Li et al. [24]. Third, we instantiated the design principles and developed a prototypical implementation called DEKNOWSE. Finally, we evaluated the prototypical instantiation in a focus group by demonstrating the prototype to DSR researchers following Tremblay et al. [38]. In the focus group design science researchers discussed the utility of the prototype, and we applied a strengths, weaknesses, opportunities, and threats (SWOT) analysis. An overview of the applied method and the underlying design cycles is illustrated in Fig. 1.

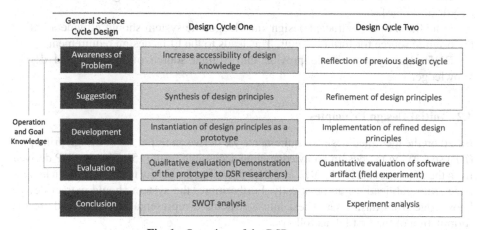

Fig. 1. Overview of the DSR process.

In a future second cycle, we plan to reflect on the first cycle and refine the proposed design. Moreover, we plan to make DEKNOWSE publicly available for researchers in order to support searching for existing design knowledge in the field of IS.

4 Design

4.1 Design Requirements

Based on the existing DSR literature introduced above, we first derive an initial set of design requirements (DR) for the class of design knowledge extraction and search systems. We use DRs in order to transfer and articulate design knowledge derived from the awareness phase [20, 41]. Practitioners, designers, and researchers can reuse the identified DRs in their designs and instantiations. One main objective of DSR projects is to generate design knowledge [19]. The gathered design knowledge is often presented in publications and described using natural language documents. We thus articulate the first design requirement as follows:

DR1: The system should capture design knowledge from natural language documents.

In the field of IS there exists a large number of publications presenting design knowledge. Additionally, this knowledge base is growing rapidly [5]. To manage the amount of data we formulate the second design requirement as follows:

DR2: The system should extract existing design knowledge automatically from natural language documents.

Existing design knowledge presented in publications does not follow a standardized knowledge representations schema and can have a wide range of different forms [9]. Therefore, we formulate the third design requirement as follows:

DR3: The system should encounter for different design knowledge representations.

In order to provide access to the collected design knowledge the system needs to provide a user interface. Thus, we formulate the fourth design requirement:

DR4: The system should provide access to the extracted design knowledge in an easy-to-use interface.

In addition to the extracted design knowledge, the system should provide a link to the original source for further details. This leads to the fifths design requirement:

DR5: The system should provide the original source of the extracted design knowledge.

4.2 Initial Design Principles

Based on the identified design requirements we derive an initial set of design principles (DP) specifying the design knowledge in an accessible form [15]. The first DP derived from the requirements DR1, DR2, and DR3 describes the ability to extract design knowledge from publications automatically. Furthermore, the system should extract design knowledge from unstructured text into a structured representation. This leads to the formulation of the first DP as follows:

DP1: The system should extract design knowledge automatically following a structured way.

The second DP is based on DR4 and DR5 and describes the accessibility of the extracted design knowledge. The system should enable searching for specific design knowledge researchers are interested in. Additionally, to the extracted design knowledge the system should provide a link to the source where the corresponding design knowledge is embedded. Therefore, we formulate the second DP:

DP2: The system should provide an interface to make the extracted as well as the source design knowledge accessible.

4.3 Instantiation

In the next step, we instantiated the two DPs and implemented a prototype called DEKNOWSE. In order to automatically extract design knowledge, we defined a design knowledge extraction template first. The template contains a set of parameters we extracted from each publication. An overview of the extraction template is illustrated in Table 1.

The extraction template is implemented in a rule-based text parser. The parser and all its functionality are implemented in python[1]. In the first step, the parser uses pdf documents as inputs and converts them to text. Next, the parser tries to find design knowledge by searching for design or meta requirements, design principles, or design

---

[1] https://www.python.org.

Table 1. Overview of the parameter descriptions of the extraction template.

Parameter	Description
Title	Title of the publication
Year	Publication year
Source	Journal or conference name of publication (e.g., JAIS, DESRIST)
Reference	Link to original source or DOI [21]
Authors	List of authors and email addresses
Tags	Tags provided in the publication
Design Requirements	Authors presented design requirements (DR) or meta requirements (MR)
Design Principles	Authors presented design principles (DP)
Design Features	Authors presented design features (DF)

feature descriptions in the converted text. Based on regular expressions and rules regarding commonly used expressions of design knowledge, the parser identifies the design knowledge in the given text documents. Design researchers use these types of descriptions to express and share design knowledge in publications [15]. The usage and syntax of DP, DF, and DR descriptions are often very similar. Typically, they start with a specifier like "DP," "DR," "MR," or "DF" followed by an index. Some examples extracted from different publications are illustrated in Table 2.

Table 2. Overview of different examples of existing design knowledge descriptions.

Example	Source
"**DP 2:** Provide features to store and categorize ideas, so that the system affords noticing and bracketing to users in environmental sustainability transformations"	Seidel et al. [35]
"**DF1:** All exercises and This design feature proved effective in implementing DR1 since many students submitted assignments are individual regular preparation and follow-up deliverables and detailed and polished baseline, target, work (DP1)"	Drechsler [13]
"**DR6:** Business model validation should be supported by systems that enable the entrepreneur to obtain rapid feedback"	Dellermann et al. [11]
"**MR3:** Provide feedback on users' attentional resource allocation to enable self-awareness."	Toreini et al. [37]

Following a rule-based approach, the parser looks for keywords, for instance, "DP" and "DP1", in the given manuscripts and extracts the type of design knowledge and the corresponding descriptions. If the text contains design knowledge descriptions, the publication information parameters title, year, source, reference, tags, and authors are extracted as well. The results of the extractions are stored in a central database using MySQL[2].

In order to provide access to the extracted design knowledge, we developed a user interface using the web framework called django[3]. Figure 2 depicts the prototypical implementation of the web application.

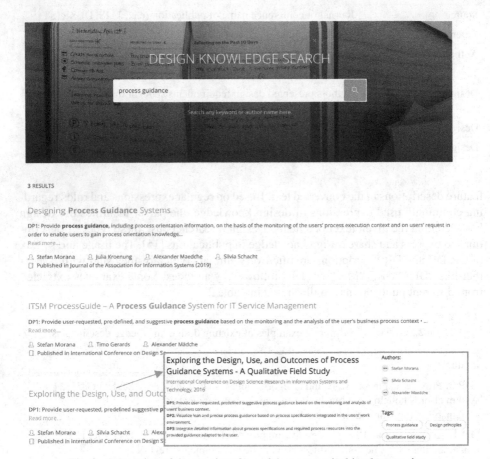

Fig. 2. Screenshot of the user interface of the prototypical implementation.

The web application provides a keyword search field and returns a list of publications containing the search key. Users can search in all the fields of the extraction templates, for example, by providing a name of an author. Each item of the search result contains the title of the manuscript, a short preview of the design knowledge description containing the search key, the authors, the journal or conference name, and the publication year. Clicking on the title or the "Read more" button expands all design knowledge items of the selected publication.

---

[2] https://www.mysql.com.

[3] https://www.djangoproject.com.

5   Evaluation

In order to evaluate the proposed design, we followed a formative evaluation strategy as suggested by Venable et al. [30]. The aim of the evaluation was to demonstrate the prototypical implementation to potential users and understand the utility of the system. We proceeded as follows. First, we collected an initial set of publications and extracted the design knowledge according to the proposed extraction template. Next, we demonstrated the initial dataset and the prototype to a group of DSR researchers in a focus group as suggested by Tremblay et al. to evaluate the design [29]. Finally, we applied a SWOT analysis and present the results in this chapter.

5.1   Design Knowledge Extraction

To create an initial set of publications we collected 462 papers from the past ten years presented at the International Conference on Design Science Research in Information Systems and Technology (DESRIST). Additionally, we collected all papers related to DSR published in the Journal of the Association for Information Systems (JAIS) published in the last ten years. By applying the search string "design science research" OR "DSR" OR "design research" we got 264 results which we added to the initial data set. In the next step, we applied the extraction template to all the collected publications and identified 63 publications containing design knowledge descriptions (DKD) in the form of design requirements, principles, and features. In these 58 papers, we extracted 349 single DKDs. To increase the quality of the design knowledge extraction, we manually compared the extraction results with the corresponding paper. If items were missing, we adapted the rules of the parser and rerun the extraction process. Table 3 provides an overview of the publications and the automatic design knowledge extraction of the last ten years.

Table 3. Overview of the initially parsed publications and the design knowledge extractions of the past ten years starting from 2012 until 2022.

Source	12	13	14	15	16	17	18	19	20	21	22	Sum
DESRIST	1	3	1	4	3	3	3	2	8	9	10	**49**
JAIS	0	0	0	1	0	0	0	3	2	2	4	**14**
DKD	3	19	8	31	10	30	12	25	32	101	71	**349**

In order to evaluate the extraction quality of the parser, we applied a precision and recall analysis [31]. Precision and recall analysis is used to measure the effectiveness of algorithms and to determine the practical usefulness [22]. We randomly selected a test sample containing 10 of the 462 collected papers and compared the extraction results with the presented design knowledge in the papers. In order to measure the performance of the extraction we created a confusion matrix for the selected papers [14]. Based on the derived confusion matrix, we calculated a precision of 0.95, a recall of 0.79, and an accuracy of 0.87.

5.2 Search Engine

In order to evaluate the prototype, we demonstrated the artifact in a focus group to five PhD students applying DSR in their thesis. The objective of the demonstration was to gain evidence of the validity of the proposed design [27]. The focus group exists of two women and three men with an average age of 29 years. We asked the participant regarding their experiences in conducting DSR projects. The average of previously conducted DSR projects of the participants was 2.5 projects. The recorded focus group session lasted 45 min and resulted in 4587 words of transcribed discussion. In the beginning, we presented them the artifact and the underlying concept of the proposed knowledge extraction. After the demonstration, the participants started to discuss the usefulness of the design knowledge extraction and the current design knowledge base. We additionally asked them about the strengths, weaknesses, opportunities, and threats of the system.

All the participants agreed on the usefulness of the system. One participant stated, *"the system enables searching for existing design knowledge which is helpful to get an overview what design knowledge already exist in the field of DSR."* Asking about the strengths of the demonstrated artifact the participants stated that the system facilitates researchers' access to existing design knowledge. One participant mentioned that *"it is a useful tool to get an overview of the current literature very efficient without studying the single studies in detail."* Furthermore, they all agreed on the ease of use of the system. However, the participants also reported some weaknesses of the demonstrated artifact and provided feedback for future features they perceived as useful. One participant stated that *"it would be helpful if the search function provides an advanced search mode, for example, a wildcard search or searching for concepts instead of keywords."* Another researcher reported that *"extracting the used kernel theory would be interesting in future developments."* Furthermore, all the participants agreed that a visual representation of the dependencies between DRs, DPs, and DFs would be helpful. Asking for opportunities the participants agreed that existing design knowledge can be accessed easily and serves as a good starting point for design researchers and for practitioners. One participant mentioned that *"the system is a rich source of examples on how to formulate DP which is helpful for less experienced design science researchers to get an impression on how others formulate design principles."* As a threat, the participants mentioned the risk of incompleteness of the underlying design knowledge database and researchers using the search engine might assume that certain knowledge does not exist in the literature if it is not included in the search results.

6 Discussion

The relevance of knowledge accumulation has increased in the past years in the field of DSR [6, 30]. In this research, we present a first step towards tool support for design knowledge accumulation and design knowledge reuse. In order to advance prior design knowledge as proposed by [6] we argue that access to design knowledge needs to be facilitated in order to foster design knowledge accumulation. In our approach, we propose collecting publications in the field of DSR and automatically extracting design knowledge from single publications. A rule-based parser identifies the design knowledge, extracts the design knowledge description, and stores the result in a central database.

This approach allows extracting and searching for existing design knowledge on a large scale.

In the demonstration and evaluation phase design science researchers stated that they perceived the proposed design knowledge database and search as useful. The implemented prototype DEKNOWSE facilitates access to existing knowledge and supports researchers in using and building on previous knowledge. Moreover, other systems can benefit from the extracted design knowledge by integrating the search API. For instance, MyDesignProcess a tool supporting design science researchers in conducting, structuring, and documenting DSR projects [7] can benefit from the knowledge base by providing access to the design knowledge during conducting DSR projects.

This study comes with several limitations. Regarding the different types of design knowledge presented by [17] the current prototypical implementation only extracts expressed and specified design knowledge such as DRs, DFs, and DPs [8, 15]. Additionally, for this first prototypical implementation, we used only DESRIST and JAIS publications to extract knowledge. Moreover, the extraction quality is limited as the data sources do not contain annotated data and need to be extracted based on parsing rules. However, in the second cycle, we plan to extend the data sources and use more journals and conferences, for instance, ICIS and ECIS, to extract more existing design knowledge. Another limitation of this study is the small number of participants in the first evaluation. Moreover, we have not included senior design science researchers in the evaluation.

Future research could also integrate a manual knowledge aggregation and editing process by inviting the authors of the publications in order to add missing design knowledge, for instance, by providing screenshots of the artifact. This approach would enhance the database and ensure the data quality of the automatically extracted design knowledge.

7 Conclusion

Systematic knowledge accumulation is one of the key concepts of scientific research in the field of IS and beyond. In this paper, we set out to investigate how a design knowledge search engine could foster design knowledge accumulation and reuse. Following the DSR process described by Kuechler and Vaishnavi [23] we reported on the first design cycle. First, we identified design requirements for a design knowledge search engine. Next, we proposed a set of design principles that we instantiated in a prototypical implementation called DEKNOWSE publicly available under the following link https://deknowse.myd esignprocess.com. Finally, we evaluated the design by demonstrating the artifact in a focus group with five design science researchers. The evaluation results showed that such a tool facilitates access to existing design knowledge to foster knowledge accumulation and reuse in the field of DSR.

As a next step, we plan to conduct a second design cycle to improve the proposed design further. More specifically, we will revise our design based on the findings of the first cycle. Additionally, we will make the revised system publicly available and evaluate the system and its usage in the field. In the long run, we believe that our approach and the system will support researchers in conducting DSR projects by facilitating access to existing design knowledge and increasing design knowledge accumulation in the field of DSR.

References

1. van Aken, J.E.: Management research based on the paradigm of the design sciences: the quest for field-tested and grounded technological rules. J. Manage. Stud. **41**(2), 219–246 (2004). https://doi.org/10.1111/j.1467-6486.2004.00430.x
2. Barquet, A.P., Wessel, L., Rothe, H.: Knowledge accumulation in design-oriented research. In: Maedche, A., vom Brocke, J., Hevner, A. (eds.) DESRIST 2017. LNCS, vol. 10243, pp. 398–413. Springer, Cham (2017). https://doi.org/10.1007/978-3-319-59144-5_24
3. Berglund, H., et al.: Opportunities as artifacts and entrepreneurship as design. AMR **45**(4), 825–846 (2020). https://doi.org/10.5465/amr.2018.0285
4. Borchers, J.O.: A pattern approach to interaction design. AI Soc. **15**(4), 359–376 (2001). https://doi.org/10.1007/BF01206115
5. Bornmann, L., Mutz, R.: Growth rates of modern science: a bibliometric analysis based on the number of publications and cited references. J. Am. Soc. Inf. Sci. **66**(11), 2215–2222 (2015). https://doi.org/10.1002/asi.23329
6. vom Brocke, J., et al.: Accumulation and evolution of design knowledge in design science research - a journey through time and space. J. Assoc. Inform. Syst. **21**, 520–544 (2020). https://doi.org/10.17705/1jais.00611
7. vom Brocke, J., et al.: Tool-Support for Design Science Research: Design Principles and Instantiation. Social Science Research Network, Rochester, NY (2017). https://doi.org/10.2139/ssrn.2972803
8. Chandra Kruse, L., et al.: Prescriptive knowledge in IS research: conceptualizing design principles in terms of materiality, action, and boundary conditions. In: Proceedings of the Annual Hawaii International Conference on System Sciences, pp. 4039–4048 (2015). https://doi.org/10.1109/HICSS.2015.485
9. Chandra Kruse, L., Nickerson, J.V.: Portraying design essence. Presented at the Proceedings of the 51st Hawaii International Conference on System Sciences, Hawaii January 3 (2018). https://doi.org/10.24251/HICSS.2018.560
10. Dann, D., et al.: DISKNET - A Platform for the Systematic Accumulation of Knowledge in IS Research. https://publikationen.bibliothek.kit.edu/1000100337. Accessed 05 March 2020
11. Dellermann, D., Lipusch, N., Ebel, P.: Developing design principles for a crowd-based business model validation system. In: Maedche, A., vom Brocke, J., Hevner, A. (eds.) DESRIST 2017. LNCS, vol. 10243, pp. 163–178. Springer, Cham (2017). https://doi.org/10.1007/978-3-319-59144-5_10
12. Denning, P., Dargan, P.: Action-centered design. In: Bringing Design to Software, pp. 105–127. Association for Computing Machinery, New York, NY, USA (1996)
13. Drechsler, A.: From synchronous face-to-face group work to asynchronous individual work: pivoting an enterprise modeling course for teaching during a COVID-19 lockdown. Commun. Assoc. Inform. Syst. **48**(1), (2021). https://doi.org/10.17705/1CAIS.04822
14. Fawcett, T.: An introduction to ROC analysis. Pattern Recogn. Lett. **27**(8), 861–874 (2006). https://doi.org/10.1016/j.patrec.2005.10.010
15. Gregor, S. et al.: Research perspectives: the anatomy of a design principle. J. Assoc. Inform. Syst. **21**, 6 (2020). https://doi.org/10.17705/1jais.00649
16. Gregor, S.: The nature of theory in information systems. MIS Q. **30**(3), 611–642 (2006). https://doi.org/10.2307/25148742
17. Gregor, S., Hevner, A.: Positioning and presenting design science research for maximum impact. MIS Quar. **37**, 337–356 (2013). https://doi.org/10.25300/MISQ/2013/37.2.01
18. Gregor, S., Jones, D.: The anatomy of a design theory. J. Assoc. Inform. Syst. **8**, 5 (2007). https://doi.org/10.17705/1jais.00129

19. Hevner, A., et al.: Design science in information systems research. MIS Q. **28**(1), 75–105 (2004). https://doi.org/10.2307/25148625
20. Holmström, J., et al.: Logic for accumulation of design science research theory. In: 2014 47th Hawaii International Conference on System Sciences, pp. 3697–3706 (2014). https://doi.org/10.1109/HICSS.2014.460
21. International Organization for Standardization: Information and documentation—Digital object identifier system (ISO Standard No 26324:2012) (2012). https://www.iso.org/standard/43506.html
22. Junker, M., et al.: On the evaluation of document analysis components by recall, precision, and accuracy. In: Proceedings of the Fifth International Conference on Document Analysis and Recognition. ICDAR '99 (Cat. No.PR00318), pp. 713–716 (1999). https://doi.org/10.1109/ICDAR.1999.791887
23. Kuechler, B., Vaishnavi, V.: On theory development in design science research: anatomy of a research project. Eur. J. Inf. Syst. **17**(5), 489–504 (2008). https://doi.org/10.1057/ejis.2008.40
24. Li, J., et al.: TheoryOn: A Design Framework and System for Unlocking Behavioral Knowledge Through Ontology Learning. MIS Quarterly (2020). https://doi.org/10.25300/MISQ/2020/15323
25. Nguyen, A., et al.: Towards ontology-based design science research for knowledge accumulation and evolution. Presented at the Hawaii International Conference on System Sciences (2019). https://doi.org/10.24251/HICSS.2019.694
26. Niederman, F., March, S.T.: Broadening the conceptualization of theory in the information systems discipline: a meta-theory approach. SIGMIS Database **50**(2), 18–44 (2019). https://doi.org/10.1145/3330472.3330476
27. Nunamaker, J.F., et al.: Systems development in information systems research. J. Manage. Inform. Syst. (1990). https://doi.org/10.1080/07421222.1990.11517898
28. Peffers, K., et al.: A design science research methodology for information systems research. J. Manag. Inf. Syst. **24**(3), 45–77 (2007). https://doi.org/10.2753/MIS0742-1222240302
29. Rai, A.: Editor's comments: diversity of design science research. Manage. Inform. Syst. Quart. **41**(1), iii–xviii (2017)
30. Reining, S., et al.: Knowledge accumulation in design science research: ways to foster scientific progress. SIGMIS Database **53**(1), 10–24 (2022). https://doi.org/10.1145/3514097.3514100
31. Roelleke, T.: Information Retrieval Models: Foundations and Relationships. Springer International Publishing, Cham (2013). https://doi.org/10.1007/978-3-031-02328-6
32. Rothe, H., et al.: Accumulating design knowledge: a mechanisms-based approach. J. Assoc. Inform. Syst. **21**, 3 (2020). https://doi.org/10.17705/1jais.00619
33. Schoormann, T., Möller, F., Hansen, M.R.P.: How do researchers (re-)use design principles: an inductive analysis of cumulative research. In: Chandra Kruse, L., Seidel, S., Hausvik, G.I. (eds.) DESRIST 2021. LNCS, vol. 12807, pp. 188–194. Springer, Cham (2021). https://doi.org/10.1007/978-3-030-82405-1_20
34. Seckler, C., et al.: Design science in entrepreneurship: conceptual foundations and guiding principles. J. Bus. Ventur. Des. **1**, 1, 100004 (2021). https://doi.org/10.1016/j.jbvd.2022.100004
35. Seidel, S., et al.: Design principles for sensemaking support systems in environmental sustainability transformations. Eur. J. Inf. Syst. **27**(2), 221–247 (2018). https://doi.org/10.1057/s41303-017-0039-0
36. Sein, M.K., et al.: Action design research. MIS Q. **35**(1), 37–56 (2011). https://doi.org/10.2307/23043488
37. Toreini, P., et al.: Designing attentive information dashboards. J. Assoc. Inform. Syst. **23**(2), 521–552 (2022). https://doi.org/10.17705/1jais.00732

38. Tremblay, M.C., et al.: The use of focus groups in design science research. In: Hevner, A. and Chatterjee, S. (eds.) Design Research in Information Systems: Theory and Practice, ISIS, vol. 22, pp. 121–143. Springer US, Boston, MA (2010). https://doi.org/10.1007/978-1-4419-5653-8_10

39. Venable, J.: The role of theory and theorising in design science research. In: First International Conference on Design Science Research in Information Systems and Technology (2006)

40. Wagner, G., et al.: Artificial intelligence and the conduct of literature reviews. J. Inf. Technol. **37**(2), 209–226 (2022). https://doi.org/10.1177/02683962211048201

41. Walls, J.G., et al.: Building an information system design theory for vigilant EIS. Inf. Syst. Res. **3**, 36 (1992). https://doi.org/10.1287/isre.3.1.36

Empowering Recommender Systems in ITSM: A Pipeline Reference Model for AI-Based Textual Data Quality Enrichment

Philipp Reinhard[1]([✉]) [iD], Mahei Manhai Li[1] [iD], Ernestine Dickhaut[1] [iD], Christoph Peters[1,2] [iD], and Jan Marco Leimeister[1,2] [iD]

[1] University of Kassel, Kassel, Germany
{philipp.reinhard,mahei.li,ernestine.dickhaut,christoph.peters,
leimeister}@uni-kassel.de
[2] University of St.Gallen, St.Gallen, Switzerland
{christoph.peters,janmarco.leimeister}@unisg.ch

Abstract. AI-based recommendation systems to augment working conditions in the field of IT service management (ITSM) have attracted new attention. However, many IT support organizations possess high volumes of tickets but are confronted with low quality, to which they train the underlying models of their AI systems. In particular, support tickets are documented insufficiently due to time pressure and lack of motivation. Following design science research, we design and evaluate an analytics pipeline to address the data quality issue. The pipeline can be applied to assess and extract high-quality support tickets for subsequent model training and operation. Based on a data set of 60.000 real-life support tickets from a manufacturing company, we develop the artifact, instantiate a recommender system and achieve a higher prediction performance in comparison to naïve enrichment methods. In terms of data management literature, we contribute to the understanding of assessing textual ticket data quality. By deriving a pipeline reference model, we move towards a general approach to designing machine learning-driven data quality analytics pipelines for attached recommender systems.

Keywords: Data Quality · Artificial Intelligence · ITSM · Recommender Systems

1 Introduction

More and more enterprises are overloaded by the vast number of technical issues regarding their infrastructure and applications [1]. They rely on IT Service Management (ITSM) to deal with downtimes and system inefficiencies by performing problem-solving tasks to keep operations going [1]. IT service desk agents are responsible for solving the tickets, which are codified user issues as support requests. They are thus faced with a constantly growing number of heterogeneous support requests and at the same time have to work more efficiently, while ensuring a high level of customer satisfaction [2, 3]. Thus, research and practice turn to AI-driven ITSM (AI-ITSM), which applies machine

© The Author(s), under exclusive license to Springer Nature Switzerland AG 2023
A. Gerber and R. Baskerville (Eds.): DESRIST 2023, LNCS 13873, pp. 279–293, 2023.
https://doi.org/10.1007/978-3-031-32808-4_18

learning and deep learning to augment the overloaded and often overworked agents [4–6]. Recently, recommendation systems based on solved IT tickets referred to as ticket recommendation systems (TRS), have gained increasing interest in research [7–9]. However, due to various reasons (e.g., time pressure or convenience) and the complexity of support services [10], support agents tend to insufficiently describe issues and summarize resolutions, which in consequence limits the capabilities of the AI-driven systems [11]. Inadvertently, data quality remains a major challenge for AI-driven cognitive IT Service Management [6] and recommendation systems in general [12, 13].

Only a few researchers have aimed at considering data quality as a key determinator of recommendation performance in the context of AI-ITSM [2, 11, 14], even though the importance of data quality for recommendation outcomes, in general, has been well-known [12, 15–17]. Currently, the literature focuses on clustering and classifying tickets (e.g., 18–22), while the role of ticket quality is largely neglected. Our work applies an approach to specify ticket documentation quality by holistically incorporating sophisticated preprocessing, clustering steps, a comprehensive set of linguistic features, as well as machine learning models. In contrast to the existing literature on data quality in recommender systems [12, 13], our research seeks to leverage existing knowledge within an organization [23] in form of solved tickets by extracting and maintaining high-quality text data to enrich TRS. Given the research motivation, we aim at answering two research questions: [RQ1]: *How can we design an analytics pipeline for considering textual ticket data quality?* [RQ2]: *How can the pipeline improve ticket recommendation systems?* We follow a design science research (DSR) approach to instantiate an analytics pipeline [24] and finally develop a pipeline reference model for data quality enrichment in AI-ITSM. Thus, we codify our design knowledge in a generally applicable reference model to make our developed knowledge accessible in new contexts.

2   Related Work

2.1   Data Quality in Recommender Systems

It is generally known that assessing data quality is important for information systems research as low data quality results in expensive data quality costs [25]. The implications for TRS are indirect quality costs such as incorrect or insufficient decision augmentation. This leads to low user satisfaction. Previous literature on recommender systems in general confirms that the quality of the underlying data has a major impact on the performance of traditional recommender systems [12, 24, 25]. The research on data management examines concepts and manifestations of data quality, although most of them do not consider unstructured text data specifically. In general, data quality is defined as a multidimensional concept [26–28]. In most methods and approaches to assess data, an individual determination of dimensions and metrics is crucial. Yet, a standardized set of data quality dimensions is not accessible due to context-specific requirements. Especially in the domain of textual data, data quality dimensions have not been widely examined. The most commonly used dimensions have been summarized by Batini et al. [29], on whose foundation Cai and Zhu [30] consolidated a concept of data quality dimensions for big data including availability, usability, reliability, relevance, and presentation quality.

The literature on recommender systems acknowledges the relevance of data quality [12, 26–28]. Researchers in that realm mainly focus on examining individual data quality dimensions. For example, Bharati and Chaudhury [26] considered data accuracy and completeness to enhance decision-making. However, most research on data quality in recommender systems focuses on analyzing the completeness dimension. Feldman et al. [25] discovered the role of incomplete data sets on a classifier and Woodall et al. [32] examined the influence of completeness on decision-support processes. Other attempts have been directed at investigating the role of completeness in terms of the number of features as well as the extent of feature values [11, 12]. By considering a multi-dimensional view of text data quality [30] and adapting the framework proposed by Heinrich et al. [11], we explore the impact of ticket data quality on TRS performance in our study.

2.2 Ticket Classification and Ticket Quality Assessment

Ticket classification is a subset of text classification, as tickets are textual data in an unstructured format. Prior research on AI-ITSM has emphasized classifying tickets according to prioritization, complexity, content, or other characteristics (e.g., [3, 29, 30]). For instance, Marcuzzo et al. [20] developed a multi-level approach for hierarchical ticket classification using BERT [31]. Revina et al. [18] classified tickets by complexity and associated effort using a set of linguistic features. Predominantly, prior research on ticket classification has shown that incorporating more complex sets of linguistic and non-linguistic features instead of naïve text classification is auspicious [10, 17]. Naïve text classification typically relics on vector representations of text such as TF-IDF, word2vec, or doc2vec. Selecting and calculating linguistic features comes with higher effort and can be more time-consuming since expert knowledge is required to determine a sufficiently sophisticated set of domain-specific features [17, 36]. In general, the use of machine learning and deep learning algorithms is being a promising tool for classifying tickets.

Assessing ticket quality is one of the subfields of ticket classification [8, 11, 32]. While there have been efforts to provide quality assessment for change request data [33], the literature on ticket quality remains limited. Baresi et al. [32] developed ACQUA, an approach for assessing the quality of issue descriptions. Thereby they removed the need for additional communications and guided users to properly describe the incident. On the other end of the agent-customer communication, Agarwal et al. [11] introduced an automated quality assessment of unstructured resolution text in IT service systems but only considers a regression model. According to their findings, high-quality resolution text involves aspects of text layout, discourse relations (contingency and expansion), and domain vocabulary. Both approaches [11, 32] try to recommend measures for improving ticket data in real time. Analogously, Zhou et al. [8] applied character-level, entity-level, semantic-level, and attribute-level features for calculating ticket resolution quality and integrating it into a resolution recommendation system. Unlike other approaches, our study considers both issue and resolution descriptions and aims at predicting ticket quality with help of machine learning models to enrich data for TRS. Additionally, we include ticket clustering approaches such as topic modeling for identifying the helpfulness of tickets. Our proposed pipeline reference model aggregates the knowledge on how to design analytics pipelines to enrich textual data quality.

3 Research Approach

This study aims to generate prescriptive knowledge types in the form of a ticket analytics pipeline [34]. Following the DSR process of Peffers et al. [35] we aim to develop domain-specific knowledge and artifacts, which includes the steps depicted in Fig. 1. We draw on existing literature and fundamentals of text analysis and data quality and include domain experts in the conceptualization of features and the labeling of domain-specific knowledge. Our design requirements are predominantly derived from literature and interviews with 17 support agents and managers who confirm the problem space. After developing an initial instantiation of the machine learning-based scoring model with a tentative set of features and conducting a first performance evaluation, we added a second iteration to improve the data labeling quality and revise our features to develop a final analytics pipeline. By extensively evaluating the pipeline and comparing it with a naïve classification pipeline, we aim to show how ticket data quality is influencing the attached recommender system performance.

In addition to the development and evaluation of our artifact, we develop a pipeline reference model, by abstracting our knowledge, making it transferable and applicable to other contexts. Thus, we address the ongoing discussion in DSR on the lack of design knowledge reusability since design knowledge is often lost after a project ends [36]. We further address the issue of DSR contributions tending to remain isolated with little to no relation to other solutions because of little abstraction of the findings [37]. Reference models offer the possibility to store knowledge in an abstract form for further use cases and to make it accessible to other projects [38].

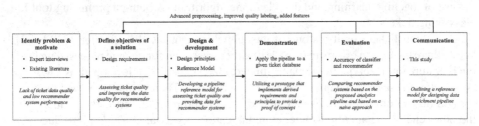

Fig. 1. Design science procedure according to Peffers et al. [35]

4 Designing a Ticket Analytics Pipeline

4.1 Problem Formulation and Objectives

Due to time constraints and a lack of motivation to create high-quality summarizations, the quality of ticket data remains a key challenge for IT support organizations [6]. Interviews with IT support agents and managers show a key goal of AI-ITSM should be to overcome inconsistent documentation, time-consuming quality assessment, inadequate quality, and inadequate knowledge base articles [2]. Intelligent quality assessment, therefore, forms the basis for improving IT support processes and augmenting the service workforce [6]. In summary, the goal of creating a knowledge repository and ensuring data quality is to improve the performance of recommender systems [12] and provide a sophisticated user experience with such TRSs. We derived the following design requirements from literature and practice (DR):

DR1: Ensure Domain-Specific Helpfulness. The included tickets in TRS should be helpful and augment the adaptation process for a new incoming incident [39]. Helpfulness should be assured by certain quality features and meaningful problem-solution pairs. It involves domain experts in conceptualizing and developing such systems [40].

DR2: Provide Transparency on Feature Importance. The pipeline should provide final sets of features, that significantly determine ticket quality. Information on the impact of certain features is of special interest. By doing so, the features and the corresponding feature values can be used to support agents to produce high-quality tickets and in general offer transparency [41, 42].

DR3: Differentiate Between Issue and Resolution Description Quality. The scoring model should be able to differentiate between issue and resolution to account for different quality characteristics [11, 32]. This requires thorough pre-processing and a dual labeling, feature engineering, and classification procedure.

DR4: Consider a Multi-Dimensional Concept of Data Quality. Features should be a set of diverse types of criteria such as linguistic and non-linguistic features to counteract the unstructured character of ticket data [43, 44]. The set of features should be able to determine the data quality of complete ticket descriptions in terms of established data quality dimensions such as reliability, relevance, and presentation quality [45–47].

DR5: Provide an Interpretable Quality Score. A readable, normalized quality score should indicate the usefulness of a ticket in terms of quality [11]. The quality score can be integrated into the TRS as complementary information for recommendation ranking and selection. However, primarily the score is utilized to filter a given data set.

4.2 Development and Demonstration

We combine machine learning models and feature engineering to predict ticket quality and gain transparency [42]. Analogous approaches have been performed on various text classification cases in the context of AI-ITSM [18, 20, 21]. Using the derived requirements from literature and practice, we describe our development and demonstration phase by elaborating on design principles in the following.

DP1 – Data Quality Conceptualization. The underlying optimization goal is to improve recommendation system performance while at the same time ensuring readability and usefulness. With reflections from the first iteration, we observed that issue and resolution descriptions possess different quality characteristics and hence as per design requirements (DR3), we differentiate between issue and resolution descriptions. Based on a workshop on ticket quality with IT support agents and quality managers, an analysis of the ticket data set, and a literature review on ticket and text analytics, we hand-selected a set of more than 30 features depending on the description type (DR4). We rely on linguistic features to address the limitation of other text representation techniques, primarily weighted words (Bag of word, TF-IDF) and word embeddings (Word2Vec, Doc2Vec) such as effortful training, incapacity of capturing word semantic similarity and limited corpus of words [18]. Additionally, linguistic features provide transparency of the characteristics of data quality (DR2).

DP2 – Data Retrieval and Preprocessing. The upstream steps of the pipeline comprise the retrieval and pre-processing of data [20, 30]. The pipeline first loads tickets from an ITSM platform, which are further filtered by default categories such as status and channel type. We rely on a set of 60,000 support tickets from 2021, which were provided by an international manufacturing company. The dataset was extracted from a ServiceNow environment and contains standard data fields for support tickets. We further anonymized sensitive information such as name, location, and mail [1]. Furthermore, pre-processing includes analyzing multiple ticket-related text fields including a short description, working notes, comments, and closing notes, and merging them into two fields: issue and resolution. For several linguistic features, our pipeline applies additional pre-processing steps such as the removal of links, attachments, and mail signatures, tokenization, lemmatization, and removal of special characters [48].

DP3 - Domain Knowledge Integration. To extract as many highly relevant tickets, and identify useful problem-solution matches (DR1), we apply a BERT-based topic modeling approach [31, 49]. Because topics could be redundant, we add an agglomerative hierarchical clustering approach [50] to aggregate topic clusters [51] and to automatically derive resolution clusters for later TRS training and testing (Table 1). The topic clusters, their keywords, and exemplary tickets indicate the quality and usefulness of the inherent set of similar tickets (DR1). The labeling process starts with labeling the topic clusters on a simple binary scale by two annotators. After annotating ten topics both annotators and the researchers discussed the results and aligned their approaches. We tested the inter-rater reliability and archived a substantial agreement (cohen's kappa = 0.682). In sum, we derived 863 topics and 215 resolution clusters for the given data set. Then, the annotators were instructed by the set of features and examples for ticket quality and were provided with a different set of labeling instructions for issue and resolution descriptions (DR3). For issue description quality we archived an agreement of 0.546 and for resolution description a cohen's kappa of 0.439. Participants of the labeling process were two researchers of TRS with expertise in the field of ITSM.

Table 1. Example of useful topics and a derived topic cluster

Cluster	Label	Topics
120	Power Bi license	**Topic 36:** pro, bi, power, fulfillment, licence, added, license
		Topic 389: pro, license, bi, fulfilment, power, pbi, premium

DP4 - Extensive Feature Engineering. Above mere feature calculation, additional goals of this stage are to eliminate constant attributes, eliminate redundant features and analyze features' influence on ticket data quality [42]. Part of feature selection spans the reduction of features, which is a common challenge in statistics [52]. First, we remove all constant or quasi-constant features (e.g., sentiment score, language confidence, and spelling mistakes) by utilizing a threshold of 0.05 for variance, which we derived by experimentally applying different thresholds and evaluating the attached model performance. Next, a correlation analysis was conducted, and we removed features that correlate strongly (> 0.95) and possess less importance (e.g., stop words count, words count). Our analysis revealed that the resolution description results in more correlating features. Random Forest Classifier revealed to possess a comparatively high performance and enables analyzing the embedded feature importance (DR2). The top features according to importance calculated with help of the SHAP framework are ranked within the following Fig. 2.

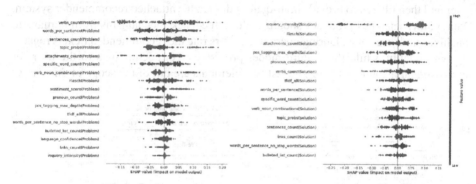

Fig. 2. Most influencing features on issue (left) and resolution (right) quality.

DP5 - Quality Scoring Model. Because deep learning-based models lack explainability and interpretability [41], we rely on certain machine learning-based models for further insights into feature importance (DR2). The analytics pipeline makes use of prior work and experiences with different ML-based classifiers in the AI-ITSM domain [18, 21]. Accordingly, common classifiers are Support Vector Machine (SVM), Random Forest Classifier (RF), Stochastic Gradient Descent Classifier (SGD), Logistic Regression (LR), and K-Nearest Neighbors (KNN) [29, 53]. Table 2 provides an overview of the applied ML-based classifiers trained on a preliminary balanced set of 160 labeled tickets differentiating between classifiers for the issue and resolution description quality (DR3). Based on the prediction we can filter the large ticket database on the highest level of quality (DR5), as shown in the evaluation part. In addition, the score can be used to influence recommendation ranking and help agents record tickets of high quality.

4.3 Pipeline Reference Model for Textual Data Quality Enrichment

Given the developed pipeline, we aggregated and abstracted our findings into a reference model for designing pipelines for data enrichment in the realm of textual data.

The pipeline reference model in Fig. 3 demonstrates a generalized view of modern machine learning-based data quality assessment for AI-enabled systems. We differentiate between four key components: the data quality model, knowledge model, feature model, and scoring and operations model following Frank [54]. The data model requires the incorporation of domain-specific knowledge regarding the context-specific quality of a text. According to the literature on data quality assessment [45], developers have to define objectives, quality dimensions, and measures in a top-down manner. The resulting data quality model informs the calculation and analysis of the measures – referred to as the feature model. Domain-specific knowledge is integrated through clustering and labeling the data. By applying methods for explainability and transparency [42], organizations can get a better understanding of the underlying data quality and can optimize their prediction models accordingly. Finally, features are transferred to the scoring and operations model, where the data set is scored based on a machine learning-based classifier and then filtered to provide high-quality data to the attached recommender system. Data quality analytics pipelines should include feedback mechanisms from humans to machines and vice versa. During operations, users rate the recommended tickets regarding data quality, while the feature model provides recommendations to the user for improving an incoming ticket. The last two elements are out of the scope of this study.

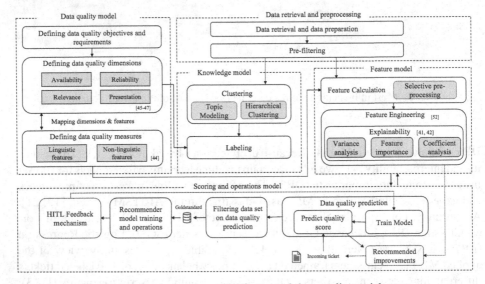

Fig. 3. Pipeline reference model for textual data quality enrichment.

4.4 Evaluation

We tested the pipeline on a dataset mentioned in Sect. 4.2. To confirm that the designed artifact, the pipeline reference model, generates a better assessment of data quality and subsequently improves the performance of the attached TRS, this study relies on a two-leveled technical evaluation (Fig. 4) [55].

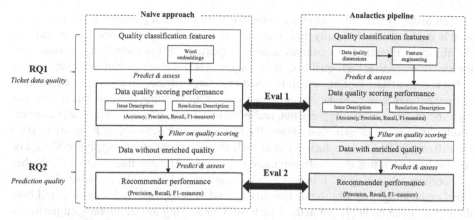

Fig. 4. Evaluation framework for the designed analytics pipeline

First evaluation (Eval 1)– Comparing Data Quality Scoring Performance

Within our first evaluation phase, we compare the performance of the scoring model of the ticket analytics pipeline with a naïve text classifier and thereby answer our first research question. The simple classifier applies a TF-IDF-based text classifier [44]. Table 2 indicates that the developed pipeline can improve the performance of text quality assessment for both issue and resolution. However, the impact is more prevalent in the case of resolution descriptions.

Table 2. Eval 1- Overall results of the first evaluation of the data quality scoring model[1].

Type	Cl.[2]	Naïve approach				Ticket analytics pipeline			
		A	R	P	F1	A	R	P	F1
Issue Description	SVM	0.794	0.481	0.410	0.442	0.762	0.637	0.662	0.646
	RF	0.810	0.490	0.411	0.447	0.786	0.688	0.702	*0.694*
	SDG	0.825	0.608	0.680	*0.626*	0.357	0.544	0.557	0.354
	LR	0.825	0.500	0.413	0.452	0.524	0.584	0.562	0.506
	KNN	0.746	0.524	0.528	0.525	0.690	0.591	0.585	0.587
Resolution Description	SVM	0.825	0.500	0.412	0.452	0.537	0.536	0.535	0.532
	RF	0.825	0.535	0.668	*0.528*	0.732	0.728	0.725	*0.726*
	SDG	0.777	0.506	0.513	0.498	0.390	0.471	0.200	0.281
	LR	0.825	0.500	0.412	0.452	0.610	0.529	0.800	0.431
	KNN	0.746	0.523	0.527	0.524	0.732	0.719	0.724	0.721

---

[1] A = Accuracy; R = Recall; P = Precision; F1 = F1-Score.
[2] Cl. = Classifier for predicting a quality score for a given support ticket.

Interestingly, the naïve approach achieves higher accuracy results. However, as the goal is to identify high-quality data, precision, and recall are more important criteria, as the ability to identify true positives is more important for the underlying problem and the aim of extracting high-quality data. We argue that it is more crucial for an automated ticket recommender system, which is based on a large dataset, to miss appropriate recommendations than to make inappropriate ones. Our pipeline outperforms the simple pipeline in terms of recall, precision, and F1 score, leading to more reliable prediction results. In the case of issue description, the ticket pipeline achieves an F1-score of 0.69 by utilizing an RFC while the naïve approach shows a score of 0.63 applying SDG. For resolution description the results are more impressive: The pipeline shows a 0.2 higher F1-score by comparing the Random Forest Classifier. Additionally, classifiers based on word embeddings cannot provide insights into what determines ticket quality and how data quality can be improved in the long term. Our scoring model not only outperforms these approaches but ensures transparency and interpretability [41, 42].

Second Evaluation (Eval 2) – Comparing Recommender System Performance
Eval 2 includes comparing recommendation systems using the prior described simple word embedding-based classifier and the here-designed enhanced analytics pipeline. In contrast to Eval 1, we do test how better data quality through filtering enables providing better recommendations. We utilize prediction performance (mean average precision, mean average recall, f-score) as the by far most established quality metric in the recommendation systems literature [56]. Accuracy, as used in Eval 1, can not be utilized for evaluating recommender systems because they output multiple options and thus are different from classification problems. From clustering topics of tickets, we derived problem-solution-pairs to evaluate the TRS. We evaluate a TF-IDF- and cosine similarity-based recommender system, that compares a given query with the set of solved tickets and proposes three tickets as possible resolutions. Given the best classifier of analytics pipeline and naïve classification (Eval 1), we filtered the data set on issue and solution description quality. Then we initiated the recommender systems on 205 problem-solution pairs. The results (Table 3) demonstrate that a prior data enrichment can slightly improve TRS performance by 0.5 points in terms of mean average precision (MAP) and can reach a total mean average recall of 0.75 and a total F-Score of 0.73. Despite showing lower accuracy values for quality scoring, the analytics pipeline outperforms a naïve method, which confirms the relevance of precision and recall.

Table 3. Eval 2 – Ticket recommender system performance evaluation

Type	Precision	Recall	F-Score
Naïve pipeline	0.667	0.713	0.689
Analytics pipeline	0.717	0.747	0.732

5 Discussion, Limitations, and Implications

Our artifact provides innovative insights into how to address the challenge of data quality and TRS performance [2, 6]. The analytics pipeline presented as a novel solution for AI-ITSM [57] in this paper is contributing to the emerging stream in data management literature to investigate machine learning techniques for auditing and curating data quality. [58]. Furthermore, we add to the research on data quality in recommendation systems [12], by revealing how the quality of ticket data affects the overall performance of recommendations. With our pipeline principles and reference model, we provide a general method and instantiation guidelines for future ticket recommender systems and answer the first research question. As a result, a comprehensive set of linguistic features and a scoring model for the ticket documentation was derived and domain-specific knowledge was incorporated through topic modeling, clustering, and labeling. The second research question was answered by evaluating an attached recommender system. Since our artifact is not based on predefined rules, it enables customizability, scalability, and effortless maintenance of data enrichment in practice. Contrary to non-transparent word embedding methods or deep learning models, the extensive feature engineering approach guarantees transparency and explainability of the ticket quality. With our paper, we show how DSR can be successfully applied to machine learning projects. Machine learning artifacts are rarely developed using DSR. However, combining a technical and a design perspective is useful to structure and guide the design project.

In addition to our designed DSR artifact and the application of DSR according to Peffers et al. [35], we codify our knowledge in a conceptual model. Reference models enable domain knowledge to be generalized and thus made transferable. Due to the generalizability, the findings are made usable for several use cases. Therefore, reference models enable what is an important criterion in the codification of design knowledge, namely the generalizability of the knowledge to be able to apply and reuse it in new situations. Being an abstract representation of domain knowledge, reference models codify prescriptive and descriptive design knowledge and facilitate the reusability of design knowledge [59].

Despite the previously mentioned contributions and implications, our research comes with certain limitations. First of all, the performance results do not improve significantly and should be improved. Further research could extend the feature selection process by more advanced feature selection techniques and consult even more relevance-related features (e.g., likes, star ratings, comments, click-rate, etc.) as well as domain knowledge after introducing an improved recommender system in IT service organizations. New approaches of ensemble methods and hybrid models of word embeddings, linguistic features, and especially large language models remain unconsidered. In addition, an evaluation with users should be conducted to validate the TRS performance in terms of usefulness. Additionally, within further research individual analysis of features and their impact on recommender performance could be conducted to improve data quality sustainability within IT support organizations and pave the way for highly performant AI-ITSM systems. Another limitation comes with the restriction to one case company. Testing the pipeline and applying the pipeline reference model to another set of IT support tickets could strengthen the here-stated results and implications. Simultaneously, further research could examine different types of machine learning mechanisms and reveal how the pipeline impacts the performance of other recommendation models above a basic TF-IDF-based similarity model.

References

1. Swain, A.K., Garza, V.R.: Key factors in achieving Service Level Agreements (SLA) for Information Technology (IT) incident resolution. Inf. Syst. Front. 1–16 (2022). https://doi.org/10.1007/s10796-022-10266-5
2. Schmidt, S., Li, M., Peters, C.: Requirements for an IT support system based on hybrid intelligence. In: Proceedings of the Annual Hawaii International Conference on System Sciences. Hawaii International Conference on System Sciences (2022)
3. Paramesh, S.P., Ramya, C., Shreedhara, K.S.: Classifying the unstructured it service desk tickets using ensemble of classifiers. In: 3rd International Conference on Computational Systems and Information Technology for Sustainable Solutions (CSITSS). IEEE (2018)
4. Al-Hawari, F., Barham, H.: A machine learning based help desk system for IT service management. J. King Saud Univ. Comput. Inform. Sci. 33(6), 702–718 (2021). https://doi.org/10.1016/j.jksuci.2019.04.001
5. Fuchs, S., Drieschner, C., Wittges, H.: Proceedings of the 55th Hawaii International Conference on System Sciences (HICSS). University of Hawai'i at Manoa Hamilton Library, Honolulu, Hawai (2022)
6. Meng, F.J., et al.: Opportunities and Challenges Towards Cognitive IT Service Management in Real World IEEE Symposium on Service-Oriented System Engineering (SOSE). IEEE (2018)
7. Ali Zaidi, S.S., Fraz, M.M., Shahzad, M., Khan, S.: A multiapproach generalized framework for automated solution suggestion of support tickets. Int. J. Intell. Syst. 37(6), 3654–3681 (2022). https://doi.org/10.1002/int.22701
8. Zhou, W., et al.: Star: A system for ticket analysis and resolution. In: Proceedings of the 23rd ACM SIGKDD International Conference on Knowledge Discovery and Data Mining, pp. 2181–2190 (2017)
9. Schmidt, S.L., Li, M.M., Weigel, S., Peters, C.: Knowledge is power: provide your it-support with domain-specific high-quality solution material. In: Chandra Kruse, L., Seidel, S., Hausvik, G.I. (eds.) The Next Wave of Sociotechnical Design. DESRIST 2021. LNCS, vol. 12807. Springer, Cham (2021). https://doi.org/10.1007/978-3-030-82405-1_22
10. Peters, C., Blohm, I., Leimeister, J.M.: Anatomy of successful business models for complex services: insights from the telemedicine field. J. Manag. Inf. Syst. 32(3), 75–104 (2015). https://doi.org/10.1080/07421222.2015.1095034
11. Agarwal, S., Sridhara, G., Dasgupta, G.: Automated quality assessment of unstructured resolution text in IT service systems. In: Sheng, Q., Stroulia, E., Tata, S., Bhiri, S. (eds.) Service-Oriented Computing. ICSOC 2016. LNCS, vol. 9936. Springer, Cham (2016). https://doi.org/10.1007/978-3-319-46295-0_14
12. Heinrich, B., Hopf, M., Lohninger, D., Schiller, A., Szubartowicz, M.: Data quality in recommender systems: the impact of completeness of item content data on prediction accuracy of recommender systems. Electron. Mark. 31(2), 389–409 (2019). https://doi.org/10.1007/s12525-019-00366-7
13. Heinrich, B., Hopf, M., Lohninger, D., Schiller, A., Szubartowicz, M.: Something's missing? a procedure for extending item content data sets in the context of recommender systems. Inf. Syst. Front. 24(1), 267–286 (2020). https://doi.org/10.1007/s10796-020-10071-y
14. Wang, Q., Zhou, W., Zeng, C., Li, T., Shwartz, L., Grabarnik, G.Y.: Constructing the knowledge base for cognitive IT service management. In: IEEE International Conference on Services Computing (SCC). IEEE (2017)

15. Konstan, J.A., Riedl, J.: Recommender systems: from algorithms to user experience. User Model User-Adap. Inter. **22**(1–2), 101–123 (2012). https://doi.org/10.1007/s11257-011-9112-x
16. Picault, J., Ribière, M., Bonnefoy, D., Mercer, K.: How to get the recommender out of the lab? In: Ricci, F., Rokach, L., Shapira, B., Kantor, P.B. (eds.) Recommender Systems Handbook, pp. 333–365. Scholars Portal, Boston, MA, (2011)
17. Sar Shalom, O., Berkovsky, S., Ronen, R., Ziklik, E., Amihood, A.: Data quality matters in recommender systems. In: Werthner, H., Zanker, M., Golbeck, J., Semeraro, G. (eds.) Proceedings of the 9th ACM Conference on Recommender Systems, pp. 257–260. ACM, New York, NY (2015)
18. Revina, A., Buza, K., Meister, V.G.: IT ticket classification: the simpler, the better. IEEE Access **8**, 193380–193395 (2020). https://doi.org/10.1109/access.2020.3032840
19. Koehler, J., et al.: Towards Intelligent Process Support for Customer Service Desks: Extracting Problem Descriptions from Noisy and Multi-lingual Texts, S 36–52
20. Marcuzzo, M., Zangari, A., Schiavinato, M., Giudice, L., Gasparetto, A., Albarelli, A.: A multi-level approach for hierarchical Ticket Classification. In: Proceedings of the Eighth Workshop on Noisy User-generated Text (W-NUT 2022), pp. 201–214 (2022)
21. Zicari, P., Folino, G., Guarascio, M., Pontieri, L: Discovering accurate deep learning based predictive models for automatic customer support ticket classification. In: Proceedings of the 36th Annual ACM Symposium on Applied Computing. ACM, New York, NY, USA (2021)
22. Agarwal, S., Aggarwal, V., Akula, A.R., Dasgupta, G.B., Sridhara, G.: Automatic problem extraction and analysis from unstructured text in IT tickets. IBM J. Res. Dev. **61**(1):4:41–4:52 (2017). doi:https://doi.org/10.1147/jrd.2016.2629318
23. Li, M.M., Peters, C., Leimeister, J.M.: Designing a peer-based support system to support shakedown. In: International Conference on Information Systems (ICIS). Seoul, South Korea (2017)
24. Zschech, P.: Beyond descriptive taxonomies in data analytics: a systematic evaluation approach for data-driven method pipelines. Inf. Syst. E-Bus Manage. 1–35 (2022). https://doi.org/10.1007/s10257-022-00577-0
25. Batini, C., Barone, D., Mastrella, M., Maurino, A., Ruffini, C.: A framework and a methodology for data quality assessment and monitoring. ICIQ, pp. 333–346 (2007)
26. Bharati, P., Chaudhury, A.: An empirical investigation of decision-making satisfaction in web-based decision support systems. Decis. Support Syst. **37**(2), 187–197 (2004). https://doi.org/10.1016/S0167-9236(03)00006-X
27. Feldman, M., Even, A., Parmet, Y.: A methodology for quantifying the effect of missing data on decision quality in classification problems. Commun. Statist. Theory Meth. **47**(11), 2643–2663 (2018)
28. Woodall, P., Borek, A., Gao, J., Oberhofer, M.A., Koronios, A.: An Investigation of How Data Quality is Affected by Dataset Size in the Context of Big Data Analytics ICIQ (2014)
29. Zicari, P., Folino, G., Guarascio, M., Pontieri, L.: Combining deep ensemble learning and explanation for intelligent ticket management. Expert Syst. Appl. **206**, 117815 (2022). https://doi.org/10.1016/j.eswa.2022.117815
30. Rizun, N., Revina, A., Meister, V.G.: Assessing business process complexity based on textual data: evidence from ITIL IT ticket processing. BPMJ **27**(7), 1966–1998 (2021). https://doi.org/10.1108/BPMJ-04-2021-0217
31. Devlin, J., Chang, M.-W., Lee, K., Toutanova, K.: BERT: Pre-training of Deep Bidirectional Transformers for Language Understanding. arXiv (2019)
32. Baresi, L., Quattrocchi, G., Tamburri, D.A., den van Heuvel, W.-J.: Automated quality assessment of incident tickets for smart service continuity. In: International Conference on Service-Oriented Computing, pp. 492–499 (2020)

33. Cavalcanti, Y.C., Da Mota Silveira Neto, P.A., do Carmo Machado I., Vale, T.F., de Almeida, E.S., de Lemos Meira, S.R.: Challenges and opportunities for software change request repositories: a systematic mapping study. J. Softw. Evol. Process **26**(7), 620–653 (2014)
34. Sonnenberg, C., vom Brocke J.: Evaluations in the science of the artificial – reconsidering the build-evaluate pattern in design science research. In: Peffers, K., Rothenberger, M., Kuechler, B. (eds.) Design Science Research in Information Systems. Advances in Theory and Practice. DESRIST 2012. LNCS, vol. 7286. Springer, Berlin, Heidelberg (2012). https://doi.org/10.1007/978-3-642-29863-9_28
35. Peffers, K., Tuunanen, T., Rothenberger, M.A., Chatterjee, S.: A design science research methodology for information systems research. J. Manag. Inf. Syst. **24**(3), 45–77 (2007). https://doi.org/10.2753/MIS0742-1222240302
36. Brendel, A.B., Lembcke, T.-B., Muntermann, J., Kolbe, L.M.: Toward replication study types for design science research. J. Inf. Technol. **36**(3), 198–215 (2021). https://doi.org/10.1177/02683962211006429
37. Chandra Kruse, L., Nickerson, J.V.: Portraying Design Essence (2018)
38. Legner, C., Pentek, T., Otto, B.: Accumulating design knowledge with reference models: insights from 12 years' research into data management. JAIS **21**(3), 735–770 (2020). https://doi.org/10.17705/1jais.00618
39. Das, A.: Knowledge and productivity in technical support work. Manage. Sci. **49**(4), 416–431 (2003). https://doi.org/10.1287/mnsc.49.4.416.14419
40. Elshan, E., Ebel, P.A., Söllner, M., Leimeister, J.M.: Leveraging low code development of smart personal assistants: an integrated design approach with the SPADE method. J. Manage. Inform. Syst. (JMIS) (2022)
41. Wambsganß, T., Engel, C.: Using Deep Learning for Extracting User-Generated Knowledge from Web Communities (2021)
42. Zacharias, J., von Zahn, M., Chen, J., Hinz, O.: Designing a feature selection method based on explainable artificial intelligence. Electron. Mark. 1–26 (2022)
43. Pitler, E., Nenkova, A.: Revisiting readability: a unified framework for predicting text quality. In: Lapata, M., Tou, N.G.H. (eds.) Proceedings of the 2008 Conference on Empirical Methods in Natural Language Processing, pp. 186–195. Honolulu, Hawai (2008)
44. Landolt, S., Wambsganss, T., Söllner, M.: A Taxonomy for deep learning in natural language processing. In: Hawaii International Conference on System Sciences, Hawaii (2021)
45. Cai, L., Zhu, Y.: The challenges of data quality and data quality assessment in the big data era. CODATA **14**, 2 (2015). https://doi.org/10.5334/dsj-2015-002
46. Pipino, L.L., Lee, Y.W., Wang, R.Y.: Data quality assessment. Commun. ACM **45**(4), 211–218 (2002). https://doi.org/10.1145/505248.506010
47. Batini, C., Cappiello, C., Francalanci, C., Maurino, A.: Methodologies for data quality assessment and improvement. ACM Comput. Surv. **41**(3), 1–52 (2009). https://doi.org/10.1145/1541880.1541883
48. Subbarao, M.V., Venkatarao, K., Suresh, C.: Automation of incident response and IT ticket management by ML and NLP mechanisms. J. Theor. Appl. Inf. Technol. **100**(12), 3945–3955 (2022)
49. Vayansky, I., Kumar, S.A.: A review of topic modeling methods. Inf. Syst. **94**, 101582 (2020). https://doi.org/10.1016/j.is.2020.101582
50. Bouguettaya, A., Yu, Q., Liu, X., Zhou, X., Song, A.: Efficient agglomerative hierarchical clustering. Expert Syst. Appl. **42**(5), 2785–2797 (2015). https://doi.org/10.1016/j.eswa.2014.09.054
51. Lee, H.J., Lee, M., Lee, H., Cruz, R.A.: Mining service quality feedback from social media: a computational analytics method. Gov. Inf. Q. **38**(2), 101571 (2021)
52. Liu, J., Zhong, W., Li, R.: A selective overview of feature screening for ultrahigh-dimensional data. Science China Math. **58**(10), 1–22 (2015). https://doi.org/10.1007/s11425-015-5062-9

53. Oliveira, D.F., Nogueira, A.S., Brito, M.A.: Performance comparison of machine learning algorithms in classifying information technologies incident tickets. AI **3**(3), 601–622 (2022). https://doi.org/10.3390/ai3030035
54. Frank, U.: Evaluation of reference models Reference modeling for business systems analysis. IGI Global, pp. 118–140 (2007)
55. Venable, J., Pries-Heje, J., Baskerville, R.: FEDS: a framework for evaluation in design science research. Eur. J. Inf. Syst. **25**(1), 77–89 (2016). https://doi.org/10.1057/ejis.2014.36
56. Shani, G., Gunawardana, A.: Evaluating recommendation systems. In: Ricci, F., Rokach, L., Shapira, B., Kantor, P. (eds.) Recommender Systems Handbook. Springer, Boston, MA (2011). https://doi.org/10.1007/978-0-387-85820-3_8
57. Gregor, S., Hevner, A.R.: Positioning and presenting design science research for maximum impact. MISQ **37**(2), 337–355 (2013). https://doi.org/10.25300/misq/2013/37.2.01
58. Chua, C., Indulska, M., Lukyanenko, R., Maass, W., Storey, V.C.: MISQ research curation on data management. MISQ Res. Curat. 1–12 (2022)
59. Schermann, M., Böhmann, T., Krcmar, H.: Explicating design theories with conceptual models: towards a theoretical role of reference models. Wissenschaftstheorie und gestaltungsorientierte Wirtschaftsinformatik, S 175–194. Springer (2009)

Education and DSR

Introduction to the Education and Design Science Research Track

Asif Gill[1] and Jean-Paul Van Belle[2]

[1] University of Technology Sydney, Sydney, Australia
asif.gill@uts.edu.au
[2] University of Cape Town, South Africa

DESRIST Education and Design Science Research (DSR) track provides a platform for discussing teaching and learning issues as a permanent concern in the DSR community. DSR is increasingly being taught in research method courses across different academic disciplines to address contemporary research problems. DSR is not only limited to academic research, but it is also being used to address teaching and learning challenges. In summary, the Education and Design Science Research track presents research, applications and experience reports on challenges and best practices in

- teaching and learning Design Science Research (DSR) as well as
- using DSR for teaching and learning.

The teaching and learning domain has faced recent unprecedented challenges which DSR has been applied to. This includes remote and global education enabled by digital and conversational AI educational technologies. The pragmatic DSR approach was proved useful to design, build, and evaluate the pedagogical conversational agents (PCAs) for addressing the difficulties in providing personalized learning material or individual learning support. Many educators may struggle to know the knowledge of their students. DSR was used to create an analytical tool for analyzing performance and identify any misconceptions around student learning. Similarly, DSR is used in research for developing a prototype national student analytics platform for supporting student success.

Scoping research questions are always challenging highlight contextual. In a DSR research work, ChatGPT is incorporated into an inquiry framework. Computational thinking is also key to DSR research; thus it has been embedded in the DSR courses in a modular way. DSR seems useful for developing new co-design models in higher education. Augmented reality is another concern, which is getting vast attraction in primary education. DSR was used to design an augmented reality app for supporting learning in primacy schools.

DSR as a method has also been proved useful in solving challenges in teaching and learning about DSR. The DSR method is also critical for research across many disciplines. The DSR method and their applications in different areas need to be examined and synthesize to inform the future of DSR. Yet many educational challenges still remain to be solved by DSR researchers, however, this Education and DSR track provides a number of examples to learn from for the present and future DSR ventures.

References

1. Winter, R.: Design science research in business research – with special emphasis on information systems. Zeitschrift für Berufs- und Wirtschaftspädagogik - Beihefte 233–246 (2014)
2. Winter, R., vom Brocke, J.: Teaching design science research. In: 42th International Conference on Information Systems (ICIS 2021), Austin, TX (2021)
3. Seckler, C., Mauer, R., Brocke, J.V.: Design science in entrepreneurship: conceptual foundations and guiding principles. J. Bus. Ventur. Des. (2022, forthcoming)
4. Romme, A.G.L.: Making a difference: organization as design. Organ. Sci. **14**, 558–573 (2003)

Inquiry Frameworks for Research Question Scoping in DSR: A Realization for ChatGPT

Oscar Díaz⬤, Xabier Garmendia(✉)⬤, Jeremías P. Contell⬤,
and Juanan Pereira⬤

University of the Basque Country (UPV/EHU), San Sebastián, Spain
{oscar.diaz,xabier.garmendiad,jeremias.perez,juanan.pereira}@ehu.eus

Abstract. Research Question (RQ) Scoping refers to defining and refining a research question before conducting research. This step is crucial for ensuring the relevance and focus of the study, particularly in Design Science Research (DSR), where problems and solutions develop gradually. Literature reviews are a traditional method for comprehending the problem and determining key questions; however, they can be time-consuming and not worth it at the onset when lashing out in the dark. NLP chatbots such as ChatGPT can serve as a cost-effective alternative to clearing the way due to their capability to interact with users in a natural language-based manner and provide intuitive responses. The requirements for RQ Scoping extend beyond conversational support to include a framework for a sustained and iterative scoping process. An inquiry framework is necessary to guide and assist students and supervisors in fully harnessing the potential of NLP chatbots. This work incorporates ChatGPT into an inquiry framework for RQ Scoping, with mind maps as the visualization and the 5 Why technique as the inquiry strategy. Contributions include Design Principles, an IT artifact, and a Technology Acceptance Model evaluation (n = 9). Regarding perceived usefulness, the results indicate agreement on the intervention's effectiveness in maintaining focus. However, there is less enthusiasm for mind maps as a communication tool. Perceived ease of use was also positive but revealed concerns about the query templates used by the framework.

Keywords: RQ Scoping · Chatbot · ChatGPT · Mind maps

1 Introduction

Research Question (RQ) Scoping refers to defining and refining the research question before beginning the research. It involves analyzing the research context and determining specific questions necessary to evaluate the investigation results effectively. This process is crucial for ensuring focused and relevant research. However, in DSR, scoping can be particularly challenging as problems and solutions evolve iteratively and gradually. If the scope is too narrow, the results may not be comprehensive or relevant to more significant problems. Conversely, if it

© The Author(s), under exclusive license to Springer Nature Switzerland AG 2023
A. Gerber and R. Baskerville (Eds.): DESRIST 2023, LNCS 13873, pp. 299–313, 2023.
https://doi.org/10.1007/978-3-031-32808-4_19

is too broad, the research may lack focus, leading to less valuable insights. This raises a 'Goldilocks issue' whereby researchers struggle to balance focused and relevant research whilst addressing topics of interest [16].

RQ Scoping is a challenging task due to its abductive nature [10]. Abductive reasoning starts with observations or experiences (e.g., empirical data that causes 'the gut feeling'). Then it seeks to find the most straightforward and likely explanations for the observations: the hypotheses [21]. This starts an exploration journey where the recently acquired hypotheses are tested, more data are generated, and a new hypothesis emerges. In this scenario, researchers are involved in continuous decision-making, beginning with discovering an interesting phenomenon to investigate. To that end, reviewing the literature is a common practice for identifying the most promising RQs and gaining a deeper understanding of the problem or opportunity. However, a literature review takes time, and its rigor and thoroughness may not pay off for preliminary questions that are initially nothing more than 'gut feelings'. Alternatively, AI-powered chatbots might be a good-enough alternative to clear out the research space, even if they lack the confidence that literature reviews offer.

This work's central tenant is that AI-powered chatbots may offer a satisfactory trade-off between effort and potential outcomes for RQ Scoping. The conversational aspect reduces effort, while AI language models increase the chances of valuable results. However, relying solely on a conversation may not be sufficient for RQ Scoping. RQ Scoping is explorative, which calls for the search to be systematic and structured to prevent losing focus. The need for such an *Inquiry Framework* increases for users who take control of their learning at their own pace [18,24]. This setting very much resembles that of doctoral students. This leads to our research question: *How could AI-powered chatbots be integrated into an Inquiry Framework (i.e., the artifact) for RQ Scoping (i.e., the task) when conducting DSR projects (i.e., the practice) conducted by doctoral students (i.e. the target audience)?*

We address this question for ChatGPT[1] as the AI-powered chatbot, the *5 Why* as the inquiry strategy, and mind maps as the recording support for the chatbot conversation. We contribute by

- exploring the capabilities and limitations of ChatGPT for RQ Scoping (Sect. 2).
- introducing *Chatin*, an inquiry framework combining ChatGPT and the 5 Why inquiry strategy (Sects. 4 and 5).
- generalization of the learning through three Design Principles for Inquiry Frameworks (Sect. 3) and comparison with sibling interventions in the inquiry-based learning literature (Sect. 6).

We start with a brief on ChatGPT.

2   A Brief on ChatGPT

ChatGPT is a chatbot based on the OpenAI GPT-3 language model. ChatGPT lets people ask questions or tell stories, and the bot will respond with answers

---
[1] https://chat.apps.openai.com/.

and topics that make sense and sound natural. ChatGPT is being fed by a huge amount of data (up to September 2021), yet its scope may not have the same breadth, depth, and timeliness of information as traditional search engines that use real-time information [5]. That said, first evaluations conclude that the use of ChatGPT "can help researchers more efficiently and effectively process and analyze large amounts of data, generate realistic scenarios for testing and evaluating theories, and communicate their findings in a clear and concise manner" [17].

ChatGPT is claimed to offer the potential to increase motivation and engagement among self-taught learners with the potential to guide and structure users' exploration of a research space [3,14]. A recent systematic review and meta-analysis on the impact of AI components on student performance ($n = 25$) support a positive impact on their performance, finding a rise in their attitude towards learning and their motivation, especially in the STEM (Science, Technology, Engineering, and Mathematics) areas [9]. More specifically, for our purposes, the advantages of self-directed learning include [7]:

- Support unique to each learner: ChatGPT can help learners in charge of their learning by adapting suggestions and responses to each learner's choices and goals. This could be very helpful for students who might not have access to more conventional support networks like a teacher or a mentor.
- Real-time feedback and direction: As self-taught learners move through the course materials and resources, ChatGPT can give them real-time feedback and direction. This can assist students in staying on task and addressing any issues or problems they might encounter.
- Accessibility: Learners who might not have access to traditional educational materials will find ChatGPT easier to use because it can be accessed through a website, a smartphone app, or a messaging service.
- Convenient and flexible learning: Autodidacts can study at their own pace and on their own terms with ChatGPT, as they can interact with the chatbot whenever it's convenient for them.
- Enhancing the use of open educational resources: ChatGPT can help self-directed learners find and use open educational materials because it can give them personalized tips and advice on using these resources well. This can allow students to use the many tools and resources for learning that are available online.
- Self-assessment and reflection: Learners can use ChatGPT to reflect on their own progress and learning and to identify areas where they may need further support or guidance.

This study investigates the potential utilization of ChatGPT in RQ Scoping.

3   Design Principles for an AI-Empowered Inquiry Framework for RQ Scoping

This section introduces a set of generalized requirements for an inquiry framework (i.e., the intervention) for AI-powered RQ Scoping (i.e., the task) in DSR-based doctoral studies (i.e., the practice). In our search for justificatory theories, we characterize RQ Scoping as a practice of inquiry-based learning, specifically, an open inquiry-based learning practice.

"Open inquiry" engages students in decision-making throughout the entire process, from identifying an interesting phenomenon to investigating. Encouraging students to take ownership of their learning, this approach can increase their self-esteem and lead to a deeper understanding of the topic being studied. [23]. However, it may present more of a challenge for some students, particularly those who struggle academically [4]. A study of over 2,800 students over three years found that many students needed assistance with scientific research, experimental techniques and procedures, and phrasing inquiry questions [25]. Overcoming interventions include:

- online forums, where students present their challenges and receive guidance from teachers and peers [25]. However, this concept is not applicable in a doctoral setting, as there are typically no peers to engage with.
- software scaffolds, like *Hypothesis Scratchpad* [20]. One problem is that noticing relevant variables in a hypothesis requires substantial conceptual domain-specific knowledge, which students may lack [15]. Without sufficient surface knowledge, engaging effectively in deeper learning activities can be difficult because the fundamental building blocks are missing [11]. It is sensible to argue that doctoral students face similar matters.

This work builds upon a software scaffold intervention, i.e., an inquiry framework. Unlike *Hypothesis Scratchpad*, RQ Scoping serves as the preliminary step for generating hypotheses by establishing domain-specific conceptual knowledge.

3.1 Inquiry Frameworks: Design Principles

We define an inquiry framework as a structured approach to problem-solving that guides the scope and analysis of a RQ [13]. We qualified an inquiry framework as 'AI-empowered' if a language-model chatbot is introduced. The next paragraphs introduce three design principles for this intervention.

RQ Scoping is exploratory, i.e., it is focused on seeking new information and gaining a general understanding of a subject rather than confirming preconceived ideas or hypotheses [12]. The difficulty lies in comprehending the range of options available so researchers can gain a comprehensive perspective. Inquiry frameworks document and track the scoping map, ensuring all pertinent information is considered. This necessitates the existence of a visual framework that enables prompt and effective visualization of the alternatives at stake, allowing students to move seamlessly among them, especially in a doctoral setting where the exploration is conducted collaboratively with the supervisor. This leads to our first design principle (DP):

(DP1) **Provide the framework with** effective visualization **in order for researchers to** get an overview of the RQ alternatives at stake to be shared with the supervisor

RQ Scoping, like the other DSR stages, is iterative. Iterative means gradually narrowing down the scope of the problem rather than cycling through possible solutions. There is a need for the inquiry framework to allow students to narrow the scope of their RQ gradually. This is when the 5 Why technique comes into play. 5 Whys is an iterative interrogative technique to explore the cause-and-effect relationships underlying a particular problem [1]. The technique is based on the premise that asking "why" five times will lead to identifying the underlying cause of a problem. The process involves asking "why" a problem happened and then using the answer to that question as the basis for the next question. The technique is simple yet effective enough to shift the focus from general concerns to their causes.

(DP2) **Provide the framework with** a searching strategy **in order for researchers to** gradually reduce the RQ scope.

The 5 Why technique focuses on explanatory questions to understand the cause-and-effect relationships of a particular phenomenon, but it says nothing about the phenomenon itself. The technique offers no help in assessing the context where "the why' is posed. Chatbots offer little help either [8]. Yet, 'context' is critical in DSR, where interventions are not general but show utility in a specific context. Indeed, Design Science is defined as "the design and investigation of artefacts *in context*" [22]. As a result, the inquiry framework should supplement the chatbot by managing its own contextual variables throughout the conversation. In a DSR setting, this may include the practice, the task, or the stakeholders that conform to the setting where the problematic phenomena arise [12].

(DP3) **Provide the framework with** a contextual state **in order for researchers to** keep the context throughout

4 Proof-of-Concept: An Inquiry Framework for RQ Scoping

This section describes *Chatin*[2], an inquiry framework for RQ Scoping using ChatGPT as the AI-powered chatbot, and MindMeister[3] as the mind-map editor. ChatGPT is considered to be at the very edge of AI technology. As for MindMeister, rationales for its selection include performance (support for large maps), popularity (25 million users at the time of this writing, as seen on the application's website), and web support. The latter is significant. MindMeister uses an online mind map editor that enables users to create, edit, share, and present mind maps right inside a web browser. No software download or update is necessary.

The rest of this section is structured along the aforementioned Design Principles.

---

[2] *Chatin* is a portmanteau of CHAtgpt-powered INquiry. The term is informally used as a friendly nickname in Spanish.

[3] https://mindmeister.com.

4.1 DP1: Provide the Framework with Effective Visualization

The 5 Why technique follows a tree-like way of conducting root-cause analysis where the next question is based on previous answers. This tree-like structure suggests the use of mind maps as a visualization approach. A mind map is a diagram used to visually organize information in a radial fashion [2]. They provide a visual overview of a topic and can help find connections, aiding comprehension, problem-solving, and decision-making. Chances are students are already familiar with this approach. Specifically, we resort to the *MindMeister* editor.

Figure 1 depicts a head start template provided by *Chatin* on top of *Mind-Meister*. Nodes are radially disposed around a root node (*"RQ Scoping"*), with two salient branches: the *"Question Model"* and the *"Scoping Analysis"*. The latter is the start of the inquiry process. *Chatin* provides a first *question node*: a RQ generated using the context variables of the Question Model (see Fig. 2 and next section). The students can edit and rephrase this question using the question variables to keep consistency. Finally, question nodes can be 'enacted', i.e., the student clicks on the magnifier icon (♀) for these questions to be transparently delivered to ChatGPT. This starts the inquiry process.

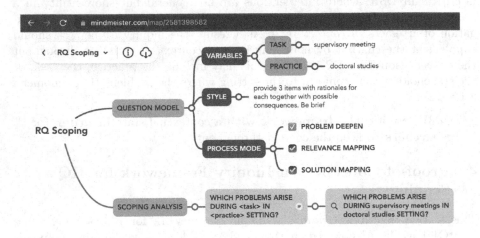

Fig. 1. A head start template provided by *Chatin* on top of *MindMeister*. The student provides the TASK and the PRACTICE variables from where *Chatin* generates the first question node in the SCOPING ANALYSIS tree. Click on this node's magnifier for this question to be issued to ChatGPT.

Chatin resorts to mind maps for structuring the conversation between the student and ChatGPT. This means that the mind map is made by putting student nodes and ChatGPT nodes next to each other. Student nodes stand for questions. ChatGPT nodes correspond to answers. *Chatin* mediates. This implies: (1) sending the student's questions to ChatGPT (through its API[4]); (2)

---

[4] https://openai.com/api/.

collecting and itemizing ChatGPT's answer; and, (3) turning each of the items into a node in the mind map. Figure 2 illustrates this: questions and answers intermingled as the map unfolds. From a rendering perspective:

- Question nodes are yellow-shaded and hold the 'magnifier' icon ($\bigcirc$). On clicking, *Chatin* constructs the prompt to be issued through the OpenAI's API, collects the answer, and transforms this answer into a set of answer nodes;
- Answer nodes are green-shaded and hold the 'activating' icon ($\blacksquare$). On clicking, *Chatin* draws a question node from the ChatGPT answers, completing the cycle.

4.2   DP2: Provide the Framework with a Contextual State

For chatbots, 'context' refers to the background information and knowledge that the chatbot uses to understand and respond to a user's input. ChatGPT keeps its own context embedded in the engine. In addition, *Chatin* makes its own context explicitly through the 'Question Model'. This model is captured as a node in the mind map (see Fig. 1). The Question Model tackles three concerns, namely:

- *Variables.* The student can set them to be used throughout the inquiry. The example shows the case of context variables of which only two have been instantiated: *task* and *practice*. This serves to define variables to be next used to write questions, and, hence, keep consistency throughout the inquiry process.
- *Style.* In our setting, ChatGPT does not target a human being but another software agent, i.e., *Chatin*. Hence, responses should be tuned to facilitate their processing. ChatGPT allows you to provide cues about how to tune your answers (e.g., itemize, number of items, special control characters, and so on). The style node serves to provide these cues in a coherent way throughout.
- *Process mode.* This mode regulates the sort of questions *Chatin* will pose to ChatGPT: WHICH PROBLEMS MIGHT ARISE DURING the task (problem statement); WHY DOES the problem OCCUR DURING the tasks (problem analysis); WHY IS the problem RELEVANT FOR task (relevance mapping); and HOW CAN the problem BE ADDRESSED FOR (solution analysis) (see next subsection). If all questions were posed right away, the mind map would quickly become unwieldy. The Process Mode allows the student to set the dimension(s) to develop at his own pace.

4.3   DP3: Provide the Framework with a Searching Strategy

The search strategy is the cornerstone of an inquiry framework. The searching strategy structures the (partial) order in which distinct types of questions are posed. We resort to a state-transition diagram for formally specifying this strategy. A state-transition diagram captures this strategy through a set of states and the events under which the strategy progresses (transitions). States might hold *entry/exit* actions to reflect events that should happen when the system transitions into or out of a particular state. For our purposes,

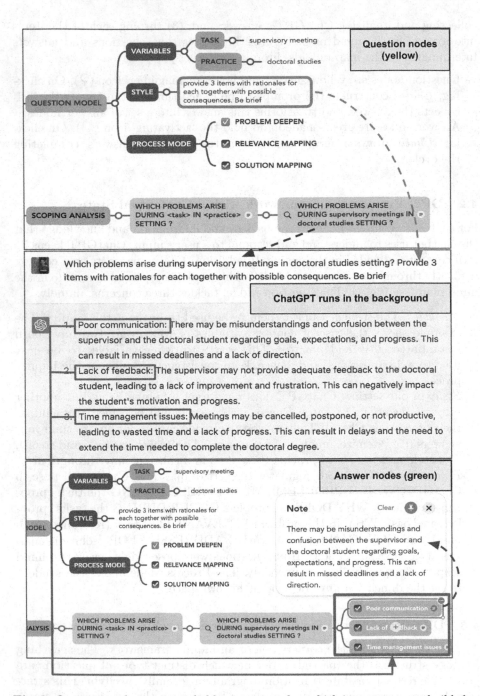

Fig. 2. Question nodes are extended by answer nodes, which in turn serve to build the next question nodes. *Chatin* takes question nodes and delivers answer nodes, and the other way around.

- *entry* actions denote preparing and issuing the query to be posed to ChatGPT (the event) when entering the state,
- *exit* actions reflect the rendering of the ChatGPT's output

Chatin's search strategy develops along with three modes that are reflect as states (see Fig. 3):

- **Problem Deepen.** Here, the student starts by setting a very first question (i.e., Problem Statement), then moves on to assess the causes of this problem (i.e., Problem Analysis). Along with the 5 Why approach, each cause can in turn become a problem in its own right (notice the 'problem deepen' interaction in Fig. 3). The student delves into the causes of the problem, till he decides to investigate the relevance of the problem at hand. This is achieved by raising the *relevance_mapping[problem]* event. Notice that it is up to the student when to rise this event;
- **Relevance Mapping.** On entry, *Chatin* queries ChatGPT about the relevance of the problem at hand, delivering ChatGPT answers as nodes in the concept map. Eventually, rising the *solution_mapping[problem]* event, the student decides to move to the next state.
- **Solution Mapping.** On entry, *Chatin* queries ChatGPT about the existence of interventions to handle the problem at hand (i.e., related work). Provided any intervention exists, the student can now shift between looking into either the EFFECTIVENESS or the FEASIBILITY of the intervention at hand (notice the namesake concurrent states in Fig. 3.)

The inquiry unfolds by moving between states by making the appropriate transitions:

- *problem_deepen[problem]*: transitions from a problem to one of this problem's causes (see Fig. 4A). Click on a problem node (green shadowed) for *Chatin* to generate a 'WHY PROBLEM' question node (yellow shadowed). The student could now rephrase the content of the question node. To investigate the causes of this cause, click on the question node's magnifier,
- *relevance_mapping[problem]*: transitions from a problem to one of this problem's consequences (see Fig. 4B). Once in a problem node, activate the 'relevance mode' in the Question Model (see next). From then on, *Chatin* will generate 'WHY RELEVANT' questions,
- *solution_mapping[problem]*: transitions from a consequence to the associated interventions (see Fig. 4C). Once in a consequence node, activate the 'solution mode' in the Question Model. From then on, *Chatin* will generate HOW questions.

This process is not inherently sequential and allows for reverting to previous stages at any moment, such as revisiting prior problems or interventions or starting afresh with a new problem statement[5].

---

[5] Figure 3's *any_scoping[previously issued]* event accounts for any event in the *Scoping* state that has already been issued once.

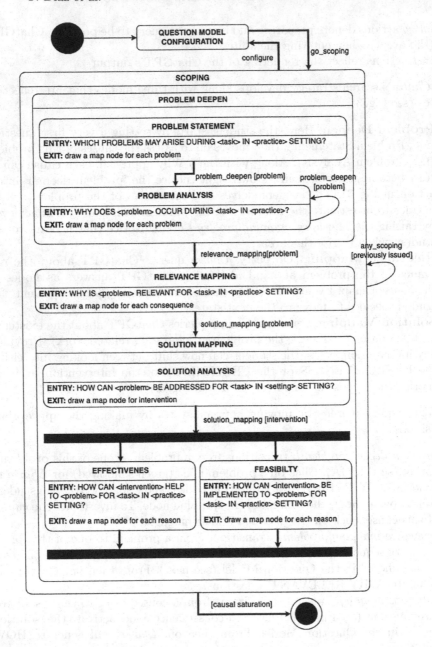

Fig. 3. State-transition diagram that governs *Chatin*'s search strategy: Problem Deepen, Relevance Mapping & Solution Mapping

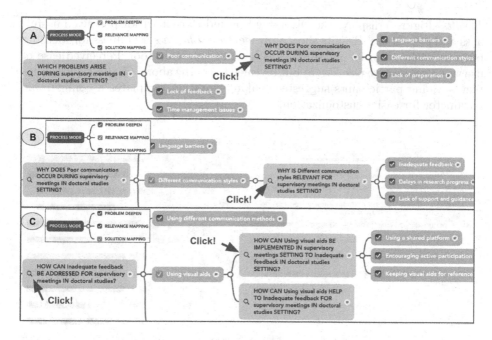

Fig. 4. *Chatin* three-mode process: PROBLEM DEEPEN transitions from a problem (*Poor communication*) to its causes (A); RELEVANCE MAPPING moves from a cause (*Different communication styles*) to study its possible relevance (B), and SOLUTION MAPPING moves from an intervention to study its effectiveness and feasibility (C). The student chooses which mode to focus on using the PROCESS MODE control variable

5   Evaluation

Goal. This study aims to *assess* the perceived ease of use and usefulness of *Chatin* with respect to *RQ Scoping* from the point of view of *researchers* in the context of *DSR projects*.

Subjects. We tap into 9 participants, all with at least one year of experience on both DSR and MindMeister.

Instrument. Given the novelty of this intervention, we opt for resorting to the Technology Acceptance Model (TAM) [19]. We extended the TAM questionnaire to refine the notions of 'usefulness' regarding the aspects involved in RQ Scoping, specifically: promoting focus, systematically refining the RQ, documenting the journey, and guiding the exploration. The TAM scores highly on internal consistency validation using various measures [19]. Our case was no exception: we got an α of 0.63 and 0.70 for usefulness and ease of use, respectively. On these premises, we consider TAM an accurate predictor of usage and adoption for *Chatin*.

Results. Figure 5 displays the Diverging Stacked Bar Chart for perceived usefulness and ease of use. Results show agreement on *Chatin*'s usefulness for focusing
but less enthusiasm for mind maps as a communication tool. Perceived ease of
use was also positive (see Fig. 5) but revealed concerns about *Chatin*'s query templates. Some participants suggested making question templates a configurable
parameter for easier customization.

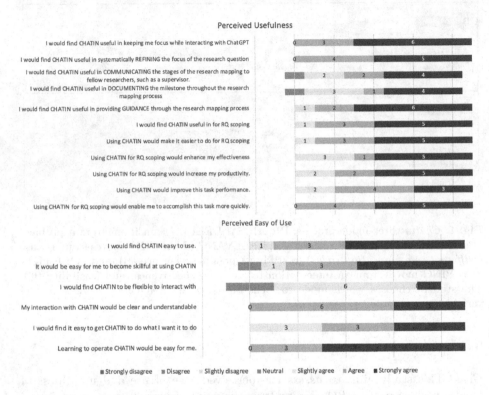

Fig. 5. Perceived usefulness and ease of use

Threats to Validity. Two primary threats exist for the findings: reduced external validity as the study's tech-savvy participants may not represent all populations, and risk of construct validity as participants may have evaluated Chat-
GPT's technology unconsciously. The participants were warned of this potentially confounding variable, but the technology's novelty may have still impacted
the results.

6   Discussion

Enholm et al. introduce a framework to place AI interventions in terms of (1)
the typologies of AI use in the organizational setting; (2) the key enablers and
inhibitors of AI adoption and use; and (3) the impacts of AI [6]. This section
places this work within this framework.

Typologies of AI Use. Enholm et al. divide AI applications into two categories: AI for automation (i.e., AI systems that replace human work) and AI for augmentation (i.e., AI systems that integrate with human expertise to improve decisions). *Chatin* is certainly AI for augmentation, specifically assisting students in developing their RQs.

Key Enablers and Inhibitors of AI Adoption and Use. The benefits that an AI intervention can bring to RQ Scoping include:

- Time efficiency: ChatGPT can provide quick and intuitive answers to RQ Scoping questions, reducing the time and effort required for traditional literature reviews.
- Cost-effectiveness: ChatGPT can serve as a cost-effective alternative to traditional methods for RQ Scoping, reducing the resources required for research.
- Accessibility: The chat-based interface and natural language interaction can make the RQ Scoping process more accessible for students and supervisors, particularly those not experts in the field.

On the downside, we envisage as main inhibitors:

- Dependence on inquiry framework: The approach's success depends on the design and effectiveness of the inquiry framework and its ability to guide and support the RQ Scoping process.
- Bias and errors. As with any AI-based system, there is a risk of bias and errors in ChatGPT's responses, which may impact the quality of the RQ Scoping process. ChatGPT's knowledge base may not be comprehensive or up-to-date, leading to inaccuracies or limitations in its ability to support RQ Scoping.
- Top Management Support. Enholm et al. note that top management support is one of the strongest determinants of AI adoption. This introduces tutors and supervisors as primary stakeholders in IA-assisted RQ Scoping. Supervisors might raise concerns not only about the accuracy of ChatGPT's answers but also the extent to which students' extensive, no-critical adoption of ChatGPT might hinder critical thinking.

We do not see ethical concerns arising in RQ Scoping. While ChatGPT can assist in mapping out the research area, it is ultimately up to the student's intuition to determine which path to take.

The Impacts of AI. How does *Chatin* change RQ Scoping, and how does this lead to competitive performance? Enholm et al. report on the AI effects on companies to identify opportunities to enter the market with new offerings. We can set parallelism here whereby students identify research opportunities to be 'bought by the research market'. Despite their limitations, models for natural language processing, such as ChatGPT, allow for more agile and flexible mapping out of blurred research areas compared to traditional bibliographic search methods.

7 Conclusions

We investigate the use of Inquiry Frameworks that mediate between students and AI-powered chatbots in the search for better structuring, tracking, documenting, and communicating student progress in pursuing the 'right RQ'. *Chatin* provides first insights using ChatGPT as the chatbot and mind maps as the representation. This initial experience serves to identify three affordances for this kind of intervention: (1) *an effective visualization* to map out the research space to share with third parties (e.g., supervisors); (2) *a search strategy* to gradually narrow down the scope of the RQ to fit the resources available; and (3) *a contextual state* to keep a presence of the searching context throughout. Though results are promising, more participants are needed for more robust conclusions.

Users of *Chatin* should be aware of the potential limitations and concerns regarding the thoroughness, accuracy, and reliability of AI technology, particularly ChatGPT. It is essential to approach AI-generated responses critically and consider seeking additional sources when necessary. The mandate is clear: *Chatin* should integrate information sources other than ChatGPT that can be checked upon request.

Finally, it is essential to remember the words of Ray Kurzweil: "The ultimate goal of AI is not to create machines that are intelligent but to create machines that make us more intelligent". *Chatin* as AI for augmentation does not endow intelligence but aims to enhance students' focus, which is necessary for manifesting natural intelligence.

Acknowledgements. Research supported by MCIN/AEI/10.13039/501100011033/ FEDER, UE and the "European Union NextGenerationEU/PRTR" under contract PID2021-125438OB-I00. Xabier Garmendia enjoys a grant from the University of the Basque Country - PIF20/236.

References

1. Andersen, B., Fagerhaug, T.: Root Cause Analysis. ASQ Quality Press (2006). https://psnet.ahrq.gov/primers/primer/10/root-cause-analysis
2. Buzan, T.: Mind maps at work: How to be the best at your job and still have time to play. HarperCollins UK (2004)
3. Cahan, P., Treutlein, B.: A conversation with ChatGPT on the role of computational systems biology in stem cell research. Stem Cell Rep. **18**(1), 1–2 (2023)
4. Chang, K.E., Sung, Y.T., Lee, C.L.: Web-based collaborative inquiry learning. J. Comput. Assist. Learn. **19**(1), 56–69 (2003)
5. Cochrane, L.: Is ChatGPT Manipulating You? (Or Are You Manipulating It?). https://logancochrane.com/blog/is-chatgpt-manipulating-you-or-are-you-manipulating-it
6. Enholm, I.M., Papagiannidis, E., Mikalef, P., Krogstie, J.: Artificial intelligence and business value: a literature review. Inf. Syst. Front. **24**(5), 1709–1734 (2022)
7. Firat, M.: How ChatGPT can transform autodidactic experiences and open education? (2023). https://doi.org/10.31219/osf.io/9ge8m

8. Følstad, A., et al.: Future directions for chatbot research: an interdisciplinary research agenda. Computing **103**(12), 2915–2942 (2021). https://doi.org/10.1007/s00607-021-01016-7

9. García-Martínez, I., Fernández-Batanero, J.M., Fernández-Cerero, J., León, S.P.: Analysing the impact of artificial intelligence and computational sciences on student performance: systematic review and meta-analysis. J. New Approach. Educ. Res. **12**(1), 171–197 (2023)

10. Hassan, N.R.: Constructing the right disciplinary is questions. In: AMCIS 2017 (2017)

11. Hattie, J.A., Donoghue, G.M.: Learning strategies: a synthesis and conceptual model. NPJ Sci. Learn. **1**(1), 1–13 (2016)

12. Johannesson, P., Perjons, E.: An Introduction to Design Science. Springer, Cham (2014). https://doi.org/10.1007/978-3-319-10632-8

13. Pedaste, M., et al.: Phases of inquiry-based learning: definitions and the inquiry cycle. Educ. Res. Rev. **14**, 47–61 (2015)

14. Qadir, J.: Engineering education in the era of chatgpt: promise and pitfalls of generative AI for education. TechRxiv. Preprint (2022). https://doi.org/10.36227/techrxiv.21789434.v1

15. Quintana, C., et al.: A scaffolding design framework for software to support science inquiry. In: The Journal of the Learning Sciences, pp. 337–386. Psychology Press (2018)

16. Rai, A.: Avoiding type III errors: formulating is research problems that matter (2017)

17. Rizzo, G., Pietrolucci, M.E., Capponi, A., Mappa, I.: Exploring the role of artificial intelligence in the study of fetal heart. Int. J. Cardiovasc. Imaging **38**(5), 1017–1019 (2022)

18. Schweder, S., Raufelder, D.: Examining positive emotions, autonomy support and learning strategies: self-directed versus teacher-directed learning environments. Learning Environ. Res. **25**(2), 507–522 (2022)

19. Turner, M., Kitchenham, B., Brereton, P., Charters, S., Budgen, D.: Does the technology acceptance model predict actual use? A systematic literature review. Inf. Softw. Technol. **52**(5), 463–479 (2010)

20. Van Joolingen, W.R., De Jong, T.: Design and implementation of simulation-based discovery environments: the smisle solution. J. Artif. Intell. Educ. **7**, 253–276 (1996)

21. Walton, D.: Abductive Reasoning. University of Alabama Press, Tuscaloosa (2014)

22. Wieringa, R.J.: Design Science Methodology for Information Systems and Software Engineering. Springer, Heidelberg (2014). https://doi.org/10.1007/978-3-662-43839-8

23. Windschitl, M.: Inquiry projects in science teacher education: what can investigative experiences reveal about teacher thinking and eventual classroom practice? Sci. Educ. **87**(1), 112–143 (2003)

24. Zhai, X.: ChatGPT user experience: implications for education. SSRN (2022). https://doi.org/10.2139/ssrn.4312418

25. Zion, M.: On line forums as a 'rescue net' in an open inquiry process. Int. J. Sci. Math. Educ. **6**(2), 351–375 (2008). https://doi.org/10.1007/s10763-006-9051-x

Design of an Augmented Reality App for Primary School Students Which Visualizes Length Units to Promote the Conversion of Units

Lea Marie Mueller[(✉)] [iD] and Melanie Platz [iD]

Saarland University, 66123 Saarbruecken, Germany
`{leamarie.mueller,melanie.platz}@uni-saarland.de`

Abstract. Insight and understanding of the structure of units can be considered one of mathematics' most important learning areas, as it is needed in everyday life. It is essential in everyday tasks, such as trading goods, which requires dealing with monetary values and, e.g., lengths, weights, volumes, or area units. In addition, students in higher education after primary school show problems with understanding units by confusing units, especially in advanced STEM subjects, e.g., physics. The paper shows how Augmented Reality (AR) technology can be used to gain insight into understanding units by visualizing units of length using an AR app. The design of the AR app will be presented, which was developed after a theoretical grounding and practical testing with an existing AR measuring tool on the app market. Design Science Research (DSR) will be used to develop a suitable content learning environment using the AR app. The learning environment will then be tested with students again and disseminated in international workshops for teachers.

Keywords: unit of length · conversion · measurement · augmented reality · design science research

1 Introduction

Measuring and dealing with units of measurement has always been an important part of the history of humans because it is necessary for everyday tasks and problems. Moreover, the topic is curricular anchored in the educational plan of the National Council of Teachers of Mathematics [1] throughout K 12 from kindergarten to grade 12, as well as, e.g., in the German educational plans for mathematics in primary and secondary schools [2–4]. Children in higher grades after primary school have difficulties applying formulas, e.g., calculating an area on which the understanding of measurement and insight into the unit system is built and should be understood. In STEM subjects, such as physics, problems arise with using units appropriately [5, 6]. Units are often used indiscriminately because of a lack of in-depth understanding of how units are constructed. Lassnitzer and Gaidoschick [7] also describe it as a kind of "gamble" that students engage when converting units without a given scheme. The difficulties usually do not end with handling measures and units but can spread to adjacent mathematical areas, such as calculating

A. Gerber and R. Baskerville (Eds.): DESRIST 2023, LNCS 13873, pp. 314–328, 2023.
https://doi.org/10.1007/978-3-031-32808-4_20

areas and volumes. This paper will present a support tool with which the unit concept can be visualized. The development of the tool is based on the interaction of theoretical approaches to build conceptual knowledge about unit systems and the findings of an empirical pilot study. For this purpose, a publicly available AR app for measuring length was tested with students to investigate the use of the app from a user-friendly perspective and mathematics didactic perspective.

2 Theoretical Background

In everyday life, we are surrounded by standardized and also non-standardized units of measurement, which we often use naturally without thinking about it (e.g., when cooking, trading goods, temperature conditions, and watering plants). In addition to everyday life, using units is also required in many professions. Especially internationally, standardized units of measurement (e.g., for lengths the scale of the metric system or the United States customary system) are of great importance since they can be compared with each other independently of time and place. This brief insight into everyday applications is one reason why dealing with measurement and units of measurement is one of the most fundamental areas in mathematics that all children and adults should understand. A comprehensive understanding of units in different size ranges requires more than procedural knowledge, such as knowing how to read the result of a measurement using a measuring instrument. It is also essential to understand the concept behind the measurement process to check the result for plausibility and understand the structure of different measurement systems.

2.1 The Concept of Measuring Lengths

According to the National Council of Teachers of Mathematics [1], the learning area of measurement includes two main areas: first, "Understand measurable attributes of objects and the units, systems, and processes of measurement" [1, p. 44], and second, "apply appropriate techniques, tools, and formulas to determine measurements" [1, p. 46]. It is important to note that all measurement systems are subject to the same scheme. Children must understand that a physical quantity is always composed of a numerical value and a unit of measurement [8, 9]. Thus, a size specification can be the same even though it consists of different numerical values and units of measurement. When converting, this becomes particularly clear in that the size specification remains the same even if one uses centimeters instead of meters but adjusts the measurement number accordingly. It is only essential that the chosen units of measurement are subject to the same system of units.

This usually starts with determining length measures in primary school because the units can be visibly marked along a distance. This makes it easier to understand the units' structure than other units of measurement, e.g., weights, time durations, or monetary values. However, this simple process of repeated recording and counting or even reading off units of measurement can lead to problems when using measuring instruments, in that the students only read off results but neglect the structure of the measuring scale. They use learned procedures such as applying a measuring device and reading the number on the scale at the end of the measured object. However, the concept behind measuring is usually not understood. For example, this can be seen in not starting to measure at zero [10] or claiming that a broken ruler cannot be used to measure [11]. Also, problems with a longer object than the measuring instrument make clear that the concept of measuring was not understood profoundly.

In the literature, several concepts exist [e.g., 12–14] which contain principles behind the concept of length measurement understanding. Zöllner [14] clearly shows that many components must be learned to comprehensively understand length and that many of them are closely connected. She cites the unit concept as one component of the concept of length measurement. This component is not to be equated with unit iteration, described as a principle in many concepts [e.g., 12, 13]. Unit iteration represents the ability to lay out a unit repeatedly along a distance to be measured. This ability is crucial for understanding units but should not be equated with the unit concept component. The unit concept accesses knowledge of unit iteration but takes it a step further by relating the measure to the unit of measurement. This means that just because students are aware that to measure a distance, it can be broken down into equal parts, it does not mean that they understand the relationship between the various conversions of the respective parts. This knowledge is necessary for the conversion of size data if students are not to learn length conversion only by "adding or deleting zeros" and "shifting the decimal point", according to Lassnitzer and Gaidoschik [7]. However, to understand the described relationship between the numerical value and unit of measurement, it is first necessary to understand the concept of units. In detail, this means that the students must have understood that a total distance can be divided into equal units. Then they can understand that the length of the sections is related to the number of sections. This means that a higher unit of measurement is needed if a smaller unit is chosen for the constant distance to be measured. They must have understood the principle that the smaller the partial steps' length, the larger the number of partial steps, and the other way around. The principle applies to standardized as well as non-standardized measurement units. This knowledge is fundamental to understanding conversions to other units in depth rather than memorizing them. In the case of standardized units, such as the metric system for lengths, the structure of the units and the relevance of naming the unit of measurement, which is often missing in student solutions, can be explained in this way. The unit of a measurement system, e.g., metric system, is then transferred to conventional measuring instruments. There are various measuring instruments that all display the metric system but use a different notation of units. For the students to be able to measure with these measuring instruments and not just read off the result as the last number of the measurement, an understanding of the unit system needs to occur. In the following, the concepts for teaching and learning the unit concept will be presented.

2.2   Learning and Teaching the Concept of Units

The length of an object can be determined in different ways. If the object is movable, it can be held against a comparison object to determine, for example, whether it is longer or shorter. Possibly the length of the comparison object is also known, and thus the length of the object to be measured can be estimated. If a direct comparison is impossible, indirect measurements can be made using standardized or non-standardized units [8, 9].

Historically, body measurements have been used to determine lengths. Often in school, this is an attempt to show the relevance of standardized units, as this is the only way to make an international comparison of a chosen unit of measurement. However, studies show that children are often unaware of this connection and that learning with self-selected units of measurement is an additional learning content [e.g., 15]. Thus, the question can be asked how else the understanding of units, the associated unit concept, and its relevance can be taught and learned. Drake [16] recommends not only using the traditional rulers that students usually get when they start school. Special rulers and measuring tapes can also be used, which, for example, visualize the metric scale only in millimeters. For this purpose, the measuring tapes and measuring results should be compared and discussed. However, he emphasizes that especially for the introduction of measurement, "rulers that show a single scale (e.g., whole centimetres [sic!]) or self-constructed rulers made of paper are all that students need to use" [16, p. 31].

Zöllner and Reuter [17] implement the recommendation by letting children in the second grade make their own ruler out of matchsticks. In doing so, the children learn that the distance must be constant. This helps children understand how consistent units are created. Whether this concept can be transferred to the different standardized units has not yet been researched. Another support approach can be made possible by using digital devices to display dynamic processes by measuring.

2.3 Learning the Concept of Units with Augmented Reality

With Augmented Reality (AR), virtual information can be displayed in the real world with the help of the camera function of digital end devices such as smartphones, tablets, or AR glasses. Thus, additional information can be faded in or out of the real world by covering it up. Many digital length measuring instruments on the market use AR as technology [18]. The AR measuring apps use the end device's camera function to scan the real environment for horizontal and vertical surfaces. If the distance to a real object to be measured is selected appropriately, most apps display a kind of crosshair with which a starting point for the measurement can be selected with a finger touch. After selecting the starting point, the digital end device can be moved slowly along the object to be measured to determine the length. The drawing function of the digital measuring tape, which happens automatically by the movement of the digital end device, updates the measurement result and displays the current numerical value with the measurement unit. The endpoint is selected with a finger touch on the display to complete the measurement, and the entire measured distance can be viewed. The measurement result is presented as a numerical value with the measurement unit in centimeters or meters and centimeters as notations with a comma. The most AR measuring instruments have this process of length measuring in common which could lead to coordination difficulties in the application due to simultaneous moving and looking. It is also known that children in Germany [19] and other countries [20] own and use increasingly digital devices, even at primary school age. Based on the fact that the functionality of AR measuring tools differs from classical games and applications on smartphones or tablets, we would like to find out which difficulties are noticeable in the handling of such AR measuring apps and how these difficulties could be solved in the design of our own developed app. In addition, a systematic analysis, according to Mueller and Platz [18], found that the vast majority of apps on the app market display the result only as a measurement value and focus less on the process of measuring. Classic analog length measuring instruments, such as a ruler or tape measure, also have the disadvantage that the procedure is often carried out, and the value read is written down without reflection, although units are available as a scale. In this context, from the mathematics didactic perspective, the aim is to determine whether children in the app only procedurally perform the act of measuring and reading the displayed result or whether they reflect the result of measurement because the app does not show how the measurement value is determined.

3   Methodology

In December 2022, a first developed learning environment was tested with students in the fourth grade. The "tape measure" AR app from Apple for iOS was used to find out how suitable the learning environment is and observe how the children handle an AR app for measuring. This should then provide conclusions for the development of essential functions of the self-developed app in addition to the theoretical background. Thus, the following research questions were posed to the study.

1. How must a learning environment be developed that allows conclusions to be drawn about students' conceptual understanding of the system of measurement units?
2. What features from the mathematic-didactics perspective does an AR app for length measuring need to promote the concept of measurement length units?
3. What essential technical features does an AR app for length measuring need to use with fourth-grade students?

The project aims to find out how to design a technology-enhanced learning environment that promotes students' conceptual understanding of units of measurement. Design Science Research (DSR) [21, 22] is a suitable approach for answering research questions, as the app is continuously developed in the interplay between theoretical findings and practical testing.

3.1   Research Design

DSR [21, 22] pursues the goal of developing and evaluating solutions to problems to codify knowledge about design sciences as design theories. The problem is that students often have procedural knowledge in the context of units of measurement and their transformation, and the concept is not understood, which is essential for a deep and flexible understanding of the structure of units of measurement. As a solution, using digital media could assist in teaching the concept and, thus, the structure of metric units of length differently, thus highlighting the need for the measurement scale and unit system. DSR usually involves the creation of an artifact and a design theory (in the case of the research interest presented here: technology-supported learning environments, including an AR app) to extend and optimize the current state of practice as well as existing research knowledge [23]. According to Platz [24], the Dortmund Model for subject didactic development research on diagnosis-guided teaching-learning processes for researching and developing teaching [e.g., 22] is combined with the DSR Methodology Process for research and developing Information System Research [e.g., 21] to be able to productively use synergy effects of both approaches for the (further) development of the technology-supported learning environment (see Fig. 1). In this context, the digital media used will be didactically reflected, and further development measures can be proposed. Related to this first empirical pilot study, the impact of a digital AR app embedded in a suitable substantial learning environment [25] was investigated as an artefact to find out whether the use of the digital tool can already contribute to the development of a conceptual understanding of length units, for example by reflecting the process of measurement.

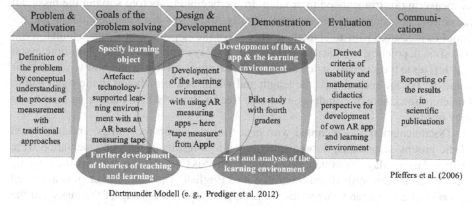

Dortmunder Modell (e. g., Prediger et al. 2012)

Fig. 1. Design Science Research Methodology Process

3.2 General Conditions

The sample consisted of nine female and ten male students in a fourth-grade primary school class in a small town in the federal state of Saarland in Germany. According to the teacher, the children had already dealt with all metric length units of millimeters, centimeters, decimeters, and kilometers in school lessons. At the time of the experiment, the children were about halfway through the fourth year of primary school. The project was carried out on the premises of one of our cooperation partners. The group of 19 pupils was divided into two groups after a joint introduction to the history of mathematics. After about 60 min, both groups swapped so that all children participated in each learning session.

3.3 Learning Tasks and Augmented Reality App

The students were asked to complete a self-developed exercise book with tasks in the field of measuring lengths and converting lengths. For this purpose, they were repeatedly given tasks they were allowed to work on alone or with the person sitting next to them. The exercise book contains twelve pages and can be divided into three sections. The first task was a classical text task for the area of conversion. The second task was another text task where they had to size conception and conversion, and finally, several tasks for conversion without factual context, which the children were allowed to work on during waiting times or at the end. The first and the second task will be described and presented in more detail in the following.

The first task was determining how many partial strings would be created for a 0.8-m-long string if 95 mm long pieces were always cut off. The students first had to calculate the task alone and then compare their solutions wither their partner and check their solutions with the help of the material provided. Therefore, every student had a pencil, an eraser, and a booklet. Together both students had a scissor, the 0.8-m-long string, and they had a ruler, a tape measure, and the tablet with the "tape measure" app as measuring instruments on their table. In the beginning, before solving the tasks, all measuring instruments were presented equally, and it was discussed again how lengths could be measured with all of them. In the case of the "tape measure" app, a joint tutorial was shown, pointing out that the app can only display centimeters and not millimeters. It was left up to the students to decide which measuring tool to use and how to check their solution. For the second task, the length and width of a whiteboard in the room had to be determined; here, the students were also free to choose which measuring instrument they used.

Documentation was recorded with observations, audio recordings, and inspection of the groups' transcripts. Subsequently, the initial results of the implementation were analyzed using Mayring's qualitative content analysis [26]. For this purpose, the acoustic recordings are transcribed and translated into English. Then the transcript is analyzed in terms of content, and categories are generated. The processing of the tasks and the manageability of the app should provide conclusions about the design of the future learning environment and the AR app.

4 First Results

The presentation of results is presented in two sections. First, general criteria for using and handling the AR app are derived. For this purpose, the editing tasks with the tablet are analyzed based on the student exercise book. Subsequently, a more detailed analysis of the procedure a pair of students for the first task is presented, and these criteria are also considered.

The analysis of the children's written results shows that only one pair of students used the tablet in the first task. The rest of the children used the analog tape measure and scissors to check the total cord length and the partial cords' determination. In the second task, 13 of the 19 children measured the length and width of the whiteboard. Nine children indicated in the exercise book that they used the tablet (iPad) as a measuring instrument. One child stated that she had used both the tablet and the traditional tape measure, and three children made no statement. The measurement results of the tablet varied considerably, although all children used the same app and tablet.

The results of the exercise book show that two of the 13 children did not specify a unit of measurement, and three children only wrote a unit for one measured value (width or height). When specifying the unit of measurement, one pair of students gave the result in centimeters instead of meters. This is interesting because the AR app displays the measurement result in the value number and appropriate unit of measurement. However, transcribing the measurement result was impossible because the students had to stand up to measure the whiteboard. After the measuring process, they returned to their table to write the result in their exercise book. Between measuring and writing down, the units could have been confused, as first, the result is shown in centimeters up to 99 cm, and then the comma notation for meters and centimeters (e.g., 1.02 m) is displayed. Overall, therefore, only six of the thirteen children who worked on the task indicated the appropriate unit of measurement for the measurement number, although even the digital tool displays the correct unit of measurement for the value number.

The variance in the results may be due to the different handling of the digital measuring instruments. Observations showed that the children sometimes moved the tablet too quickly, making the measurements inaccurate. Some results deviated strongly from the actual measurement result of the whiteboard width and height. In one observation, for example, it was found that a pair of students had measured 70 cm for the width of the board, although it was 1.80 m long. The children were about to write the result in their exercise book when the teacher approached the pair again and asked them if this measured value could be correct. Only on this occasion did the students reflect on their results and measure again with the tablet and the traditional tape measure. On the one hand, this shows that the results found are not necessarily reflected and simply assumed to be true, and on the other hand that, analogous to other materials, the use and handling of digital applications must also be learned and should not be taken for granted. Often the feedback from the AR app "tape measure" in the form of text (e. g. move slower, reduce distance, etc.) was either not perceived, ignored, or not understood by the students. The more detailed analysis of a talk between a group of two boys showed similar results by using the AR app. As the only pair of students, the two boys decided to use the tablet to check their calculations of the first task. Before they can start measuring, however, some difficulties arise in using the app. These will be analyzed below using an excerpt of the transcript (see Table 1).

The transcript shows that the students are waiting for a signal that the measurement can start (see Table 1, line 4). Therefore, a crosshair becomes visible, and a starting point can be selected. However, the tablet must first scan the room, so it must be moved back and forth slowly. This could be why the students get the feedback from the tablet that it has to be moved slower (see Table 1, lines 9, 12, 14). The conversation shows that they are trying to follow the instruction, but they still do not know the problem of why they cannot start measuring. Student 2 (S2) gives the approach to move the tablet back and forth again (see Table 1, line 11) or to change the distance to the object to be measured (see Table 1. line 15). The teacher (T) also provides this as an aid. At the end of the dialog, the button's function to select the starting point is explained. Here, the start point must be fixed with the crosshairs through the camera, and then, at the same time, a button placed on the right side of the display must be pressed to select the start point. This might have caused a problem for student 1 (S1) by trying to click directly on the crosshair instead of the button, and thus a selection was not possible (see Table 1, line 27). They have problems keeping the proper distance to the object to be measured and timing when they are allowed to begin measuring.

Table 1. Transcription of a group of two boys, which uses the AR app "tape measure"

01	S1:	the cord (.) there we have to#
02	S2:	#no first move a bit in space (..) she said
03	S1:	< (S1 clicks on the tablet)
04	S1:	<no S2 (..) first move in the room (.) then when the signal comes#
05	S1:	#move in the room (.) ok (4s)
06	S2:	may I just/
07	S1:	no (.) I do move in the room
08	S2:	but I want to try out something briefly
09 10	S1:	No (.) It says slow down (..) this is supposed to be the surface (.) is that correct/
11	S2:	(..) back and forth like this
12	S1:	it says slow down
13	S2:	yees (...)
14	S1:	it says **slow down**
15	S2:	Maybe you have to go a little further away/
16	S1:	hm (..) table (not understandable)
17	S2:	may I now too S1/
18 19	T:	(T1 goes to the children) maybe it works better if you go a little further away
20 21 22	S1:	I don't understand this tablet (...) there's another thing now (.) that doesn't work (.) it says slow down all the time (.) ah (.) move the surface (.) eh move iPad
		[…]
23	S1:	< I do move it (.) yes I do move it
24	S2:	oh man (.) I know yet
25	S1:	<no (.) it says iPad continues to move (.) oh man
26	S2:	so I think you should press on it
27	S1:	what do you think I'm doing/ not pressing it or what/
28	S2:	oh (.) may I not just take a look too/

(interrupt = #; speaking directly = <; questing = /; breaks: (.) = 1 sec., (..) = 2 sec., (...) = 3 sec., more than 3 sec. = (number of seconds)

In total, it took the two students four and a half minutes until they could start with the first measurement. This is mainly because although the app displays feedback on how to use it, it is very general. They were aware of the app's instructions but did not know how to implement them correctly, as the app did not give them any visual or auditive feedback. This should be considered in the developed app so that the students can start measuring independently and initial frustration is counteracted.

In general, it can be stated that the used AR app has a very clear design in the presentation of the functions. The students had no problems with the process of measuring. Only before they could start with the measurement, it was noticed that the information in text form led to excessive demand. This was particularly evident in the misunderstandings between the two boys, who repeatedly tried to implement the instructions. This succeeded, however, only very slowly after a larger duration with repeated trying out. The results of the experiment with the students combined with the knowledge of the theoretical background will be used to adapt the design in the form of additional or modified features that a proposed AR app should have to promote conceptual understanding of units of length in a technically supported learning environment.

5   Proposed Augmented Reality App

To present the proposed AR app, we will first look at the technical modification with a focus on the experiment with the students. From practical experience and our investigation, it can be stated that children can be distracted quickly. For this reason, it is important to mention as an essential requirement that our app receives only necessary functions compared to many AR measurement tools existing on the market. In addition, information displayed to children in text form can be overwhelming. This was also evident in the results, in that children often did not know what to do with prompts such as "move slowly" or "reduce distance." They were confused about at what point they were allowed to start measuring. In the new app's design, this problem will be improved by using colors to signal when it is allowed to begin measuring. The classic signal colors red, yellow, and green are used for this purpose. If the color is red, no measurement can take place because the environment has not been scanned long enough or the distance between the digital end device and the object to be measured is too great. The color yellow indicates that, for example, the distance has been reduced, and measurement will soon be possible, and in the case of green, the measurement can be started. This way, the user gets feedback at any time on whether an approximate measurement can succeed or whether something needs to be adjusted. The colors could either be displayed by a bar above the screen or based on the app "AirMeasure - App-Messausrüstung" [27] as a circle directly around the starting point of the measurement (see Fig. 2). The advantage of this is that the students look at the starting point before the measurement anyway. It would therefore be visible directly at the same time. Figure 2 shows an ideal-typical illustration of how the measurement can work.

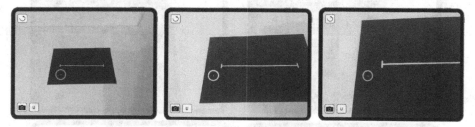

Fig. 2.   Visualization of the starting point with colors (inspired by Laan Labs [27])

The point in the middle serves as the starting point of the measurement touching on it. This was chosen to counteract the simultaneous coordination of selecting the starting point and pressing a button separately, as it works in the AR app "tape measure". After the starting point of the measurement has been determined, a digital measuring tape is displayed. From a mathematics-didactic perspective and to answer the second research question, the presentation of the measurement result without a unit scale did not lead the children to wonder whether the indicated result of the digital device was truly correct. A check, e.g., with the help of an analog measuring tape provided, was only chosen by one pair of two students, which were, however, made aware of this. All the other children entered the result without checking it. The display of the appropriate unit, which could be easily read and memorized with the help of the AR app and then written down in the notebook, was only considered by slightly less than half of the children. With the inclusion of existing theories and teaching approaches to the unit concept of lengths, it was decided that units, as with an analog ruler, the children themselves must take the measurement result using the length scale. However, the advantages of AR should be used so that the developed digital measuring tape can dynamically adjust the scale of the measurement units (see Fig. 3).

For this purpose, the smallest unit of measurement, starting with millimeters, is displayed until the next larger unit can be displayed. That means first nine millimeters are displayed (see Fig. 3a). From the tenth millimeters, one centimeter is shown (see Fig. 3b). Then, millimeters follow again until the next centimeter (2 cm) is displayed (see Fig. 3c). We decided that ten centimeters should not be used to indicate one decimeter since children from the second grade onwards first learn millimeters and centimeters. In addition, decimeters are no longer a topic in many mathematics schoolbooks in Germany. Nevertheless, we see the relevance of continuing to teach decimeters since the structure of the metric system of units is comprehensible. However, it could lead to confusion at this point. To discuss decimeters anyway, it was decided to display the view of conversions after completing the measurement process. So, when the end of the measurement has been set with the end of the measuring tape, the entire measurement can be viewed, as with almost all apps, by having the user move the digital end device away from the object (see Fig. 3d).

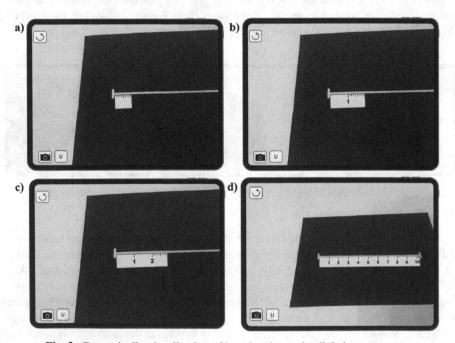

Fig. 3. Dynamically visualization of length units on the digital tape measure

To pick up standardized metric units of measurement, the AR measurement app is to be developed so that desired units can be shown and hidden so that conversions of measurement numbers and units of measurement are visualized (see Fig. 4). For this purpose, there will be a button with which the length units millimeters, centimeters, decimeters, and meters are faded in. By pressing the buttons, the scale can be flexibly changed, and individual units of measurement can be shown (see Fig. 4a). With this function is possible to show the scale of the measuring tape in decimeters and faded out millimeters and centimeters (see Fig. 4b).

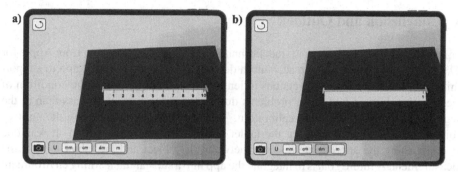

Fig. 4. Visualization of the conversion of length units

Another issue for the students was dealing with inaccuracies in the app's measurement results. The students are only used to inaccurate measurements with a ruler or tape measure, which they cause themselves by, e.g., inaccurate application. However, with the digital AR app, other factors independent of the user can influence the measurement result, such as light influences or the app's program. Of course, the user can also affect the measurement result by, e.g., performing the measurement too quickly or changing the distance during the measurement. To reduce these problems as far as possible, it is essential that the children first learn how to use the AR measuring tape. In addition, the issue of dealing with inaccuracies can be reduced by visualizing the units. Thus, the units of the analog ruler can be compared with the digital tape measure's digital units to see if they are consistent. In addition, the tasks of the learning environment should be adapted in the future so that it is more about the understanding of units and the conversion of measurement units than about exact measurements of objects.

Consequently, the tasks in the example must be adapted because they relied on exact measurements to solve the first task correctly. When working on the second task, somewhat approximate results were required. If we look at the results again, it is noticeable that the students did not reconsider the results read from the AR tape measure but mostly just used them. This could be a starting point for a joint discussion and support basic representations. Related to the answer to the first question, how a learning environment should be designed, it can be stated that by itself the measured result is not checked for the use of units. Consequently, the one additional common reflection must be stimulated to draw attention to the need for units. Suppose a student receives a very unrealistic result due to incorrect use and assumes this result to be correct. In that case, it could be concluded that he or she does not have sufficient support point ideas to estimate the result down to an approximate value. Subsequently, the result of different measuring instruments could be compared in discussion with the child or all children in the class. Validation, which an overarching competence for assessing and verifying results, could be promoted. Accordingly, with the pure use of the tape measure app, it can be assumed that most students will only question a reflection of the determined values with the digital tool if an additional occasion is provided. The revised app will attempt to create this context by allowing the measurement process to be discussed during the selection of units and their visualization.

6 Conclusion and Outlook

This study aimed to find out how students handle the "tape measure" app from Apple for iOS to take the knowledge into account in developing an optimized AR app to support children in understanding conversions in length units. It shows that in the condition of the app, the children had fewer problems during the measurement process than at the beginning of the measurement calibration. This was not due to selecting the starting point by simultaneously moving the tablet and clicking the start button. It was due to establishing the appropriate distance between the object and the tablet to start the measurement. A future goal is to integrate the app into a substantial learning environment where the children use it as much as possible independently to make their mathematical explorations. However, this means that to enable independent use we must ensure that children know when to start measuring.

Looking back at the tasks of this study, tasks with approximated measurement results should be selected for the use of AR measurement instruments existing on the market since the measurement instruments display the measurement result and do not focus on the measurement process [18]. It can be deduced that the tasks of the learning environment must be chosen appropriately. In this study, the first task would require a precise measurement to arrive at a result. However, the digital AR measuring instrument is not designed for this purpose. The different applications depending on the length measuring instrument must be discussed with the students, e.g., by comparing and discussing the measurement results. This, in turn, means that the learning environment must be designed so that the students' findings should be reflected together afterwards. In this regard, Drake [16, p. 30] says, "giving classroom rulers to students and teaching how to use them is not enough-rulers are simply too variable for a 'one size fits all' approach. Students must develop conceptual understanding. […] Contexts for measurement should also be carefully chosen as length measurement is a situated activity; that is, the choice of tool and unit depends on what is being measured." Consequently, measurement tools and the tasks of a learning environment must be appropriately chosen. If the measurement process and the unit system's structure are to be visualized to establish conceptual understanding, then the app should be extended. To this purpose, the app should be further developed by exploiting the full potential of AR technology by allowing it to fade units in and out individually. From a future perspective, other unit systems (e.g., the United States customary system) could be visualized or, in secondary school, unit squares for area content or unit cubes for volume [28]. However, it should be emphasized again that the analog material is never replaced, but only another form is used as a new measuring instrument besides the conventional ones. To what extent does the visualization of the units change? We will test the insight into the unit concept in future studies.

References

1. National Council of Teachers of Mathematics (NCTM): Principles and Standards for School Mathematics. NTCM, Reston (2000)
2. Kultusministerkonferenz (KMK): Bildungsstandards im Fach Mathematik für die allgemeine Hochschulreife. Beschluss vom 18.10.2012. (2012). https://www.kmk.org/fileadmin/veroef fentlichungen_beschluesse/2012/2012_10_18-Bildungsstandards-Mathe-Abi.pdf. Accessed 26 March 2023
3. Kultusministerkonferenz (KMK): Bildungsstandards im Fach Mathematik für den Primarbereich. Beschluss vom 15.10.2004 i.d.F. vom 23.06.2022. Luchterhand, München (2022a). https://www.kmk.org/fileadmin/veroeffentlichungen_beschluesse/2022/2022_06_23-Bista-Primarbereich-Mathe.pdf. Accessed 26 March 2023
4. Kultusministerkonferenz (KMK): Bildungsstandrds für das Fach Mathematik. Erster Schulabschluss (ESA) und Mittlerer Schulabschluss (MSA) (2022b). https://www.kmk.org/fileadmin/ veroeffentlichungen_beschluesse/2022/2022_06_23-Bista-ESA-MSA-Mathe.pdf. Accessed 26 March 2023
5. Cebesoy, Ü.B., Yeniterzi, B.: 7th grade students' mathematical difficulties in force and motion unit. Turkish J. Educ. **5**(1), 18–30 (2016). https://doi.org/10.19128/turje.06150
6. Jua, S.K., Sarwanto, S., Sukarmin, S.: The profile of students' problem-solving skill in physics across interest program in the secondary school. J. Phys. Conf. Ser. **1022**(1), 1–8 (2018). https://doi.org/10.1088/1742-6596/1022/1/012027
7. Lassnitzer, E., Gaidoschik, M.: Größen: Messen – Schätzen – Umwandeln. Sicherheit durch Begreifen – Anregungen für einen verständnisorientieren Unterricht. http://www.rec heninstitut.at/mathematische-lernschwierigkeiten/fordertips/umwandeln-von-maseinheiten/. Accessed 26 March 2023
8. Reinhold, S., Franke, M.: Didaktik der Geometrie, 3rd edn. Springer, Heidelberg (2016)
9. Franke, M., Ruwisch, S.: Didaktik des Sachrechnens in der Grundschule, 2nd edn. Spektrum, Heidelberg (2010)
10. Bragg, P., Outhred, L.: Students' knowledge of length units: Do they know more than rules about rulers? In: Nakahara, T., Koyama, M. (eds.) Proceedings of the 24th Conference of the International Group for the Psychology of Mathematics Education, pp. 97–104. Hiroshima, Hiroshima University (2000)
11. Kloosterman, P., Rutledge, Z., Kenney, P.: Exploring results of the NAEP: 1980s to the present: results of the long-term trend assessment (LTT) for middle grades show positive advancement. Math. Teach. Middle School **14**(6), 357–365 (2009). https://doi.org/10.5951/ MTMS.14.6.0357
12. Stephan, M., Clements, D.H.: Linear and area measurement in prekindergarten to grade 2. In: Clements, D.H. (ed.), Learning and teaching measurement, pp. 3–16. National Council of Teachers of Mathematics (2003)
13. Clements, D.H., Samara, J.: Learning and Teaching Early Math: The Learning Trajectories Approach. Routledge, New York, London (2009)
14. Zöllner, J.: Längenkonzepte von Kindern im Elementarbereich. Springer Fachmedien Wiesbaden, Wiesbaden (2020). https://doi.org/10.1007/978-3-658-27671-3
15. Peter-Koop, A.: Messkompetenzen und Längenvorstellungen entwickeln. Mathematik differenziert **4**, 6–8 (2011)

16. Drake, M.: Learning to measure length. The problem with the school ruler. Austral. Prim. Math. Classroom **19**(3), 27–32 (2014)
17. Zöllner, J., Reuter, F.: Wie messen Kinder? Überlegungen zur Einheit beim Messen. Fördermagazin Grundschule **4**, 19–24 (2018)
18. Müller, L.M., Platz, M.: Von den Ellenstäben hin zu Augmented Reality. Vergangenheit, Gegenwart, Zukunft – Die (Weiter-)Entwicklung von Messinstrumenten. In: Digitaler Mathematikunterricht in Forschung und Praxis. Tagungsband zur Vernetzungstagung 2022, Mathematiklernen mit digitalen Medien 3, Universität Siegen (in print)
19. Medienpädagogischer Forschungsverbund Südwest (mpfs): KIM-Studie 2020. Kindheit, Internet, Medien (2022). https://www.mpfs.de/fileadmin/files/Studien/KIM/2020/KIM-Stu die2020_WEB_final.pdf. Accessed 26 March 2023
20. Baller, S., Dutta, S., Lanvin, B.: The Global Information Technology Report 2016. Innovating in the Digital Econonmy (2016). https://www3.weforum.org/docs/GITR2016/WEF_GITR_F ull_Report.pdf. Accessed 26 March 2023
21. Peffers, K., et al.: The design science research process: a model for producing and presenting information systems research. In: Proceedings of the First International Conference on Design Science Research in Information Systems and Technology, pp. 83–106 (2006)
22. Prediger, S., Link, M., Hinz, R., Hußmann, S., Thiele, J., Ralle, B.: Lehr-Lernprozesse initiieren und erforschen – Fachdidaktische Entwicklungsforschung im Dortmunder Modell. Der mathematische und naturwissenschaftliche Unterricht **65**(8), 452–457 (2012)
23. Vaishnavi, V., Kuechler, W., Petter, S.: Design Science Research in Information Systems. January 20, 2004 (updated until 2019 by Vaishnavi, V. & Kuechler, W.) (2019). http://www.desrist.org/design-research-in-information-systems/. Accessed 26 March 2023
24. Platz M.: „Forscher spielen" und mathematisches Beweisen in der Primarstufe. transfer Forschung - Schule 2020 **6**, 30–43 (2020)
25. Wittmann, C.E.: Design und Erforschung von Lernumgebungen als Kern der Mathematikdidaktik. Beiträge zur Lehrerbildung **16**, 329–342 (1998)
26. Mayring, P.: Qualitative Inhaltsanalyse. Grundlagen und Techniken. Beltz, Basel (2010)
27. Laan Labs: AirMeasure - App-Messausrüstung. iOS App Store (2020)
28. Mueller, L.M., Platz, M.: Visualization of area units with augmented reality. In: Immersive Learning Research Network (iLRN) Online Conference Proceedings, pp. 143–145 (2022)

Know the Knowledge of Your Students: A Flexible Analytics Tool for Student Exercises

Sören Aguirre Reid[ID], Frank Kammer[ID], Daria Schüller[ID], Markus Siepermann[ID], and Jonas Wölfer[✉][ID]

Technische Hochschule Mittelhessen, Wiesenstraße 14, 35390 Gießen, Germany
{Soeren.Aguirre.Reid,Frank.Kammer,Daria.Schueller,Markus.Siepermann, Jonas.Woelfer}@mni.thm.de

Abstract. Intelligent tutoring systems (ITS) have the power to influence lecturers' practices in the classroom and to improve students' learning. Many ITS provide standardized analytical methods to evaluate classroom performance or the results of the exercises. But they lack more sophisticated, flexible and individual analyses. This paper presents an e-learning Analytics Tool (EAT) for an ITS that provides a dashboard with key figures and a flexible analytics board (FAB). This enables lecturers to analyze students' performance in detail and identify misconceptions. For instance, the FAB allows us to classify student solutions, reveal conceptual errors in exercises, and analyze each part of an exercise. By this, common mistakes can be identified, and tailored feedback can be given to the students. Following the design science approach, the platform is designed in a general way so that it can be used for different types of exercises (e.g., Math, Excel, SQL). To assess the artifact, we conducted group interviews with German University lecturers from various courses. The results show that lecturers require a good overview of the submitted student solutions to provide timely feedback. They also appreciate the flexible analytics tool for detailed analyses of student solutions to understand student mistakes better. The employed architecture allows general analyses of exercises and the content of students' solutions. In addition, the EAT is not bound to a specific kind of exercise, but can cope with different kinds like SQL and Excel.

Keywords: Intelligent Tutoring System · ITS · Learning Analytics and Evaluation · Dashboard · Flexible Analysis

1 Introduction

E-Learning platforms mainly support five different kinds of tasks: (1) course administration, (2) provision of course material, (3) communication and cooperation, (4) providing exercises for practicing, as well as (5) assessment and grading [36]. Platforms for categories 1 and 2 like Blackboard, Canvas, Moodle, Ilias, or WEB-CT exist for many years. By and by, they have been extended with additional features of categories 3, 4 and 5. However, particularly category 4 still

A. Gerber and R. Baskerville (Eds.): DESRIST 2023, LNCS 13873, pp. 329–344, 2023.
https://doi.org/10.1007/978-3-031-32808-4_21

remains underdeveloped. Mostly, simple types of exercises are implemented like multiple-choice or fill-in-the-blank. More sophisticated exercises are left to specialized platforms, known as Intelligent Tutoring Systems (ITS). ITS provide challenging exercises that are mostly specialized to a certain field of application like mathematical conversion (e.g. [29]), graphical modeling (e.g. [35,37]), or SQL (e.g. [27]) etc. Nowadays, students' submissions are no longer just classified as correct or wrong. Students receive a detailed analysis of their submission stating which parts are incorrect and why. Such a detailed analysis helps students to better understand the learning subject so that they can improve their skills.

While students are the number one addressee of ITS, also the needs of lecturers are considered beyond the possibilities of easily providing exercises, which are automatically reviewed and assessed. This certainly relieves lecturers from a huge amount of recurring standard tasks. But apart from that, ITS can accommodate lecturers with information about students, courses, and exercises. No matter what kinds of exercises are provided, there is a lot of data concerning the usage of the system or the processing of the exercises by students. Provided that this data is analyzed in the right way, valuable insights concerning the learning behavior of students, their level of knowledge and individual performance in the course, the general status of courses but also concerning single exercises and subsequently the knowledge transfer of lectures can be generated. Already the detailed analysis of individual student submissions helps lecturers with providing feedback on students' performance. This in turn improves and accelerates students' learning processes and empowers them as self-regulated learners [31].

However, most ITS provide only general (meta-)information concerning courses [4,16,32], students and exercises [10,23]. The students' solutions are usually not analyzed and interpreted. Although ITS try to "understand" the content of a student solution so that they can give detailed feedback to students, they hardly use the content of students' solutions for advanced analyses (see also next section). The most advanced analysis of data collected by ITS consists in the forecast of possible grades based on the historic performance a student has shown during a course [10,18]. This is quite surprising as Business Intelligence methods are mature, widely known and applied in business applications ([5], p. 1–3). There exist standard procedures that can be adapted to the context of e-learning [34]. Whatsoever, existing ITS do not compare student solutions, do not provide any filter for a deeper analysis of solutions not to mention an analysis of which solutions parts are often done wrong.

Interestingly, although general metrics like the number of attempts, or the average processing time, cannot only be used for one course or exercise, but on an aggregated level for a set of courses and among exercises used in different courses, existing ITS even do not provide this feature. Yet, such information on an aggregated level and/or as a time series can provide interesting insights to lecturers. Lecturers usually try to improve their teaching and change explanations and teaching methods. In addition, courses may be divided into subgroups taught by different lecturers. Hence, information aggregating different courses and/or exercises over time can be helpful to lecturers to better adjust their teaching methods. Thus, this paper aims to answer the following research questions:

RQ1: Which kind of analyses of student solutions are useful for lecturers?
RQ2: How can such analyses be realized in a generalized analytics tool?
RQ3: How can different exercises be analyzed in a unified way?

To answer these research questions, we developed an e-learning Analytics Tool (EAT) that acts as an add-on for ITS. Our implementation is open source and can be found at github [14]. Particularly, EAT is built for SQL and Excel exercises but can be adapted to analog kinds of exercises like programming or mathematical transformations. EAT is an IT-artifact that provides general key performance indicators (KPI) concerning courses, exercises, and students and allows sophisticated analyses of the student solutions with regard to their content. It consists of two parts: a dashboard that displays pre-calculated KPIs and a flexible analytics board with which it is possible to analyze student solutions in detail concerning solution parts that were done right or wrong. The analyses can be done for courses, exercises, students, and different time periods without limitations in any of those dimensions. They are not bound to a specific kind of exercise, but can easily be transferred to new types of exercises. However, we will demonstrate EAT for SQL exercises. In addition, the analyses are flexible and can be defined by any lecturer. The analyses are oriented to classic BI systems and therefore allow the commonly known BI functions like drill-down etc. To the best of our knowledge, EAT is the first analytics tool that provides BI analyses to lecturers which focus on the content of student solutions and not only the metadata of courses, exercises, and student performance.

For the development of the IT-artifact, we used the design science approach (DSA) introduced by Hevner et al. [19]. For this, we orientated to the DSA processes of Conboy, Gleasure, and Cullina [8] and Peffers et al. [30] as well as to the recommendations given by Gregor and A. Hevner [17]. Hence, the remainder of this paper is organized as follows: In the next section, we review the related literature and which analytic tools have already been introduced in ITS. In Sect. 3, requirements for the IT-artifact are derived, and the architecture of EAT is presented. Particularly, as the analyses of EAT are not restricted to a special kind of exercises, a general representation of e-learning exercises has to be developed. Additionally, some technical solutions are chosen. Section 4 introduces the IT-artifact in detail which is evaluated in Sect. 5 by interviewing 16 lecturers. The paper closes with a discussion of the results and an outlook on future developments.

2   Related Work on Intelligent Tutoring Systems

2.1   Structured Literature Review

For the structured literature review [38,39], we developed the relevant key terms for the search string and identified the database for our structured literature review in the first step. In the second step, we run the literature review with the following search string for published journal papers and conference proceedings between 2010 and 2021: *"("Intelligent Tutoring System OR Learning Analytics*

("Intelligent Tutoring System" AND "Learning Analytics") OR ("Learning Analytics" AND "Dashboard") OR ("Intelligent Tutoring System" AND "Dashboard") OR ("Intelligent Tutoring System" AND "Education") OR ("Learning Analytics" AND "Education") OR ("Intelligent Tutoring System" AND "Feedback") OR ("Learning Analytics" AND "Feedback") OR ("Dashboard" AND "Education")".
In total, we identified 393 publications. After excluding duplicates and non-peer-reviewed papers, the analysis of title and abstract reduced the number of papers to 64 that were read entirely. Of these 64 papers, only 16 papers are relevant for our study. An additional backward and forward search found four additional publications leading to a total of 20 relevant publications.

2.2 Literature Discussion

Former studies investigated the application of an analytics tool for e-learning exercises in different courses like math courses [1, 20, 28, 42], information system courses [3, 4, 9, 21], computer science and programming courses [2, 10, 16, 18, 23, 32] and general science courses [6, 7, 11, 13, 25, 26]. However, all studies used generic KPIs for the analysis like the number of participants, downloaded course material, the number of text messages between students [4, 16, 32], usage of group work or comment options [6, 7, 10, 16, 23, 32, 42], students course working activity in hours, the processing time for an exercise, results (correctness) of students submission, or the number of code posts or commits [10, 23]. Although such generic KPIs are applicable for different courses or exercises, none of the former studies investigated this aspect of aggregation but solely on one single course.

Furthermore, former studies neither tried to analyze the content of student solutions nor utilized flexible adjustable metrics (e.g., drill-downs). Subsequently, analyses of multiple exercises types (e.g., Excel, SQL) also do not exist. In contrast, EAT focuses on the content of student solutions and analyzes for example the different parts of a submitted SQL query. This helps lecturers identify typical mistakes like students' misunderstanding of the GROUP BY clause. Instead, platforms of former studies can only sort students' results according to their exercise performance (pass or fail) [1, 2, 4, 7, 10, 11, 13, 18, 20, 21, 28, 32, 42], filter exercises which create the most problems generally [20, 42], calculate average performance of students regarding the exercises [20, 42], count the number of trials, or show the course progress of students [2, 4, 13]. Only two studies [10, 18] utilized a more sophisticated approach to forecast the students' final result based on their current course performance.

3 Objectives, Requirements and Architecture

3.1 Objectives

The main goal of EAT is to support lecturers with useful information about their courses and to provide them with a flexible analytics tool with which it is possible to examine the content of student solutions in depth. An EAT shall help lecturers to get a complete picture of students' knowledge and summarize the evaluation and assessment of student solutions. The assessment of student solutions (e.g. by running SQL queries on test databases, comparing the structure and formulas of an excel sheet, or executing unit tests on student programs) is not done by EAT but provided to EAT by the underlying ITS.

In more detail, the requirements can be distinguished into *general requirements* and *specific analysis abilities*. The *general requirements* comprise usability and technical factors. An ITS should be user-friendly, ease of use and simple [24]. But, usability does not only mean that the tool is easy to use but content wise that it delivers immediate benefits for the lecturer with standard analyses (e.g., overview of processing rates of exercises) which answer typical questions of the lecturer (see Sect. 4.1). Often, standard analyses can be tailored with the help of further parameters. But too many such parameters make a frontend confusing. Hence, parameters should initially be set to useful default values. Only in a separate display, additional parameters should be adaptable. (For similar reasons, almost all search sites have a standard search and an advanced search [40]) Then, individual, flexible in-depth analyses can start from this second display on [32]. Like business information, e-learning data and the according in-depth analyses can become very complex ([5], p. 113). Also, the data volume is quite big. During one course, it is not uncommon that several ten thousand data sets are generated. Hence, suitable methods are necessary to cope with this complexity. Business Intelligence (BI) has brought up several techniques like Pivot Tables and Pivot Charts with which it is possible to summarize, analyze, explore, and present complex data accordingly. Therefore, an EAT for ITS should orientate to these well-established methods (see Sect. 3.2) in order to ensure acceptable performance of analyses within a few seconds ([5], p. 112).

This also helps to deal with different exercise types. The EAT presented in this paper is not bound to one but several types (e.g. SQL, Excel, mathematics). Thus, the user interface, the underlying analysis architecture and data structure have to be generic so that different data can be stored, processed and analyzed.

The specific *analysis abilities* concern the content of analyses, i.e. what kind of information should be provided so that lecturers are supported in the teaching task. Besides a quick overview of what happens in courses (e.g. [7]), answers to the following questions are frequently demanded.

- Which mistakes occur most often? What is the share of students who understood the topic? [20,42]
- How many attempts and time do students need for solving an exercise? [7]
- How many students have solved which exercises? Which are difficult? [20]
- What are the expected (final) results of students based on their current performance concerning the exercises? [10,18]

3.2 Evaluation Platform Architecture

A main requirement for the analytics tool is to deal with different kinds of exercises. This can be compared with an integration of different information systems into one analytics solution. In both cases, the data of the different sources may differ greatly. Therefore, a generic architecture is needed with which it is possible to incorporate all the different data from different sources. A common approach to solve this problem is to use a reference architecture. However, in the area of learning analytics, we only found the concept of a value chain [34] which does not suit the needs of EAT.

Therefore, we employ a so-called data warehouse used for BI systems to get a single point of view (SPOT) combining all relevant data. A common reference architecture for BI systems is described in [33]. It consists of so-called *source systems*, a *data warehouse system* and a *BI platform* for data analyses. The *source systems* are the systems that generate the data to be analyzed. The *data warehouse system* is composed of four layers. First, incoming data is loaded from a *staging area* and restructured/corrected in a *cleansing area* before being stored in a *core* in a subject-oriented manner. In preparation for evaluation data is aggregated and stored in *data marts*. In addition, the architecture consists of a meta-data manager that stores information on all operations with a timestamp.

Comparing the BI reference architecture with our use case EAT, the source systems are represented by the different exercise types which are realized by so-called checkers in the underlying ITS. These contain the business logic for assessing student exercise submissions and provide the results in a database. APIs to the ITS are the staging area in EAT. The cleansing area has the goal to prepare the data. In other words, the process consists of two core aspects. The first is the detection and correction of defects within the data. Much more important is the second point, the transfer into a generic data schema. Technically, the cleansing area of a BI system and EAT is very similar.

The part of EAT corresponding to the BI core is the database where all information is stored. The data scheme is depicted in Fig. 1. Exercises belong to courses which lie in the responsibility of lecturers. Students can submit solutions to an exercise. As exercises can be of different subjects (e.g. SQL, Excel) with different structures, solutions (i.e. submissions) to an exercise are generically deconstructed into their basic parts, called attributes. Attributes are subject specific. In the case of SQL exercises (e.g. "SELECT * FROM employees"), a possible attribute can represent the table names of an SQL query. Thus, the characteristic "attribute" of the class "Attribute" gets the value "tables". The tables that are really used in a solution are then stored in the characteristic "values", in our example, characteristic "value" has the value "employees". Whether the attribute can be used to get a valid solution is stored in the "status" field. This helps to analyze if parts of solutions are correct or wrong. With this deconstruction of exercise parts, it is possible to represent different exercise types within the model and to analyze the exercises then in a unique way.

The counterpart of data marts in the BI world, is the analytics level of EAT. First, analysis-related subsets are extracted from the core and made available. Aggregated key figures are calculated in order to make them instantly available. As is also common in BI systems, there is also a metadata management in place. This is important, for example, in order to record the checker versions used to evaluate the student solutions. In this way, the evaluation of student solutions can be updated if a better checker is available. Furthermore, the evaluation data

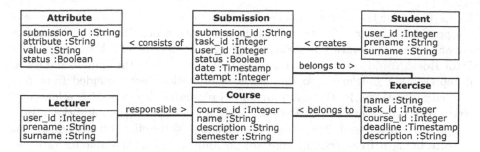

Fig. 1. Generic Data Model

is considered as a so-called *slowly changing dimension* of *Type 2* where a BI system stores history data on all information. In doing so, the progress in the checkers can be analyzed, too.

3.3 Capabilities for an E-Learning Analytics Tool (EAT)

For the realization of the functional requirements, several technical solutions already exist that differ in several aspects. Therefore, the following technical requirements have been set up to choose an application that suits EAT:

Embedding. The application should be able to be integrated into an existing web application in order to be able to use EAT within the ITS.

Customizing. In particular, it is important that the graphical components can be adapted to the existing design in the ITS system. In addition to visual integration, the product must be technically integrable into the existing frontend.

Data Volume. Various interface options should allow for the connection of any data source. Data size should not be a limiting factor in any way that confines the usability of potential data sources.

License Model. The application should be free of charge as this increases the attractiveness and usability and because the existing ITS is also open source.

Functional Requirements. The application should enable the graphical display of data, the visualization in the form of tables as well as complex filtering without having to resort to other applications.

Based on these requirements, KNIME (Individual)[1], Grafana (Free)[2], PlotlyJS[3], ChartJS[4], WebDataRocks[5], and Plotly Dash[6] were analyzed to evaluate their usage for EAT. Any available paid functions were not taken into account.

---

[1] https://www.knime.com/.
[2] https://grafana.com/.
[3] https://plotly.com/javascript/.
[4] https://www.chartjs.org/.
[5] https://www.webdatarocks.com/.
[6] https://plotly.com/dash/.

In particular the license model is a limiting factor. KNIME and Grafana cannot provide the desired functions in the free variants. Since PlotlyJS and ChartJS are only charting libraries, these must be supplemented by a table function. Web Data Rocks could serve as such a table tool, but due to the limited data size it represents a bottleneck so that these combinations are excluded from further considerations. PlotlyDash provides all requested features. It is a low-code framework programmed with Python. Being not an application, additional programming efforts result. Nonetheless, this has a positive effect on customization. Despite being a free version, there are no limitations on the amount of data. These large quantities can also be processed efficiently and in real time. The Dash DataTable module enables pivot tables to be displayed, which offer a second form of analysis in addition to the integrated graphics. The development of the prototype is therefore carried out in Plotly Dash.

4   The E-Learning Analytics Tool (EAT)

4.1   Dashboard for General Information

The first part of EAT consists of a dashboard where standardized information about courses is presented in a Pivot Table and via a Pivot Chart (see Fig. 2). In the first step, the course(s) and the exercise(s) have to be selected for the analysis. Then, a key figure is chosen and the details of which are displayed in the Pivot Chart. For simplicity, data is not displayed in a time series. Instead, the analysis can be restricted to different time periods (number of attempts, date, semester week) with the help of a slider. This helps to check exercises done during a lesson or to monitor the learning progress during a semester by changing the slider and observing the changes in key figures. The key figures below are supported.

Processing Rate, Average Attempts and Facility Index. These key figures are presented in a matrix showing students (possibly grouped by tutorial, degree program, etc.) in the rows, exercises (possibly grouped by learning target, issue time, etc.) in the columns and the key figures in the cells. At a glance, you can see which exercises are solved by which students and how many attempts students have needed. Student and exercise groups in the matrix allow us to focus on different tutorial and learning goals, respectively. The difficulty index is defined similarly to [15] as the ratio of correct to incorrect submissions. This provides lecturers with an indication if exercises have an appropriate level of difficulty.

Earned Points and Grades. The gradings of the student solutions are also shown in a matrix. Exercises can be subdivided into mandatory, voluntary, and bonus exercises as well as grouped by learning goals, weekly, etc. Moreover, rules can be set up to define when an exam admission or course is passed. For each student, the grading overview shows the result from evaluating the rules and summarizes the points in one exercise group, but one can also see the detailed points.

Typical Errors. To identify typical weaknesses of students and to be able to align a course more precisely to the individual students, lecturers can have a look at the frequency of errors students made when solving exercises. The errors

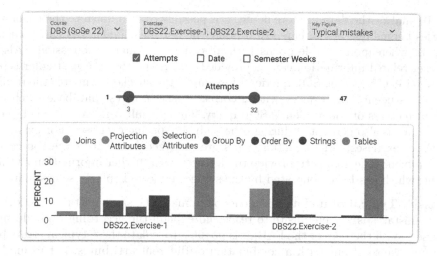

Fig. 2. Dashboard

investigated in the dashboard are specific to an exercise type like SQL or Excel. They correspond to the attributes described in the previous section. For each selected exercise, a bar chart is generated, displaying the percentage of errors for each attribute. There are various additional parameters for better insights.

4.2 Flexible Analytics Board

The Flexible Analytics Board (FAB) allows lecturers to dive deeper into the data than it is possible with the dashboard. Similarly to the dashboard, filters can be defined for courses and exercises. Additionally, it is possible to use filters on subject-specific characteristics. The example shown in Fig. 3 shows a flexible analysis for SQL exercises where the possible SQL-specific attributes are displayed as filters. For Excel, attributes such as specific operators (e.g. sum) are displayed. Regardless of the subject-specific exercises, the various attributes can be moved to a so-called background filter or to the columns.

Background Filter. By adding a background filter, it is possible to set conditions for the displayed data. For example, all erroneous GROUP BY-clauses can be filtered on the condition that the used STRING-comparisons are correct. Thus, attributes GROUP BY and STRING are placed in a background filter. Another background filter is the possibility to filter by the attempts (e.g., consider only attempts 1–3) or by time aspects. This is done similarly to the dashboard but displayed in Fig. 3.

Columns. Attributes can be further analyzed with the help of a bar chart. If one attribute is selected, one bar displays the number of correct and another one the number of incorrect student solutions. If several attributes are included as columns, there is a bar for each possible combination of the attributes.

To analyze the data in more detail, it is possible to drill down to the concrete entries behind one of the bars. To do this, the bar must be clicked (first bar in Fig. 3), whereupon a table opens with all concrete student submissions. Also, checker related information can be provided that is specific to a particular type of exercise. Concerning SQL queries for example, the checker compares the result set of a student's SQL query with a correct query in a test database to check the correctness of the student's SQL query. These result sets can be displayed. Such data is also generated during other subject-specific exercises. For example in Excel exercises, consequential errors are analyzed to identify the source of the problem. The goal is to provide the lecturer with further information at this point, which has been generated by the subject review. Typical use cases are:

Classify Typical Solutions. Students often make the same mistakes. To know these mistakes is a prerequisite to react and explain the according topic during courses. With the help of the FAB, it is possible to isolate these typical errors by filtering the solutions with a combination of different attributes. For example, Fig. 3 shows that students make frequent errors on the Joins attribute. Digging deeper and looking additionally at the tables used in a query, the join mistakes

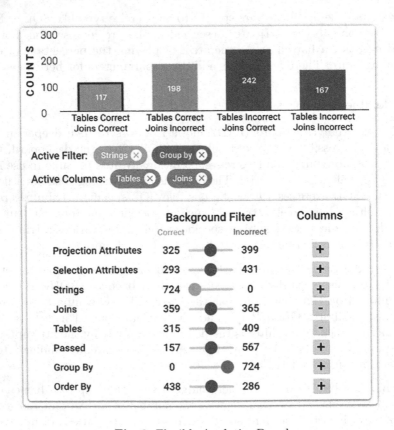

Fig. 3. Flexible Analytics Board

also appear when the correct tables are used. Hence, a misconception of the join clause is quite likely.

Focus on Important Errors and Hide Unimportant Errors. Student mistakes stem from different causes. While some mistakes reveal a lack of understanding of the general concepts, some mistakes are read or transcription errors. To distinguish between these categories, solutions can be filtered by fixing the value of an attribute and moving this attribute to a background filter. Looking again at the example in Fig. 3, before focusing on the join operator, it should be clear that the correct tables are used in the SQL query. Otherwise, the join operator can hardly be correct without using the correct tables. Thus, it makes sense to set tables to "correct" in a background filter before analyzing the joins. In the field of Excel, this function can help to detect the source of errors in case of subsequent errors.

Show Concrete Solutions and/or Explanations. Often, mistakes can easily be seen when looking directly at the student solution. Hence, for SQL, the comparison between the result sets on the test database of a student solution and a correct solution can be very helpful. For Excel, the incorrect fields should be shown with additional information. This includes, for example, a comparison of the dependency structure in the student solution and a correct solution.

5   Evaluation

Following the design science approach, we evaluate the validity and utility of our proposed artifact [17]. The evaluation was conducted in two ways: First, we collected lecturers' comments regarding the artifact with a semi-structured group interview [12]. The group interviews were conducted by two researchers and lasted 10 between 20 min. In each interview, five lecturers participated. Five interviews were conducted online via zoom and seven in presence. Second, after the group interviews, each participating lecturer was invited to fill out the standardized questionnaire regarding the perceived usefulness and value of the artifact. In total, 16 lecturers from two different modules (business administration and information systems: 4; database systems: 12) participated in the group interviews and the questionnaire.

In the group interview section, the lecturers were asked to evaluate their expectations and personal options regarding EAT. Generally, the lectures demand the provision of a good overview of EAT (e.g., to see the submitted exercise or processing time of each student for each exercise). They also expect a high level of ease of use so that their interaction with the artifact is clear. Lecturers want to make only a few settings (e.g., select filters) to analyze students' exercise solutions. Hence, aside from usability, EAT should help them to quickly analyze students' submissions. Moreover, lecturers want to analyze exercises according to the level of difficulty with an accurate error display. In particular, they highly expected a detailed analysis of students' typical mistakes to promote students' learning progress. Additionally, the lecturers also expected that the EAT should be suitable for various courses at the university.

Most of the interviewed lecturers have a positive opinion about the EAT (average score for each statement of the questionnaire in parentheses). The lecturers assessed EAT as useful in general. They agreed that the dashboard interface is intuitive (3.6) and not overloaded with information (4.2). Moreover, they consider the interface as easy to understand (3.7). In their eyes, EAT provides a good overview which helps to identify what needs to be improved in the learning content and in optimizing existing exercises (average 4.2). They regard EAT as being useful for tracking students' learning progress so that they can determine how they can help students to improve their learning outcomes (3.8) and individually give students more efficient feedback related to their learning situation (3.6). The lecturers valued the flexible filtering options like filtering for students' attempts or the time period (e.g., the third week in a course) as being useful to carry out flexible analyzes for individual students or tasks (3.6) and to better understand and evaluate the solutions that have been submitted (4.2) (e.g., detailed filtering for part of an SQL query). Nevertheless, criticism was also expressed, namely the missing design aspects (e.g., front, labels unclear), or the inappropriateness of the color scheme for people with red-green color blindness.

6   Conclusion

To answer our research questions, we developed an IT artifact (EAT) that aims to analyze different kinds of exercises. Following the design science approach, several iterations of design, development, and evaluation have been run through leading to a gradually improved system according to the needs of lecturers.

Concerning *RQ1: Which kinds of analyses of student solutions are useful for lecturers?*, the results of our two surveys show that standard analyses as well as flexible analytics options are expected and valued by lecturers in equal measure. With regard to standard analyses, this aligns with former studies which highlighted the necessity of a good overview with exercise-related information like processing time, results (correctness) of students' submission [10,23], sorting students' results according to their exercise performance (e.g., [1,2,4,7]) or counting the number of trials [2,4,13]. In contrast, flexible analytics options have been investigated for the first time and were considered as highly practical and helpful. Lecturers valued the possibility to better assess their students' domain knowledge (e.g., what the students need to know) and in particular the flexible filtering option. This helps lecturers to understand students' mistakes better and subsequently to tailor their feedback on students' performance and how to proceed, which is extremely valuable for the student's learning process [22].

The answer to *RQ2: How can such analyses be realized in a generalized analytics tool?* consists in the usage of a reference architecture that is derived from BI applications. Already one kind of exercise like SQL is composed of a variety of elements, not to speak of several kinds (see RQ3 below). In addition, different courses contain a plethora of different exercises. To successfully cope with this situation, the BI concept was employed to the e-learning analytics tool. For this, a generic data schema was developed which disassembles exercises into their basic parts. This not only allows general analyses of exercises on a dashboard concerning average attempts, processing time, or facility index for example like in many other e-learning tools [1,2,4,7,13,18,20,21,28,32,42], but also analyses of the content of students' solutions with the help of a flexible analytics board. For the first time, profound analyses of student mistakes are possible with the help of drill-down functions.

With regard to RQ3: *How can different exercises be analyzed in a unified way?*, a side effect of the generic data schema is that the analytics tool is not bound to a specific kind of exercise but can cope with different kinds like SQL, Excel, or mathematics. The reason is that the exercise structure is disassembled into its basic parts and generalized. These basic parts are called attributes. For example, in SQL exercises, the joins are an attribute while in Excel exercises an attribute may be the color scheme of cells. This approach opens the analytics board to a variety of exercises. Each exercise type just needs to be decomposed into its parts. Integrating EAT into ITS creates a single touchpoint for lecturers. Student submissions are collected and evaluated within a single tool. EAT relieves lecturers from a huge amount of recurring standard tasks with the standard and flexible analyses. It accelerates the evaluation process of student submissions as submissions are automatically assessed by the ITS and lecturers can directly make use of the analytics functions to intervene in a course's learning process and improve their teaching. The flexible analyses enable tailored feedback to single students and the whole course. This in turn improves students' learning outcomes and empowers them as self-regulated learners.

Future developments concern lecturers as well as students. For students, notification functions are planned which remind students to keep up with their learning (e.g., continue with your course-related exercise) or which highlight knowledge gaps (e.g., "you need to improve your understanding of the GROUP BY clause"). Additionally, due to the positive effect of learning partners [41] a recommendation function for possible learning partners shall be integrated which is based on students' performance. For lecturers, downloads of anonymized reports shall be available that can be used for example in lectures to show and discuss common mistakes (e.g., If function problems in Excel). Regarding the limitations of our study, first, the data sample revealed vital aspects for the development of our tool, but is also small and needs to be increased in future research. Second, we only interviewed lecturers from the information system context. Future studies should include lecturers from different subjects like mathematics.

References

1. Aleven, V., Xhakaj, F., Holstein, K., McLaren, B.M.: Developing a teacher dashboard for use with intelligent tutoring systems. Technology **34**, 44–50 (2010)
2. Ali, L., Hatala, M., Gašević, D., Jovanović, J.: A qualitative evaluation of evolution of a learning analytics tool. Comput. Educ. **58**(1), 470–489 (2012)
3. Alzoubi, D., Kelley, J., Baran, E., B. Gilbert, S., Karabulut Ilgu, A., Jiang, S.: Teachactive feedback dashboard: using automated classroom analytics to visualize pedagogical strategies at a glance. In: CHI EA 2021 (2021)

4. Arnold, K.E., Pistilli, M.D.: Course signals at purdue: using learning analytics to increase student success. In: LAK 2012, pp. 267–270 (2012)
5. Baars, H., Kemper, H.G.: Business Intelligence & Analytics - Grundlagen und praktische Anwendungen: Ansätze der IT-basierten Entscheidungsunterstützung. Lehrbuch, Springer Vieweg (2021)
6. Barr, J., Gunawardena, A.: Classroom salon: a tool for social collaboration. In: SIGCSE 2012, pp. 197–202 (2012)
7. Cobos, R., Gil, S., Lareo, A., Vargas, F.A.: Open-dlas: an open dashboard for learning analytics. In: L@S 2016, pp. 265–268. ACM (2016)
8. Conboy, K., Gleasure, R., Cullina, E.: Agile design science research. In: Donnellan, B., Helfert, M., Kenneally, J., VanderMeer, D., Rothenberger, M., Winter, R. (eds.) DESRIST 2015. LNCS, vol. 9073, pp. 168–180. Springer, Cham (2015). https://doi.org/10.1007/978-3-319-18714-3_11
9. Dawson, S., Bakharia, A., Heathcote, E., et al.: SNAPP: realising the affordances of real-time SNA within networked learning environments. Networked Learning (2010)
10. Diana, N., Eagle, M., Stamper, J., Grover, S., Bienkowski, M., Basu, S.: An instructor dashboard for real-time analytics in interactive programming assignments. In: LAK 2017, pp. 272–279 (2017)
11. Dickler, R.: An intelligent tutoring system and teacher dashboard to support mathematizing during science inquiry. In: Isotani, S., Millán, E., Ogan, A., Hastings, P., McLaren, B., Luckin, R. (eds.) AIED 2019. LNCS (LNAI), vol. 11626, pp. 332–338. Springer, Cham (2019). https://doi.org/10.1007/978-3-030-23207-8_61
12. Döring, N., Bortz, J.: Forschungsmethoden und evaluation. Springer, Wiesbaden (2016)
13. Dourado, R.A., Rodrigues, R.L., Ferreira, N., Mello, R.F., Gomes, A.S., Verbert, K.: A teacher-facing learning analytics dashboard for process-oriented feedback in online learning. In: LAK 2021, pp. 482–489 (2021)
14. Feedbacksystem: Intelligent, personalized feedback for students using artificial intelligence. https://github.com/thm-mni-ii/feedbacksystem
15. Gamage, S.H.P.W., Ayres, J.R., Behrend, M.B., Smith, E.J.: Optimising moodle quizzes for online assessments. Int. J. STEM Educ. 6(1), 1–14 (2019)
16. Govaerts, S., Verbert, K., Duval, E., Pardo, A.: The student activity meter for awareness and self-reflection. In: CHI EA 2012. ACM (2012)
17. Gregor, S., Hevner, A.R.: Positioning and presenting design science research for maximum impact. MIS Q. 37(2), 337–355 (2013)
18. Herodotou, C., Maguire, C., McDowell, N., Hlosta, M., Boroowa, A.: The engagement of university teachers with predictive learning analytics. Comput. Educ. 173, 104285 (2021)
19. Hevner, A.R., March, S.T., Park, J., Ram, S.: Design science in information systems research. MIS Q. 28(1), 75–105 (2004)
20. Holstein, K., Xhakaj, F., Aleven, V., McLaren, B.: Luna: a dashboard for teachers using intelligent tutoring systems. Education 60(1), 159–171 (2010)
21. Hu, X., Hou, X., Lei, C.U., Yang, C., Ng, J.: An outcome-based dashboard for moodle and open edx. In: LAK 2017, pp. 604–605 (2017)
22. Keuning, H., Jeuring, J., Heeren, B.: A systematic literature review of automated feedback generation for programming exercises. ACM Trans. Comput. Educ. 19(1), 1–43 (2019)
23. Leony, D., Pardo, A., de la Fuente Valentín, L., de Castro, D.S., Kloos, C.D.: Glass: a learning analytics visualization tool. In: LAK 2012, pp. 162–163 (2012)

24. Li, D., Zhou, H.H.: An intelligent tutoring system with an automated knowledge acquisition mechanism. In: 2015 IEEE International Conference on Computational Intelligence & Communication Technology, pp. 88–91. IEEE (2015)
25. Martinez-Maldonado, R.: A handheld classroom dashboard: teachers' perspectives on the use of real-time collaborative learning analytics. Int. J. Comput. Support. Collab. Learn. **14**(3), 383–411 (2019)
26. Martinez Maldonado, R., Kay, J., Yacef, K., Schwendimann, B.: An interactive teacher's dashboard for monitoring groups in a multi-tabletop learning environment. In: Cerri, S.A., Clancey, W.J., Papadourakis, G., Panourgia, K. (eds.) ITS 2012. LNCS, vol. 7315, pp. 482–492. Springer, Heidelberg (2012). https://doi.org/10.1007/978-3-642-30950-2_62
27. Mitrovic, A.: An intelligent SQL tutor on the web. Int. J. Artif. Intell. Educ. **13**(2–4), 173–197 (2003)
28. Molenaar, I., Knoop-van Campen, C.A.N.: How teachers make dashboard information actionable. IEEE Trans. Learn. Technol. **12**(3), 347–355 (2019)
29. Patel, A., Kinshuk: Intelligent tutoring tools-a problem solving framework for learning and assessment. In: Fie 1996, vol. 1, pp. 140–144 (1996)
30. Peffers, K., Rothenberger, M., Tuunanen, T., Vaezi, R.: Design science research evaluation. In: Peffers, K., Rothenberger, M., Kuechler, B. (eds.) DESRIST 2012. LNCS, vol. 7286, pp. 398–410. Springer, Heidelberg (2012). https://doi.org/10.1007/978-3-642-29863-9_29
31. Sadler, D.R.: Formative assessment: revisiting the territory. Assess Educ. **5**(1), 77–84 (1998)
32. Santos, J.L., Govaerts, S., Verbert, K., Duval, E.: Goal-oriented visualizations of activity tracking: a case study with engineering students. In: LAK 2012, pp. 143–152 (2012)
33. Schnider, D., Jordan, C., Welker, P., Wehner, J.: Data Warehouse Blueprints: Business Intelligence in der Praxis. Hanser (2016)
34. Shankar, S.K., Prieto, L.P., Rodriguez-Triana, M.J., Ruiz-Calleja, A.: A review of multimodal learning analytics architectures. In: ICALT 2018, pp. 212–214. IEEE (2018)
35. Siepermann, M.: Lecture accompanying e-learning exercises with automatic marking. In: E-Learn: World Conference on E-Learning in Corporate, Government, Healthcare, and Higher Education, pp. 1750–1755. Association for the Advancement of Computing in Education (AACE) (2005)
36. Siepermann, M., Börgermann, C., Lackes, R.: Question-and-answer based explorative elearning exercises. In: ECGBL2010, p. 360. Academic Conferences Limited (2010)
37. Thomas, P., Smith, N., Waugh, K.: Automatic assessment of sequence diagrams (2008)
38. Vom Brocke, J., Simons, A., Riemer, K., Niehaves, B., Plattfaut, R., Cleven, A.: Standing on the shoulders of giants: challenges and recommendations of literature search in information systems research. Commun. Assoc. Inf. Syst. **37**(1), 9 (2015)
39. Webster, J., Watson, R.T.: Analyzing the past to prepare for the future: writing a literature review. MIS Q. **26**(2), xiii–xxiii (2002)
40. White, R.W., Morris, D.: Investigating the querying and browsing behavior of advanced search engine users. In: Kraaij, W., de Vries, A.P., Clarke, C.L.A., Fuhr, N., Kando, N. (eds.) SIGIR 2007, pp. 255–262. ACM (2007)

41. Woolf, B.P., et al.: The effect of motivational learning companions on low achieving students and students with disabilities. In: Intelligent Tutoring Systems (1), pp. 327–337 (2010)
42. Xhakaj, F., Aleven, V., McLaren, B.M.: Effects of a dashboard for an intelligent tutoring system on teacher knowledge, lesson plans and class sessions. In: André, E., Baker, R., Hu, X., Rodrigo, M.M.T., du Boulay, B. (eds.) AIED 2017. LNCS (LNAI), vol. 10331, pp. 582–585. Springer, Cham (2017). https://doi.org/10.1007/978-3-319-61425-0_69

Designing Pedagogical Conversational Agents for Achieving Common Ground

Antonia Tolzin[1]([⊠]) [iD], Anita Körner[1] [iD], Ernestine Dickhaut[1] [iD], Andreas Janson[2] [iD], Ralf Rummer[1] [iD], and Jan Marco Leimeister[1,2] [iD]

[1] University of Kassel, Kassel, Germany
{antonia.tolzin,anita.koerner,ernestine.dickhaut,rummer,
leimeister}@uni-kassel.de
[2] University of St. Gallen, St. Gallen, Switzerland
{andreas.janson,janmarco.leimeister}@unisg.ch

Abstract. As educational organizations face difficulties in providing personalized learning material or individual learning support., pedagogical conversational agents (PCAs) promise individualized learning for students. However, the problem of conversational breakdowns of PCAs and consequently poor learning outcomes still exist. Hence, effective and grounded communication between learners and PCAs is fundamental to improving learning processes and outcomes. As understanding each other and the conversational grounding is crucial for conversations between humans and PCAs, we propose common ground theory as a foundation for designing a PCA. Conducting a design science research project, we propose theory-motivated design principles and instantiate them in a PCA. We evaluate the utility of the artifact with an experimental study in higher education to inform the subsequent design iterations. We contribute design knowledge on conversational agents in learning settings, enabling researchers and practitioners to develop PCAs based on common ground research in education and providing avenues for future research. Thereby, we can secure further understanding of learning processes based on grounding communication.

Keywords: common ground · conversational agent · design science research · education

1 Introduction

Software-based dialogue systems, known as conversational agents (CAs), are common in our everyday lives as they enable communication between humans and computers and aim to simulate human conversations [1]. These dialogue systems show "humanlike behavior" and interact with users through natural language [2]. In the domain of higher education, pedagogical conversational agents (PCAs) can make it easier for learners to study independently at any given place or time. Digital education can be extended to a large audience but in consequence the interaction between learner and educator decreases and it is challenging to replace this interaction. Here, PCAs may mitigate this

A. Gerber and R. Baskerville (Eds.): DESRIST 2023, LNCS 13873, pp. 345–359, 2023.
https://doi.org/10.1007/978-3-031-32808-4_22

problem by providing natural interaction to support learners similar to educators [3, 4]. New digital tools, like PCAs, are increasing didactical possibilities and can improve learning processes and outcomes [5, 6].

Apparently, the perception of CAs in general is shifting from tools to teammates [7]. Therefore, collaboration between humans and CAs is gaining more importance, indicating the need for investigating their conversational aspects for successful interactions. As conversational interactions are fragile, especially in learning situations that mimic teacher-student interactions, they can easily fail after misunderstandings during the dialogue and impact the effectiveness between learners and PCAs [8, 9]. The most common reason for conversational breakdowns is a collapse of the natural language processing and the interpretation by the PCA [10]. PCAs sometimes provide none, wrong, or incomprehensible responses which leads to discomfort, annoyance, and questioning of the capabilities of the PCA, which can end in usage discontinuance and disruption of learning processes and outcomes [11, 12]. Thus, improving the communication between learners and PCAs and a common ground about the learning material is an important goal for researchers and practitioners [13].

Dialogue understanding is an inherently interactive process and understanding each other and the anticipated conversational grounding is a key element for language-based interactions between humans and computers [14]. The interactive process to achieve dialogue understanding is called conversational grounding and describes the coordinative process of dialogue partners to establish a shared understanding also known as common ground [15], which is fundamental for fruitful communication and successful learning. Following, we define common ground as a shared understanding resulting from a coordination process between conversational partners [16]. Nevertheless, identifying the needs and capabilities in human-computer interaction (HCI) and developing presumptions about what the PCA can do and understand is a great challenge [17]. Conversely, it is difficult for programmers and system designers to guess, how the human part of the dialogue will act [15, 16, 18]. While there is ample discussion and research on the *why* of grounding and shared understanding, there is little literature and a lack of research about the *how* [14, 19]. With successful CA interaction through effective conversations based on grounding in the domain of higher education, learning outcomes could be increased [14]. Consequently, this study aims to contribute to improving our understanding of common ground in human-agent interaction and to design components to increase common ground in educational contexts by specifically exploring the following research question:

RQ: How can we design a PCA that builds common ground and improves learning outcomes of students?

The goal of our research is to present a theory-driven design approach to provide a set of design principles to achieve common ground when utilizing a PCA for students in higher education. Hence, we implemented and evaluated a PCA for higher education. To achieve this research goal, we follow the design science approach [20, 21]. Therefore, our research provides a theory of design and action as an improvement for known problems [22]. We designed a prototypical PCA prototype and evaluated the first instantiation in a fully randomized field experiment.

2 Theoretical Background

2.1 Pedagogical Conversational Agents

CAs include all types of software that allows people to have a conversation with a computer and have a long history, with memorable representatives like ELIZA, ALICE, Claude, and HeX. They are part of the educational domain as PCAs since the early 1970s [23]. CAs can include voice as an interaction channel [24], for example Amazon´s Alexa, and typically make use of natural language interfaces and machine learning techniques, which allow them to take on tasks more successfully, assisting the users [25]. In contrast, text-based CAs are based on a set of established rules or flow to react to specific queries posed by users. As interactions between learners and PCAs are usually textually mediated [26], we focus on text-based PCAs in this study.

PCAs show great potential to transform education by individualizing and personalizing learning processes, supporting educators, giving insights into learners´ behavior, and engaging learners [3]. This is why we can observe an increasing interest in PCA research in education [27]. PCAs can be seen as a type of intelligent tutoring systems, where they interact with learners through natural language conversations [27, 28]. Through PCAs it is possible to provide learning support to all learners in a personalized way, which is a crucial part of the individualization of learning processes. PCAs can help to keep up motivation during the learning process throughout the interaction, they can improve meta-cognitive skills and help the learner to structure their knowledge actively [29]. In large online classes and where personalized support from educators to learners is not possible, PCAs can facilitate learning, for example by promptly providing students with rehearsal questions [30], assignments [31], course content [32], and study resources [33].

The design of PCAs includes considerations of cognitive, social, emotional and pedagogical elements [34]. Kuhail et al. [3] discovered principles used to design chatbots in education. Most chatbots included personalized learning, some included experimental learning, social dialogue, and collaborative learning, and only few studies included affective learning, learning by teaching, and scaffolding. They can be used in a broad application area because they can act in different human roles like teaching agents, peer agents, teachable agents, and motivational agents [3, 35].

2.2 Common Ground as a Kernel Theory

It is well investigated that senders adapt to the supposed needs and capabilities of the recipient in a dialogue [36]. That is why people speak differently to children, friends, foreigners, and colleagues. Dialogue understanding is an interactive process, aiming to resolve misunderstandings and building shared understanding. Especially, in learning contexts, this shared understanding is crucial to gain procedural and factual knowledge [37]. The process can be improved through additional signals of mutual understanding to individual turns [36]. Thus, we introduce common ground as a kernel theory for our design science research endeavor. We define common ground as a shared understanding resulting from a coordination process between conversational partners [16]. Common Ground contains the background knowledge on which the communication planning of the conversational partners builds on and can be divided into the global knowledge (all knowledge about the conversational partner and their knowledge requirements) and the situational knowledge (knowledge about the mutual perception conditions and the communication protocol).

Grounding processes lead to a coordination of the background knowledge of the conversational partners [16, 36]. Identifying the needs and capabilities in the context of HCI and developing presumptions about what the PCA can do and understand is a great challenge for most people. The dialogue must therefore be appropriate for the conversational setting including conversational partners, prior dialogue, task context, and lexical context. It is crucial to acknowledge that the recipient has understood the sender [38] through different verbal and non-verbal information (e.g., saying "yes" or "okay", nodding) [39]. Verbal grounding does not bring new information or arguments to the conversation. It is more like a semantic mechanism to check that both dialogue partners received and understood the sender's contribution.

Dialogue partners have different ways to provide evidence of their understanding, which could be explicit acknowledgements (words), display of what has been understood, continued attention, and continuing with next steps [40]. Responses can get interconnected and contingent on what has been said previously by mutually grounding the conversational partner's input [41]. Successful grounding results in a shared context, guided comprehension, instant feedback, and enhanced processes in conveying intent [42]. In essence, we expect that the incorporation of common ground as a kernel theory for the design of a PCA is an important scaffold in the dialogical interaction with a learner. In the following, we outline this design process in detail.

3   Design of a PCA based on Common Ground

3.1   Research Method and Context

For the design of the PCA with the consideration of common ground, we draw on a theory-driven design approach [43, 44] following Peffers et al. [21] on engineering our IT artifact. Therefore, we base our subsequent design decisions on our phenomena of interest and the related theory concept (problem identification and motivation phase). We focus on common ground as an ancillary phenomenon and learning outcomes as the focal phenomenon. We claim that the successful usage of natural language processing in human-computer communication depends on a design that reflects human conversational grounding processes so that each contribution to the ongoing dialogue can be appropriately grounded by both the learner and the PCA (objectives of a solution). Grounding measures are associated with achieving common ground in a learning scenario when utilizing a PCA. Hence, we want to design a PCA that improves common ground and ultimately learning outcomes (design and development phase). For the further design of these grounding elements, we derive requirements from theory and practice [45]. In a first step, we derived requirements from common ground mechanisms and theories found in the literature (T). In a second step, we derived requirements from learners. For this purpose, we presented a mockup of a chatbot learning tutor in a mobile application to 33 students and asked them for user requirements that also relate to the use and utility for learning with PCAs [46] (demonstration phase). The answers and requirements given by the students were clustered and requirements (L) were derived. Afterwards, we addressed all requirements by design principles that should influence the common ground with a PCA and linked phenomena like [47] learning outcomes. Ultimately, we present our implementation for the first design iteration that was subject for evaluation (see Sect. 4) in Western-European lecture (evaluation phase) (Fig. 1).

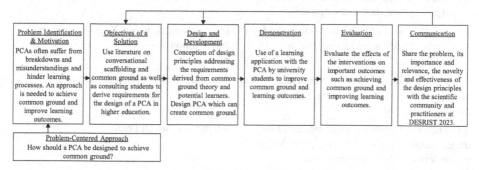

Fig. 1. Research Approach for PCA Development. Adapted from [21].

3.2   Requirements From Common Ground Theory and Practice

In this section, we will describe how we gathered the preliminary requirements from literature and practice to address the first two parts of the objectives of the solution phase of the design science approach of Peffers et al. [21]. The problem formulation (step one), described in the introduction, serves as the foundation for the derivation of the requirements. First, we derived requirements to design our PCA from common ground theory and literature.

Examining more closely the grounding processes, two different ways have been suggested as the mechanism responsible for grounding: Alignment [48] and complementarity [16, 49]. Alignment theory emphasizes increasing alignment and similarity between dialogue partners over time [48], which can be achieved through mimicking different language characteristics of each other (e.g., on phonetic, lexical, or syntactic levels) [14]. Studies proved that alignment could enhance human-computer interaction [50, 51] and surprisingly humans align more to computers than they align to other humans. In contrast, complementarity emphasizes the complementarity between dialogue partners. This theory assumes, that the mutual understanding is grounded in dissimilar contributions, which supportively relate to each other and therefore create a greater whole. Complementarity can be distinguished into two subtypes, interpersonal synergy and audience design. Rothwell [14] showed a consistent advantage of the two complementarity theories, considering that syntax seems to be essential and indicates evidence for the alignment model.

Furthermore, in a prior systematic review we identified five mechanisms to achieve common ground in the interaction with CAs [52]. Embodiment (1) describes the presentation of an identifiable conversational counterpart [53–55]. Learners are more willing to put effort into establishing common ground if the interaction resembles a human-to-human interaction. Social Features (2) are needed to show authenticity: the CA has to

Table 1. Requirements from Theory and Practice.

Requirements from Common Ground Theory (T) and Learners (L)	Common Ground Mechanisms
T1) The PCA should be transparent concerning its purpose, goals, intentions, and abilities	Social Features, Joint Action, Mental Model
T2) The PCA should elaborate, "close-the-loop" constantly regarding the shared goal and knowledge	Interpersonal Synergy, Knowledge Base, Joint Action
T3) The PCA should check the understanding of communication and the learning material constantly	Audience Design, Mental Model
T4) The PCA should integrate signals of mutual understanding by acknowledging that the learner has understood the sender and task	Alignment, Social Features
T5) The PCA should make the background knowledge transparent and motivate the learner to do so	Knowledge Base
L1) The PCA should indicate if a misunderstanding/breakdown is appearing	Practice & Audience Design, Alignment, Social Features
L2) The PCA should inform the learner about what it can do (and what not) and what to expect from it	Practice & Inoculation Theory, Mental Model

be transparent concerning its purpose, abilities, and knowledge, must be able to learn from experiences and remember the communication protocol [56–58]. Joint Action (3) describes that in a collective task the goals and intentions of the dialogue partners need to be salient. Common Ground is what both dialogue partners know in a transparent way [59, 60]. The Knowledge Base (4) refers to the knowledge organisation of the CA: To establish common ground, it is crucial that all dialogue partners suppose the others have access to the same information [61]. Lastly, it is desirable that learners develop a Mental Model of the CA (5) [62, 63]. This influences learners' expectations of the CA and whether the CA interaction is effective and therefore whether it is worth putting effort into establishing common ground. Hence, a shared mental model is a sign of common ground. Through these mechanisms, common ground can be achieved to improve learning outcomes.

Based upon the above-described theoretical tenets and the requirements derivation with learners, we identified seven requirements (T1-T5 and L1–2 in Table 1) to establish common ground with a PCA. The first requirement from theory (**T1**) refers to the transparent goals (see Joint Action, [52]), purpose, intention, and abilities of the PCA as these are typical social interaction elements and support the development of an appropriate mental model. The second requirement (**T2**) deals with the mechanisms of interpersonal synergy [14] and joint action [52] and proposes that common ground is based on complementary actions. A PCA must contain a constant elaboration and references to the dialogue partners' contributions. During joint actions, common ground can be achieved by sending relevant information to the dialog partner, verifying what each partner knows, establishing or negotiating shared meaning, requesting information or repairing insufficiencies in shared knowledge. Moreover, it has been shown, that good teams "close the loop" more often than bad teams [64]. The third requirement (**T3**) refers to the mechanisms of audience design [14] and mental model of the PCA [52], emphasizing that the learner uses theory of mind and perceives that their dialogue partner possibly does not share their perspective and knowledge. The sender develops assumptions of their partner's perspective and can adjust their contribution. To achieve an internal representation of the dialogue partner's perspective, constant checking of each other's perspective is fundamental. The next requirement (**T4**) deals with the interactive alignment mechanism [14, 48] and social features [52], in which shared understanding results in imitation of the partner's language characteristics as a signal of mutual understanding by acknowledging this understanding, which is a key element of conversation. The last requirement (**T5**) is based on the mechanism of the knowledge base [52]. To achieve common ground, the PCA needs to adapt to the learner's level of knowledge and the level of common ground between them. Therefore, transparency of the partner's background knowledge is needed.

In addition to the theory requirements, we address the second part of the objectives of a solution phase of the design science approach by deriving requirements from Learners (L). In a large-scale lecture, we identified the needs, wishes, and expectations of 33 learners considering the PCA. The clustered answers and considerations of the students resulted in two requirements (L1 and L2 in Table 1). Students required information about the possible arising of a misunderstanding (**L1**), which can be linked to the mechanisms of audience design, alignment and social features as constant checking of the understanding and indicating if something is going wrong is an essential part of successful human communication. The second requirement (**L2**) can be seen as a prevention strategy for possible conversational breakdowns as inoculation messages can prevent breakdowns [12]. By informing the learner about its abilities, the PCA can foster the learner's development of an appropriate mental model of the PCA.

3.3 Design Principles to Achieve Common Ground

In this section, we will describe how we derived the design principles (DPs) addressing the design and development phase of the design science approach. The goal is to develop DPs that consider common ground for PCA interactions as a key driver of learning processes. In Table 2 we describe four DPs derived from requirements from theory and learners and describe how these DPs were implemented in the PCA prototype. Figure 2 shows how the different DPs are instantiated in the evaluated PCA prototype. We argue that a PCA that instantiates our DPs improves common ground between learners and the PCA, therefore resulting in increased learning outcomes. To evaluate our design, we developed a PCA based on the derived DPs.

The first design principle (**DP1**) considers an active communication protocol and the repetition of personalized information ("what was said previously") so that responses become contingent and the knowledge of the PCA is more transparent. This design principle was implemented through different answers of the PCA depending on the type

Table 2. Design Principles for Pedagogical Conversational Agents.

Title	Design Principle	Req
DP 1) Active Communication Protocol	Provide a PCA that makes its knowledge transparent and is grounding the learner's contributions in order to interconnect conversational responses, so they become contingent on what had been said previously	T3, T4, T5
DP 2) Introduction	Provide a PCA that initial informs the learner about what it can do and what to expect from it in order to make its purpose, (shared) goals, and abilities transparent and show authenticity	L2, T1, T2
DP 3) Student Question Generation	Provide a PCA that instructs students to practice question generation to make students' knowledge transparent and show the boundaries of common ground	L1, T2, T3, T5
DP 4) Re-check	Provide a PCA that includes agreements, questions, and rewordings to avoid misunderstandings, breakdowns, and make the knowledge of the dialogue partners salient	L1, T2, T3, T5

of information (question, explanation, definition, example) required from the student and given before (see Fig. 2). The second design principle **(DP2)** addresses the need for detailed instruction by the PCA with information about what it can do (and what not) and what learners can expect from it. In the introduction part of the conversation the abilities of the PCA are stated and a shared goal of the interaction is built. The PCA prototype started the conversation with an introduction of itself, in which its abilities (You can ask me questions and determine what information I give to you; My ability to understand natural language is unfortunately limited) and goal (equal understanding of what aspects of theories increase or decrease falsifiability) became transparent. The third design principle **(DP3)** refers to the importance of student question generation which has positive effects on learning [65]. Moreover, student question generation makes students' knowledge transparent and shows the boundaries of the common ground. At the end of every learning unit, the PCA prototype encouraged the students to generate a question before the next learning unit started. The last design principle Re-check **(DP4)** relates to the establishment of a common ground as a result of agreements, questions, and rewordings. This prevents misunderstandings and makes the knowledge of the dialogue partners salient. This DP was implemented through repeated questions about the deeper understanding of the learning material and joint agreements about the further course of the conversation and the given information.

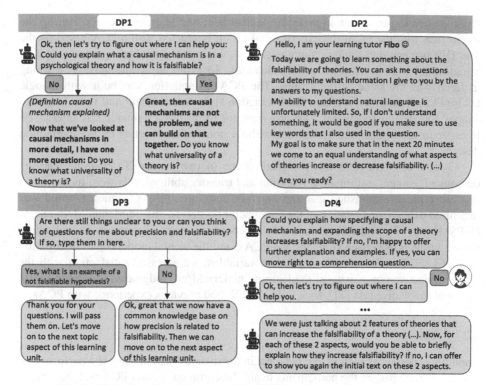

Fig. 2. Exemplary Conversations of the PCA based on the Design Principles.

4 Demonstration and Evaluation of the PCA

4.1 Demonstration

We demonstrate the prototypical instantiation in a fully randomized field experiment. In our evaluation, we followed the DSR evaluation frameworks proposed by [66] and adopt a formative ex-post evaluation approach [66, 67]. This approach will allow us to iteratively refine and improve the design of our method in the early stages of its development. We conducted an online experiment in a lecture at a Western European university. The students who participated majored in psychology, were enrolled in the course "General Psychology I", and were undergraduates (freshmen). The learning material (falsifiability of theories) presented by the PCA was part of the curriculum for this course. 71 students started the study. From these, we collected 54 valid data sets in total, of which only 33 participants completed all learning performance questions. Therefore, evaluations are based on 54 participants, and learning performance on 33 participants. The sample consisted of 24 female students and seven male students (and two who did not want to answer this question) with an average of 21 years.

The experiment consisted of three main parts: 1) a pre-test, 2) the interaction with the PCA, and 3) a post-test. The pre- and post-tests were identical for all participants. The pre-test took place before the use of the PCA and captures the student knowledge level of the learning material. The post-test was conducted at the end of the implementation phase to investigate common ground establishment and learning success. During the interaction with the PCA, the experimental group interacted with a PCA based on the four DPs presented to achieve common ground, while the control group interacted with a traditional PCA without grounding elements. To avoid any confounds, all learning material was the same across groups. The PCA instantiation was built with Google DialogFlow. Moreover, we kept the interaction style transactional and thus, language simple and design functional. Our aim was not to design a humanic CA interaction in order to investigate our hypotheses without potential confounds by the interaction design.

43 students were randomly assigned to one of two groups. To examine learning outcomes, learners' information retention and transfer ability levels were measured as this are typical, established learning outcome measures [68]. Common Ground was measured using a modification of the Five Factor Perceived Shared Mental Model Scale (5-PSMMS) [73], as there are no widely accepted measures of common ground, either among humans or between humans and PCAs, and the mental model is part of common ground [22]. Besides our key dependent variables, we assessed satisfaction with the PCA, subjective complexity of the learning material [69], judgments of learning [70], personal innovativeness [71], trust in PCA [72], and previous experience with PCAs.

4.2 Results

Previous experiences with PCAs, personal innovativeness and pre-test test performance did not differ between the participants using the common ground PCA and the control PCA, indicating that the two groups of participants were similar concerning their previous knowledge and relevant experiences. When evaluating their experience with the PCA, satisfaction and judgments of learning did not differ significantly between the two groups.

However, participants who used the common ground (vs. control) PCA spent more time with the PCA, $t(51) = 2.11$, $p = .02$, $d = 0.58$. Additionally, participants who used the common ground (vs. control) PCA evaluated the common ground between themselves and the PCA as higher, $t(50) = 1.73$, $p = .045$, $d = 0.46$. The common ground scale consisted of four subscales concerning shared representations concerning communication, task performance, mental models, and content of learning materials. Participants interacting with the common ground (vs. control) PCA especially judged their and the PCA's understanding of the content of the learning materials, such as central terms and concepts, to be more similar, $t(51) = 2.53$, $p = .007$, $d = 0.69$. However, this did not lead to increased trust in the PCA or greater liking of the PCA for the common ground compared to the control version. Concerning the learning success, there was a non-significant tendency towards better performance for participants with the common ground compared to the control PCA, $t(27) = 1.33$, $p = .097$, $d = 0.47$, indicating that with a larger sample size, the common ground PCA might facilitate learning success compared to a control PCA.

5   Contributions, Limitations, and Future Work

Common ground is a key element of human dialogue and a necessary capability for PCAs. Overall, this study should help designers to implement CAs, especially in educational contexts. As it is important to address the mechanisms of common ground, focus on domain (e.g., education) specific requirements for PCA design, and derive DPs, this study aims to fill this gap. We provide the first steps of designing a PCA to achieve common ground and improve learning outcomes. As our contribution, we provide a new solution to the problem of conversational breakdowns and unsatisfactory learning processes with PCAs to counteract poor learning outcomes. In terms of design science research, our research can be classified as an improvement according to Gregor and Hevner [22] since we address a known problem with a new solution. We contribute to theory by systematically considering theory-driven requirements to achieve common ground in the design of a PCA. That is how we can secure further understanding of learning processes based on grounding communication. We enable practitioners to design PCAs based on common ground and enhance learning processes. We present a theory-driven design of PCA to achieve common ground. Thus, we demonstrate and evaluate the design according to Peffers et al. [21]. The results provide deeper insights into the different ways how common ground could be successfully implemented in human-agent interaction by presenting design solutions in the form of DPs and one possible instantiation. With our study, we provide a first design iteration that consider common ground mechanisms. Thus, future research should use the evaluation results to re-design the PCA, e.g., aiming at different educational contexts.

A limitation for the examination of common ground is that there are no widely accepted measures of degree of common ground, neither between humans nor between humans and PCAs. In dyadic conversations, explicit acknowledgments (e.g., how often feedback occurs of having perceived, understood, and accepted the other's message) have been assessed [40]. However, explicit acknowledgments might not seem necessary when all conversational partners are sure that common ground has been established. Here, we therefore employed an adapted version of the Five Factor Perceived Shared Mental Model Scale (5-PSMMS) [73]. Shared mental models are one aspect of common ground. As common ground violations can go undetected, however, such a subjective measure can also lead to biased common ground assessments. Therefore, a measure that assesses the conceptual content on which common ground is necessary for the respective conversation would be desirable.

Our PCA-prototype yielded promising results. However, the sample size in our evaluation study was too small to draw firm conclusions. Moreover, the sample was also too small to examine how usage of the PCA influences learning success. A larger study is necessary to gain a detailed understanding of which design features meant to enhance common ground are most successful and most conducive to learning success.

Acknowledgments. The results presented in this article were developed in the research project Komp-HI funded by the German Federal Ministry of Education and Research (BMBF, grant 16DHBKI073). The fourth author acknowledges funding from the Basic Research Fund of the University of St. Gallen.

References

1. Bittner, E.A.C., Oeste-Reiß, S., Leimeister, J.M.: Where is the Bot in our Team? Toward a Taxonomy of Design Option Combinations for Conversational Agents in Collaborative Work. HICSS (2019)
2. Vassallo, G., Pilato, G., Augello, A., et al.: Phase coherence in conceptual spaces for conversational agents. In: Sheu, P.C.-Y. (ed) Semantic computing. IEEE Press; John Wiley & Sons, Piscataway, NJ, Hoboken, N.J., pp. 357–371 (2010)
3. Kuhail, M.A., Alturki, N., Alramlawi, S., et al.: Interacting with educational chatbots: a systematic review. Educ. Inf. Technol. (2022)
4. Winkler, R., Söllner, M.: Unleashing the Potential of Chatbots in Education: A State-Of-The-Art Analysis. Proceedings 2018, 15903 (2018)
5. Mikic Fonte, F.A., Burguillo, J.C., Nistal, M.L.: An intelligent tutoring module controlled by BDI agents for an e-learning platform. Expert Systems with Applications (2012)
6. Hayashi, Y.: Gaze awareness and metacognitive suggestions by a pedagogical conversational agent: an experimental investigation on interventions to support collaborative learning process and performance. Int. J. Comput.-Support. Collab. Learn. 15(4), 469–498 (2020)
7. Seeber, I., Bittner, E., Briggs, R.O., et al.: Machines as teammates: a research agenda on AI in team collaboration. Information & Management 57, 103174 (2020)
8. Benner, D., Elshan, E., Schöbel, S., et al.: What do you mean? a review on recovery strategies to overcome conversational breakdowns of conversational Agents. ICIS (2021)
9. Luger, E., Sellen, A.: Like having a really bad PA. In: Kaye, J. (ed) Proceedings of the 2016 CHI. ACM, New York, pp. 5286–5297 (2016)
10. Myers, C., Furqan, A., Nebolsky, J., et al.: Patterns for how users overcome obstacles in voice user interfaces. In: Mandryk, R. (ed.) 2018 CHI, pp. 1–7. ACM, NY (2018)
11. Chakrabarti, C., Luger, G.F.: Artificial conversations for customer service chatter bots: architecture, algorithms, and evaluation metrics. Expert Syst. Appl., pp. 6878–6897 (2015)
12. Weiler, S., Matt, C., Hess, T.: Immunizing with information – inoculation messages against conversational agents' response failures. Electron Markets (2021)
13. Meredith, J.: Analysing technological affordances of online interactions using conversation analysis. Journal of Pragmatics, 42–55 (2017)
14. Rothwell, C.D., Shalin, V.L., Romigh, G.D.: Comparison of common ground models for human--computer dialogue. ACM Trans. Comput.-Hum. Interact. 28, 1–35 (2021)
15. Koulouri, T., Lauria, S., Macredie, R.D.: Do (and Say) as i say: linguistic adaptation in human-computer dialogs. Human-Computer Interaction 31, 59–95 (2016)
16. Clark, H.H.: Using language, Sixth printing. [ACLS Humanities E-Book]. Cambridge University Press, Cambridge (1996)
17. Diederich, S., Brendel, A.B., Morana, S., et al.: On the design of and interaction with conversational agents: an organizing and assessing review of human-computer interaction research. JAIS 23, 96–138 (2022)
18. Montemayor, C.: Language and Intelligence. Mind. Mach. 31(4), 471–486 (2021)
19. Khosrawi-Rad, B., Rinn, H., Schlimbach, R., et al.: Conversational agents in education – a systematic literature review. ECIS 2022 Research Papers (2022)
20. Hevner, A.R., March, S.T., Park, J., et al.: Design science in information systems research. MIS Q. 28, 75–105 (2004)
21. Peffers, K., Tuunanen, T., Rothenberger, M.A., et al.: A design science research methodology for information systems research. JMIS 24, 45–77 (2007)
22. Gregor, S., Hevner, A.R.: Positioning and presenting design science research for maximum impact. MIS Q. 37, 337–355 (2013)

23. Laurillard, D.: Rethinking University Teaching: A Conservational Framework for the Effective Use of Learning Technologies, 2nd edn. Taylor & Francis, London (2002)
24. Schmitt, A., Zierau, N., Janson, A., Leimeister, J.M.: Voice as a Contemporary Frontier of Interaction Design. ECIS 2021 Research Papers (2021)
25. Budiu, R.: The User Experience of Chatbots. www.nngroup.com/articles/chatbots/ (2018)
26. Song, D., Oh, E.Y., Rice, M.: Interacting with a conversational agent system for educational purposes in online courses. HSI. IEEE, pp. 78–82 (2017)
27. Hobert, S., Meyer von Wolff, R.: Say Hello to Your New Automated Tutor – A Structured Literature Review on Pedagogical Conversational Agents. WI (2019)
28. Gupta, S., Bostrom, R.: Technology-mediated learning: a comprehensive theoretical model. J. Association for Inf. Syst. pp. 686–714 (2009)
29. Gabriel, C., Hahne, C., Zimmermann, A., et al.: The virtual tutor: tasks for conversational agents in online collaborative learning environments. In: Bui, T. (ed): HICSS (2021)
30. Sinha, S., Basak, S., Dey, Y., et al.: An educational chatbot for answering queries. In: Mandal (ed) Emerging Technology in Modelling and Graphics, Singapore, pp. 55–60 (2020)
31. Ismail, M., Ade-Ibijola, A.: Lecturer's apprentice: a chatbot for assisting novice programmers. IMITEC, pp. 1–8 (2019)
32. Cunningham-Nelson, S., Boles, W., Trouton, L., Margerison, E.: A review of chatbots in education: practical steps forward. AAEE: Educators Becoming Agents of Change: Innovate, Integrate, Motivate, pp. 299–306 (2019)
33. Mabunda, K., Ade-Ibijola, A.: PathBot: an intelligent chatbot for guiding visitors and locating venues. In: 2019 ISCMI, pp. 160–168 (2019)
34. Gulz, A., Haake, M., Silvervarg, A., et al.: Building a social conversational pedagogical agent. In: Perez-Marin, D., Pascual-Nieto, I. (eds): Conversational agents and natural language interaction: Techniques and effective practices. IGI Global, pp. 128–155 (2011)
35. Kerly, A., Hall, P., Bull, S.: Bringing chatbots into education: towards natural language negotiation of open learner models. Knowl.-Based Syst. **20**, 177–185 (2007)
36. Clark, H.H., Brennan, S.E.: Grounding in communication. In: Resnick, L.B., Levine, J.M., Teasley, S.D. (eds) Perspectives on socially shared cognition. APA, pp. 127–149 (1991)
37. Trede, F., Higgs, J., Rothwell, R.: Critical transformative dialogues: a research method beyond the fusions of horizons. forum qualitative sozialforschung: qualitative social research, (2009): Qualitative Research on Intercultural Communication (2008)
38. Jurafsky, D., James, M.: Dialog Systems and Chatbots. Speech and Language Processing (2017)
39. Richardson, D.C., Dale, R.: Grounding dialogue: eye movements reveal the coordination of attention during conversation and the effects of common ground. Proceedings of the Annual Meeting of the Cognitive Science Society (2006)
40. Dillenbourg, P., Traum, D.: Sharing solutions: persistence and grounding in multimodal collaborative problem solving. J. Learning Sci. **15**, 121–151 (2006)
41. Sundar, S.S., Qian, X., Bellur, S.: Designing interactivity in media interfaces: a communications perspective. CHI 2010: Perspectives on Design, pp. 2247–2256 (2010)
42. Brennan, S.E.: The grounding problem in conversations with and through computers. Social and Cognitive Approaches to Interpersonal Communication. Fussell, S.R., Kreuz, R.J. (Eds.), 201–225 (1998)
43. Briggs, R.O.: On theory-driven design and deployment of collaboration systems. International Journal of Human-Computer Studies, 573–582 (2006)
44. Gehlert, A., Schermann, M., Pohl, K., et al.: Towards a research method for theorydriven design research. Wirtschaftinformatik Proceedings 2009 (2009)
45. Dickhaut, E., Janson, A., Söllner, M., et al.: Lawfulness by Design – Development and Evaluation of Lawful Design Patterns to Consider Legal Requirements. EJIS, 1–28 (2023)

46. Brenner, W., Karagiannis, D., Kolbe, L., et al.: User, use & utility research. Bus. Inf. Syst. Eng. **6**, 55–61 (2014)
47. Serban, I.V., Sankar, C., Germain, M., et al.: A Deep Reinforcement Learning Chatbot. arXiv (2017)
48. Pickering, M.J., Garrod, S.: Toward a mechanistic psychology of dialogue. Behav. Brain. Sci. **27**, 169–90; discussion 190–226 (2004)
49. Fusaroli, R., Rączaszek-Leonardi, J., Tylén, K.: Dialog as interpersonal synergy. New Ideas Psychol. **32**, 147–157 (2014)
50. Branigan, H.P., Pickering, M.J., Pearson, J., et al.: Linguistic alignment between people and computers. J. Pragmat. **42**, 2355–2368 (2010)
51. Cowan, B.R., Branigan, H.P., Obregón, M., et al.: Voice anthropomorphism, interlocutor modelling and alignment effects on syntactic choices in human–computer dialogue. Int. J. Hum Comput Stud. **83**, 27–42 (2015)
52. Tolzin, A., Janson, A.: Mechanisms of Common Ground in Human-Agent Interaction: A Systematic Review of Conversational Agent Research. HICSS (2023)
53. Corti, K., Gillespie, A.: Co-constructing intersubjectivity with artificial conversational agents: People are more likely to initiate repairs of misunderstandings with agents represented as human. Comput. Hum. Behav. **58**, 431–442 (2016)
54. Pustejovsky, J., Krishnaswamy, N.: Embodied Human Computer Interaction. Künstl Intell. **35**, 307–327. https://doi.org/10.1007/s13218-021-00727-5#auth-James-Pustejovsky (2021)
55. Maybin, J., Mercer, N., Stierer, B.: 'Scaffolding' learning in the classroom. In: Norman K (ed) Thinking Voices: Thework of the National Oracy Project. Hodder Arnold (1992)
56. Clark, L., Pantidi, N., Cooney, O., et al.: What makes a good conversation? In: Brewster, S., Fitzpatrick, G., Cox, A., et al. (eds.) 2019 CHI, pp. 1–12. ACM, New York, NY, USA (2019)
57. Neururer, M., Schlögl, S., Brinkschulte, L., et al.: Perceptions on authenticity in chat bots. MTI **2**, 60 (2018)
58. Cassell, J.: Negotiated collusion: modeling social language and its relationship effects in intelligent agents. User Model. User-Adap. Inter. **13**, 89–132 (2003)
59. Bernard, D., Arnold, A.: Cognitive interaction with virtual assistants: from philosophical foundations to illustrative examples in aeronautics. Comput. Ind. **107**, 33–49 (2019)
60. Pinhanez, C.S., Candello, H., Pichiliani, M.C., et al.: Different but Equal: Comparing User Collaboration with Digital Personal Assistants vs. Teams of Expert Agents (2018)
61. Blache, P.: Dialogue management in task-oriented dialogue systems. In: Chaminade, T., Interaction ASIGoC-H (eds) Proceedings of the 1st ACM SIGCHI International Workshop on Investigating Social Interactions with Artificial Agents. ACM, , pp. 4–8 (2017)
62. Frijns, H.A., Schürer, O., Koeszegi, S.T.: Communication models in human–robot interaction: an asymmetric model of alterity in human–robot interaction (AMODAL-HRI). Int J of Soc Robotics (2021)
63. Kiesler, S.: Fostering common ground in human-robot interaction. In: Robot and Human Interactive Communication, 2005. ROMAN 2005. IEEE International Workshop on. IEEE, pp 729–734 (2005)
64. Fischer, U., McDonnell, L., Orasanu, J.: Linguistic correlates of team performance: toward a tool for monitoring team functioning during space missions. Aviat Space Environ. Med. **78**, B86-95 (2007)
65. Yu, F.-Y.: Learner-centered pedagogy + adaptable and scaffolded learning space design— online student question-generation. International Conference on Computers in Education 2012 (2012)
66. Venable, J., Pries-Heje, J., Baskerville, R.: FEDS: a framework for evaluation in design science research. Eur. J. Inf. Syst. **25**, 77–89 (2016)
67. Mettler, T., Eurich, M., Winter, R.: On the use of experiments in design science research: a proposition of an evaluation framework. CAIS **34** (2014)

68. Soderstrom, N.C., Bjork, R.A.: Learning versus performance: an integrative review. Perspect Psychol. Sci. **10**, 176–199 (2015)
69. Gupta, S., Bostrom, R.: Research note —an investigation of the appropriation of technology-mediated training methods incorporating enactive and collaborative learning. Inf. Syst. Res. **24**, 454–469 (2013)
70. Rhodes, M.G.: Judgments of learning: methods, data, and theory. In: Dunlosky, J., Tauber, S.K. (eds) The Oxford handbook of metamemory. Oxford University, New York (2016)
71. Agarwal, R., Prasad, J.: A conceptual and operational definition of personal innovativeness in the domain of information technology. Information Syst. Res. (1998)
72. Schmitt, A., Wambsganss, T., Janson, A.: Designing for Conversational System Trustworthiness: The Impact of Model Transparency on Trust and Task Performance. ECIS 2022 Research Papers (2022)
73. van Rensburg, J.J., Santos, C.M., de Jong, S.B., et al.: The five-factor perceived shared mental model scale: a consolidation of items across the contemporary literature. Front Psychol. **12**, 784200 (2021)

Computational Thinking for Design Science Researchers – A Modular Training Approach

Eva-Maria Zahn[1](✉) iD, Ernestine Dickhaut[2] iD, Mark Vonhof[2],
and Matthias Söllner[1] iD

[1] Information Systems and Systems Engineering, University of Kassel, Kassel, Germany
{zahn,soellner}@uni-kassel.de
[2] Information Systems, University of Kassel, Kassel, Germany
ernestine.dickhaut@uni-kassel.de, mark.vonhof@wi-kassel.de

Abstract. Addressing and solving challenges by designing innovative artifacts is one of the main objectives of design science research (DSR). However, to achieve this goal, learning the theory of DSR and its methodology alone is not enough. We argue that computational thinking (CT) is an important skill set for design science researchers, since it helps to understand and structure problems from a computational point of view, which is an important basis for developing effective and innovative information system artifacts. CT consists of four core components: (1) dividing the problem, (2) abstraction, (3) pattern recognition, and (4) algorithmic thinking. Therefore, it is a skill set that can support DSR researchers in a broad way. However, so far, CT is rarely taught and trained and mainly not part of DSR courses. To close this gap and to train CT comprehensively, we develop a course based on low code programming, in other words, programming with little to no code. Our training can be embedded in DSR courses in a modular way. Thus, during a DSR course, students and researchers can develop and improve various prototypes with little effort and transfer the acquired competence to new design projects. As a central contribution of our study, we show how the training of CT can be applied in a modular way in DSR courses.

Keywords: Transferable Skills · Computational Thinking · Design Science Research

1 Introduction

Design science research (DSR) is a suitable approach for designing new digital systems. The main objective of DSR is to create innovative artifacts for addressing and solving various challenges. However, to achieve this goal, learning the theory of DSR and its methodology alone is not enough. As described in the fundamental thoughts of DSR by Hevner et al., knowledge and understanding of a problem domain and its solution are achieved through building artifacts [1]. Design science researchers focus on specific problems in the problem space and investigate the contexts to elaborate solutions in the

A. Gerber and R. Baskerville (Eds.): DESRIST 2023, LNCS 13873, pp. 360–374, 2023.
https://doi.org/10.1007/978-3-031-32808-4_23

solution space [2]. Thus, successful DSR researchers and developers should acquire so-called transferable skills, especially computational thinking (CT), to effectively adapt their existing knowledge and skills to new circumstances and situations.

Transferable skills are frequently used as an umbrella term for nontechnical skills such as problem-solving, creativity, or communication [3, 4]. Those skills are domain independent and portable between different jobs, tasks, and situations and allow to quickly adapt to new environments. Consequently, using these skills, design science researchers can understand the complex challenge process that needs to be solved faster and more comprehensively. Apart from managing economic challenges, transferable skills also help an individual to deal with social and personal issues and to be agile researchers and learners [5, 6]. Especially the skill set of CT is one of the most important nowadays, since nearly everybody is affected by it – directly or indirectly [7].

Consequently, we argue that CT is an important skill set for design science researchers, since it helps to understand and structure problems from a computational point of view, which is an important foundation for developing effective and innovative information system (IS) artifacts. CT relates to various transferable skills (e.g., problem-solving, creativity, adaptivity) and consists of four core components: (1) dividing the problem, (2) abstraction, (3) pattern recognition, and (4) algorithmic thinking [7]. However, training CT is challenging, since skills are subjective and action oriented [8]. Previous studies already used the approach of DSR for training CT [9, 10], but trainings especially for DSR researcher, particularly in combination with new settings, such as low code programming, are missing. Studies already showed that lightweight co-construction activity can be a promising approach for teaching transferable skills, such as CT [e.g., 11, 12]. Nevertheless, CT is a skill set that can support DSR researchers in a broad way. However, so far, CT is rarely taught and trained and mainly not part of DSR courses. To close this gap and train CT comprehensively, we develop a CT training based on low code programming, in other words, programming with little to no code. Our paper is based on the following research question:

RQ: *How can computational thinking be trained within design science research courses?*

Our training can be embedded in DSR courses in a modular way. Thus, during a DSR course, students and researchers can develop and improve various prototypes with little effort and transfer the acquired competence to new design projects. Here, a main aim and novelty of our study is highlighted: CT as a central skill set for DSR researchers in combination with low code programming. Therefore, as a central contribution of our paper, we show how the training of CT can be applied in a modular way in two university courses to support the application of DSR. Furthermore, we provide recommendations for practitioners and researchers to address important requirements for building skill trainings or implementing such a training into their DSR approach.

This paper's composition is structured as follows: In the first step, we clarify the concept of CT and its relation to transferable skills and competencies, as well as how to train these skills, in the theoretical background. Second, we illustrate the DSR process of Peffers et al. [9] to integrate CT into the design and development phase. Afterward, the development of our CT training based on low code programming is highlighted before we present and discuss the results. Finally, we discuss the results and give contributions and an outlook for further research.

2 Theoretical Background

Since there is no unique definition for skills and competencies, they are often used as synonyms, although they differ in their meaning and role [14]. Generally speaking though, a competence relies on three components: knowledge, skills, and attitude [15, 16]. All three parts influence competencies and interact with each other (see Fig. 1). Additionally, competencies connect the characteristics of an individual with the current challenge the individual deals with in work and life contexts [16]. Therefore, competencies are subjective and action oriented [8].

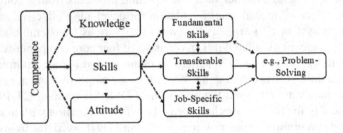

Fig. 1. The Distinction between Competencies and Skills.

Especially skills have become more significant in recent years, so we primarily focus on this component in our study. Skills can be divided into fundamental, technical, or job-specific, and nontechnical or transferable skills. Fundamental skills address skills such as reading or writing, while technical/job-specific skills are, for example, marketing [5]. However, so-called transferable skills, including CT skills, are particularly essential nowadays because they can be a key catalyst for helping the workforce adapt [17]. To better comprehend CT, we first want to clarify the structure of transferable skills before going into the skill set of CT in greater detail.

2.1 Transferable Skills in the 21st Century

Transferable skills, also known as 21st century skills, soft skills, core skills, or cross-cutting skills, are nontechnical skills such as communication or problem-solving [5, 18, 19]. The term "transferable skills" is frequently used as an umbrella term for skills that can be portable between different professions, jobs, and tasks [3, 4]. Therefore, they help an individual to adapt to new environments quickly and consequently enable learners to cope with different economic, personal, or social challenges [5].

Since transferable skills are part of many disciplines and no unique framework exists, we draw on a widely spread framework that clusters three subcategories of transferable skills: cognitive, metacognitive, and socio-emotional skills [5]. However, they still interact and influence each other [5].

Cognitive skills include abilities such as focused attention, identifying correlations in a problem or task, and the ability to conclude. Moreover, metacognitive skills are necessary to organize, control, and guide one's own actions, thinking, or learning processes. This category includes, for example, problem-solving, decision-making, communication, or critical thinking skills. The third category addresses socio-emotional skills that enable learners to regulate their behavior and emotions. Therefore, socio-emotional skills influence the acquisition and use of cognitive and metacognitive skills. Socio-emotional skills include abilities such as emotional regulation, collaboration (incl. Empathy, trust, cooperation), open-mindedness (incl. Creativity, tolerance), engaging with others (incl. Sociability), and task performance (incl. Self-control, responsibility [20]. However, combining various transferable skills is necessary for training the skill set of CT.

Computational Thinking. In the 21st century, the skill set of CT influences most parts of our society, since digital technologies and data analyzing are omnipresent [11, 12]. CT already has an immense impact on many research agendas in different disciplines, such as science, engineering, and the humanities [22, 23]. Consequently, CT is one of the most important skill sets students need to develop nowadays [24].

Computer science professor J. M. Wing mainly characterized the research field around CT in the last two decades, and she defined CT as a process that involves "formulating a problem and expressing its solution(s) in such a way that a computer – human or machine – can effectively carry out" [25]. The skill set of CT includes various transferable skills from all three categories (cognitive, metacognitive, and social-emotional skills), such as problem formulation or critical thinking [13]. Moreover, the skill set consists of three main aspects: problem-solving, designing systems, and understanding human behavior [21]. So, CT is not only the ability to solve complex problems. Even if CT involves primarily cognitive and metacognitive skills, socio-emotional abilities such as creativity, cooperation, and empathy are also important to reach a high level of CT [7].

In the process of CT, the learner needs to consider four main dimensions: (1) decomposition, (2) pattern recognition, (3) pattern generalization and abstraction, and (4) algorithm design [7, 26]. The abstraction dimension is the most critical process of CT. Therefore, the third dimension is an essence of CT that requires thinking at multiple levels of abstraction [21, 22]. Other aspects like defining patterns (dimension 2), generalizing from specific instances (part of dimension 3), and parameterization, are necessary for executing the abstraction dimension.

CT is not only a crucial requirement to model new and more complex computer systems. The skill set also helps to analyze and understand the massive amounts of generated data [7]. Therefore, CT is one of the most crucial skill sets nowadays.

2.2 Training Transferable Skills

As learning happens throughout life and in various scenarios, informal learning environments are more relevant nowadays – particularly for training transferable skills [27]. Moreover, skills are subjective and action oriented [8], so individual and action-oriented learning processes are necessary to generate the most significant output [28, 29]. Additionally, the benefit of individual learning/training concepts is being able to adapt the learning content and procedure to the learner. So, the learners' respective skills or knowledge levels can be addressed. Beside the requirement of individuality, the action-oriented aspect for effective skill training needs to be comprised. In particular, interactive learning approaches are promising for achieving the highest learning success possible. The "Interactive, Constructive, Active, Passive" (ICAP) Framework enables this by highlighting that interactive learning sections like discussing with other learners can generate an exceptionally high learning outcome [30].

Hence, suitable instructions for training complex skills are required. Therefore, in the first step, it is necessary to analyze how the skill to be learned can be trained in the best way possible. In a nutshell, for adequate skill learning settings, the learning instructions need to be adaptive, personalized, and oriented towards real-world tasks [31].

Training Computational Thinking. A training process for computational thinking skills can occur in several ways. The instructions can be computer guided in digital environments, but it is also possible to learn CT in a more classical learning setting without digital technologies [32]. Even though digital technologies are not necessary, various studies have already demonstrated that, nevertheless, technologies offer suitable opportunities to learn CT effectively and in a personalized way [25-27]. Studies highlighted that learning settings based on gamification could be one suitable approach for learning the CT skill set [24, 33]. Moreover, other skill-oriented approaches like project-based or experimental learning are frequently linked with real-world tasks. Consequently, they can improve the learning outcomes and the learners' engagement [34, 35].

Although various studies have developed computer-based learning processes for CT skills, we want to highlight that these studies are mostly very specific and do not address CT from a comprehensive perspective of competencies with different sub-skills, knowledge, and attitude.

3   The Computational Thinking Training

Before presenting our CT training and its development, we want to highlight that the training is based on the three components of competencies. After addressing the development of the training, we illustrate the application of the CT training and, furthermore, the integration of the CT training in the DSR approach.

3.1   Integration of a Computational Thinking Training in a DSR Process

We follow the DSR process of Peffers et al. [13] to integrate CT into the design and development phase (see Fig. 2). In many DSR projects, the focus is on action and design. Thus, projects usually develop new artifacts to solve pre-identified problems in this phase. Peffers et al. describe the main activity of the design and development as follows: *"This activity includes determining the artifact's desired functionality and its architecture and then creating the actual artifact. Resources required for moving from objectives to design and development include knowledge of theory that can be brought to bear in a solution."* [9, p. 55].

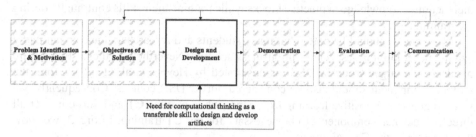

Fig. 2. Integration of CT Training in the DSR Process

Through modular integration into the DSR process, we enable CT training to be flexibly integrated into the DSR course. While some DSR courses start with a theory part, others start with practical insights, but at the core of every DSR course should be the application of the methodology. While DSR literature supports the process of DSR courses, the design and development phase is mostly unstructured.

We argue that the training of a CT skill set during the practical application enables DSR researchers to develop better artifacts. In addition, the theory-driven structure to train the four core elements during the design and development phase provides the overall learning concept of DSR courses. Thus, DSR researchers can use the course to train and practice CT skill sets that others learn through their training as software developers.

3.2 Conceptual Development of the Computational Thinking Training

As CT supports the understanding and structuring ability of problems from a computational point of view, it is an important foundation for developing effective and innovative IS artifacts. As many DSR researchers do not have any or fewer programming abilities, our training should not require any previous knowledge in programming. Therefore, our training focuses on the acquisition of CT for a wide range of participants – e.g., university students and DSR researchers.

For training CT effectively, besides the skill acquisition, our course also needs to address the participants' knowledge and abilities [8]. Another important factor in training skills successfully is to design the training in an action oriented manner [8]. Hence, we follow an experimental learning approach [36] implemented in a real-world problem scenario, so learners solve small tasks or problems while training CT. To implement this in an application-oriented and real-world-oriented way, we decided to use a low code programming platform (Mendix), since participants can develop their own systems without extensive programming capabilities. The CT training is designed in a way that it can also be applied to other low code platforms, such as VoiceFlow.

To develop a CT training on such a platform, we use the theoretical concept of competencies as a foundation. Consequently, our training is structured by the three components of competencies: knowledge, skill, attitude (see Fig. 1). Especially for the acquisition of CT, these components are important aspects. Since our training addresses participants without previous knowledge, it is necessary to teach underlying facts about low code and programming itself. After building foundation knowledge of low code, the participants need to solve a task. Here, they develop a homepage for an app and apply their acquired knowledge in practice blocks while training their skills continually during the training.

Moreover, it should be noted that many students and researchers have an antipathy against programming, especially in business schools. Nevertheless, these students are precisely the target group of DSR, as postulated by Hevner et al. [1]. Therefore, the attitude component should also be considered during DSR courses. Consequently, we want to generate a positive learning experience when training CT and thus consider all three competence components to be necessary for our CT training. In Fig. 3, we show the structure of the CT training.

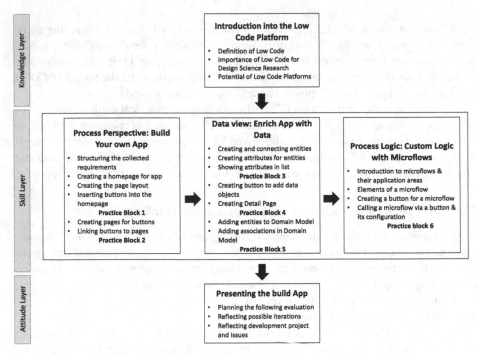

Fig. 3. Layers and Steps of the developed Computation Thinking Training

Knowledge Layer. First, the participants need to receive fundamental knowledge of low code programming and programming in general. Since we do not want to presuppose any experience in using low code platforms or programming, the explanation of basic terms is necessary. Here, the training conveys the core characteristics of low code, how to use these platforms and their importance for DSR. Moreover, the participants learn the distinction between low code and no code. For a more comprehensive and application-oriented understanding, the training covers the low code platform Mendix' structure and functions. After providing factual knowledge about low code, the participants should nevertheless understand the basic concept of programming. Therefore, our course explains the most important aspects of programming, such as variables, loops, data types, functions, and parameters. Furthermore, as already mentioned, the participants need to complete a task. This task includes developing a homepage for an app.

In addition to focusing on low code, this phase includes an introduction to the design and development process of DSR. The design and development phase is important for the outcome but also for the success of the DSR project. This knowledge is also integrated into building the knowledge layer.

The overall aim of the knowledge layer is to provide the participants with the fundamental knowledge they need to solve their own projects. The knowledge layer is located in the first box in Fig. 3.

Skill Layer. We focus on the skill layer while the participants are starting the design phase. This phase focuses on the acquisition of a CT skill set. For the acquisition of CT, we design the skill layer based on an experimental learning approach [36]. For this, the participants go through different phases, which include the following steps that are arranged in a circular procedure: concrete experience (doing), reflecting (reviewing/reflecting on the experience), abstract conceptualization (learning from the experience), and active experimentation (trying out what was learned) [36].

For a more structured approach, the skill layer is clustered into three main parts (process perspective, data view, and process logic). The aim is to split the app development into single steps, so the task can be solved comprehensively and instructed. The single parts are constructed by various blocks, including learning, practice, and a short reflection section. In each block, the participants first receive an introduction by observing an expert and creating concrete experiences for the respective block. This is followed by an active practice part in which the participants need to reflect on the introduction and consider the knowledge for their own problem/use case. This is followed by the core element of each block, where the participants implement the taught and abstracted knowledge in their own app development via the low code platform. In a nutshell, every practice block (six overall) consists of an expert observation, an active practice, and a reflecting step. Generally speaking, while solving the different blocks, the participants train their CT by considering the core characteristics of this skill set (decomposition, pattern recognition, pattern generalization and abstraction, and algorithm design).

The skill layers' first part addresses the process perspective, where participants can build the first version of their own app. This part is divided into two blocks. The first section addresses the basics for building a homepage on a low code platform. Therefore, structuring previously collected requirements, creating a homepage and the page layout as well as inserting buttons into the homepage are necessary contents (see Fig. 3). Especially in this first block, the participants train important characteristics of CT, such as decomposition and pattern recognition. Also, the training of different transferable skills, e.g., problem-solving and critical thinking, is addressed, since such skills are necessary to structure and analyze requirements in a goal-oriented way. Another necessary transferable skill is creativity in order to create the page layout, for example. Therefore, combining various transferable skills is considered when solving the practice blocks.

Moreover, creating pages for buttons and linking buttons to pages are substances of practice block two.

After finishing the process perspective, the data view phase can start (see Fig. 3). Here, the main content is to enrich the app with data, which is trained in three blocks. In block three, participants create and connect entities, create attributes for the entities and show these attributes in a list. Thus, characteristics of CT, such as decomposition, can be trained while structuring the generated entities.

Furthermore, creating a button to add data objects and a detail page is the content of block four. As an example, the step of creating a detail page is quite similar to creating the page layout from practice block one. Here, the aim is to abstract a previously learned acquirement and apply it to a new problem. Since the step of abstraction is one of the most important ones in CT, we have integrated this procedure for training abstraction several times in the skill layer. Another example is the task of creating buttons to add data objects (practice block 4) compared to the tasks of practice block two (see Fig. 3).

However, the data view section closes with practice block five, where adding entities to a domain model and adding the associations in a domain model are in focus. The last section in the skill layer addresses the process logic and contains all the CT characteristics learned so far in order to train CT comprehensively. Therefore, block six starts with a short introduction to microflows and their application areas. Afterward, the participants need to adapt their existing knowledge and acquired skills step by step to the new problem (custom logic of microflow).

During the training and the practical application blocks, the complexity and the demand for the problem to be solved increases. Thus, the participants practice algorithmic thinking, starting with small problems to be solved clearly, transferring what they have learned to new problems and solving new complex problems. While at the beginning the practical tasks to be solved were divided relatively clearly and in small steps, the last applications required creativity and presented the participants with new challenges in terms of problem division. However, the participants are guided to solve problems in a structured way and to acquire algorithmic thinking.

Attitude Layer. After solving all six practice blocks, the third layer starts. Here, the participants' attitude is in the focus. Even if the participants' attitude is a relevant aspect during the whole training, especially at the end of our concept, it builds an autonomous layer. In the third layer, we put the CT training back into the overall context of DSR. As a next step, the participants think about possible evaluations and iterations to improve their artifacts.

Moreover, the main part of the last layer is to present the developed artifact and to reflect on the development procedure. This includes reflecting on the development project and issues, as well as possible interactions. Since many learners' and researchers have an antipathy against programming, we want to respond to the practitioners' attitudes in greater detail. One aim of our training is that participants can collect positive learning experiences while developing their own digital systems on a low code platform. Thus, the small steps in the second layer should prevent a negative learning experience caused by a task overload or less input information. Since we assume that most participants have no or less experience in programming, we want to provide an ongoing feeling of success. Moreover, participants can ask the teachers/supervisors during the whole process to minimize a negative attitude. Here, an overcharging reflection is one desired outcome to provide a positive influence attitude at the end of the CT training.

3.3 Reflecting and Evaluating the Computational Thinking Training

After developing our CT training concept theoretically to integrate it into DSR courses, in the following we will reflect on the training and its concept. Thus, we applied the CT training in a bachelor university course. Our evaluation was implemented in a design-oriented course for two weeks with 21 participants (n = 21). Here, the training is an intervention to measure the acquisition of CT and the attitude toward programming. Therefore, we used a quantitative pre-test and post-test to measure our dependent variables (research subjects), and the low code training represents the independent variable. Of our participants, 57.14% had programming experience before the training.

Because of COVID-19 and online lectures, the training was divided into an online teaching section via Zoom (one day) and two weeks of an autonomous practice section. The online teaching section started with an introductory presentation highlighting the training procedure followed by the first learning video to address fundamental information on low code programming.

Afterward, the participants received a link for filling out the pre-questionnaire online. The presentation of the remaining learning videos and a subsequent time slot for questions via Zoom followed this. Here, the participants had the opportunity to ask questions about the low code training and the further procedure. During this two-week period of the practice section, the trainers were available to answer the participants' comprehension questions. After the autonomous practice section, the participants had to complete the post-survey questionnaire.

In our evaluation, we focus on the impact of CT training on attitude. The affection (describes the emotions to programming) significantly improved by 11.81% due to the training (see Table 1). While affection ($t = 2.979$; df = 20; $p = 0.557$) was moderately high in the pre-questionnaire, it was high in the post-questionnaire. We did not find any significant differences in cognition (opinion about programming). This remained equally high between pre-questionnaire and post-questionnaire ($t = 0.187$; df = 20; $p = -0.474$). In addition to measuring changes in CT, we gave participants the opportunity to reflect on the training and the format to measure subjective perceptions of the training. Overall, the training was well received, with 95.24% of the participants saying they would recommend the training to others. As a matter of fact, 42.86% of the participants think that the training has an influence on their further professional career, which in turn is reflected in the future application of DSR and the design of artifacts in low code platforms.

4 Discussion

In the following, we discuss our approach to designing the CT training and the developed training. First, we derive recommendations for how to train CT in DSR courses, based on our findings in combination with the previous literature. Second, we reflect our CT training und present limitations and room for future research.

Table 1. Evaluation Data.

Variable	p	t	df
Affection	0.557*	2.979	20
Cognition	0.187 n.s	−0.474	20
Behavior	0.255 n.s	0.587	20
Attitude towards programming (CPAS scale)	0.790**	1.852	20

*: $p < 0.05$; **: $p < 0.01$; n.s.: not significant (one tailed)

4.1 Recommendations

One of the study's aims was the iterative development of the CT training, so in the following we present recommendations that can be used to train the CT skill set in DSR projects.

To structure our training, we used the three characteristics of competence and derived the three basic layers of our training from this (knowledge layer, skill layer, attitude layer, see Fig. 3). Since we believe that knowledge and the participants' attitudes are also relevant for comprehensive skill and competence building, the triad provides a suitable basis. This enabled us to convey basic knowledge in order to introduce the participant to the topic of low code platforms. However, we have to note that the teaching of low code and programming information in the knowledge layer was not sufficient. For a more comprehensive understanding, basic knowledge about the skill to be trained should also be taught from the beginning in a revised training. It is important to teach the participants what the main characteristics of the trained skill are and how to improve them. In our case, the participants should receive a basic understanding of the four characteristics of CT (decomposition, pattern recognition, pattern generalization and abstraction, algorithm design [7]). This leads to the first recommendation:

Recommendation 1: *The knowledge input for the training needs to cover basic information about the use case/the problem to be solved as well as the main characteristics of the skill that needs to be trained.*

Next, we divided the main task of developing a homepage for an app into smaller parts. Therefore, the sub-tasks in the skill layer started with small work packages that became increasingly extensive. The aim of increasing the size of the work packages was that the participants could first solve the small steps in a well-prepared way without having to apply the main characteristics of CT at the same time. The larger the work packages become, the more they have to draw on their CT abilities and break down the work packages into smaller steps themselves to solve the package. Independent of the work package size, every task is pre-structured into sections on input/observation, practice, and reflection. This segmentation and decomposition of the tasks lead to our second recommendation:

Recommendation 2: *Divide the sub-tasks into small work packages that become more comprehensive as the training progresses and divide them into an introduction/observation, a practice, and a reflection section.*

Since a skill can only be trained through repeated and multiple executions, the main characteristics of CT are applied repeatedly and partially in an unstructured way in the single sub-tasks. Thus, e.g., algorithm thinking needs to be trained several times in the learning process. Furthermore, it is important to apply what has been learned in different contexts and to test it in an action-oriented way in real-world scenarios. Accordingly, it is important for DSR researchers to carry out multiple design processes and thus train CT for different problems.

Recommendation 3: *Provide the ability to transfer CT to new contexts and improve them over a long period of time.*

Furthermore, some DSR researchers do not design and build new systems, so they often end up developing design principles in their research. This is where we want to start with our training and minimize the antipathy to programming with the help of low code programming and thus promote the participants' attitude. With the approach of low code, a faster sense of achievement can be generated, and programming is more abstract than with classical programming languages such as C + + or Python. In this way, the attitude and the motivation to program can be promoted.

Recommendation 4: *Motivate students or DSR researchers to design and develop systems so that the fear of programming can be taken away – low code programming is one suitable approach here.*

4.2   Limitation and Further Research

Our study and the development of CT training are not without limitations and offer room for further research. With our CT training, we have developed a theory-based concept that is based on low code platforms. In general, the training is limited to one low code platform but can also be applied to other platforms. A transfer without technology-based design is also possible but requires adjustments in the concept.

In general, not every problem in DSR is equally easy to solve, and the design requires many different factors, such as creativity, necessary knowledge, and the CT skill set. Several challenges in teaching DSR are identified in the literature. Winter and vom Brocke [37] have identified, for example, progress of the field, diversity of the field, critical thinking, and action competence. With our training, we do not have the possibility to fully prepare DSR researchers for these problems. However, we can introduce them to the design and development phase of DSR to a certain extent and train the basic CT skill set, which needs to be consolidated and extended further on. For example, action competence can be trained and interdisciplinary differences can be countered through low code platforms.

With our application of the CT training, we have demonstrated in a course how the training can be used. Further research could look at other course levels and specific DSR courses. Here, adaptations of the content might be necessary. In addition, we have not yet integrated the course into a larger DSR course. Thus, future research should investigate the integration into different DSR course formats and make necessary adjustments.

CT, in general, is very difficult to make tangible. There are scales that measure CT, but each problem remains a new problem, and interdisciplinary problems, such as those often encountered in DSR, are very difficult to compare. Therefore, future research should look at measuring and improving CT through the training.

5 Conclusion

The aim of our study was to develop a computational thinking training for DSR courses. For this purpose, we developed a CT training based on a low code platform, so participants without any previous knowledge and experiences can take part. Our course content is divided into three layers (knowledge, skill, and attitude) to comprehensively cover the main characteristics of our CT training. This approach for reaching our aim highlights the novelty of our study. Furthermore, we can give two main implications for practitioners and researcher. First, a practical contribution of our study is a modular course where the course structure and main content can be adapted to other low code platforms and problems. Second, we can give another implication by providing four recommendations for DSR researchers and researchers in general who want to build skill training or implement it into their DSR approach. In summary, our study shows how a developed CT training can be implemented in the DSR approach and improve the training of DSR researchers in the future.

References

1. Hevner, A.R., March, S.T., Park, J., Ram, S.: Design science in information systems research. MIS Q. **28**, 75–105 (2004)
2. vom Brocke, J., Winter, R., Hevner, A., Maedche, A.: Accumulation and evolution of design knowledge in design science research - a journey through time and space. J. Assoc. Inf. Syst. **21**, 520–544 (2020)
3. Chan, C., Fong, E.: Disciplinary differences and implications for the development of generic skills: a study of engineering and business students' perceptions of generic skills. Eur. J. Eng. Educ. **43**, 1–23 (2018)
4. Olesen, K.B., Christensen, M.K., O'Neill, L.D.: What do we mean by "transferable skills"? a literature review of how the concept is conceptualized in undergraduate health sciences education. HESWBL. **11**, 616–634 (2021)
5. UNICEF: Global Framework on Transferable Skills. UNICEF. 3 United Nations Plaza, New York, NY 10017. Tel: 212–326–7000; Fax: 212–887–7465; http://www.unicef.org/education (2019). (visited on 02/01/2023)
6. Bridges, D.: Transferable skills: a philosophical perspective. Stud. High. Educ. **18**, 43–51 (1993)
7. Wing, J.: Computational thinking and thinking about computing. Philosophical Transactions. Series A, Mathematical, Physical, and Engineering Sciences **366**, 3717–3725 (2008)
8. Erpenbeck, J., von Rosenstiel, L.: Handbuch Kompetenzmessung: erkennen, verstehen und bewerten von Kompetenzen in der betrieblichen, paedagogischen und psychologischen Praxis. Schaeffer-Poeschel Verlag fuer Wirtschaft Steuern Recht, Stuttgart (2007)
9. Dolgopolovas, V., Dagiene, V., Jasute, E., Jevsikova, T.: Design science research for computational thinking in constructionist education: a pragmatist perspective. Problemos. **95**, 144–159 (2019)
10. Apiola, M., Sutinen, E.: Design science research for learning software engineering and computational thinking: Four cases. Computer Appl. Eng. Educ. **29** (2020)
11. Laato, S., Pope, N.: A Lightweight Co-Construction Activity for Teaching 21st Century Skills at Primary Schools (2019)
12. Walden, E., Browne, G., Oboyle, M.: Computational Thinking: Changes to the Human Connectome Associated with Learning to Program. In: ICIS 2015 Proceedings (2015)

13. Peffers, K., Tuunanen, T., Rothenberger, M.A., Chatterjee, S.: A design science research methodology for information systems research. J. Manag. Inf. Syst. **24**, 45–77 (2007)
14. Dezhgahi, U.: Die Auswahl von Schulleitern in einem Assessment Center: Eine theoretische und empirische Analyse eines Eignungsfeststellungsverfahrens. Springer VS, Wiesbaden Heidelberg (2021). https://doi.org/10.1007/978-3-658-32387-5
15. Rychen, D.S.: E2030 Conceptual Framework: Key Competencies for 2030 (DeSeCo 2.0) (2016)
16. Weinert, F.E.: Concept of competence: A conceptual clarification. In: Defining and selecting key competencies, pp. 45–65. Hogrefe & Huber Publishers, Ashland, OH, US (2001)
17. ILO: Global framework on core skills for life and work in the 21st century. (2021)
18. Elliott, S., Epstein, J.: Selecting the future doctors: the role of graduate medical programmes. Intern. Med. J. **35**, 174–177 (2005)
19. Succi, C., Canovi, M.: Soft skills to enhance graduate employability: comparing students and employers' perceptions. Stud. High. Educ. **45**, 1–14 (2019)
20. Chernyshenko, O.S., Kankaraš, M., Drasgow, F.: Social and Emotional Skills for Student Success and Well-Being: Conceptual Framework for the OECD Study on Social and Emotional Skills. OECD, Paris (2018)
21. Wing, J.M.: Computational thinking. Commun. ACM. **49**, 33–35 (2006)
22. Wing, J.: Computational thinking's influence on research and education for all. Italian J. Educational Technol. **1** (2017)
23. Bundy, A.: Computational Thinking is Pervasive. Presented at the (2007)
24. Hooshyar, D., Malva, L., Yang, Y., Pedaste, M., Wang, M., Lim, H.: An adaptive educational computer game: effects on students' knowledge and learning attitude in computational thinking. Comput. Hum. Behav. **114**, 106575 (2021)
25. Wing, J.M.: Computational thinking benefits society. 40th Anniverssary Blog of Social Issues in Computing **26** (2014)
26. Lin, P.-H., Chen, S.-Y.: Design and Evaluation of a Deep Learning Recommendation Based Augmented Reality System for Teaching Programming and Computational Thinking. IEEE Access. (2020)
27. Siemens, G.: Connectivism. (2017)
28. Denton-Calabrese, T., Mustain, P., Geniets, A., Hakimi, L., Winters, N.: Empowerment beyond skills: computing and the enhancement of self-concept in the go_girl code+create program. Comput. Educ. **175**, 104321 (2021)
29. Lin, Y.-N., Hsia, L.-H., Hwang, G.-J.: Promoting pre-class guidance and in-class reflection: a SQIRC-based mobile flipped learning approach to promoting students' billiards skills, strategies, motivation and self-efficacy. Comput. Educ. **160**, 104035 (2021)
30. Chi, M.T.H., Wylie, R.: The ICAP framework: linking cognitive engagement to active learning outcomes. Educational Psychologist **49**, 219–243 (2014)
31. van Gog, T., Ericsson, K.A., Rikers, R.M.J.P., Paas, F.: Instructional design for advanced learners: establishing connections between the theoretical frameworks of cognitive load and deliberate practice. ETR&D. **53**, 73–81 (2005)
32. Moreno-Leon, J., Roman-Gonzalez, M., Robles, G.: On computational thinking as a universal skill: a review of the latest research on this ability. In: 2018 IEEE Global Engineering Education Conference (EDUCON), pp. 1684–1689. IEEE, Tenerife (2018)
33. Rowe, E., et al.: Assessing implicit computational thinking in Zoombinis puzzle gameplay. Comput. Hum. Behav. **120**, 106707 (2021)
34. Gunawan, G., Sahidu, H., Harjono, A., Suranti, N.M.Y.: The effect of project based learning with virtual media assistance on student's creativity in physics. Jurnal Cakrawala Pendidikan. **36**, 167–179 (2017)

35. Lyz, N., Lyz, A., Neshchadim, I., Kompaniets, V.: Blended learning and self-reflection as tools for developing it-students' soft skills. In: 2020 V International Conference on Information Technologies in Engineering Education (Inforino), pp. 1–4 (2020)
36. Kolb, D.: Experiential Learning: Experience As The Source Of Learning And Development (1984)
37. Winter, R., vom Brocke, J.: Teaching Design Science Research. In: ICIS 2021 Proceedings. Austin, TX (2021)

Human Safety and Cybersecurity

Human Safety and Cybersecurity Track

Mala Kaul[1], H. Raghav Rao, and Paolo Spagnoletti

[1] University of Nevada, Reno
mkaul@unr.edu
[2] University of Texas, San Antonio
hr.rao@utsa.edu
[3] Luiss University, Roma
pspagnoletti@luiss.it

Abstract. The human safety and cybersecurity track for DESRIST 2023 invited studies contributing to design knowledge at the intersection of information systems and security. We accepted one paper that offers a novel Business Process Modelling Notation for monitoring security-aware processes and compliance in Industrial IoT demonstrating that design science can be effectively used in the industrial automation and control systems. We propose that the increased convergence of operational and information technology, which creates the need for supporting cybersecurity and human safety through human-centered, sustainable, and resilient systems, provides opportunities for designing novel socio-technical systems.

Keywords: Design science research · Cybersecurity · Human safety research

The digital revolution, often referred as the fourth industrial revolution, has been transforming industries and business through connectivity, advanced analytics, human-machine interaction, and advanced engineering. As industries and businesses are increasingly becoming more connected through the convergence of Operational Technology and Information Technology, technology such as IoT, Industrial IoT, and analytics is becoming more integrated into industrial and business processes[1]. These advances in connected industries, and cyber-physical systems leads not just to cybersecurity, but also human safety as a grand challenge. This is now paving the path for Society 5.0 and against this backdrop, the opportunity to design sustainable, human-centered, and resilient solutions. New ways of integrating technology, IoT, artificial intelligence, robotics, and other technologies, provide various pathways for *smart* Design Science Research (DSR) as a means of rigorously examining challenges at the intersection of security and digital innovation, and contributing to knowledge about solving human safety and cybersecurity problems

---

[1] Lyytinen, K. (2022). Innovation logics in the digital era: a systemic review of the emerging digital innovation regime. Innovation: Organization and Management, 24(1), 13–34. https://doi.org/10.1080/14479338.2021.1938579

through the design of novel socio-technical systems. For example, stronger medical cybersecurity leads to better patient safety by protecting patients' health information. Stronger manufacturing cybersecurity leads to better worker safety by protecting against cyber-attacks that cause equipment to malfunction and stronger financial cybersecurity leads to greater fiscal safety by preventing fraud amongst customers of financial institutions. This is an area that provides rich opportunities for using design science research to address critical safety and security challenges that have a high societal impact.

Track Reviewers

Oluwafemi Akanfe (oaakanfe@uab.edu), Assistant Professor, University of Alabama, Birmingham
Jonna Järveläinen (jonna.jarvelainen@utu.fi), Adjunct professor, University of Jyväskylä; University lecturer, Turku School of Economics
Wael Soliman (wael.soliman@uia.no), Associate Professor, University of Adger, Norway
Tiziano Volpentesta (tvolpentesta@luiss.it), Doctoral Candidate and Teaching Assistant, Luiss University
Alan Yang (alanY@unr.edu), Assistant Professor, University of Nevada, Reno

SIREN: Designing Business Processes for Comprehensive Industrial IoT Security Management

Markus Hornsteiner$^{(\boxtimes)}$ and Stefan Schönig

University of Regensburg, Regensburg, Germany
{markus.hornsteiner,stefan.schoenig}@ur.de
https://go.ur.de/iot

Abstract. The Industrial Internet of Things (IIoT) paradigm means that "things" in an industrial context are equipped with connectivity. The convergence of formerly isolated Operational Technology with IT provides disruptive opportunities for organizations but is also vulnerable to cyberattacks. To mitigate these risks, the IEC62443 standard was developed, which will be mandatory for critical infrastructure organizations due to the EU Cybersecurity Act. This standard demands various requirements for the technology and organizational aspects of organizations. To implement the standard's technical requirements and demonstrate compliance, applications can be used. This paper utilizes Design Science Research (DSR) to design, develop, and demonstrate *Security Iiot pRocEss Notation (SIREN)*, an approach based on Business Process Model and Notation (BPMN) to model and monitor processes and compliance. Previous research have yet to cover the IIoT explicitly and lack the monitoring of the modeled attributes. Therefore, a novel specialized approach is presented, enhancing the model with monitorable attributes based on the standard. Thus, this paper presents a BPMN-based approach to model and monitor security-aware processes in IIoT.

Keywords: Industrial Internet of Things Security · Process Aware Monitoring · Security Aware Processes · Security Aware Modeling

1 Introduction

The Industrial Internet of Things (IIoT) offers a broad compendium of technologies from the Internet of Things (IoT) to automate and network production systems [7]. This networking is achieved by connecting industrial operational technology (OT) with information technology (IT). The resulting convergence leads to more efficient systems and enables new solutions.

This work is funded by the "Bavarian Ministry of Economic Affairs, Regional Development and Energy" within the project *INduStrial IoT Security Operations CenTer (INSIST)*.

However, the convergence of IT and OT has a significant drawback: machines and plants become vulnerable to external attacks. In the context of digital production systems, it is essential to understand that cyber security is a joint and overarching task of both IT and OT areas. Therefore, security aspects for IIoT environments require special attention, while also new solutions for maintaining cyber security are necessary [29].

For this reason, there are regulatory efforts to establish the implementation of security measures like IEC62443 in the EU as a standard [13]. According to this standard, respective organizations should follow a "security by design" paradigm [12]. In this respect, to conduct meaningful and sustainable security management, it is crucial to know and define corporate assets, their operative processes, and their information needs. Based thereon, risks can be identified, protective measures can be taken, and security incidents can be monitored. Against this background, the discipline of Business Process Management (BPM) offers numerous established methods, concepts, and technologies for systematic modeling of operational IIoT processes that can also be exploited for improving IIoT security [1,30,33]. How SIREN differs from these is thoroughly discussed in Sect. 3.2. Also an in-depth analysis has already been published [11]. While there is already research on the integration of IoT and BPM technology in general [14,24,25,27,28], we claim that BPM methods represent an unexploited source for improving cyber security in manufacturing companies [26].

A formally defined process modeling notation, like the de-facto standard Business Process Modeling and Notation (BPMN) [20], is a fundamental means for implementing a BPM-based security by design approach. However, since the IIoT security requirements from the IEC62443 standard are not yet supported, a method must be created to represent security requirements and possible protective measures accordingly. While some notations already exist for security aspects in the IT domain [3,15,34], a specialized approach for the IIoT with its unique requirements is still missing.

In this paper, strictly following DSR, we develop *Security Iiot pRocEss Notation (SIREN)*, a BPMN-based modeling approach for specifying IIoT processes enhanced with security requirements compliant with the IEC62443 standard. Our notation is based on clearly defined functional requirements and security levels extracted from the IEC standard. SIREN uses standard BPMN elements to map security aspects without requiring language extensions and therefore remains completely executable and monitorable. Additionally, as depicted in Fig. 1, we present tool support that enables automated mapping of SIREN-based process models to computer-interpretable security rules that can be monitored within an intrusion detection system. Therefore we deem SIREN comprehensive, because it supports the entire process lifecycle, from identification to monitoring [26]. The evaluation of our approach is twofold: first we applied the notation within a real-life industrial use case, and, based thereupon, we extensively evaluated the artifact with experts from various fields, based on a 4-episode evaluation schema.

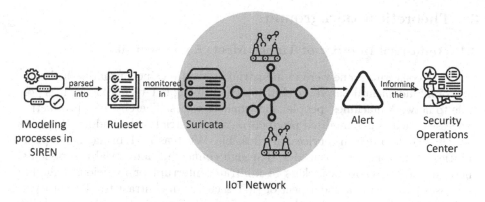

Fig. 1. Overview of IIoT security management with SIREN

The remainder of this paper is structured as follows: in Sect. 2, the research method that guided this paper is discussed. Followed by Sect. 3 in which the underlying concepts and technologies for the suggested approach is discussed, related work is explained, and the design objectives that guided the development are presented. This is followed in Sect. 4 with the design and development of the approach. After that in Sect. 6, we extensively evaluate the approach with various experts.

2   Research Method

This paper is based on the DSR Methodology that aims at creating valuable artifacts within the information systems discipline. [10] To enable systematic and rigorous research, the established procedure model of [21] has been applied, which provided methodological guidance. It consists of six iterative phases, including (i) the identification and motivation of the underlying problem, (ii) the definition of the objectives of the solution, (iii) the actual design and development, (iv) the demonstration, (v) an evaluation, and (vi) the communication to an appropriate audience. While the identification and motivation have already been outlined in Sect. 1, a set of fundamental design objectives are discussed in Sect. 3 that have been derived from the formulated research questions. These design objectives form the basis for subsequent design and development decisions performed iteratively. As a proper evaluation is crucial within any DSR endeavor, a comprehensive evaluation strategy has been created, based on Venable et al. [31]. This strategy included formative and summative evaluation episodes performed before and during (ex-ante) and after (ex-post) the design and development phase. Objective evaluation criteria (cf. Prat et al. [22]) were defined to measure conformance with the design objectives. The design of the artifact follows Moody [19].

3   Theoretical Background

3.1   Industrial Internet of Things Meets Cybersecurity

The IIoT constitutes a new era in industrial production since it marks the beginning of a fundamental paradigm shift [6]. By utilizing IoT technologies, it is possible to network machines, people, and whole factories. Thereby, new production processes, such as personalized products on an industrial scale, and new business models, like data-driven services, are possible. Whereas IIoT brings new opportunities, it also has its downsides. Through connecting industrial components, there are new ways for attackers to infiltrate, interrupt or maliciously modify processes [5,6]. One unique aspect of IIoT security, in contrast to IT security, is that it is mainly concerned with the security of OT and in that the availability [29]. To ensure that, in industrial standards like the IEC62443, the security by design paradigm is required [12]. That means the security of processes and components must be ensured as early as in the design stage. To consider security in industrial processes, there is a need for an inclusive modeling approach of security- and IIoT-aware processes [26].

3.2   Related Work

During the development of SIREN, we have made several design and development steps. Initially, we conducted an extensive systematic literature review (SLR) for knowledge curation. The detailed paper is already published [11]. In the following, this paper only discusses the implications that the SLR raised.

IIoT Extensions for BPMN. In science, the importance of IIoT is already recognized, and by that, a lack of a modeling language to represent IIoT aware processes [16]. For that an EU-funded research project developed a comprehensive BPMN extension that covers sensors, IIoT-specific tasks, and cloud devices. [16–18]. However, it doesn't address security or executability. [9] closes this gap by explicitly considering the execution of modeled processes, but doesn't cover security.

Security Extensions for BPMN. BPMN has been extended to represent security in processes, including classic goals like confidentiality, integrity, and availability [1], encrypted messages [23], and delegation/binding of duty [30]. However, only one paper explicitly deals with an industrial use case [33], but from a business perspective. No explicit integration of IIoT security into BPMN has occurred and there are no concepts for executing secure processes. This paper aims to address these gaps by presenting a BPMN extension that considers the IIoT and enables execution of modeled processes.

Previous work has not explicitly addressed security in IIoT environments, and transforming process models into monitorable rules is, to the best of our knowledge, a novelty. Therefore, our contribution includes using BPMN for IIoT security and transforming process models into monitorable rules.

3.3   Design Objectives

Based on the research question **how can BPMN be used to model processes in IIoT cybersecurity aware and to monitor compliance with the rules**, the following design objectives (DO) emerge. These serve as guidance during development and are used to measure development completion, as described in Sect. 6. The four main objectives are defined and described in the following.

- **DO 1: As little as possible, as much as necessary.** When developing notations, such as SIREN, it is necessary to keep the complexity as low as possible to maximize comprehensibility [19]. Therefore, the first requirement for the artifact is that it contains only essential information.
- **DO 2: Specialized for the IIoT.** As shown in Sect. 3.2, there are already security extensions for BPMN. However, these are either generic or specialized for specific use cases. So far, none explicitly addresses the IIoT, which is why we see a gap in the research here. Therefore, the second requirement for the artifact is that it explicitly addresses IIoT security.
- **DO 3: Relevant, useful and applicable in practice.** A fundamental goal of DSR projects is to create an artifact that is relevant and applicable in the real world [2]. Herefore, the third goal of the artifact is that it is advantageous for the real world, i.e., the IIoT environment.
- **DO 4: Compliance with rules for comprehensibility.** To ensure that the artifact is understandable and thus accessible to people with disabilities, it should comply with standard rules for understandability and readability.

4   Notation Design and Development

4.1   Building the Theoretical Foundations

As shown in Sect. 3, research already enhances BPMN with security attributes, but these lack the specific challenges of the IIoT [11]. In order to establish security requirements for the IIoT, specific requirements must be taken into account. IEC62443 is a comprehensive standard that defines how the security of industrial communication networks can be increased [12]. The standard is divided into three perspectives, manufacturers, integrators, and operators. On the manufacturer side, research already supports compliance with the standard [8]. SIREN focuses on the operator's perspective. SIREN contributes to three corners of security in organizations. i) documentation of processes and security attributes to gain and keep an overview. ii) communication of information so processes can be discussed, optimized, or adapted graphically with various stakeholders, and compliance with regulations can also be proven externally. iii) monitor modeled processes to detect, e.g., intrusions or malicious activities in the network.

Fundamental Requirements (FR). The seven FRs of IEC62443 refer to the security of industrial automation and control systems (IACS) and their components. A list of system, component, network devices, embedded devices, host devices, software application requirements, and requirement enhancements specifies the FR. This paper will limit the focus to the Fundamental and System Requirements described in more detail in Sect. 4.2. In the following, the FR are listed with their respective definitions.

- **FR1 - Identification and authentication control.** Identify and authenticate all users (humans, processes, devices), and grant access to the IACS.
- **FR2 - Use Control.** Enforce the assigned privileges of an authenticated user (human, process, or device) to perform the requested action on the system or assets and monitor the use of these privileges.
- **FR3 - System Integrity.** Ensure the integrity of information on communication channels and in data repositories to prevent unauthorized actions.
- **FR4 - Data confidentiality.** Ensure the confidentiality of information on communication channels and in data repositories to prevent dissemination.
- **FR5 - Restricted data flow.** Segment the system via zones and conduits to limit the unnecessary flow of data
- **FR6 - Timely response to events.** Respond to security violations by notifying the proper authority, reporting needed forensic evidence of the violation, and taking timely corrective action when incidents are discovered.
- **FR7 - Resource Availability.** Ensure the availability of the system or assets against the denial of essential services.

Security Levels (SL). The FR and their specifications are categorized into four security levels. Each represents a specific attacker with the respective motivation, capabilities, and resources. SIREN supports these by allowing the security level to be annotated to entities. An alert can be triggered in the event of deviations from the defined security level and attached monitoring annotations. However, this exact functionality is outside this work's scope.

4.2 Technical Aspects of SIREN

Tool Supported Development. The extension is implemented in Camunda Modeler[1]. This is an extensible open-source modeling tool for BPMN 2.0. It offers two perspectives on the BPMN model. One is a graphical display of the modeled process, and the other is a text editor to display the underlying Extensible Markup Language (XML). Python is used for parsing the rules modeled in BPMN. Parsing means they are translated into monitorable rules. Therefore the XML from Camunda is read and processed by the Python scripts. The exact workflow is described in Sect. 5. Suricata[2] is used to implement network monitoring. Suricata is an open-source network analysis and threat detection tool whose behavior can be configured with self-defined rules. The open-source platform Wazuh[3] is used in this paper for the Security Operations Center (SoC). An SoC is a centralized unit that combines security-related data from multiple sources to provide a comprehensive view of the current cybersecurity status [32].

---

[1] https://camunda.com/de/download/modeler/.
[2] https://suricata.io/.
[3] https://wazuh.com/.

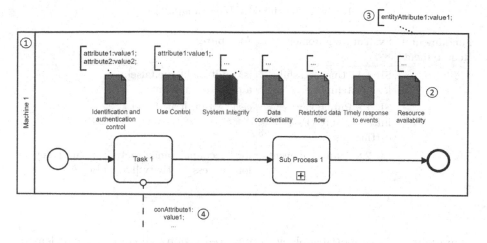

Fig. 2. Example IEC62443-aware process model based on SIREN.

Elements of the Notation. The process shown in Fig. 2 contains numbered circles. These reference to the descriptions of SIREN elements given below, each with an explanation of their use. These indicators are also given in the industrial use cases Fig. 3.

1. **Pools.** The participants of a SIREN process are network entities. These entities are each represented by a pool. Security requirements and entity attributes can extend each entity.
2. **Security Requirements with Attributes.** Data objects are used to extend the entities with the requirements described in Sect. 4.1. Each entity is assigned all requirements with a unique color and name. The requirements are represented in the standards order, and attributes can be added via TextAnnotations which indicate characteristics to fulfill each requirement.
3. **Participant Attribute.** To extend an entity with basic information, TextAnnotations are used, which are attached to it. This information can be, e.g., IP addresses, targeted security levels, or similar.
4. **Network Connection.** The network communication between the entities is represented by MessageFlows. These MessageFlows correspond to a communication connection between two entities and can be enriched with information via TextAnnotations.

Physics of the Notation. Following Moody [19], three different levels of visual distinction are used. First, arrangement, which means that each element has a fixed place in the set of the seven requirements, following the structure of the FR (cf. Sect. 4.1). Secondly, each element is provided with a label that names the FR. The third level of distinction is color. The colors are based on the WCAG

Table 1. Shortened table of mappings.

Fundamental Requirement	System Requirement	Attributes
FR 1	SR 1.11 Unsuccessful login attempts	isMonitored:[true,false]; auth_attempts:int;
	SR 1.8 Public key infrastructure (PKI) certificates	cert_valid: [true;false]
FR 2	SR 2.8 Auditable events	log_reconnaissance_activity:[true;false]; log_access_activity:[true;false];
FR 3		

2.0 guidelines[4] to support people with impaired vision. All colors have at least a Contrast Ratio of 3, so AA conformance is the minimum. However, color is only one of the three levels of distinctiveness, so if, e.g., the model is printed in black and white, the position and the text remain distinguishing features.

5 Implementation and Rule Monitoring

5.1 From Process Modeling to Rule Monitoring

The workflow shown in Fig. 1 is the path of a SIREN user from modeling to monitoring a process. At first, the process is modeled with its participants, dependencies, relationships, and attributes. Various sources can be used for this, e.g., existing documents, process mining, or interview methods [4]. The modeler then enriches the process with the security attributes. These are in a catalog with information about which attributes are needed for a specific security level. After creation, the SIREN parser reads the underlying XML. This parser extracts the required information from the model. The data structure is object-oriented and accordingly creates classes for the entities, which should increase traceability and adaptability. The SIREN rule builder then derives rules based on this information. These can currently be divided into communication and entity rules. Example rules are shown in Listing 1. These rules are then fed into Suricata. This monitors the network based on the rules and examines the data packets for deviations. If it detects some, it informs the SoC.

5.2 Mapping of Security Requirements to Model Attributes

Section 3-3 of IEC62443 is the fundamental of SIREN, which focuses on security requirements for industrial control systems. In the following each requirement is named, followed by a brief description and an example of how SIREN can support it.

---

[4] https://www.w3.org/TR/2008/REC-WCAG20-20081211/0.

- **FR1 - Identification and Authentication Control.** To meet this requirement, e.g., the control systems must be able to identify and authenticate all users (cf. IEC62443-3-3 SR1.1). To detect unauthorized access attempts, rules can monitor login attempts. SIREN contains a rule that tracks login attempts and triggers an alert after a certain threshold is reached.
- **FR2 - Use Control.** The control system shall provide the ability to generate audit records relevant to security. For activities such as access restrictions, operating system events, backup or restore events, and potentially malicious activities on the network (cf. IEC62443-3-3 SR2.8). Continuous network monitoring supports this capability, e.g., unusual activities can be recorded and detected. In addition, records of security-relevant events, such as unusual access activities, are continuously created.
- **FR3 - System Integrity.** To ensure system integrity, control systems shall provide the ability to detect, prevent and minimize the impact of malicious code (cf. IEC62443-3-3 SR 3.2). For this purpose, SIREN can integrate publicly available libraries, which detect malicious operations in the network and can trigger an alert in the SoC if so. This means that these can be detected and prevented at an early stage.
- **FR4 - Data Confidentiality.** Confidentiality should be ensured for data exchanged or stored between control systems (see IEC62443 - SR 4.1, SR 4.3). To ensure this, SIREN can monitor the network traffic of entities and check if secure protocols and encryption are used. If a deviation from the specification is detected as an alert can be raised.
- **FR5 - Restricted Data Flow.** The control system should provide the possibility to separate networks according to task and security level and monitor this separation (cf. IEC62443 SR 5.1, 5.2). SIREN can support this in that it offers a visualization option in the first step and can monitor the separation of the networks in the second step. If an exchange of packets from entities of different, independent networks is detected, the SoC is alerted.
- **FR6 - Timely Response to Events.** The control system should provide the ability to continuously monitor activity on the network to allow for rapid intervention if needed (cf. IEC62443-3-3 SR 6.2). By continuously monitoring the network, depending on the configuration, with intrusion detection and detection of suspicious traffic, requests, and packets, SIREN can support this requirement on a network basis.
- **FR7 - Resource Availability.** To fulfill this requirement, the control systems should not stop working in case of a DDOS attack, and unused ports, functions, and protocols should be disabled (cf. IEC62443 3-3 SR7.1, SR7.7). In addition, a permanent inventory of the network components should be made (cf. IEC62443 3-3 SR7.8). In order to fulfill this requirement, SIREN offers the possibility of quickly detecting DDoS attacks, including affected systems, through its continuous monitoring. In addition, alerts can be triggered in the SoC when unknown protocols, ports, or services are used. In addition, SIREN informs the SoC about unknown participants.

```
------------------
Network rules
pass OPCUA 192.168.95.1 22 > 192.168.95.25 24
pass OPCUA 192.168.95.25 any > 192.168.95.1 any
------------------
Entity rules
alert tcp any any -> 192.168.95.25 any (msg:"More than 3 login
↪    attempts!"; content:"admin"; flowint: usernamecount, +, 1;
↪    flowint:usernamecount, >, 3;)
```

Listing 1: Automated generated rules.

To add attributes to each FR in the monitored model, a mapping table was created. The table contains attributes that can be inserted into the model. Currently, the table has limited examples which will be expanded in future development stages. A shortened version of the table is shown in Table 1. For example, the two attributes, *isMonitored* and *auth_attempts*, can monitor failed login attempts. The former sets a Boolean value to indicate if login attempts should be monitored, while the latter sets a threshold for how many consecutive failed attempts should trigger an alert in the SoC.

5.3   Automatically Generating Monitorable Rules

The BPMN model with added attributes is parsed and transformed into monitorable rules using Python programs called xml_parser and rule_generator. The xml_parser extracts relevant information from the BPMN XML and the rule_generator generates monitorable rules based on this information, using the open-source intrusion detection system Suricata. Examples of generated rules from Fig. 3 are given in Listing 1. SIREN is developed modularized to allow the integration of different monitoring systems and is thus not limited to Suricata. In this paper, Suricata serves as a proof of concept.

5.4   Monitoring Security Within IIoT Networks

The last step is monitoring the rules generated in the previous step. For this purpose, they are fed into Suricata. Based on this, Suricata then monitors the network and provides the central SoC, based on Wazuh, with information. If, e.g., deviations from the defined process are detected, Suricata reports this to the SoC. Decisions or countermeasures can then be taken in the SoC to ensure or restore the network's security.

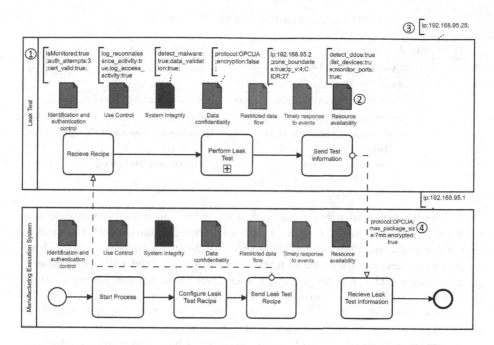

Fig. 3. An abbreviated process of an automotive supplier modeled in SIREN.

6 Evaluation

6.1 Demonstration in Industrial Use Case

For the evaluation, a finishing process of an automotive supplier was modeled in SIREN. An abbreviated representation of this process is shown in Fig. 3. The overall process checks components for specific criteria. Various systems and equipment are involved in this process. In the abbreviated version included in this paper, a manufacturing execution system prepares a so-called recipe, and sends it to the Leak Test machine. A recipe is an instruction with precise information about the test. After processing the recipe, the machine send the result to the central system. Communication takes place via the OPC-UA protocol.

6.2 Execution of the Evaluation

The evaluation was divided into five episodes, as shown in Table 3. The first four have already been carried out, and the fifth is planned after the completion of the overall project. Four evaluation criteria were selected based on the DO. *(i) Conciseness:* The notation contains only essential components, *(ii) Efficacy:* The artifact meets the design objectives established in Sect. 3.3, *(iii) Operational feasibility:* Experts believe that SIREN is usable and helpful for them in their everyday work, and *(iv) Effectiveness:* SIREN proves the achievement of the design objectives in reality.

Table 2. Participants of the Evaluation.

Participant Id	Job Title	Work/Company
1	Cyber Security Associate	Big 4 Consulting (1)
2	Assistant Manager Cyber Security	Big 4 Consulting (2)
3	Security & Senior Security Engineer	International Automotive Supplier
4	Information Security Consultant	Leading Business and IT Consulting
5	Consultang Cybersecurity (Industrial Sector)	Leading Business and IT Consulting
6	Cybersecurity Expert	Automation Technology

The evaluation was carried out as follows. First, an example use case was modeled (cf. Fig. 3), and the authors discussed the compliance with the evaluation criteria of conciseness and efficacy (EV 1). Once the authors decided these criteria were met, semi-structured interviews were conducted with eight experts on compliance with the criteria. Expert interviews are a well-established method for gathering insights from knowledgeable individuals in a specific field [22]. The Interviews revealed that version 1 of the artifact was too complex and overloaded, raising doubts about its feasibility. As a result, the decision was made to regress from the evaluation phase to the design phase and intensify efforts to meet the four design objectives and evaluation criteria. After Version 2 reached, in the authors opinion, the status of meeting the evaluation criteria (EV 3), the experts listed in Table 2 were invited for unstructured interviews. These were carried out according to the following scheme:

Step 1. Request contextual information such as familiarity with IEC62443, cybersecurity domain knowledge, and process modeling experience.
Step 2. (If needed) Brief introduction of the IEC62443 standard.
Step 3. Presentation of the components of SIREN and the workflow.
Step 4. Open question/discussion with the guiding questions:
  – Do you think all important elements are included/is anything missing?
  – Do you think SIREN is easy to apply?
  – Do you think you could work with SIREN?
  – Do you think it would be helpful for the company to use SIREN?
  – What do you think might be challenging in using it?
  – What should be added in the future?

All survey participants found the tool concise and usable, with a solid practical relevance due to its focus on IEC62443 (participants 1, 3, 4, 5, and 6). Future challenges include embedding the artifact in a structured cycle, clarifying its limited organizational cybersecurity coverage, mapping additional requirements, and testing it in a real-world deployment. Following expert confirmation of the evaluation criteria in EV 4, the monitoring attributes will be extended, and a large-scale practical test is planned in EV 5 with a partner company.

Table 3. Performed and planned evaluation episodes.

Evaluation episode	Why?	How?			What
	Function	Environment	Timing	Method	Criteria
EV 1	Formative	Artificial	Ex-ante	Static analysis	Conciseness, Efficacy
EV 2	Formative	Artificial & naturalistic	Ex-ante	Semi-structured interviews	Conciseness, Efficacy, Operational feasibility
EV 3*	Formative	Artificial	Ex-ante	Static analysis	Conciseness, Efficacy
EV 4	Formative	Artificial & naturalistic	Ex-ante	Semi-structured interviews	Conciseness, Efficacy, Operational feasibility
EV 5	Summative	Naturalistic	Ex-post	Real-world use	Effectiveness

Restart of the development after EV2.

7   Conclusion

While IIoT security is becoming increasingly important, and the process perspective is an essential part of security by design, research lacks modeling possibilities. In particular, one cannot use modeling as a basis for effective monitoring.
To fill this research gap, this paper presents SIREN, a BPMN based modelling
notation which enhances industrial processes with attributes of IEC62443 and
transforms them to monitorable rules. This novel approach has been shown to be
effective in practice in accompanying surveys. In order to further develop SIREN
and increase its usability, future work will focus on the following aspects:

- **IEC62443 conformance** SIREN needs to expand its capabilities beyond
  IEC62443 3-3 to include, for example, section 4-2. Additionally, the rule gen-
  erator must be further developed to support security levels, such as detecting
  deviations from the desired security level to the actual security level. The
  rules presented in Sect. 5 are just an example to explain the basic approach
  of SIREN and therefore, they need to be extended.
- **Scalability** SIREN represents one monitoring device for one industrial plant.
  SIREN should provide the possibility of equipping entire factories. Therefore
  an scalabe architecture for SIREN must be developed, so that is is capable
  of larger tasks.
- **Real world usage** SIREN must be used in practice to further evaluate its
  usability. According to EV 5 (cf. Sect. 6 a large spanned evaluation of SIREN
  in an real world scenario must be done, to gather insights on its capabilities
  in the IIoT environment.

As representing assets, processes, and security infrastructure is crucial for organizations seeking IEC62443 certification, we hope to offer added value by providing
SIREN's comprehensive attribute representation.

References

1. Altuhhova, O., Matulevičius, R., Ahmed, N.: An extension of business process model and notation for security risk management. IJISMD **4**(4), 93–113 (2013)
2. vom Brocke, J., Hevner, A., Maedche, A.: Introduction to design science research. In: vom Brocke, J., Hevner, A., Maedche, A. (eds.) Design Science Research. Cases. PI, pp. 1–13. Springer, Cham (2020). https://doi.org/10.1007/978-3-030-46781-4_1
3. Chergui, M.E.A., Benslimane, S.M.: Towards a BPMN security extension for the visualization of cyber security requirements. IJTD **11**(2), 1–17 (2020)
4. Dumas, M., Rosa, M.L., Mendling, J., Reijers, H.A.: Fundamentals of Business Process Management, 2nd edn. Springer, Heidelberg (2018). https://doi.org/10.1007/978-3-662-56509-4
5. Empl, P., Pernul, G.: A flexible security analytics service for the industrial IoT. In: Proceedings of the 2021 ACM Workshop on Secure and Trustworthy Cyber-Physical Systems, SAT-CPS 2021. ACM (2021)
6. ENISA: Good Practices for Security of Internet of Things in the context of Smart Manufacturing. European Union Agency for Cybersecurity (2018)
7. Feki, M.A., Kawsar, F., Boussard, M., Trappeniers, L.: The internet of things: the next technological revolution. Computer **46**(2), 24–25 (2013)
8. Fockel, M., Merschjohann, S., Fazal-Baqaie, M., Förder, T., Hausmann, S., Waldeck, B.: Designing and integrating IEC 62443 compliant threat analysis. In: Walker, A., O'Connor, R.V., Messnarz, R. (eds.) EuroSPI 2019. CCIS, vol. 1060, pp. 57–69. Springer, Cham (2019). https://doi.org/10.1007/978-3-030-28005-5_5
9. Gallik, F., Kirikkayis, Y., Reichert, M.: Modeling, executing and monitoring IoT-aware processes with BPM technology. In: International Conference on Service Science, ICSS 2022, Zhuhai, China, 13–15 May 2022. IEEE (2022)
10. Hevner, A.R., March, S.T., Park, J., Ram, S.: Design science in information systems research. MIS Q. Manag. Inf. Syst. **28**(1), 6 (2004)
11. Hornsteiner, M., Stoiber, C., Schönig, S.: Towards security- and IIoT-aware BPMN: a systematic literature review. In: Proceedings of the 19th International Conference on Smart Business Technologies - ICSBT. SciTePress (2022)
12. IEC: Cybersecurity for Operational Technology in Automation and Control Systems. Standard, International Electrotechnical Commission, Geneva, CH (2009)
13. International Society of Automation: United Nations commission to integrate ISA/IEC 62443 into Cybersecurity Regulatory Framework. InTech Magazine (2019)
14. Janisch, C., Koschmider, A., et al.: The internet-of-things meets business process management: a manifesto. IEEE Syst. Man Cybern. Mag. **6**(4), 34–44 (2020)
15. Maines, C.L., Zhou, B., Tang, S., Shi, Q.: Adding a third dimension to BPMN as a means of representing cyber security requirements. In: DeSE (2016)
16. Mayer, S.: Internet of Things Architecture IoT-A Project Deliverable D2.2 - Concepts for Modelling IoT-Aware Processes. IoT-A Project (2012)
17. Meyer, S., Ruppen, A., Hilty, L.: The things of the internet of things in BPMN. In: Persson, A., Stirna, J. (eds.) CAiSE 2015. LNBIP, vol. 215, pp. 285–297. Springer, Cham (2015). https://doi.org/10.1007/978-3-319-19243-7_27
18. Meyer, S., Ruppen, A., Magerkurth, C.: Internet of things-aware process modeling: integrating IoT devices as business process resources. In: Salinesi, C., Norrie, M.C., Pastor, Ó. (eds.) CAiSE 2013. LNCS, vol. 7908, pp. 84–98. Springer, Heidelberg (2013). https://doi.org/10.1007/978-3-642-38709-8_6

19. Moody, D.: The "physics" of notations: toward a scientific basis for constructing visual notations in software engineering. IEEE TSE **35**(6), 756–779 (2009)
20. OMG: Business Process Model and Notation (BPMN), Version 2.0 (2011)
21. Peffers, K., Tuunanen, T., Rothenberger, M.A., Chatterjee, S.: A design science research methodology for information systems research. JMIS **24**(3), 45–77 (2007)
22. Prat, N., Comyn-Wattiau, I., Akoka, J.: A taxonomy of evaluation methods for information systems artifacts. JMIS **32**(3), 229–267 (2015)
23. Sang, K.S., Zhou, B.: BPMN security extensions for healthcare process. In: ICCIT; UBICC; DASC; PICom (2015)
24. Schönig, S., Ackermann, L., Jablonski, S., Ermer, A.: IoT meets BPM: a bidirectional communication architecture for IoT-aware process execution. Softw. Syst. Model. **19**(6), 1443–1459 (2020)
25. Schönig, S., Aires, A.P., Ermer, A., Jablonski, S.: Workflow support in wearable production information systems. In: Mendling, J., Mouratidis, H. (eds.) CAiSE 2018. LNBIP, vol. 317, pp. 235–243. Springer, Cham (2018). https://doi.org/10.1007/978-3-319-92901-9_20
26. Schönig, S., Hornsteiner, M., Stoiber, C.: Towards process-oriented IIoT security management: perspectives and challenges. In: Augusto, A., Gill, A., Bork, D., Nurcan, S., Reinhartz-Berger, I., Schmidt, R. (eds.) Enterprise, Business-Process and Information Systems Modeling, vol. 450, pp. 18–26. Springer, Cham (2022). https://doi.org/10.1007/978-3-031-07475-2_2
27. Stoiber, C., Schönig, S.: Digital transformation and improvement of business processes with internet of things: a maturity model for assessing readiness. In: 55th Hawaii International Conference on System Sciences, HICSS, pp. 1–10 (2022)
28. Stoiber, C., Schönig, S.: Improving business processes with the internet of things - a taxonomy of IIoT applications. In: 30th European Conference on Information Systems - New Horizons in Digitally United Societies, ECIS (2022)
29. Tange, K., De Donno, M., Fafoutis, X., Dragoni, N.: A systematic survey of industrial internet of things security: requirements and fog computing opportunities. IEEE Commun. Surv. Tutor. **22**(4), 2489–2520 (2020)
30. Turki, S.H., Bellaaj, F., Charfi, A., Bouaziz, R.: Modeling security requirements in service based business processes. In: Bider, I., et al. (eds.) BPMDS/EMMSAD-2012. LNBIP, vol. 113, pp. 76–90. Springer, Heidelberg (2012). https://doi.org/10.1007/978-3-642-31072-0_6
31. Venable, J., Pries-Heje, J., Baskerville, R.: FEDS: a framework for evaluation in design science research. Eur. J. Inf. Syst. **25**(1), 77–89 (2016)
32. Vielberth, M., Glas, M., Dietz, M., Karagiannis, S., Magkos, E., Pernul, G.: A digital twin-based cyber range for SOC analysts. In: Barker, K., Ghazinour, K. (eds.) DBSec 2021. LNCS, vol. 12840, pp. 293–311. Springer, Cham (2021). https://doi.org/10.1007/978-3-030-81242-3_17
33. Zareen, S., Akram, A., Ahmad Khan, S.: Security Requirements Engineering Framework with BPMN 2.0.2 Extension Model for Development of Information Systems. Appl. Sci. **10**(14), 4981 (2020)
34. Zarour, K., Benmerzoug, D., Guermouche, N., Drira, K.: A BPMN extension for business process outsourcing to the cloud. In: Rocha, Á., Adeli, H., Reis, L.P., Costanzo, S. (eds.) WorldCIST'19 2019. AISC, vol. 930, pp. 833–843. Springer, Cham (2019). https://doi.org/10.1007/978-3-030-16181-1_78

Co-design and Collective Creativity for Addressing Grand Challenges

Co-design and Collective Creativity for Addressing ´Grand Challenges Track

Leona Chandra Kruse[1] and Pascal LeMasson[2]

[1] University of Liechtenstein
Leona.chandra@uni.li
[2] MINES ParisTech
pascal.le_masson@mines-paristech.fr

Addressing grand challenges lies at the heart of contemporary design initiatives. Such initiatives rely on effective collaboration – on co-design and collective creativity. The increasing sophistication and interconnectivity of digital systems creates vast possibilities for co-designers, provided they have the necessary tools, structures, and knowledge. This means co-designers must develop collaborative processes and systems that allow them to harness insights from a range of actors, such as technology specialists, artists, managers, and of course, the intended users. How can one promote both rigor and collective creativity at the same time? Moreover, co-designers must capture and harness the different outputs of their collective creativity. When presenting and evaluating design initiatives, we tend to focus only on the final outputs, such as prototypical implementations, deployed artifacts, and design knowledge. However, intermediary outputs and unfinished solutions play an important role in fostering collective creativity and shaping the final outputs. How can one avoid losing these invaluable assets? This track demonstrates out-of-the-box research on co-designers and their approaches to foster collective creativity in order to address grand challenges.

This track presents three papers that illustrate the importance of co-design and collective creativity in addressing grand challenges. They also demonstrate methods and approaches for supporting designer teams in their co-design efforts. The two papers demonstrate the application of co-design to harness collective creativity in providing viable solutions. Lina Lukusa, Ulrike Rivett, Tom Sanya and Shallen Lusinga, narrates an approach to co-designing a platform for water-sensitive urban design in Africa. The second paper is about capturing collective creativity in an idea management system which has been implemented in a national train maintenance center. This paper is co-authored by Honorine Harlé, Pascal Le Masson, Benoit Weil, Tony Bourlier and Yann Veslin. The last paper, co-authored by Alicia Roschnik and Stéphanie Missonier, sheds light on how to co-design visual inquire tools.

We thank our reviewers for their constructive assessments. Their collective effort has contributed significantly to the development of each paper.

What Does the Factory's Suggestion Box Reveal?

An Analysis of the Design Capabilities of a Train Maintenance Center from Its Idea Management System

Honorine Harlé[1] , Pascal Le Masson[1]([✉]) , Benoit Weil[1], Tony Bourlier[2],
and Yann Veslin[2]

[1] Mines Paris- PSL, Mines Paris – PSL, Centre de Gestion Scientifique (CGS), i3 UMR CNRS 9217, Chaire Théorie & Méthodes de la Conception Innovante, Paris, France
pascal.le_masson@minesparis.psl.eu
[2] SNCF, Technicentre TER Pays de la Loire, 44000 Nantes, France

Abstract. Suggestion boxes have been used in factories to improve processes through a continuous improvement approach. From this perspective, the ideas with direct and quick implementation and visible results are favoured. This paper investigates the nature of design activities hidden behind the ideas suggested. The authors sort 132 ideas from a suggestion box of a French train maintenance center and highlight differences in the processing of the ideas through the suggestion box. The paper shows that a part of the ideas should have been rejected, as they present a gap in the design to be directly implemented. However, they are kept and collectively re-worked to be well adapted to the factory. This enriches literature on creativity and crowd sourcing for and by manufacturing. In particular, it gives a design perspective to innovation and continuous improvement in factory by revealing different design types in the box to fit the production system.

Keywords: Factory · Design · Suggestion box

1 Introduction

In manufacturing, the shop floor operators are often involved in the performance of the production, especially in the continuous improvement approach [1]. For this reason, they have to detect the problems and the losses that become sources of potential gains when they are solved. Among the tools used to foster continuous improvement in a participative way, the suggestion box, physical or virtual, is classically used [2, 3]. The operators, as users of the production line, are better placed to propose ideas and to implement them. They receive their prize in function of the effect of the improvement of the production performance. However, this tool faces a major ambiguity: it is at the same time a tool to optimize the production process by involving operators in the continuous improvement process [4], but it is also expected for more radical innovation [5]. This later aim could appear contradictory to a production context. Indeed, when used in factories, suggestion systems meet the constraints inherent to the shop floor production: the factory is a place of execution and not ideation; operators are highly prescribed, their objectives and the

A. Gerber and R. Baskerville (Eds.): DESRIST 2023, LNCS 13873, pp. 397–411, 2023.
https://doi.org/10.1007/978-3-031-32808-4_25

guidance, and time for processes are very precise and let a little place for innovation [6]. Moreover, the factory's performance should be maintained and cannot suffer from troubles caused by experimentation.

This article intends to overcome the conflict between the manufacturing impossibility to change and design new rules and the wish to make them evolve through the suggestion box. The authors went to a train maintenance center of the French railway company SNCF, and questioned the design opportunities and practices that the digital suggestion box could offer. They provided a new comprehension of the factory's digital suggestion box through a design perspective. The study shows that, even if the digital suggestion box of the maintenance center is designed to collect ready-to-implement solutions in a continuous improvement manner, it also admits derogations. A collective design action is launched to validate the conformity with the factory's rules and/or change them. Hence, this article explains how a digital platform which intends to collect and validate (or not) ideas with strict decision criteria is finally used to organize an ambitious design activity of the production rules. It contributes to information system literature by providing a comprehension of the design mechanisms and effects hidden behind a digital suggestion system in a manufacturing context. The results finally offer a method [7] to support, reinforce, and open new ways of using this type of digital collaborating system fostering the design capabilities of the factory.

2 Literature Review

2.1 A Short Genealogy of Suggestion Systems

Suggestion systems emerged and were developed during the 19th century in the manufacturing industry [8]. Eastman Kodak was one of the famous first examples of a US company implementing a suggestion box for its employees to foster their creativity and raise their commitment [9]. Funding the scientific organization, F.W.Taylor separated the design and production activities, isolating the execution function on the shop floor. This organization led to high productive gains. However, the innovation function was not expected from the operators but from the engineering office. Nevertheless, suggestion systems were tested in Taylorian factories to support the shop floor performance: the French company Michelin, one of the first French enterprises to import and implement Taylorian ideas, already collected the operators' ideas in a physical box in the 1920s. At the same time, a suggestion engineer was in charge of motivating them to post and implement the suggestions. However, the suggestion box was given up on after few years [10]. Later, the suggestion systems principle was re-introduced in factories as a way to make the work more participative. The suggestion box has been a tool of first importance for continuous improvement (the Kaizen approach) in the Toyota production system ([11] [12]) and in lean manufacturing (e.g., [4]). Indeed, one of the principles of continuous improvement is the contribution of all the employees to the productive performance, including those working on the shop floor. Hence, according to [13] the functions of the suggestion box are various: to collect employees' opinion, to be more democratic, and to stimulate employees' engagement and their creativity.

The paper [3] insists on the fact that suggestion systems did not remain confined to the manufacturing field but appeared in other fields. Idea management, and more particularly the collection of ideas for innovation, were systematized and developed in companies [8]. The functions are multiple: e.g., to catch customers and collaborators' ideas to foster innovation and develop new products or to solve problems [8]. [14] comments the digitalization of the innovation tools: collaboration and idea management tools are facilitated under digital form. [15, 16] argue that digital platforms can be accelerator for innovation. However, one of the risks is to consider the suggestion system as a passive tool. Following this idea,[16] proves that in academic literature, innovation management and information system researches are only partially connected. Studying the design of intrapreneurship platforms that foster employee driven ideas, as in [17], is one of the means to address this research gap. Moreover, the specificity of industry and the precise mechanisms by which digital platforms transform industry are yet poorly known [14].

2.2 The Contribution and Known Problems of Suggestion Systems

Suggestion systems and, more generally, participative approaches to collect employee's ideas constituted a pillar of the continuous improvement and gains in productivity in factories. However, it can suffer from many problems: e.g., suggestions systems are given up on after a certain time of implementation, and they do not collect qualitative ideas [3] or people are not motivated to post new ideas [18]. The literature gives a lot of insights into organizing and designing a system that collects ideas efficiently, by improving the collection of ideas with an adapted management or by making the process transparent and rapid with a rewarding system that provides enough incentive [3].

As a manufacturing tool, the suggestion box has been viewed as a means to foster innovation. However, the type of innovation that is possible as a result of a participative system in a factory is unclear. In particular, [19] shows that the suggestion box is efficient for small innovation and continuous improvement: according to [20] it brings forth solutions to optimize the performances on the production line, whereas more elaborate suggestion systems are used in product development to screen radical innovation. However, there are calls for radical changes across the industrial world to answer present and future challenges (e.g., cleaner production systems, mass customization, and so on). The transition towards industry 4.0 [21], sustainable manufacturing [22], agile factory [23], and more, generally towards creating a desirable future for factories will require significant efforts and not merely continuous improvement.

2.3 The Selection of Directly Implementable Ideas

The generation of numerous improvements was encouraged, but the very original or new ideas for which the implementation is not direct do not fit into the industrial frame and cannot be accepted. In this configuration, the criterion of evaluation of the ideas is often implicit and not highlighted in the literature: the ideas are validated if they are implementable without any risk of perturbation of the system and rejected otherwise (for instance, in [24]). Thus, the validation criterion for this type of industrial suggestion system is a yes/no criterion based on the probability of success of the idea. Then, a more elaborated scale is used to sort the ideas and decide the reward to grant.

In a larger perimeter than manufacturing, for instance in the new product development or engineering design, suggestion systems are also used to enable the participation of people and the decentralization of the idea collection e.g. [20]. In this context, the validation criterion remains but can be enriched. [25] argues that idea management concerns different types of ideas: some are ready to implement, whereas others show a design gap before being developable and require a different development process. Then, during the collection of ideas, one should pay attention to the "false negatives" that are not considered as innovation and are put aside to be given up since they are not in the core business of the company. On the contrary, those ideas should have raised attention of the management since they could be relevant for the future of the company [26]. [5, 27] explain that a particular selection, treatment, and validation process is needed for the "out of the box" ideas. In particular, the criteria to differentiate them from the "in the box ideas" should be adapted. In [5] the differentiation between the ideas is made by experts assessing the novelty compared with the resources and the capabilities of the company. If the idea is considered to be "out of the box", it will be treated like a radical innovation project. In other terms, according [28], companies should have an ambidextrous process for the collection of ideas: a specific procedure should be designed for the exploration ideas to distinguish them from the exploitation ones and to finally bring the appropriate support to bridge the design gap.

Nevertheless, this last selection and process used in new product development appear to be not suitable for a factory. A factory focuses mainly on the preservation of the production; a change can put the manufacturing system at risk [6]. The notions used previously to characterize innovation, such "out of the box" or "exploration ideas," are not directly comprehensive for a manufacturing context: how can an idea be "out of the box" if it goes against or beside the industrial rules? Regarding the complexity of an industrial system and the numerous constraints in it, the factory's suggestion box is designed to select the ideas that are implementable in a straightforward manner.

3   Research Questions

This article intends to test this later hypothesis: the suggestion box, due to its manufacturing context, rejects not-directly implementable solutions. Alternatively, the factory's suggestion box accepts a wider range of ideas. It also collects solutions that present a design gap before their implementation and that need to be treated separately, as the former paragraph suggests for the field of new product development.

Research questions: What types of ideas can be found and processed in a factory suggestion box? How could this tool be improved to foster the potential of innovation and of collective creativity in manufacturing?

To answer to these questions, the paper evaluates both the idea types and the added design step necessary before implementation. Thus, this research highlights the role of this digital suggestion system to organize a design activity hidden in factory. The context of this study is very specific: it focuses on suggestion systems in production, which constitutes, as shown in the literature review, their roots, but at the same time their limitation. First, the manufacturing sector requires ready-to-use solutions from the operators; it is not organized to liberate time and development means for the operators to design more ambitious and impacting solutions on the shopfloor [6]. Second, in production, the processes, organization, standards, etc. rule the activity in order to produce complex outputs at a chosen quality level in a repeatable way. In this context, a minor change can put the production system at risk and cause significant failures. Hence, design activity in manufacturing is dedicated to improve and optimize the rules (methods, processes, organization, etc.) in place but not to change them [29]. All these constraints are not present in other sectors where there is a place to test, try, and implement new approaches, products, services, organization, etc. Then, the implementation, the management, and the effect of a suggestion system are different between a productive and an administrative department. [30].

4 Methodology

In order to answer these research questions, the authors conducted an in-depth case study [31] in the maintenance center of regional trains at Nantes (France). The next parts gives the details of the material and the method used.

4.1 Research Context: The Nantes SNCF Maintenance Center

The maintenance center, located in Nantes, is dedicated to the maintenance of regional trains of the French railway company SNCF, for the trains linking the cities of the region around Nantes (the region "Pays de la Loire").

The maintenance center employs about 150 people, with various technical qualifications: electric specialists, heating specialists, interior systems technicians, mechanics, and so on. The center can operate up to seven trains at the same time, with three shifts around the clock. It performs the maintenance of 35 trains each day. The technicenter operates the control of the trains and undertakes preventive actions according to the methods department's rules; it also makes small repairs on the trains. An innovative manager is in charge of the continuous improvement and innovation of the site. Among his tasks, he animates the suggestion system of the technicenter, that is to say, he follows the process of the good treatment and implementation of the ideas. His work and tasks correspond to those of the "continuous improvement officer," a manufacturing classic, who supports continuous improvement implementation. However, the term "innovation" marks the wish of the SNCF to deeply change its maintenance centers to address the big industrial challenges of the future (e.g., more sustainable, smarter, and so on).

This field was very relevant to study innovation since it has a very long history of continuous improvement. For instance, the 5S method is implemented, the QCDS (Quality Cost Delivery Safety) is narrowly followed in daily briefings, and, among other tools, the suggestion box was officialized in the SNCF maintenance center in 1954 and has been used ever since [32]. On the other hand, in this center, the nature of the activity of the train maintenance evolves at the rhythm of the automatization of the systems in the trains, which makes the maintenance skills evolve train generation after train generation. Hence, this center is the result of a long heritage of rules, practices, and know-hows in train maintenance.

The authors were in narrow partnership with the maintenance center's director and innovation manager. They visited and came to the technicenter 3 times. Eight two-hour meetings took place between the industrial partners and the researchers to guide the exploration and discuss the partial results. They corresponded by calls and emails when precisions were required. This determined the design methodology based on the study of the suggestion box, and complemented the reading and the comprehension of the panel of the 132 ideas investigated by the authors.

4.2   A Sample of 132 Ideas from the Suggestion Box of the Maintenance Center

This digital suggestion box received about 170 ideas in 2019. It is daily animated by the direct managers of the work groups in the briefing at the beginning of each shift: the managers encourage the operators to post good ideas in the suggestion box. They also follow the idea process and its implementation with the operators. If the idea is not rejected, the operator earns a minimum of 30€, and the financial incentive is scaled in function of the QCDS results of the idea after implementation. Each month, an "innovator of the month" is nominated in the center and each year a national competition chooses the best suggestions from among the various similar SNCF technicenters.

An idea is an electronic form including the date, the innovator(s) name(s), and the decider's name. The forms include the following categories: description of the problem, description of the solution, advantages, manager(s)' comments; then, a category "recommendation for the implementation" can be added, where the manager can add specifications of the solution. Finally, a category labelled "treatment step" appears, where the successive status of the idea are written, and comments can be added to the status. Hence, the reading of the idea informs the nature of the idea as well as all the potential comments of different managers and experts while the idea was processed.

The box has existed for a long time, is well known and used in the factory, and has a manager dedicated for its proper working. Its digitalization consisted in a platform which gathers pre-structured idea forms to be digitally fulfilled. Generally speaking, there is no problem of giving up or lack of motivation or implementation of ideas. Second, the suggestion box gathers the innovation of the technicenter and makes it visible and comprehensive from an external point of view. It seems to be a good instrument to capture the meaning of innovation and continuous improvement for a train maintenance center.

The sample of the 132 ideas contains the following characteristics. It covers the period between 1st January 2019 and the 30th September 2019. There are 93 contributors, over 150 people in the center. On average, each author published 1.9 ideas. 68% of the contributors (63 people) published only one idea, while 3 people published 6 or 7 ideas. In majority, the ideas are written by an author alone or with a colleague: 73% of ideas are written by only one author and 20% of the ideas are written in duo. The box was used by the operators throughout the year, with an average of 14,6 ideas per month. July was a particularly remarkable month as an operator decided to post 7 ideas at the same time. There were 3 ideas that remained not fully completed by their author. Moreover, 11 were not accepted, as the solution was already studied or another solution had already been proposed or because it was not considered as an idea (for instance, somebody who would complain about the organization).

4.3 Steps of Analysis of the Sample

Step 1: Filtering the ideas presenting at first a lack in design
First, the authors picked the 132 ideas from January to September and looked at the history of comments at the end of the idea forms. Some comments were just the validation or the appreciation of the idea (e.g., "good idea that improved the maintenance delay"; "implemented a month ago and works well"; and so on). Others showed an investigation step to design the solution (e.g., an expert is called, the design goes on in a dedicated team with a supplier, for example, and so on). The authors sorted the ideas between those without investigation comments and those with investigation comments. In this manner, instead of making assumption about the degree of novelty or the innovativeness of ideas to conduct their analysis, the authors filtered the ideas which were supposed to be rejected from the process (as not directly implementable ideas).

Step 2: Determining the nature of the supplementary design and resources required
To have a better understanding of the supplementary design and management required before the acceptation of the ideas, the authors identifies 5 categories of investigation comments. Thus, the ideas with these comments were coded. The authors carefully discussed with the innovation manager and the director's center during two semi-directive interviews of one-and-a-half hours to understand the resources and the organization devoted to the idea treatment, especially when a supplementary design step was necessary.

5 Analysis and Results

5.1 The Two Hidden Categories of a Unique Suggestion Box

The authors sort the ideas in two categories: the ideas with or without investigation comments, as described in the former section.

A first category of ideas: the tricks directly implementable
The category gathered ideas that include only validation comments or do not include any comments. A validation comment is a manager's comment that underlines the quality of the idea, e.g., "good idea," "too be implemented soon," "to be awarded," and so on. It does not improve or change the nature of the idea itself. 101 ideas (77% of the ideas) belong to this category. Hence, this category includes ideas that are directly implementable. Examples of this category are: a tool for a better ergonomics (e.g., by adding a handle, or colouring in yellow to increase the visibility), a best storage organization to save time, a change in the garbage place so as to put them nearer the operations, a trick not to lose the security keys between two shifts, and so on.

Qualitative analysis and comment:. The ideas of this category look like a standardized form to be checked and stamped. Indeed, the solutions are directly implementable without any specifications and present observable and direct results. They rely on the slight modifications of organization and techniques to improve the processes in term of security, ergonomics, cost, and so on. They use the common sense or the employees' creativity applied on technical gestures, the tricks found by the operators. For these ideas, the solutions were not far from the existing one, the effects could be observed immediately and the validation was direct. This is an expected result in factory: the innovation relies on continuous improvement in which the employees have a major role. The innovations captured by this system includes the improvements that enable the better implementation the rules and optimize the prescription, in accordance to the traditional gap between the real and prescribed in factory [33].

A second category of ideas: the ideas with design gap

The authors took all the ideas that had investigation comments and gathered them in a category. An investigation comment is a comment where the manager investigates the solution, such as the following:

- The written solution can be considered as not sufficiently detailed nor specified to have a decision about its implementation; "What diameter, length, would you need?"; "Do you have any reference of this solution in a catalogue?", "Do you have any picture of its implementation where else?".
- The manager calls a SNCF expert who gives precision on the form (on the technical characteristics or on the rules). "We saw the health and safety committee, who advised to avoid this solution."
- The manager asks for a quotation to a supplier and finishes the specifications and the design with him.

Of all the ideas, 31 were noticed to have investigation comments and thus belong to the second category. Among the 31 ideas, the 7 ideas with the status "in-depth investigation" received investigation comments. The comments were precision to the necessary investigation (Manager 1 to Manager 2): "Can you tell me if this innovation is taken into account in the rules?"; (Manager 2) "Relayed to the supplier"; for another idea: "Does it exist somewhere? (pictures, catalogue, references)". The solution is considered as not implementable, and the design is not finished. The 3 ideas with the status "closed and failed" indicates that the idea was judged good, and awarded but failed in the implementation. Two of them received comments about a future study to be launched ("there is no system for this problem"). One of them noticed in the comments that the idea was good but already explored; the technicenter was not able to decide alone (cf. Example in part 2), but the idea was considered good enough not to be rejected.

Qualitative analysis and comment: Finally, the investigation comments show the following elements: the managers commented the solutions and suggested other ones, debated via the form with other managers on the solution, or made checks into the rules and changed the solutions afterward. In other cases, the solution was explicitly given to design with the supplier, and the design work went on between the operator, the manager, and the supplier. Thus, the ideas could not be validated immediately but needed changes, verifications, an expert's advice, or the supplier's intervention. The authors called "**design gap**" this complementary investigation. Hence, the criterion used by the managers of the suggestion box is a "pass or fail" criterion. However, the criterion "pass" is richer than the direct implementation. It encompasses various situations. In particular, 23% of ideas are denoted "pass" with a design gap. At first sight, this design gap necessary to complete the solutions can be viewed as undesirable in a factory where the solutions should be implementable directly. One can consider that 31 ideas in this category is a low number to assess the phenomenon that the authors are investigating. However, ideas of this category are highly unexpectable in this suggestion box (they do not fit with the rules of the tool) and should not have been processed. From this point of view, 23% of the ideas is a significant amount, and this category should be analyzed more carefully.

5.2   The Nature of the Investigation Necessary to Complete the Design

The idea with design gap were analyzed. An illustrative example is detailed.

An illustrative example: the "Fake" platform

An operator indicates that the tool to control the good working of the sensors of the automatic doors is not reliable. He suggests to adopt another process to control the sensors, by testing the doors in real conditions on the recent storage platforms of the maintenance center. The manager answers that it was a good idea, but suggests a new tool-platform on wheels.

The history of the comments written on the idea form was the following:

5th July:. (innovation manager to the tool manager) Hello, Tool Manager! Can you help the author on this idea? Thank you! The idea would consist of doing a "fake platform" on wheels and using it on the platforms x, y, z.

12th July:. (Tool manager to innovation manager): Hello, Innovation Manager. A fake platform on wheels, why not. But there is no use to limit it to the platforms x, y, z. We could use it on other platforms. But, if I understood well, the idea would be to realize a true platform on the storage platform. To be discussed with the author directly.

18th July:. (Manager N + 1) approved. The author has to make a drawing of the fake platform, with the help of the tool manager.

In the following months, the idea's author, the tool responsible, the innovation manager, and a supplier created and produced a new "fake platform" on wheels to test the automation system of the doors. In this example, the idea's author highlighted a problem in a tool and proposed a solution. His managers considered the solution but found another one, apart from the idea form, in a collective design effort.

The type of comments clarifies the nature of the design gap

The comments can be classified in 5 categories. All the investigation comments fit in one or more category of comments.

Category 1:. The comments that imply another person than the direct manager N + 1:

"The operator should consult the tools manager to implement its idea"; "see with the supplier"; [Manager N+1 to manager 2] "Dear Manager 2, could you study the idea?"

Category 2: The comments that question the solution and that show that there is a lack of details or specification: "Relevant idea. (…) Can you give an example of the beacon (pictures) and find an adequate storage space?"; "What are the visits concerned by this dimension measurements? What are the series concerned? How to do with the dimension measures with tolerance?".

Category 3: The comments that show that the solution is not satisfying, implying that the problem remains: "This idea would be difficult to implement. But it is indeed a problem to have to isolate 6 batteries"; "After discussion with Manager Y, it is rather a no from our part."; "Already tested. See for another solution".

Category 4: The comments that make an explicit check in the system of rules to validate (or invalidate) the solution: "The rule asks to each agent who would need to work locked out to protect himself."; "a form does already exist, the form "Y", which explains the eco- parking process.

Category 5:. The comments that mention an explicit change in the rules: "The whole file has to be transmitted to the technical department in order to maintain this relevant tool"; "Do you think that the rules should be modified or a mere verbal opinion by the hierarchy would be enough?".

The authors completed in the following table (Table 1) the nature of the comments found in each idea form. One comment can belong to several categories.

Table 1. The coding of the investigation comments for the ideas with a design gap (extract)

Idea number	more people	more details	the problem remains	explicit check in the rules	explicit change in the rules
1		X			
2		X			
3				X	
...	...	...	...	...	...
31	X				
total	21	10	6	8	2
total in % of the 31 ideas	68%	32%	19%	26%	6%

Qualitative Analysis and Comments

All the investigation comments are included in one or more categories. These comments can be interpreted as marks of the design process necessary to fill the design gap. Indeed, they give evidence of the necessity to build the solutions with more people, including experts. There is a concern about the feasibility of the solution, technically but also in compliance with the industrial rules. This appear to be a particularity of innovation in the factory: the prescription, i.e. the good realization of the production, at the standards of performances in terms of quality, cost, delay, safety, gives a fixed frame to the novelty. In contrast, the ideas that are in this frame can be directly implementable, a design process step has to be added for the ideas that present an incertitude or ambiguity or incompleteness relative to the rules. To sum up, the nature of the comments provides insights on the type of investigation carried outside the form, in the maintenance center.

The design activity requires a collective action, rigorous specifications of solutions to be validated and inserted in the production system, and a new phase of ideation to tackle the problem. This design activity also presents an effect on the maintenance rules since the rules are checked and evolve, if necessary.

5.3 Results: A Hidden Design Activity to Change the Manufacturing Rules Emerged from the Suggestion Box

Finally, this study demonstrates that the selection of ideas from the suggestion box is not based solely on a binary pass/fail criterion, as supposed at a first glance. The box is used by the managers to check the idea's validation conditions, to look for rules, and ensure that the solution adheres to the rules. The re-discovery of the system of rules is implied by this exploration. For some of the ideas that do not directly fit with the rules, the technicenter organizes teams to design the validation of the new rules (or its change) implied in the ideas. Thus, this study also highlights the nature of design activity occurring in the maintenance center: beyond the radicality of the ideas, it deals with the revision of the rules.

Consequently, the suggestion box's management and design could have resembled those of a gate: a list of defined criteria and a decider who checks and validates the criteria. However, unlike a gate, the SNCF suggestion box reveals another organization around it. In the technicenter, new actors congregate and discuss ideas, new knowledge about the rules is shared, and the inquiry and validation phases begin with the idea form. A new room was built for the innovation teams to investigate broad concepts and questions in collaboration with other actors; partnerships with local actors (universities, public labs in cities) were formed to design, test, and prototype; and a network of SNCF experts was formed to answer technical questions. The innovation manager and the director of the technicenter were heavily involved in following the innovations, allocating a dedicated budget, creating an innovation workshop to pursue the ideas, and rewarding the creative employees.

6 Discussion, Managerial and Design Implications for Suggestion Systems

6.1 The Nature of Design in Factory: Re-discussing the Notion of Radicality

This research enriches the understanding of the "novelty" (or the "radicality") of the ideas (vs "the marginal," "the continue") in the factory, according the well-known distinction [34]. The "radical ideas" are not radical themselves, but the radicality can be understood as a distance to the existing solutions. Slightly differently, the article invites to re-think the nature of the distance for a factory. Indeed, an idea can be near the existing solution, and at the same time very far from validation, because it does not exactly fit to the production rules. Hence, the distance to validate and, consequently, the design gap is high. What remains to design is not another idea newer and more radical but the validation of the idea in the factory. This is also true while reflecting in term of ambidexterity [35]: the article shows that the routine can be an object of re-discovery and the design of a solution among the routines is neither properly an exploitation problem, nor an exploration problem, hence refining [28]. It mixes both of them to explore the routines and validate the solutions regarding them or rethinking them. This refinement could be supported by the notion of creation heritage [36], which indicates the capacity for an existing system ("the heritage") to innovate and to achieve a transformation within itself ("creative"). The article indicates that the novelty and so-called radicality is made possible by a careful attention and rework on the rules. The digital suggestion system, gathering employees who post ideas, manager who assess the conformity of the ideas to the rules, and other technical and rule experts, becomes a medium through which this activity can be organized. In this view, the article contributes to the research on the innovation mechanisms derived from digital platforms in industry [14].

6.2 Design Principles and Managerial Implications for Suggestion Systems in Constrained Environments

In accordance to the design principles for digital suggestion systems, a recommendation can be derived from this study [17]: the evidence that a special process does exist for not directly implementable ideas claims for designing digital suggestion systems in coherence with this fact. In the validation process, the digital system should incorporate an explicit category for these ideas, and visible process steps for them. Thus, the ideas could be considered as entire collective projects, requiring appropriate means, and not only as derogations. This is coherent with the design principles of transparency of the process and the identification of informal roles identified in [17].

On the managerial level, this study highlights an idea management system in a factory that involved all levels of the hierarchy in a design approach. The studied suggestion box is an example of a traditional manufacturing tool that was developed in the nineteenth century to recognize and encourage employees' creativity while also involving them in the production process on an individual or group level. Following investigations, this tool allows for more than just the collection of tricks. It also coordinates an intensive and collaborative design process involving a wide range of stakeholders, including the idea's creator, the supplier, various experts and specialized managers, engineers from the local or national material center, and the innovation manager. They each have a role to play in the design process. Wide ideas or concepts that could be new axes of exploration for the maintenance center and its partners can be found on the outskirts of the suggestion box. Because many rules are compatible with this design activity, this significant organization for a continuous design activity in a factory could be found in other factories and other suggestion boxes. The system's management rules gave the managers various degrees of freedom in this study, including the ability to add comments, improve the solution, call various experts to check the rules, and finally, time, place, and financial resources dedicated to this goal.

6.3 Limits and Further Research

This article relies on a study of a particular digital suggestion box in a maintenance center. The sample of 132 ideas allowed the authors to conduct a detailed analysis of the process followed by ideas, beyond what was expected by the suggestion box. 31

ideas (20% of the sample) were found to be out of the classical scope of this tool. The methodology used by the authors could be used in other factories and in other contexts to increase their generality. In the same way, the design principles for the suggestion systems could be tested in further research, as well as the management and organization needed in addition to these systems to drive the design activity.

This research discusses the innovation tools and information systems available in the factory. If the factory design is able to explore the rules and re-discuss them, tools and management adapted for this property are needed. This analysis is also true for innovation in industry 4.0, which is often viewed as a technological change to implement [37], potentially implemented by a central technologic or innovation team in the manufacturing engineering department [21, 38], whereas this article implies a wider spread of the design activity among the teams, a new inventive regime with a reasoning on the system of rules. Other environments, which also deal with constrained rules (administrative services, enterprises, etc.), could have the same relation to radicalness, and the same need for adapted suggestion systems. Other research works could be undertaken to enrich this argument and understand this design activity.

References

1. Iwao, S.: Revisiting the existing notion of continuous improvement (Kaizen): literature review and field research of Toyota from a perspective of innovation. Evolutionary Institutional Econ. Rev. **14**(1), 29–59 (2017)
2. Pizam, A.: Some correlates of innovation within industrial suggestion systems. Pers. Psychol. **27**(1), 63–76 (1974)
3. Fairbank, J.F., Williams, S.D.: Motivating creativity and enhancing innovation through employee suggestion system technology. Creativity Innov. Manage. **10**(2), 68–74 (2001). https://doi.org/10.1111/1467-8691.00204
4. Moica, S., Harea, C.V., Marian, L.: Effects of suggestion system on continuous improvement: a case study. In: 2018 IEEE International Conference on Industrial Engineering and Engineering Management (IEEM), IEEE, pp. 592–596 (2018)
5. Sandstrom, C., Bjork, J.: Idea management systems for a changing innovation landscape. IJPD **11**(3/4), 310 (2010). https://doi.org/10.1504/IJPD.2010.033964
6. Castagnoli, R., Stal-Le Cardinal, J., Büchi, G., Cugno, M.: Industry 4.0 management: preliminary design implications. In: Proc. Des. Soc., **2**, pp. 121–130 (2022). https://doi.org/10.1017/pds.2022.13
7. Offermann, P., Blom, S., Schönherr, M., Bub, U.: Artifact types in information systems design science – a literature review. In: Winter, R., Zhao, J.L., Aier, S. (eds.) DESRIST 2010. LNCS, vol. 6105, pp. 77–92. Springer, Heidelberg (2010). https://doi.org/10.1007/978-3-642-13335-0_6
8. Gerlach, S., Brem, A.: Idea management revisited: a review of the literature and guide for implementation. Int. J. Innov. Stud. **1**(2), 144–161 (2017). https://doi.org/10.1016/j.ijis.2017.10.004
9. Carnevale, D.G., Sharp, B.S.: The old employee suggestion box: an undervalued force for productivity improvement. Rev. Public Personnel Administration **13**(2), 82–92 (1993)
10. Tesi, F.: Michelin et le taylorisme. Histoire, économie & société, vol. 27e année, no. 3, pp. 111–126 (2008). https://doi.org/10.3917/hes.083.0111
11. Yasuda, Y.: 40 years, 20 Million Ideas: the Toyota Suggestion System. Productivity Press (1991)

12. Recht, R., Wilderom, C.: Kaizen and culture: on the transferability of Japanese suggestion systems. Int. Bus. Rev. **7**(1), 7–22 (1998). https://doi.org/10.1016/S0969-5931(97)00048-6
13. Thom, N.: Idea management in Switzerland and Germany: past, present and future. Die Unternehmung **69**(3), 238–254 (2015)
14. de Reuver, M., Sørensen, C., Basole, R.C.: The digital platform: a research agenda. J. Inf. Technol. **33**(2), 124–135 (2018). https://doi.org/10.1057/s41265-016-0033-3
15. Benbya, H., Leidner, D.: How allianz UK used an idea management platform to harness employee innovation. MIS Quarterly Executive **17**(2) (2018)
16. Opland, L.E., Jaccheri, L., Pappas, I.O. Engesmo, J.: Utilising the innovation potential-a systematic literature review on employee-driven digital innovation. In: ECIS (2020)
17. Reibenspiess, V., Drechsler, K., Eckhardt, A., Wagner, H.-T.: Tapping into the wealth of employees' ideas: design principles for a digital intrapreneurship platform. Inf. Manage. **59**(3), 103287 (2022). https://doi.org/10.1016/j.im.2020.103287
18. Buech, V.I.D., Michel, A., Sonntag, K.: Suggestion systems in organizations: what motivates employees to submit suggestions? Euro J. Inn Mnagmnt **13**(4), 507–525 (2010). https://doi.org/10.1108/14601061011086311
19. Carrier, C.: Employee creativity and suggestion programs: an empirical study. Creativity Innov. Manage. **7**(2), 62–72 (1998). https://doi.org/10.1111/1467-8691.00090
20. Detterfelt, J., Lovén, E., Lakemeond, N.: Suggestion systems for engineering designers - a case study. DS 58–9: Proceedings of ICED 09, the 17th International Conference on Engineering Design, Vol. 9, Human Behavior in Design, Palo Alto, CA, USA, 24.-27.08.2009, pp. 135–146 (2009)
21. Alcácer, V., Cruz-Machado, V.: Scanning the industry 4.0: a literature review on technologies for manufacturing systems. Eng. Sci. Technol., an Int. J. **22**(3), 899–919 (2019). https://doi.org/10.1016/j.jestch.2019.01.006
22. Malek, J., Desai, T.N.: A systematic literature review to map literature focus of sustainable manufacturing. J. Clean. Prod. **256**, 120345 (2020)
23. Gunasekaran, A., Yusuf, Y.Y., Adeleye, E.O., Papadopoulos, T., Kovvuri, D., Geyi, D.G.: Agile manufacturing: an evolutionary review of practices. Int. J. Prod. Res. **57**(15–16), 5154–5174 (2019)
24. Neagoe, L.N.: Employee Suggestion System (Kaizen Teian) The Bottom-Up Approach For Productivity Improvement, **10**(3), 6 (2009)
25. Boeddrich, H.-J.: Ideas in the workplace: a new approach towards organizing the fuzzy front end of the innovation process. Creativity Innov. Manage. **13**(4), 274–285 (2004). https://doi.org/10.1111/j.0963-1690.2004.00316.x
26. Chesbrough, H.: Managing open innovation. Res. Technol. Manag. **47**(1), 23–26 (2004)
27. Herrmann, T., Binz, H., Roth, D.: Necessary extension of conventional idea processes by means of a method for the identification of radical product ideas. In: DS 87–8 Proceedings of the 21st International Conference on Engineering Design (ICED 17) Vol 8: Human Behaviour in Design, Vancouver, Canada, 21–25.08. 2017, pp. 079–088 (2017)
28. Herrmann, T., Roth, D., Binz, H.: Framework of an ambidextrous process of idea management supporting the downstream product development process. In: Proceedings of the Design Society: DESIGN Conference, Cambridge University Press, pp. 587–596 (2020)
29. Harlé, H., Le Masson, P., Weil, B.: A model of creative heritage for industry: designing new rules while preserving the present system of rules. Proceedings of The Design Society **1**, 141–150 (2021)
30. Ostrowski, D., Jagodziński, J.: Operation of an employee suggestion system in administration and production departments of a remanufacturing company. J. Remanufacturing **11**(2), 107–120 (2020). https://doi.org/10.1007/s13243-020-00095-7
31. Eisenhardt, K.M.: Building theories from case study research. Acad. Manag. Rev. **14**(4), 532–550 (1989)

32. Janssoone, D.: De la boîte à idées... à l'innovation. Revue Generale des Chemins de Fer **1999**(9), 11–19 (1999)
33. de Terssac, G., Soubie, J.-L., Neveu, J.-P.: Systèmes experts et transferts d'expertise. sotra, **30**(3), 461–477 (1988). https://doi.org/10.3406/sotra.1988.2418
34. Dewar, R.D., Dutton, J.E.: The adoption of radical and incremental innovations: an empirical analysis. Manage. Sci. **32**(11), 1422–1433 (1986)
35. March, J.G.: Exploration and exploitation in organizational learning. Organ. Sci. **2**(1), 71–87 (1991)
36. Hatchuel, A., Masson, P.L., Weil, B., Carvajal-Perez, D.: Innovative design within tradition - injecting topos structures in C-K theory to model culinary creation heritage. Proceedings of the Design Society: International Conference on Engineering Design **1**(1), 1543–1552 (2019). https://doi.org/10.1017/dsi.2019.160
37. Veile, J.W., Kiel, D., Müller, J.M., Voigt, K.-I.: 4.0 Implementation in the German Manufacturing Industry p. 21 (2019)
38. Lass, S., Gronau, N.: A factory operating system for extending existing factories to Industry 4.0. Comput. Ind. **115**, 103128 (2020). https://doi.org/10.1016/j.compind.2019.103128

Operationalising Co-design: Development of an ICT Platform to Facilitate Stakeholder Engagement in Water Sensitive Design

Lina Ntomene Lukusa[1]([✉]) [iD], Ulrike Rivett[1] [iD], Tom Sanya[2] [iD],
and Shallen Lusinga[1] [iD]

[1] Department of Commerce, Information Systems, University of Cape Town, Cape Town, South Africa
{Ulrike.rivett,Shallen.lusinga}@uct.ac.za
[2] School of Architecture, Planning and Geomatics, University of Cape Town, Cape Town, South Africa
Tom.sanya@uct.ac.za

Abstract. Co-design is considered a critical success method for designing efficient solutions. However, this method presents challenges when working with wicked problems because participants come from different backgrounds and disciplines. Through a case study review, this study describes the operationalisation of the co-design approach to develop an Information Communication Technology (ICT) platform to address the complex, wicked problem faced in Water Sensitive Design (WSD), namely stakeholder engagement. The ICT platform aimed to integrate data from different disciplines to facilitate the collaboration and engagement of WSD stakeholders. Participants were involved in five different co-design cycles to reach a strategic solution. This study aimed to fill the gap of the co-design method regarding its operationalisation from project inception to delivery.

The study adopts a pragmatism philosophy to demonstrate how co-design could be executed entirely online using a sequential and evolving series of co-design workshops following the cycles developed by Ssozi-mugarura, Blake, and Rivett [37] and the factors for effective co-design developed by Yokota et al. [33]. Previous studies conclude that the two theoretical frameworks are feasible, convenient, and efficient due to their simplicity. However, relying solely on the co-design cycles without the aid of factors for effective co-design would not be sufficient to operationalise the co-design of an ICT platform from project inception to completion, as the two do not serve as complete instructional models on their own. Hence, a comprehensive model was created that combines these two models systematically and thoroughly. This study makes significant theoretical and methodological contributions, guiding future researchers and practitioners to run co-design sessions online with multiple and cross-sectoral stakeholder teams.

Keywords: Co-design · Water Sensitive Urban Design · ICT Platform · Stakeholder Engagement

A. Gerber and R. Baskerville (Eds.): DESRIST 2023, LNCS 13873, pp. 412–429, 2023.
https://doi.org/10.1007/978-3-031-32808-4_26

1 Introduction

Water is globally threatened by poor governance, maladministration, depletion, and contamination [1]. These threats have always caused a debate on centralisation versus decentralisation in water management [1]. They necessitated the review of stakeholders' roles in water resource management by different water forums around the globe [1]. These international forums have developed strategies stressing the importance of stakeholders' participation at all levels of water governance and management [2]. Among these strategies is developing an Information and Communication Technology (ICT) platform to bring together representatives from different interest groups to give them a role and voice in the governance process and solve complex water conflicts [3].

ICT platforms bringing diverse stakeholders together adopt different names across industries, including Multi-Stakeholder Platforms (MSPs), multi-stakeholder initiatives, collaborative platforms, partnerships, and forums [5]. Developing a usable and valuable ICT platform to solve a challenging environment requires input from stakeholders from various disciplines because no actor alone has the resources, capacity, and know-how to develop such a platform effectively [6]. As such, the co-design method has been considered suitable in this study for designing an ICT platform that accommodates different WSD stakeholders.

The co-design method is a methodology for actively engaging a broad range of stakeholders in exploring problems across the process of designing and implementing solutions [7]. This method allows the generation of design concepts that are valuable and original for users [8]. The co-design method is of interest in the current environment because it enables the development of products and services that are purposefully and collaboratively created with stakeholders to match their needs [7, 8]. These stakeholders come from different disciplines and backgrounds to contribute to the content and design process by sharing their experience and knowledge [8].

Various potential frameworks on co-design were discovered in both academic and grey literature [48, 49, 50]. Many of these frameworks were carefully researched and even field tested and validated. Although previous studies, such as [48, 49], and [50], have made significant contributions to the field of co-design, there is still much to be explored in the water context regarding how co-design activities can be effectively conducted and integrated into the overall project lifecycle. Hence, instead of creating a new framework from scratch, the Yokota [33] study on the factors for effective co-design and the Ssozi-mugarura, Blake, and Rivett [37] study on co-design cycles were chosen in this research to contribute to the existing taxonomy of co-design methods. The Yokota [33] study was chosen because it provides a comprehensive overview of the factors that contribute to effective co-design, synthesising findings from a range of existing literature. Meanwhile, the Ssozi-mugarura, Blake, and Rivett [37] study was chosen because it presents a specific co-design method that includes relevant steps such as co-design workshops, prototype development, and testing which are beneficial to the design of the ICT platform.

Accordingly, the researchers set out to achieve three objectives. First, to examine, and understand the Ssozi-mugarura, Blake, and Rivett, [37] method and the factors for effective for effective co-design informed by Yokota et al. [33]. Second, to work with stakeholders to implement the existing co-design method and framework to understand how the co-design process could be operationalised spanning from the initiation of the project to its completion. Operationalisation is the process of defining and implementing a research method to make it measurable and observable [9]. It is also defined as a precise concept that is measured through specific indicators [10]. For this study, operationalisation refers to a process of defining and implementing a method so that it is measurable and observable. The third objective was to develop a conceptual framework that informs co-design operationalisation to develop an ICT platform from inception to delivery.

This study used a case study to inform the operationalisation of co-design to develop an ICT platform from inception to delivery to address stakeholder engagement issue in Water Sensitive Design (WSD) - a holistic approach to water management. The present study has a theoretical and practical contribution, providing detailed stages to operationalise the co-design method. The conceptual framework may serve as a roadmap for future researchers and practitioners to conduct co-design sessions with stakeholders from diverse disciplines and backgrounds.

2   Literature Review

2.1   Water Sensitive Design (WSD)

WSD is a water management approach that integrates the management of an urban water cycle with the "roles and interactions of the various institutions and local stakeholders involved in its management." WSD allows the development of suitable solutions for water management to address both water quantity and water quality issues [13].

WSD considers design as an act that involves social, governance, and engineering aspects in minimising the hydrological impacts of urban development on the surrounding environment [12]. This is of importance in the South African context as WSD has the potential to bridge previously divided communities and settlements by: "linking open spaces and promoting these spaces to showcase water; providing the blue-green infrastructure; and creating 'liveable' cities" [12].

2.2   Water Sensitive Design Challenges in South Africa

WSD in South Africa faces significant challenges, including social constraints and fragmentation within institutional structures [11]. Stakeholder involvement is lacking, even though decisions should consider their viewpoints [15]. Daily operational decisions are not connected to scientific analysis conducted by experts [15]. There is a disconnection between the stakeholders who use water resources management systems and scientific experts who have created them [15]. Therefore, it results in a "tragedy of the commons", meaning that water availability and quality continue to degrade, even if each stakeholder is genuinely attempting to decrease its impact and moderate its consumption [15].

The successful implementation of WSD is also hindered by the "wicked" nature of water [16]. Wicked problems are public issues involving many stakeholders with conflicting interests [17, 18]. Due to the complex nature of wicked problems, no single stakeholder has sufficient knowledge to address the challenges effectively [19]. Additionally, stakeholders' understanding of the issues tends to be limited to their perspectives, and any solution created on a single view will generate undesired consequences. The over-segmentation in WSD and the wicked nature of water supports the necessity for engaging all stakeholders in having a mutual responsibility for water management and adopting effective coordination mechanisms [20].

2.3 ICT Platform for Multi-stakeholder Engagement in WSD

Many world water forums have highlighted the importance of multi-stakeholder engagement in water resources management [20].

For instance, at the World Water Forum in Marseille in 2012, thought leaders in the water sector highlighted the need for multi-stakeholder platforms to support the effective management of water services and resources [21]. Similarly, many international laws on public participation have increased, which envisaged public involvement in developing, implementing, and enforcing environmental policies and regulations [20, 21]. In South Africa, a constitutional provision exists that obligates the government to establish public participation systems and structures [22]. In terms of sections 59(1) (a), 72(1) (a) and 118(1) (a) of the South African Constitution, public participation is not a privilege but a Constitutional right [23]. Public participation in the WSD must thus be pursued to comply with legislative prescriptions and ensure good corporate governance [23, 24]. The Water Research Commission (WRC), the premier water knowledge hub in South Africa, recognised ICT platforms for multi-stakeholder engagement as creative and integrative ways to enable effective water management [25]. Platforms centred on a deliberative dialogue involving diverse stakeholders identified based on their stakes and cognitive frames are considered common strategies to ensure stakeholder engagement in a challenging environment such as WSD [17]. MSP is essential to define the issue, share a common understanding of the wicked issue and identify short-term and partial solutions [17, 27].

2.4 The Co-design Method

Co-design is a method for actively engaging stakeholders from different fields during the design and implementation of a project [26]. According to Sanders and Stappers [51], co-creation, another naming for co-design, emphasises the importance of understanding user needs and integrating those needs into the design process. Thus, co-design refers to a user-centered Design (UCD) approach [27]. Many UCD exist, such as design thinking, open design thinking, and participatory design [27].

Co-design is about advancing scientific theory and understanding. It is also about grounding a solution on the understanding that scientific knowledge combined with lived experience is a powerful agent of change [28].

Benefits of the Co-design Method

The co-design method offers many benefits, such as generating more valuable ideas from people's perspectives, better knowledge of end-users' requirements and creating better-fit solutions that meet stakeholders' needs [29].

Two broadest benefits are associated with the co-design method [30]. The first one is the co-design's ability to generate design concepts that are valuable and original for users. The second benefit is the co-design ability to enhance the overall quality of products [30]. Therefore, co-designed solutions can result in more effective services, commitment, and higher levels of responsiveness [32].

Challenges of the Co-design Method

Despite its benefits, co-design could be more challenging to adopt than other methods with homogenous participation [28]. It could be hard to bridge the gaps between real-world practice and scientific theory [33]. One of the most frequently mentioned challenges is communication and, as many put it, the time-consuming process of finding a common language because of the co-design transdisciplinary nature [28, 33]. The challenges go beyond becoming familiar with each other's practice-specific jargon or discipline [28]. Communication challenges may lead to misunderstandings between participants and jeopardise the co-design process [28]. These challenges can thus slow down the co-design process because addressing misunderstandings takes time away from the principal goals.

Continuous participation and interest of all participants are critical success factors for the co-design research project [34]. However, unexpected events, such as time constraints or personal problems, can undermine participants' continued participation [34, 35].

Key Elements of the Co-design Method

The key elements of the co-design method identified are the co-design cycles [36]38 and the factors that influence the effectiveness of co-design [33]. The co-design cycles and the factors for co-design effectiveness are defined below.

Co-design Cycles

The co-design cycles are series of events that use creative and participatory methods [39]. These cycles involve step-by-step series of actions required to conduct the co-design method [38].

Barbier et al. [53] highlight the importance of transdisciplinary collaboration and the need for iterative co-design cycles that involve both technical and social dimensions. The iterative co-design cycles allow to alternate between action and critical reflection [37]. They also have other positive effects such as the discovery and correction of flaws, the exploration of concepts and the possibility of development under conditions of change, uncertainty, and complexity [40].

Key Factors for Effective Co-design

Factors that ensure the effectiveness of co-design refer to different elements that enable and support the success of co-design activities [33, 41]. Examples of co-design factors include elements such as mutual understanding, stakeholders' commitment, trust, and empowerment, among others [2].

These factors should be considered in a co-design activity to ensure the project's sustainability and achieve the goal of the co-design activity [2]. They help to ensure that the process is inclusive and productive. They promote inclusivity, collaboration, empowerment, innovation, participatory, and efficiency [2].

3 Research Method

This paper was part of the Liveable Neighborhood (LN) project, a transdisciplinary research project aiming to redesign the existing neighbourhood of Hangberg in Hout Bay through a suitable WSD approach. The project started in 2019 and comprised inputs from anthropology, architecture, information systems, urban design, urban planning, and engineering.

The study used a pragmatic approach and employed abductive reasoning, moving between induction and deduction. Data was collected through both one-on-one and team discussions. One-on-one discussions were conducted with each participant in November 2020 and constituted the primary data collection method for gaining an understanding of the situation. The team discussions, held in May and June 2021, aimed to clarify the concepts emphasised in the one-on-one discussions and deliberate on the features and requirements that the researcher needed to consider while developing the collaborative platform.

The participants involved in this study were members of the LN project who also acted as gatekeepers by providing in-depth information about their field and introducing the researchers to three other experts involved in the WSD space. However, due to time constraints, these three participants had to discontinue their participation. The final sample consisted of a total of six participants (n = 6) involved in the project. The participants were divided into two teams, with each team comprising of three participants.

In this study, thematic analysis was used to analyse the data. To ensure validity and reliability, the following verification strategies were employed: appropriate sample selection, utilisation of 'rich' and 'thick' verbatim quotes from participants [47], reflexivity [47], and consultation of multiple data sources [46].

4 Development of the Conceptual Framework and Reflections

This section describes the co-design cycles informed by Ssozi-mugarura, Blake, and Rivett, [37] and the factors for effective co-design informed by Yokota et al. [33]. It also presents the conceptual framework created from the main shortcoming of the method and conceptual framework.

4.1 Cycles of Co-design

The co-design cycles informed by Ssozi-mugarura, Blake, and Rivett, [37] is an iterative process comprising five co-design cycles that are alternated between action and critical reflection (See Fig. 1). These cycles are situational analysis, problem identification, collaborative design, prototype development, and prototype evaluation [37].

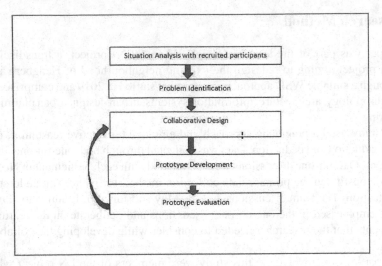

Fig. 1. Cycles of Co-Design Method [37]

The following Table 1 explains these co-design cycles.

Table 1. Cycles of co-design method

Cycles	Explanation
Situational Analysis	This cycle aims to understand the existing problems and to evaluate existing systems through community discussions [2]
Problem Identification	In this stage, participants identify the causes of problems and brainstorm solutions [2]
Collaborative Design	Participants collectively refine needs and requirements and develop an initial prototype based on the collaborative design [2]
Prototype Development	In this stage, the researcher designs the ICT platform based on the feedback received from the collaborative design. Then, the researcher deploys the platform's first version [2]
Prototype Evaluation	Participants collectively identify areas that need to be changed, and the researcher responds to requests for design changes. Collective redesign and implement new changes. Deploy the new version [2]

4.2 Key Factors for Effective Co-design

The conceptual framework developed by Yokota et al. [33] involves seven factors that influence the effectiveness of the co-design method (see Fig. 2). These factors are: (1) Team-oriented personality and characteristics of stakeholder leaders: Highly open, trust, high awareness; (2); Effective coordinators; (3) Mutual understanding and agreement on long term plan, protocol, and budget; (4) Stakeholder's commitment; (5) Empowerment of research staff and participants; (6) Continuous effort to engage stakeholders through meetings, consultations, and discussions and; (7) stakeholder's trust.

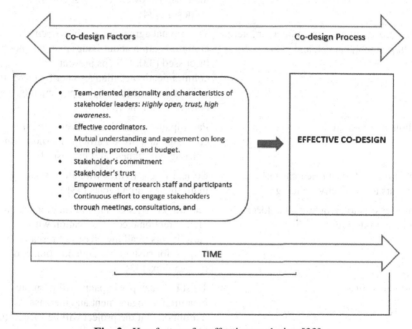

Fig. 2. Key factors for effective co-design [33]

The following Table 2 describes and explains these seven factors.

4.3 Proposed Co-design Operationalisation Framework

The co-design method informed by Ssozi-mugarura, Blake, and Rivett, [37] describes only the co-design iterative steps. The co-design framework developed by Yokota et al. [33] highlights only the key factors that facilitate effective co-design. This method and the conceptual framework are practical guides to conducting the co-design method. However, they do not explicitly present and discuss the preparation, planning process and recruitment of participants even though these processes were found to be of great importance when operationalising the co-design method. Several authors who have studied UCD approaches, such as design thinking, participatory design, and co-design studies, have recognised the preparation and planning process as a critical step [42, 49, 50].

Table 2. Factors that facilitate effective co-design

Factors	Definition
Team-oriented personality and characteristics of stakeholder leaders	Participants' agreeableness, openness, and favourable characteristics are vital elements for adequate knowledge and information sharing [33]
Effective coordinators	Coordinators who understand the project's objective and local situations are essential for the initiative overall, not just effective co-design [34]
Mutual participant agreement on a long-term research protocol, budget, and plan	The mutual agreement enables open communication about issues that may not be discussed [33]. It helps prevent communication challenges later by providing written documentation that participants can consult over time [35]
Stakeholders' commitment	Participants' commitment is essential in co-design activities. Participants should show a strong willingness and interest [33]
Empowerment of local research staff and participants and capacity-building	Co-learning activities with all of stakeholders in all the research cycles [33]
Continue efforts to involve stakeholders throughout co-design	Sharing knowledge and information through multidirectional communication with participants in all the phases of research is helpful for sustainable collaboration and partnerships [33]
Stakeholder's trust	Trust between participants will promote meaningful engagement and increase the likelihood that the project will be successful [35]

In this study, the preparation and planning process helped the researchers to become acquainted with the project and develop an environment for the co-design sessions to succeed. The recruitment process facilitated the selection and enlistment of suitable participants to achieve the paper's objective. As a result, these crucial processes were grouped together under the pre-codesign stage.

The factors for effective co-design were deemed crucial by the researchers to be observed and implemented during each co-design cycle. This is because these key factors, such as stakeholder engagement, trust-building, communication, shared understanding, and co-creation, are critical in developing solutions that cater to users' needs and enhance their experience [33]. These factors are significant in ensuring that the co-design process produces tangible outcomes that meet the expectations and requirements of stakeholders.

On the other hand, the co-design cycles consist of iterative steps designed to engage all stakeholders in the design process and facilitate the rapid prototyping and testing of design solutions. When combined with the co-design factors, it allows for an effective collaborative and user-centered design process. Failure to integrate these critical factors may result in co-design falling short in producing innovative solutions that cater to the needs of all stakeholders. Thus, the integration of Ssozi-mugarura, Blake, and Rivett's [37] co-design cycles with Yokota et al.'s [33] framework on co-design factors is crucial for successful co-design that produces tangible outcomes with a lasting impact.

A new phase was created following this merge which was named "the co-design stage". The pre-codesign and co-design stages introduced in this research led to the development of a new conceptual framework termed the co-design operationalisation framework (see Fig. 3).

The co-design operationalisation framework serves as a valuable tool for effectively implementing the co-design process. It integrates the essential elements of effective co-design factors with co-design cycles, resulting in a thorough and organised approach to co-design. With the aid of this framework, stakeholders can ensure that they are following a process designed to deliver meaningful outcomes aligned with their needs and expectations.

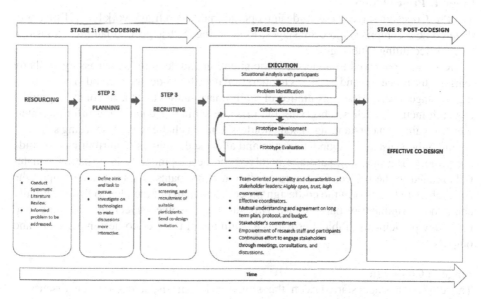

Fig. 3. Co-design operationalisation framework

The co-design operationalisation framework comprises three stages: pre-codesign, co-design and post-codesign. Table 3 summarises these three stages.

Table 3. Stages of the co-design operationalisation framework

Stages	Definition
Pre-codesign	It is a basic management process when operationalising the co-design method, which involves a preparatory, planning, and recruitment process. It consists of brainstorming and developing processes, practices and settings in which the co-design method must be implemented
Co-design	It is a stage in which the researcher collaboratively designs the ICT platform with participants by following the iterative co-design cycles and implementing the key factors for effective co-design
Post-codesign	It is the final stage of the co-design operationalisation in which the ICT platform is ready to be used for its intended purpose. The researcher assesses the lessons learned and the impact of the developed platform. All deliverables are finalised, and the documentation is signed off, approved, and archived

4.4   Operationalisation of Co-design

Stage 1: Pre-codesign
The Pre-Codesign stage in the co-design operationalisation framework for ICT platform development comprises three substages: Resourcing (Substage 1), Planning (Substage 2), and Recruiting (Substage 3).

Resourcing allowed to understand the situation and acquire the necessary skills by learning the processes and practices to operationalise the co-design method. The resourcing substage involved the consultation of preliminary studies and the use of ethnographic research methods such as observing the practice setting or conducting informal interviews to gain an understanding of stakeholders' current challenges. Resourcing substage should only be used as a foundation step and allow stakeholders' contributions to guide the project. The planning substage involved the development of informational materials related to the project for future co-design participants. This substage helped the researchers to brainstorm the co-design process and map out the plan to follow. Finally came the recruitment of participants. This substage involved selecting, screening, and recruiting participants. Table 4 provides a summary of the pre- co-design activities and outputs.

Stage 2: Co-design
The co-design stage started with the situational analysis, a one-on-one discussion between the researchers and participants. The situational analysis differs from the resourcing substage, as the former sought to learn from lived experience by consulting directly with stakeholders. The latter involved a systematic collection, study findings, and informal interviews to help researchers familiarise themselves with the problem before starting the co-design sessions [42]. A topic guide was used in this substage to guide the conversation and keep the focus on the challenges encountered by stakeholders regarding the engagement between them. Participants pitched their ideas and organised

Table 4. Summary of pre-codesign activities and outputs.

Substages	Activities	Outcomes and outputs
Resourcing	• Field observation • Conduct a systematic literature review • Decide on the project's focus and goal	• Understanding of the current state • Understanding of existing organisational workflow and barriers • Narrow the topic • Data from literature
Planning	• Define aims and tasks to pursue • Development of informational materials Technologies investigation	• Development of materials for Design Session workshops • Developmentofsharedvisionfor technology design and implementation
Recruiting	• Selection, screening, and recruitment of suitable participants • Send co-design invitation	• Participants' recruitment and involvement in the project • Build an understanding of the project's objective among every participant

data together asynchronously on a board as the co-design was conducted online (see Fig. 4).

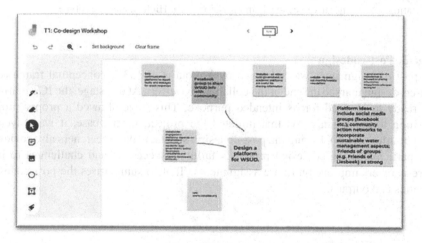

Fig. 4. Collaborative design

Participants' stories helped the researchers to understand what had to be changed and how it had to be changed. With this new knowledge, the researchers designed the ICT platform based on the requirements articulated by participants and within the constraints of what was possible regarding the project's budget, the scope of work and timeline. The co-design participants finally evaluated the ICT platform developed by the researchers. Table 5 summarises the co-design activities and outputs.

Table 5. Summary of co-design activities and outputs.

Substages	Activities	Outcomes and outputs
Situational Analysis	• Framing the situation to develop a mutual understanding • Brainstorming, journey and context mapping	• Develop a shared vision of the project • Describe participants' experience • in-depth understanding of the situation • Data from people with lived experience. Build trust, connections, and capacity for design
Problem Identification	• Brainstorming • Identification of the problem	• In-depth understanding of the problem
Collaborative Design	• Generative design work • Artefactsdevelopmentand storytelling • Brainstorming and solutions	• Establishcommunity-definedsuccess metrics • Generate features and core components of the ICT platform • Design artefacts that the researcher will use as wireframes
Prototype Development	• Select technology • Implement artefacts and outputs from collaborative design	• Design team uses to the prototype • Low-fidelity prototype
Prototype Evaluation	• Inquiry • Iterative Feedback and revision	• Implement revision • High-fidelity prototype

Stage 3: Post-codesign

The post-codesign stage was informed by Yokota et al. [33]'s conceptual framework. Post-co-design marked the end of the collaborative effort. At this stage, the ICT platform was ready to be used for its intended purpose. This stage allowed a proper project transition to the organisation that initiated the project; in this case, it was Liveable Neighbourhood (LN). During the post-codesign substage, the researchers also reviewed with participants the co-design process's failures, successes, and challenges to help the researchers improve on future assignments. Table 6 summarises the post-codesign activities and outputs.

Table 6. Summary of co-design activities and outputs.

Stage	Activities	Outcomes and outputs
Post-Codesign	• End of the collaborative effort • Review the co-design process's failures, successes, and challenges with participants • Allow a proper project transition • Stakeholders provided the final sign-off and approval	• Ready to be used for its intended purpose • Improve on future assignments • Future users of the ICT platform have the resources, training, and information necessary to manage and use the ICT platform successfully • A formal closing process

5 Discussion

The key strengths of the proposed framework are the integration of the pre-co-design phase and the combination of the factors that promote effective co-design with the co-design cycles.

Numerous studies have recognised the significance of pre-co-design as an essential phase in the design process. This phase lays the groundwork for the project by determining its objectives, constraints, and design parameters [42, 49, 50].

In this study, the pre-codesign phase facilitated the creation of topic-specific design tools to be used in the co-design sessions and the planning for unforeseen circumstances that may arise during the co-design process (such as conflicts, participant disengagement or drop-out, technology configuration issues, and so on). Failure to formalise the pre-co-design stage as an integral part of the co-design operationalisation may pose challenges.

The co-design cycles and factors for effective co-design, on their own, do not form comprehensive instructional models that can allow co-design operationalisation throughout a project's entire lifecycle. The study showed that these two elements are mutually reinforcing, as the former provides a roadmap for iterative design, while the latter offers practical instructions for carrying out the work. It can be challenging to execute the co-design cycles without taking into account the factors that promote its effectiveness. By incorporating these factors, the researchers were able to make incremental progress towards ensuring the project's sustainability. Consequently, the co-design operationalisation framework developed in this study provides valuable guidance for incorporating stakeholders' perspectives, eliciting their viewpoints, and distilling practical considerations for operationalising the co-design approach.

It is important to note that participants involved in a co-design activity generally have different interests, and expectations because they have different standpoints. These differences can impact the co-design factors and thus extend the agenda if they are not moderated effectively [52]. For instance, the lack of commitment of participants not part of the LN project revealed that participants are more committed to a co-design project when they have a certain interest in the project. Pirinen [41] supports this notion, suggesting that commitment is influenced by one's level of interest and ownership of the project's goals. Therefore, it is crucial to develop a mutual understanding so that participants can determine if they have a genuine interest in the project.

Several studies have highlighted a significant positive correlation between co-creation, user satisfaction, and ICT platform usage [43–45]. This suggests that involving stakeholders in the co-design process can improve the quality of the platform and increase user acceptance, ultimately leading to greater usage of the ICT platform [43]. Therefore, the ICT platform co-designed in this study was an invaluable tool that better aligned with stakeholders' requirements.

6 Conclusion

This study provided a detailed step-by-step explanation of how the co-design method could be operationalised to develop an ICT platform from the beginning until the end of a project in the WSD context. It also provides a conceptual framework describing the operationalisation of the co-design method to develop an ICT platform. The conceptual framework can guide future researchers or practitioners in incorporating stakeholders' voices in the design process.

7 Limitations and Proposals for Future Research

One of the many limitations is the power dynamics between participants in co-design activities. These power dynamics stem from differences in levels of knowledge among participants. As a result, some participants had more to say and share than others. It is important to implement facilitation techniques that promote equal participation and ensure that all voices are heard.

References

1. Meijerink, S., Huitema, D.: The challenges and pitfalls of decentralisation in water resources management. http://hdl.handle.net/2066/152795
2. Grzybowski, M., Glińska-Lewczuk, K.: Principal threats to the conservation of freshwater habitats in the continental biogeographical region of Central Europe. Biodivers. Conserv. 28(14), 4065–4097 (2019). https://doi.org/10.1007/s10531-019-01865-x
3. Adom, R.K., Simatele, M.D.: The role of stakeholder engagement in sustainable water resource management in South Africa. Nat. Resour. Forum 46, 410–412 (2022). https://doi.org/10.1111/1477-8947.12264
4. Sigalla, O.Z., Tumbo, M., Joseph, J.: Multi-stakeholder platform in water resources management: a critical analysis of stakeholders' participation for sustainable water resources. Sustainability 13(16), 9260 (2021). https://doi.org/10.3390/su13169260
5. UnitedNations (UN). The Seventeen (17) Sustainable Development Goals, New York, USA (2015). https://sdgs.un.org/goals. Accessed 09 Jan 2023
6. Dentoni, D., Bitzer, V., Schouten, G.: Harnessing wicked problems in multi-stakeholder partnerships. J. Bus. Ethics 150(2), 333–356 (2018). https://doi.org/10.1007/s10551-018-3858-6
7. Burkett, I.: An introduction to co-design (2011). http://www.csi.edu.au/

8. Siew, T.F., et al.: Transdisciplinary research in support of land and water management in China and Southeast Asia: evaluation of four research projects. Sustain. Sci. **11**(5), 813–829 (2016). https://doi.org/10.1007/s11625-016-0378-0

9. Babbie, E.R.: The practice of social research: cengage learning (2016). https://www.worldcat.org/title/practice-of-social-research/oclc/939265246. Accessed 26 March 2023

10. Peters, B.: Qualitative methods in monitoring and evaluation: concept formation and operationalization, America University Washington DC (2022)

11. Fisher-Jeffes, L., Carden, K., Armitage, N., Borwa, A.: A water sensitive urban design framework for South Africa. Town Reg. Plann. **71**(1), 1 (2017). https://doi.org/10.18820/2415-0495/trp71i1.1

12. FutureWater. Water Sensitive Design. FuturebWater (2022)

13. Adeyeye, K., Tram, D.: Integrated water sensitive design: opportunities and barriers to implementation, pp. 214–217 (2016). https://www.watefnetwork.co.uk/files/default/resources/Conference2016/Session_Eight/47-TRAM.pdf. Accessed 27 May 2022

14. Barraclough, B.C.L., Bio, R.P., Lucey, W.P., Bio, M.S.R.P, Urban, W.: Water-sensitive urban design (2008)

15. Hidaka, C.E., Kolar, H.R., Williams, R.P., Hartswick, P.G., Foong, S.B.: Collaboration platforms in water management. Water Pract. Technol. **6**(3) (2011). https://doi.org/10.2166/wpt.2011.062

16. Anna, S.T., Krozer, Y.: Wicked Water Systems: A Review of Challenges and Opportunities. IntechOpen (2017). https://doi.org/10.5772/intechopen.71914

17. Simon, J.W.: Stakeholder analysis and wicked problems. In: Farazmand, A. (ed.) Global Encyclopedia of Public Administration, Public Policy, and Governance, pp. 1–6. Springer, Cham (2017). https://doi.org/10.1007/978-3-319-31816-5_2710-1

18. Sanya, T.: Freshwater: towards a better understanding of a wicked problem. Int. J. Environ. Sci. Sustain. Dev. **5**(2), 48 (2020). https://doi.org/10.21625/essd.v5i2.759

19. Dewulf, A.: Contrasting frames in policy debates on climate change adaptation. Wiley Interdiscip. Rev. Clim. Change **4**(4), 321–330 (2013). https://doi.org/10.1002/wcc.227

20. OECD. Stakeholder engagement for inclusive water governance (2015). https://www.riob.org/sites/default/files/IMG/pdf/Stakeholder_Engagement_for_Inclusive_Water_Governance_clean_24dec2014.pdf. Accessed 26 May 2022

21. WorldWaterForum. World Water Forum (2022). https://worldwaterforum.org/. Accessed 09 Jan 2023

22. Rivett, U., et al.: Community engagement in drinking water supply management: a review. Wrc K5/2114, pp. 1–67 (2014). ISBN 978-1-4312-0506-8

23. Nyati, L.: Public participation: what has the constitutional court given the public? (2008). https://www.saflii.org/za/journals/LDD/2008/15.pdf. Accessed 27 May 2022

24. McNaughton, J.: Water sensitive design - an interview with Tony Wong, Kaitiaki Wai (2022). https://www.wellingtonwater.co.nz/kaitiaki-wai/blog/water-sensitive-design-making-cities-of-the-future-places-where-people-want-to-live-and-work/. Accessed 02 July 2022

25. WRC. Water research commission corporate plan (2019). https://www.wrc.org.za/wp-content/uploads/WRC_Corporate-Plan_final.pdf. Accessed 27 May 2022

26. NCOSS. Principles of co-design (2017). https://www.ncoss.org.au/wp-content/uploads/2017/06/Codesign-principles.pdf. Accessed 02 July 2022

27. Pinkston, R.: Participatory design thinking, the social design toolkit (2022). https://socialdesigntoolkit.com/process/participatory-design-thinking/. Accessed 09 Jan 2023

28. Moser, S.C.: Can science on transformation transform science? Lessons from co-design. Curr. Opin. Environ. Sustain. **20**, 106–115 (2016). https://doi.org/10.1016/j.cosust.2016.10.007

29. Steen, M., Manschot, M., de Koning, N.: Benefits of co-design in service design projects (2011). http://www.ijdesign.org/index.php/IJDesign/article/view/890. Accessed 08 May 2022
30. Cockbill, S.A., May, A., Mitchell, V.: The assessment of meaningful outcomes from co-design: a case study from the energy sector. She Ji **5**(3), 188–208 (2019). https://doi.org/10.1016/j.sheji.2019.07.004
31. Magnusson, P.R.: Benefits of involving users in service innovation. Eur. J. Innov. Manag. **6**(4), 228–238 (2003). https://doi.org/10.1108/14601060310500940
32. Trischler, J., Dietrich, T., Rundle-Thiele, S.: Co-design: from expert- to user-driven ideas in public service design. Public Manag. Rev. **21**(11), 1595–1619 (2019). https://doi.org/10.1080/14719037.2019.1619810
33. Yokota, F., et al.: Lessons learned from co-design and co-production in a portable health clinic research project in Jaipur district, India (2016–2018). Sustainability **10**(11), 1–16 (2018). https://doi.org/10.3390/su10114148
34. Page, G.G., et al.: Co-designing transformation research: lessons learned from research on deliberate practices for transformation. Curr. Opin. Environ. Sustain. **20**, 86–92 (2016). https://doi.org/10.1016/j.cosust.2016.09.001
35. Lang, D.J., et al.: Transdisciplinary research in sustainability science: Practice, principles, and challenges. Sustain. Sci. **7**(Suppl. 1), 25–43 (2012). https://doi.org/10.1007/s11625-011-0149-x
36. Leinonen, T.: Designing learning tools for learning by design (2010). https://www.academia.edu/2722657/Designing_Learning_Tools_for_Learning_by_Design. Accessed 31 Dec 2022
37. Ssozi-mugarura, F., Blake, E., Rivett, U.: Codesigning with communities to support rural water management in Uganda. CoDesign **0882**, 1–17 (2017). https://doi.org/10.1080/15710882.2017.1310904
38. Reponen, S.: Co-design framework, learning layers results (2018). http://results.learning-layers.eu/methods/co-design/#:text=development%20when%20applicable.-,Theoretical%20framework%20for%20co%2Ddesign%20process,best%20possible%20artifact%20or%20tool. Accessed 08 May 2022
39. Peacock, A.: Difference between co-design & Participatory design. Passio, vol. 10 (2020). https://passio.co.uk/2020/09/10/difference-between-co-design-participatory-design/. Accessed 09 Jan 2023
40. Wynn, D.C., Eckert, C.M.: Perspectives on iteration in design and development. Res. Eng. Design **28**(2), 153–184 (2016). https://doi.org/10.1007/s00163-016-0226-3
41. Pirinen, A.: The barriers and enablers of co-design for services boundary-crossing collaboration and organisational change (2016). www.ijdesign.org
42. Trischler, J., Kristensson, P., Scott, D.: Team diversity and its management in a co- design team. J. Serv. Manag. **29**(1), 120–145 (2018). https://doi.org/10.1108/JOSM-10-2016-0283
43. Bano, M., Zowghi, D.: A systematic review on the relationship between user involvement and system success. Inf. Softw. Technol. **58**, 148–169 (2015). https://doi.org/10.1016/j.infsof.2014.06.011
44. Bano, M., Zowghi, D., da Rimini, F.: User satisfaction and system success: an empirical exploration of user involvement in software development. Empir. Softw. Eng. **22**(5), 2339–2372 (2016). https://doi.org/10.1007/s10664-016-9465-1
45. Harris, M.A., Weistroffer, H.R.: A new look at the relationship between user involvement in systems development and system success. Commun. Assoc. Inf. Sys. 24(1), 739–756 (2009). https://doi.org/10.17705/1cais.02442
46. Buchan, J., Bano, M., Zowghi, D., MacDonell, S., Shinde, A.: Alignment of stakeholder expectations about user involvement in agile software development. In: Proceedings of the 21st International Conference on Evaluation and Assessment in Software Engineering, pp. 334–343 (2017)

47. Noble, H., Smith, J.: Issues of validity and reliability in qualitative research. Evid.-Based Nurs. **18**, 34–35 (2015)
48. Della Rossa, P., Mottes, C., Cattan, P., Le Bail, M.: A new method to co-design agricultural systems at the territorial scale - application to reduce herbicide pollution in Martinique. Agric. Syst. **196**, 103337 (2022). https://doi.org/10.1016/j.agsy.2021.103337
49. Bird, M., et al.: A generative co-design framework for healthcare innovation: development and application of an end-user engagement framework. Res. Involv. Engagem. **7**, 1–12 (2021). https://doi.org/10.1186/s40900-021-00252-7
50. Greenhalgh, T., et al.: Frameworks for supporting patient and public involvement in research: systematic review and co-design pilot. Health Expect. **22**(4), 785–801 (2019). https://doi.org/10.1111/hex.12888
51. Sanders, E.B.N., Stappers, P.J.: Co-creation and the new landscapes of design. In: TEI 2020 - Proceedings of the 14th International Conference on Tangible, Embedded, and Embodied Interaction, pp. 799–809. Association for Computing Machinery (2007). https://doi.org/10.1080/15710880701875068
52. Naqshbandi, M., Harris, S.B., Macaulay, A.C., Comeau, J., Piché, J., Montour-Lazare, D.: Work-in-progress & lessons learned lessons learned in using community-based participatory research to build a national diabetes collaborative in Canada (2011)
53. Barbier, R., Yahia, S.B., Masson, L.E., Weil, B.: Co-design for novelty anchoring into multiple socio-technical systems in transitions: the case of earth observation data (2022)
54. Plutynski, A.: Four problems of abduction: a brief history. HOPOS: J. Int. Soc. Hist. Philos. Sci. **1**(2), 227–248 (2011). https://doi.org/10.1086/660746

Co-designing a Visual Inquiry Tool

Alicia Roschnik and Stéphanie Missonier

Faculty of Business and Economics (HEC), University of Lausanne, 1015 Lausanne, Switzerland
{alicia.roschnik,stephanie.missonier}@unil.ch

Abstract. Grand challenges may be considered as wicked problems. These wicked problems are best addressed with social and visual methods rather than linear and analytical ones. One type of management tool that allows to do so is the visual inquiry tool. Their rise has been observed and a design theory to design them has been proposed. The latter provides design principles but does not however provide concrete guidance on how to operationalise them. Meanwhile, co-design has been suggested as a way to address wicked problems by using the collective creativity of the users who are experts of their own everyday activities. This paper sets out to explore the design of visual inquiry tools with co-design practices. To do so, we present the design journey of a visual inquiry tool named the "Agile Culture Transformation Canvas" (ACTC). The ACTC aims to help teams work together on their culture in the context of an agile transformation. This paper deep-dives into three different co-design events we conducted with agile practitioners to design the ACTC. From these events, we extract insights regarding what went well, and what did not go so well. Based on this, we formulate suggestions regarding how one may operationalise the design principles from the design theory for visual inquiry tools using co-design practices. This adds to the prescriptive knowledge regarding the design of visual inquiry tools. In addition to the formulated suggestions, this paper presents the current version of the ACTC. Namely, the one resulting from the three co-design events we conducted with agile practitioners.

Keywords: Visual inquiry tools · Co-design · Wicked problems · Agile culture · Agile culture transformation canvas

1 Introduction

A grand challenge can be defined as wicked problems. A wicked problem is a problem that is complex, intangible and unique [8]. It is impossible to solve in a way that is simple or final, and for which intervention in one realm yields unexpected results elsewhere [22]. Related to strategic and management approaches, such a problem cannot be addressed by using linear analytical techniques and instead calls for social approaches to address it [14]. On that note, Avdiji et al. [5] have suggested that wicked problems can be tackled with a new type of management tool: the visual inquiry tool. Built on design thinking techniques (e.g., visual thinking, prototyping and ideation), a visual inquiry tool allows its users to jointly and visually explore a problem space and ideate on possible solutions [5]. The Business Model Canvas [19] and the Team Alignment Map [4] are examples

A. Gerber and R. Baskerville (Eds.): DESRIST 2023, LNCS 13873, pp. 430–444, 2023.
https://doi.org/10.1007/978-3-031-32808-4_27

of such tools. Another example is the Agile Culture Transformation Canvas (ACTC) that we are currently developing within the Design Science Research (DSR) paradigm and using the design theory for visual inquiry tools as prescriptive knowledge [5]. The design theory provides three design principles to guide the design of a visual inquiry tool: 1) develop a conceptual model framing the wicked problem, 2) instantiate it into a shared visualisation, and 3) formulate directions of use. In the design journey of the ACTC we have already addressed the first design principle by developing and evaluating a conceptual model of agile culture [23, 24]. Hence, in this paper we solely focus on the operationalisation of the second and third design principles. In that regard, although the design theory proposes design principles to guide the design of a visual inquiry tool, it falls short in suggesting how to concretely operationalise them. In respect to the ACTC, we decided to use co-design practices because it allows to extend the understanding of the problem faced by the stakeholders and access greater creativity and generate further design ideas [15]. Co-design can be understood as including the stakeholders who are not necessarily design experts in the design process of an artefact [27]. Therefore, in light of the rise in contributions pertaining to visual inquiry tools [38], added to the unfortunate lack of concrete guidance regarding how to design them, along with the merits of co-design, this paper sets out to explore co-design in relation to visual inquiry tools. We accordingly pose the following research question: *"How is co-design considered in relation to visual inquiry tools?"*.

To answer this question, we present the design process of the ACTC and specifically focus on the three co-design events we conducted with agile practitioners. The three co-design events are a prototyping workshop, an exploratory focus group and a one-on-one workshop. Respectively, the objective of these events was to instantiate the conceptual model of agile culture previously designed [23, 24] into a shared visualisation and elaborate the directions of use (i.e., second and third design principles of the design theory [5]) and subsequently, test, evaluate and iterate them. From these three co-design events we then extracted insights regarding how one may operationalise the design principles two and three of the design theory [5] using co-design. Based on what went well, and what did not go so well, we additionally formulated suggestions to guide future visual inquiry tool designers. This reflection on what went well – or not so much, during a design process has been mentioned by Purao et al. [21] in the context of design principles. The authors refer to this as the *"blind alleys in a design process"* (ibidem, p. 185). Therefore, to continue the analogy, with the insights and resulting suggestions on how to operationalise the design principles two and three using co-design practices, we light up the alley of the design journey of visual inquiry tools. This feeds into the prescriptive knowledge regarding visual inquiry tools and therefore acts as the first contribution of this paper. The second contribution is the resulting artefact, namely the ACTC. The ACTC aims to help teams in organisations collaboratively and visually work on their culture. Using the theory of organisational culture proposed by Schein [29] as kernel theory and having been co-designed with practitioners whilst integrating the ethical notions of co-design into it [31], the ACTC is an improvement [12].

The remainder of this paper is structured as follows: we present the background literature in Sect. 2. In Sect. 3 we present the design journey of the ACTC along with the extracted insights and formulated suggestions. We describe the artefact in Sect. 4 and finally conclude in Sect. 5.

2 Background Literature

2.1 Co-design

Co-design can be used to, amongst others, enhance the generation of new ideas, foster collaboration with stakeholders, improve their satisfaction, and promote creativity [31]. It is frequently discussed in conjunction with participatory design, user-centred design, and co-creation. Because a deep understanding of what co-design entails is necessary for the remainder of this paper, we hereunder introduce co-design by positioning it against participatory design, user-centred design, and co-creation.

Participatory design for IS development emerged in the 1970s [17, 27] from an association between academics and trade unions [30] in Scandinavia and the United Kingdom [17]. According to Spinuzzi [30], the core of participatory design rests in tacit knowledge [30]. To uncover such knowledge, participatory design is collaborative and focuses on the mutual learning of the involved parties with the intent to co-build the artefact [15, 17]. In doing so, the involved parties further define the problem, whilst simultaneously designing the artefact. This deepens the knowledge regarding the addressed problem [1]. Regarding the distinction between participatory design and co-design, Steen [31] notes that the two differ by their very nature: while the former relates to a methodology, the latter relates to a design process. Co-design has also been compared to user-centred design and co-creation. Regarding the former, Sanders and Stappers [27] argue that the difference between the two rests in the degree of involvement of the user. In user-centred design, the user's involvement is slighter because they are indirectly solicited for their inputs through interviews for example. Whereas in co-design the user is considered the expert and takes an important role in the design process, thus being fully included. The user can be included by using different techniques and tools such as: scenario centres, focus groups, bags of stuff [e.g., 3], scenario-based design [e.g., 25], mock-ups, and storyboards [e.g., 6]. Regarding co-creation, Sanders and Stappers [27] point out that they have been used as synonyms, but according to them, co-design is a part of co-creation.

Regarding the definition of co-design, Steen [31] uses two central terms: design thinking and joint inquiry. Steen [31 p.13] suggests that co-design is "a process of collaborative design thinking: a process of joint inquiry and imagination in which diverse people jointly explore and define a problem and jointly develop and evaluate solutions.". Design thinking is described by the author as a way by which a problem and its solutions are explored iteratively where the exploration of the problem co-evolves with the exploration of the potential solutions. This contrasts itself to a linear problem-solving process where the steps are sequential and where the problem is identified prior to finding the unique best solution to it. Design thinking is a means to address wicked problems [8, 31]. A wicked problem is a problem that is ill-defined, where the information regarding it is incomplete and complex [8]. According to Coyne [10], one may consider that most problems are in fact wicked. In addition to design thinking, joint inquiry is another central term used in Steen's definition of co-design. Joint inquiry is a process where together, people explore a problem space and learn from one another [31]. Steen [31] notes that joint inquiry is only one part of co-design. The second part of co-design is imagination. It is the imagination component that brings the creativity element into the co-design. Overall, similarly to Sanders and Stappers [27], we will henceforth understand co-design as a process through which "collective creativity" is put to good use during the entire design process of an artefact.

Finally, on another note, Steen [31] suggests adding an ethics dimension to co-design. The author does so by leveraging the pragmatist discourse of Dewey (1850–1952) and suggests that they are part of the process of co-design. More precisely, Steen claims that if the parties involved in the co-design process can express themselves, are empathetic towards one another when doing so, and together, can build a suitable solution to their problem, then co-design is ethical. Steen argues in favour of explicitly integrating the ethics dimension into the co-design process and suggests doing so by making the involved parties attentive to what they are thinking and feeling, thus being more in touch with themselves and their needs.

2.2 Design Theory for Visual Inquiry Tools

A visual inquiry tool is a visual management tool in the format of a canvas. It acts as a boundary object [9] and allows its users to jointly inquire into a wicked problem, and ideate on its potential solutions. Vom Brocke and Maedche [38] have noted an increase in suggestions towards such canvases in varying fields. Concurrently, Avdiji et al. [5] have theorised their design by formulating a design theory. The design theory builds on the elements that we have presented above and suggests three design principles: 1) develop a *conceptual model* of the wicked concept, 2) instantiate it into a *shared visualisation* by transforming the components of the conceptual model into empty design blocks, and finally, 3) define *directions of use* of the tool that sustain joint inquiry. The design theory does not however suggest how a designer ought to operationalise the proposed design principles. By that, we mean that it does not indicate what activities the designer must concretely do to design and evaluate the visual inquiry tool in view of the proposed design principles. Considering this gap, in the next section, we present the activities taken to co-design a visual inquiry tool with its stakeholders.

3 The Design Science Research Journey

For the design of the ACTC we follow the process model proposed by Peffers et al. [20] and Fig. 1 presents a simplified version of the journey. We hereunder briefly present the identified problem and resulting objectives of the ACTC and as per de posed research question, we subsequently cover its design journey by focusing on the three co-design events.

3.1 Problem Identification and Objectives of the ACTC

Agile Culture as a Wicked Problem. When conducting an agile transformation, a fundamental aspect to consider is the culture of the organisation because, as noted by both

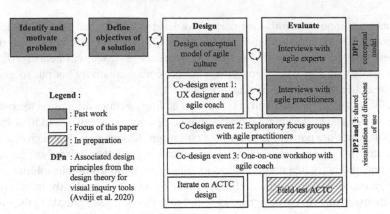

Fig. 1. Overview of ACTC DSR project

scholars [e.g., 16] and practitioners [11], the culture may act as a blocker in the transformation. We refer to a culture that sustains agile practices and methods as an *agile culture*. Amongst others, an agile culture nurtures psychological safety, cooperation, open communication, continuous learning and improvement, and feedback [34]. Although an agile culture is often associated with the values in the Agile Manifesto [7], from a 9-month field study [24], we identified that what is meant by having an agile culture varies from one group to another and confusion exists when describing what an agile culture means to them. Hence, although many agree that an agile culture stems from similar roots (i.e., the Agile Manifesto), it is not a one-size fits all type of situation.

Because there is not one unique agile culture, and even less one single path to get there, we can consider it as being a wicked problem. As reported in the literature review of this paper, such type of problem is best approached visually and in joint inquiry through, for instance, visual inquiry tools. However as reported in Roschnik and Missonier [24], such a tool does not − yet − exist. Therefore, from our empirical findings motivated by the existing literature, we were able to articulate the problem by using the concepts proposed by Maedche et al. [18]. To summarise, the two main stakeholders impacted by the design of the ACTC are its users and the facilitator. The users are members of a team (i.e., a group of people that work together) that are in an organisation undertaking an agile transformation. The facilitator is the agile coach (i.e., an agile-certified person that is hired by organisations to help with the agile transformation) that brings the ACTC to the team and helps them use it during a workshop.

We drew up the requirements for the ACTC by leveraging a kernel theory [i.e., 29] as well as broader justificatory knowledge [12]. The requirements, structured following the template for natural language requirements [26], and associated theoretical justification can be found in Table 1. The kernel theory is the one of organisational culture proposed by Schein [29]. It describes the three levels within which organisational culture exists. Namely, 1) artefacts, which is the most visible and tangible level that includes elements that can be seen, heard, or felt 2) values, which would for example include goals or social principles, and finally 3) underlying assumptions. This third layer is the deepest and encompasses the taken-for-granted assumptions which define how information is interpreted. Schein suggests that to act on culture, it is easier to act on the most tangible layer, namely by concentrating on practices. Additionally, according to Schein, one must first identify the characteristics of both the current and the desired cultures to then perform a gap analysis between the two.

From the requirements, we then formulated a first set of design principles for the ACTC by following the design theory for visual inquiry tools [5]. Subsequently, as suggested in [21], we refined the design principles based on the insights gained from the co-design events presented in the following section. All of the design principles relate to both the artefact and the associated user activity [13].

Table 1. ACTC requirements and design principles

Requirement	Justificatory knowledge	Design principle
R1: When being used in an agile transformation, the ACTC should allow teams to inquire about their culture jointly and visually	When addressing such type of wicked problem, it is important to visualise the big picture [5]	To allow teams to inquire on their culture jointly and visually during an agile transformation, the ACTC should be a visual inquiry tool [5] that follows the 5 phases for joint inquiry (Dewey in [31]) and act as a boundary object [9]
R2: When being used, he ACTC should allow teams to co-design their desired agile culture (i.e., to-be)	Knowing the characteristics of the desired culture is essential in a culture change initiative [28]. Meanwhile, the definition of an agile culture is nebulous and context-dependent [24]	To allow teams co-design their desired agile culture during an agile transformation, the ACTC must embody the key pillars of an agile culture by being based on a conceptual model of agile culture [5]
R3: When being used, the ACTC should allow teams to identify their current culture (i.e., as-is), the gap between the as-is and to-be and formulate everyday actions to close the gap	To act on culture, individuals must first identify the current and the desired cultures, to then identify the gap. To close the gap, an everyday reframing through the internalisation of new practices is recommended [2, 28]	For the ACTC to allow teams to identify the characteristics of their as-is culture, the gap between the as-is and desired to-be cultures, and formulate everyday actions to close the gap, it must contain visual spaces for those elements, enact the proper flow of use (design principle added from the co-design event 1) and act on practices [28]

3.2 Artefact Co-design

We decided to co-design the ACTC with agile practitioners because it allows us to learn more about the faced problem and to broaden our ideas regarding the potential solutions by using collective creativity and diversity. Additionally, co-designing a solution with the potential users increases the likelihood of them liking and thus committing to it [5]. To co-design the current version of the ACTC, we conducted three co-design *events* that each include several co-design *activities* (Table 2). We conducted all three events with agile experts (i.e., coaches and practitioners) rather than the end-users (i.e., members of the team) because we wanted to leverage the different scenarios the former had lived whilst working with agile. In the next steps, we will also evaluate the ACTC with the end-users. It is worth noting that because we concentrate on the co-design perspective, we disregard (for the sake of this paper) the multiple expert interviews we conducted to evaluate the different versions of the ACTC and solely discuss the activities relating to co-design. As suggested by Thoring et al. [33], during the co-design events we collected data by observing and noting the participant's behaviours, dialogues and interactions. When it was possible (i.e., during the exploratory focus group), we additionally audio and video recorded the event. At the end of each event, we analysed the produced artefacts (e.g., sketches, notes, mock-ups) along with the notes and, when applicable, recordings. We manually coded the elements bottom-up to uncover the recurring themes. From the themes, we consolidated the new design choices.

Table 2. ACTC co-design events

Co-design event and date	Purpose of event	Co-design activity	Participants	Outcome from co-design event
Prototyping workshop 11.05.22	Instantiate conceptual model into shared visualisation with directions of use	Ideation, Paper prototyping, sketching	One agile coach, one UX designer	ACTC V1
Exploratory focus group 9.06.22	Test the functioning of ACTC V1, evaluate and improve it	Mock-up, scenario-based design, ideation	13 agile coaches/practitioners, one UX designer	ACTC V2
One-on-one workshop, 4.12.2022	Evaluate and improve the flow of use of the ACTC V2	Ideation, paper sketching	One agile coach	ACTC V3 (Fig. 2)

Co-design Event 1 – Prototyping Workshop. The objective of this first event was to instantiate the conceptual model of agile culture [23, 24] into a first version of the ACTC. To do so, we conducted a prototyping workshop. The workshop included an agile coach (4 years of experience) and a user experience (UX) designer (5 years of experience) and lasted two hours. Each professional designer has their own area of expertise [27], and the one of a UX designer is the interaction between the user and the designed artefact. The UX designer was therefore invited to this first co-design event to help us think about the use case outside the box. We began the prototyping workshop by presenting the conceptual model of agile culture to the participants. The conceptual model has eight components representing the key elements of an agile culture that are structured around the three levels of organisational culture [29]. Using the conceptual model as starting point, together, with the agile coach and UX designer, we ideated on ways to instantiate the conceptual model into a shared visualisation. Ideation is a process of generating ideas and we did so by using paper and pens to prototype different preliminary versions of the ACTC and eventually converge towards the first version of the ACTC (Table 1). *Insights and Suggestions.* The trickiest part was figuring out how to represent the flow of use of the ACTC. The design theory suggests turning the components of the conceptual model into empty design spaces (i.e., the boxes of the canvas) and visually arranging them in a way that implies their relations. However, by doing so, the first requirement (R1 Table 1) was met but it left out R2 and R3. As a reminder, R2 states that the solution must allow for co-design of the desired agile culture and R3 notes that the solution must allow to identify the as-is culture, the gap between the as-is and to-be cultures and formulate everyday actions to close the gap. R2 and R3 therefore suggest sequential steps in the use of the ACTC. To reflect this flow of use, we consequently had to go beyond the design principles and not only instantiate the components of the conceptual model into empty design spaces but also include additional spaces to reflect the different steps the users will have to perform. We can extend this insight by suggesting to future designers to instantiate the conceptual model into a shared visualisation with a UX designer and an expert in the topic at issue. This helps envision and craft the flow of use of the visual inquiry tool.

Co-design Event 2 – Exploratory Focus Group. The objective of this second co-design event was to test, evaluate, and improve the ACTC V1. In essence, a focus group is a group discussion led by a moderator [32]. Tremblay et al. [35] adapted this technique to design science research and accordingly proposed two types: exploratory focus groups that aim to refine an artefact and confirmatory focus groups that aim to evaluate the artefact in the field. Because the purpose of this event was to test and improve the ACTC, we conducted an exploratory focus group [35] and introduced co-design activities (i.e., mock-up, scenarios and ideation) into it. We held the focus group with 13 agile practitioners. We decided on 13 (one group of six and one of seven) because, as noted by Tremblay et al. [35], if the participants are asked to handle the artefact, as in our case, large groups are complicated to manage. Conversely, we did not want too few participants either because we aimed for richness in backgrounds, ideas and more generally, personalities to enhance the generation of design ideas. During the exploratory focus group, we asked the participants to use the ACTC and then give us feedback regarding it. To do so, we conducted scenario-based design [25] where the participants were given a scenario and roles with which they had to fill in the ACTC. By grounding the activity with a scenario, we made the design activities more concrete [25]. We randomly distributed roles to the participants. In their role description, we included the years of experience the person had, their responsibilities, age, and expertise. The participants were divided into two groups and one participant per group was asked to facilitate the workshop, thus acting as the agile coach. The other participants played the role they had been given. During the event, we observed and noted the dialogues and interactions between the participants as well as the interactions between the participants and the ACTC [33]. Once the participants had filled in the ACTC, we asked them what they had liked and what they did not like as much. We then ideated on how the ACTC could be improved, resulting in the ACTC V2 (Table 1). *Insights and Suggestions.* Regarding the ACTC, the participants commended its flow of use. This relates to R3. Concerning R2 which states that the ACTC must allow its users to co-design their desired agile culture, participants noted that the ACTC allowed them to do so. Regarding the elements that can be improved, the participants brought up that the visual layout of the ACTC was confusing. From our observations, we additionally noticed that too much responsibility in terms of facilitation weighed on the shoulders of the agile coach. This poses a problem for two reasons: firstly, as a reminder, the objective of the ACTC is to encourage interaction between the participants. However, because it was the facilitator that was prompting the participants, the interactions were mainly between the participants and the facilitator. Thus, failing to meet R1. The second reason is that because the use of the ACTC relies a lot on the facilitator, it largely depends on his or her skills. Finally, concerning the co-design process, the participants were confused regarding the scenario and the role description they had been given. Hence, concerning the scenario and role-based design, we would suggest to future designers to elaborate detailed scenarios to frame the co-design session as close to the intended use's context as possible. This will avoid confusion among the participants.

Co-design Event 3 – One-on-one Workshop. The purpose of the third co-design event was to evaluate and improve the layout of the flow of use of the ACTC (R3). The reason behind this purpose is that, in the co-design event 2, although the participants liked the general flow, they had noted that the corresponding layout was confusing and thus, not optimal. Consequently, to review the flow of use of the ACTC, we conducted a two-hour one-to-one workshop with an experienced (5 years of experience) agile coach. We refer to workshop in the sense of Thoring et al. [33] that have suggested workshops as a way to design and evaluate artefacts in design science research. During these two hours, we dove deep into the ACTC and ideated on the flow of use, the names of the agile culture components, and the layout of the boxes of the ACTC. To do so, we printed the ACTC V2 on an A0-size poster and stook it on the wall. This allowed us to have a general view of the ACTC. We then used sticky notes and crayons to add to the ACTC when ideating. This allowed us to remove, shift, and add elements as much as we wanted. *Insights and Suggestions.* This workshop demonstrated the added value of co-designing with an agile coach, who is an agile expert. Because of his years of practice and thus having been exposed to many different contexts of use, he was able to foresee them and accordingly enlighten us about them. Together, we adapted the ACTC to best prepare for the different contexts of use. Additionally, as per the objective of this co-design event, we reorganised the arrangement of the components to better reflect R3. We suggest conducting a one-on-one ideation workshop with an expert on the topic at issue to rethink and improve the shared visualisation and directions of use. Doing so allowed us to challenge the current version of the ACTC against the experiences of an expert and adjust the design accordingly.

4 Artefact Description

In this section, we present the current version of the ACTC (Fig. 2), namely the one resulting from the three co-design events presented above.

Acting as a boundary object [9], the ACTC is a tool that allows its users to work on their culture in joint inquiry in the context of an agile transformation. To do so, it offers a space to discuss and collaboratively analyse the current as-is culture, co-design the desired to-be agile culture, identify the gaps and formulate action to close the gaps. The users (i.e., a team) use the ACTC in joint inquiry and write their answers on sticky notes and stick them on the ACTC in the corresponding section.

The ACTC may be used at any given moment of an agile transformation. Whether it be at the beginning or when the transformation has been going on for quite some time. It can for example be used when something is not working quite right, and a re-alignment is needed in the team, or simply to do a team check-up.

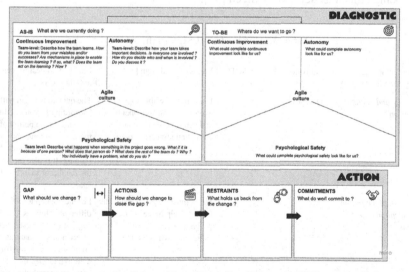

Fig. 2. The Agile Culture Transformation Canvas (ACTC) version 3

It is composed of two parts, each including a set of steps. The first part is called *diagnostic* and includes three steps: Step 1 – as-is: in joint inquiry, users answer the guiding questions around the three key pillars of an agile culture. Step 2 – to-be: users co-design the desired agile culture around the same three key pillars of an agile culture.

Step 3 – gap analysis: users compare the answers in steps 1 and 2. If they are in line, they keep the sticky note in the as-is section. If they are not, they move the sticky note to the section named "gap". The second part of the ACTC is named *action* and includes three additional steps: Step 4 – actions: for the sticky notes in the gap section, the users ideate to identify what they can do to change it. Step 5 – restraints: up until now, the users have been asked to concentrate on practices. In this fifth step, users go a step further a identify what would stop them from performing the practices they have just written down in step 4. According to Schein [28], this step allows to access the deeper layer of culture. Finally, in this last 6th step named commitments, the users draw up changes they will commit to doing until the next time they will use the ACTC. The aim is to, given the restraints they have identified, formulate actionable and precise commitments to close the gaps.

The ACTC is not meant to be used only once as a consulting tool. Rather, it is meant to be a living tool, that reflects the evolution of the agile (culture) transformation. The aim is to use the ACTC a first time and go back to it regularly to review and reassess the commitments (e.g., where they respected? If not, why? If yes, did they close the gap?), the as-is and the desired to-be. The logic is to iterate, inspect and adapt by reflecting and changing the sticky notes accordingly.

Finally, we integrated the elements of ethics of co-design in the conception of the ACTC. For each phase of joint inquiry and imagination of Dewey, Steen [31] adds an ethics discourse. As showcased in Table 3, the ACTC reflects both the phases of joint inquiry and the dimension of ethics. In other terms, the ACTC enables joint inquiry whilst being ethical as defined by Steen [31].

Table 3. Ethics of co-design in the ACTC

Phases of joint inquiry (Dewey cited in [31 p.7])	Equivalent phase in ACTC	Ethics of co-design [31]	Ethics of co-design integrated into the ACTC
"Exploring and defining the problem"	Diagnostic	Users must be able to both express themselves openly and safely as well as be empathetic towards others	The questions begin with "according to you…" this encourages the notion of there is no wrong nor right. Rather, each expresses their opinion. It is also the role of the facilitator to install a safe space
"Perception of the problem and conception of possible solutions"	Action	Users must be given adequate tools to help perceive the problem and conceive different possible solutions	For the conception of different solutions, the ACTC suggest that the users use sticky notes to mark as many solutions as possible (in action) and then filter the actions out with the restraints box
"Try-out and evaluation solutions"	Try out the commitments	Users must be able to question and test the solutions	The users must try out the commitments and inspect and adapt the next time round

5 Discussion and Conclusion

Grand challenges may be considered as wicked problems. These wicked problems are best addressed with social and visual methods rather than linear and analytical ones [14]. Visual inquiry tools are a type of management tool that allows us to do just that. Due to their growing number, a design theory to design them has been proposed [5]. However, although the theory suggests design principles, it does not propose how they can concretely be operationalised. On another note, co-design is a practice whose merits to address wicked problems have been noted [31]. It does so by leveraging the collective creativity of the users who, although not design experts, are the experts of their own everyday activities [37]. Given the latter, we have suggested that the design principles of the design theory for visual inquiry tools [5] can be operationalised with co-design practices. To further explore the matter, we asked the following research question: *"How is co-design considered in relation to visual inquiry tools?"*.

To answer this research question, we have illustrated the design process of the ACTC and particularly focused on the three co-design events that we conducted to operationalise the design principles two and three of the design theory. From these three co-design events, we gained insights on how to operationalise the design principles through co-design and distilled them into three suggestions for future visual inquiry tool designers. The first suggestion is to instantiate the conceptual model into a shared visualisation along with directions of use with a UX designer and an expert on the topic at issue. This helps craft the flow of use of the visual inquiry tool. The second one is to test and improve the designed artefact with exploratory focus groups with a scenario and roles as close to the intended use context as possible. However, we suggest making them detailed to avoid confusion among participants. Finally, the third suggestion is to conduct a one-on-one ideation workshop with an expert in the matter at hand to dive deep into the different scenarios.

Overall, by suggesting operationalising the design principles of the design theory with co-design and formulating suggestions regarding how to do so, we have provided concrete guidance on how the design principles can be operationalised. Thus, adding to the prescriptive knowledge regarding how one may design a visual inquiry tool. Considering we are today confronted with many wicked problems and can note a rise in contributions towards visual inquiry tools developed to address them [38], this refinement and extension of the design theory to design such type of tool is particularly useful for future designers. This serves as the first contribution of this paper.

The second contribution of this paper is the ACTC. The ACTC is a visual inquiry tool co-designed with field experts and future users. Having embodied the ethics of co-design Steen [31] into its conception, it aims to help its users work in joint inquiry on their culture in an agile transformation. Using the theory of organisational culture as kernel theory [29], the ACTC helps by offering a visual space for its users to collaboratively characterise their current culture, co-design their desired agile culture and formulate actions to close the gap between the two. The aim of the ACTC is not to provide a formal definition of what an agile culture is, nor is it to provide an established set of steps to take to get there. Rather, similarly to what Visser et al. [37] have noted, the objective is to bring people together, allow them to discuss their culture, explore and co-design where they want to go and how they want to get there. Overall, because of the value co-design brings in addressing wicked problems, added to the lack (and need) of such a tool [24] for addressing culture change in an agile transformation, the ACTC is the second contribution of this paper. It can be considered as an improvement [12].

At this stage, this study has several limitations. The first limitation concerns the lack of evaluation of the ACTC. It has not (yet) been tested and evaluated in naturalistic settings [36] (i.e., by a team in an organisation conducting an agile transformation). This is however an ongoing design science research project, and we are currently planning on conducting confirmatory focus groups [35] in naturalistic settings [36]. The second limitation concerns co-design as a process, and specifically the suggestions regarding how to operationalise the design principles of the design theory. We have formulated suggestions from having extracted and subsequently extended the insights from the design journey of the ACTC. Although it is our objective, we cannot claim that their relevance may apply to all future designers. We can however recommend to future designers to apply the design principles with the co-design events and suggestions presented in this paper to further build on them. This would allow us to make a claim regarding their effectiveness in other contexts. Finally, in spite of its limitations, this paper aims to be a catalyst for a further and broader reflection on the design of visual inquiry tools. In particular in terms of integrating the voices of the intended users and field experts in the design process. Additionally, the topic of ethics in co-design, and how one integrates it into the core of the design of the visual inquiry tool is an important issue and will require further research. In particular given the omnipresence of wicked problems [10], and the responsibilities we hold as designers to design artefacts that will contribute to a more positive future.

References

1. Ågerfalk, P.J., Wiberg, M.: Pragmatizing the normative artifact: design science research in scandinavia and beyond. Commun. Assoc. Inf. Syst. **43**, 68–77 (2018). https://doi.org/10.17705/1cais.04304
2. Alvesson, M., Sveningsson, S.: Changing Organizational Culture. Routledge, Taylor & Francis Group, New York (2008)
3. Ashktorab, Z. Vitak, J.: Designing cyberbullying mitigation and prevention solutions through participatory design with teenagers. In: CHI 2016: Proceedings of the 2016 CHI Conference on Human Factors in Computing Systems, pp. 3895–3905 (2016)
4. Avdiji, H.: Supporting the challenges of cross-boundary teamwork through design science research. University of Lausanne, Lausanne (2018)
5. Avdiji, H., Elikan, D., Missonier, S., Pigneur, Y.: A design theory for visual inquiry tools. J. Assoc. Inf. Syst. **21**, 695–734 (2020). https://doi.org/10.17705/1jais.00617
6. Ayobi, A., et al.: Co-designing personal health? Multidisciplinary benefits and challenges in informing diabetes self-care technologies. In: Proceedings of the ACM on Human-Computer Interaction, New York, pp. 1–26 (2021)
7. Beck, K.M., et al.: Agile Manifesto for Software Development (2001)
8. Buchanan, R.: Wicked problems in design thinking. Design Iss. **8**, 5–21 (1992)
9. Carlile, P.R.: A pragmatic view of knowledge and boundaries: boundary objects in new product development. Org. Sci. **13**, 442–455 (2002). https://doi.org/10.1287/orsc.13.4.442.2953
10. Coyne, R.: Wicked problems revisited. Design Stud. **26**, 5–17 (2005). https://doi.org/10.1016/j.destud.2004.06.005

11. Digital.ai, 15th State of Agile Report, p. 23 (2021)
12. Gregor, S., Hevner, A.R.: Positioning and presenting design science research for maximum impact. MIS Q. **37**, 337–355 (2013). https://doi.org/10.25300/MISQ/2013/37.2.01
13. Gregor, S., Kruse, L., Seidel, S.: Research perspectives: the anatomy of a design principle. J. Assoc. Inf. Syst. **21**, 1622–1652 (2020). https://doi.org/10.17705/1jais.00649
14. Hawryszkiewycz, I.T.: Visualisations for addressing wicked problems using design thinking. In: European Conference on Information Systems (ECIS) Proceedings, Tel Aviv, pp. 1–12 (2014)
15. Joshi, S.G. Bratteteig, T.: Designing for prolonged mastery. On involving old people in participatory design. Scand. J. Inf. Syst. **28** (2016)
16. Kischelewski, B., Richter, J.: Implementing large-scale agile - an analysis of challenges and success factors. In: European Conference on Information Systems (ECIS) Proceedings, pp. 1–17. Virtual (2020)
17. Lukyanenko, R., Parsons, J., Wiersma, Y., Sieber, R. Maddah, M.: Participatory design for user-generated content: understanding the challenges and moving forward. Scand. J. Inf. Syst. **28** (2016)
18. Maedche, A., Gregor, S., Morana, S., Feine, J.: Conceptualization of the problem space in design science research. In: Tulu, B., Djamasbi, S., Leroy, G. (eds.) DESRIST 2019. LNCS, vol. 11491, pp. 18–31. Springer, Cham (2019). https://doi.org/10.1007/978-3-030-19504-5_2
19. Osterwalder, A., Pigneur, Y.: Business Model Generation: a Handbook for Visionaries, Game Changers, and Challengers. Wiley, New Jersey (2011)
20. Peffers, K., Tuunanen, T., Rothenberger, M.A., Chatterjee, S.: A design science research methodology for information systems research. J. Manag. Inf. Syst. **24**, 45–77 (2007). https://doi.org/10.2753/MIS0742-1222240302
21. Purao, S., Kruse, L.C., Maedche, A.: The origins of design principles: where do... they all come from? In: Hofmann, S., Müller, O., Rossi, M. (eds.) DESRIST 2020. LNCS, vol. 12388, pp. 183–194. Springer, Cham (2020). https://doi.org/10.1007/978-3-030-64823-7_17
22. Rittel, H., Weber, M.: Dilemmas in a general theory of planning. Policy Sci. **4**, 155–169 (1973). https://doi.org/10.1007/BF01405730
23. Roschnik, A., Missonier, S.: A framework proposal to evaluate conceptual models framing wicked managerial concepts. In: European Conference on Information Systems (ECIS) Proceedings, Timişoara, pp. 1–16 (2022)
24. Roschnik, A., Missonier, S.: From a traditional to an agile culture: towards the construction of a crossable bridge. Association Information and Management, pp. 1–15. Virtual (2021)
25. Rosson, M.B., Carroll, J.M.: Scenario-based design. In: Sears, A., Jacko, J.A. (eds.) Jocko Human-Computer Interaction. CRC Press, Boca Raton (2002)
26. Rupp, C.: Systemanalyse Kompakt. Springer, Berlin (2013)
27. Sanders, E.B.N., Stappers, P.J.: Co-creation and the new landscapes of design. CoDesign **4**, 5–18 (2008). https://doi.org/10.1080/15710880701875068
28. Schein, E.H.: The Corporate Culture Survival Guide. Wiley. Jossey-Bass, Wiley, San Francisco (2009)
29. Schein, E.H.: Organizational Culture. Sloan School of Management. MIT (1988)
30. Spinuzzi, C.: The methodology of participatory design. Tech. Commun. **52**, 163–175 (2005)
31. Steen, M.: Co-design as a process of joint inquiry and imagination. Design Iss. **29**, 16–28 (2013). https://doi.org/10.1162/DESI_a_00207
32. Stewart, D.W., Shamdasani, P.N., Rook, D.W.: Focus Groups: Theory and Practice, 2nd edn. Sage Publications, Newbury Park (2007)
33. Thoring, K., Mueller, R.M., Badke-Schaub, P.: Workshops as a research method: guidelines for designing and evaluating artifacts through workshops. In: Proceedings of the 53rd Hawaii International Conference on System Sciences, pp. 5036–5045 (2020)

34. Tolfo, C., Wazlawick, R.S., Ferreira, M.G.G. Forcellini, F.A.: Agile methods and organizational culture: reflections about cultural levels. J. Soft. Maint. Evol. Res. Pract. **23**, 423–441 (2011). https://doi.org/10.1002/smr.483

35. Tremblay, M.C., Hevner, A.R., Berndt, D.J.: Focus groups for artifact refinement and evaluation in design research. Commun. Assoc. Inf. Syst. **26**, 599–618 (2010). https://doi.org/10.17705/1CAIS.02627

36. Venable, J., Pries-Heje, J., Baskerville, R.: FEDS: a framework for evaluation in design science research. Eur. J. Inf. Syst. **25**, 77–89 (2016). https://doi.org/10.1057/ejis.2014.36

37. Visser, S.F., Stappers, P.J., Van der Lugt, R., Sanders, E.B.N.: Contextmapping: experiences from practice. CoDesign **1**, 119–149 (2005). https://doi.org/10.1080/15710880500135987

38. vom Brocke, J., Maedche, A.: The DSR grid: six core dimensions for effectively planning and communicating design science research projects. Electron. Mark. **29**(3), 379–385 (2019). https://doi.org/10.1007/s12525-019-00358-7

Sustainability and Responsible Design

Introduction to the Sustainability and Responsible Design Track

Johann Kranz[1], Nigel P. Melville[2], and Nicolas Prat[3]

[1] University of Munich
kranz@lmu.de
[2] University of Michigan
npmelv@umich.edu
[3] ESSEC Business School
prat@essec.edu

In Society 5.0, complex and interconnected technologies and systems enable myriad new business opportunities. From a sustainability perspective, examples include decarbonization, sustainable energy systems, and the circular economy. From a responsibility perspective, important characteristics include fairness, inclusiveness, transparency, explainability, accountability, security, safety, and robustness.

Design science research can develop artifacts that address the challenge of sustainability. In addition to its potential contributions to sustainability through the development of artifacts, design science research should ensure that the design process is sustainable and responsible. This may be achieved, for example, through the development of design theories or principles.

The Sustainability and Responsible Design track of DESRIST addresses this research opportunity by advancing design science research that promotes and proposes artifacts that directly address these societal challenges. The accepted papers provide a sense of design science research's potential to significantly contribute to the achievement of the goals of sustainability and responsible design, with one paper focusing on explainable AI in medical imaging, and the other on the design of sustainable safe spaces in immersive learning environments.

However, it is also clear that significant challenges exist for applying design science research to achieve the goals of sustainability and responsible design in Society 5.0, and we identify two such challenges.

First, engaging early in the development and implementation of emergent digital technologies bears the potential for design science research to actively contribute to this development. This can help to both support sustainability and responsibility related to the technologies' design as well as to their application to implement sustainability and responsibility at individual, organizational, and societal levels. Key contemporary examples include emergent applications of AI and Internet of Things technologies.

Second, value judgements about what constitutes "good" design need to consider multidimensional evaluation criteria—such as the aforementioned fairness, inclusiveness, transparency, explainability, accountability, security, safety, and robustness. These

evaluation criteria need to be constantly questioned and adjusted to the evolving requirements of sustainability and responsibility under consideration of the wider institutional
context at regional, governmental, and international levels. Beyond immediate utility,
the long-term impact of artifacts needs to be evaluated.

A Mid-Range Theory for Designing Sustainable Safe Spaces of Immersive Learning Environments: A Design-Science Based Gamification Approach

Amir Haj-Bolouri[1]([✉]) [iD], Jesse Katende[1] [iD], and Matti Rossi[2] [iD]

[1] School of Economics, Business, and IT, University West, Trollhättan, Sweden
amir.haj-bolouri@hv.se
[2] Information Systems, Aalto University, Espoo, Finland
matti.rossi@aalto.fi

Abstract. Gamification provides a prominent technique that can be used to provide Immersive Learning Environments (ILEs) for domains, where it is dangerous or expensive to learn in real environments. Especially industrial organizations (e.g., manufacturing, mining, construction) are a promising domain for implementing ILEs that combine gamification concepts with a pedagogical design to facilitate safety training under secure circumstances. Although there are design research studies that exemplify the utility of gamification of learning activities, or how to improve organizational safety training through gamification, there is a need to address how sustainable safe spaces can be designed for enhanced safety training in ILEs. Safe spaces are key elements of a successful safety training experience in ILEs as they provide safe and secure training environments, which in the physical world are typically considered too dangerous with high risk of injuring the training participants. This study reports findings from an ongoing DSR project that stresses the design of ILEs for sustainable safety training. Within the project, an artifact for immersive fire safety training in virtual reality has been designed, developed, and evaluated together with employees of a train operator company. The research responds to the need of producing design knowledge that moves beyond the highly contextualized designs principles that are particular for IVR applications. We use gamification concepts as a kernel theory for developing a mid-range theory of designing immersive virtual safety training environments.

Keywords: Immersive Learning Environments · Virtual Reality · Safe Spaces · Design Science, · Gamification · Sustainability · Mid-Range Theory

1 Introduction

The immersive human interface brought forth by innovation and technological development, resulted from the intricate connection of Virtual reality (VR) technology [1]. VR has, over time, continued to evolve into Immersive Virtual Reality (IVR) technology [2]. Typically, the IVR technology is constructed into Head Mounted Devices (HMD) that

A. Gerber and R. Baskerville (Eds.): DESRIST 2023, LNCS 13873, pp. 449–469, 2023.
https://doi.org/10.1007/978-3-031-32808-4_28

users equip to transport their senses to a reality beyond the physical one [3]. As such, the IVR experience becomes an absorbing experience based on immersion, an increased sense of embodied presence, and high level of interactivity [4]. Consequently, the application of IVR technology has had significant implications in facilitating Immersive Learning Environments (ILEs) for organizations and schools, which has led to scholars to explore the design of ILEs [5, 6].

Traditionally ILEs consist of a mix of different approaches to facilitate learning in an immersive way [7]. The feeling of 'immersion' is an experiential mode of becoming absorbed by the virtual reality through an increased sense of 'being-there', also known as embodied presence [8]. The experiential attributes that ILEs consist of vary heavily with respect to learning objectives, learning scenarios, pedagogical design (e.g., learning methods), and design features [9]. The design features of ILEs are thus constituted through properties that convey a narrative for learning, whether it is through simulation, visualization, and/or more typically, through a gamified approach that makes the immersive learning highly interactive for the participants [10]. Previous research advocates that the gamification provides a prominent collection of techniques that can be applied to incorporate game elements into ILEs (e.g., [11]. Especially industrial organizations (e.g., manufacturing, mining, construction) have showcased to be a prominent domain for implementing ILEs that combine gamification concepts with a pedagogical design to facilitate safety training [12, 13].

Recent research within the field of IS (e.g., [3, 14–16]) calls for prescriptive design knowledge that informs the design process of ILEs through game elements [17]. In the paradigm of Design Science Research (DSR) in IS [18, 19], scholars follow an inherent tradition of producing design knowledge that balances rigorous scientific output (e.g., design principles, design theories) with viable artifacts [20]. And although there are DSR studies that exemplify the utility of gamification of learning activities in general (e.g., [21, 22]), and studies about how to improve organizational safety training through a gamification approach (e.g., [23]), there exists a current need to address how 'safe spaces' can be designed for ILEs that facilitate safety training [24]. Safe spaces are considered to be key elements of a successful safety training experience in ILEs because they provide secure virtual training features that, in the physical world, would typically be considered as dangerous with high risk of injuring the training participants.

In light of the given background above, this study reports findings from an ongoing DSR project that stresses the design of ILEs for sustainable safety training. Within the project, an instantiated artifact for immersive fire safety training in virtual reality has been designed, developed, and evaluated together with employees of a Swedish train operator company. The design of the IVR artifact provides a basis for exploring the possibilities for extracting design knowledge that can be transferred from the current design context to a context that share similar challenges and characteristics. Such kind of aspiration lies in the heart of the constitution of a DSR project [18, 20, 25]. Hence, this study incorporates current learning outcomes from the project and attempts to extract design knowledge that advances the research towards addressing the following research question:

- *How can sustainable safe spaces be designed for gamified Immersive Learning Environments to facilitate safety training?*

The research question responds to the need of producing design knowledge that moves beyond the highly contextualized designs principles that are particular for IVR applications. In order to address the research question, this study employs a design science approach that employs a synthesized body of knowledge on gamification concepts into a kernel theory for developing a mid-range theory [26]. As such, the contribution of this study is a mid-range theory for designing sustainable safe spaces of ILEs, and the implications of the mid-range theory are targeted to: (1) advance DSR and gamification for training in VR (e.g., [21, 22]); (2) advancing an ongoing DSR project by developing design goals for sustainable safe spaces as constitutive parts of the mid-range theory; and (3) discussing the added value of safe spaces for the discourse of sustainability in the IS field [27–29], with a specific interest for research that urges to inform how innovative technologies can be designed to help resolving environmental, social, and economic issues over [30, 31].

The rest of this paper is organized as follows. First, a section of related research on ILES, IVR and safety training, along with sustainability in the IS field, is outlined. Second, the design science-based gamification approach along with the empirical setting of the ongoing DSR project is presented. Third, the preliminary findings of this study are presented. Fourth and finally, a section on concluding remarks and an outlook for future research is presented.

2 Related Research

2.1 Research on Immersive Learning Environments and Safety Training

Safety training (also referred to as 'safety education') is a special form of learning experience that integrates the development of procedural skills (e.g., how to accomplish something) through hands-on exercises that are heavily task-dependent and can expose the training participants to potential risks [32]. Moreover, practical safety training exercises can also require expensive, fragile, or rare equipment, which could be difficult to secure for real-life training experiences [33]. A particular field that is affected by such issues is that of industrial training, where operators must be prepared to work with potentially hazardous systems (e.g., robotic manipulators, electrical machinery) [34], or dangerous situations that might affect other people such as fire safety training (e.g., [35]). However, thanks to the rapid development of IVR technology, organizations can today create high-detailed simulations of real-life training scenarios that, given also the widespread availability of low-cost devices, can be easily exploited to safely facilitate safety training in ILEs [36, 37].

ILEs are based on IVR technology, and they are gaining traction as innovative bundles of technology for facilitating safety training experiences in the virtual reality [15]. One of the major reasons why ILEs are prominent for safety training is their high practicality, low risk, and low cost, as well as their capacity to ensure both safety and efficiency during learning processes [38]. ILEs are mainly based on pedagogical design features and experiential modes of learning through simulation, visualization, and/or gamified learning scenarios [39]. As such, ILEs employed for safety training purposes allow workers to actively participate in scenarios that represent the actual conditions of real-life scenarios, enhancing and strengthening safety awareness and allowing them to experience the learning activities, under secure circumstances [40]. Application areas include emergency preparation [41], fire prevention [42], and first aid [43], and preparation for managing workplace accidents [15, 44, 45]. However, with increasing possibilities of organizing and facilitating safety training in ILEs, come ideas about how such learning experiences become meaningful for the individual employees' life-long learning process [46], and what their implications are for organizations' strategies of increased sustainability through safe spaces that eliminate unsafe practices and increase the safe performance of dangerous training tasks [47].

2.2 Research on Sustainability and Safe Spaces

Sustainability issues are one of our times' main concerns and include a complex set of interconnected environmental, social, and economic problems. The sustainable development goals (SDGs) set by the United Nations (UN) for 2030 involve the three dimensions (environmental, social, and economic), requiring, at the same time a massive reduction of resources' use and their accessibility to the whole global population. This radical transformation determines a need to educate citizens, organizations, and professionals, increase their awareness, and ultimately support a behavior change towards sustainable choices. To this purpose, IVR technology, that constitute the technological foundation for ILEs, has been identified as a prominent for tackling all three dimensions of sustainability in the context of safety training by increasing employees' industrial skills with a particular emphasis on enhanced safety awareness [15]. Organizing and conducting safety training in ILEs is considered to be a sustainable approach because of the safe spaces that focus the environmental dimension by reducing heavy pollution and environmental issues [24] and supporting the socio-economic dimensions of sustainability by reducing costs for training initiatives and increasing behavioral skills and safety awareness of participants under secure circumstances [48].

Currently, there are no universal definitions of what a safe space is. However, as a concept, safe spaces have typically been employed in IVR to promote education and learning experiences that feel safe for participants that want to experiment with their personal identities [49]. This includes safe spaces for provoking new ideas for learning that might be controversial [50], and/or to provide low skilled novice workers with a safe environment to learn through experience and perform actions that might be costly or embarrassing to do in the physical space [51]. Safe spaces provide thus a secure virtual space that allow and encourage end-users of ILEs to navigate freely, experiment with behaviors and actions, and iterate around learning objectives through a safe trial-and-error process. Moreover, safe spaces focus trigger warnings that raise negative reactions among training participants. Such trigger warnings could for instance be related to certain sounds, imagery, or behaviors that create an uncomfortable atmosphere in the physical space. As such, safe spaces are feasible for organizations that want to experiment with training scenarios through low-cost initiatives and secure circumstances that are efficient for developing meaningful learning experiences that do not lead to traumatic experiences or physical injuries [37, 38, 52]. This includes designing a safe space in virtual reality that facilitate learning activities for development of situational awareness through procedural skills (how to accomplish something), descriptive skills (how to define/describe something), and behavioral skills (how one can behave in a given situation).

And while many frameworks and models have been developed to support design for sustainable behavior and decision improvements among organizations in general [40–43, 53, 54], to this day, there is a lack of design knowledge that guide and support the design of sustainable safe spaces in ILEs that facilitate safety training across a variety of safety training contexts [14, 44, 54]. With 'sustainable', we are referring to the need of mapping design elements with safety training objectives that resolve sustainable issues that traditional safety training initiatives consist of [55]. Such issues include high consumption of natural resources, limited flexibility to various fields and areas of training, lack of adaptability for experimentation and repetition of training scenarios, and high risk for injury in safety operations. Although it is evident that ILEs provide safe spaces a remedy towards resolving such issues [56], there is still a need for producing design knowledge that explicate the mapping of design elements that increase the internal and external motivation of learning experiences. One way of pursuing to address such gap, is through gamification in DSR.

2.3 Research on Gamification and Design

Gamification applies knowledge from gaming theory and flow theory [56–58] to nongaming contexts. As such, gamification is *"[...] the application of lessons from the gaming domain in order to change stakeholder behaviors and outcomes in non-game situations"* [59]. Although gamification emerged from the flow literature as it is applied to gaming, scholars have not reached a consensus regarding gamification's definition [58]. Similarly, in IS research, scholars such as Liu et al. [62, p. 3] concluded that:

> *"The common themes that emerge from the various definitions over the past decade are: gamified systems must have a specific user engagement and instrumental goals, and the way to achieve these is by the selection of game design elements."*

Another key gamification concept is that a game-like user experience activates the end-users' individual motives and make the learning experience meaningful for them [61, 62]. However, Bui et al.'s [63] review of gamification disclosed that most gamification studies do not explain the design elements of the gamified artifact, such as how these artifacts foster gamification for meaningful learning experiences, and that there is a:

> *"[...] large gap in research of potential relevance to organizations... more research is needed on employees interacting with group systems resulting in collaboration dynamics and longer-term behavioral outcomes."* [63].

Moreover, gamification is difficult to design for a variety of reasons, most prominent of which is that: (1) the inspirational source of gamification design [64]; games, are complex, multifaceted, and thus, difficult to generally design and let alone transfer to other environments [65, 66]; (2) the goal of gamification is to affect behavior and not only to entertain – as it is primarily the intention of games [67]. Hence, the design of gamified ILEs should not be equaled with developing games in general. Otherwise, transferring game elements to the meaningful learning experience in safe spaces, may lead to the design of ILEs that provide a level of entertainment, but might not lead to a behavioral change as is intended from gamification; (3) the serious learning context in which gamification is applied provides requirements, which may limit the design space drastically compared to games [68]; and (4) in order to affect behavioral change through gamified learning experiences, gamification involves motivational development of design knowledge which entails the understanding of how to incorporate synthesized game elements into the immersive learning experience [69].

However, so far, only a few sources exist that provide methodological insights and practical guidance into how to gamify IT artifacts (e.g., [70–72]), gamification of immersive learning experiences in VR (e.g., [38, 73, 75]), or how to systematically incorporate gamification into the design process of a DSR project (e.g., [21–23, 76]). As a response, we propose that gamified safety training represents a natural opportunity to apply a design-science based gamification approach that advances the development of a mid-range theory for designing sustainable safe spaces of ILEs.

3   The Design Science-Based Gamification Approach

In order to support our design science-based gamification approach, we adhered to a methodology that closely follows the framework advocated by [26], which emphasizes mid-range theories as: theories that lie between the minor but necessary working hypotheses that evolve in abundance during day-to-day research and all-inclusive systematic efforts to develop a unified theory [77, 78]. Whereas grand theories are all encompassing in their nature, mid-range theories are bounded by their subject matter and therefore offer the kind of detail that can only come from an in-depth focused on contextualized design science research [79]. Consequently, mid-range theory building is suggested to be more specific to accommodate empirical data from a sub-range of the phenomenon covered by a general theory [80]. In other words, a mid-range theory of DSR in IS, shall attempt to strongly link kernel theory constructs with design facets of artifacts [81]. But what is a 'kernel theory'?

A 'kernel theory' is per definition a body of theoretical knowledge (e.g., concepts, principles, theories) that is drawn from natural or social sciences to govern design requirements [82, 83]. In design science, kernel theories can be employed to underpin and inform the design process of artifacts [20], by providing justificatory knowledge [84] that explain how and why the design of an artifact is sufficient for its purpose and scope. However, a common challenge with using kernel theories in DSR, is the difficulty to discern the relationship between high-level abstracted kernel theories with design goals of a mid-range theory development project [26, 84]. Another challenge of developing mid-range theories as to do with the difficulty of using existing frameworks for design theory development (e.g., [83]) to explicate design-related knowledge from kernel theories [26]. As a consequence, unlike the management, medical, sociology, and engineering literatures, where mid-range theories are frequently developed, the IS literature provides a modest quantity of examples on mid-range theories that were developed through DSR projects (e.g., [26, 85]).

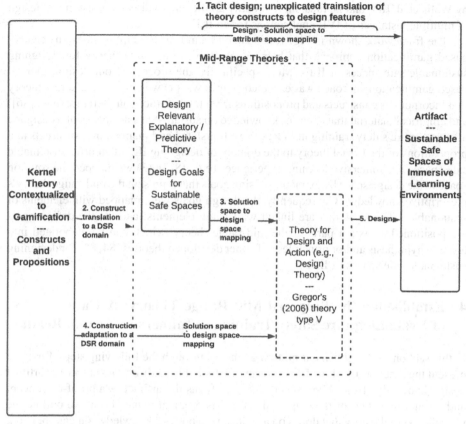

Fig. 1. Overview of a Proposed Mid-Range Theory for Designing Sustainable Safe Spaces of ILEs (adapted from [26])

As a way of advancing the discourse on developing mid-range theories through DSR in IS, for this study (as shown in Fig. 1), we focused on developing mid-range theories in form of Design Relevant Explanatory/Predictive Theories (DREPTs) proposed by Kuechler & Vaishnavi [26].

A DREPT is a mid-range theory that formally captures the translation of a kernel theory constructs (derived from both within and outside of IS) to the design realm of an artifact [26]. In other words, a DREPT augments the 'how' information of a theory for design and action [78] with explanatory information explaining why an instance artifact as the effects it does for the design space. Subsequently, the reason this study focused on developing a mid-range theory in form of DREPTs, is because of a number of reasons. First, DREPTs capture knowledge generated during a DSR project that is not captured into a high-abstract design theory [83, 84], but instead link the captured knowledge with explanations about a phenomenon that is derived from a kernel theory that incorporate design goals for the theory. Second, a mid-range theory of this kind, explains how and why design goals based on the theory achieve their intended novelty across contexts of artifact design [20]. And third, DREPTs is more abstract than a design theory proposed by Walls et al. [83] and is, thus, more broadly applicable to directly assist in the design of multiple instances of IVR applications for an ILE.

The framework shown in Fig. 1, is adapted from [26] to employ a design science-based gamification approach that help us develop a mid-range theory for designing sustainable safe spaces of ILEs. More specifically, the process of our design science-based gamification approach was executed as follows: (1) we employed a kernel theory that incorporates constructs and propositions from the gamification literature (e.g., [86]) and empirical material that captures knowledge on sustainable safe spaces of a designed artifact for fire safety training in IVR; (2) we translated and mapped the constructs and propositions of the kernel theory to the domain of designing ILEs that offer sustainable safe spaces for immersive learning experiences (e.g., [87]); (3) we mapped the solution space to the design space by extracting design goals that represent the mid-range theory's prescriptive knowledge. Consequently, the design goals were mapped with elements of sustainable safe spaces that are linked with game elements; and (4) the design goals are positioned as extant parts of the mid-range theory, which can be elaborated into testable hypothesis and/or principles of further developed theories [84, 85] for designing sustainable safe spaces of ILEs.

4 Establishing the Proposed Mid-Range Theory: A Case of Evaluating Fire Safety Training in Immersive Virtual Reality

In this section, we establish our mid-range theory through the following steps. First, we present the case setting of the DSR project of which this study extracted specific artifact design knowledge from. More specifically, we focus the artifact as a proof-of-concept and discuss its value for the empirical setting as proof-of-value. Then, we outline the identified kernel theory that draws on a synthesized body of knowledge on gamification. Thereafter, we operationalize the kernel theory into a set of the design goals that, together with constructs of our kernel theory, inform the prescriptive aspects (e.g., addressing the how-part of our research question) of our proposed mid-range theory.

4.1 The Empirical Case Setting: An IVR Learning Experience of Fire Safety Training

The empirical case setting of this study took place within a project of evaluating an IVR learning experience of fire safety training. The empirical case is a design science project following the Action Design Research (ADR) method [25] and was executed at one of the headquarters for the biggest train operator company in Sweden, named SJ. The cycle of evaluating the IVR learning experience, was manifested through a specific focus on evaluation of a designed IVR application for fire safety training, which is intended to become an integrated part of a future ILE for safety training. The IVR application had undergone two iterations of design and evaluation for Alpha and Beta versions.

More specifically, the evaluation process focused on establishing proof-of-concept and proof-of-value by: (i) evaluating the IVR learning experience of individual end-users/participants with an interest for how safe they felt during the training exercise; and (ii) evaluating the sustainable implications of conducting fire safety training in

IVR. Consequently, the evaluation phase took place between 2021–2022 and was conducted through direct observations of the IVR learning experience combined with semi-structured group interviews [88]. A total of 4 training sessions were observed and a total of 26 participants were interviewed. Subsequently, the training sessions were performed individually by each participant and the interviewees consisted of end-users (e.g., training participants) and organizational stakeholders (e.g., instructors), which were asked questions such as "In what ways did you feel safer in virtual reality than in physical reality when extinguishing fire?", "Why do you think it is better for the organization to do fire safety training in virtual reality?", or "How will the organization continue with safety training in virtual reality?". As a result of the observations and the interviews, we could establish proof-of-concept and proof-of-value, as justification for our kernel theory and as an empirical basis for establishing the mid-range theory.

Fig. 2. Proof-of-Concept: Instantiated IVR Artifact for Fire Safety Training

In DSR, a **proof-of-concept** is the point at which evidence exists to show that the described conceptual design of an artifact is feasible and promising, at least in a limited context [18, 20]. For the proof-of-concept of this study, we applied gamification to carefully extract and propose the gamification design implications that serve as the bridge between the artifact's functionality and meaningful engagement [60]. A **proof-of-value**, on the other hand, is achieved when IS researchers show that an IT artifact actually works for its purpose in the context it is implemented [89]. Both concepts were incorporated into the kernel theory.

For establishing a **proof-of-concept** we reviewed the overall impressions and thoughts among participants (end-users) of the IVR safety training sessions. We went to the organization where the proof-of-concept was established and interviewed the participants (e.g., train operators, train drivers, instructors of the training sessions) to see how pleased they were with their learning experience in IVR. The instantiated IVR artifact that mediated the immersive learning experience, was based on IVR technology in form of HTC Vive Pro Headset and a replica of a fire extinguisher that was connected to the IVR training environment (shown in Fig. 2). Through observations and interviews, we perceived an overall positive impression among the participants. In terms of their learning experience, they found meaning in conducting safety training a virtual environment in front of a physical one:

"The experience felt safer than doing it physically. I did not feel any threat from the fire and still I could learn how to use the fire hose to extinguish the fire" (Train Operator 1)

"It was a different kind of experience, much more fun and motivating than, you know, looking at a powerpoint or something. This felt more like a video game... I could fail over and over again and still learn more" (Train Driver 1)

And when the participants were asked whether or not they would like to do other kind of safety training exercises in virtual reality, some of them answered:

"I mean, we feel safer doing dangerous stuff in a virtual reality... it still feels quite real, and we recognize the exercises, scenarios and so... also, it seems that we can do this individually without any organized effort as well, that is good!" (Train Operator 2)

"It is difficult to say for sure... hm, well, I think so, I mean, it is much safer and that is comfortable and perhaps that makes us calmer when a dangerous thing happens in reality... there are other scenarios, such as dealing with threats from passengers... that could be realistic to exercise in a safe space as well" (Train Operator 3)

Additionally, for establishing a **proof-of-value** for this study, we interviewed instructors (the organizational stakeholders) from the organization, who expressed a positive view on continuing with training their staff in IVR, by extending the repertoire:

"I definitely feel that this is the future, you know, especially because it is so safe to do things wrong without getting hurt in the virtual reality. People feel safe and they are not afraid to do wrong because it is also fun to practice like this. Little bit like a video game, you must finish your assignment and then you can do it over and over again in a rather entertaining way." (Instructor 1)

"Many of them [referring to the participants] felt safer to do this kind of training like this. I have done traditional fire safety training with them and that was much more stressful and demanding." (Instructor 2)

Finally, when asked about providing an outlook into the future of the organization's need of using IVR technology for safety training purposes, more systematically, the instructors answered:

We can see the value of doing more training in virtual reality, more systematically perhaps, if that is possible... the virtual reality is much safer for the participants, especially when we do safety training, they can fail without getting hurt. That is very appreciated" (Instructor 1)

"We have other training activities that might benefit from doing them in virtual reality because it is safe, secure, does not take time for transportation and it is quite fun. I can see that our, eh, employees think this is different and fun and quite realistic, I think so too as well... also I feel good that it is safer for everyone to train like this." (Instructor 2)

4.2 Structure of the Mid-Range Theory: Contextualization of Game Elements and Design Goals into the Mid-Range Theory

Having established a proof-of-concept and proof-of-value, we now move on to explicate the structure of our mid-range theory by focusing its constructs as design goals, and their relationship with constructs of our kernel theory. Previous DSR studies have largely lacked a systematic DSR approach to how concepts of gamification can be synthesized into constructs and propositions of a kernel theory [23, 63]. As such, the key role of using gamification as a kernel theory for this study was to contextualize gamification concepts in a way that informs the explanatory statements of our mid-range theory. Here, we followed Kuechler & Vaishnava's [26] guidelines for how to express the constructs and propositions of a mid-range theory. This allowed us to map the prescriptive elements of our mid-range theory with the explanatory statements of the kernel theory deriving from the literature on Gamification. At this stage, however, the proposed mid-range theory does not include any predictive elements because the theory's utility has not been verified across multiple contexts and can thus not yet be proposed to predict any specific outcomes.

Table 1 depicts the constructs, propositions, and contextualization of gamification concepts (e.g., game elements, game features) with elements of safe spaces in ILEs, whereas a detailed presentation of each design goal is provided below Table 1.

From the kernel theory propositions shown in Table 1, we infer (as the arrows in between the columns indicate) gamification concepts to inform the formulation of four design goals that constitute the prescriptive knowledge of our mid-range theory. The gamification concepts were inferred from reviewed literature on gamified safety training in IVR (e.g., [75, 90–92]). Moreover, the literature review informed specific game elements that are important to take into consideration when designing gamified learning environments for increasing extrinsic/intrinsic motivation among end-users. As such, we propose that the design goals are achieved by incorporating the linked game elements shown in Table 1. Consequently, the development of the design goals was supported by the DSR case through a number of ways: (1) the case helped us contextualize the design goals within a hands-on IVR training scenario; (2) the case helped us derive the prescriptive statements of the design goals from features of the fire safety training artifact; and (3) the case helped us evaluate the immersive learning experience in order to motivate a gamified approach for safety training procedures that are sustainable over time.

The **first design goal** was extracted based on kernel constructs that emphasize 'flow' as a central concept of gamification [75]. The reviewed literature on gamification explicated flow as a psychological experience that end-users of IVR enjoy, the more they engage with training activities over time [92]. Experiencing and seeking flow is similarly why end-users engage with games in a committed, repetitive, and safe way [90]. On this basis, we can reason that the literature provides examples on game elements that we map with designing for intrinsically rewarding repetitions through the accomplishments of missions and mastery of levels, which help stimulating a sense of flow in safe spaces of an ILE. For instance, simulation of missions, similar to missions in games that are exciting and fun to accomplish, can be defined to support immersion and sense of increased embodied presence in IVR [39]. The length and speed of an assignment can,

Table 1. Structure of Mid-Range Theory: Gamification Concepts, Game Elements, and Design Goals

Kernel Construct/ Gamification Concept(s)	Game Element Example(s)	Mid-Range Construct/ Design Goal(s)	Descriptions
Sense of Flow	- Simulation - Missions - Levels - Speed	DG1. Design for Intrinsically Rewarding Repetitions	Games tend to indicate to end-users that they have succeeded or failed in a simulated mission as well as what levels and expertise they have gained from their experience. Hence, designing for intrinsically rewarding repetitions require a safe space for control of speed and self-efficacy (e.g., person's belief in their abilities), which enables repeated engagement with activities in the IVR space
Entertaining Utilitarianism	- Quests - In Game Rewards - Roleplay - Virtual helpers	DG2. Design for Increased Situational Awareness	Games promote end-users with utilitarian motivations through quests and in game rewards, which increase situational awareness through incentives of positive actions and increased safety skills. Hence, designing for increased situational awareness can promote an entertaining form of utilitarianism that is extrinsically motivated through roleplays and virtual helpers (e.g., avatars) that enable a safe space for guidance and learning
Meaningful Narratives	- Reminders - Customization - Narration - Clear Goals - Direct Feedback - Theme	DG3. Design for Experimental and Interactive Storytelling	Games provide end-users interactive spaces for safe experimentation through customizable narratives and reminders of objectives. Hence, designing for experimental and interactive storytelling can provide clear goals through an exciting theme that facilitate meaningful learning experiences (e.g., valuable, and significant for the user's professional identity)
Motivational Autonomy	- Tasks - Increased Difficulty - Badges - Performance Stats - Performance Feedback	DG4. Design for Flexible Level of Mastery	Games offer end-users the freedom of choosing what challenges to undertake without becoming punished or risking embarrassment. Hence, designing for motivational autonomy need to provide end-users a safe space to explore increased difficulty of tasks, and evaluate their performance through direct or post performance feedback/stats that generate indicative rewards (e.g., badges) for increased autonomy over time

for example, be designed according to the difficulty of a training assignment; length is defined according to the number of objectives and given steps that need to be followed in order to achieve the objectives, whereas speed is measured according to how fast the assignment must be solved [93]. Additionally, the entire training experience is designed into different levels, which signify how far in the gamified training process the end-user has advanced [94], which provide them a sense of safety and control of self-efficacy.

The **second design goal** was extracted based on kernel constructs that emphasize 'utilitarianism' in an entertaining way. The utilitarian aspect is here defined as the aspect that mediates the achievement of a goal according to its applied fields (e.g., efficiency in training). As such, the aspect is based on a pragmatic inquiry of actions, consequences, and their values for a given training assignment [95]. On this basis, we can reason the main purposes of game elements are to achieve utilitarian goals supported by gamified behaviors and features in the IVR safe space [93]. For instance, in game rewards are game elements that the safe space can incorporate to engage end-users in utilitarian quests that are guided by virtual safety training helpers (e.g., embodied avatars) [35]. Here, role plays can be employed to provide end-users a comfortable way of increasing their situational awareness, without losing motivation due to the risk of feeling ashamed or embarrassed for failing their assignments [38]. Consequently, the elements can be designed to increase end-users' situational awareness through possibilities for explicit interaction with safety tools that help end-users to understand the situation [96], or implicit interaction through safety signages that simulate their awareness of understanding a utilitarian behavior in the situation [97].

The **third design goal** was extracted based on kernel constructs that emphasize 'meaningful narratives' that can be customized together with reminder of objectives (e.g., indicator of accomplished and not accomplished training tasks), which end-users encounter in a safe IVR training space [98]. The 'meaningfulness' of narratives derive from how intelligible the training scenario is framed and presented to the end-users. In other words, the scenario must make sense to the end-users, and as such, the framing of the training scenario gets more meaningful if the goals of the training scenario are presented clearly before and during the IVR training experience [99]. On this basis, we can reason that the narration of a safety training scenario needs to incorporate a given theme with clear goals that is conveyed through a creative and interactive form of storytelling, which allow the users to experiment in their safe IVR training space [38, 100]. Here, direct feedback is essential to incorporate through multimodal training features (combination of sound, visuals, animation, avatar behavior) that afford a safe atmosphere to increase the external and internal motivation of the end-users by demonstrating the validity of creative experimentation through a learning by doing [101].

The **fourth design goal** was extracted based on kernel constructs that emphasize 'motivational autonomy' that stimulates the end-users learning process and development of procedural skills, over time. 'Autonomy' is here defined as the condition or quality of being self-govern and self-determined [102], whereas it becomes motivational when the IVR training experience enables a safe space with the freedom of choosing the complexity of challenges and training tasks [103]. On this basis, we can reason that motivation and autonomy are afforded through game elements that allow the training tasks' difficulty to increase adaptably, depending on the sufficiency of users' performances [15]. Elements such as performance feedback and stats, accompanied with badges (e.g., ranking depending on quality of performance), are thus crucial to take into consideration when designing for flexible level of mastery that gets evaluated and refined in a safe IVR training space [74].

In summary then, the design goals can be achieved by DSR scholars together with design practitioners that develop ILEs for safety training purposes. The next step of operationalizing the design goals would thus be to follow the explanatory statements and contextualize the prescriptive elements of gamification, in order to gamify either a present or future ILE artifact. Moreover, the proposed design goals need to be achieved by following the prescriptive statements of safe spaces as a means for realizing ILEs that are not only gamified, but also secure for conducting safety training procedures. Together, the design goals can then be evaluated against settings that are in need of safety training procedures that support the sustainable development of organizations, with a particular emphasize on reducing physical injuries during safety training, increasing the well-being of training participants by preparing them under safe and secure circumstances of training, and eliminating the amount of pollution that is usually an implication of hazardous situations in the physical training space.

5 Discussion

Given the outline of establishing our proposed mid-range theory for designing sustainable safe spaces of ILEs, we discuss that our theory has implications for both practice and theory. Hence, in this section, we start by discussing the practical implications of the mid-range theory, with a particular focus on the design goals and their implications for designing safe spaces in ILEs that support organizations' safety training initiatives in a sustainable way. After that, we discuss the theoretical implications of our proposed mid-range theory, with an emphasis on how it contributes to the area of design science and gamification of IVR safety training.

5.1 Implications for Practice

If we start by discussing the implications of the design goals, we can see that all four goals put a strong emphasis on employee involvement in safety, such as raising their level of situational behaviour awareness by advocating gamified safe spaces that are designed to reduce the likelihood of workplace accidents and improve the effectiveness of safety management [38]. Many enterprises and organizations, as well as the general public, are advocating for a stronger emphasis on safety education and training to limit the potential for human error and consequently improve workplace safety [35], something that the design goals echo through their empirical illustrations from the case presented in Sect. 3. As the data material from the empirical case indicated, both the organization and their employees expressed to see a value in conducting safety training that is safe in IVR. This was confirmed through the established proof-of-concept, whereas the proof-of-value provided a snapshot into a potential of conducting additional safety training exercises in safe spaces of ILEs that are sustainable.

At this stage of our research, we understand that the design goals can support organizations to employ ILEs that support the social dimension of sustainability by providing their employees a learning experience that feels safe, and that increase diversity in participants' skills and performances [15]. Moreover, the design goals provide prescriptive knowledge [20], which can support organizations to target the environmental dimension of sustainability by reducing the risk of injuries, energy consumption, and pollution in situations where experimentation is needed but is dangerous and hazardous, such as for instance in the context of fire safety training [35]. Finally, we think that the design goals can support the economical dimension of sustainability by making the learning experience safe over time without risking to overconsuming organizational resources (financial, humans, technology). This is in particular a tedious task when increasing situational awareness in physical training environments, which are limited to budget and technological constrains, such as for instance in health care or safety education [38, 100].

Secondly, the gamified approach to designing sustainable safe spaces of ILEs, might increase the sense of motivation among end-users, by showcasing how their competence, autonomy, and relatedness, is augmented through enjoying and engaging tasks through meaningful training narratives [98, 99]. For example, game elements such as quests and missions have been proven to increase the lust and motivation for experimenting with the virtual surrounding and the affordances they provide [75]. These elements can be designed to confirm the embedded safety of the ILEs through for instance training assignments that are generally dangerous to experiment with in the physical reality, such as experimenting with training assignments in the manufacturing industry [75, 101]. And although the empirical case of this study supports that safety training in IVR might become more interesting when it is fun and exciting, which is a central tenet of gamifying IVR safety training experiences [64, 97], one case alone cannot justify the level generalizability among the gamified design goals of this research. It should thus be noted that we are not implying that all aspects of safety training in ILEs should be gamified, but rather, we propose the design of ILEs for safety training to incorporate game elements that increase safety and sense of autonomy among end-users. Furthermore, evaluating improvement in end-users' motivation is not a simple and straightforward thing to design for [60], Hence, as part of the design science approach [20, 26], it will be necessary to determine how to evaluate this in order to determine the practical viability of our proposed design goals.

5.2 Implications for Theory

Promoting gamification through a design science approach, and vice versa, has implications for how design science outputs [20] can be developed as mid-range theories [26] for designing a class of IVR safety training artifacts as ILEs. Gamification concepts can be used to guide the design of safe spaces in ILEs, which leads to meaningful IVR learning experiences that is theoretically informed through the mid-range theory's kernel theory constructs. As such, the proposed mid-range theory of this study was pragmatically driven from the serendipitous confluence of design science goals and gamification concepts. We not only were able to demonstrate the empirical connection of our theory with the synthesized body of kernel constructs, but we also did so in a manner that can contribute to theory development beyond DSR.

Our first key contribution here is the extension of mere IVR safety training to gamified safe spaces for training in a sustainable way. To do so, we combined constructs from the gamification literature that is adhered to increase behavioral change (e.g., [67, 69]), methodological insights and practical guidance on how gamify IT artifacts in general (e.g., [71, 72]), with literature on security gamification [23] that distills gaming elements for theorizing characteristics of sustainable safe spaces. Given that *safety* is essential to our gamification context and the proposed mid-range theory, we also suspect that safety would not have a beneficial relationship a non-gamified safe space that is immersive. Hence, beyond proof-of-concept and proof-of-value, we suggest that an extension of this research needs to examine each game element involved in designing sustainable safe spaces of ILEs. Our second key contribution is the novelty of our mid-range theory, which synthesizes elements of safe spaces with gamification concepts to improve the sustainable quality of safety training in ILEs. The novelty lies in the prescriptive and explanatory nature of the synthesis, which goes beyond design knowledge that is merely constrained to gamified ILEs alone or immersive training environments that are not gamified nor emphasize the importance of incorporating safe spaces that improves the sustainable development of organizations' safety training procedures.

Another consideration that needs to be examined is the proof-of-use, which in DSR (e.g. [19]) is demonstrated when the outputs seek to create self-sustaining and growing communities of practice around a generalizable solution, which in our case would be an ILE that provide sustainable safe spaces for safety training. Thus, proof-of-use is perhaps the greatest limitation and future research opportunity for this research. The first obvious issue and opportunity here is that of generalizability, in terms of further developing the mid-range theory into a design theory [84]. Although our mid-range theory is both theoretically and empirically grounded, it is not established across many organizations which limits the generalizability of our current results. We therefore encourage future DSR to employ our mid-range theory to other contexts that share similar characteristics and needs as the one we illustrated through the empirical case of this study.

6 Conclusion

In this paper we proposed a mid-range theory for designing safe spaces for safety training in immersive learning environments. The goal was to give context sensitive design guidance for especially designing training in hazardous or otherwise potentially dangerous environments. Our study advances a mid-range theory of gamifying the experiences of such training and proposes a set of design goals for developing such gamified learning environments. Consequently, we synthesize a body of knowledge on gamification into a kernel theory that informs the design process and justifies the underlying knowledge of our proposed mid-range theory. Moreover, we target the contributions of this study as sustainable for organizations and practitioners as we offer design guidance and proof-of-value of implementing immersive learning environments that are cheaper, safer, and easier to implement than traditional approaches of safety training. This allows for repeated training with less cost and no real danger for the trainees, without compromising with motivational factor of the learning experience The gamification approach should thus enhance the development of the skills that are trained and encourage repeated training by the participants. As a result, we think that a sustainable approach to safety training in IVR, should over time lead into better trained workers and better overall safety. The limitation of this study, however, is that we have not tested the proposed mid-range theory in other similar contexts. Hence, for future research, we propose to test the mid-range theory to evaluate its level of generalizability, validity, and empirical usefulness across contexts that are interested in designing and implementing safety training in immersive learning environments that are safe and sustainable.

References

1. Aukstakalnis, S.: Practical augmented reality: A guide to the technologies, applications, and human factors for AR and VR. Addison-Wesley Professional, Boston (2016)
2. Vergara, D., Extremera, J., Rubio, M.P., Dávila, L.P.: Meaningful learning through virtual reality learning environments: a case study in materials engineering. Appl. Sci. 9(21), 4625 (2019)
3. Hageman, A.: Virtual reality. Nursing 24(3), 3–3 (2018). https://doi.org/10.1007/s41193-018-0032-6
4. Martín-Gutiérrez, J., Mora, C.E., Añorbe-Díaz, B., González-Marrero, A.: Virtual technologies trends in education. Eurasia J. Math. Sci. Technol. Educ. 13(2), 469–486 (2017)

5. Carruth, D.W.: Virtual reality for education and workforce training. In: 2017 15th International Conference on Emerging eLearning Technologies and Applications (ICETA), pp. 1–6. IEEE (2017)
6. Feng, Z., González, V.A., Amor, R., Lovreglio, R., Cabrera-Guerrero, G.: Immersive virtual reality serious games for evacuation training and research: a systematic literature review. Comput. Educ. **127**, 252–266 (2018)
7. Beck, D., Morgado, L., O'Shea, P.: Finding the gaps about uses of immersive learning environments: a survey of surveys. J. Univ. Comput. Sci. **26**, 1043–1073 (2020)
8. Mütterlein, J.: The three pillars of virtual reality? Investigating the roles of immersion, presence, and interactivity. In: Proceedings of the 51st Hawaii International Conference on System Sciences (2018)
9. Bizami, N.A., Tasir, Z., Kew, S.N.: Innovative pedagogical principles and technological tools capabilities for immersive blended learning: a systematic literature review. Educ. Inf. Technol. **28**, 1–53 (2022)
10. Ahmed, A., Sutton, M.J.: Gamification, serious games, simulations, and immersive learning environments in knowledge management initiatives. World J. Sci. Technol. Sustain. Dev. (2017)
11. Frasson, C.: A framework for personalized fully immersive virtual reality learning environments with gamified design in education. In: Novelties in Intelligent Digital Systems: Proceedings of the 1st International Conference (NIDS 2021), Athens, Greece, 30 September–1 October 2021, vol. 338, p. 95. IOS Press (2021)
12. Gulhane, A., et al.: Security, privacy and safety risk assessment for virtual reality learning environment applications. In: 2019 16th IEEE Annual Consumer Communications & Networking Conference (CCNC), pp. 1–9. IEEE (2019)
13. Ip, H.H.S., Li, C.: Introducing immersive learning into special education settings: a comparative review of two studies. In: Creative Collaborative Learning Through Immersion, pp. 135–150 (2021)
14. Dincelli, E., Yayla, A.: Immersive virtual reality in the age of the Metaverse: a hybrid-narrative review based on the technology affordance perspective. J. Strateg. Inf. Syst. **31**(2), 101717 (2022)
15. Radhakrishnan, U., Koumaditis, K., Chinello, F.: A systematic review of immersive virtual reality for industrial skills training. Behav. Inf. Technol. **40**(12), 1310–1339 (2021)
16. Radianti, J., Majchrzak, T.A., Fromm, J., Wohlgenannt, I.: A systematic review of immersive virtual reality applications for higher education: Design elements, lessons learned, and research agenda. Comput. Educ. **147**, 103778 (2020)
17. Gardner, M.R., Elliott, J.B.: The immersive education laboratory: understanding affordances, structuring experiences, and creating constructivist, collaborative processes, in mixed-reality smart environments. EAI Endorsed Trans. Future Intell. Educ. Environ. **1**(1) (2014)
18. Bichler, M.: Design science in information systems research. Wirtschaftsinformatik **48**(2), 133–135 (2006). https://doi.org/10.1007/s11576-006-0028-8
19. Nunamaker, J.F., Jr., Briggs, R.O., Derrick, D.C., Schwabe, G.: The last research mile: achieving both rigor and relevance in information systems research. J. Manag. Inf. Syst. **32**(3), 10–47 (2015)
20. Gregor, S., Hevner, A.R.: Positioning and presenting design science research for maximum impact. MIS Q. 337–355 (2013)
21. Cheong, C., Cheong, F., Filippou, J.: Quick quiz: a gamified approach for enhancing learning (2013)
22. El-Masri, M., Tarhini, A., Hassouna, M., Elyas, T.: A design science approach to gamify education: from games to platforms. In: ECIS (2015)
23. Silic, M., Lowry, P.B.: Using design-science based gamification to improve organizational security training and compliance. J. Manag. Inf. Syst. **37**(1), 129–161 (2020)

24. Joshi, S., et al.: Implementing virtual reality technology for safety training in the precast/prestressed concrete industry. Appl. Ergon. **90**, 103286 (2021)
25. Sein, M.K., Henfridsson, O., Purao, S., Rossi, M., Lindgren, R.: Action design research. MIS Q. 37–56 (2011)
26. Kuechler, W., Vaishnavi, V.: A framework for theory development in design science research: multiple perspectives. J. Assoc. Inf. Syst. **13**(6), 3 (2012)
27. Pan, S.L., Carter, L., Tim, Y., Sandeep, M.S.: Digital sustainability, climate change, and information systems solutions: opportunities for future research. Int. J. Inf. Manage. **63**, 102444 (2022)
28. Seidel, S., et al.: The sustainability imperative in information systems research. Commun. Assoc. Inf. Syst. **40**(1), 3 (2017)
29. Zeiss, R., Ixmeier, A., Recker, J., Kranz, J.: Mobilising information systems scholarship for a circular economy: review, synthesis, and directions for future research. Inf. Syst. J. **31**(1), 148–183 (2021)
30. Seidel, S., Chandra Kruse, L., Székely, N., Gau, M., Stieger, D.: Design principles for sensemaking support systems in environmental sustainability transformations. Eur. J. Inf. Syst. **27**(2), 221–247 (2018)
31. Zeng, F., Lee, S.H.N., Lo, C.K.Y.: The role of information systems in the sustainable development of enterprises: a systematic literature network analysis. Sustainability **12**(8), 3337 (2020)
32. Lamberti, F., De Lorenzis, F., Pratticò, F.G., Migliorini, M.: An immersive virtual reality platform for training CBRN operators. In: 2021 IEEE 45th Annual Computers, Software, and Applications Conference (COMPSAC), pp. 133–137. IEEE (2021)
33. Conges, A., Evain, A., Benaben, F., Chabiron, O., Rebiere, S.: Crisis management exercises in virtual reality. In: 2020 IEEE Conference on Virtual Reality and 3D User Interfaces Abstracts and Workshops (VRW), pp. 87–92. IEEE (2020)
34. Zhang, H., He, X., Mitri, H.: Fuzzy comprehensive evaluation of virtual reality mine safety training system. Saf. Sci. **120**, 341–351 (2019)
35. Çakiroğlu, Ü., Gökoğlu, S.: Development of fire safety behavioral skills via virtual reality. Comput. Educ. **133**, 56–68 (2019)
36. De Lorenzis, F., Pratticò, F.G., Repetto, M., Pons, E., Lamberti, F.: Immersive virtual reality for procedural training: comparing traditional and learning by teaching approaches. Comput. Ind. **144**, 103785 (2023)
37. Pirker, J., Dengel, A., Holly, M., Safikhani, S.: Virtual reality in computer science education: a systematic review. In: 26th ACM Symposium on Virtual Reality Software and Technology, pp. 1–8 (2020)
38. Seo, H.J., Park, G.M., Son, M., Hong, A.J.: Establishment of virtual-reality-based safety education and training system for safety engagement. Educ. Sci. **11**(12), 786 (2021)
39. Adami, P., et al.: Effectiveness of VR-based training on improving construction workers' knowledge, skills, and safety behavior in robotic teleoperation. Adv. Eng. Inform. **50**, 101431 (2021)
40. Park, J., Lee, S.H., Kim, S.H., Won, J.H., Yoon, Y.C.: A study on safety information provision for workers using virtual reality-based construction site. J. Korean Soc. Saf. **35**(1), 45–52 (2020)
41. Pinheiro, J., de Almeida, R.S., Marques, A.: Emotional self-regulation, virtual reality and neurofeedback. Comput. Hum. Behav. Rep. **4**, 100101 (2021)
42. Zhu, M., et al.: Haptic-feedback smart glove as a creative human-machine interface (HMI) for virtual/augmented reality applications. Sci. Adv. **6**(19), eaaz8693 (2020)
43. Fromm, J., Radianti, J., Wehking, C., Stieglitz, S., Majchrzak, T.A., vom Brocke, J.: More than experience?-On the unique opportunities of virtual reality to afford a holistic experiential learning cycle. Internet High. Educ. **50**, 100804 (2021)

44. Chryssolouris, G., Mourtzis, D., Stavropoulos, P., Mavrikios, D., Pandremenos, J.: Knowledge management in a virtual lab collaborative training project: a mini-formula student car design. In: Bernard, A., Tichkiewitch, S. (eds.) Methods and Tools for Effective Knowledge Life-Cycle-Management, pp. 435–446. Springer, Heidelberg (2008). https://doi.org/10.1007/978-3-540-78431-9_24
45. Mavrikios, D., Papakostas, N., Mourtzis, D., Chryssolouris, G.: On industrial learning and training for the factories of the future: a conceptual, cognitive and technology framework. J. Intell. Manuf. **24**(3), 473–485 (2013)
46. Kim, S.H., Leem, C.S.: Factors affecting the transfer intention of VR construction safety training: a task-technology fit perspective. Glob. Bus. Adm. Rev **17**, 300–318 (2020)
47. Benbelkacem, S., Belhocine, M., Bellarbi, A., Zenati-Henda, N., Tadjine, M.: Augmented reality for photovoltaic pumping systems maintenance tasks. Renew. Energy **55**, 428–437 (2013)
48. Toyoda, R., Russo-Abegão, F., Glassey, J.: VR-based health and safety training in various high-risk engineering industries: a literature review. Int. J. Educ. Technol. High. Educ. **19**(1), 1–22 (2022)
49. Naseem, M., Younas, F., Mustafa, M.: Designing digital safe spaces for peer support and connectivity in patriarchal contexts. Proc. ACM Hum.-Comput. Interact. **4**(CSCW2), 1–24 (2020)
50. Acena, D., Freeman, G.: "in my safe space": social support for LGBTQ users in social virtual reality. In: Extended Abstracts of the 2021 CHI Conference on Human Factors in Computing Systems, pp. 1–6 (2021)
51. Freeman, G., Acena, D.: "Acting Out" queer identity: the embodied visibility in social virtual reality. Proc. ACM Hum.-Comput. Interact. **6**(CSCW2), 1–32 (2022)
52. Al Farsi, G., Yusof, A.B.M., Rusli, M.E.B.: A review of meaningful learning through virtual reality learning environment. J. Hunan Univ. Nat. Sci. **48**(9) (2021)
53. Cao, Y., Ng, G.W., Ye, S.S.: Design and evaluation for immersive virtual reality learning environment: a systematic literature review. Sustainability **15**(3), 1964 (2023)
54. Salah, B., Abidi, M.H., Mian, S.H., Krid, M., Alkhalefah, H., Abdo, A.: Virtual reality-based engineering education to enhance manufacturing sustainability in industry 4.0. Sustainability **11**(5), 1477 (2019)
55. Scurati, G.W., Bertoni, M., Graziosi, S., Ferrise, F.: Exploring the use of virtual reality to support environmentally sustainable behavior: a framework to design experiences. Sustainability **13**(2), 943 (2021)
56. Csikszentmihalyi, M.: Flow and education. NAMTA J. **22**(2), 2–35 (1997)
57. Csikszentmihalyi, M.: The contribution of flow to positive psychology (2000)
58. Treiblmaier, H., Putz, L.M., Lowry, P.B.: Setting a definition, context, and theory-based research agenda for the gamification of non-gaming applications. Assoc. Inf. Syst. Trans. Hum.-Comput. Interact. (THCI) **10**(3), 129–163 (2018)
59. Robson, K., Plangger, K., Kietzmann, J., McCarthy, I., Pitt, L.: Understanding gamification of consumer experiences. ACR North American Advances (2014)
60. Liu, D., Santhanam, R., Webster, J.: Toward Meaningful Engagement: a framework for design and research of Gamified information systems. MIS Q. **41**(4) (2017)
61. Crossler, R.E., Johnston, A.C., Lowry, P.B., Hu, Q., Warkentin, M., Baskerville, R.: Future directions for behavioral information security research. Comput. Secur. **32**, 90–101 (2013)
62. Lowry, P.B., Gaskin, J., Moody, G.D.: Proposing the multi-motive information systems continuance model (MISC) to better explain end-user system evaluations and continuance intentions. J. Assoc. Inf. Syst. **16**(7), 515–579 (2015)
63. Bui, A., Veit, D., Webster, J.: Gamification–a novel phenomenon or a new wrapping for existing concepts? (2015)

64. Huotari, K., Hamari, J.: A definition for gamification: anchoring gamification in the service marketing literature. Electron. Mark. **27**(1), 21–31 (2016). https://doi.org/10.1007/s12525-015-0212-z

65. Deterding, S.: The lens of intrinsic skill atoms: a method for gameful design. Hum.-Comput. Interact. **30**(3–4), 294–335 (2015)

66. Rigby, C.S.: Gamification and motivation. The gameful world: Approaches, issues, applications, pp. 113–138 (2015)

67. Hamari, J., Koivisto, J., Sarsa, H.: Does gamification work?–a literature review of empirical studies on gamification. In: 2014 47th Hawaii International Conference on System Sciences, pp. 3025–3034. IEEE (2014)

68. Herger, M.: Enterprise gamification. Engaging People by Letting Them Have Fun. Book, 1 (2014)

69. Hamari, J., Koivisto, J.: Why do people use gamification services? Int. J. Inf. Manage. **35**(4), 419–431 (2015)

70. Marache-Francisco, C., Brangier, E.: Process of gamification. In: Proceedings of the 6th Centric, pp. 126–131 (2013)

71. Robson, K., Plangger, K., Kietzmann, J.H., McCarthy, I., Pitt, L.: Is it all a game? Understanding the principles of gamification. Bus. Horiz. **58**(4), 411–420 (2015)

72. Werbach, K., Hunter, D.: For the Win: How Game Thinking Can Revolutionize Your Business Wharton Digital Press (2012)

73. Bucchiarone, A.: Gamification and virtual reality for digital twins learning and training: architecture and challenges. Virtual Reality Intell. Hardware **4**(6), 471–486 (2022)

74. Cavalcanti, J., Valls, V., Contero, M., Fonseca, D.: Gamification and Hazard communication in virtual reality: a qualitative study. Sensors **21**(14), 4663 (2021)

75. Ulmer, J., Braun, S., Cheng, C.T., Dowey, S., Wollert, J.: Gamification of virtual reality assembly training: effects of a combined point and level system on motivation and training results. Int. J. Hum.-Comput. Stud. 102854 (2022)

76. Morschheuser, B., Hassan, L., Werder, K., Hamari, J.: How to design gamification? A method for engineering gamified software. Inf. Softw. Technol. **95**, 219–237 (2018)

77. Gregor, S.: The nature of theory in information systems. MIS Q. 611–642 (2006)

78. Merton, R.K.: The matthew effect in science: the reward and communication systems of science are considered. Science **159**(3810), 56–63 (1968)

79. Hassan, N.R., Lowry, P.B.: Seeking middle-range theories in information systems research. In: International Conference on Information Systems (ICIS 2015), Fort Worth, TX, December, pp. 13–18 (2015)

80. Goldkuhl, G.: Design theories in information systems-a need for multi-grounding. J. Inf. Technol. Theory Appl. (JITTA) **6**(2), 7 (2004)

81. Arazy, O., Kumar, N., Shapira, B.: A theory-driven design framework for social recommender systems. J. Assoc. Inf. Syst. **11**(9), 2 (2010)

82. Venable, J.: The role of theory and theorising in design science research. In: Proceedings of the 1st International Conference on Design Science in Information Systems and Technology (DESRIST 2006), pp. 1–18 (2006)

83. Walls, J.G., Widmeyer, G.R., El Sawy, O.A.: Building an information system design theory for vigilant EIS. Inf. Syst. Res. **3**(1), 36–59 (1992)

84. Gregor, S., Jones, D.: The anatomy of a design theory. Association for Information Systems (2007)

85. Nelson, D.G.K., Frankenfield, A., Morris, C., Blair, E.: Young children's use of functional information to categorize artifacts: three factors that matter. Cognition **77**(2), 133–168 (2000)

86. Falah, J., et al.: Identifying the characteristics of virtual reality gamification for complex educational topics. Multimodal Technol. Interact. **5**(9), 53 (2021)

87. Radhakrishnan, U., Chinello, F., Koumaditis, K.: Immersive virtual reality training: three cases from the danish industry. In: 2021 IEEE Conference on Virtual Reality and 3D User Interfaces Abstracts and Workshops (VRW), pp. 1–5. IEEE (2021)

88. Kallio, H., Pietilä, A.M., Johnson, M., Kangasniemi, M.: Systematic methodological review: developing a framework for a qualitative semi-structured interview guide. J. Adv. Nurs. **72**(12), 2954–2965 (2016)

89. Vance, A., Lowry, P.B., Eggett, D.: Increasing accountability through user-interface design artifacts. MIS Q. **39**(2), 345–366 (2015)

90. Hassan, L., Xi, N., Gurkan, B., Koivisto, J., Hamari, J.: Gameful self-regulation: a study on how gamified self-tracking features evoke gameful experiences (2020)

91. Mohd, N.I., Ali, K.N., Bandi, S., Ismail, F.: Exploring gamification approach in hazard identification training for Malaysian construction industry. Int. J. Built Environ. Sustain. **6**(1), 51–57 (2019)

92. Zhao, Z., Toh, D.J., Ding, X., Ng, K.C., Sin, S.C., Wong, Y.C.: Immersive Gamification Platform for Manufacturing Shopfloor Training (2020)

93. Hamari, J., Shernoff, D.J., Rowe, E., Coller, B., Asbell-Clarke, J., Edwards, T.: Challenging games help students learn: an empirical study on engagement, flow and immersion in game-based learning. Comput. Hum. Behav. **54**, 170–179 (2016)

94. Chen, P.Z., Chang, T.C., Wu, C.L.: Effects of gamified classroom management on the divergent thinking and creative tendency of elementary students. Think. Skills Creat. **36**, 100664 (2020)

95. Koivisto, J., Hamari, J.: The rise of motivational information systems: a review gamification research. Int. J. Inf. Manage. **45**, 191–210 (2019)

96. de Oliveira, T.R., et al.: Virtual reality system for industrial motor maintenance training. In: 2020 22nd Symposium on Virtual and Augmented Reality (SVR), pp. 119–128. IEEE (2020)

97. Erten, B., Oral, B., Yakut, M.Z.: The role of virtual and augmented reality in occupational health and safety training of employees in PV power systems and evaluation with a sustainability perspective. J. Clean. Prod. **379**, 134499 (2022)

98. Karagiannis, P., Togias, T., Michalos, G.S., Makris, S.: Operators training using simulation and VR technology. In: Procedia CIRP, Proceedings of the 8th CIRP Global Web Conference (CIRPe 2020), Patras, Greece, 14–16 October 2020, pp. 290–294. Elsevier, Amsterdam (2021)

99. Upadhyay, A.K., Khandelwal, K.: Metaverse: the future of immersive training. Strateg. HR Rev. **21**(3), 83–86 (2022)

100. Le, Q.T., Pedro, A., Park, C.S.: A social virtual reality based construction safety education system for experiential learning. J. Intell. Rob. Syst. **79**(3), 487–506 (2015)

101. Gupta, A., Vargheseb, K.: Scenario-based construction safety training platform using virtual reality. In 37th International Symposium on Automation and Robotics in Construction, Kitakyushu, Japan (2020). https://doi.org/10.22260/ISARC2020/0123

102. Deci, E.L., Ryan, R.M.: The support of autonomy and the control of behaviour (2000)

103. Santhanam, R., Liu, D., Shen, W.C.M.: Research Note—Gamification of technology-mediated training: Not all competitions are the same. Inf. Syst. Res. **27**(2), 453–465 (2016)

Designing User-Centric Explanations for Medical Imaging with Informed Machine Learning

Luis Oberste[1(✉)] [iD], Florian Rüffer[1] [iD], Okan Aydingül[1] [iD], Johann Rink[2] [iD],
and Armin Heinzl[1] [iD]

[1] University of Mannheim, Mannheim, Germany
{loberste,frueffer,oaydingu,aheinzl}@mail.uni-mannheim.de
[2] University Medical Centre Mannheim, Mannheim, Germany
johann.rink@medma.uni-heidelberg.de

Abstract. A flawed algorithm released in clinical practice can cause unintended harm to patient health. Risks, regulation, responsibility, and ethics shape the demand of clinical users to understand and rely on the outputs made by artificial intelligence. Explainable artificial intelligence (XAI) offers methods to render a model's behavior understandable from different perspectives. Extant XAI, however, is mainly data-driven and designed to meet developers' demands to correct models rather than clinical users' expectations to reflect clinically relevant information. To this end, informed machine learning (IML) utilizes prior knowledge jointly with data to generate predictions, a promising paradigm to enrich XAI with medical knowledge. To explore how IML can be used to generate explanations that are congruent to clinical users' demands and useful to medical decision-making, we conduct Action Design Research (ADR) in collaboration with a team of radiologists. We propose an IML-based XAI system for clinically relevant explanations of diagnostic imaging predictions. With the help of ADR, we reduce the gap between implementation and user evaluation and demonstrate the effectiveness of the system in a real-world application with clinicians. While we develop design principles of using IML for user-centric XAI in diagnostic imaging, the study demonstrates that an IML-based design adequately reflects clinicians' conceptions. In this way, IML inspires greater understandability and trustworthiness of AI-enabled diagnostic imaging.

Keywords: Explainable Artificial Intelligence · Informed Machine Learning · Action Design Research · Medical Image Analysis · User-Centric Design

1 Introduction and Problem Statement

Advances in artificial intelligence (AI) have led to human-level performance in time-consuming routine tasks such as medical image analyses, which is highly beneficial for more efficient and qualitative medical diagnostics [1]. However, the lack of interpretability, known as the 'black-box' challenge, faced by medical AI raised fears of having

A. Gerber and R. Baskerville (Eds.): DESRIST 2023, LNCS 13873, pp. 470–484, 2023.
https://doi.org/10.1007/978-3-031-32808-4_29

unintended as well as unethical consequences. Thus, it has become a serious barrier to its widespread adoption in clinical routine [2]. A flawed algorithm in this high-stake domain can cause large-scale harm to patients [3]. Meanwhile, frameworks have been proposed to develop and apply AI in an ethical, legal, and morally responsible manner [4]. These ascribe a fundamental role to explainability for a safe clinical application of AI [5]. Since clinicians must be able to justify their decisions, supporting the output of a model with explanations that they can fully understand and trust is of vital importance for clinical application [6, 7]. Explainable artificial intelligence (XAI) involves several techniques to render models' behaviors and outputs understandable from different perspectives. Despite the surge of developed XAI methods and their potential to realize responsible AI, their utility in healthcare is still questioned [8]. One critic is that current XAI designs purely rely their results on the features, examples, or patterns detected in the input data, e.g., through attribution-based methods to generate heat maps. These do not reveal the reason why exactly a model found an area useful for a diagnosis decision [8]. Such data-driven explanations have been claimed by clinicians as inadequate to identify appropriate interventions [9] and mismatching human conception [10]. To make matters worse, current XAI initiatives do not pay enough attention to whom the explanations are targeted [11], and mostly only meet developers' demands, e.g., to debug and enhance models [12].

Clinicians, in contrast, expect explainable systems to leverage validated and clinically relevant information that reliably supports their medical decision-making [9]. Meanwhile, it has been concluded that integrating prior knowledge into machine learning systems is essential for improved explanations of their functioning [13]. Techniques from informed machine learning (IML) have been developed to learn from both data and a separate source of knowledge [14]. While it lacks understanding of their precise effect on explainability [15], they bear the potential to integrate medical information for more informed explanations. Thus, this paper aims to answer the following research questions: *How can IML be used to provide more clinician-centric explanations for medical image analysis? How can effective explanatory information be integrated to help clinicians make more informed diagnosis decisions?*

There is a lack of studies involving respective users in the design process and evaluations within real applications [16]. However, evaluating medical XAI's effectiveness requires human-in-the-loop experiments [7]. Therefore, we will follow an Action Design Research-based approach to facilitate our interdisciplinary collaboration with radiologists [17, 18] and aim to develop a novel IML-based system for explainable diagnostic image analysis. On this basis, we aim to contribute to the XAI challenge by designing user-centric explanations that are congruent to clinical users' expectations and evaluating the effectiveness in a true-to-life setting in a team of real clinicians.

2 Theoretical Background and Related Work

2.1 AI-Enabled Computer-Aided Diagnosis Systems

Based on predictive statistical models, AI-enabled tools can support clinicians in diagnosis decisions with a second objective opinion [19–21]. So-called computer-aided *diagnostics* (CADx) flourished in disciplines that rely on the interpretation of images, including radiology [22]. In contrast to conventional CADx designs, deep architectures of contemporary AI have been able to overcome the highly specialized and effortful feature extraction by learning features from input images by themselves [21, 23]. During technological progress, human-AI collaboration is leading to various new forms of interaction, with research and clinical implementations in their infancy [2, 24, 25]. Successfully translating AI-enabled CADx into practice requires purposeful designs of clinician-AI interactions that build conviction and trust [20, 26]. For fostering clinical trust, transparency has emerged as a crucial element, as even accurate diagnoses that are not understood are likely to be ignored by clinicians [2, 27].

2.2 Explainable Artificial Intelligence in Healthcare

Explainability (or interpretability) is associated with the extent to which a user of an AI system is able to understand the reasoning behind an output generated by it [20, 28]. Such techniques attempt to explain a model's prediction, uncover its inner workings, or represent it using coherent expressions [29]. Typically, one can develop XAI either by designing an intrinsically interpretable model or by complementing a black-box model with a post-hoc explanation method, offering local or global explanations [20, 30]. Among the most used explainability techniques in various medical imaging tasks and modalities are heat maps [31]. These highlight how much each region of an image influences a model's disease prediction [22]. Like most XAI techniques, these are *data-driven* [32] since the explanations are generated purely from the data underlying the ML pipeline. These do not offer any information on how salient regions contribute to the result, and the same regions can be highlighted for contradicting predictions [20]. Any highlighted region leaves it up to the clinician to find an explanation, e.g., whether an airspace opacity, the shape of an organ, or a particular pixel has triggered the decision [33]. Moreover, *post-hoc* XAI methods (like heat maps) are based on approximations which cannot ensure complete accountability [20]. Complementing data-driven models with validated medical knowledge is thus a key to enhanced interpretability of medical imaging predictions [34, 35].

2.3 Informed Machine Learning

Integrating prior knowledge into ML can increase performance, robustness, and lower demands for large amounts of data [36]. While data-driven models might not conform to the knowledge of the domain and context, IML uses a separate source of information and integrates it into an ML pipeline [15]. It has been recently revisited to provide users with more meaningful and useful explanations [13, 37]. According to recent reviews [14, 15, 37], the spectrum of IML approaches ranges from the integration of scientific knowledge via common sense to expert knowledge in the respective field of application, based on various representations such as logical rules, equations, or knowledge graphs. A common way to integrate prior knowledge is to add a regularization term to a model's loss function which guides its learning toward desired outcomes. In healthcare, IML techniques are particularly promising to utilize the medical knowledge already available, such as disease-symptom relations or expert decision criteria, ultimately improving human understanding of ML models [30].

2.4 User-Centric Design

Clinical users have different expectations of the appropriateness of information than systems designers [38]. Their sustained use of predictions depends, among others, on effectiveness rather than the amount of information, and whether these anticipate a clinically significant change in a patient's condition. This implies to only report relevant results and avoid repeated or uncertain prompts, e.g., by using thresholds. However, clinical users are often not included in the development process [27], leading to unexpected dynamics and ambiguity when having the tools implemented into the high-judgment work of radiologists [39]. Information systems (IS) research has recognized that user-centric design is one of the central challenges for XAI to meet the needs of users who are typically domain but not technical experts [12]. Notable studies revealed that XAI models should reflect an analytic process like that of evidence-based medical decision-making [40], allow users to connect outputs to existing clinical processes [9, 41], and allow novices to become experts [42]. Hence, developing and evaluating user-centric XAI requires application-grounded experiments to justify whether goals are achieved in real-world settings [43].

3 Research Method and Process

3.1 Action Design Research-Based Approach

Design Science Research is concerned with designing and evaluating innovative IT artifacts for practically relevant challenges and with deriving prescriptive design knowledge [44, 45]. In particular, Action Design Research (ADR) places special emphasis on the interaction with stakeholders during artifact development [17]. That is, the interaction between researchers and stakeholders (here: radiologists) is reflected in the artifacts' redesign and the evaluation takes place in continuous interaction throughout each design cycle [18]. While XAI systems have been driven primarily by technological capabilities [39, 46], ADR helps us to intertwine XAI development and its integration into the highly loaded clinical routine, by closely collaborating with a clinic of radiology and nuclear medicine at a cooperating university hospital. The original ADR concept offers many opportunities for interpretation of how to conduct the 'build, intervene, and evaluate' engagement [18]. Critics argue that in different stages of the intervention, various artifact creations emerge gradually from which design knowledge should be captured at all levels. Hence, we conducted an elaborated ADR (eADR) process with all ADR activities in each intervention [18]: *problem formulation and planning, artifact creation, evaluation, reflection, and learning.*

The first activity aims to identify and conceptualize the research object [17]. Initial interviews concerned (a) the clinical background of radiology imaging, (b) problematic diseases and the help of XAI, (c) existing CADx support, as well as (d) appropriate modes and desired characteristics of explanations. We also conducted a refined literature search to identify solution possibilities and plan the design. Artifact creation is the essential building activity of various forms like models, tools, principles, features, or instantiations, depending on the current stage of the process [18].

The artifact was continuously evaluated and iteratively refined according to meeting expert expectations in practice [17, 47], through biweekly on-site presentations for ad-hoc feedback and semi-structured interviews for each ADR stage. All interviews were conducted with two resident radiologists (3 and 4 years of work experience), prior to half-hour job shadowing. Finally, the implementation stage was also evaluated in an informal expert group of radiotherapists, physicists, radiologists, and CADx software developers. Reflection and learning activities shift from a case-specific solution to broader medical XAI research: First, we constantly compared our artifact to the literature streams of IML and medical imaging to plan the next ADR cycles. To overcome the limited design knowledge accumulation observed in the IS community [44], we have aimed at comple-mentary design knowledge. To this end, we collected meta-requirements (MRs) from prior research as theory-derived MRs are abstract and valid for more than one artifact [48]. We then derived generalizable learnings and formalized them as design principles (DPs), a set of prescriptive instructions for an artifact design that addresses MRs and follows established templates [48].

To avoid common inconsistencies in DPs, we derived 'action and materiality ori-ented' design principles that state *what* an artifact should provide and *how* it should be built to reach that [49]. Iterations are divided by eADR into *diagnosis, design, imple-mentation*, and *evolution* stages. As the problem domain is largely identified and XAI models generally need to explain *how* and *why* the system generated a particular output [28], we chose an *objective-centered* entry point. To begin with the solution design, we explored options based on IML to develop user-centric and effective explanations for medical practice. After the diagnosis stage was conducted in July 2022, we started the ADR project with a design stage in August 2022, which evolved into an implementation stage in November 2022 and ended in January 2023.

4 Results of Designing a User-Centric XAI System

4.1 Synthesizing Literature for a Theory-Informed Artifact Design

In this diagnosis stage, we derived MRs from literature a priori to artifact instantiation [49], to guide the eADR process and inform the artifact design. As our study addresses user-centric explanations in medical imaging, we selected the key concepts of AI-enabled CADx, XAI, IML, and user-centric design to derive MRs and validated them in expert interviews, in line with ADR [48, 49]. For each concept, we constructed MRs that are abstract and tied to the solution objective [48], based on frequently cited studies as well as recent reviews within the respective communities (e.g., [22, 29, 32, 33], respectively) to build the knowledge base (cp. Sect. 2).

MR1 – Practically-Evaluated Diagnosis Support. AI-enabled CADx systems are highly accurate but require purposefully designed human-AI collaboration [25]. Thus, practical solutions and testing in clinical routine contexts are necessary [22].

MR2 – Inherent Explainability. Trustable and successful AI interactions require clin-icians' understanding [20, 26]. A trustworthy XAI design in healthcare must embody an inherently explainable model to avoid pitfalls of post-hoc interpretability [20] and to overcome unimodal, data-driven XAI workflows [22, 33].

MR3 – Informed Machine Learning Component. Integrating medically relevant knowledge in machine learning models can overcome the limits of data-driven systems and enable knowledge-informed explanations [13, 15].

MR4 – User-Centric System Design. A user-centric XAI design must involve end-users from early on in development [27]. Clinician-centric XAI should provide information that is useful for patient-specific decision-making, and leverage validated medical knowledge [6, 11, 34, 35]. The explanations should mirror clinicians' way of thinking and integrate cleanly with their diagnostic workflow [40, 41], as well as provide information that users can connect to existing clinical processes [9, 42].

4.2 Design of a Conceptual XAI Prototype for Image Analysis

As it lacks knowledge on how IML can help to design user-centric and effective explanations for diagnostic imaging, we initiated the eADR process with a design stage.

Problem Formulation and Planning. Job shadowing and expert interviews helped us refine the problem and explore the design space of the artifact. After the radiologists validated the MRs, we pursued chest CT as an essential diagnostic tool across all patient populations. Thereby, pulmonary nodules are always a critical concern, as they occur in all age groups and are examined on every CT scan. The diagnostic difficulty consists of the detection of benign nodules as a sign of early lung cancer. The cooperating radiology clinic did not have an explainable CADx system in place. Instead, systems assist with the automated detection of nodule candidates and the semi-automated measurement of nodule size. As it is highly important to make a provable decision on whether a nodule has a risk of being malignant or not on the part of radiologists, we selected pulmonary nodules as a research case to explore XAI assistance. To guide the artifact, we reviewed key literature on PubMed, Google Scholar, and AIS eLibrary, using search terms (and a wide range of synonyms) related to disease prediction, medical imaging, XAI, and IML techniques. The search was restricted to English articles published between 2016 and 2022. Articles were included if they explain an image diagnosis by integrating, enriching, or combining a dataset with a separate source of medical knowledge, resulting in 11 relevant papers.

Prior AI studies of lung nodules are unable to explain the predicted malignancy [50]. One type of XAI extracts high-level concepts learned by deep learning [37], called concept attribution. It links model units, e.g., convolutional neural network (CNN) channels, with a separate set of human-friendly semantic concepts. The attribution, however, represents global post-hoc explanations (contrary to MR2) [51].

Other IML techniques build predictions based on pre-defined concepts [52]. These, however, rely classification only on a few expert-defined clinical concepts annotated to entire images, without combining deep image-based features. Another technique is multi-task learning (MTL) that learns multiple outputs simultaneously [37]. It has been used to learn diagnostic criteria jointly with the diagnosis, e.g., a dermoscopic 7-point checklist for skin cancer prediction [53]. As there are no connections between high-level outputs, one cannot extract mutual influence, e.g., between criteria and diagnosis [54].

One study overcame this by arranging two-tier predictions in a hierarchical CNN with a global loss function [55]. Here, the intermediate predictions of low-level semantic properties and learned image features of the CNN were concatenated into a high-level subnetwork for final diagnosis prediction. This way, the model learned from hybrid information, i.e., image and semantic features, both inherently influencing diagnosis prediction. Diagnostic criteria (e.g., the pattern or composition of nodules) are intuitive to radiologists since they are educated to apply them to chest images (MR4). Thus, we adapted a two-tier CNN [55] to not only predict whether a criterion is fulfilled but also provide its influence on a particular malignancy result.

Artifact Creation. Given an image of a possible nodule, our first intended IML prototype predicted intermediate characteristics and the final malignancy risk. Hereby, we integrated all low-level characteristics of nodules reported in the related literature, including subtlety, internal structure, calcification, sphericity, margin, lobulation, spiculation, as well as texture [23]. To increase transparency, we used more granular labels per criterion (e.g., non-solid, partly-solid, or solid texture) compared to the binary labels used in [55]. To extract their numerical importance for nodule malignancy, we adapted the integrated gradients XAI technique since it applies to any differentiable model and does not require modifications of the original network [56].

Evaluation. We gathered feedback from the clinicians on the usefulness of information integrated into the conceptual prototype (MR1) and the correspondence to the diagnostic workflow (MR4). First, radiologists had differing opinions and prioritizations regarding explanatory criteria (explanators). The size, number, localization, texture, as well as morphological features of nodules (shape and margin) were most important across all interviews. Notably, the first three features were not covered by our artifact, though being highly relevant. We attributed this to the fact that reviewed XAI approaches applied classification to individual nodule regions rather than overall lung volumes due to intended performance advancements. Thereby, ML was utilized to only predict features that conventional CADx could not provide rather than using them jointly. Second, radiologists validated that these criteria were effective to explain malignancy. Some of them were perceived as "an ultra-detailed perspective (...) of a very small structure." Though granularity was appropriate, it likely differs from other medical specialties. Another radiologist suggested that explanators should not be too detailed as a patient may have *many* nodules. Hence, relevant diagnostic criteria should be highlighted, and information overload must be avoided.

Reflection. The patient-wise and diagnostic nature of explanations were approved. Though, two important explanators (number and position of nodules) could not be predicted when classifying individual nodule images. This turned out problematic: If radiologists let the AI classify regions of supposed nodules, they already have made a preselection (using diagnostic criteria) and the explanations would become redundant.

Learning. We could generalize the learnings from a lung nodule-related design to medical imaging tasks as design principles that address MRs as follows.

DP1: In order to provide appropriate explanations, AI tasks need to be designed in an end-to-end manner. As indicated, integrating medical knowledge for malignancy prediction (MR3) did not per se render explanations appropriate. Applying classification to image regions implied that a radiologist had to preselect problematic areas. Consequently, explanations become obsolete. Thus, explanations should provide information unknown to clinicians (MR1) and perform both detection and classification.

DP2: In order to provide diagnostically relevant information, the system should provide criteria tailored to users' medical specialties. Finding the right information to be integrated into IML was not trivial (MR2). Morphological criteria of lung nodules were appropriate for the domain of radiologists in which they are practically applied (MR4). Other explanators (e.g., the number and size of nodules) aim at a more common medical understanding and are helpful to general practitioners assessing chest CT images. Thus, designing informative explanations requires adjustment to the medical understanding and analytical decision-making of the specialty (MR2, MR4).

4.3 Implementation of a Conceptual XAI Prototype for Image Analysis

We continued with development-centered activities and aimed to implement a functional IML artifact to demonstrate a useful instantiation of the solution class.

Problem Formulation and Planning. In this stage, we dealt with the additional automated detection of nodules and the refinement of the explanators based on the end-to-end design. CNNs can successfully be applied end-to-end (from the input of a raw CT volume to the classification), whereas determining the right network input for medical imaging is very complex: One way is to extract slides from the 3D volume as usual 2D inputs [57]. Then, slices are analyzed independently and many of them are not informative. Region of interest-based inputs are only useful to diseases that do not span over multiple areas. One can also apply 3D CNNs directly to a whole CT volume. This fully integrates spatial information but is prone to overfitting due to one-per-patient samples. Hence, we planned to use 3D patches for creating a nodule detection model, prepended to the explainable classification task. This has resulted in a larger sample size since many 3D patches can be extracted and used as input to a single CNN model. Reflecting on the novel set of possible explanators with radiologists, patient details, such as demographics and clinical history, were found inappropriate as they had been already known before image interpretation. Radiologists found "recommendations using the Fleischner table" more useful, as this guideline is referred to determine follow-up biopsy or CT intervals depending on the texture, number, and size of nodules. Thus, we planned to provide Fleischner-related criteria to increase artifact utility and facilitate follow-up decision-making.

Artifact Creation. As an IML artifact, we implemented a functional prototype consisting of nodule detection (Fig. 1, upper lane) and classification (lower lane). Both tasks were implemented in python based on PyTorch and pylidc libraries, using ConvNet architectures[1]. From the public LIDC-IDRI dataset[2], 1,017 low-dose lung CT scans associated with 1,012 (both positive and clean) patients and 1,388 nodules (each annotated from at least three physicians) were taken. CT scans were transformed to

---

[1] https://github.com/facebookresearch/ConvNeXt.
[2] https://wiki.cancerimagingarchive.net/x/rgAe.

Hounsfield scale, filtered [−1000, 500], and scaled to [0, 1]. To prevent data leakage, we used patient-level splits for training, validation, and test data (75%, 10%, and 15%). Both models were separately trained using PyTorch's 'AdamW' optimizer.

Model 1 (detection). For voxel-wise training of the nodule candidate detector (Fig. 1, top left box), we selected 1,095 positive (and applied thirtyfold random shift augmentation) and 116.4k random negative (i.e., nodule-free) 3D patches, in the size of 40 × 40 × 40 mm. We trained the model using binary cross-entropy loss. To detect final nodule locations, we applied the model to whole lung CT volumes using a sliding window, as common in medical imaging [58]. From the outputs in different windows, we kept the bounding boxes of ones with a sigmoid probability above 0.98. If two neighboring boxes are predicted as positives, we only kept the median one. Final locations were used as input to subsequent classification (Fig. 1, lower left box).

Model 2 (IML-based classification). Each detected candidate nodule is classified like [55]. It was trained based on the positive instances from the dataset used for model 1 (class distribution: 11.1%, 11%, 45.8%, 18.5%, and 13.6%, from benign to malignant), using a common classification loss (cross-entropy). We discarded internal structure, lobulation, and subtlety to match identified criteria. We added a size feature (nodule diameter) which we binned analogous to Fleischner guidelines [<4, 4–8, 8–20, 20–30, > 30]. Low-level image features (ConvNet output) were used to compute each nodule-level diagnostic criterion through fully connected layers (Fig. 1, blue lines). Image and criteria representations were merged and fed into another block of fully connected layers to compute the malignancy probability (golden lines).

XAI Output. To generate lung-level explanations, we extracted the number and position (positive bounding boxes) of nodules from model 1 (green lines). From model 2, we used diagnostic features, along with brief corresponding labels as well as their numerical importance, and malignancies as nodule-level explanations. The combination of both levels was used for patient-level summarization: Overall malignancy risk reported at least one malignant nodule being present and, if yes, the average malignancy. As favored by the radiologists, only the most malignant nodule was initially explained, and less malignant ones were displayed on request. Rule-based recommendations were added as per Fleischner guidelines, e.g., multiple 6–8 mm large nodules with solid texture and low malignancy risk should be CT screened after 3–6 months.

Evaluation. In semi-structured interviews, we used exemplary diagnosis explanations and validated complexity, medical relevance, and the effect on the routine. Radiologists advocated the multi-level approach, i.e., regarding overall malignancy as well as each nodule candidate. They perceived nodule-specific criteria and their importance as satisfactory to understand malignancy results, whereas one preferred even shorter explanations. All positively stressed that they can quickly compare criteria with their assessment and adopt them for documentation in case they agree. Overall, the system was found as a quality-enhancing cross-check to not overlook any nodes, with helpful explanatory information. It offered well-prepared characteristics, helping both residents to justify diagnoses as well as chief residents to verify reports. From an organizational view, this can qualitatively improve follow-up activities since high-risk patients could automatically be referred to further imaging or biopsy for confirmation.

For a quantitative evaluation, we applied metrics commonly used in image classification [57]. In detection (model 1), we achieved an F-score of 0.71, accuracy of 0.99, precision of 0.62, and recall of 0.84. Although the precision is relatively lower (probably due to the realistic test dataset), our detection is still highly accurate with comparably few false positives, compared to state-of-the-art results in deep learning [50]. The downstream model yielded a root-mean-square error (RMSE) of 0.79 for malignancy classification, which is low compared to the feature's standard deviation of 1.19. For performance comparison, we also binarized the features to match [55]. Malignancy (0.86), calcification (0.92), margin (0.77), texture (0.88), and sphericity (0.59) all resulted in equal or higher binary classification accuracy compared to [55]. Size and spiculation were predicted with an accuracy of 0.93 and 0.86, respectively.

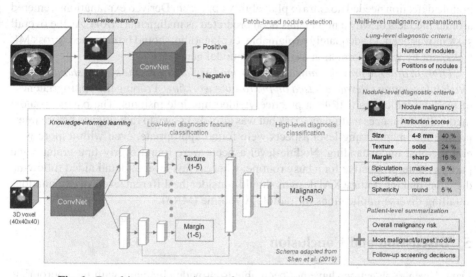

Fig. 1. Resulting user-centric XAI for lung nodule analysis based on IML.

Overall, the two-tier artifact (Fig. 1) provided higher granularity of explanators including their numerical influence, improving the practical relevance of explanations. Compared to binary nodule classification [55], IML is equally performant while ensuring radiologist-informed explainability. We have also gained a more realistic performance estimate and mitigated data leakage through patient-level holdout data.

Reflection. Contrary to initial assumptions, diagnostically relevant information with which clinicians are familiar was not automatically meaningful. Instead, definitions in close collaboration with clinicians showed context-specific usefulness. IML as a tool for knowledge integration was beneficial to clinician-centric and effective explainability. Not only could nodule classification be enhanced with informative explanations, but the detected characteristics also assisted in creating follow-up screening rules, further reducing manual work in nodule-related decision-making.

Learning. Further strands of image analyses, such as Alzheimer's disease detection, are seeking diagnostic-focused explanations [59]. Our developed artifact, therefore, may apply to any disease whose diagnosis relies on image interpretation. Among others, oncological diseases such as liver and bone metastases could also benefit from the proposed design of explanatory information as they adhere to structured diagnosis criteria, too. Thus, we could embody the IML-based solution within the general black-box problem of AI-based CADx systems. For the goal of designing user-centric and effective XAI for medical image analyses, we generalize two more learnings.

DP3: In order to provide useful explanations, the system should span medical explanations across ML tasks instead of model-driven explanations. Unlike common XAI approaches, model-specific explainability was not useful (MR1). In contrast, the mere nodule detection needed no extra explainability approach. Derived explanations centered around the facts of why a nodule has been predicted as malignant (MR4). As the overall system was deemed adequately explainable, explanations should be designed across ML tasks, not by what information a single ML model generates.

DP4: In order to provide knowledge-informed explanations, the system should distinguish information relevance based on the routine workflow. Probing the appropriateness of medical indicators (MR4) in practice yielded multiple insights. The patient context medically influences malignancy risk but was already known to radiologists before interpreting the image. Lung-level aspects were found appropriate, even with a more general medical understanding. Nodule-level aspects were found overly fine-grained and partly counterproductive for a busy routine, whereas this level of detail aided follow-up decision-making. Future XAI designs should consider the different levels of explanations entailing diverse implications for radiology routine (MR3).

5   Discussion and Conclusion

Data-driven explanations have not been able to provide clinicians with the appropriate understanding of AI-powered results. We hope to further contribute to the medical XAI challenge by actively involving clinicians in building a CADx system for image analysis. Our findings suggest that IML can surpass data-driven and post-hoc XAI and directly derive explanations from the inference process. Such 'intrinsic interpretability' benefits from desirable properties such as faithfulness, trustworthiness, and fidelity [60] since no black box needs to be approximated. While competitive performance could be achieved, IML involved a complex design of the network input to make end-to-end image detection and additional feature classification possible.

Another challenge entailed by IML is that explanatory benefits are not often readily apparent. While the two-tier hierarchy allowed for explainable feature predictions, other techniques such as knowledge graph integration may have less obvious effects.

Thanks to eADR, we have been able to gain valuable practical insights into malignancy assessment to constantly refine our artifact design. While quality frameworks are being developed and attribute many possible properties to explanations (e.g., [28]), our findings strongly support observations that explanations do not need to be exhaustive but must ensure usability when implemented in healthcare [5]. Radiologists did not find all diagnostically relevant information meaningful but preferred actionable factors, though in dissenting granularity. Meanwhile, we provided explanations that span over two ML tasks, which ensured that the XAI system's purpose was useful. Consequently, workflow-level utility and system-level explainability were mutually dependent. In contrast to suggestions to additionally utilize patient demographic data [50], we observed that these were medically but not practically adequate. After all, we identified explanators that mimic radiologist diagnostics and integrate cleanly with the workflow. Considering the broader medical XAI field, we identified diseases of other specialties, including but not limited to oncology and neurology that are assessable through similar diagnostic criteria. These are very likely to benefit from IML, too. The proposed architecture provides flexibility to change the detection component to other diseases, intermediate features to other medical indicators, and follow-up rules. Ultimately, we proposed hands-on principles that facilitate the design of corresponding explanations. Nevertheless, our study has two limitations. First, nodule classification could encounter a consequential error if the first model produces a false detection, so the estimated performance may be optimistic. However, we expect this to have only a minor impact on the performance of our instantiation as we observed relatively few false positives. Second, the qualitative feedback on the explanatory information as part of our evaluation was limited to experts from one institution with many years of experience. Hence, we encourage research to practically test and evaluate the principles of IML design and resulting explainability methods in various healthcare settings. As the communication format may also affect explanation understanding, the variants to arrange such information within an interface could provide further important insights into the demands of clinical users.

For practically designing explanatory information in medical imaging, our study faced heterogeneous information according to what CADx systems semi-automatically obtain, what radiologists desire, what is obsolete due to the workflow, as well as what medical guidelines suggest. The order of importance was also different. In summary, we encourage future developments to unite the medical knowledge available with user-centric XAI purposes. Through a proposed multi-level explanation approach, medically relevant and actionable criteria could and should be consolidated. It follows that identifying the correct intersection areas may also reduce the manual efforts required to document image interpretation and aftercare decision-making.

References

1. Pumplun, L., Fecho, M., Islam, N., Buxmann, P.: Machine learning systems in clinics – how mature is the adoption process in medical diagnostics? In: Proceedings of the 54th Hawaii International Conference on System Sciences (2021)
2. Johnson, M., Albizri, A., Harfouche, A.: Responsible artificial intelligence in healthcare: predicting and preventing insurance claim denials for economic and social wellbeing. Inf. Syst. Front. (2021)
3. Topol, E.J.: High-performance medicine: the convergence of human and artificial intelligence. Nat. Med. 25(1), 44–56 (2019)
4. Wiens, J., et al.: Do no harm: a roadmap for responsible machine learning for health care. Nat. Med. 25(9), 1337–1340 (2019)
5. Arbelaez Ossa, L., Starke, G., Lorenzini, G., Vogt, J.E., Shaw, D.M., Elger, B.S.: Re-focusing explainability in medicine. Digital Health 8 (2022)

6. Markus, A.F., Kors, J.A., Rijnbeek, P.R.: The role of explainability in creating trustworthy artificial intelligence for health care: a comprehensive survey of the terminology, design choices, and evaluation strategies. J. Biomed. Inform. **113** (2021)
7. Payrovnaziri, S.N., et al.: Explainable artificial intelligence models using real-world electronic health record data: a systematic scoping review. JAMIA **27**(7), 1173–1185 (2020)
8. Fernandez-Quilez, A.: Deep learning in radiology: ethics of data and on the value of algorithm transparency, interpretability and explainability. AI Ethics **3**(1), 257–265 (2022)
9. Jacobs, M., et al.: Designing AI for trust and collaboration in time-constrained medical decisions: a sociotechnical lens. In: Kitamura, Y., Quigley, A., Isbister, K., Igarashi, T., Bjørn, P., Drucker, S. (eds.) Proceedings of the 2021 CHI Conference on Human Factors in Computing Systems, pp. 1–14. ACM, New York (2021)
10. Li, X., Qian, B., Wei, J., Zhang, X., Chen, S., Zheng, Q.: Domain knowledge guided deep atrial fibrillation classification and its visual interpretation. In: Zhu, W., et al. (eds.) International Conference on Information and Knowledge Management, pp. 129–138. ACM, New York (2019)
11. Ribera, M., Lapedriza, A.: Can we do better explanations? A proposal of user-centered explainable AI. In: Proceedings of the IUI Workshops. ACM, New York (2019)
12. Bauer, K., Hinz, O., van der Aalst, W., Weinhardt, C.: Expl(AI)n it to me – explainable AI and information systems research. Bus. Inf. Syst. Eng. **63**(2), 79–82 (2021). https://doi.org/10.1007/s12599-021-00683-2
13. Gaur, M., Faldu, K., Sheth, A.: Semantics of the black-box: can knowledge graphs help make deep learning systems more interpretable and explainable? IEEE Internet Comput. **25**(1), 51–59 (2021)
14. Beckh, K., et al.: Explainable Machine Learning with Prior Knowledge (2021)
15. von Rueden, L., et al.: Informed machine learning - a taxonomy and survey of integrating prior knowledge into learning systems. IEEE Trans. Knowl. Data Eng. **35**(1), 614–633 (2021)
16. Doshi-Velez, F., Kim, B.: Considerations for evaluation and generalization in interpretable machine learning. In: Escalante, H.J., et al. (eds.) Explainable and Interpretable Models in Computer Vision and Machine Learning. TSSCML, pp. 3–17. Springer, Cham (2018). https://doi.org/10.1007/978-3-319-98131-4_1
17. Sein, M.K., Henfridsson, O., Purao, S., Rossi, M., Lindgren, R.: Action design research. MIS Q. **35**(1), 37–56 (2011)
18. Mullarkey, M.T., Hevner, A.R.: An elaborated action design research process model. EJIS **28**(1), 6–20 (2019)
19. Fernández-Loría, C., Provost, F., Han, X.: Explaining data-driven decisions made by AI systems: the counterfactual approach. MIS Q. **46**(3), 1635–1660 (2022)
20. Salahuddin, Z., Woodruff, H.C., Chatterjee, A., Lambin, P.: Transparency of deep neural networks for medical image analysis: a review of interpretability methods. Comput. Biol. Med. **140**, 105111 (2021)
21. Cheng, J.-Z., et al.: Computer-aided diagnosis with deep learning architecture: applications to breast lesions in US images and pulmonary nodules in CT scans. Sci. Rep. **6**, 1–13 (2016)
22. Rajpurkar, P., Chen, E., Banerjee, O., Topol, E.J.: AI in health and medicine. Nat. Med. **28**(1), 31–38 (2022)
23. Hancock, M.C., Magnan, J.F.: Lung nodule malignancy classification using only radiologist-quantified image features as inputs to statistical learning algorithms. J. Med. Imaging **3**(4), 044504 (2016)
24. Grüning, M., Trenz, M.: Me, you and AI - managing human AI collaboration in computer aided intelligent diagnosis. In: SIGHCI 2021 Proceedings (2021)
25. Hinsen, S., Hofmann, P., Jöhnk, J., Urbach, N.: How can organizations design purposeful human-AI interactions: a practical perspective from existing use cases and interviews. In: Proceedings of the 55th Hawaii International Conference on System Sciences (2022)

26. Alam, L., Mueller, S.: Examining the effect of explanation on satisfaction and trust in AI diagnostic systems. BMC Med. Inform. Decis. Making **21**(1), 178 (2021)
27. Braun, M., Harnischmacher, C., Lechte, H., Riquel, J.: Let's get physic(AI)l - transforming AI-requirements of healthcare into design principles. In: ECIS 2022 (2022)
28. Vilone, G., Longo, L.: Notions of explainability and evaluation approaches for explainable artificial intelligence. Inf. Fusion **76**, 89–106 (2021)
29. Tjoa, E., Guan, C.: A survey on explainable artificial intelligence (XAI): toward medical XAI. IEEE Trans. Neural Netw. Learn. Syst. **32**(11), 4793–4813 (2021)
30. Oberste, L., Heinzl, A.: User-centric explainability in healthcare: a knowledge-level perspective of informed machine learning. IEEE Trans. Artif. Intell. 1–18 (2022)
31. Saporta, A., et al.: Benchmarking saliency methods for chest X-ray interpretation. Nat Mach Intell **4**(10), 867–878 (2022)
32. Li, X.-H., et al.: A survey of data-driven and knowledge-aware explainable AI. IEEE Trans. Knowl. Data Eng. (2020)
33. Ghassemi, M., Oakden-Rayner, L., Beam, A.L.: The false hope of current approaches to explainable artificial intelligence in health care. Lancet Digit. Health **3**(11) (2021)
34. Zihni, E., et al.: Opening the black box of artificial intelligence for clinical decision support: a study predicting stroke outcome. PLoS ONE **15**(4) (2020)
35. Sun, Z., Dong, W., Shi, J., Huang, Z.: Interpretable Disease Prediction based on Reinforcement Path Reasoning over Knowledge Graphs (2020)
36. Choi, E., Bahadori, M.T., Song, L., Stewart, W.F., Sun, J.: GRAM: graph-based attention model for healthcare representation learning. In: ACM SIGKDD, pp. 787–795 (2017)
37. Deng, C., Ji, X., Rainey, C., Zhang, J., Lu, W.: Integrating machine learning with human knowledge. iScience **23**(11) (2020)
38. Lahav, O., Mastronarde, N., van der Schaar, M.: What is interpretable? Using machine learning to design interpretable decision-support systems (2018)
39. Lebovitz, S.: Diagnostic doubt and artificial intelligence: an inductive field study of radiology work. In: ICIS 2019 Proceedings (2019)
40. Tonekaboni, S., Joshi, S., McCradden, M.D., Goldenberg, A.: What Clinicians Want: Contextualizing Explainable Machine Learning for Clinical End Use (2019)
41. Evans, T., et al.: The explainability paradox: challenges for xAI in digital pathology. Futur. Gener. Comput. Syst. **133**, 281–296 (2022)
42. Pazzani, M., Soltani, S., Kaufman, R., Qian, S., Hsiao, A.: Expert-informed, user-centric explanations for machine learning. In: AAAI, vol. 36, no. 11, pp. 12280–12286 (2022)
43. Das, A., Rad, P.: Opportunities and Challenges in Explainable Artificial Intelligence (XAI): A Survey (2020)
44. vom Brocke, J., Winter, R., Hevner, A.R., Maedche, A.: Special issue editorial –accumulation and evolution of design knowledge in design science research: a journey through time and space. JAIS **21**(3), 520–544 (2020)
45. Peffers, K., Tuunanen, T., Niehaves, B.: Design science research genres: introduction to the special issue on exemplars and criteria for applicable design science research. EJIS **27**(2), 129–139 (2018)
46. Chari, S., Seneviratne, O., Gruen, D.M., Foreman, M.A., Das, A.K., McGuinness, D.L.: Explanation ontology: a model of explanations for user-centered AI. In: Pan, J.Z., et al. (eds.) ISWC 2020. LNCS, vol. 12507, pp. 228–243. Springer, Cham (2020). https://doi.org/10. 1007/978-3-030-62466-8_15
47. Gilpin, L.H., Testart, C., Fruchter, N., Adebayo, J.: Explaining Explanations to Society (2019)
48. Möller, F., Guggenberger, T.M., Otto, B.: Towards a method for design principle development in information systems. In: Hofmann, S., Müller, O., Rossi, M. (eds.) DESRIST 2020. LNCS, vol. 12388, pp. 208–220. Springer, Cham (2020). https://doi.org/10.1007/978-3-030-64823-7_20

49. Chandra, L., Seidel, S., Gregor, S.: Prescriptive knowledge in IS research: conceptualizing design principles in terms of materiality, action, and boundary conditions. In: Proceedings of the 48th Hawaii International Conference on System Sciences, pp. 4039–4048 (2015)

50. Jassim, M.M., Jaber, M.M.: Systematic review for lung cancer detection and lung nodule classification: taxonomy, challenges, and recommendation future works. J. Intell. Syst. **31**(1), 944–964 (2022)

51. Bau, D., Zhou, B., Khosla, A., Oliva, A., Torralba, A.: Network dissection: quantifying interpretability of deep visual representations. In: IEEE Conference on Computer Vision and Pattern Recognition, pp. 3319–3327 (2017)

52. LaLonde, R., Torigian, D., Bagci, U.: Encoding visual attributes in capsules for explainable medical diagnoses. In: Martel, A.L., et al. (eds.) MICCAI 2020. LNCS, vol. 12261, pp. 294–304. Springer, Cham (2020). https://doi.org/10.1007/978-3-030-59710-8_29

53. Murabayashi, S., Iyatomi, H.: Towards explainable melanoma diagnosis: prediction of clinical indicators using semi-supervised and multi-task learning. In: International Conference on Big Data, pp. 4853–4857. IEEE (2019)

54. Lucieri, A., Dengel, A., Ahmed, S.: Deep learning based decision support for medicine—a case study on skin cancer diagnosis (2021)

55. Shen, S., Han, S.X., Aberle, D.R., Bui, A.A., Hsu, W.: An interpretable deep hierarchical semantic convolutional neural network for lung nodule malignancy classification. Expert Syst. Appl. **128**, 84–95 (2019)

56. Sundararajan, M., Taly, A., Yan, Q.: Axiomatic attribution for deep networks. In: Proceedings of the 34th ICML, vol. 70, pp. 3319–3328. PMLR (2017)

57. Wen, J., et al.: Convolutional neural networks for classification of Alzheimer's disease: Overview and reproducible evaluation. Med. Image Anal. **63**, 101694 (2020)

58. Wu, J., Qian, T.: A survey of pulmonary nodule detection, segmentation and classification in computed tomography with deep learning techniques. J. Med. Artif. Intell. **2**, 1–12 (2019)

59. Dyrba, M., Hanzig, M., Altenstein, S., Bader, S., Ballarini, T., Brosseron, F., Buerger, K., et al.: Improving 3D convolutional neural network comprehensibility via interactive visualization of relevance maps: evaluation in Alzheimer's disease. Alzheimer's Res. Ther. **13**(1), 1–18 (2021)

60. Pintelas, E., Livieris, I.E., Pintelas, P.: A grey-box ensemble model exploiting black-box accuracy and white-box intrinsic interpretability. Algorithms **13**(1), 17 (2020)

Author Index

A. Gerber and R. Baskerville (Eds.): DESRIST 2023, LNCS 13873, pp. 485–486, 2023.
https://doi.org/10.1007/978-3-031-32808-4

Printed in the United States
by Baker & Taylor Publisher Services

Printed in the United States
by Baker & Taylor Publisher Services